The Oregon Literature Series

General Editor: George Venn
Managing Editor: Ulrich H. Hardt

Volume 5: Oregon Folk Literature

A project of the Oregon Council of Teachers of English

The Stories We Tell
An Anthology of Oregon Folk Literature

Suzi Jones & Jarold Ramsey

 Oregon State University Press
Corvallis, Oregon

Cover art: Detail from Beaded Bag, Plateau, Umatilla, c. 1915
Cover design: John Bennett
Text design: Jo Alexander
Permissions: Susanne Shotola
Art photographer: Susan Seubert

The paper in this book meets the guidelines for permanence and durability of the Committee on Production Guidelines for Book Longevity of the Council on Library Resources and the minimum requirements of the American National Standard for Permanence of Paper for Printed Library Materials Z39.48-1984.

Library of Congress Cataloging-in-Publication Data
Jones, Suzi.
    The stories we tell : an anthology of Oregon folk literature / Suzi Jones, Jarold Ramsey.
        p. cm. — (Oregon literature series ; v.5)
    Includes bibliographical references (p.) and index.
    ISBN 0-87071-379-5 (cloth : acid-free paper) —ISBN 0-87071-380-9 (paper : acid-free paper)
        1. Folklore—Oregon. 2. Folk literature, American—Oregon. 3. Tales—Oregon. I. Ramsey, Jarold, 1937- . II. Title. III. Series.
GR110.07J67 1994   94-5078
398.2'09795—dc20   CIP

Acknowledgments

Without steady collaboration by many individuals, agencies, and institutions, the *Oregon Literature Series* would never have appeared in print. We wish to recognize those who contributed support, time, and resources here—more or less in the order in which their contributions were received—and knowing even now that the real evidence of our gratitude lies open before all of them.

In 1986, the Executive Committee of the Oregon Council of Teachers of English (OCTE) began to discuss the idea of publishing a collection of Oregon literature. We wish to identify the members of that Executive Committee and thank them for their pioneering role: Lauri Crocker, Joe Fitzgibbon, Robert Hamm, Ulrich Hardt, Michelann Ortloff, and Ed Silling. Under then-OCTE President Ulrich Hardt, the Publications Committee was given the goal to further develop the idea of a state-based literary collection.

In 1988-89, the Executive Board of OCTE approved the pilot study by George Venn which became the *Oregon Literature Series*. We would like to recognize the members of that distinguished professional group of teachers by listing them here: Brian Borton, Sister Helena Brand, Suzanne Clark, Darlene Clarridge, Elaine Cockrell, Edna De Haven, Joe Fitzgibbon, Robert Boyt Foster, David Freitag, Debra Gaffney, Tim Gillespie, Irene Golden, Robert Hamm, Ulrich H. Hardt, Martha House, Ilene Kemper, Debbie LaCroix, Bill Mull, Thomas Nash, Debby Norman, Michelann Ortloff, Phyllis Reynolds, Eldene Ridinger, Mei-Ling Shiroishi, Andy Sommer, Daune Spritzer, Kim Stafford, Lana Stanley, Kathy Steward, Paul Suter, Nathaniel Teich, Linda Vanderford, George Venn, Michael Wendt, and Barbara Wolfe. Many members of that board gave many extra hours to reviewing the design, editorial guidelines, rationale, and budgets for that pilot project and other documents.

We would also like to acknowledge the following individuals from Oregon's literary and humanities community who reviewed the pilot proposal, made valuable suggestions, and gave their endorsement in 1988 to the idea of a collection of the best Oregon writing: Richard Lewis, Oregon Council for the Humanities; Brian Booth, Oregon Institute of Literary Arts; Peter Sears, Oregon Arts Commission; Jo Alexander, Oregon State University Press; Bruce Hamilton, Oregon Historical Society. OCTE President in 1988, Tim Gillespie, and Joe Fitzgibbon, OCTE President Elect, also reviewed the pilot proposal and made important contributions not only in these early stages but throughout the project.

When we presented the completed proposal for the *Oregon Literature Series* to the Editorial Board of Oregon State University Press in 1989, they broke with all precedent by signing a guaranteed publication contract and by agreeing to turn over editorial control of the content of the *Oregon Literature Series* to OCTE editors and appointees. We want to thank both press editors, Jeff Grass and Jo Alexander, and the members of that board who voted unanimously in favor of this project: Pat Brandt, Larry Boersma, Richard Maxwell Brown, Bill Denison, Gordon Dodds, Mike Strelow, Dave Perry, Sandy Ridlington, and the late Marilyn Guin. Without their vote for collaboration and its implicit vote of confidence in us, we would have found it difficult to continue this project.

Our first financial support beyond OCTE was provided by a pilot grant from Eastern Oregon State College, School of Education. Specifically, we wish to thank Deans Jens Robinson, Gerald Young, and James Hottois for their willingness to grant a sabbatical and three years of part-time appointments to George Venn so that this project could be undertaken. At Portland State University, we want to thank Dean Robert

Everhart, School of Education, for his steadfast support. He granted Ulrich Hardt a sabbatical to help launch the project, and he continued that support throughout the four years of the project. At Portland State University, we also want to acknowledge Interim Provost Robert Frank and Provost Michael Reardon for the faith they showed in the project by assigning graduate assistant Susanne Shotola to help us.

When we drafted our "Call for Editors" in 1989, we received helpful critiques from Kim Stafford, Edwin Bingham, Paul Suter, Sister Helena Brand, Edna DeHaven, Daune Spritzer, Lana Stanley, Michelann Ortloff, as well as other members of the OCTE Executive Board. When it was time to mail that "Call for Editors" to all Oregon libraries, newspapers, and other regional and national media, Lana Stanley assisted us. When it was time to select Volume Editors, these Publications Committee members assisted us: Robert Hamm, Marti House, Ilene Kemper, Debbie LaCroix, Mei-Ling Shiroishi, Michael Wendt, and Linda Vanderford. We'd like to thank them for the many hours they gave to evaluating the applications of 130 highly qualified individuals from Oregon and across the U.S. who applied for or were nominated for editorships.

When we needed to verify that these anthologies would, indeed, be both needed and used in the public schools, Portland State University School of Business Administration faculty member Bruce Stern gave us important assistance in designing a survey instrument which demonstrated a clear demand for the *Oregon Literature Series* in Oregon schools and homes. When we needed public relations expertise during editorial appointments, Pat Scott in the Portland State University Public Relations Office provided it.

When we needed legal advice, Leonard DuBoff and his firm of Warren, Allan, King, and O'Hara were more than helpful in contributing their contractual expertise.

As the project began to take a clear and definite shape in 1989, we received formal endorsements from these individuals whose confidence in the project made it possible to continue in spite of meager funding: Wes Doak, Oregon State Librarian, and Director, Center for the Book; Brian Booth, Director of Oregon Institute of Literary Arts; Kim Stafford, Director of the Northwest Writing Institute at Lewis and Clark College; Jennifer Hagloch, President of the Oregon Museums Association; Richard Lewis, Executive Director, Oregon Council for the Humanities; Joanne Cowling, President of the Eastern Oregon Library Association; Leslie Tuomi, Executive Director of the Oregon Arts Commission; Peter Sears, Oregon Arts Commission; Michael K. Gaston, President, Oregon Library Association; John Erickson, State Superintendent of Public Instruction; Carolyn Meeker, Chair, Oregon Arts Commission; Carolyn Lott, Chair, National Council of Teachers of English (NCTE) Committee on Affiliates; Shirley Haley-James, president-elect of NCTE; William Stafford, Oregon's past poet laureate; and Terry Melton, Director of the Western States Arts Foundation.

Essential financial support after 1989 came first from a generous allocation by the OCTE Executive Board. Later, we received modest one-time contributions from the Oregon Center for the Book and the Jackson Foundation. We would also like to state that this project was made possible—in part—by two minor grants from the Oregon Arts Commission.

Our sustaining patrons in the final three years (1990-93) of the project have been five; each of them contributed amounts in five figures so that the *Oregon Literature Series* could be completed in a timely and professional manner: (1) the OCTE Executive Board, who sustained and underwrote us when regional foundations failed us; (2) the Oregon Council for the Humanities, an affiliate of the National Endowment for the Humanities, which made and honored an exemplary three-year commitment ably administered by Robert Keeler; however, no funds from NEH or OCH were used to support volume 5, Oregon Folk Literature; (3) the National Endowment for the Arts, Literature Program, which assisted us at a time when we had been sent begging by all but one of the private foundations in Oregon; (4) Portland State University, which granted multi-year support for graduate assistant Susanne Shotola to help with the many details of the publication of this six-volume series; (5) Oregon State University Press, where Jo Alexander and Jeff Grass contributed the vital tasks agreed to in 1989—designing, printing, and distributing these volumes. OSU Press set a national precedent by becoming the first university press in the United States to publish a multi-volume, comprehensive collection of a state's literature in the same state as the university press.

When we came to recommending graphics and cover designs for the *Oregon Literature Series* in 1992, we welcomed the generous and expert advice of three of Oregon's most knowledgeable art historians: Ron Crosier, Portland Public Schools; Gordon Gilkey, Curator, Portland Art Museum; and Nancy Lindburg, arts consultant and former staff member of the Oregon Arts Commission. Some of the works they recommended were selected by them from the slide inventory in Oregon's Percent for Art in Public Places Program. Other works were chosen from the Gordon and Vivian Gilkey Collection of Prints and Drawings at the Oregon Art Institute, and from the Institute's collection of photographs. Petroglyph images were provided by James L. Hansen from sites flooded by The Dalles dam. In addition to those three individuals, we were also fortunate to attract the services of John Bennett, book designer and publisher at Gardyloo Press in Corvallis, who collaborated on all features of the graphic design, and created covers for these volumes.

No literary project of this magnitude can be accomplished without skillful and reliable staff. The General and Managing Editors would like to express their profound appreciation to Susanne Shotola and Barbara Wiegele—both of Portland State University—for their patient, professional, and timely attention to thousands of pages of details during the past four years: keeping accurate records, handling all permissions and finances, doing all the copying, typing, and mailing. We thanked them during the project and here we want to thank them again.

Unfortunately, this naming of our benefactors will be incomplete. We cannot list here all of those writers, families, and institutions who waived permissions fees, those innumerable librarians, archivists, storytellers, and historians who have safeguarded many of these pieces of writing for more than 100 years, those many who sent us notes of encouragement, those members of the public press who considered this project worthy of coverage. What we can say, however, is that every contribution moved us one page closer to the volume you now hold in your hands. Those others who failed us when we needed them most—they may eat—well?—cake?

Finally, George Venn would like to thank his wife, Elizabeth, who has tolerated great financial sacrifice for four years and who has begun to wonder about this tough, miserly Oregon muse her husband seems to have been serving at the expense of his art and her budget. Also, Ulrich Hardt would like to thank his wife, Eleanor, for her insights and interest in this project as Social Studies Specialist for Portland Public Schools, and for being more patient than could have been expected and tolerant of being alone many evenings and weekends while he was occupied with editorial responsibilities.

Ulrich Hardt, Managing Editor   *George Venn, General Editor*
Portland State University   *Grande Ronde Valley, Oregon*
Portland and Stuttgart
               September 1992

Editors' Acknowledgments

One of the special gratifications of working with folklore and oral literature is the generosity and camaraderie of those who share a love of such things—and in editing this collection we have been greatly helped and fortified in our work by many generous people, in Oregon and beyond. If we had space to tell it, the story behind *The Stories We Tell* would be mainly a cheering tale of sound advice, constructive criticism, and support given to us by friends and interested strangers: may they recognize their contributions here, in the book's strengths!

Early on, the project profited from the attentions of members of our editorial advisory committee for this volume: Walter Bolton, Prineville; Keith Clark, Redmond; Joanne Mulcahy, Portland; Lynn Sconchin, Chiloquin; Twilo Scofield, Eugene; Cynthia Stowell, Portland; Donald Tyree, Portland, Elizabeth Woody, Portland; and Julie Quaid, Warm Springs. At every stage, our colleagues and fellow editors in the *Oregon Literature Series*—Shannon Applegate, Stephen Dow Beckham, Gordon Dodd, Glen Love, Terence O'Donnell, Primus St. John, and Ingrid Wendt—have helped us with new leads and wise queries. They have been a grand editorial brain-trust, with a wonderful joint wealth of Oregon erudition and savvy to place at the disposal of each volume in the series. For this happy editorial arrangement and for many other advantages along the way, we are deeply indebted to George Venn, General Editor of the Series, and to Ulrich Hardt, Managing Editor: "Theirs the dream, and theirs the road to build whereon to reach it."

The range and diversity of the materials in this book would surely have suffered without the help of many individuals who came forward as sources and sources-of-sources, notably Louie Attebery, Gordon Bettles, Brian Booth, Olivia Cadaval, Hal Cannon, Eva Castellanoz, Edwin Coleman, Jan deWeese, Ed Edmo, Janet Gilmore, Meg Glazer, Archie Green, Sunny Hancock, Bess Hockema, Dell and Virginia Hymes, Paula Johnson, Jody Lorimer, Jens Lund, Dan Macy Sr., Steven Martin, Robert McCarl, Judith McCulloh, Darrell Millner, Cecil C. Moore, Nancy Moore, Leslie Ramsey, Robert Sayers, John Scharff, Dolores Helfrich Scott, Steve Siporin, Gary Snyder, Kim Stafford, the late William Stafford, Theodore Stern, Jim Strassmaier, Caryn Throop, George Wasson, Susan Wasson Wolgamott, Roger Weaver. We would also like to thank Daniel Sheehy and Twilo Scofield for their assistance with musical transcriptions and Norma Cantú for help with *corrido* translation.

In addition, the editors would also like acknowledge the generous assistance of the staff of several archives and libraries in helping us locate stories: Nancy Nusz and the staff of the Oregon Folk Art program; Sharon Sherman, Bill Goldsmith, Carol Lichtenstein, and Brennan Washburn of the Randall V. Mills Archives of Northwest Folklore, Department of English, University of Oregon; Barre Toelken and Barbara Walker, Fife Folklore Archives, Utah State University; Joseph Hickerson, Archive of the American Folklife Center, Washington, DC; Alden Mobers and the staff at the Oregon State Library Archives; and the staff at the Oregon State Historical Society Library and Archives. Our thanks to one and all.

For encouraging her to listen to the stories we tell and teaching her to recognize their importance in literature and in life, Suzi Jones would like to thank her first teachers of folklore, Louie Attebery of the College of Idaho and Barre Toelken, then at the University of Oregon, now at Utah State University.

Finally, on the grounds that gratitude like charity ought to begin and end at home, Suzi Jones would like to thank her parents, Genevieve and Wallis Jones, her brother and sister-in-law, Charles and Susan Jones, and her nieces, McKenna and Kakki—who always have lots of good stories. Jarold Ramsey would like to thank his mother, Wilma Mendenhall Ramsey, his brother and sister-in-law, Jim and Diane Ramsey, his children Kate, Sophia, and John, and especially his wife Dorothy, whose patient support warrants a story all its own. Let me tell you . . .

Contents

Oregon's Folk Heroes and Characters

Tales of Hunting and Fishing

Coyote and Other Tricksters

General Introduction

The idea for the *Oregon Literature Series*, six anthologies of the best Oregon writing, was first proposed to the Oregon Council of Teachers of English (OCTE) in 1988. At that time, OCTE decided to depart from the conventional state literary anthology—a monolithic tome put together by a few academic volunteers and generally intended for libraries and adult readers. Instead, OCTE decided to create six shorter, genre-based anthologies: prose, poetry, autobiography, folk literature, letters and diaries, and short fiction. OCTE would publish a public "Call for Editors," and the most qualified individuals would be hired for their expertise and treated professionally—honoraria, expenses, research assistance, travel, etc. The anthologies would be intended as classroom/reference texts for students and teachers, and as introductory readers for the general public. Books would be designed to be easily held, carried, and read.

Numerous arguments were raised against this innovative proposal—most of them signaling Oregon's 150-year status as a literary colony. *No one had ever done this before. Oregon's literature was non-existent. There wasn't much writing of merit. Most scholars and critics have ignored Oregon literature—even in the best histories of Western literature. There's no literary history of Oregon. It will take years to find this work. In Oregon, literature has the least financial support of all the major arts. We had no publisher. It might rain.*

Nevertheless, in 1989, Ulrich Hardt and I were appointed by OCTE to complete the *Oregon Literature Series*. The work began when we signed a publication contract with Oregon State University Press, our first and most important professional collaborator. Next, from a pool of 130 applicants, OCTE chose these editors to discover Oregon's literary heritage: Shannon Applegate, Stephen Dow Beckham, Gordon B. Dodds, Primus St. John, Suzi Jones, Glen A. Love, Terence O'Donnell, Jarold Ramsey, and Ingrid Wendt. Appointed in August 1990, those individuals began the search for Oregon writing that eventually spread beyond every corner of the state—from ranch houses to university archives, from oral storytellers in longhouses to Chinese miners in museums, from Desdemona Sands to Burns. Some editors traveled thousands of miles. Others corresponded with hundreds of authors. Most read thousands of pages. Poets, historians, folklorists, critics, scholars, teachers, and editors—they all benefited from and shared their research expertise. Even though honoraria were small, editors gave generously of their time. While the editors looked for Oregon writing, Ulrich Hardt and I sought out and received endorsements from many major cultural and arts organizations. Financial support was like rain in the time of drought, but we attracted a few wise, faithful, and generous patrons, as the Acknowledgments record.

Once the editors had discovered this vast, unstudied, and unknown body of writing, they assembled their manuscripts by using the following guidelines—guidelines that required them to choose writing—in its broadest sense—that might reveal the Oregon experience to both students and the public:

1. The volume must include a representative sample of the best Oregon writing from all periods, regions, occupations, genders, genres and sub-genres, ethnic, religious, political, and cultural backgrounds.

2. Oregon birth should not be used as a single criterion for inclusion. Oregon residence is important, but no arbitrary length of stay is required for a writer to be included.

3. Works about experience in Oregon are preferred, but editors are not limited to that criterion alone.

4. "Oregon" will be defined by its changing historical boundaries—Native American tribal territories, Spanish, Russian, British, U.S. Territory, statehood.

5. One or more translations and original from non-English languages should be included when appropriate to show that linguistic multiplicity has always been a part of Oregon.

6. Controversial subjects such as sexism and racism should not be avoided. Multiple versions of events, people, and places should be included when available.

7. Length of works must vary; limit the number of snippets when possible. Meet the need for diversity in reading, from complex to simple.

8. New, unknown, or unpublished work should be included.

9. Works will be edited for clarity but not necessarily for correctness. Editors may invent titles, delete text, and select text as appropriate and with appropriate notation.

Once assembled in draft, most of these manuscripts were two to three times longer than could be published by Oregon State University Press, therefore much fine writing had to be omitted, which all editors and our publisher regret. After being reduced to the requisite size, the manuscripts passed through two separate reviews: first, a different Advisory Board for each volume read and rated all selections; second, the Editorial Board composed of all fellow editors read, responded, and eventually voted to adopt the manuscript for publication. At all stages, both Ulrich Hardt and I worked closely with editors in many ways: readers, critics, fundraisers, administrators, arbitrators, secretaries, grant writers, researchers, coordinators, pollsters.

Now, we hope that these books will create for Oregon literature a legitimate place in Oregon schools and communities, where the best texts that celebrate, invent, evaluate, and illuminate the Oregon condition have been invisible for too long. Here, for the first time, students will have books that actually include writing by Oregonians; teachers can find original, whole, local, and authentic texts from all regions, periods, and peoples in the state; librarians will be able to recommend the best reading to their patrons; the new reader and the general reader can find answers to the question that has haunted this project like a colonial ghost: "Who are Oregon's writers, anyway?"

Let it be known that an Oregon literary canon is forming—rich, diverse, compelling. Here we give this sample of it to you. Let your love of reading and writing endure.

George Venn, General Editor
Grande Ronde Valley, Oregon
September 1992

Oregon Folk Literature

Folk Literature and Oregon's Literary Heritage

This first anthology of Oregon folk literature bears a special relationship to the other five volumes in the *Oregon Literature Series*. For here, if we have done our job well, you will find examples of the kinds of cherished traditional stories and songs, myths, and sayings from many Oregon groups and communities that have nurtured and continue to nurture the state's best *writings*. In their distinctive styles, writers like H.L. Davis, Ken Kesey, William Stafford, Ursula Le Guin, Barry Lopez, and Beverly Cleary all owe much to what Oregonians have told and sung and kept in memory, in kitchens and sweat-lodges, on the range and on the street, in canneries and convention centers, in schools, bunkhouses, and funeral parlors.

Even if our oral traditions from Native American myths to jokes about the spotted owl were somehow declared off-limits to Oregon authors—*No Trespass!*—they would surely, at this point in our state's history, be worth collecting and enjoying anyway. But the happy fact is that what we call folk literature is like a fertile soil to the talents and imaginative ambitions of individual writers, just as surely in a place called Oregon as in places known as New York, Chicago, and Moscow. Read through this collection and see if it doesn't enhance your understanding and appreciation of what is distinctively "Oregonian" in Oregon's *written* literary heritage!

What Is Folk Literature?

Properly understood, folk literature is the collective traditional verbal art of a community (meaning any kind and size of grouping, from a rural or urban neighborhood, to a kind of occupation or work, to a linguistic or ethnic or racial community, to a geopolitical entity like Oregon). Folk literature usually entails *oral* performance and transmission—things told, recited, sung, from memory: myth-narratives, legends, tall tales, anecdotes, poems, ballads and song lyrics, jokes, proverbs and sayings, set-speeches, verbal rituals, word-games, and the like. *Literature* here specifies imaginative, evocative uses of language and the expression of subjective truths in conventional forms (ballads, origin myths, riddles, and so on); folk *history,* by contrast, seeks to document facts and circumstances relating to "the way it was." Not that the two forms of discourse don't sometimes overlap, of course: oral histories often contain examples of folk literature within them, and folk literature is often taken as a source of oral history, providing glimpses into the way people felt about "the way it was."

A community's folk literature is its distinctive way of talking to itself through time and change and of reaffirming its collective identity: "We are the people who know these stories and songs." Hence folk-literary repertories (the whole kit-and-caboodle of things to be told or sung) are likely to be *ethnocentric*—that is, they deal imaginatively with what the people know and care about habitually; everything else is foreign.

Thus, in the traditional Klamath creation myth, creation takes place around Klamath Lake—how other places, the High Desert or the Coast Range, say, came to be, are subjects for other people's mythologies. And when Eastern Oregonians tell stories about buck-feverish Portland hunters ("Burnsiders") bagging Holstein venison on Opening Day of deer season, they are likewise confirming the ethnocentric, culturally self-conscious tendencies of folk literature.

This is not to say, of course, that the elements of folklore are rigidly limited as to place or time. Quite the contrary—if folk tales weren't adaptable and subject to variation and adaptive change, then this anthology would lack all the expressively "Oregonized" versions of Scots-Irish, Hispanic, African-American, and other stories that we've brought here with us as newcomers. And for all the distinctiveness and exclusivity of Indian oral literatures, embedded as they have been in the state's twenty-plus Native languages, there is much over-lapping of story-types and episodes, both because tribes appropriated each other's stories through contact, and because some stories (like "The Star Husbands" and many Trickster episodes) are apparently so old that versions of them have been part of individual Indian cultures since they split off from some common parent culture.

Thus, because folk stories and songs figure intimately in people's lives on a local, daily, oral basis, entertaining, consoling, instructing them over the years, it is the very essence of folk literature to be *dynamic,* endlessly subject to variation. Through the flexible outlines of traditional stories, people can imagine the changes in their lives, as well as the continuities—as happens in the Basque story, "The Coyote, the Bear, and the Moon" (p.296), in which the Spanish-born storyteller has added a coyote from the Oregon desert to the traditional plot of his tale!

The eminent folklorist J. Barre Toelken (who lived and taught in Oregon for many years) argues that "all folklore participates in a distinctive, dynamic process. Constant change, variation within a tradition, whether intentional or inadvertent, is . . . a central fact of life for folklore" (*The Dynamics of Folklore,* p. 10).

How the Contents of This Book Were Selected

As editors, we agreed from the outset that the decision to include a book like this in the *Oregon Literature Series* created a wonderful set of opportunities to advance the study and recognition of Oregon's folklore—more opportunities, in fact, than any one volume could hope to realize, but maybe we could point a way. Consequently, we've sorted through haystacks and silos of printed and archival material, pestered friends and colleagues, harassed each other with possible leads (Ramsey concentrated on Native American materials, Jones on non-Indian, but there has been much crossing over), and gone back to look again.

What have we been looking for, in what now seems to us more than ever the embarrassment of riches that is our state's folklore? Mostly it has been those combinations of imaginative power and emotional truth conveyed in vivid language that mark the work of great novelists and great storytellers alike. We wanted texts that were verbally expressive and reasonably true to their origins in spoken performance, accessible to general readers, and, taken together, indicative of the varieties of Oregonian experience—racial and ethnic, bioregional, economic, sexual, and so on.

Here is as good a place as any to acknowledge that we have included some folk texts whose language and underlying attitudes may be offensive to modern readers, on racial, ethnic, or sexual grounds. No editorial offense is intended by such material—but surely it *is* important, in understanding where we have come from, to know what our Oregon forebears were capable of saying and telling. To omit once-popular stories from a collection like this because they contain expressions that we now rightly reject as racial insults or sexual slurs is to trivialize an important link with our past, when we should be endeavoring to grasp it whole, the better to avoid the prejudices and errors of those who came here before us.

We want to acknowledge, too, that as this collection is based largely on archival sources, it reflects their strengths and weaknesses. In particular, we have not been able to locate texts that reflect the full ethnic diversity of Oregon. We discovered that a much broader range of ethnic folklore has been collected and recorded in categories such as customs, popular beliefs, home remedies, and foodways than for any of the genres of folk literature. Undoubtedly, this situation reflects the nature of the complex relationship between language and literature, the history of native language retention by various immigrant groups in Oregon and the acquisition of the language by succeeding generations, as well as the short-term nature of many field collecting projects of university students, most of which have dealt with items of folklore that could be collected in English. Clearly, there is much more field work to be done in Oregon, and on a broader basis of race, ethnicity, and gender than heretofore.

In addressing the question of gender diversity in the anthology, we believe that we have assembled a fair representation of texts from and about both women and men, although we note that several thematic sections—heroes and characters, hunting and fishing, and the chapter on occupational folk literature—are predominantly male oriented. The latter section reflects the abundance of texts from those occupations traditionally associated with Oregon—logging, mining, fishing, and ranching. The relative scarcity of female-oriented texts here should not be taken as a sign that women did not work or tell stories as such, but only that few such stories have so far been recorded. This is an area of folklore study that should be receiving greater attention as a result of the emphasis on women's studies.

In sum: if both the strengths of this book and its limitations spur others—teachers and students, writers, local archivists, tribal historians—to go forth in pursuit of Oregon's oral traditions as they carry on today, right now, in Paulina and Portland, in retirement homes and offices and on playgrounds, we'll be gratified indeed. The poet William Carlos Williams, who chose to stay home and write in Rutherford, New Jersey, when most of his contemporaries were setting up as expatriates after World War I, once asserted that "the local is the only thing that is universal. The classic is the local fully realized, words marked by a place." ("Kenneth Burke," *Selected Essays,* p. 114) Whether or not these selections are "classics" of Oregon folk literature is not our concern, but we believe that their wordings are vividly marked by the places, physical and mental, of Oregon; and we believe, too, that as stories and songs they can only hint at the full richness of what Oregonians have told and sung to each other over the years.

How This Book Is Organized

Our editorial aim from the beginning has been to represent Oregon's folk literature heritage as fairly, accessibly, and accountably as possible, so that both general readers and members of the specific communities represented here can engage that heritage both as a vital, ongoing whole and in its parts.

Consequently, against the usual practice of presenting Indian and non-Indian oral materials separately, or of organizing traditions by ethnic groups, we have freely intermixed them throughout, in the hope that Native and non-Native, indigenous and immigrant traditions will "talk to each other"—as indeed they have throughout our state's history. Storytelling conventions do of course differ radically on some points, and we have tried to address these differences, so that they aren't blurred or ignored altogether. But knowledge of distinctive differences between these stories will, we hope, accentuate what they have in common, as "Oregon stories." The best way to read through this book, then, is *comparatively.*

Moreover, we have not arranged this collection strictly by genre, which would entail, for example, placing myths in one section and tall tales in another. While such an arrangement would be possible and would certainly highlight the forms of folk literature, we have chosen, instead, a thematic approach that focuses more directly on the expressive ways Oregon is represented in and by the stories, songs, and sayings. In some cases, we have clustered similar story types together, e.g., the Münchhausen tales of Hathaway Jones, B.F. Finn, and Tebo Ortego; and, in most cases, we have identified texts by genre. For those interested in the different genres of folk literature, we have included a brief glossary with the definitions of the genres.

The thirteen headings which divide the contents are mostly thematic categories, but they have not been imposed upon the material arbitrarily; instead, they have emerged naturally as we have sifted through the material. No doubt, readers will think of other categories and headings (an organization according to Oregon's *regions* would be workable), and, for sure, a collection of this kind of, say, New York or North Dakota folk literature would require a very different scheme of chapters. But for Oregon and its oral traditions as we have surveyed them, the best scheme turned out to be this one. And one of its virtues is that it should promote thematic and formal comparisons among the selections, and also between them and the examples of Oregon's written literature presented in other volumes in this series.

About Tellers and Tellings, Transcriptions, Translations, and Texts

As instances of folk literature, nearly all of the selections in this book are *transcriptions*—renderings in print—of originals which traditionally have existed wholly in oral performance, constantly being recomposed out of memory for different occasions and audiences, every performance thus likely to be different from every other. So to find them here mostly in neat written English sentences and paragraphs, looking like short stories in standard English, can be very misleading. Yet to read these pieces carefully (best of all, to read them aloud) is to rediscover at least something of their origins in colloquial speech, as indicated by emphasis on dialogue, evocative sound-effects, the kinds of narrative repetition-with-change that all good storytellers rely on, dramatic creation of scenes in place of elaborate description, and so on. We have tried where possible to avoid texts in which such oral features have been "written off," as in summaries,texts edited into standard English, and self-consciously "literary" retellings—but inevitably there is a wide range of presentational styles here, from the rather literary "rewritten" texts from the WPA folklore files to the stenographic roughness and immediacy of more modern folkloric transcriptions, like those taken from the Randall Mills Archives, and Theodore Stern's transcript of Lulu Lang's telling of the Klamath story "Lulu'laidi" (see p. 220).

The headnote for each text will indicate its source and to what extent it reflects an oral performance.

In many of our selections, of course—from Native American tradition, and also from Hispanic and other non-English sources—the texts are the product not only of transcription but of *translation* as well. The Italians have a dour proverb that to translate something is to betray its essential meaning—but we have been zealous to include only scholarly, accountable translations. The work of Dell Hymes on Clackamas and other Chinookan stories is worth noting here. Not only has Hymes's long, patient work on Chinookan languages enabled him to make superb new translations of the Clackamas stories that Victoria Howard told to Melville Jacobs in 1929-30, but it has also led to the development of new ways of presenting these texts in English as a kind of dramatic poetry, corresponding to the poetically measured forms of the originals. (See pp. 34-42 and 258-260) Indeed, Hymes, Dennis Tedlock, and other scholars and poets in the ethnopoetic movement have questioned whether what we recognize as prose adequately conveys any form of oral performance—in any language.

Wherever possible, we have identified the tellers whose voices (and gestures and facial expressions!) brought these texts into existence. We have done so not only to serve the needs of scholarship, and to give credit where credit is due, but also to counter a common misconception about oral/traditional literature and its human sources: that the latter are merely "informants," only passive vehicles of unchanging tradition, and that the art of folk tales lies mainly, impersonally in the traditions, and hardly at all in the narrators. Anybody lucky enough to have heard and seen Lulu Lang of Chiloquin or Tebo Ortego of French Glen or Reub Long of Fort Rock or Verbena Greene of Warm Springs, knows how wrong-headed this notion is, in denying artistic authority to the tellers. Degrees of skill and creative originality differ widely, of course, and no doubt the stories in this collection reflect such differences and inequalities—but the fact remains that it is the artistry and imaginative generosity of storytellers that has kept Oregon's folk literature alive in people's minds all these years.

A Note on Reading Traditional Indian Stories

Like all the selections in this book, the traditional Indian stories presented here originally lived in local oral *tellings*—first, perhaps for thousands of years, in Oregon's Native languages, like Wasco Chinookan, Klamath, and Nez Perce Sahaptin, and then, more uncertainly, in English. As printed texts to be read, Indian stories may seem at first reading at times cryptic, abrupt, puzzling—and indeed like all traditional folktales they often do assume "insider" cultural information that as "outsiders" we don't possess. Thus, to take just one example, in the Klamath creation story (p. 2), all Klamath listeners would know without being told that the setting is Klamath Lake, and that the tribes named at the end were the Klamaths' traditional neighbors. Such information is often available in anthropological studies known as *ethnographies*—systematic descriptions of individual Indian cultures. For the Klamaths, two such works are Leslie Spier's *Klamath Ethnography* (1930), and Theodore Stern's *The Klamath Tribe* (1965). A full listing of ethnographic sources for Oregon Native groups can be found in J. Ramsey, "Resource Bibliography for the Study of Native Americans," pp. 62-67.

Very often, traditional Indian stories puzzle readers because, in obeying Native literary conventions and "rules," they don't behave like Euro-American narratives. We need more "literary ethnography" than we now have, certainly, but keeping the following conventions in mind will help you to understand and enjoy Native stories like those offered in this collection:

•Indian myths and stories are *not* to be conceived of as "children's stories"—although often they are very appealing to children's imaginations. In their original settings, they were told to and enjoyed by all ages together.

•Many Indian narratives are *myths*, dealing with the beginnings of the world, and thus set in a "Myth Age," when reality was still unfinished, and crucial precedents good and bad were being set for the real People yet to come, by figures like Coyote as they traveled around. Often in myths, sacred happenings occur in very earthy, even (we might be tempted to say) obscene circumstances, notably when Old Man Coyote is involved. The strict separation of "sacred" and "profane" in Judeo-Christian culture is not recognized in traditional Indian cultures: not that their devotion to the sacred is any less strong than with Anglos, but that sacredness to them is very much connected to earthly life and the here and now.

•Like all oral narratives, Indian storytelling relies insistently on *repetition*. Important events happen in sequences of repetition, building up to the "last time," which is decisive—generally, the number of repetitions is five, because five is the sacred or ceremonial number for most of Oregon's Native groups.

• Especially in translation, the presentational style of Indian stories tends to be sparse, unelaborated, more dramatic (emphasizing dialogue) and less descriptive than in Anglo narratives.

• Characterization in these stories tends to be conventional rather than innovative or individualized; stock characters like Coyote (trickster and transformer), Eagle (right-thinking leader), Grizzly Bear (unpredictable, dangerous), and Raccoon (spoiled brat) appear and reappear throughout a tribe's repertory of stories. Tricksters like Coyote (over much of Oregon), Kamukamts (Klamath and Modoc), and South Wind (Tillamook) are central figures in Indian storytelling. Reckless, self-seeking, and capable of anything, from shabby tricks that often backfire to important deeds like freeing the salmon in the Columbia River, when Coyote and his kind turn up in a story, "the plot thickens."

• Apart from what they say, characters' emotions usually must be inferred from the situation. Motivation is often left undefined; action is more important than motive. In general, Natives who knew their tribe's whole "mythbody" (as the Nez Perce scholar Archie Phinney called it) from childhood on, undoubtedly had a much richer and more subtle understanding of characters in the stories than we can have, knowing only a few of their exploits.

But despite such cultural differences and difficulties, Oregon's Indian story-heritage *is* accessible to study and enjoyment, if we use our wits. What's the imagination for, if not to find out understanding and kinship in difference? It helps that these Indian stories—many of them probably very ancient—are located imaginatively in Oregon landscapes we still know and love today; it also helps that gifted Indian writers like Elizabeth Woody, Ed Edmo, Gloria Bird, Vince Wannassay, and Phil George are adapting the old Oregon stories to new realities in their work—proving the continuing vitality and relevance of Oregon's share of what has been rightly called "the first American literature."

Late in his life, the pioneer folklorist Jeremiah Curtin could still recall the awe he felt in 1884 on hearing the stories of an elderly Modoc woman named Koalak'aka or "Hard Working Woman": "She had more stories in her head than I dreamed it possible for anyone to learn and keep without aid of books." (*The Memoirs of Jeremiah Curtin*, p. 335). Let Koalak'aka and what Curtin calls her "tenacious memory" stand for all Oregon tale-spinners, then and now, with wonderful stories in their heads to tell—and let this be a book to celebrate their tellings.

J.R., Rochester/Madras
S.J., Washington D.C./Ontario

This Place
Is Home

One way we make ourselves at home in a region is by telling stories about it—about its climate, its weather, its landmarks and wildlife, and the expressive ways people react to these "natural features." The territory that is now the State of Oregon is remarkably diverse environmentally, and in each of the following stories and songs from Native American and European-American settlers' traditions, the main character is really the *setting*: whether the Oregon coast, with its fogs and storms, or the game-rich marshes and hills around Klamath Lake, the rainy terrain of the Willamette Valley or the high desert country east of the Cascade Mountains. What was new country to cope with to early European-American settlers, of course, was a richly storied and familiar landscape to Oregon's Indians, but in their different ways both the state's first inhabitants and those who came later vividly exercised their imaginations on the features of the land where they lived, and thus made it "home." Reflecting an intimate sense of place, these narratives are expressions of local knowledge—and attitude— and so we may read them as well for what they reveal of the character of Oregon's peoples and how they understood their relationship to the land. They are a good place to begin.

Cornhusk Bag. Early twentieth century, Plateau, maker unknown. Hemp, cotton, string, cornhusk, and yarn.

Creation of the Klamath Country

In this creation myth, told by S'mausic, "Long Wilson," to Edward Curtis around 1920, the main features of the Klamaths' world are laid down for all time, through a genial competition between Kamukamts (the Klamath Trickster/Creator) and Pocket Gopher. The real winners of this contest are the Klamath people, who by the end of the story are already living the good life in their bountiful homeland around Klamath Lake.—From Edward Curtis, *The North American Indian*, Vol. 13, p. 210.

There was no land, only a great lake. Kamukamts came from the north in a canoe. It floated along. It stopped. He shook it, but could not move it. He looked down, and in the water he saw the roof of a house. It was the house of Pocket Gopher. Gopher looked up. Then Kamukamts went down into the house, and they talked.

Kamukamts said, "You had better be thinking of what is the best thing to do."

"Yes, I am thinking of that now," replied Gopher.

"If you can plan anything better than I can do, you shall be the elder brother," promised Kamukamts. "What kind of food are we going to have?"

Gopher opened his mouth to yawn, and fish, roots, and berries came forth.

"It seems that you will be the elder brother," said Kamukamts.

That night Gopher caused his companion to sleep, and he burrowed under the bottom of the lake and made it bulge up into hills and mountains, which raised their tops above the surface. In the morning he said, "You had better go and look around!" When Kamukamts went out he was astonished. Gopher asked what should become of his house, and Kamukamts replied, "It will always remain as the oldest mountain [Modoc Point]."

"What will our children have for amusement?" asked Kamukamts. They played the game of throwing spears at a mark. They threw them, and their targets were hills. Kamukamts's spear knocked off the top of Bare Island, and so it is today. Then they invented all the other games.

Gopher asked, "What will live on the mountains?"

"Mountain lions, bears, elk, deer." Kamukamts named all the animals, both beasts and birds.

"What will grow in the mountains?" asked Gopher.

"I will walk over the earth and see what I can do," replied Kamukamts. So he went about and selected homes for the different tribes, and in each territory he placed something which was to characterize that particular tribe, such as obsidian in the Paiute country, marble in the Shasta country, and tules in the Klamath country. Then he looked about and saw smoke.

Kamukamts said, "What is the matter, I wonder? I see smoke here and there."

And Gopher replied, "You have beaten me. You are the elder brother." For he knew that the smoke was from the fires of people brought into being by Kamukamts. They listened, and heard the sound of people talking, and of children laughing and playing. The people increased very rapidly, and the animals and plants on the mountains multiplied.

The Origin of Black Butte, Medicine Rock, Eagle Rock, and Mt. Jefferson

Natural landmarks on and around the present Warm Springs Reservation are mythically established in this Wasco/Warm Springs story about War Eagle's troubles as a lover. Such narratives don't serve to "explain" natural features so much as to *locate* them imaginatively and morally in story-form. This earliest recorded version of the story was told by Donald McKay, a Wasco military scout and medicine show performer, in English around 1900 (McKay Papers, Pendleton Library). The story is still known and told today on the Warm Springs Reservation.

There was a young fellow living in Te-ni-no who did not think there was a being on earth like himself and that there was only one woman on the face of the globe good enough for him to marry. This was a young woman who lived in the south at a place known as Mt. Shasta.

Woman after woman had been to see this young warrior but without avail. Finally this young woman from the south made up her mind to journey to this great man, and as was the custom the bride took with her great quantities of berries which they called sal-lal and quantities of nuts, fish, and dried meats. She also brought with her what they called *o-wont*, which is a pearlshell of great value to the Indians.

After journeying the great distance and encountering many difficulties she arrived at this young warrior's tent at night, which she entered and waked him. On discovering it to be a woman and supposing it to be one of the many who were always after him, he drove her off and as she went away crying, her tears dropped in the shape and form of the valuable *o-wont*. He, on waking in the morning, discovered from these pearls that the only woman he had ever loved had been to his bedside and he had driven her away. He immediately buckled on his bow, arrows, and shield and drum and started on her trail.

After journeying for several days he discovered her when he arrived at what is now known as the Warm Springs Agency. She being at Um-ba-net Mountain, he became disgusted and wished the mountain to disappear, and when he threw down his shield and drum [they] turned into stone and [are] now known as Medicine Rock. Seeing he could not get her he wished her to turn to stone, which she did right where she was, and she is now known as Black Butte.

On this mountain you will find all kinds of sal-lal which she carried, and nuts and game. On this mountain you will always find berries where there is not a berry for miles around. To this day on this mountain you will find the head-waters of the swift river which is called Ma-don-ias [Metolius] (which means the place where the fish try to work their tails in the crevices of the rocks), and the water flowing from the crevices is supposed to be the water flowing from her body.

Another woman, thinking to be revenged for this War Eagle's folly, journeyed from the south and on arriving at Wish-ram opposite Te-ni-no on the Columbia River (which was their great sporting grounds where the different tribes met once a year and gambled and raced after the old Indian fashion) she looked across the river to the table-land for War Eagle. Instead, Grey Eagle, his brother, saw her and knowing she came to marry his brother he went up to her saying he was expecting her, so [he] took her to the table-land above, to what is known as Bed Rock, where they lay together as was the marriage custom.

War Eagle, knowing that it was time for her to come, got uneasy and commenced hunting for her, at which Grey Eagle got scared and taking his new bride flew away. War Eagle, knowing that some trick had been played on him, pursued them and the farther he went the more angry he grew until he discovered them when he arrived at Mutton Mountain. He wished them to turn into mountains which they did, she becoming Mt. Jefferson and Grey Eagle, Eagle Rock, or as the Indians call it, Pattu-pattu, which means smaller of the two. As you stand and look at this rock you can see the top covered with snow and ice, and under his wings it is always warm and no snow or ice can stay there.

Oregon as Paradise

One theme that runs through many Oregon texts is the notion of Oregon as a paradise. Literally a "promised land" for pioneers, Oregon became as well the promised land in a metaphorical sense, and the verdant Willamette Valley evoked the Garden of Eden. We know that early land developers promoted Oregon as "paradise," but it's also true that the Willamette Valley must have truly seemed like paradise to those who had trudged across so many miles of less hospitable territory en route, and their feelings are reflected in song, story, and saying.

The WPA Oregon Folklore Project contains several pieces from Oregon newspapers that convey the theme of Oregon as paradise. The first is from the *Corvallis Gazette* (August 11, 1882), and the second anecdote was found in the *Arlington Record* (October 13, 1904).

The following was written on an immigrant wagon which was passing through La Grande recently:

> In God we trusted,
> In Nebraska we busted,
> And now we are bound for the promised land.

❈ ❈ ❈

An editor dreamed that he died and, of course, went to heaven and seeing a man chained to a post inquired if it was necessary to punish people that way in heaven. "That man," said St. Peter, "is from Oregon. We always have to keep Oregonians chained up for a while in order to keep them from going back."

Abraham "Oregon" Smith in the "Land of Milk and Honey"

When many in the Midwest were catching the "Oregon Fever," Abraham Smith left his farm near Bloomfield, Illinois, about 1852 and headed for Oregon. In Illinois, newspapers were full of propaganda about Oregon, the "land that flows with milk and honey." Smith farmed and practiced medicine for several years in Linn County, but in 1859 he moved back to Indiana, where he quickly gained notoriety as "Oregon" Smith for the stories he told about the wonders of Oregon. "Oregon" Smith was a marvelous taleteller—some would say "liar." In fact, several recall that he was "churched," called to account in a regular church trial for his "lies" about Oregon. The stories of Abraham "Oregon" Smith circulated widely and were later collected by folklorist William Hugh Jansen for his study, *Abraham "Oregon" Smith: Pioneer, Folk Hero, and Tale Teller.* This information and these tales from Smith's much larger repertoire are from Jansen.

Oh, yes, he had lots of stories about Oregon . . . . He used to tell how big the potatoes grew out there in Oregon. He raised lots of them, boatloads of them, in fact. His potato field was on an incline leading down to a river where he had a boat tied up along the bank. Those potatoes grew to the size of your head— or a gallon bucket, Abe would say. He'd say, "We wouldn't even bother to pick them up if they were the size they grow back here [Illinois]." How'd he gather them? Well, he'd dig them up, but instead of sacking them, he'd just roll them down the hill to his boat. (Albert Wilkin, Vermilion, IL, February 18, 1947, pp. 295-296)

He used to claim that out in Oregon the pumpkins grew so big that all you had to do was cut holes in the ends, hollow them out, and you could make barns out of them. He said the corn grew so high in Oregon that you had to use a ladder to climb up to reach the ears, and each of them was three feet long. (Harry A. Axtell, July 1944, pp. 294-295)

Oregon trees grew so tall that an eagle in the top branches looked like an English sparrow. Oregon fish grew so large that a trout was liable to reverse the usual procedure and pull a fisherman into the river. Oregon rabbits grew so powerful that hunting dogs were often accidentally killed by a rabbit's kick. (B. W. Bradfute, August 23, 1944, pp. 296-297)

Now, I never heard these stories told by Oregon himself, but everyone told Oregon's tales. This was one I was told as a boy, or a young man maybe. In Oregon, he never had to worry about butter. There was a cataract [waterfall] in the river near Oregon's cabin where the buffalo would rush across the river. A little milk would leak out, you know, and it would get churned at the bottom of the cataract, and then Smith would go and collect it a little at a time whenever he needed it. (Will I. Fee, Bloomington, January 9, 1947, p. 224)

Oregon Suits Me

Closely related to the theme of Oregon as paradise is the theme of the self-satisfied Oregonian. Here, in lyrics to be sung to the tune of "The Battle Hymn of the Republic," the narrator, an emigrant from Missouri via Kansas and North Dakota, has at last found satisfaction in Oregon. This song, from the Pacific Northwest Farm Quad Collection 345, Fife Folklore Archives, is one of many folksongs submitted to an "Old Songs" column of *The Farmer,* a magazine published in several western states.

I have lived in old Missouri,
    In that good old show-me state;
Where they feed you on corn dodgers,
    Buttermilk and sweet potates.
I have lived 'way out in Kansas,
    On the broad and rolling plain—
        But Oregon suits me.

Chorus:
    I am satisfied with Oregon,
    I am satisfied with Oregon,
    I am satisfied with Oregon,
    The good old webfoot state.

I have lived in North Dakota,
    Where the thunders rip and roar,
Where the wind is never silent,
    And there's ice and frost galore;
Where you have to stoke the heaters
    Fully half a year or more—
        But Oregon suits me.

Oregon Land

Orlo Flock

This folk song made its way across North America with the settlers, its lyrics changing to fit the circumstances and discomforts of pioneer life. Sung to the tune of the familiar hymn, "Beulah Land," which depicts the fertile wealth of heaven, these parodies offered an ironic comment on the often less than heavenly realities of the "promised land" in places such as Kansas, South Dakota, New Mexico, and Oregon. The original hymn begins, "I've reached the land of corn and wine/ And all its riches now are mine." In South Dakota, settlers sang, "We've reached the land of dying wheat/ Where nothing grows for man to eat"; those who arrived in the Willamette Valley began, "I've reached the land of rain and mud."

This version was sung by Orlo Flock (1913-90) of Powell Butte, Oregon, and recorded by Walter Bolton of Prineville, on February 14, 1969 (RVMA). Orlo Flock's great-great-grandfather and great-grandfather emigrated to Oregon from Pennsylvania and settled on a 640-acre Donation Land Claim on Fall Creek, near Oakridge, in 1853. Mr. Flock's family included five generations of musicians, and the house his grandfather Warner, a fiddler, built on Fall Creek even had a dance floor upstairs. Orlo himself began playing the fiddle at dances when he was twelve, and he learned a fine repertoire of ballads and folksongs from his mother. His childhood was spent on the "west side," before he moved to central Oregon where he worked as a log scaler.

Another Oregon variant titled "Webfoot Land," submitted to the "Old Songs" scrapbook of *The Farmer* by Pearl R. Huring of Med. Springs Stage, Baker, can be found in the Pacific Northwest Farm Quad Collection 501, Fife Folklore Archives.

I've reached the land of rain and mud
Where trees and flowers so early bud
And where it rains the blessed day
For in Oregon it rains always.

Chorus:
Oh! Oregon, wet Oregon
As through the rain and mud I run
I look about, behind, around
And see the rain soak in the ground
I look about and see it pour
And wish it wouldn't rain anymore.

A sweet perfume is on the breeze.
It comes from fir and alder trees
And flowers that in the springtime grow
And many shrubs that bud and blow.

Chorus:
Oh! Oregon girls, sweet Oregon girls
With sparkling eyes and dainty curls.
They sing and dance both night and day
'Til some webfooter comes their way.
They meet him at the kitchen door,
Saying clean your feet or come no more.

South Wind Marries Ocean's Daughter

The distinctively tempestuous weather of the northern Oregon Coast is mythically chartered in this Nehalem Tillamook story. For South Wind—fittingly, the Tillamook trickster—to marry into Ocean's family guarantees that sudden storms and rough seas will be part of the Tillamook reality permanently.—Told by Mrs. Clara Pearson to Elizabeth Jacobs in Garibaldi in 1934: *Nehalem Tillamook Tales*, pp. 92-93.

South Wind [*As'ai'yahahl*] traveled in the winter. It was always stormy then. He had many different headbands. He would say, "I will put on my headband with which I run on trees. I will travel only on the limbs of trees." That was the time when the limbs broke off the trees. The limbs broke off and fell down when he walked on them. Sometimes he would say, "Now I will wear this headband with which I break off the tree tops." He had still another headband which he wore when he felled whole trees, just as if they had been chopped down. Very rarely he would start out saying, "This time I will wear the headband with which I pull trees up by the roots."

In his travels he always saw a beautiful girl on the ocean beach. She would be sitting by the waves at the edge of the beach. He was always attempting to catch her. But just as he almost touched her she would disappear. Ah, he thought about her. He wanted so much to catch her. He had seen her many times, but he did not know what kind of a girl she was. Finally Blue Jay told him, "Well, South Wind, do you still want to catch that girl?"— "Yes, aunt," he replied, "would you tell me how to do it?" She told him, "When you see her, if you attempt to catch her, do not blink your eyes. Just keep staring straight at her until you seize her with your hand. Then it will be all right. You will have caught her. Do you know who she is?"—"No!"—"She is that Ocean's daughter. Ocean is the chief of chiefs." South Wind had often destroyed things for Ocean to receive.

He found her the next time he went forth. He did as he had been advised, and he caught hold of her. He took her home, he took her south. He made her his wife. That girl did not like it. She said, "Oh, I have never had a home like this! My bed at home is soft. I did not sleep on a hard bed at home." South Wind had a wooden bed. After a while he asked her, "Do you want me to take you home to your father? Shall we go and stay with your father a while?" Yes, she wanted to go home. She was very pleased.

He took her home. He saw many different things there. His father-in-law had everything! All sorts of living things were his pets. Those whales and many unattractive animals were his pets. They talked together. South Wind said, "Well, we will work together for the remainder of time. I will destroy things for you, so you can possess them. You must do your part. When I travel, you will be angry and drift things and drown things. In that way we will work together forever." Then he took his wife to his own home again. She took her belongings from her father's place since she was to remain with South Wind.

South Wind had one wife already when he was trying to catch that girl. She was continually getting angry and jealous. She would decide, "I will leave. I am not going to live with him any more. I am going away." She would start in the night and travel, travel as long as she could. She would then think, "Well, I must be far away now." South Wind would arise in the morning and notice that his first wife was gone. He would look, there in the far corner of the room he would see her. There she would be, with her belongings scattered around, and her bed made there. She was never able to travel far enough to get out of South Wind's house. The whole world was South Wind's house!

That is ended.

Origins of *Webfoot*

No one knows for certain when the term *webfoot* was first applied to Oregonians, but according to Hazel E. Mills ("The Constant Webfoot," pp. 153-164), evidence suggests that it was first used by Californians during the gold rush of 1848-49 to express their dislike of Oregonians, who reached the California gold fields early, worked hard, and took their gold with them back to the rainy Willamette Valley. The term *webfoot* appeared in California newspapers as early as 1853 but did not come into wide usage in Oregon papers until the mid-1860s, by which time it had been adopted by Oregonians as a humorous acknowledgment of their soggy climate. Before long it had become a "term of pride and affection" for those Oregonians who lived west of the Cascades.

The folklore that has grown up around the origins of the term *webfoot* takes the form of a legend describing a traveler's discovery of the webbed toes of an Oregon-born baby. This story was popularized in print in the 1870s by the writer, Frances Fuller Victor, in several pieces. The version that follows is Victor's account as it first appeared in *All Over Oregon and Washington*, pp. 179-180. *Webfoot* was first used by University of Oregon students in 1901, and *Webfoots* was adopted as the official nickname for the school's athletic team in 1932. (N. B., the proper plural of *webfoot* is *webfoots*.)

Two tributaries enter the Wallamet between Corvallis and Eugene—the Muddy, from the east, and Long Tom from the south-west. The country on the Long Tom is celebrated for its fertility, and for the uncompromising democracy of its people. . . . It is also claimed for Long Tom, that it originated the term "Webfoot" which is so universally applied to Oregonians by their California neighbors. The story runs as follows: A young couple from Missouri settled upon a land-claim on the banks of this river, and in due course of time a son and heir was born to them. A California "commercial traveller" chancing to stop with the happy parents overnight, made some joking remarks upon the subject, warning them not to let the baby get drowned in the unusually extensive mud-puddles by which the premises were disfigured; when the father replied that they had looked out for that, and, uncovering the baby's feet, astonished the joker by showing him that they were *webbed*. The *soubriquet* of Webfoot, having thus been attached to Oregon-born babies, has continued to be a favorite appelative ever since.

About the Word *Oregon*

The Mystery of Its Origin

The origin of the name *Oregon* puzzled scholars for many years, and numerous theories along with less plausible conjecture have at various times proposed that *Oregon* derived from French, Spanish, and several Native American languages—Shoshone, Mohawk, Mohegan, and Santee. Some of the more fanciful—and erroneous—hypotheses were that the name of the state of Oregon was derived from Spanish words—from *oregano*, an herb that does grow in Oregon; from *oreja* (ear) because the Spanish explorers thought the indigenous people had large ears; from *orejon* (slice of dried apple); and, according to writer Joaquin Miller, from the Spanish phrase, *oye agua* (hear the water). However, there is no evidence to support any of these hypotheses in the records of the early Spanish explorers.

The "most plausible" explanation of the source of the name *Oregon*, according to the 1974 edition of McArthur's *Oregon Geographic Names* is the explanation originally proposed by Professor George R. Stewart in *American Speech* (April 1944). Professor Stewart's investigations show that the name *Oregon* may be the consequence of an eighteenth-century mapmaker's error. In 1709 a map miscopied "Ouisconsing"—which is the way "Wisconsin" appears on early French maps—as "Ouaricon-sint," with the "sint" printed offset below "Ouaricon-." Thus anyone using this map could easily have misread the Wisconsin River, known as the "River of the West," as the "R. de Ouaricon," and, in fact, we find that Major Rogers, an English army officer posted in the Great Lakes area, used the name "Ouragon" or "Ourigan" in a petition he wrote in 1765 requesting permission to explore the territory west of the Great Lakes. The earliest known document with the spelling "Oregon" is Jonathan Carver's 1778 *Travels through the Interior Parts of North-America,* his account of his 1766-67 expedition to the West in which he writes of "the River Oregon, or the River of the West."

It was many years, however, before *Oregon* became the term used for the northwest part of the United States. It was not used by the explorers Vancouver or Gray, nor does it appear in the journals of Lewis and Clark, published in 1814-17. Its most notable appearance and the apparent source of its later usage was in the poem "Thanatopsis," published in 1817 by William Cullen Bryant:

> . . . Take the wings
> Of morning, pierce the Barcan wilderness,
> Or lose thyself in the continuous woods
> Where rolls the Oregon. . . .

Oregon in the Vernacular

European-Americans began settling in Oregon in the 1840s, and by the 1850s the word *Oregon* had entered our vocabulary as an adjective. Sometimes it simply served as a specific geographical marker, but it often indicated other qualities as well. We find several examples of this in a general word list compiled by Randall V. Mills, one of Oregon's pioneering folklorists and scholar of Oregon's speechways. Mills cited newspapers, fiction, diaries, and oral informants as the sources for these terms from the Oregon Country.

Oregon bed stead: two cross sticks between logs meeting at a corner post; tick placed on slats (1851)
Oregon cure-all: infusion of dogwood and chittim bark
Oregon mist: hard rain (1853)
Oregon style: vituperative journalism
Oregon tea: yerba buena (1891)
Oregon winter: steady rain (1850)

Oregon in the Woods

Forester Walter F. McCulloch cites nine examples of the occurrence of *Oregon* in the terminology of loggers and foresters in the Northwest in his monumental dictionary, *Woods Words*.

Oregon block: a stump used instead of a block to change the direction of a line.
Oregon fir: Douglas-fir
Oregon larch: Noble fir, a very fine timber tree at higher elevations in the Coast and Cascade regions.
Oregon lead: Same as Oregon block—using a stump to change the direction of a line instead of hanging a block; applied mostly when moving a donkey, as in swinging the nose around to change the lead.
Oregon pine: The name given to Douglas-fir by Dr. John McLoughlin as early as 1833 when shipping timber to the Sandwich Islands. He felt that fir was an unknown word, whereas pine was a well-understood term and would make the cargo sell better. Oregon pine was used by loggers and lumbermen as late as 1910, and the term is still known in foreign ports.
Oregon spruce: Sitka spruce
Oregon white cedar: Port Orford white cedar
Oregon white pine: Ponderosa pine
Oregon wrench: cold chisel and hammer, carried by old-time steam engineers.

Oregon on Horseback

Ramon F. Adams' dictionary of the American West, *Western Words*, provides additional entries for our *Oregon* lexicon from the occupational folk speech of those who work with horses.

Oregon diamond hitch: A packer's knot formed by not bringing a loop of the running rope under and forward of the standing rope; so called because it was widely used in Oregon Territory.

Oregon puddin' foot: A type of horse produced by crossing a riding horse with a draft horse, such as a Percheron or Clydesdale. This type was developed to some extent in Oregon for mountain work. Also called *Oregon bigfoot.*

Oregon short line: A name used in the Northwest for *fraid strap.* [A *fraid strap* is defined by Adams as "a strap buckled around the fork of the saddle which a rider holds while riding a bucking horse. A good rider considers it a disgrace to use a fraid strap."]

The Girl with the Striped Stockings

Several folksong collectors recorded this song from Clarice Mae Judkins of Eugene, Oregon, in the 1950s and 1960s. Born in Iowa, Mrs. Judkins moved to Oregon in 1890 and attended school in Crow and Springfield. She was a well-known traditional singer in Lane County, performed at many local gatherings, and is said to have had a repertoire of more than 250 songs. According to Russell M. Harrison, who collected this song from Clarice Mae Judkins in 1951, she had learned it from her father who had come from England ("Folk Songs from Oregon," p. 174). In a 1966 interview with folklorist Barre Toelken, Mrs. Judkins explained that this song is set in Boston, and she believed it was one of the oldest songs in her repertoire. She thought that it had been transplanted from the east coast but became popular in Oregon because it "rains in every verse." She noted that a professor who learned this song from her had taught it to his glee club, which then sang it in concerts throughout the state. Toelken discusses this song in his essay, "Northwest Regional Folklore," in Edwin R. Bingham and Glen A. Love, eds., *Northwest Perspectives*, p.36, and in *The Dynamics of Folklore*, pp. 371-372.

$\mathbf{O}$ne rainy day, I'll ne'er forget
The prettiest girl that I ever met.
And as she raised her skirt to the wet,
I saw she had striped stockings on.

Chorus:
Oh! She was always out if the wind blew high.
If the weather was wet she'd walk or die.
By the raising of her dress as she passed by,
I saw she had striped stockings on.

Oh the color of her hose was red and yeller.
Said she, "I think you're a mighty fine feller."
I escorted her home under my umbrella—
The girl with the striped stockings on.

Chorus

And when we parted in the rain
She said, "We'll never meet again."
And so she took my watch and chain.
The girl with the striped stockings on.

Chorus

Alsea Girls

Like "Oregon Land," this is a song that existed elsewhere in regional variants; for example, Utah versions warned the girls not to marry the "Mormon boys" for "johnny cakes and babies" is all they'll see. Through the processes of regionalization and oral transmission, the lyrics have been changed to accommodate the Oregon condition (Alsea is located between Corvallis and the Oregon coast). In this Oregon variant, the "Alsea girls" are advised not to marry the "Oregon boys" for "johnny cakes and venison" is all they'll see. Sung by an outsider, this song would have been insulting, but it's an insider's song, and as such it allows Oregonians to laugh among themselves about their own hardships with humor and affection. The bluntness of its closing lines—"Some gets little and some gets none,/ And that's how things in the Oregon run"—are a useful antidote to nostalgic and romanticized views of the "good old days." This text was published by Suzi Jones in *Oregon Folklore*, p. 11.

Come you Alsea girls and listen to my noise,
Don't you marry the Oregon boys,
If you do your fortune it'll be,
Cold johnny cakes and venison is all you'll see.

They'll take you to a side-hewed wall
Without any windows in it at all;
Sandstone chimney and a button door,
A clapboard roof and a puncheon floor.

Every night before you go to bed
They'll build up a fire as high as your head,
Rake away the ashes and in they'll throw
A great big chunk of old sourdough.

When they go a-milkin' they milk in a gourd,
Strain it in the corner and hide it with a board.
Some gets little and some gets none,
And that's how things in the Oregon run.

Oregon's Healthy Climate

Published in 1871 in *The Democratic Era* (Vol. 1, no. 11), this newspaper story is a well-known tall tale which has been cast in an Oregon locale. Nineteenth-century newspapers are a great source of folktales and legends from oral tradition, often printed like this one, as a sketch with dialogue and a folksy dialect. This is just one of many newspaper sketches of folk material that were copied for the Oregon WPA Folklore Project. An earlier version of this tale from the New Orleans *Weekly Delta,* January 15, 1849, where it is reported as a conversation between the popular Yankee stage actor, Dan Marble, and a newly returned Californian describing the wonders of that state, may be found in Dorson's *American Folklore* (pp. 66-67).

While strolling along the wharves of Boston I met a tall, gaunt-looking figure, a Webfoot from Oregon, and got into conversation with him. "Healthy climate, I suppose?"

"Healthy, it ain't anything else. Why, stranger, you can choose there any climate you like—hot and cold—and that without travelin' more than fifteen minutes. Just think o' that the next cold mornin' when you git out o' bed. There's a mountain there—Mount Hood, they call it—with a valley on each side of it, the one hot, the other cold. Well, git on the top of that mountain with a double-barreled gun, and you can without movin' kill either summer or winter game, just as you will."

"What, have you ever tried it?"

"Tried it often—and should have done pretty well, but for one thing."

"Well, what was that?"

"I wanted a dog that would stand both climates. The last dog I had froze off his tail while pintin' on the summer side. He didn't git entirely out of the winter side, you see. Trew as you live!"

Getting the Wash Done Oregon Style

Like the hunter in the previous sketch, the woman in this anecdote also takes advantage of—or has to contend with, depending on your point of view—the climate on both sides of Oregon's Cascade range. The source cited for this anecdote from the Oregon WPA collection is the *Corvallis Gazette*, February 5, 1892, p. 2.

The purser of the *Lurline* tells a story which illustrates the difference between eastern and western Oregon. About two years ago an old lady got on the boat at the Cascades, on her way to the valley, and a friend sang out: "Hello, Mrs. Blank. Where are you going?"

"Going to where there is water enough to wash my clothes; we don't have enough for that in eastern Oregon," was the reply.

About a month after she was a passenger on the *Lurline* going back. The purser said: "How do you do, Mrs. Blank? Have you got your washing done?"

"Yes," said the old lady, "I have, and now I am going back east of the mountains to get my clothes dry."

Oregon Sayings, West and East

West of the Cascades

—From Helen Pearce, "Folk Sayings in Pioneer Family in Western Oregon," pp. 229-242. The family came overland to the Salem area in the 1850s, with roots in England, Ireland, Maryland, and Illinois.

That looks like a saddle on a hog.
It's root, hog, or die. [Desperate efforts are required.]
That'll never show on a galloping horse. [To a woman who is excessively fussy about her appearance.]
She's got a hen on. [Hatching a scheme]
It looks like the last run of salmon. [Something on its last legs]
That looks like last year's bird nest. [Ditto]
She'd ask you the width of the hem on your skirt. [Of a nosey person]
She knows everybody and why they left Missouri. [Ditto]

He's on his uppers now. [Someone on the edge of financial ruin: the soles of his shoes are gone, and he's reduced to walking on his "uppers"]

He got his moccasins sunned. [Someone turned upside down in his life, so that his feet face the sun]

The back of one is the face of another. [A succession of lovers]

He got the camas knocked out of him. [Indian borrowing? The bulb of the camas was a Willamette Valley Indian staple]

He's off the reservation! [Someone running wild]

She's got eight acres of hell in her. [A wildcat]

He hasn't got a Chinaman's chance. [Re: notorious exploitation of Chinese laborers in the West in the nineteenth century]

That's only small potatoes and few to the hill. [Puny, "underwhelming"]

He salts everything down he can get his hands on. [A miser]

He can see through the hole in a grindstone. [Has good sense]

He's as crooked as a rail fence. [Early fences in Western Oregon ran in zig-zags—no fence-posts needed!]

A woodsman is known by his chips.

Her sickness will fall into her arms. [Sarcasm about a woman's "indisposition" signifying pregnancy]

Busy as a cranberry merchant. [Re: a distinctive Oregon crop]

It's a good day for ducks. [Valley weather!]

All signs fail in Oregon. [On the settlers' need to re-interpret all the folk "signs" —weather, planting, etc.—they brought with them from their homelands, according to the new reality of Oregon]

East of the Cascades

—Recorded by the editors from Madras and elsewhere.

It was hot as the hubs of hell, and I was sweating like a trooper.

It was as cold as a blue flujeon.

I'm still kickin', but I'm not raisin' much dust.

I'll do it, but I'll be draggin' both hind feet. [Reluctance]

She's got the collywobbles and probably the epizootic, and she's lookin' mighty green around the gills.[(Undiagnosed illness]

Going to have to fire the hired man, he's work-brittle. [Lazy, averse to hard labor]

He was about as handy around the ranch as a ribbon-clerk. [Consider the skills and temperament of someone in this line]

They're tryin' to make a living on hell's half-acre. [Of someone whose home-stead location was ill chosen]

That pickup of his is as worthless off-road as tits on a boar.

You look like you've just smelled a wolf! [Of someone who's been startled and/or has tousled hair]

Fred and me have decided to *renovolate* the whole house! [A special degree of renovation?]

Hard-shell Baptists [Devoted to baptism by immersion]

From the looks of your hands and face, you must be a Methodist. [To an unwashed child—refers, probably from a Baptist perspective, to the Methodist practice of baptism by merely sprinkling]

Reub Long on the Oregon Desert

Reub Long

One of Oregon's greatest raconteurs was Reub Long (1898-1974), a rancher and sagebrush philosopher from the Fort Rock area. His parents moved from Lakeview to homestead at Christmas Lake when he was two years old, and his lifetime of experiences on the Oregon Desert became the subject of many of his stories, some borrowed, many original. *The Oregon Desert*, a book he wrote with E. R. Jackman, has become an Oregon classic, and the tall tales and anecdotes he included are integral to the sense of place Long so convincingly creates.

About a quarter of Oregon, 24,000 square miles of it, is a high desert. Jackrabbits, mule deer, antelope, rattlesnakes, coyotes and other "varmints" are at home among the juniper and sagebrush of the Oregon Desert. Water is scarce in this part of Oregon, wind and dust frequent. Several of Reub Long's stories from *The Oregon Desert* deal with these elemental matters.

Once a stranger stopped to ask about the country. His interest was stirred by the utter absence of anything in sight to show it had rained around Fort Rock. He said, "Has it *ever* rained here?"

I told him, "Yes, once. Do you remember how Noah, the first long-range weather forecaster, built the ark and floated it during forty days and nights of rain?" He said he had knowledge of that. I told him, "That time we got a quarter of an inch." (p. 348)

In this big desert area of Oregon . . . we have a vast inland basin where no water *ever* reaches the sea. We have some pretty respectable rivers, such as the Chewaucan and the Donner and Blitzen, but the farther they flow the smaller they get, until they peter out or flow into shallow lakes with no outlet. On my own place and the government land, where I pay for pasturing, amounting to maybe fifty thousand acres, there is not one stream, no lakes, no water on the surface at all. Every drop of water my cattle and horses drink and every drop my wife Eleanor and I drink, is pumped by windmill or power. We measure humidity by the amount of sand in the air. When it rains, we keep our hired man in—we want all of the water on the land. (p. 347)

Water is often the subject of conversation in our country. It is the basis for neighborhood quarrels and lawsuits. The owner of a water hole is in a different situation than the man without one. In well-watered counties, peacemakers try to settle heated arguments by saying, "There's no reason to get bothered by this matter—it's all water gone under the bridge." Our peacemakers say, "It's sand over the dune." (pp. 347-348)

The worst hardship was the dust. A little breeze would start around Bend to the northwest, would get into the spirit of the thing, whip itself into a frenzy, and by the time it got to Christmas Lake, it would be blowing the quills off the porcupines. Reub tells about one wind that blew a sage hen against a rock cliff and just held her there until she laid eleven eggs. Easter occurred during this time and two were Easter eggs. (p. 62)

The reason I've been able to produce some fast horses is that, where I graze them, they have to feed at thirty miles an hour to get enough to eat. (p. 385)

There are numerous scholarly books upon the wild horses of the West. They are written by anthropologists, historians, and humanitarians, whereas I am a sagebrush desert rancher. I dreamed once that I went to Heaven. St. Peter looked me over more than casually.

St. Peter: Where you from, cowboy?

I: The Fort Rock desert.

St. Peter: Well—all right, you can come in, but I can tell you right now, you ain't a-goin' to like it, because it ain't a bit like Fort Rock. (p. 74)

Southeastern Oregon Weather

Just as Willamette Valley folks joke about the constant rain, so ranchers in eastern Oregon happily explain the truth about their weather through clever lies about the lack of precipitation, the constant wind, and the dust. The first three entries were collected in 1971 by Mardi Wilson from her mother and brother at their Mann Lake ranch near Princeton (Mardi Wilson, RVMA, February 1971). The last four appeared in the "Liars' Forum" of the *Sunday Oregonian,* February 9, 1936.

We got an inch of rain today—an inch between drops.

One time a couple of guys went out to dig some post holes down at Mann Lake, but it got dark before they finished so they went home and left their tools behind so they could finish the next day. Well, it blew so hard that night that the next day they found that the tools and post holes had blown to Nevada.

At the Alvord Ranch [located at the foot of the Steens Mountains] there's a big tall pole with a ten-foot-long log chain hanging off of it. When the chain's hangin' straight out, it's a gentle breeze. When the links start snappin' off the end, then the wind's blowin'.

In the first place, the country is so dry that you have to be primed before you can spit.

The word "dew" has been dropped from the vocabulary, and the children under 10 have heard it only as part of the expression, "Dew tell—"

A man hoarded some water in the bottom of a 12-foot well and doled it out to his family like gold dust. But he forgot and left the cover off one day and a little twister came along. It corkscrewed that water clean out of the well, and it disappeared so fast in the dry air that only one drop fell to the ground. That drop hit one of the children. It was such a surprise that he fainted, and it took two buckets of sand to bring him back to normal.

An average rainfall of less than eight inches a year has produced many irregularities not only of behavior but even of physiognomy. Even the domestic fowl and livestock of the region are altered. Barnyard ducks lose their web feet in the second generation, and the fourth generation is actually afraid of water. They forget how to take a dust bath, as they don't need to ruffle their feathers in a hole any more. They simply turn tail to the dust storm and let her riffle.

Valley Rabbit and Mountain Rabbit

A favorite of Nez Perce children, judging from the number of recorded versions of it, the droll tale of the Valley Rabbit and the Mountain Rabbit parallels in form and meaning the Euro-American tale, "The City Mouse and the Country Mouse." In Oregon's diverse climate and terrain, home is where . . . you're at home. —Told by Mrs. Dave Isaac to Dell Skeels around 1950: Skeels, *Style in the Unwritten Literature of the Nez Perce Indians.* Vol. 1, pp. 268-269.

So the Valley Rabbit visited the Mountain Rabbit. So he came to a big mountain. He saw a big tipi made out of bark from a big pine tree, and he went in. There was his friend lying on his bed. He said, "Hello." And he said, "I've come to visit and see your country, what kind of living you have in the wintertime and what you eat." And Mountain Rabbit said, "I have all kinds of grass that grows on these cliffs and moss and the roots of plants and small bark." He said to Valley Rabbit, "I wish you could stay here with me. We'll have a lot of fun together." He said, "Take a good look at where you came from, how hot a place you've got, how smoky it is."

And he [Valley Rabbit] answered him, he said, "I want you to come along and stay with me." And he [Mountain Rabbit] said, "I'll only go home with you for a visit." And he did. He came down to the valley, so they came to his camp. He had a camp made out of bunch grass in an oak, and he had grass mats, too, and he told this Mountain Rabbit to stay there. "We'll have a lot of fun together. You can have green grass all year round and all the greens along the streams you can eat. There'll be two kinds of rabbits in the valley and no rabbits in the mountains." The Mountain Rabbit said, "I think I prefer to stay in the mountains, so we'll be there when the humans come, and one will be Mountain Rabbit and another Valley Rabbit, so we'll split up. You keep your country and I'll keep mine." So he went home, and that is how they split up.

First Contacts
and
Other Encounters

The stories in this section reveal how Oregonians of various identities and at different times reacted to the shock of *newness,* things unforeseen and unintelligible to customary understanding.

There is something mythic in first encounters, signaling both beginnings and endings in our experience, and whether we are Indians seeing for the first time the white-skinned strangers of legend and rumor, or we are immigrants to the Oregon country meeting our first Natives face-to-face, we tend to make memorable stories out of our surprise and curiosity, and sometimes our fear.

"Nez Perce on Horseback" from Signal sketchbook. University of Oregon Collection.

The First Ship Comes to Clatsop

Charles Cultee

Given what happened to the Native way of life after the arrival of the Anglos in force, it's hardly surprising that many Indian narratives of "first encounters" with the newcomers are, like this one, tinged with a sense of impending doom. Whoever the shipwrecked sailors are—Russians? Spanish?— the Clatsop people have heard rumors of their kind, but the actual arrival of the strangers is traumatic, bound up in the old woman's grief over her dead son: "Oh, my son is dead, and the thing about which we have heard in tales is on shore!" The wonderful metallic objects (in Chinook Jargon, *skookum iktahs*) in the ship replace the native currency, and the Clatsops wrangle amongst themselves over ownership of the surviving sailors, portending worse trouble to come.

—Told by Charles Cultee in the Clatsop Chinook language to Franz Boas in 1893, in Bay Center, Washington: Boas, *Chinook Texts,* pp. 278-279.

The son of an old woman had died. She wailed for him for a whole year and then she stopped. Now one day she went to Seaside. There she used to stop, and she returned. She returned walking along the beach. She nearly reached Clatsop; now she saw something. She thought it was a whale.

When she came near it she saw two spruce trees standing upright on it. She thought, "Behold! it is no whale. It is a monster!" She reached the thing that lay there. Now she saw that its outer side was all covered with copper. Ropes were tied to those spruce trees, and it was full of iron. Then a bear came out of it. He stood on the thing that lay there. He looked just like a bear, but his face was that of a human being. Then she went home. She thought of her son, and cried, saying—"Oh my son is dead and the thing about which we have heard in tales is on shore!"

When she (had) nearly reached the town she continued to cry. (The people said), "Oh, a person comes crying. Perhaps somebody struck her." The people made themselves ready. They took their arrows. An old man said, "Listen!" Then the old woman said again and again, "Oh, my son is dead, and the thing about which we have heard in tales is on shore!" The people said, "What can it be?" They went running to meet her. They said, "What is it?"—"Ah, something lies there and it is thus. There are two bears on it, or maybe they are people."

Then the people ran. They reached the thing that lay there. Now the bears, or whatever they might be, held two copper kettles in their hands. The people were arriving. Now the two persons took their hands to their mouths and gave the people their kettles. They had lids. The men pointed inland and asked for water. Then [the] two people ran inland. They hid themselves behind a log. They returned again and ran down to the beach.

One man [of the people from the town] climbed up and entered the thing. He went down into the ship. He looked about in the interior; it was full of boxes. He found brass buttons in strings half a fathom long. He went out again to call his relatives, but they had already set fire to the ship. He jumped down. Those two persons had also gone down.

It burned just like fat. Then the Clatsop gathered the iron, the copper, and the brass. Then all the people learned about it. The two persons were taken to the chief of the Clatsop. Then the chief of the one town said, "I want to keep one of those men with me!" The people almost began to fight. Now one of them [sailors] was returned to one town, and the chief there was satisfied. Now the Quinault, the Chehalis, and the Willapa came. The people of all the towns came there. The Cascades, the Cowlitz, and the Klickitat came down the river. All those of the upper part of the river came down to Clatsop. The Quinault, the Chehalis, and the Willapa went. The people of all the towns went there. The Cascades, the Cowlitz, and the Klickitat came down river. . . .

Strips of copper two fingers wide and going around the arm were exchanged for one slave each. A piece of iron as long as one-half the forearm was exchanged for one slave. A piece of brass two fingers wide was exchanged for one slave. A nail was sold for a good curried deerskin. Several nails were given for long dentalia. They bought all this and the Clatsop became rich. Then iron and brass were seen for the first time. Now they kept those two persons. One was kept by each [Clatsop] chief, one was at the Clatsop town at the cape.

The Nez Perce Meet Lewis and Clark

The virtual rescue of the Lewis and Clark Expedition by a band of Nez Perce at Weippe, Idaho, in late summer 1805, after the explorers had struggled through early snowstorms over the Bitterroot Mountains, is well documented in the journals of the Expedition. This Nez Perce account of the meeting was recorded in the 1890s by a Presbyterian missionary and teacher, Kate Macbeth, at the Lapwai Mission. She gives no source, and appears to have condensed and retold what may well have been a lengthy and detailed oral tradition amongst the Nez Perce. Still, even in this form the story conveys the Native point of view expressively, indicating the Indians' consternation and curiosity in encountering Thomas Jefferson's explorers. In the pathetic figure of Wat-ku-ese, Lewis and Clark found their second female savior, the first, of course, being the Shoshone woman Sacajawea. —H.S. Lyman, "Items from the Nez Perces," pp. 295-296.

A Nez Perce woman, Wat-ku-ese, was taken captive by a tribe, who, while on their return to their own land, fought with still another tribe, and the Nez Perce woman was again captured, and carried farther and farther away: and it was while there, still a captive, that she was the first Nez Perce to look upon a white face.

Some time afterwards, with her child upon her back, she made her escape, and along the way met with much kindness from the whites, whom she called "So-yap-po," or the crowned ones (because of the hat). Her child died, and she buried it by the way in the Flathead country. There she was fortunate in finding some of the Nez Perce, who brought her home, a poor, diseased woman. She had much to tell about the strange people with the white eyes, who had been so kind to her.

Later on this poor woman was with a great company of Nez Perce on their best camas ground, at Weippe, when Lewis and Clark came over the Lo Lo trail and surprised them there. Their first impulse was to kill the white strangers. Wat-ku-ese lay dying in her tent, but was told about the strange people who were on the ground. She at once began to plead for them, saying: "Do not harm them, for they are the crowned ones, who were so kind to me. Do not be afraid of them; go near to them."

Cautiously they approached, and the whites shook their hands; this they had never done before, and in surprise they said to one another, "They dandle us." Wat-ku-ese died that same day, but had lived long enough to keep Lewis and Clark from being put to death by . . . the Nez Perce. Their fear of the palefaces soon vanished and they became friends.

Some of the Nez Perce guided the explorers into their beautiful Kamiah Valley, and on down the Clearwater River. At North Fork the Indians presented the leaders with some very fine fish. Lewis or Clark carefully unrolled a package containing a piece of cloth, the first they had seen—they now think it was a flag—and tearing a red band from it, wound it around the head of the man who had given the fish, and by this act was the first Nez Perce chief made. They separated at [the site of] Lewiston, Lewis and Clark intrusting many things of value to them, and found them safe when they returned the following year [from their stay at the mouth of the Columbia River].

"Goldilocks on the Oregon Trail"

"Goldilocks on the Oregon Trail" was the title of a 1962 lecture given by Dr. Francis Haines, Sr., then professor emeritus of history at Oregon College of Education, in which he describes a type of story that is found repeatedly in the reminiscences of families who made the 2,000-mile journey to Oregon over the Oregon Trail. As the story is usually told, a wagon train is stopped by some Indians who take notice of grandmother, then a young, blonde, blue-eyed girl. The Indians want to buy her, offering a large number of horses in exchange. The offer is refused, and the young girl goes on with her family to the Willamette Valley, where she grows up and has children and grandchildren of her own. As Haines points out, this story is not to be found in the daily journals kept by pioneers; it only began appearing thirty to fifty years later, when old timers told stories at annual pioneer picnics or published their reminiscences in pioneer society publications. Haines notes that "all of these stories are based on two common misconceptions of the Anglo-Saxon: first, the firm belief that all other people on earth envy him his fair children and women; second, that all Indians buy their wives." Pointing out the longevity of such folklore, Haines reminds us of the stories told in England a century earlier with the Gypsies as the dark-skinned people who wanted the blond children. Haines's lecture was published in *Idaho Yesterdays*, pp. 26-30.

The first example of this legend is from Haines's article and tells the story of Nellie Jane Earp, the two-year-old daughter of Virgil Earp, who came west in 1864 with her mother and stepfather. The second account is from an 1896 letter from Bartlett Cave to George Himes (Mss 1500, Oregon Historical Society). The third and longest story, told at an Oregon pioneer reunion, was published as "A Brave Pioneer Girl," by J. A. Buchanan in 1901 (*Pacific Monthly*, Vol. 6, p. 162). It was collected for the WPA Project by Eugene Woods, December 10, 1940.

Nellie Jane Earp

As they were passing through Idaho, the wagon train had an opportunity to do some trading with Chief Joseph and his braves. Not having seen a tow-headed youngster before, Chief Joseph caught a glimpse of little Nellie Jane and immediately set out to try to trade for her. He wanted to have her as his daughter and would trade more ponies and skins than were ever offered by him on any occasion of trading. Of course the offer was refused. During their stay at this site of trading Chief Joseph came many times to play with and hold the little girl who was to become my great-grandmother.

Postscript: Francis Haines writes: "Chief Joseph actually had been familiar with little blond girls since the birth of Alice Clarissa Whitman at Waiilatpu Mission in 1837, and by 1864 he had seen hundreds of white children among the thousands of people who had invaded the Nez Perce reservation following the discovery of gold in 1860. Also the Nez Perce had no Oregon Trail trading place in Idaho at any time. When they did meet the wagon trains for the purpose of trade, it was in Powder River Valley or the Grande Ronde."

Moses Eads's Red-Headed Daughter

Looking Glass. Apr 24th, 1896
Mr. Geo. H. Himes

Dear Sir

being very young when I crossed the plains cannot speak of any incident in regard to myself, but I remember of a little trouble that we had with the Indians at Deschutes River. There was a family by the name of Moses Eads in the train that had a red-headed daughter. The Indians took great fancy to her. They ferried one half the immigrants across and refused to take the rest over unless they would give up the girl. This they would not do, and the Indians threatened to massacre the train, but fortunately the young lady's father Moses Eads and a big stout buck Indian got into a single-handed combat. It was a hard fight. All the time the fight was going on there was two ministers standing by shouting, "Hit him underhanded, Brother Moses."

Brother Moses finely got the best of the battle and the Indians seemed to consider the trouble decided. They crossed us over and we went on our way.

Yours Truly,
B. Cave
(in haste)

Mary Walker, a Brave Pioneer Girl

At every reunion of the Pioneers of Oregon new stories are told and old stories retold. . . . As many of the deeds done were never known to any but the perpetrators, so also many of the stories of those times have never seen the light of the printed page. The following story is of that class.

One summer afternoon a covered wagon drawn by an ox-team, was slowly wending its way down a beautiful river valley. The occupants, a family named Walker, had somehow become separated from the train with which they crossed the mountains. The family was from Missouri; the mother and father, Robert, 15, Mary 13, and a baby brother.

One more day of travel and they would reach the settlement. They were cheerful for they anticipated meeting old friends and built beautiful air castles filled with bright hopes for the future.

The father busied himself preparing camp and the mother was cheerfully preparing the evening meal when six Indian warriors in full war paint rushed up the bank uttering their war crys. The father, taken by surprise, grasped a stout club and fought with the energy of despair, but soon a tomahawk went crashing through his skull. Robert and his mother were killed in the same manner. Mary who was in the wagon when she heard the war cries took the baby and hid in a large trunk.

She heard two or three of the savages climb into the wagon. She heard them rummaging through the goods with cries of surprise and delight. Presently the trunk was opened and the little girl and helpless baby were dragged ruthlessly from their hiding place.

"We will keep the white girl," said the chief, "but the child must be killed. If he grows up he will be our enemy and kill many of our people." Upon hearing the order a savage took the child by the head and dashed its head against the tree. As they were leaving the scene, her dog, Rover, that had been under the wagon whining, came bounding out to accompany her. She was not bound, but he pointed to his tomahawk, reminding her that if she attempted escape she would be killed. Only a short time elapsed from the beginning of the attack to the departure. Until past midnight they continued to the south. Then they built a fire, secured their prisoner and slept until morning. After breakfast they resumed their march. When they halted for the night Mary gathered fire wood and cooked the venison.

Before leaving the scene of the massacre, Mary had managed to secrete in her clothing a bottle of whiskey and a small vial of laudanum, which had formed part of their stock of medicines. Pouring the contents of the vile [vial] into the bottle of whiskey, she awaited developments.

That night after they had eaten, the Indians sat around the fire smoking. Being well satisfied with their expedition, they were laughing and boasting. When the merriment was at its height, Mary produced the bottle of whiskey. They each drank in turn until the bottle was empty.

The drug soon had its effect. One by one the savages dropped over in a profound slumber. Mary took the chief's tomahawk and dealt him a blow on the temple with all her strength. The others were soon dispatched in a like manner.

She, then, took some of the Indians' provisions, and calling Rover struck out into the forests towards where she thought the settlements ought to be. All night she kept steadily on.

When morning broke she was afraid to continue on her way, and she crept into a hollow log preceded by her dog.

She slept peacefully until past noon when some bear hunters found her. Mary Walker lived to be the mother of a large family.

A Sampling of Chinook Jargon

As they did elsewhere, Northwest Indians probably used some form of Chinook Jargon for trading and diplomatic purposes amongst themselves before the coming of the whites. But with the arrival of explorers, trappers, evangelists, and farmers, the need for a simplified "esperanto" or universal language became acute, and—fortified considerably by loan words from English and especially from French—the Jargon became indispensable in Oregon and elsewhere, well into the twentieth century. Basically a 500-word vocabulary, and for the most part lacking a conventional grammar and syntax, Jargon operated *metaphorically,* and often with considerable ingenuity: for example, the fork, apparently unknown to Northwest Indians before Contact, was given the Jargon name *opitsah yakha sikh,* meaning "the (girl) friend of the knife" (*opitsah*).—See *A Dictionary of the Chinook Jargon or Indian Trade Language* and E.H. Thomas, *Chinook, a History and Dictionary.*

Ah-ha: Yes
Ahn-kut-te: Formerly (with the first syllable prolonged, "a long time ago")
Bos-ton: American
Chuck: Water (hence, *salt chuck* = "sea"; *skookumchuck* = "rapids")
Coo-ley: To run
Cul-tus: Worthless
Eh-kah-nam: Tale or story
E-lip: First (*elip tillikum* = "the first people")
Ha-lo: None, absent
Hee-hee: Laughter, amusement
Huy-huy: To barter or trade
Hy-as: Large, great, very
Hy-iu: Much, many, plenty (*hyiu tillikum* = "a crowd")
Ik-tah: What, something (*skookum iktah* = "something strange, powerful")
Il-la-hee: The ground, the earth (*saghalie illahee* = "mountains")
In-a-ti: Across (*inati chuck* = "across the river")
Kah-ta: Why (*kahta mika mamook okook* = "why do you do that?")

Kam-ooks: Dog
Kel-a-pie: To turn or return (*kelapie tumtum* = "to change one's mind")
Klah: Free or clear from
Kla-how-ya: How do you do or goodbye
Kla-ta-wa: To go
Klo-nass: Uncertainty, doubt
Klootch-man: A woman; female
Klo-she: Good, well
Ko-ko: To knock (*kokostick* = woodpecker)
Koo-sah: The sky
Kum-tuks: To know or understand
La-mah: The hand (from French, *le main*)
Mah-kook: To buy or sell
Mam-ook: To make, to work
Mem-a-loose: To die, dead
Me-sah-chie: Bad, wicked
Mow-ich: Deer
Nan-itsch: To see, look
O-lal-lie: Berries (esp. huckleberries)
O-pit-sah: Knife (*opitsah yakha sikh* = "fork, the friend of knife")
Pel-ton: Foolish, crazy
Pi-ah: Fire, cooked
Po-lak-lie: Night (*tenas polaklie* = early evening)
Pot-latch: A gift, to give
Sagh-a-lie: Up above, high (*Saghalie Tyee* = "God")
Si-ah: Far off
Si-wash: Indian
Skoo-kum: Strong, powerful (often in the sense of spirits)
Sol-leks: Anger, angry
Stick: Tree, anything wooden (*stick skin* = "bark")
Tal-a-pus: Coyote
Ta-mah-no-us: Magic, spiritual
Te-nas: Few
Ti-li-kum: People
To-ke-tie: Pretty
Tum-tum: Heart (*sick tumtum* = "grief, jealousy")
Ty-ee: Chief
Wa-wa: To talk, speak (*cultus wawa* = idle chatter)
Yak-wa: Here, this side of
Yi-en: To relate, to tell (as of a story, *yi-en ehkahnam*)

The Sun's Myth

The work of Dell Hymes (a native of Portland) has both enriched and altered the course of Native American literary studies. Hymes's "ethnopoetic" approach (working from knowledge of Native languages and a scrupulous understanding of cultural contexts) has revealed that in Chinookan culture (and probably in others) verbal performance was poetically *measured*, in units of lines, "stanzas," and scenes. Hence, in Hymes's view, traditional Native narratives should be presented not in prose form, like short stories, but as dramatic poetry.

Like "Seal and her Younger Brother Lived There" (p. 258), "The Sun's Myth" illustrates Hymes's methods in recovering in printed English the poetic structure of a Chinookan myth. And the story itself, as performed for Franz Boas by Charles Cultee, is thereby revealed as a work of great dramatic power, *composed*, not merely "transmitted," by a gifted literary artist. In its starkly tragic vision, "The Sun's Myth" seems to express Cultee's understanding of what has happened to his people since the coming of the Anglos with their wonderful assortment of "shining things," each in its way as potentially harmful as the mysterious, irresistible *iktah* of this story. The Indians' calamity, as terrible as it is in the story and in history, must be reckoned with by the victims without self-excuse or denial of responsibility: in the unbearably stern words of the sun-woman to her broken protege, "Why do you weep?/It is you who chose . . ."

Perhaps, given our reckless fondness for all sorts of material "shining things" in modern life, "The Sun's Myth" is a signifying fable for us all.—Told by Charles Cultee in Kathlamet Chinook to Franz Boas in 1894: Boas, *Kathlamet Texts*, pp. 26-33; retranslated by Dell Hymes and first published in "Folklore's Nature and the Sun's Myth," pp. 345-369.

They live there, those people of a town.
Five the towns of his relatives, that chief.

In the early light,
    now he used to go out,
      and outside,
      now he used to stay;
        now he used to see that sun:
        she would nearly come out, that sun.
Now he told his wife:
    "What would you think,
      if I went to look for that sun?"

She told him, his wife,
     "You think it is near?
     "And will wish to go to that sun?"

Another day,
     again in the early light,
         he went out;
             now again he saw that sun:
             she did nearly come out there, that sun.
He told his wife:
     "You shall make ten pairs of moccasins,
     "You shall make me leggings,
         leggings for ten people."
Now she made them for him, his wife,
     moccasins for ten people,
         the leggings of as many.
Again it became dawn,
     now he went,
         far he went.
He used up his moccasins,
     he used up his leggings;
         he put on others of his moccasins and leggings,
Five months he went,
     five of his moccasins he used up,
         five of his leggings he used up.
Ten months he went—
     now she would rise nearby, that sun—
         he used up his moccasins.
Now he reached a house,
     a large house;
he opened the door,
     now some young girl is there;
he entered the house,
     he stayed.
Now he saw there on the side of that house:
     arrows are hanging on it,
     quivers full of arrows are hanging on it,
     armors of elkskin are hanging on it,
     armors of wood are hanging on it,
     shields are hanging on it,

axes are hanging on it,
warclubs are hanging on it,
feathered regalia are hanging on it—
all men's property there on the side of that house.
There on the other side of that house:
mountain goat blankets are hanging on it,
painted elkskin blankets are hanging on it,
buffalo skins are hanging on it,
dressed buckskins are hanging on it,
long dentalia are hanging on it,
shell beads are hanging on it,
short dentalia are hanging on it,—
now, near the door, some large thing hangs over there;
he did not recognize it.

Then he asked the young girl:
"Whose property are those quivers?"
"Her property, my father's mother,
she saves them for my maturity."
"Whose property are those elkskin armors?"
"Our property, my father's mother (and I),
she saves them for my maturity."
"Whose property are those arrows?"
"Our property, my father's mother (and I),
she saves them for my maturity."

"Whose property are those wooden armors?"
"Our property, my father's mother (and I),
she saves them for my maturity."
"Whose property are those shields,
and those bone warclubs?"
"Our property, my father's mother (and I)."
"Whose property are those stone axes?"
"Our property, my father's mother (and I)."

Then again on the other side of that house:
"Whose property are those buffalo skins?"
"Our buffalo skins, my father's mother (and I),
she saves them for my maturity."
"Whose property are those mountain goat blankets?"
"Our property, my father's mother (and I),
she saves them for my maturity."

"Whose property are those dressed buckskins?"
    "Our property, my father's mother (and I),
        she saves them for my maturity."
"Whose property are those deerskin blankets?"
    "Our property, my father's mother (and I),
        she saves them for my maturity."
"Whose property are those shell beads?"
    "Our property, my father's mother (and I),
        she saves them for my maturity."
"Whose property are those long dentalia?"
"Whose property are those short dentalia?"
    "Her property, my father's mother,
        she saves them for my maturity."

He asked her about all those things.
    He thought:
        "I will take her."
At dark,
    now that old woman came home,
        now again she hung up one (thing).
He likes that,
    that thing (is) shining all over;
        he stayed there.

A long time he stayed there;
    and now he took that young girl.
They stayed there.
In the early light,
    already that old woman was gone.
In the evening,
        she would come home;
    she would bring things,
        she would bring arrows;
    sometimes mountain goat blankets she would bring,
        sometimes elkskin armors she would bring.
Every day like this.

A long time he stayed;
    now he felt homesick.
        Twice he slept,
        he did not get up.

That old woman said to her grandchild:
    "Did you scold him,
        and he is angry?"
    "No, I did not scold him,
        he feels homesick."
Now she told her son-in-law:
    "What will you carry when you go home?"
    "Will you carry those buffalo skins?"
He told her,
    "No."
"Will you carry those mountain goat blankets?"
He told her,
    "No."
"Will you carry all those elkskin armors?"
He told her,
    "No."
She tried in vain to show him all that on one side of the house.
    Next all those (other) things.
        She tried in vain to show him all, *every*thing.
He wants only that,
    that thing which is large,
        that (thing) put up away.
When it would sway,
    that thing put up away,
        it would become turned around,
        at once his eyes would be extinguished;
            that thing shining all over,
            now he wants only that thing there.

He told his wife:
    "She shall give me one (thing),
        that blanket of hers, that old woman."
His wife told him:
    "She will never give it to you.
    "In vain people continue to try to trade it from her;
    "She will never do it."
Now again he became angry.

Several times he slept.
Now again she would ask him:
    "Will you carry that?"
        she would tell him.

She would try in vain to show him all those things of her,
    she would try in vain to show him all those men's things,
        she would try in vain to show him all.
She would reach that (thing) put up away,
    now she would become silent.
When she would reach that (thing) put away,
    now her heart became tired.
Now she told him:
"You must carry it then!
    "Take care! if you carry it.
    "It is you who choose.
    "I try to love you,
    indeed I do love you."
She hung it on him,
    she hung it all on him;
        now she gave him a stone ax;
            she told him:
                "Go home now!"

He went out,
    now he went,
        he went home;
    he did not see a land;
        he arrived near his father's brother's town.
Now that which he had taken throbbed,
    now that which he had taken said:
        "We two shall strike your town,
        "We two shall strike your town,"
            said that which he had taken.
His reason became nothing:
    he did it to his father's brother's town,
        he crushed, crushed, crushed it,
            he killed all the people.
He recovered—
    all those houses are crushed,
        his hands are full of blood.
He thought:
    "Oh I am a fool!
    "See, that is what it is like, this thing!
    "Why was I made to love this?"

In vain he tried to begin shaking it off,
    and his flesh would be pulled.

Now again he went,
    and he went a little while—
Now again his reason became nothing—
    he arrived near another father's brother's town.
Now again it said:
    "We two shall strike your town,
    "We two shall strike your town,"
In vain he tried to still it,
    it was never still.
In vain he would try to throw it away,
    always those fingers of his would cramp.

Now again his reason became nothing,
    now again he did it to his father's brother's town,
        he crushed it all.
He recovered:
    his father's brother's town (is) nothing,
        the people all are dead.
Now he cried.

In vain he tried in the fork of a tree,
    there in vain he would try squeezing through it;
In vain he would try to shake it off,
    it would not come off,
        and his flesh would be pulled;
In vain he would keep beating what he had taken on rocks,
    it would never be crushed.

Again he would go,
    he would arrive near another father's brother's town;
Now again that which he had taken would shake:
    "We two shall strike your town,
    "We two shall strike your town."
His reason would become nothing,
    he would do it to his father's brother's town,
        crush, crush, crush, crush;
    all his father's brother's town he would destroy,
        and he would destroy the people.

He would recover,
he would cry out,
   he would grieve for his relatives.
In vain he would try diving in water;
  in vain he would try to shake it off,
   and his flesh would be pulled.
In vain he would roll in a thicket;
  in vain he would keep beating what he had taken on rocks;
   he would abandon hope.
Now he would cry out.

Again he would go.
Now again he would arrive at another town,
  a father's brother's town.
Now again what he had taken would shake:
  "We two shall strike your town,
  "We two shall strike your town."
His reason would become nothing,
  he would do it to the town,
   crush, crush, crush, crush;
    and the people.
He would recover:
  all the people and the town (are) no more,
   his hands and arms (are) only blood.
He would become
  "Qa! qa! qa! qa!"
   he would cry out.
In vain he would try to beat it on the rocks,
  what he had taken would not be crushed;
In vain he would try to throw away what he had taken,
  always his fingers stick to it.

Again he would go.
Now his too, his town,
  he would be near his town.
In vain he would try to stand, that one,
  see, something would pull his feet.
His reason would become nothing,
he would do it to his town,
   crush, crush, crush, crush;
  all his town he would destroy,
   and he would destroy his relatives.

He would recover:
> his town (is) nothing,
>> the dead fill the ground.

He would become
> "Qa! qa! qa! qa!"
>> he would cry out.

In vain he would try to bathe;
> in vain he would try to shake off what he wears,
>> and his flesh would be pulled.

Sometimes he would roll about on rocks;
> he would think,
>> perhaps it will break apart;
>>> he would abandon hope.

Now again he would cry out,
> and he wept.

He looked back.
Now she is standing near him, that old woman.
"You,"
> she told him,
>> "You.

In vain I try to love you,
> "In vain I try to love your relatives.

"Why do you weep?
> "It is you who choose;
>> "Now you carried that blanket of mine."

Now she took it,
> she lifted off what he had taken;
> now she left him,
>> she went home.

He stayed there,
> he went a little distance;
>> there he built a house,
>> a small house.

Gishgiu's Escape

This story is told by George B. Wasson, a Coquelle Indian, about his great-grandmother's experiences in the nineteenth century at a time when she and other Indians in southwestern Oregon were "herded up to the concentration camp" at Yachats by government agents, where they were kept in miserable conditions. As Wasson indicates, he heard his father and his aunts tell the story of "Gishgiu's Escape" often when he was growing up. The "escape" story is followed by a second Wasson family story about Gishgiu, which George describes as a "classic example of how she fit right in and served the family well." Both of these stories are about "encounters," but of a very different kind.

The word *Coquille* is French, meaning *shell*, but there is strong evidence that the Native people who lived along the Coquille River and its outlet called themselves *Coquelle*—pronounced *ko-kwel*—as the Wasson family and others still do. As happened elsewhere, the Indian word seems to have been replaced in pronunciation and spelling by a Caucasian homonym. See McArthur, *Oregon Geographic Names*, p. 48.

—These texts are from a speech given by George Wasson at the annual meeting of the American Folklore Society in Eugene on October 28, 1993. (All rights reserved.)

My great-grandmother, Gishgiu (affectionately called "Gekka" by her grand-children), went with the American soldiers in good faith, first to the concentration camp at Reedsport and then on to Yachats, because she believed that the treaty which had been signed by her husband, Kitzu-Jin-Jin, would eventually be honored. Unfortunately, conditions were so bad there that she finally lost faith in the word of the American government and ran away.

My father, Aunt Lolly, Aunt Daisy, and Aunt Mary often told me the story of "Gekka" running away and coming back to South Slough. Diving into the ocean, she swam around the major headlands such as Cape Perpetua and the Sea Lion Caves to avoid the soldiers on the trail above. After hiding in the bushes during the daytime, she walked the long beaches at night, arriving at Coos Bay through the sand dunes. At the turn of high-tide, Gishgiu entered the water and swam with the ebb-flow until it carried her across and down to South Slough. There she walked up the slough to near her daughter's home and made herself a comfortable den in a hollow log not far away.

At night "Gekka" made contact with her daughter, Susan "Adulsah," who gave her food. They met secretly that way until grandfather [who was not an

Indian] became suspicious of his wife talking to someone in her Indian language, late at night. He usually thought nothing of grandmother getting up and doing things in the middle of the night, but this became more secretive, and when he discovered that his mother-in-law was living not far away in a hollow log, he became indignant and insisted that she move into the house with them where she belonged. However, the soldiers from Fort Yamhill had orders to round up those run-away Indians, and a detachment was sent out to scour the country where they might be hiding.

One day when grandfather was out in the logging woods with his bull-team, word came to the house that soldiers were headed there to take "Gekka" back to Yachats. Quickly, the women emptied the storage space behind the living-room staircase, and tiny Gishgiu crawled back under the bottom step. Then all the boxes and trunks were shoved into place as though nothing more could possibly be under there.

While the soldiers were ransacking the house looking for Gishgiu, some of the younger kids, caught up in the excitement of a fun game with real soldiers, were running around pointing to the bottom step of the stairs saying "Gekka, Gekka." Fortunately, those soldiers had no idea what the kids were saying and just pushed them out of their way as they hurried with their search, nervously pounding the floor with their rifle butts, looking for loose boards under which the old woman could be hidden.

Swiftly, one of the older children raced through the woods to summon Grandpa for help. Now they say that Grandpa Wasson was a big man, and no two soldiers could possibly stand up to his fury. He marched into his house, grabbed them both by the back of their necks, and threw them out into the yard (some say that he threw them through the parlor room window). He told them never to come back, and, needless to say, they didn't.

Gishgiu lived out the remainder of her days with the family, mending clothes, which she could do even though she was blind by then, yet doing all the things any old grandmother would need to do while sitting in the dark.

Gishgiu and the Sugar Thief

Grandmother (Susan Adulsah) had begun to notice that things seemed to be missing from the store room, which was a small log outbuilding just to one side of the main house, with loosely fitted log rails barring the entrance. Anyone could crawl through if they wanted inside. The items which seemed to be rapidly disappearing were sugar, syrup, and dried apples, which were stored in large wooden barrels, just as they came off the ship from San Francisco. It seemed that the only possible explanation was that a run-away Indian was sneaking in there and stealing the food, as no other white families lived nearby at that time. Grandfather said that something had to be done—"they are always fair when treated right." So it was decided that someone who could speak all of the languages in southern Oregon should wait in hiding for them to show up and talk to them in words they could understand. It would probably be best to try to catch them at night, when the stealing seemed to occur. So Gishgiu was elected to wait up in there all night since she could speak more languages than anyone else. Also, she was blind, and the dark wouldn't even bother her at all.

The next night, with a bed made for her up in the far corner, "Gekka" crawled in there to wait for the thief to show up. Sure enough, along in the night she heard them climbing through an opening in the logs. She thought, "I don't want to frighten them. I'll just let them get good and started, then I'll talk to them just a little." There was a scratching noise, as if they were trying to light matches and they were probably damp. Soon she heard them in the sugar barrel and decided, "now is the time." She had waited until they were way down inside scraping near the bottom when she spoke to them, at first in her own language. She said loudly, "Listen to me, whoever you are. You don't have to steal from my son-in-law. He is a good and generous man and would never refuse you anything." There was no response. The digging in the barrel stopped for just a moment, as though the thief paused to listen, yet there was no answer to her words. When they went back to scraping again, she tried another language, saying her son-in-law would help them if they would only answer her and identify themselves. Again there was no response. They just went back to scraping sugar. Gishgiu tried all the languages she knew, finally scolding them in Chinook Jargon, "Why don't you talk, why don't you answer me?" Still they made no response. "Well," she said to herself, "they just deserve to be punished. I'll call my son-in-law." She yelled loudly for grandfather to "come quickly, they are stealing the sugar and pay no heed to me." Grandfather came rushing in with a lantern in one hand and his faithful Winchester in the other. There, digging into the sugar barrel, was a big black bear. Grandfather was a good shot, so there was short work of the sugar thief.

Indians Speculate on White Ladies' Bustles

In this anecdote from an 1851 newspaper, a Mr. Russell describes the conversation among a group of Oregon Indians, perhaps Clackamas Chinook, trying to make sense of one of the more puzzling aspects of the settlers' way of life: the bustles worn by white women. As in much of the writing of the time, Indians are stereotyped as "warriors" and "squaws" and the sound of their languages as "grunts." Nonetheless, it is not the Indians who are shown to be the foolish ones in this story. (A transcript of this story in the WPA Oregon Folklore Project indicates that it was copied from the *Weekly Times,* Portland, Oregon, December 13, 1851, originally from the *California Courier.*)

Mr. C. T. Russell relates his experience among the Indians of the Northwest, when attending the fishing ceremonies at the mouth of the Columbia. Having attended it with a party of ladies and gentlemen from Astoria and Portland, he noticed the effect of the ladies' bustles on the Indians. Some time later, having gone to their lodges with the Indians, he relates, "Imagine an immense lodge, in which were seated in a circle the whole tribe. At length a squaw rose up, and taking a bag of feathers, tied them around her waist with a string. She then walked up and down the lodge to show how the white women walked. She then sat down and the rest gave a grunt of satisfaction. A warrior arose and stated that he thought its use was to catch fleas, for, said he, when they get to the string, they will walk around to see what it is and will fall into the bag, and when it is full, they take the bag off and burn it. He sat down and received a general grunt. Another arose and gave his opinion, that it was to catch the perspiration, for when it meets the string, it runs into the bag, and when it is full they empty it. Another grunt. At last the old doctor—the medicine man—from whose decision there is no appeal, gave the signal for silence and then said that the white women did not have so good forms as the Indian women, and wore these bags to make the white men think that they were well formed." He sat down amid repeated grunts, in which Mr. R says he had to join.

An Encounter between Miners and Indians

The *Oregonian* newspaper ran a weekly contest for the best true pioneer stories in the 1930s. This story would be seen by some readers as an example of "Indian cunning" and by others as an example of what happens to the white man who is certain that he knows it all. Originally published September 22, 1935, in the *Oregonian*, this story was included in Erik Bromberg's "Frontier Humor: Plain and Fancy," pp. 340-341.

It was just after the Civil War . . . and a young fellow by the name of Day had landed in San Francisco after a journey around the Horn. There he met a fast talker who convinced him that he not only knew Oregon, all the Indians there—their languages and habits—but he knew just where the gold was. If only Day would grubstake the pair he would escort them directly to the Oregon El Dorado.

After the pair had panned along the Sacramento for a couple of months and then stumbled into the Klamath country of Oregon, Day was sure that his companion had less knowledge about gold, Indians, and Oregon than he. The pay-off came one hot day in the wastelands of Klamath. Provisions were running low and they hunted all day with no luck. Then came the discovery that they had no water nor could they find any.

There was an encampment of Indians nearby. These were neither friendly nor hostile, so Day's selfsure partner approached them in search of water. He waved his arms wildly and shouted all sorts of gibberish at them.

"No savvy," shrugged the Indians.

So the white man went into his routine again.

And once more said the Indians, "No savvy."

A third time the prospector went at it. This time there was a gleam of understanding in one face. The Indian led them to a spring.

One taste of the stuff was plenty. It was warm and sulphurous, and required a mental ramrod to get it down. Even in coffee it tasted horrible. But they choked it down, and after a while rolled up for the night.

The next morning they were drinking the concoction once more, when the Indian who pointed out the spring wandered into their camp. He watched them drink for a while and then finally asked, "You likem?"

Both prospectors denied this with vehemence. And at this the Indian led them to a cool bubbling spring a short distance away.

"Why didn't you tell us about this last night?" demanded Day indignantly.

The Indian shrugged and pointed at the partner.

"Him say him wantum bath," he grunted. "Indians bathe in other spring."

Donald McKay

The Origin of Horses in Oregon

This plausible-sounding account of the sensation created in Cayuse/Umatilla country by the appearance of the first horse (in the early eighteenth century?) was dictated around 1900 by Donald McKay, a Wasco notable. —McKay Papers, Pendleton Library.

The Cayuse Indians who occupied the country north of the Snake and Columbia rivers were always at war with some of the other tribes. Now at this time they went to war with the Im-a-tell-ar [Umatilla] against the Snake Indians. They got as far as the Burnt or Mailer [Malheur] River, and they sent out spies to the bluffs overlooking the river, where they discovered their enemy riding on what they took to be an elk or deer. They went back to their Chief Oc-oc-tuin [Umatilla] and reported what they saw. He sent others who discovered the footprints were not that of a split hoof but that of a round solid hoof. Oc-oc-tuin then concluded to make a treaty with the Snake Indians, which he accomplished, also getting from them a stud horse [for the Umatillas] and [for] the Cayuse a mare, after which the Snake Indians went back to their own country.

The next year when it came time for the sports they met at Ft. Wallula, and when the stud saw the mare which had dropped a colt and was in season again, he immediately got into action which greatly scared the Indians until it was over, after which they concluded it was all right. Then every man, woman, and child there had to ride on the wonderful animals. One would ride and the other lead the horse. It was concluded then that they would make another war against the Snake Indians for the purpose of obtaining more horses, which they did, and obtained a great many more from which they have continued to breed.

Bill McBride's Race Horse

This is a version of a story that appears to be fairly widespread in the Northwest. It involves an Indian entering a horse race, placing a bet on his horse, and winning, sometimes through substituting one horse for another in the final race. Whether or not such an event ever happened, the folklorist is most interested in trying to understand why these stories became so popular. In these stories the Indian behaves almost like a trickster figure and uses his wits to get the better of the whites, who think they already have him beat. This account about Bill McBride was told by Shirley Susac, who was raised in central Oregon, to her daughter, Cathryn, on March 14, 1971. You can find another version of this story by E. R. Jackman in *The Oregon Desert*, p. 58.

When I was a child, one of the big things was going to the fair, the county fair. My most very favorite person was an Indian named Bill McBride. He was everything an Indian should be. He had long braids and was very, very straight. The only thing I think he had ever done in his life was raise race horses, and the big treat of his year was to bring his horses to the fair. When I was really little I remember the story about Bill.

He lived up at the top of the reservation [Warm Springs], somewhere around Simnasho, and so he came into the fair and brought all his race horses. He had a race horse that looked beautiful. It was a coal black horse with one white stocking. So the first day of the fair, everyone always expected Bill McBride to win the Indian horse race, and the first day of the fair he ran his horse, and his horse came in last. And so he told everyone he just didn't know, he had brought his horse all the way into Redmond to this fair, and he just couldn't tell his horse that he was disgracing him. So, second day, he ran his horse and he came in last. He looked very dejected, and I guess his braids hung down.

So that night he went around and told everyone this: By golly, he wasn't going to let his horse know how disappointed he was. He said just to prove his faith in his horse, he was going to bet every cent he could get his hands on, and then he told everyone he didn't want to disillusion his horse. He didn't want him to get some kind of complex, and so, of course, everyone thought, Ho, Ho, Ho. And they gathered up all the money they had, and Bill McBride gathered up all the money he had. The next day they had just a match race between Bill McBride's horse and another horse. And the two horses lined up at the starting gate, and Bill McBride's horse just absolutely ran away from the other horse. And the one thing I remember about Bill McBride—and I can still see him just doing the same thing—he always got so far ahead he always turned around and looked to see the other horses behind him, and evidently he must have really had to look back to see the other horse. So he gathered up all his money, and with a huge, beautiful smile on his face, went back to the reservation. What no one really knew, but everyone suspected, was that he had completely matching horses, and he had run the dog first and then come up with his real race horse the last day of the fair.

The Joke Was on the Whites in Pendleton

This story is older than the story about Bill McBride's race horse, but it is similar in its portrayal of Indians liking to bet, the whites assuming they'll win the race and the bets, and Indians winning the race. These stories are also a reflection of the common belief in the West, still prevalent today, that Indians are excellent horsemen. This story was copied from the *Oregonian*, February 28, 1873, p. 1, and included in the WPA Oregon Folklore Collection.

The people, that is, the sporting portion of them at Pendleton, have been preparing for a grand horse race at that place, to come off on Washington's birthday. The managers declared the track "free for all horses," hoping, perhaps, to give their friends a chance to gobble up a few dollars and some ponies from the Nez Perce Indians, who live on a reservation nearby. The Indians didn't bite at first, but at length entered a certain horse belonging to one of their number and staked a considerable amount of coin and a number of ponies on the event of his winning the race. The whites thought they had a good thing, and bantered Lo to double the pot. Get an Indian to bet and he'll stake his bottom dollar every time, and Lo doubled and "went two better," and the stake was enlarged until the loose coin in the pockets of the whites was pretty near all up. The horses were brought out, the start given, and the way the Nez Perce horse swooped down the track was only equaled by the way the Nez Perce themselves swooped down on the stakes. Next time they have a race there the Nez Perce will be ruled out on account of color.

Histo and the Carnation Man

The following anecdote from Warm Springs is a kind of "First Contact" story in reverse: it has obviously never occurred to the canned-milk salesman until he meets Histo that Indians could be world travelers in the late nineteenth and early twentieth centuries, as featured players in Wild West shows, Buffalo Bill Cody's and others'. Histo's great predecessor in this would be Sitting Bull, who grandly toured with Cody in the 1880s; closer to home, the Warm Springs/Wasco leader Donald McKay parlayed his role as a scout in the Modoc War into success as the star attraction of several "Indian Medicine" shows, touring nationally. (See Keith and Donna Clark, eds. *Daring Donald McKay.*)—Told to Jarold Ramsey by Dan Macy Sr. at Macy's Store in Warm Springs, August 13, 1991.

When I first started working here in the store at the Agency [in the late '20s], a lot of the old Indian fellers would come in as soon as we opened in the morning, and sit around and talk things over, tell stories and "score" off each other all day. Old Histo, he was very old and nearly blind—when it got to be lunch-time, he'd hammer on the floor with his stick, and that was my signal to ask him in Jargon, "What do you want, Histo?" And he'd answer, "Want little fish (he meant sardines) and crackers, and red pop." So I'd fix it up and he'd have his lunch. It was part of my job.

Old Histo never had much to say at the best, and some days we'd know he was in an especially low mood because he'd come in with his reservation hat down over his eyes, and never look up all day. It happened to be one of those days when the Carnation Milk salesman came by—and all the while he was bringing in the cartons of cans and writing up orders, he was complaining about how remote Warm Springs was, how dangerous it was for him to drive down the Mecca Grade, and on and on. All of a sudden he sees old Histo over there in the corner, and says, "Hi there grandpa! Have you ever been anywhere?" Old Histo didn't look up from under his hat, just grunted. "Ever been to Portland, grandpa?" Another grunt. "Even to *Madras*?" Grunt. So the Carnation man turns to me and says, "Well, I think that's just terrible—why doesn't the Tribe or somebody raise some money to send these poor old guys to see a little of the world?"

At this old Histo lifts his hat with his finger and stares at the Carnation man for a while. Then he says, "I been lotsa places. I been to London before the King and Queen! I been to Copenhagen, Madrid, Rome, and Barcelona! Where *you* been, white-eyes?"

All the other old-timers had a good laugh at this, and finally one of them explained to the Carnation man that as a young buck Histo had gone off the Reservation for ten years to travel all over the world as a rider with the Buffalo Bill Wild West Show! That Carnation salesman, he just folded up his order-forms and went off talking to himself.

Wong Sam's Phrase Book

Nineteenth- and early twentieth-century Chinese immigrants to Oregon and other Western states made good use of an English/Chinese phrase book, compiled by "Wong Sam and Assistants," and first published and distributed in 1875 by Wells, Fargo. The phrases come in "sets," partly based on commercial needs, partly on the difficulties of coping in a strange and often hostile Anglo society.

你有乜貨物出賣	What goods have you for sale?
樣樣都有	I have all kinds.
我想買條好褲	I want to get a pair of your best pants.
你愛點樣價銀	What do you ask for them?
你舡減少些	Can you take less for them?
先生　不舡	I cannot, sir.
沒肯賣賒欵麼	Will you sell them on credit?
我賣現銀　先生	No sir, I sell for cash.
佢強搶我物	He took it from me by violence.
我無意打佢	I struck him accidentally.
佢無事打我	He assaulted me without provocation.
你肯去我包沒回	I guarantee to bring him back, if he will go.
此人欲撺工銀	The men are striking for wages.
我身分足用	I am content with my situation.
你同佢鬭欵	You contend with him about the account.
裝滿箱蘋果	The box contains apples.

佢詐病	He feigned to be sick.
我綁起此麥	We bind the wheat up.
我綁治個瘡	We bound up the wound.
汝毀了窗門	You break windows.
我毀了刀	I broke my knife.
他毀了國法	They have broken the laws of the State.
丟佢下水	Cast him into the water.
我捉個人入監今日	We cast a man into prison today.
人他放出去	They have cast the man out.
我貨物從唐山載來	All our goods were imported from China.
幾時我鋪滿期通知	Tell me when the lease of my store is expired.

Does Anyone Speak Finnish Here?

One of the difficult challenges many immigrants to a new land face is language, and a common type of story traditionally told in many immigrant families relates, often with humor, the experiences a grandmother, father, or other relative had trying to communicate. This story, told by Mrs. Ray Maggard of Bremerton, Washington, is about the arrival of her mother from Finland to Astoria, Oregon, at the turn of the century. This story appears in an article by Erik Bromberg, "Frontier Humor: Plain and Fancy," pp. 261-262.

Late in the last century Mrs. Maggard's mother embarked from Finland, alone and not possessing a word of English. She arrived in Astoria and looked over the crowd expectantly, but saw no one familiar.

The young immigrant stood in the busy street keeping back tears and fright. At last she gained courage to step up to one of the through passengers who was on the platform stretching his legs before the train departed.

"Can you direct me to Auntie Rosie?" she asked in Finnish.

But the poor girl had accosted a Native American, and he shook his head vigorously to indicate he did not understand.

She tried another, and another. All by some freak chance were itinerant, non-Finnish Americans.

She was about to sit down and bawl when a Chinese who was nearby came up.

"Who are you seeking?" he asked in flawless Finnish.

The girl gaped at the Mongolian stranger.

"Who are you seeking?" he repeated.

Gathering her wits, she asked for directions to Auntie Rosie's house and received them. Then she asked, "You're not Finnish. I can see that. But how do you know our language?"

"Lady," said the Chinese, who ran a local laundry, "in Astoria one either knows Finnish or one starves rapidly."

When Basque Herders First Arrived in the Owyhee Region

Like every other immigrant group to the United States, the Basques who immigrated from Spain's northern provinces to the Owyhee region of southeastern Oregon and Idaho to work in the sheep industry have stories about the difficulties the newly arrived herders experienced learning new ways and a new language. Although many of these stories are now recounted by Basques with humor, some second-generation Basques also remember times from their childhood when there were rules against speaking Basque on the school playground and they were punished for doing so, even though many who were raised on ranches had no opportunity to learn English until they got to school.

The following anecdotes about Basque herders' experiences with English were collected by Sarah Baker Munro in the 1970s around Jordan Valley ("Basque Folklore in Southeastern Oregon," pp. 159-175).

They tell of Domingo Aldecoa that he came into a restaurant at Mountain Home [Idaho] on evenings, listening intently for the sound and meaning of the words of his adopted neighbors, only to discover after a few weeks of bewilderment that he was trying to learn not English but Chinese. In those days there were only Chinese restaurants. (p. 170)

A Basque went to a ranch to get some chickens. He had been living in cattle country and his English was more complete in dealing with cattle than with chickens. At the ranch he was being given only hens. Protesting but not knowing the word "rooster," he shouted, "No, I want bull-hens, bull-hens." (p. 170)

A ranger in Emmett [Idaho] once wanted his non-English-speaking Basque herder to move his camp. He could not make the herder understand where he was to move his camp. Finally he gave up in disgust and muttered, "Oh, go to Hell." "Take a lunch?" the herder inquired. (p. 173)

Dad's Embarrassment

This story was collected by George Venn from Angie Tsiatsos, a Greek-American student at Eastern Oregon State College in La Grande in 1989. She notes that "this story was first told to me by my father when I was ten years old. We had company at our house that day for dinner. After dinner, my father and his friends always tell stories of their pasts. We laughed at him for a long time after he told that story. I think that's the most embarrassed I've ever seen my dad." She continues, "Our family tells stories like this quite often, just for entertainment. It was my father's way of telling us that he, too, could get embarrassed."—From Venn Collection, Eastern Oregon State College.

My father came from Greece when he was sixteen years old. He had been supporting his family since he was thirteen, when his father had been killed in the war by guerillas. He came to America to earn money to send back to his family in Greece. He had an aunt and uncle here in La Grande that offered their hospitality to him as long as he needed it.

He came to La Grande the first part of November. His birthday was on the eleventh, as was Veterans' Day. There was a parade in town that day, and my father didn't understand why because he didn't know any English. His cousin explained to him that La Grande was so happy to have him here in the U. S. on his birthday that they wanted to help him celebrate it, so they had a parade for him. For the whole next year, my father thought that the parade was for him, until the next year, when there was another parade again, [and] he thought it was for him. He was extremely embarrassed to find out the real reason for the parade.

How Masuo Yasui Found Hood River

Masuo Yasui, a Japanese immigrant (*issei*) in 1903, who became a prominent businessman and orchardist in Hood River, often told this tale to his family. Whatever its basis in fact, it vividly conveys how his discoveries in the new world of Oregon were shaped and colored by his memories of "home" in Japan.—In Lauren Kessler, "Spacious Dreams: A Japanese Family Comes to the Pacific Northwest," p. 163.

Masuo Yasui liked to tell his children that as a young man he heard about a place called *shin-shin-no-chi*, the Japanese pronunciation of Cincinnati, which translated as *new, new land*. Fascinated by the name and what the city might hold, he boarded a train in Portland heading east for Ohio. But—and here he would pause for dramatic impact when narrating the story later—as the train snaked through the Columbia River gorge approaching Hood River, he stared out the window and was transfixed by the beauty of the passing scenery. The dense, green valley sloping back to touch the base of a snow-capped peak that resembled the beloved Mt. Fuji reminded him so much of Japan that he got off the train then and there, declaring Hood River his new home.

Golden America

Just as overland emigrants to Oregon were seeking "paradise," European immigrants to America in the nineteenth century believed that America was a land of such economic opportunity that it was described metaphorically as "golden," or with "streets paved of gold." The following story was told by John Klobas, a second generation Slovenian, of Eugene, Oregon, to folklore student Nancy Beplat in August 1971 (RVMA). John Klobas explains that it is about a young man who came to America "maybe with my father."

In the old country all the time people heard America, "*Zlatna Amerika*." Gold, with golden streets. Gold in America. You just bend down and you pick it up.

One time this lad came to America. A young one who came, maybe with my father, who knows? But they came, and they came—y'know, they came on the ship, in the hold of a ship. And there wasn't much space, and there wasn't much food, and the water was green and dirty, and people stole from them, and they came in between decks, and they got to Ellis Island.

And at Ellis Island was still waiting more bad things and horrors. They got to Ellis Island, and they got checked to see if they had glaucoma in the eyes, to see if they had tuberculosis, to have a blood test. Did they have enough money? Sometimes they, even they had to borrow money—to get past the gates, to go into this free America with the gold.

[Nancy: You could rent money, couldn't you?]

You could rent money, even. Oh, *ja*, for a sum, you could rent-—for maybe your coat, a sheepskin jacket, or a hat, or some dinara, or some zlato, or gold- —you could rent money. But finally this one guy, this one who came, he finally got through all the indignities and made it from the village-—he made it to the seaport, and he changed his money, and he got his ticket.

And he came to New York, and he went to Ellis Island, and he got through Ellis Island, and he came out to New York. New York! Past the Statue of Liberty, where we have freedom and equality, and where we take the world's hungry, huddled masses. And he saw this, and he saw the picture, and he saw the statue.

And he came out on the gangplank to New York, and he stepped on solid ground. And he said, "Aha! so this is my golden America." And he looked down from the gangplank, and *oi-yo*, what should he see, coming from the gangplank, but y'know what, a "double eagle." Now the double eagle in the old times was a gold piece. A single eagle was ten dollars, a half-eagle was five dollars, and a double eagle was a twenty-dollar gold piece. And he looked down, and he saw a double eagle—like a wagon wheel lying there on the end of the gangplank. And y'know, he bent over, and he said, "Aha! The first one."

And he bent over to pick it up, but bent over he thought: Aha! Why for all this trouble I go to. This is only one. Eh, I will wait. And he straightened up. And he said again to himself: Hah! I will wait until they get thicker to fill my sack so I can go back to the old country. Aha!

But then they tell his story later. That was the first double eagle and the last double eagle that he saw for free. The rest he paid for in sweat, and in blood, and in tears. That was the first one and the last one he saw in this America. To go back home for free, this double eagle.

Oregon's Folk Heroes and Characters

With the exception of the culture heroes that exist in Native American oral literature, Oregon's folk heroes of the nineteenth and twentieth centuries—like American folk heroes in general—are historic figures and *local* heroes. They are individuals whose remarkable antics have been commemorated and embellished through storytelling traditions, sometimes of their own creation. The qualities that make a "folk hero" vary. The local character whose own wit and storytelling abilities are of heroic proportions and the town strong man are two of the primary types of folk heroes. Occasionally an individual's bravery or kindness (Lou Southworth, Aaron Meier) results in the development of a local narrative tradition. And, of course, there will always be stories told about the anti-hero— the badman or outlaw. In Oregon we can find all these folk hero types alive and well, although the editors failed to uncover many narratives of female heroes or outlaws. Oregonians have probably also heard of the mighty Paul Bunyan; however, his reputation really owes much more to professional writers than to folklore and oral tradition. While Oregonians learn of folk heroes like Hathaway Jones, B.F. Finn, and Tebo Ortego from hearing stories about them, their acquaintance with Paul Bunyan most likely occurred in an elementary school classroom with a book and not through the tales told by Oregon's loggers.

"Bear and Buckskin" by Lloyd Reynolds. Wood engraving, date unknown.

Chiloquin

Chiloquin is a prominent Klamath family name, and also the name of the tribal center of the Klamath people. When the ethnographer Leslie Spier studied the Klamath culture in the 1920s, he recorded a set of anecdotes about a nineteenth-century leader named Chiloquin, whose heroic exploits embody great strength, courage, and hardihood—nobody could out-do Chiloquin!—Spier, *Klamath Ethnography*, pp. 37-38.

Chiloquin was a short man, deep-chested, powerful, and exceptionally hardy. It is related that he overtook a party camped in the deep snows atop the Cascades. Not being properly equipped, he lay beside a fire covered only with a single blanket. In the morning he was covered with frost but apparently had not suffered.

Somewhere in the north, possibly Warm Springs, was a man who owned a big slave who was very much a bully. While the slave was absent Chiloquin traded three horses for the master's best horse. When the slave returned he inquired for the horse and sent a man to demand it. That man went twice but each time Chiloquin sat quietly sewing and did not reply. Then the slave himself went out and demanded its return but Chiloquin paid no attention. When the slave went to untie the horse, Chiloquin tripped him. The slave struck at him with his hatchet but missed. Then Chiloquin wounded him and he retreated.

Chauchau, a northerner, wanting Chiloquin's daughter, offered horses and other valuables. The latter refused. He came to Chiloquin at night and fought with him till daybreak. Chiloquin clung to Chauchau's hair despite the beating he was receiving. Chauchau came again the next night and again they fought. This performance kept up through the whole winter. When spring came, Chauchau acknowledged his defeat: "Yes, Chiloquin, you are fierce," and they were again friends.

Again in the north some northern shamans went into a sweatlodge. They wanted a shaman among their Klamath visitors to accompany them. None was present so the Klamath insisted on Chiloquin joining them. One after the other each northern shaman sprinkled water on the hot rocks as he sang his song, hoping to force the others out. Some, overcome by heat and steam, had to be dragged out. Once outside they wondered what had become of Chiloquin; he was nowhere to be seen. They thought he must have died. After a long time he began to talk, throwing water on the rocks. When he was quite ready he came out and walked to his own people. He had bested the shamans.

How Fish-Hawk Raided the Sioux

Fish-Hawk

Like Chiloquin, Fish-Hawk was a historical figure, a Cayuse warrior whose feats of derring-do in the 1870s and '80s with a band of Cayuse and Nez Perce comrades (known as the *us-ka-ma-tone,* or "The Brothers") became the stuff of heroic legends, still told by his people. For a detailed study of this stirring narrative and other tales about the *us-ka-ma-tone,* see Jarold Ramsey, "Fish-Hawk and Other Heroes," in *Reading the Fire: Essays in the Traditional Indian Literatures of the Far West,* pp. 133-151. The story was told in Nez Perce Sahaptin by Gilbert Minthorne to Morris Swadesh in Pendleton in 1930, and adapted from Swadesh's interlinear notebook translation by Jarold Ramsey for publication in *Coyote Was Going There,* pp. 24-25. Gilbert Minthorne claimed to have heard the story from Fish-Hawk himself: it's interesting to note that although the Cayuse had vanished as a distinct tribal and linguistic entity before 1900, being absorbed into the Nez Perce and Umatilla tribes, the perspective of Minthorne's telling of the story is distinctly, proudly pro-Cayuse.

A long time ago, when many Nez Perce and Cayuse lived to the east, they used to go buffalo hunting. Once a man dreamed of the Sioux, he saw them in his sleep, and he told the village men, "Now I am going on the war-path day after tomorrow, and I shall travel to the Sioux." He was a tough man; many times he had fought and come out all right. His name was Fish-Hawk. Four Cayuse men and two Nez Perce men were going, the one named Fish-Hawk and one named Come-with-the-dawn and one named All-alighted-on-the-ground and one named Charging Coyote, and two Nez Perce men. Fish-Hawk took the lead, he held the pipe, he was the thinker in travels.

They all had red jackets, they were on the war-path, all six of them. They traveled and it snowed, it snowed like winter on the prairie. They traveled on horseback and they came upon the prairie, and went down into a canyon. Many Sioux lived close by there. Fish-Hawk stopped and he turned around towards his friends—"We've come right into camp, see, here are the tents, and they don't know we're here." Tents were all around, maybe two hundred or more, they saw the tents.

Then the Sioux discovered them and yelled in Sioux! Fish-Hawk said, "Brothers, think good, and take it easy—they are going to try and take us." And now they swept the Sioux horses along with them, they drove them along a little way, and then they all turned. "They are catching up with us," he told the others, the pipe-leader told them. "Younger brothers, move on from here, don't shoot yet, for soon they will try and take us. Look, there is brushy ground ahead, there we will dismount, and soon they will try and get us. We shall not desert each other; look to your guns," and the Sioux chased them along.

Fish-Hawk, the people's chief in battle, turned his horse and he waved at the Sioux, he told them: "I am Cayuse, we all are; come on, you are three hundred or more. You are Sioux and you are just like old women, you never will kill us, we are Cayuse!"

So they yelled at the Sioux during the chase, and shot at them, they killed them as they went, and he told his brothers, the pipe-leader, "Now turn your horses loose," and they got off and they took off the bridles and took off their jackets and left it all behind and took only the guns and bullets into the brush, among the cottonwoods. He told them, the pipe-leader, he told them, "Younger brothers, look: we can dig trenches and fight well from there." They dug out the ground and crossed cottonwoods over the trenches and got under it all. They yelled at the Sioux, the Sioux yelled back at them and hurled insults, they yelled back again. They were killing Sioux.

Now one of the Sioux used up his bullets and he came up to them, one Sioux, a tough man, dog-disguised, he came towards them, he came up singing. Fish-Hawk said, the tough one, "Little brothers, now he comes, take good aim"—and they hit him close by the trench. He came on, and now he shot at Fish-Hawk with a bow and arrows. Fish-Hawk cried, "Little brothers, he shot me!" He got mad, the one named Fish-Hawk. He told them, "Friends, now watch your leader, now! He shot one of us, now know me, now I am going after him and I am going to drag him right into the trench"—and he stood up suddenly and threw himself out of the trench and they yelled, the Sioux, they shot at him, and he hopped, he grabbed the Sioux warrior by the legs and dragged him along, he threw him into the trench and he hit him. They took his bullets and gun, and scalped him.

Fish-Hawk told them, "Little brothers, maybe I am dying, now pull out the arrow"—and they pulled it out, and the pipe-leader, chief in war, breathed good again, but he was bleeding and getting weak and they tied up the wound. He started shooting again, he told them, "Little brothers, think carefully; look, they are trying to get us, try to shoot straighter," and they yelled.

He saw now that there was fire all around them, below and up above, and he told them, "Now, look, it's burning, they are trying to kill us by burning. Dig deeper now, we are going to be burned, they're scared and that's why they are trying to burn us to death. But we will never die of fire, we are younger brothers, tough ones with guns, they can't get us killed, and they will never kill us with fire."

So he told them, and when night came he gathered them in the middle of the thicket, he told them: "We killed many Sioux, now we're going, we're going out. We're in the midst of them but with my knowledge, soon we will get through anyway." And he told them, "A little wind will come up presently, now get ready, little brothers, let's travel!" And it came, the whirlwind, and they got out of the trench. When the fire flared up, they went down, they passed the Sioux by unseen, they traveled on.

Dawn came. The Sioux said, "Now, look they're all burned up," and they went to the trench. When they got there they found nobody. The Sioux were surprised. "Where are they? How could they live? On which side of us did they pass?" They were greatly surprised, and as they went home, they cried on their way, they took many bodies home.

The Cayuse got out from the trench all right and from there they traveled without pants, shirt-less, pants-less, shoe-less—all they had were guns, and he told them, the Chief, the pipe-leader, he told them, "Younger brothers, now we have traveled far, and one of us is getting cold and can travel no further." It was Charging Coyote; he told them,"Friends, now leave me, I will be too much bother, I'll stay right here. My forefathers died too, I'll just rest." Then the others told him, "It's the same with all of us, without shoes, without pants, without shirts, somehow we will all get back."

Then they came upon a buffalo bull, and Fish-Hawk told them, "We have traveled far without eating, now kill it." And they killed two buffalo; and from them they made shoes and pants and shirts, and they ate buffalo meat. But they had no tents, they got black from freezing and were awful to look at: thus they came back to their own tents.

This is all of the story about the raid on the Sioux: now they told it at the big war-dance at celebration-time, how this man, Fish-Hawk, the pipe-leader, went on the warpath, he was the man! "Only six of us, and you couldn't get us killed, only six, and maybe you were three hundred and maybe more . . . ." Thus they told the story, and now all the people know it. This is a true story, now there, we have made it, and it will always be the same story.

Patrick Dooney and the Bear Dooneys

Irish heroic pride takes root in Oregon in these family legends about Pat Dooney the strong man. They were told by Michael E. Brophy, a second-generation Irish American from Portland, Oregon, to Paul Feist, a University of Oregon folklore student. (RVMA, Feist, February 1980)

The Bear Dooneys

The Bear Dooneys date from a cousin of mine named Patrick Dooney who lived down in Astoria . . . . He was a logger and walking through the woods one day on a narrow path a bear came the other way and the bear apparently growled, expecting Pat to get out of the path so he could get by. Pat wasn't about to . . . get out of the way for any bear or man, so, ah, he got into a wrestling match with the bear, and strangled the bear with his bare hands. And somebody actually has the skin of that bear somewhere in the family. He actually did kill a bear with his bare hands. Word got back to Ireland, so . . . the Dooneys who settled in Oregon became known as the "Bear Dooneys."

Pat Dooney Beats the Russians

Another story about Pat Dooney was when he was working as a longshoreman. He was a very large man. Pat was about six feet four, weighed around 230 and had worked all his life as a logger, a longshoreman, jobs that take strength and build strength in the process . . . a very strong man and a character that would not back down to anybody. He had very little education, in fact he couldn't read or write, but . . . highly respected as a man. And he was helping unload a Russian ship one time here in Portland, fifty, sixty years ago, when he noticed that there were some [very heavy] weights in one package. The Russians that were working with the weights made a bet that none of the Americans on the ship, the longshoremen, could do what they could do with the weights. So he [one of the Russians] proceeded to pick up the weights and press it over his head. I never did hear how much it was, but nobody was even interested in trying, except that somebody told Pat and says, "Are you going to let a Russian outdo you?" And that was all it took. Pat got down to pick up the weights . . . when he attempted to lift up the weights he couldn't get it up off the floor, and decided no Russian was going to outdo him so he stayed at it. Finally he got it off the floor and over his head and won the bet, but in the process he snapped all the rawhide laces in his boots. Estimates seem to be in vicinity of 400-500 pounds of weight.

Neshukulayloo

When Clara Pearson told this Nehalem Tillamook story (in English) to Elizabeth Jacobs in Garibaldi in 1933, she concluded by telling Mrs. Jacobs, "This happened before my great-great-grandfather's time, but it is true." Neshukulayloo (the name has not been translated) is a Native Amazon, a female hero who fiercely defends her independence against male prerogatives and masculine envy. —*Nehalem Tillamook Tales,* pp. 178-180.

Neshukulayloo was the only one like herself all over. She was too brave, too strong to marry. No man could handle her. She lived right here [at Garibaldi], not at Nehalem. She had no sister; she was the only girl in the family. Her brothers were just common men, not strong like her. She could do anything with her great strength. Her bow required two men to bend it. Her arrows were immense. No one could marry her, she would not have them. She was not too large, not fat, simply exceedingly strong. She did a man's work. She made dams in the river, she made and tended basket traps. No ordinary woman could ever do that.

She had two grown brothers and one younger one. She always allowed her younger brother to accompany her. She would say, "You carry my bow and arrows for me." She was ever alert, always ready. If anyone tackled her, she killed them. She and her little brother would go and look at her fish trap. One day she felt that someone was watching her. Her brother was sitting close by her. She said, "Hand me my quiver." She took out her bow, she pointed her arrow in every direction. (Those devils, just because she was different from other people, they thought they ought to kill her.) She was so brave that those people who were near there feared to do anything. They left, the men who had been after her. She did not harm anyone, her brothers harmed no one, but the men were all jealous of her strength and angered because she did not want anyone for a husband.

Soon again those men gathered together saying, "Let us go there." They went to her house while she and her little brother were away at the trap. Her two older brothers were at home. Those men arrived there and killed her two brothers just to hurt her. The two brothers had wives. That group of men went in the house and killed those two brothers and their wives. Then those devils went away again. They did not care, they thought she would not know who had done it.

Neshukulayloo was not feeling quite right that day. Earlier than usual she said to her young brother, "We must go home now." They went home, found her two brothers killed, her two sisters-in-law dead. She told her brother, "You come along. We will follow them, we will catch them." She hurried along on foot with her little brother. She said, "I do not believe they have already gone downriver. If they have already gone, that is my bad luck. But I think they have not yet." She stopped at a bend of the river. She broke off brush so she could see clearly.

After a while she heard loud talking. People were laughing, saying, "I guess that Neshukulayloo has not come home yet. She does not know what has happened at her home." She looked, she whispered, "Oh, they are the ones who killed my brothers." There was a whole canoeload of men just coming in sight around the bend. She was angry enough to eat rocks. She told her brother, "Hand me my quiver." She took her bow and arrow, she waited until they were at the best shooting distance. She thought, "I will not bother shooting any persons, but I will split that canoe so they can drown. Then those that swim around I can shoot through the head at my leisure." She did that. She shot that canoe right on the bow, the canoe split in two. Those men had to swim. Some held on to the pieces of the canoe, some tried to swim ashore; she shot them through the heads and they sank in the water. She allowed just two old men to swim ashore; they got away and walked all the way home.

She stood there. Presently another canoe came along. Their talk revealed them to be part of the same gang. "Oh, I wonder what Neshukulayloo will think when she gets home." She did the same thing. She shot that canoe on the bow, splitting it. Those men were swimming around; she shot them all through the heads. Now she was satisfied. She turned to her young brother, "Well, we will have to go home now and put our brothers away."

Those two old men arrived home. They said, "All of those people who killed her brothers were killed." She had let those two go because they were old people. After that Neshukulayloo moved farther down the valley. No one ever bothered her again. She never married, her young brother lived with her, he was her company. She had never harmed anyone. It was just Indian style to be jealous of her strength.

This happened before my great-great-grandfather's time, but it is true.

The Revenge against the Sky People

Versions or analogues of this weird and rousing heroic narrative exist in the recorded repertories of tribes all over the Northwest, attesting to the popularity and significance of the basic story of the revenger's courage, cleverness, and self-control in carrying out his "mission impossible" against the Sky People. The storytelling art of this Coos version is striking: notice how major events are foreshadowed (as in the hero's interview with his brother's killer's wife), and how intimate we become with his desperate situation disguised as the wife in the killer's household, until, in the climactic scene, the point of view shifts and we see our hero from the perspective of the unwitting Sky People as "she/the woman." For a study of this story and its relationship with the Clackamas Chinook horror-story, "Seal and Her Younger Brother Lived There" (p. 258 in this volume), see Ramsey, "The Wife Who Goes Out Like a Man, Comes Back as a Hero," in *Reading the Fire*, pp. 76-95. The Coos story originally appeared in Leo J. Frachtenberg, *Coos Texts*, pp. 149-157.

A man lived in Kiweet. He had an elder brother, who was always building canoes. Once he was working on a canoe, (when) a man came there to him. "What do you do with your canoes after you finish them?"—"I always sell my canoes." He kept on working, with his head bent down, while the man was talking to him. Alongside the man who was building lay his dog. All at once he [the stranger] hit the neck of the man who was building, and cut off his head. He took his head home.

The man who was building did not come home, and they went out looking for him. He lay in the canoe, dead, without a head. The little dog was barking along-side the canoe. The dog would look upwards every time it barked. Straight up it would look. So they began to think, "(Someone) from above must have killed him!" Then the next day the man's younger brother looked for him. The young man shot an arrow upwards, and then would shoot another one. He was shooting the arrows upwards. Every time he shot, his arrow would join (to the other); and as he kept on shooting this way, the arrows reached [down] to him.

Then he climbed up there. He went up on the arrows. He saw people when he had gotten up, and he asked, "From where do you come?" They were taking home a man's head. "We are [going to dance] for it," they said. They were taking home his elder brother's head. They said to the young man, "At a little place [nearby] the wife of the killer is digging fern-roots. Every forenoon she digs fern-roots there." So he went. He did not go very far. Suddenly, indeed, [he saw] a woman digging fern-roots. There was a big river.

So he asked the woman, "Do you have your own canoe?"—"Not so."—
"Who ferries you across the river? " "My husband ferries me across."—"What
do you do when he ferries you across?"—"He does not land the canoe. I usually jump ashore."—"What does he do afterward?"—"He usually turns back.
Then, when it is almost evening, I go home. He again comes after me. A little
ways off [shore] he stops the canoe. Then I jump in with my pack. I get in
there all right."—"What do you do with your fern-roots?"—"I usually dry
them."—"What do you do with your fern-roots after they are dry?"—"I usually give some of them to all the people who live here. A little ways off in the
next house, there live an old man and an old woman. I never give them any
fern-roots."—"What do you usually do?" —"Then I cook the roots in a big
pot."—"What do you do (then)?"—"I stir them with my hands."—"Doesn't
your hand get burned?"—"Not so." —"Does your pot boil? Don't you ever
say 'It hurts my hand!'?"—"No, it doesn't hurt me."—"What does your husband do when you lie down?"—"I lie a little ways off from my
husband."—"Does your husband usually fall asleep quickly?"—"Yes, he usually falls asleep quickly."

Now he asked her all [these questions], and then killed her. He skinned the
woman, and put on her hide. Indeed, he looked just like the woman. Then he
took her load and packed it. He saw the husband coming. The husband was
crossing. A little ways off in the river he stopped the canoe. Thus he [the
young man] was thinking, "I wonder whether I shall get there if I jump! I will
try it from this distance." He packed the load and jumped. One leg touched
the water. He pretty nearly did not get there. Thus spoke the man [husband],
"Is that you, my wife?" Thus he spoke: "I am tired, this is the reason why I
almost did not get (there). My pack is heavy." He [the husband] did not think
about it any more.

Whatever the woman had told him, the young man (did it) that way. He
made only one mistake. He gave fern-roots to those old people. He opened
their door. The two old people saw him when he entered. They did not take
the fern-roots which he held in his hands. Then one [of them] shouted, "Someone from below gives us something!" They did not hear it in the next house.

When the thing he was cooking began to boil, he stirred it with his hand.
"Ouch! It burned my hand!" The husband heard it. "What happened to you?"—
"My finger was sore, this is the reason why I [yelled]." And he [the young
man] was looking at the head that was fastened to the ceiling. It was his elder
brother's head. He cried there because he saw his elder brother's head. The
husband said: "You seem to be crying."—"There is so much smoke, my eyes
are sore." He [the husband] no longer paid any attention to it.

Now it got to be evening. The woman was going upstairs. Thus spoke the [husband's little brother], "My sister-in-law (looks) like a man!" His grand-mother said to him, "The women where she comes from (look) just like men. You must keep quiet!" Nobody again thought about it. From everywhere people (came) there to the murderer to help him. They were dancing for the head. For it they were dancing. Blood was dropping (from) the head (that) was hanging (there).

Then it got (to be) evening and they went to bed. . . . She [the "woman"] had a big knife under her pillow. The husband went to bed first. The woman was walking outside. She bored holes in all the canoes in the village. Only in the one in which she intended to cross she did not bore a hole. As soon as she was finished, she went inside. Then she went to bed a little ways from her husband. At midnight the husband was fast asleep. She got up on the sly. She cut off the head of the husband, and seized her elder brother's head. Then she ran away, and crossed over alone in the canoe.

His (the husband's) mother was sleeping under their bed. The blood dripped down on her, and the old woman lighted a torch. "Blood! Blood! What have you done? You must have killed your wife!" She heard nothing. So everybody woke up. Then they saw the man lying on his bed, without a head. His wife had disappeared, and the head that was hanging from the ceiling was gone. "The woman must have killed her husband."—"It was not a woman," [said the little boy].

Then they followed him. [They] shoved the canoes (into the water), but they kept on filling up with water, and they could not follow him.

Then [the young man] went down on his arrows, on which he had climbed up. Then he returned there (home). He brought back his elder brother's head. He assembled all his folks. Now, it is said, they were going to join his elder brother's head. Now they commenced to work. A small spruce tree was stand-ing there. Against that small spruce tree they were joining his head. They danced for it. His head climbed a little bit on his body, and then fell down. Four times it happened that way. His head would go up a little bit, and then fall down again. The fifth time, however, his head stuck on. . . . Then he [the young man] said to his elder brother, "Now you are all right. . . ."

These are the Woodpecker people; this is why their heads are red today. The blood on their necks, that's what makes the head red. [Someone] said to them, "You shall be nothing. You shall be woodpeckers. The last people shall see you."

Black Harris and the Putrefied Forest

Moses "Black" Harris (on the left)

Moses Harris, widely known on the frontier as "Black" Harris, was a celebrated African-American mountain man (James Beckwourth was another), whose career of adventures took him all over the Rockies and into Oregon Country in the 1830s and 1840s. He served as a guide to the Whitman party in 1836, for example, guided the Nathaniel Ford wagon train to Oregon in 1844, and helped rescue the lost Meek Cut-off emigrant train of "Blue Bucket" gold fame (see p. 189) in 1845. Between 1844 and 1847 he lived in a cabin on the Luckiamute River (Polk County), before returning to Missouri, where he died of cholera in 1849.

Black Harris was renowned, even among yarn-spinning mountain men, as a master storyteller. The artist Alfred Jacob Miller, who drew his only known portrait, shown above, wrote that "This Black Harris always created a sensation at the campfire, being a capital *raconteur,* and having had as many perilous adventures as any man probably in the mountains." (Quoted in LeRoy Hafen, ed. *The Mountain Men and the Fur Trade of the Far West,* Vol. IV, p.109; see also Verne Bright, "Black Harris, Mountain Man, Teller of Tales," pp. 3-20.)

Alas, no verifiable first-hand accounts of his tales have survived, but the following episode from *Life in the Far West* (1849), by the English writer Frederick Ruxton, who traveled widely with the mountain men and may have known Harris, probably catches something of the way he entertained listeners in pioneer Oregon and elsewhere. An old trapper "frames" Harris's story—

The darndest liar was Black Harris—for lies tumbled out of his mouth like boudins [cuds] out of a buf'ler's [buffalo's] stomach. He was the child as saw the putrefied forest in the Black Hills. Black Harris come in from Laramie; he'd been trapping three year an' more on Platte and the other side; and, when he got into Liberty, he fixed himself right off like a Saint Louis dandy. Well, he sat to dinner one day in the tavern, and a lady says to him—

"Well, Mister Harris, I hear you're a great trav'ler."

"Trav'ler, marm," says Black Harris, "this nigger's no trav'ler; I ar' a trapper, a mountain man, wagh!"

"Well, Mister Harris, trappers are great trav'lers, and you goes over a sight of ground in your perishinations, I'll be bound to say."

"A sight, marm, this coon's gone over, if that's the way your stick floats. I've trapped beaver on Platte and Arkansa, and away up on Missoura and Yaller Stone; I've trapped on Columbia, and Lewis Fork, and Green River; I've trapped, marm, on Grand River and Heely [Gila]. I've fought the Blackfoot (and damned bad Injuns they are); I've raised the hair of more than one Apache, and made a Rapaho 'come' before now; I've trapped in heav'n, in airth, and hell; and scalp my old head, marm, but I've seen a putrefied forest."

"La, Mister Harris, a what?"

"A putrefied forest, marm, as sure as my rifle's got hind sights, and *she* shoots center. I was out of the Black Hills, Bill Sublette knows the time—the year it rained fire—and everybody knows when that was [1833, the year of a spectacular meteor shower]. If thar wasn't cold doins about that time, this child wouldn't say so. The snow was about fifty foot deep, and the bufler lay dead on the ground like bees after beein'; not whar we was, tho', for *thar* was no bufler, and no meat, and me and my band had been livin' on our moccasins (leastwise the parfleche) for six weeks; and poor doins that feedin' is, marm, as you'll never know. One day we crossed a canyon and over a divide, and got into a peraira, whar was green grass, and green trees, and green leaves on the trees, and birds singing in the green leaves, and this in February wagh! Our animals was like to die when they saw the green grass, and we all sung out, "Hurraw for summer doins!"

"Hyar goes for meat," says I, and I jest ups old Ginger [rifle] at one of them singing birds, and down comes the critter elegant; its darned head spinning away from its body, but never stops singing; and when I takes up the meat, I finds it stone, wagh! "Hyar's damp powder and no fire to dry it," I says, quite skeared. "Fire be dogged," says old Rube. "Hyar's a hoss, as'll make fire come," and with that he takes his axe and lets drive at a cottonwood. Schr-u-k goes the axe agin the tree, and out comes a bit of the blade as big as my hand. We looks at the animals, and thar they stood shaking over the grass, which I'm doggone if it wasn't stone too. Young Sublette comes up, and he's been clerking down to the fort on Platte, so he'd know something. He looks and looks, and scrapes the trees with his butcher knife, and snaps the grass like pipe-stems, and breaks the leaves a-snappin like Californy shells.

"What's all this, boy?" I asks.

"Putrefactions," says he, looking smart: "putrefactions, or I'm a nigger."

"La, Mr. Harris," says the lady, "putrefactions! Why did the leaves and the grass smell badly?"

"Smell badly, Marm!" says Black Harris; "would a skunk stink if he was froze in stone? . . . ."

Hathaway Jones, Rogue River Münchhausen

Some folk heroes are self made, creating for their listeners a cycle of stories of their own adventures and misadventures, real and otherwise. Their tall tales are so entertaining that they get told and retold by future generations, ensuring the gifted raconteur a solid place in the local lore. Folklorists call such storytellers *münchhausens,* naming them after Baron Münchhausen (Rudolph Eric Raspe, 1720-97), an early yarn spinner whose *Narratives of His Marvelous Travels and Campaigns* exemplify grand exaggeration recounted with straight-faced veracity.

One of Oregon's notable münchhausens was Hathaway Jones (1878-1936), who worked as a contract mail carrier, traveling by mule in the Rogue River Wilderness area. In the 1930s and 1940s, WPA writer Arthur Dorn captured a large number of Hathaway Jones tales, and folklore students at the University of Oregon were still recording them from residents of the Rogue area in the 1970s, when historian Stephen Dow Beckham assembled and published a major study, *Tall Tales from Rogue River, The Yarns of Hathaway Jones.* However, as Beckham notes, it was not folklorists but the public who contributed to Jones's reputation as the "biggest liar in the country" as "guides, miners, packers and settlers told and retold his tales."

We can catch a glimpse of Hathaway Jones in Claude Riddle's account of meeting Hathaway Jones in 1903 in the Rogue Canyon when Riddle was on a mining expedition.

> We were busy assembling our outfit, when we heard the jangle of bells and the scuffle of horses' feet on the trail. Some unintelligible human calls were heard from the approaching cavalcade. It was Hathaway directing his animals. The file of horses and mules meandered down from the trail to the flat where we had our camp, and Hathaway appeared in person.
>
> He was small and short and walked with a forward stoop. His arms were long and his hands seemed to swing ahead below his knees. . . . He wore a conical little black hat with a buckskin string woven in for a headband. His heavy blue flannel shirt was open and black hair decorated his throat and breast. A narrow leather belt held his pants about his slim hips and it looked like he might come apart in the middle at any time. Hathaway's speech was most peculiar—a cross between a hairlip and tonguetie. His pronunciation of some words was intriguing, and he always seemed in dead earnest. (*In the Happy Hills,* p. 1)

The Hathaway Jones stories that follow are typical in their emphases on Hathaway's clever feats, his great strength, his hunting prowess, and his experiences with mules. Some tales are original with Hathaway; others, "Hathaway's Marvelous Hunt," for example, are popular tales that circulate widely and are adapted by narrators in all parts of the country. These Hathaway Jones stories provide an occasion for comparing oral and written style in storytelling since some are direct transcriptions from audio recordings and others bear the marks of the writer (Dorn) recomposing in a more formal literary style the stories he once heard.

Hathaway's Father Builds a Fireplace

Another thing that Hathaway Jones was proud of was his father, and he felt that his father was a real builder of fireplaces. . . . One day—let us let Hathaway Jones tell it—his father had just completed a fireplace. Picture, if you will, an old ramshackle log cabin with a clapboard door, small porch outside to which was tied a hound dog, and you have the setting.

Hathaway Jones tells it this way: "Pa, he built this fireplace, and boy, did that fireplace draw. You never seen a fireplace draw like that. He shut the door and built a fire in this fireplace, and the first thing it did, it drew the door right off the hinges, sent it up the chimney. The old hound dog was about to have puppies, was tied to the post of the porch, and then she came right behind that door—it pulled four pups right out of her, and before we could put out the fire, we had two more. That's drawing." (Collected by Linda Barker on May 25, 1969, from Joel Barker, Grants Pass, Oregon. [RVMA])

Hathaway's Own Fireplace

You heard about old Hathaway. He's wantin' to build a fireplace when he was a kid. An' he was sixteen years old an' there's quite a trick to buildin' a fireplace. But the old man was afraid it wouldn't have enough draft. By gosh, ol' Hathaway got rocks and built the fireplace an' he went outside an' cut up some kindlin' to start the fire with, an' he went inside an' built the fire, and then all of a sudden—whammo!—the wood was sucked right into the cabin 'n' loaded itself. After that, all they'd have to do anytime they wanted wood in the fireplace was open the door an' it'd suck it right in offa the wood pile. (Collected by Penny Lee Colvin, Gold Beach, Oregon, from Rogue River boat pilot, Court Boice, near Agness on July 25, 1975. [RVMA])

Hathaway's Great Strength

Upon one of the rare visits to Gold Beach indulged in by Hathaway Jones he was accosted by a stranger, and a "dude" at that. He was pointed out to the city man who had been making inquiries respecting Jones, whose reputation had spread far and wide from the wilds of the lower Rogue, until whispers concerning him were beginning to be heard in the great cities throughout the land. Hathaway was young in years but old in the ways of the mountains. He was retiring and bashful in the presence of strangers, especially dudes, whom he held in contempt. He did not respond in a cordial manner to the stranger's advances.

Ignoring the dude's proffered hand, Hathaway continued slowly toward the saloon, permitting the stranger to do all the talking. But when the man asked Hathaway if he could lead him to a place where they served good drinking liquor, the ice was broken, and over their drinks, which the stranger paid for, they soon became at ease with each other.

After the fifth or sixth drink the city man asked Hathaway where he was working, to which inquiry the latter answered that he never worked. "Why not?" pursued the stranger, with apologies for his temerity.

Hathaway merely answered: "Can't."

"Why not?" persevered the dude.

"'Tain't good for me," answered Hathaway.

"What does work do to you?" persisted the dude.

Whereupon Hathaway, helping himself to another drink for which the dude paid, stated that he was a mass of scars caused by his efforts to work; that he liked to work, and was very down-hearted about his unfortunate condition. "Look at my gold mine," he declared in accents forlorn. "Boat load of gold a week if I could work, and here I am broke. Ranch work behind, wood to chop for winter, hogs to kill, dad old and weak, brothers all worthless, and all I can do is stand around like a wooden Indian."

"You look pretty strong and healthy," observed the stranger.

"Strong! Healthy! You bet I'm healthy and strong. I'm the strongest and healthiest man on the lower Rogue," exclaimed Hathaway.

"Then why can't you work?" queried the stranger.

So Hathaway explained that work was exercise, and that whenever he exercised his muscles developed so fast they split through the skin from one end to the other. (Arthur Dorn, "Folklore: Lower Rogue River," WPA Oregon Folklore Project.)

Packing a Bear Home

Right here at the cabin, Hathaway kept a string of mules. Favorite animal was Buckshot, his old mule. One day he took him across the river to go bear huntin'. Pretty soon they found a good one, about a five-hundred pounder, and killed it.

Well, under protest, he loaded it on the mule with the mule kickin' 'n' snortin' 'n' bitin' at the old man pretty bad. Well, he led the mule down to the edge of the river. The mule refused to go any farther. The old man kicked him in the stomach a couple times.

Finally, he pulled the bear off a his pack and loaded it onto his own shoulders and started across the river. Hathaway was a darn good swimmer. He didn't have any problems until he got about halfway across and started runnin' into trouble, deeper and deeper down into the water. Finally he got to the other side. Coughin' an' sputterin' for air, he crawled out onto the bank. Looked over his shoulder and there was that damn mule, Buckshot, ridin' on top of the bear. (Told by Timothy O'Dwyer, a Rogue River boat pilot, during a passenger boat trip from Gold Beach to Agness, July 25, 1975, to Penny Lee Colvin, Gold Beach. [RVMA 8/1975])

Hathaway's Marvelous Hunt

He told that one about an awful storm, when he just stayed there in that cabin. He just about starved, so he just had to go and get some meat. Well, he had to cross this stream, he said. When he got on the other side, why oh, his pockets was just so full of fish that the button flew off, he said, and killed a rabbit. And then he started on. He seen a whole lot of turkeys, wild turkeys up on a limb, so he thought, "Well, if I just split that limb. . . ." So he split that limb, and it caught all their toes in that crack. While he was gatherin' up the turkeys, why it was just drippin' honey out of there, dripped in his face. It was all honey.

Let's see, then he went home then. Took his turkeys and his fish and his rabbit. Went home and he got this old mare, and he made buckskin tugs, see, for the harness. So he took a barrel and a sled, and he went back, and he filled that up with honey. Well then, he just went home, and while he was there the sun come out. When he got to the cabin, why he had the horse all right, but the sled wasn't there. He got something to eat. It got a little warm, you know, and he went out and thought he'd have to go back when here come the sled. Tugs was drawin' up in that sun. Here comes his honey over the hill. (Told by Zahnie Crockett, Pistol River, Oregon, to George Wasson and Suzi Jones, spring 1975.)

Hathaway Shoots His Old Mare

He had this old mare, and he didn't want to let her die there in the winter, so he thought he'd just shoot her, save her from suffering. And he got up there on the hill. He had an old muzzle loader, and he brought the powder and cap, but he never had any lead, so he just—he had a peach seed in his pocket, so he just took that peach seed—it made him feel so bad—he just shot her and turned around and left.

When he come back in about ten, twelve years, he looked up there, 'n' there was a peach tree in bloom, 'n' he knew it wasn't ever there before. He went up there, 'n' it was growin' out of that old mare's back. He said it was just right; he just cut it off and he had a perfect pack saddle. He used that old mare.

When he started in she was old enough to die. Oh, he tells some of the damnedest yarns. Tells 'em so much though, a fella'd just get disgusted with him. (Told by Zahnie Crockett, Pistol River, to George Wasson and Suzi Jones, spring 1975.)

Shooting Geese

He shot a bunch of geese one time.

[The geese] come down 'n' lit in a gulch, right down in a ditch in a straight row. So he got the rifle—and he was a good shot, he said—but this time he made a bad shot. They all flew away. So he went up there to take a look. And he said, "You know, I just pulled off a little bit, and I picked up a whole basket of bills." (Collected from Larry Lucas, Agness, Oregon, on April 15, 1972, by Dwight L. Clarke, Eugene, Oregon. [RVMA])

The Black Powder Bullet

He was tellin' about when the black powder was goin' out, and they were usin' smokeless, which is so much quicker [than] the old black powder. He went out huntin' 'n' shot at this buck 'way off, 'n' he made a mistake and put in a black powder shell, 'n' the old buck stood there. So then he put in a smokeless powder shell and shot 'n' he said, "God, the buck [*gesturing with his hand*] fell down." And he run down there, and he grabbed his knife and bent over to cut his throat. And he said [*imitating Hathaway's speech*], "Wham, somethin' hit me right there" [*grabbing his upper thigh*]. He said, "That was that black powder bullet. It just got there." (Told by Larry Lucas, age 72, Agness, Oregon, April 15, 1972, to Dwight L. Clarke, Eugene. [RVMA 6/1972])

A Nimble Mule

Some fellow down there at court week at Gold Beach, when people collected there, wanted to—some fellow wanted to see Hathaway Jones, 'n' he was in town there, and so they pointed out Hathaway. The fellow run over 'n' got alongside of him, 'n' walked down the sidewalk 'n' got him in conversation. Well, he wanted to get a story or somethin' from him like that. So he got to askin' him about the mules 'n' stuff, 'n' if he'd ever had mules, 'n'—it got to the point where Hathaway got tellin' about one special mule he had, very nimble, very nimble little mule. Said he rode it down the trail at night—in the evening toward the river, ridin' along, gun across the saddle, 'n' he said [*imitating Hathaway's speech*], "—rode up face to face with a big cougar," he said, "that little mule just turned a flipflop backwards and hit in the trail a runnin'." He said, "I never even dropped the gun—I just got the top of my hat a little bit dusty."

I don't know about the mule, but the man was a good rider, wasn't he? (Told by Larry Lucas, Agness, Oregon, April 15, 1972, to Dwight L. Clarke, Eugene. [RVMA 6/1972])

Hathaway Mixes Up His Mules

Well, the last time I saw him, he got mixed up with the mules. I had some people with me, went up to Illahe early in the morning. We walked up from the river, went up in the boat. He led this mule out. He was gettin' ready to go on the mule train, you know. And he got 'em mixed up. He had several gray mules that just looked alike, [but] one of 'em was partic'lar—he couldn't ride it at all. He packed it all.

And he led him out there, in this barnyard, 'n' we come along early in the morning. He sprinted, spunky old guy, 'n' he just led this gray mule out. He had the wrong one. And, he just got on the mule right in front of us, you know. Well, that mule just bucked like mad, and into the dust and horse manure he hit, kerplop, and the dust just flew. Hurt him. Kinda knocked the wind out of him. And he rolled over—he had a cleft palate; he couldn't talk too good—but he looked at the mule, and he said, [*imitating Hathaway's speech*] "What the hell's the matter with you, you damned old fool, don't you know I got rheumatism?" (Told by Larry Lucas, Agness, Oregon, on April 15, 1972, to Dwight L. Clarke, Eugene, Oregon. [RVMA 6/72])

Benjamin Franklin "Huckleberry" Finn

According to several sources, the only thing that mattered as much to Benjamin Franklin Finn as his claim that he was the original "Huckleberry Finn" was his reputation as the "biggest liar on the McKenzie River." B. F. Finn (b. 1823 or 1832, d. 1919), a Civil War veteran and bricklayer by trade, left Missouri and settled with his wife and seven children in the McKenzie River Valley near Leaburg in 1871. He later made his living distilling turpentine but earned his place in Oregon's literary history for his remarkable skills as a raconteur, a münchhausen of the first order. Finn's tales are still widely told, now mostly in the third person, and one of the largest collections of his stories was gathered by folklore student Susan Mullin in 1962 from Arthur Belknap, Finn's grandson and a retired McKenzie River guide.

Finn Upholds His Reputation as a Liar

They was some newspaper men come up by stage coach from Eugene to see Grandad an' they stopped and called him to come out. Grandad, he come out on the porch, and they says, "Mr. Finn, we heard that you're the biggest liar on the McKenzie River, and we come up to ask you to tell a lie for us. We'd like you to tell us a big lie." Well, Grandad, he stepped down off the porch an' he says, he says, "Boys," he says, "I'd like to tell you a lie today, but the truth is," he says, "I've just lost my best friend. Old Man Pepiot died yesterday and I've set up all night with his corpse. I'm just on my way now to build him a coffin. Any other time I'd be glad to tell you a lie, boys, but I just don't feel up to it today. You come around some other time and I'll be glad to tell you a lie." Well, them fellas left Grandad then and drove on down the road, and when they got to the top of the hill, why the first one they seen was the Old Man Pepiot! (Collected from Arthur Belknap by Susan Mullin in 1962. Published by Mullin in "Oregon's Huckleberry Finn: A Munchhausen Enters Tradition," p. 20.)

Moving Finn Rock

Susan Mullin: We've heard a story about your Grandad that says he's the one who moved Finn Rock over to where it is now. There was something about using a buckskin harness, but since he had to drive the mules out cross the river, the harness got wet and stretched; but he just tied it to a tree and when it dried out, it pulled the rock over to where it is. Can you tell us that story, so we'll have it straight?

Arthur Belknap: Oh no, you got it all wrong. Grandad moved Finn Rock over for Emma Dunavan. She was sister to Harvey Scott, who had the *Oregonian*. See, they called that place Pillow Point 'cause of all the rocks, and Mrs. Dunavan wanted to get a wagon through. So Grandad just put a chain around Finn Rock, got his mules, and moved it that way. (Susan Mullin, "Oregon's Huckleberry Finn: A Munchhausen Enters Tradition," p. 23. Mullin notes that "Finn Rock is a formation which lies between the McKenzie River Highway and the river itself; it has quite obviously never been moved by anybody." And "Emma Dunavan" must be none other than Abigail Scott Duniway.)

Trapped in a Honey Tree

Grandad had bees, you know, down on the old Finn place, and he was a great one to go out and find a tree of honey. One time he found a bee tree and crawled in to eat the honey. He ate so much he couldn't get back out of the tree so he had to go home and get the axe and chop hisself out.

Caught in a Stump

One time he was out plowin' and he hit a stump. He split the stump wide open, and when he pulled the plow out of it, the stump caught his overcoat. Had to go all the way back to the house and get a axe to cut hisself loose.

Making Turpentine

Grandad was on the summit [McKenzie Pass] makin' turpentine one time. It was in the summer and pretty hot, I guess. Anyway, he couldn't sleep at night 'cause the mosquitoes was so bad. So Grandad, he got one of his big copper kettles and put that over his head to keep the mosquitoes out. Well, the mosquitoes just drilled right through that copper kettle, so Grandad, he got hisself a hammer, and when them mosquitoes drilled through the kettle, why Grandad just cinched their beaks over with that hammer. Pretty soon it got so's they was so many mosquitoes that they flew away with his kettle.

(All three of these tales are from "Oregon's Huckleberry Finn: A Munchhausen Enters Tradition," pp. 19-25.)

Finn and the Muzzle Loader

You know, another time he says they were having a dance upstairs at his place. He was sitting downstairs when a flock of ducks landed on the river. He took the old muzzle loading shotgun down, put a cap on the nipple, poured a bunch of powder in, tamped a load of paper in on top of that, poured a handful of shot in and went to tamp a wad on top of the shot, and he jarred it a little too much, and the hammer fell down on the cap. He said he had the hardest time holding that load in there 'til he could get over to the window where he could let loose of it without hurting anybody. (Collected from retired lumberman, George McCornack, Dexter, Oregon, on June 5, 1970, by folklore student, Charlene Walker, Dexter. [RVMA])

The Big Fish

Grandad was quite a one to fish, too, you know. He'd fish for Dolly Varden [trout]. They're pretty big. One day Grandad was fishing, and he hooked something and his line broke. So he got a stouter line, and then he hooked something and his hook broke. So he got a bigger hook, and then his line broke again, so he got a half-inch rope and went down to the blacksmith's and built him a big hook. And he used some kind of big bait. Well, he tied one end to an alder tree and went away.

When he come back that old alder tree was just a-whippin' the water. He pulled on it and finally pulled the fish out. It was three and a half foot between the eyes [*pauses for laughter*]. Well, his trouble wasn't over then. Booth Kelly [a local logging firm] was havin' a log drive, and when Grandad pulled that fish out of the water, why the level went down and beached all their logs, and he had a lawsuit on his hands. (Susan Mullin, "Oregon's Huckleberry Finn: A Munchhausen Enters Tradition," p. 22.)

The "Kalarup" Gun

When he got to be an old man they used to have him around the hotel to lie to the tourists as they came through. One fella came up there with a new Winchester automatic rifle which he was very proud of and did a lot of bragging about. After he'd talked himself out, old Finn says, "You know, them damned 'kalarup' guns is no good. My boy Willie had one. We went across the river the other day, and I sat on the river, and he said he'd go and chase one into me. He went up the ridge about a half a mile, and he jumped one and shot at it. It come right down the ridge to me. You know, when that deer went by me that bullet was still three feet behind him, and there was drops of sweat as big as your fist a-falling off that bullet, and it just couldn't catch him. I tell you, them damned 'kalarup' guns is no good." (Collected from George McCornack, Dexter, Oregon, on June 5, 1970, by Charlene Walker, Dexter. [RVMA])

Finn and the Game Warden

There's a fellow name of Fitzhenry was down there staying at O'Brien's. O'Brien had an eating place this side of the wagon bridge. Fitzhenry and Grandad was talkin' one time. Fitzhenry was tellin' huntin' stories to a couple of other fellas that was there. Grandad says, he says, "By God," he says, "I went up there back of my place the other day," he says, "and I killed two big bucks." And he told how he dressed 'em out and brought 'em down and all this and that, and finally one of these men says, "Do you know who we are?" "By golly, no." "Well," he says, "we're state game wardens." Grandad says, "Well, you know who I am?" "No." "Well, I'm the biggest liar on the McKenzie!" (From "Oregon's Huckleberry Finn: A Munchhausen Enters Tradition," p. 21.)

Tebo Ortego, *Vaquero* Münchhausen

Tebo Ortego

On September 4, 1991, Marcus Haines made a recording of stories about Prim "Tebo" Ortego for the Harney County History Project, Harney County Historical Society, Burns, Oregon. Haines, who had been a personal acquaintance of Ortego's, noted that Prim Ortego, better known as "Tebo," "was known for the big stories he told and the things he could do. Some people said he was a Mexican, others said he was a pure-blooded Spaniard. But anyway, he was a little dried up fellow—he didn't weigh much over a hundred pounds—but he certainly remembered his stories, and he had a great memory, there was no question about that . . ."

Haines provided information on Tebo's background by quoting a statement that had been given by Prim Ortego when he was a witness in a trial held in Burns in 1931:

I am sixty-eight years of age and was born at Red Bluff, Tehama County, in California, and raised in Colusa County in California. I came to Harney Valley in 1873 with Pete French. I knew him before I came here. When I arrived here I went to work on the P Ranch that is up in the Blitzen River. I have worked there since that time up to now, and I'm still working there. Generally my work consisted of riding after stock. I was foreman at one time, for a short time. My work took me around Malheur and Harney Lakes a good deal from

1877, when I first saw the lakes, up to the recent years. I was down there almost every year. I have seen it in the spring, and I have seen it in the fall, and I've seen it in the winter.

Marcus Haines described Tebo's place on the P Ranch as follows:

Tebo was kind of an honored student, you might say, of Pete French's. He let him run cattle, and as near as we know, he was the only one that ever did that. He [Tebo] had his own brand and run a few cattle. And I think he had a race horse or two, too. And then when they made the drive down to Winnemucca—that's where they marketed these cattle—well, Tebo would go along and he'd sell his cattle. . . .

Tebo went with the sale of the French holdings. It occurred two times prior to the purchase of the property by the Fish and Wildlife Service, as it is known now, for the Wildlife Refuge in February 1935. And Tebo went with that sale too. And he was housed at the P Ranch with Arthur Paige, a civil engineer for the government. Both Tebo and Arthur Paige died with pneumonia in January 1937. Arthur was 52, and Tebo was in his early 70s, probably 74 or 75.

Haines recalled attending a picnic at the P Ranch on the Fourth of July in 1935 where Tebo entertained the crowd with card tricks, stunts, and rattling the bones—

that used to be one of the methods of creating a little music. Somebody would sing and rattle the bones. We didn't have radios and TVs and phonographs and all that stuff. And Tebo would cut four bones about six inches long, as I remember, out of a dried cow rib bone, and then he would put these two bones in between his fingers on each hand, and he'd just rattle them and keep time with the music, or whatever. It sounded kind of like a drummer, you know. I used to play the accordion at dances in the early 1930s at Frenchglen, and Tebo would play with me until he got tired, and then he'd go back to the P Ranch.

The Tebo Ortego stories that follow are tales that Marcus Haines remembered from the time he spent two or three nights in the bunkhouse at the P Ranch in the fall of 1929 and Tebo entertained.

Kiger Gorge

First, we'll start with the one about Kiger Gorge. He said he was riding up there in the spring of the year and rode up and he looked off into Kiger Gorge, and he said there was a monstrous rock right near by. It was just all ready to fall into the canyon. So he said he got a pry pole, and he finally broke it loose, and down the hill it went and up the other side, and rolled right back up from where Tebo had started it. So Tebo watched it for awhile, but he had to leave, and he didn't get back up there until fall. So he thought he would ride over and look off into Kiger Gorge again. And he said that rock was still rolling, but he said it was about the size of a basketball then. And I suppose if it had been a little later on, it would have gotten down to a baseball, but anyway, it was a basketball at that time.

Tebo's Mosquito Stories

And then he had some good mosquito stories too. And he tells about one night there the mosquitoes were real bad. And so he got a big cast iron kettle that all the ranches had back in those days. It would hold twenty, thirty gallons of water, I guess. And they used them to render lard and to heat water in when they butchered hogs in the fall of the year—they scalded them to get the hair off of them. So he turned that upside down and got under it with a hammer to kill what mosquitoes went under there with him. So he said that pretty soon the bills started coming through this cast iron kettle. So he'd just reach up with his hammer and he'd clinch the bill. And he said, "By gosh, all of a sudden away went the kettle." He said, "I just clinched too many bills and the mosquitoes flew off with it."

And then he tells another one about—I guess this happened at the P Ranch too—he said there was a couple mosquitoes come in when he was in bed. One of them set on the head of the bed, the other one was on the foot of the bed. And one said to the other, he said, "What will we do, eat him here or take him off down to the swamp?" And, well he answered, he said, "We had better eat him here. We take him down to the swamp, those big fellows will take him away from us."

Tebo's Pet Fish

And then he said that he had a fish there one time that he got out of the river, and [Tebo] taught him to follow around like a dog. And he said he did, he followed him out to the barn, and he followed him here, and he followed him there, just like a dog would do. He said he had a little foot log there across the river. He started to cross there one day with the fish behind him. He [the fish] fell off and drowned before Tebo could get him out.

Birds Freeze in the Lake

And he tells about the water flooding the meadows there one spring. And the birds came in there by the thousands, and was around in this water. And he said it just turned terribly cold, and it froze those birds right in the water. He said they never got away there, they just froze right there. He said they weren't dead. He said they were just floundering around there trying to get out, but they were froze in there. So he said, "We shod some horses and hooked up to the mowing machines and raised the sickle bars up about six inches," and he said, "We just went out there and mowed their heads off, and that kept them from dying of starvation."

The Fast Palomino Stallion

Then he tells about a horse there, a palomino stud, he said, "a beautiful horse." He didn't know too much about him, other than he came down to the place there to get a drink of water at ten o'clock every morning. So he decided he would catch him. And so he made a rope, a rawhide rope—a *riata*—and he braided it out of cowhide and made it about a hundred feet long. And he slipped down there to the big boulder nearby where this horse came in, and he roped him. But he got away from Tebo, rope and all, and away he went. Tebo jumped on his horse and took after him, but he couldn't begin to keep up with him. But after so long a time he run onto a sheepherder, and he asked him, said, "Did you see a horse come by here with a rope on?"

"Yeah," he said, "he went by here awhile ago." He said, "I never saw a horse run so fast." He said, "That rope was just standing right straight out in the air behind him, wasn't touching the ground anywhere." And he said, "It was covered with horseflies, as near as I could tell." He said, "Well, what happened there?"

"Well," Tebo said, "there was a lot of horseflies on him when I roped him alright, and they kept falling off, but they'd catch that rope coming along, so they were still going on for the ride."

The Horses Have a Rodeo

And he said they were branding calves out in Catlow Valley one time. And he said they got up one morning to go to work and their *caviata* (group of horses used on a drive or on a job) was gone. They didn't know what had happened, but they could see a big dust out in the valley there a ways. So they went out to see what was going on. He said there they were, the *caviata* had gone out there, and they rodeoed these cattle. And they had the young horses holding a rodeo, and the old horses were working out the cows and the calves.

A Night at Buena Vista

The last story I think that I can remember at the present time—he said that he came down to Buena Vista one time. Now that was one of Pete French's headquarters, and it is at the present time—it's the headquarters or maintenance station for the Fish and Wildlife Service. It's right near the road going to Frenchglen, just a big white building there, and big high trees, and a house. You can see it real plain. And the story had it that in previous years there had been some treasures buried around there. People have tried to find them, but they hadn't had any luck. . . .

Well, anyway, Tebo got his supper, and there was nobody there. He got his supper and went upstairs and went to bed. And he closed the door, and [was] just about to go to sleep when the door flew open. So he got up and he closed it again and got back in bed. And it just flew open again, nearly before he got in bed. So there was a dresser nearby, so he slid this dresser over against this door and got back in bed. And away went the dresser, and the door was open again. So he said, "Well, I'll fix this." So he closed the door again and shoved his bed up against it, and just got in bed, and away went his bed, and the door was open again. And he said that he looked out there at the opening, and he said there stood the most beautiful woman he had ever seen in his life, standing there in the nude, and she was beckoning to him. So he said, "Well, I might just as well follow her along here and see what's going on." So she took him out on the east side of the house and went to one of the big trees that you see there now and pointed down and made a motion for him to dig. So he said he got down on his hands and knees and found a soft spot and was digging down there and got down a foot or so, and he just got his hand in what felt like a fruit jar without a lid on top of it.

And then Tebo would stop, he wouldn't say any more. He noticed everybody was kind of on the edge of his chair listening to this, you know, a pretty good story. "Well, what happened then, Tebo?"

"Oh," he said, "that's when I woke up." He said, "I had my hand in my mouth trying to pull my teeth out."

Bill Brown

William Walter Brown, known as Bill Brown, or Wagontire Brown, raised sheep and horses around Wagontire Mountain west of Burns in the early part of this century. Although rugged as the next man, Brown had some habits that set him off from his contemporaries. According to Giles French (*Cattle Country of Peter French,* p. 12), Brown's worst expletive was "shucks, confound it," and once, when he killed a herder "after being threatened and fired upon, he then rode to the nearest county seat to report it, and was soon exonerated." Brown was known for his generosity, and one of his most memorable habits was writing checks on whatever was handy. This story about Bill Brown was collected by Cathryn Susac from her grandfather, Arthur W. Tuck, who lived in Redmond for many years. (RVMA, Susac, 3/71)

You know Papa and a couple other old fellows—well, they weren't so damned old then—they practically built that Methodist Church down there [in Redmond], and they had it almost finished. They ran out of money so they were short about two thousand dollars—or twenty-three hundred, or something—that'd take to finish it. So they started looking for some donations. So Papa said he'd drive out and see Old Bill Brown out there at Buck Creek out north of Burns. And they said, "No use seeing him. He wouldn't give you anything."

So he rode out there; told him what he needed—or, what they were doing. He said, "How much do you need to finish it? How much do you figure for a contribution?" He didn't expect him to buy the darn thing, but he hauled out his old checkbook and wrote a check for the whole damned thing.

One time the bank in Burns had checks he'd written on pine bark, and tomato can wrappers, for thousands of dollars. He'd write them on anything. They had those checks all plastered all over the bank.

And he had a store. He just had a sign up saying: "Help yourself." And a little box there for collecting money.

Aaron Meier and the Darning Needle

Aaron Meier

The hero in this narrative is Aaron Meier, a Jewish immigrant from Germany in 1855, who became one of the founders of the well-known Oregon department-store firm, Meier and Frank, and was the father of Oregon governor Julius Meier (1931-35). Although this version of the story is obviously the work of a writer rather than a storyteller, the editor's note describes it as "an example of pioneer folklore, a story told and retold by old-timers. Most of the story was told by Mary Drain Albro of Portland. Howard M. Corning has verified enough of the facts to convince us that the incident could have occurred in [the 1850s]."—Helen Krebs Smith, ed. *With Her Own Wings*, pp. 117-120.

Grandmother Drain had a darning needle, and it was the only darning needle among the settlers in Pass Creek Canyon. The folks who lived in Pass Creek Canyon had come across the plains by wagon train. By the time they got to the top of the Cascades, they were so eager to end their journey they settled at the first likely spots as they went down the west slopes. Every natural clearing close to water was the site of a land claim. Pass Creek Canyon was quite thickly settled, at least there were ten or fifteen families living within a few miles of each other, and they neighbored back and forth, sharing what they had. In those days families had to get along with each other. No one knew when he might need help. Grandmother Drain's darning needle was one of the most cared-for possessions in the community, because it was the only one, and clothes had to be patched and mended until new ones could be secured, and who knew when that would be? The women learned to make pins out of slivers of dogwood, but for mending nothing was so handy to use as the darning needle. Women in the lower canyon shared the needle for a day or two, then women up farther would take turns catching up on the family mending.

All went well until the day Mrs. Chitwood sent the needle back to Grand-mother Drain's by Jimmy.

Jimmy was eight years old, and he was a responsible boy—boys had to be responsible and do their share of the work.

Mrs. Chitwood put a long red ravelling through the eye of the needle and knotted it, then she put the needle into a potato so that Jimmy could carry it safely to the Drain cabin.

Jimmy walked through the canyon trail in the spring morning sunshine which filtered through the tall firs. He paid no attention to rabbits and squirrels that crossed the path in front of him. He scarcely looked up when bluejays scolded. He stopped for a moment when a doe raced a few yards down the trail as though being chased, but he did not leave the trail. He was on an errand with the only darning needle in Pass Creek Canyon.

But when a mother bear with two cubs came into sight, he jumped from the trail and hid behind a serviceberry bush to watch them. He was not afraid, he said to himself, because bears didn't harm, but of course a mother bear was different when she had cubs. No, he was not afraid, but it was best to hide just the same. He stood behind the bush, then stooped down. It would be nice, he thought, if father were here to see the bears, too. He was not afraid, but he wished the bears would hurry along on their way. And after a bit they did.

Jimmy stood up again and went back onto the trail. He walked a little, thinking of the bears and wishing that sometime he might have a cub all his own, without a mother bear. Then he remembered the darning needle! He looked down at his hand. The potato and the needle were gone! "Oh, I lost it in the bushes," he thought. "I'll have to go find it." He went back as fast as he could, but he could not find the serviceberry bush. "Here are those bracken, and here was where I came out to the trail again, but where is the bush? What shall I do?" He ran down the trail as fast as he could and told his mother. Mrs. Chitwood was alarmed.

"Oh, Jimmy!" she exclaimed. "To think it had to be lost when we had it. Well, we'll just have to find it. Go tell your father."

Jimmy ran to the edge of the clearing where his father and some other men were trimming logs. When Jimmy told what he had done, the men stuck their axes into the logs and went with Jimmy. "We'll have to help, too," they said.

The men and Jimmy went to the cabin. Mrs. Chitwood had sent word to the other neighbors, and they all went up onto the trail where Jimmy thought he had seen the bears.

They looked for bear tracks and found one or two, but the earth was dry. They all looked for the serviceberry bush Jimmy had hidden under, but there were many serviceberry bushes, and where was that one?

Everyone was worried, but no one scolded Jimmy except his sister. She was ten, and she said, "You won't be a good woodsman if you can't even remember landmarks. Don't you know you should always have landmarks?" Jimmy was white and tearful, but he tried to show his mother exactly where he had been. After a while, he said, "I know there was a stump under the bush. A funny stump." All the men and women, and children, too, began looking for a red ravelling near a stump under a serviceberry bush.

Suddenly Jimmy left the others. He said nothing but walked through a bramble of bracken. When he came out, he went straight to his mother and handed her the potato with the red ravelling hanging from it.

"It was by the stump," he said.

"Why, Jimmy," replied his mother, "you are a woodsman, and a reliable boy, to find what you lost. Give it to Grandmother Drain. Quick! before you lose it again."

Everyone, and that was about twenty-five people, came together to share the joy of finding the needle. Then the men went back to trimming logs, the women went home to get their suppers, and the children went back to their play. The darning needle was found, and it was kept all that summer and into the fall, but one day when Grandmother Drain was sewing, the head of the needle broke off, and all the women had to make neat piles of clothing to be mended, hoping that before long, someone would come from Fort Vancouver or the East with a needle. Each time women were together they talked of their sewing and hoped that another needle would soon be provided. One day, about Thanksgiving time, a peddler with a mule came over the pass and down through the canyon. The children playing school on some logs saw him and ran to tell their mothers a visitor was coming. The mothers, one by one, hurried to see the goods the peddler had brought and to hear news of people to the east. Several hurried to buy combs. One bought a china doll's head. Two women enthusiastically bought dress goods before they thought of needles and thread to sew it with. Then one of the mothers said, "Oh, do you have any needles? We'll have to have a needle."

"Oh," said Mrs. Chitwood, "how could we forget when it is the one thing we need most—a good needle with a large eye! We need one at least, now that Grandmother Drain's needle is broken." Mrs. Chitwood told the story of the lost darning needle, glancing occasionally at Jimmy who was stroking the mule's neck and pretending not to notice.

Those standing around talked, too, and the peddler listened. Then he reached into his inside pocket.

"My people do not celebrate Christmas," he said, "but I suppose you good people will soon be having a holiday with presents. Are you going to give any presents, sonny?" asked the peddler.

Jimmy looked up quickly. "Oh, yes, sir, that is, I guess I will."

"Well," said the kind-faced man, "suppose you and I give the ladies of Pass Creek Canyon each a Christmas present right now, shall we?"

Jimmy looked puzzled. The peddler opened the thin package he had taken from his pocket. "Here are some darning needles, all I have, but I believe there will be enough for every family in the canyon to have one."

No one said anything for a moment, then there was a gasp of astonishment. The women smiled to each other, "He's a good man."

The peddler and Jimmy passed out the needles to those gathered around, and the next day Jimmy delivered the rest of the needles up and down the canyon. The peddler left, and no one saw him again for many months, but that was just the first of many kindnesses shown the women in Pass Creek Canyon by Aaron Meier who later founded the store of Meier and Frank in Portland.

Lou Southworth of Waldport

Lou Southworth

Louis Southworth was born into slavery in Tennessee around 1830, and emigrated to Oregon with his mother and his master in 1851. After buying his freedom by working in the Jacksonville gold mines, and serving in the Rogue River Indian Wars, he homesteaded with his wife in 1879 at Tidewater, four miles upriver from Waldport on the Alsea River. A storyteller and the subject of affectionate stories in the Alsea country, Southworth died in Corvallis in 1917, proud of being an African American, a Lincoln Republican, and an expert fiddler.—From M. Hays, *The Land That Kept Its Promise*, pp. 105-106; see also Elizabeth McLagan, *A Peculiar Paradise: A History of Blacks in Oregon 1788-1940*, pp. 83-84.

Lou Southworth was once a member of a very strict church congregation in Waldport—so strict that the other members dropped him from the church rolls for playing the violin.

"The brethren wouldn't stand for my violin, which was all the company I had most of the time. They said it was full of all sorts of wicked things and that it belonged to the devil. I inquired if there's music up in heaven and they told me that there is. But when I asked them if I could play a little of it here below, they couldn't answer that to suit a fellow like me. And it hurt me a good deal when they told me that playin' a fiddle is unbecomin' to a Christian and the sight of the Lord. So I told them [the only way] to keep me in the church would be with my fiddle. I couldn't think of partin' with my ole friend.

"They turned me out, and I reckon my name isn't written in their books here any longer. But I somehow hope it's written in the big book up yonder in the land of golden harps where they aren't as partic'lar about an ole man's fiddle. And sometimes I think when you go up yonder and find my name, to your suprise, in the big book, you'll meet many a fellow who remembers the old fiddler who played "Home Sweet Home," "Dixie Land," "Arkansaw Traveler," "Swanee River," and other tunes for the boys who were far away from home the first time. And they'll talk over the days when there was no society for men like them out West; when there wasn't any Bible and hymn books were unknown; when playin' poker and buckin' faro were the only schoolin' a fellow ever got; when whiskey ran like water and made the whites and Indians crazy; when men didn't go by their right names and didn't care what they did. And when they have talked over those early days, the fellows will say, 'Where you all been and what'd we all done in the mines but for Uncle Lou's fiddle, which was most like a church of anything we had?' For the boys used to think the good Lord had put a heap of ole-time religion music into my fiddle, and the ole-time religion music is good enough for an old man who's done some mighty hard work in his 85 years. . . ."

At the Southworth home, [Abraham Lincoln's] photo hung over the fire-place, and Lou never failed to vote in an election. On the day of the Presidential Election in 1880 [James Arthur vs. Winfield Hancock] a southwest storm battered Alsea Bay and everyone feared rowing over to Lutgens, the polling place to vote, except Lou Southworth, who said, "Boys, Abe Lincoln's on trial every time there is a big election in this country; so I'm goin' to cross the bay to vote, or drown in the attempt."

And go he did. He fastened two large oil cans astern and in the boat's bow. The others watched nervously as the boat appeared and disappeared in the wave troughs. No one expected Lou to reach the opposite shore until they saw him standing on the dock waving his hat and perhaps yelling three cheers for Abraham Lincoln. Lou Southworth was the only man who had the courage to cross the Bay to vote that day.

Jack Dalton Pays His Bill

Jack Dalton and his wife

Legends of outlaws have occupied a place in European and American folklore for a long time, especially stories that reveal the outlaw's good side—treating women kindly, donating his ill-gotten gold to the poor, or, as in this central Oregon legend about "Jack Dalton," paying his bills. This story was told to Cathryn Susac on March 9, 1971, by her grandfather, Arthur W. Tuck, a native of Redmond. (RVMA, Susac, 3/71)

You know, the funniest thing was that one time, one of the Daltons, Jack Dalton, stopped at Burns. He'd bought a bunch of land up there by Silvies River above Burns, and he had quite a crew. He had about twenty men working up there to clear up this ranch and get it ready to go. So he was under the name of Robinson, and he had quite an account down there at Archie McGowen's store there at Hines. They had a general store, and, of course, those days that's the way people operated—come in a new country and they just start operating on the cuff. They didn't have credit checks like they do now or everybody would have been broke, and they'd starve to death.

Anyway, this Robinson had a cook, and the boys were all complaining about him, so he went to town and hired some woman to do the cooking. So he brought her home, back up, and this cook blew a fuse—he told her she'd have to do that kind of work. She said she'd be damned if she would—she was a cook and nothing else.

So then the cook got his shootin' pole and said, "I'm going to shoot the old so-and-so." Everybody, they egg him on. They wanted to see a good shooting scrape. So they told him, "Go ahead, go ahead." So he went up and accosted Dalton. So Dalton talked him out of it, and he went back down to the saloon, but the fellows made fun of him for chickening out, so he got a few more drinks and a little more courage, 'til this time—"I'll get him."

So he went out this time and hauled out his old hogleg and started shooting. But of all the people to start shooting at was one of the Daltons—he mowed him down. So they sent to Canyon City for the sheriff. So he came over. 'Course he cleared Dalton 'cause of self-defense. Well, when he [the sheriff] was there, he noticed the team Dalton was driving was stolen from Canyon City, among other things. So Dalton jumped in the buckboard and took off for his ranch and outran the sheriff. Well, apparently he wasn't too hard to outrun. When they found out who he was, he wasn't hard to outrun. So he got away.

And the next thing they heard of him way up on the Dalton Trail in Yukon, Alaska, in the gold rush days. So McGowen thought he'd pull a sneaky, so he sent his bill up to: Address: Jack Dalton, Seattle. In just a few weeks, by God, he got the money back. He'd paid every nickel of his bill. He was honest. Steal the occasional team of horses, but, by God, he paid his bill.

A similar tale turns up in Mike Hanley and Ellis Lucia, Owyhee Trails: The West's Forgotten Corner, *pp. 296-297. Notice how many of the details differ in the two accounts.*

There are countless amazing stories, tall tales, and exciting legends concerning the I-O-N [Idaho-Oregon-Nevada] country. Take Jack Miller, for instance. Miller was a Texan, a tough hombre who had a thriving timber operation in the Blue Mountains. His crew consisted of a half-dozen men, among them a cook named Matt Egan.

When Miller fired Egan, the cook took off for Burns in a bitter frame of mind. He swore that Miller canned him for a woman cook, whose company he liked better. He began drinking heavily, and the more he drank, the more he brooded. One day he accosted Miller on a Burns street and all hell broke loose. Egan pulled a gun, there was a struggle, Miller got his own gun free and pumped four bullets into Egan's stomach.

Jack wrenched the weapon from the dead man's hand and brandishing both guns, strode up the street to the saloon where several toughs, possibly friends of Egan, were eyeing him in challenge.

"If any of you sons-of-bitches don't like what I've done, get right out here and try your hand," Miller declared.

Nobody stepped forward. And the shooting was ruled justifiable homicide.

But a short time later, a warrant was on Miller's head for horse stealing. He got out of Burns ahead of the sheriff, cutting the telegraph lines on the way. He dropped from sight, not to be heard from again until the Klondike Stampede of 1898. Suddenly, he was back in the limelight under a new name—Jack Dalton. He formed a partnership with Ed Hanley, Uncle Bill's brother, and John Malony to drive cattle from eastern Oregon to the Yukon, making them a fortune.

"I got here all right with my cattle," wrote Ed Hanley to his brother and sister in December 1898. "They averaged three hundred dollars and a little better. We did real well out of them."

The cattle and horse herds bound for the Yukon were put together in eastern Oregon. And the route became known as the famous Dalton Trail. . . .

Old Blue

Outlaw narratives often appear in ballad as well as in legend. This ballad was discovered by Alta and Austin Fife in their search for folklore texts in old issues of the *Pacific Northwest Farm Quadrant* (Fife Folklore Archives, Utah State University). It was published in the "Old Songs" column, and the letter that accompanies the text explains the origin of the song.

To the editor: I saw a request in the Old Songs column for the song entitled "Old Blue." I am rather curious just who should have made this request and would like for the party to write to me as there would scarcely be any one living now who would know the song except myself and John Bare, a son of the man who composed it.

Old Blue's real name was Bruce Evans, and he was a real gangster and outlaw who operated in Wallowa County, Oregon, from about 1884 until probably '89 or '90. He and his gang, aside from stealing horses and cattle by wholesale, murdered a man on Snake River, only 16 miles from where we lived, for some gold bricks the man had. This man's name was Douglas. They also killed 27 Chinamen on Deep Creek, only two miles from where they killed Douglas for the gold they had placered from Snake River. This place is near the mouth of Imnaha River and is 60 miles above Lewiston. When Evans and his gang were ready to kill the Chinamen they sent a 16-year-old boy to Enterprise to buy ammunition and the boy stayed at our place, both going and coming. This boy told my father that they were going out on a big hunt. This job cost the United States one thousand dollars per Chinaman, $27,000 in all. I remember almost every man who was with Evans and also the sheriff, whose name was Tom Umphrey.

The man who composed this song was our nearest neighbor at the time and was typical old frontiersman and a natural-born poet and an exceptionally smart man, but entirely without education. I doubt if he could write his own name.

At the time of Evans's arrest, the jail was at Joseph, which was then the county seat of Wallowa County, and the jail was a little wood construction, so Evans talked thru the jail at night to his friends on the outside and told them to leave a brace of pistols under the table in the spring house, where he was permitted to go for water each day by the sheriff, while the sheriff waited at said door for Evans's return. Of course, Umphrey let him do this once too often, and Evans walked away. Evans was never apprehended after the murdering scrapes.—NEWELL STUBBLEFIELD, Stites, Idaho.

'Tis not long since I've learned, by the laws of our land,
Our law-abiding citizens have taken in hand,
By a well-known desperado and a horse-brander, too,
He is known on the trails as our Captain, Old Blue.

They took him to justice, bold action to try,
And he thought for a moment his time had come to die,
But the Vit was plain and the OK, too,
So they tried and bound over our Captain, Old Blue.

Now Blue, he is an outlaw; the sheriff he stands
With a pair of cocked pistols gripped tight in each hand.
Go take a walk, Tommy, I'm telling you true,
Take a walk for your health and bother old Blue.

Stay at home, don't go, don't go if you can,
Stay close to the ranch with your sweet Mary Ann,
For there is Tity so tricky and Homar Larue
Will take off your scalp if you bother Old Blue.

There is Homar, the ranger, he sails on the trails,
Equipments are graceful, he uses horsehide for sails,
He is fond of wild life and a bold buckaroo,
By life or by death, he will stay with Old Blue.

He went down on Snake River, no horse could he find,
And he thought of his dear friends he had left far behind.
His limbs they got weary, he was darned hungry, too,
A-prowling around on the trails for Old Blue.

But now he is with them and comfort he finds,
And he cares not for the dear friends he left far behind.
He is a night eagle and a bold buckaroo,
And he works to perfection on the line with Old Blue.

The roundhouse at Mackies is filled every night
With horse thieves and bummers of all description in sight;
No rags on their backs, in their pockets no bills,
An yet they are rambling around in the hills.

There is Tommy, the orphan, who has passed in his checks [chips]
By smearing fat cattle too much round his lips;
He gave him a chase and he gave it in true,
But he failed to connect on the line with Old Blue.

The Ballad of Archie Brown

Notes accompanying this ballad state that "it was composed in prison by Archie Brown sometime before 1880," according to the aunt of Miss Cecilia E. Tenney, who communicated the song to William L. Alderson in 1944. It is one of two versions of the ballad in the William L. Alderson Papers, Special Collections, University of Oregon Library. The contributor of the second version, Mrs. Michael Cawley, Portland, notes that "Brown was apprehended in the Lewis River country (Cowlitz County, Wash.) where he had taken a job cutting wood, after fleeing from Portland. He and Johnson were hanged on a gallows erected for them next to the Portland jail. Seward, who turned state's evidence, was sentenced to life imprisonment."

I'm a daring highwayman,
My name is Archie Brown.
I've robbed in every city,
In village and in town;
I've robbed the rich and poor,
As you may understand.
'Twas down in California
I was leader of a band.

I came to Portland city
To see that lively place
I purchased there some blankets—
Which proved my great disgrace.
I instantly did pay for them,
And that without delay,
Unto the noble broker
Whose name was Walter O'Shay.

As he was counting out the change—
'Twas with a glancing eye—
On peering through the showcase
Some jewelry I did spy.
From underneath my coatsleeve
Cold iron I did haul.
Three taps I gave him on the head,
Which quickly made him fall.

As Walter lay upon the floor,
All bleeding in his gore,
I robbed him of his jewelry,
But still I wanted more.
I hunted for his money
But didn't have long to stay;
Five gold watches I did pin
To tell the time of day.

There were Seward, myself and Johnson,
And we were all the same;
But Seward being young and cowardly,
He failed to play the game.
And off to California
Poor Johnson ran away.
But soon was overtaken
To become a hangman's prey.

Now we are all in prison,
All in the county jail,
Loaded down with irons,
Our sorrows to bewail.
My day has come, my race is run,
My robbing days are o'er.
When you receive these deathly lines,
Poor Archie'll be no more.

Farewell, my loving sister,
Relations, too, likewise,
When you receive this letter,
It will you all surprise.
Farewell, my aged mother,
These lines to you I write.
I'm nearly broken-hearted,
I write by candlelight.

Tales of Hunting and Fishing

Oregon's popular image as a sportsman's paradise goes back to the earliest episodes of exploration and settlement in the nineteenth century—but of course for the Chinookan Indians netting salmon on the Columbia River, or the Klamaths hunting a winter's supply of deer and elk near Yamsi Mountain, it was no "image," this natural bounty, but rather the basis of their way of life on the land. Hence a fundamental difference between Anglo and Indian narratives about hunting and fishing: whereas the Anglo tales accentuate the *adventure* of going out into the wilds after game, the bigger and more fantastic the better (the teller is *expected* to exaggerate), the Indian stories typically emphasize what to do and what not to do in the woods and on the river. Their perspective is, as we now say, "ecological," but it is more than that, it is *religious:* to live within the natural order; the people had to know the rules, the rituals and taboos, of harvesting their food.

"Celilo." Photograph by H.M. Prentiss, c. 1900.

A Hunter's First Kill

The Native American concept of hunting as a kind of *sacramental* activity, in which respect and gratitude for the animals being hunted must be maintained, is well expressed in this account of a Paiute "first kill" ceremony, reported to Isabel Kelly by Joshua Brown.—Kelly, "Ethnography of the Surprise Valley Paiutes," p. 80.

A man told his son, "Do not eat the first deer you kill. Butcher it and hang it up. Then let me know. I will go with you to bring back the meat."

Once I killed a deer up above Lake City [California]. My father came and asked me, "What kind of tree would you like? Service?" I said, "Yes, that is stout; maybe it will make me strong." Then we cut green service to make a ring. I pulled over the stem and my father cut it, saying, "I cut you." Then he sliced thin meat from inside the deer's ribs and twisted it around that service ring.

Then my father said, "Take off your shirt, your moccasins. Take the beads from your neck." I took off my clothes. My father said, "Step in this ring. Do it carefully; be sure not to touch it." I did that, and he lifted the ring up over my head and then let it down, and I stepped out. Then he put it over my head and pulled it down. I stood still. "Step over," he said. Every time my father did this he called all kinds of game—goose, swan, mountain sheep, bear, elk, and otter.

This is called *natsa'-tiha'niu* ["skinning an animal"], and afterwards a person will always be lucky. My father said, "You can eat this meat tomorrow." I wanted some that day, but I waited.

The Redwood Canoe

The strict code of dos and don'ts that governed Native hunting and fishing (and still does, for the most part) is dramatized in this story from Coquelle family tradition by George Wasson. The old Indian taboos and restrictions are giving way to Anglo pragmatism: as a result, a whole boat-load of valuable salmon is wasted.—George B. Wasson, personal communication to the editors, December 10, 1991; all rights reserved.

Redwood was held in such high regard among coastal peoples that one time when someone carved a large canoe out of such an honored driftwood log, all the people around South Slough on Coos Bay considered it dangerous and extremely bad luck to touch or even look at it. Sometime, around the turn of the century, my grandfather, George R. Wasson, evidently didn't take the taboos of the local people very seriously and quite matter of factly took the canoe out fishing. He caught a large amount (some say he had the canoe full of salmon) and took them home to my Grandmother Susan Adulsah, for her to clean and smoke or dry for the winter. He learned his lesson well about taking Indian traditions and taboos seriously, when my small but strong-willed grandmother adamantly refused to even touch or look at them, leaving the whole catch of salmon to spoil right where he left them, contaminated in the "bad luck" canoe.

The Hunter Who Had an Elk for a Guardian Spirit

Like all the other Indian communities in the Oregon Country, the Wasco Chinookans believed that the identity and special powers of each individual were shaped by contact (usually obtained through "spirit quests" during adolescence) with one or more guardian spirits. In this starkly tragic Wasco story, the guardian Elk-spirit actually seeks the young man out with his gift of hunting prowess, in exchange for a vow of humility and prudence.

As must have happened in real life, the young hunter is caught between two figures of authority—his secret guardian spirit, and his irresponsibly pushy, lying father. For the hunter to be so sternly punished for his wasteful hunting might seem to us unjust—after all, he has acted out of ignorance, both of his father's motives and of the strict terms of his pact with the Elk: "how much killing is too much?" But in the Native ecological scheme, the hunter is guilty of violating the spirit of his promise to his guardian spirit, and thus abusing the natural order: as we are learning painfully today, Nature does not obligingly tell us when we are "going too far"! The young man's loss of power and death constitute a personal tragedy, and also imply a *social* calamity: how will his people survive without his hunting prowess? (For a discussion of this story in its Native literary and cultural context, see Ramsey, *Reading the Fire,* pp. 60-75.) —Told by Donald McKay or Charlie Pitt to Jeremiah Curtin on the Warm Springs Reservation in 1885: "Wasco Tales and Myths," in *Wishram Texts,* pp. 257-259.

There was a man at Dog River [Hood River] in days gone by, whose wife was with child. Pretty soon she gave birth to a boy. While she was sick, the man carried wood, and one day a piece of bark fell on his forehead and cut him.

When the boy was large enough to shoot, he killed birds and squirrels; he was a good shot. One day, however, his father said to him, "You don't do as I used to. I am ashamed to own you. When I was of your age, I used to catch young elk. One day when I killed a young elk, the old one attacked me and made this scar you see on my forehead."

Then the boy had a visit from an elk, and the elk said, "If you will serve me and hear what I say, I will be your master and will help you in every necessity. You must not be proud. You must not kill too many of any animal. I will be your guardian spirit."

So the young man became a great hunter, knew where every animal was—elk, bear, deer. He killed what he needed for himself, and no more. The old man, his father, said to him, "You are not doing enough. At your age I used to do much more." The young man was grieved at his father's scolding. The elk, the young man's helper, was very angry at the old man. At last [he] helped the young man to kill five whole herds of elk. He killed all except his own spirit elk, though he tried without knowing it to kill even [that one]. This elk went to a lake and pretended to be dead; the young man went into the water to draw the elk out, but as soon as he touched it, both sank.

After touching bottom, the young man woke as from a sleep, and saw bears, deer, and elk without number, and they were all persons. Those that he had killed were there too, and they groaned. A voice called, "Draw him in." Each time the voice was heard, he was drawn nearer his master, the Elk, until he was at his side. Then the great Elk said, "Why did you go beyond what I commanded? Your father required more of you than he himself ever did. Do you see our people on both sides? These are they whom you have killed. You have inflicted many needless wounds on our people. Your father lied to you. He never saw my father, as he falsely told you, saying that my father had met him. He also told you that my father gave him a scar. That is not true, He was carrying fire-wood when you were born, and a piece of bark fell on him and cut him. He has misled you. Now I shall leave you, and never be your guardian spirit again."

When the Elk had finished, a voice was heard saying five times, "Cast him out." The young man went home. The old man was talking, feeling well. The young man told his two wives to fix a bed for him. They did so. He lay there five days and nights, and then told his wives, "Heat water to wash me, also call my friends so that I may talk to them. Bring five elk-skins." All this was done.

The people came together, and he told them, "My father was dissatisfied because, as he said, I did not do as he had done. What my father wanted grieved the guardian spirit which visited and aided me. My father deceived me. He said that he had been scarred on the head by a great elk while taking the young elk away. He said that I was a disgrace to him. He wanted me to kill more than was needed. He lied. The spirit has left me, and I die."

Coyote and the Talking Fish Trap

In this Kalapuya tale, Coyote the Transformer, having created Willamette Falls and the good fishing sites along the river, invents a magical fishing-machine, but typically botches his invention. Oregon's Native peoples had fish traps in the olden days, but this story may allude to the elaborate, "automatic" fishwheels that Anglos installed on Northwest rivers at the end of the last century, seriously threatening the salmon population, until they were banned—only to be followed by the far worse threat of the great hydroelectric dams. —Recorded in the 1890s by H.S. Lyman from Louis Labonte, a very old French Canadian who settled in the French/Indian community of French Prairie after service with the Hudson's Bay Company: Lyman, "Reminiscences of Louis Labonte," pp. 183-184.

Coyote came to that place [around Oregon City] and found the people there very hungry. The river was full of salmon, but they had no way to spear them in the deep water. Coyote decided he would build a big waterfall, so that the salmon would come to the surface for spearing. Then he would build a fish trap there too.

First he tried at the mouth of Pudding River, but it was no good, and all he made was the gravel-bar there. So he went on down the river to Rock Island, and it was better, but after making the rapids there he gave up again and went farther down still. Where the Willamette Falls are now he found just the right place, and he made the Falls high and wide. All the Indians came and began to fish.

Now Coyote made his magic fish trap. He made it so it would speak, and say *Noseepsk!* when it was full. Because he was pretty hungry, Coyote decided to try it first himself. He set the trap by the Falls, and then ran back up the shore to prepare to make a cooking-fire. But he had only begun when the trap called out, *"Noseepsk!"* He hurried back; indeed the trap was full of salmon. Running back with them, he started his fire again, but again the fish trap cried *"Noseepsk! Noseepsk!"* He went again and found the trap full of salmon. Again he ran to the shore with them; again he had hardly gotten to his fire when the trap called out, *"Noseepsk! Noseepsk!"* It happened again, and again; the fifth time Coyote became angry and said to the trap, "What, can't you wait with your fish-catching until I've built a fire?" The trap was very offended by Coyote's impatience, and stopped working right then. So after that the people had to spear their salmon as best they could.

Goose Hunting Near McMinnville, Fishing at Meadow Lake

Interviewed by Sara B. Wrenn for the WPA Oregon Folklore Project on March 10, 1939, A. J. Howell of Oswego, Oregon, told these stories about hunting and fishing. Howell was born January 15, 1851, near Bowling Green, Kentucky; he moved to Illinois in 1856 and to Oregon in 1872. Howell's account of his fishing experience at Meadow Lake is a version of one of America's favorite tall tales, first recorded in the United States in 1809 in Vermont. Also popular in Europe, the tale usually begins with a hunting expedition. For another Oregon version of this tale type, see "Hathaway's Marvelous Hunt," on p. 75.

When I firs' come here, there was a narrow gauge railroad that run to McMinnville. It was a perty crooked right-of-way, an' I remember when the conductor would tell hunters that was travellin' out that way, that if they wanted to get off the train an' go through the field, they could, an' he'd meet 'em further up the line. Many's the time I heard him tell that.

An' that reminds me of once when I went after wild geese. Out 'round McMinnville the wild geese was thick then. I heard a big flock of 'em honking one night. It was in the evenin', an' they sounded like they had lighted. I didn't have no gun, but I borrowed a single-barrelled shotgun from my father-in-law, an' next morning I started out for my geese. I went where I thought I heard 'em, but nary a goose. Then, perty soon I heard 'em. They was 'bout a quarter of a mile away. I made up my mind I was goin' have goose or know why. So, so's they wouldn't see me, I crawled nearly the whole way. Perty soon I come to an ol' snake fence row—that's a rail fence all growed up with weeds an' grass; an' I peeked through, an' sure enough, close by, was my geese—a lot of 'em. I put my gun on the old rail fence, took a good sight, an' pulled the trigger. The trigger snapped, an' that was all! The gun didn't go off, but the geese heard the snap, an' up they went! I was perty mad. There was a lot o' feathers droppin', an' I pulled the trigger again, an' this time she worked. I climbed over the fence an' went after my goose, an' I picked up eleven! Yep, that's what I got, 'leven geese with one shot. "B'lieve it or not," as Ripley says.

If you think that's wonderful, here's a real story. (I ought to belong to the Liar's Club, huh!) This happened out at Meadow Lake, west of Carlton, in Yamhill County. Ol' Yamhill, the Yamhillers al'ays call it, an' I guess they're right. Anyway, this day I was goin' fishin'. I wore my ol' fishin' clothes an' my ol' fashioned wide-leg gumboots. I was goin' along, an' the fish was jumpin' good, I see. An' perty soon I cast my line, an' right away I caught a fish. Nice big fish it was, too. I pulled in my line an' flung it over my shoulder, an' the fish come off the hook and landed in the fern back o' me. Well, I'll be derned if that fish didn't land right in the nest of a grouse, an' the minute the hook an' bait let go from the fish, the ol' grouse hen grabbed it! 'Course then that ol' grouse hen started to fly, an' she hit me square in the back an' knocked me in the water. That ol' grouse hen was caught good an' plenty on my hook, an' I hung on tight to my fish pole. By and by, when the line give out, I floundered out to where the grouse was in some rushes, an' I got the grouse and brung her in. An' then I pulled off my boots to get the water out. An' when I emptied the water out, derned if I didn't empty out 13 fish that had got caught in my boots goin' after that grouse. Yep, I al'ays thought that a perty lucky fishin' trip, when you figger that with one cast an' one bait I got 14 fish (countin' the first one), one grouse hen an' the nine grouse eggs that was in the nest.

The Biggest Catch

Cannon Beach was where Peter Lindsey recorded this story from seventy-three-year old Emmett Wallace in May 1971. Lindsey notes that this story was prompted by his own tale about a Tennessee mountain man who always put salt in his black powder "to keep the game he shot from spoiling, since his long rifle shot so far, he often had to walk for days before he caught up to it." (RVMA, Lindsey, 1971)

[That's just like] a fisherman up here at Astoria. Two old fishermen were tellin' how big a fish they caught. This one ol' fisherman said he caught a Chinook salmon weighed over a hundred and forty pounds. The other old fisherman set there and spit out a gobbet of snoose. He says, "I don't believe that."

"Well, I did."

He says, "That's nothin'." He says, "I was fishing here the other day, caught onto somethin," says, "I drug it around, and brought it up, and it was an old ship's light."

"An old ship's light?"

"Yeah."

"Well, what's that? What's an old ship's light? Heck, that could have been near ever'thing."

"But," he says, "the light was still burning in it."

"Oh, the light was not burnin'."

"Well," he says, "Tell you what you do. You knock about a hundred pounds off the fish, and I'll blow the light out a the lantern."

Boiled Owl

Part of hunting and fishing entails the preparation of the game after it has been caught. Recipes for wild game are often family traditions, passed down from one generation to the next. This recipe for owl, a bird few think is edible, has something in common with the other tall tales. It was published in the *Forest Log,* the Oregon State Department of Forestry publication, in 1934, and collected as part of the WPA Oregon Folklore Project.

One of the CCC camp superintendents recently found an old timer who insists that the owl is an edible bird. Here's his recipe:

"Some folks think they ain't no way to cook a owl. I hev a old receep that's dandy an' works every time if carried out properly. Here it is: Remove the feathers, entrails, head, etc., as you would a chicken. Be sure to get the gall bladder as it spoils the meat. Stuff the owl with yer favorite dressing—mine is quartered apples and raisins. Get a deep kettle, iron preferred. Fill it with water and toss in plenty of salt and pepper. Put in the owl after the water begun to boil; an' to keep him from bobbing around on top, tie one of his hind legs to a piece of railroad iron—sort of a sinker.

"To dee-cide when the owl's done, take yer fork in hand—and when the iron bar's soft enough to stick with the fork, the owl's ready ter eat."

A Good Hunting Dog

One subcategory of hunting tall tales contains the yarns spun about exceptionally talented hunting dogs, as we shall see in this story about hunting chukars, a kind of partridge widely hunted in the high desert country of eastern Oregon. This story was originally collected in Baker, Oregon, by Melissa Oestreich for the Randall V. Mills Archives of Northwest Folklore, it was published in *Oregon Folklore*, p. 61.

Don was out hunting one day, you see, and then his dog was out ahead of them there, and he was running a bunch of chukars. He was on the scent, you know, and he was tracking them down. And they went over this little ridge. The dog disappeared over it, and Don starts walking up on this ridge, and all of a sudden this chukar flies up, and Don shoots the thing. And he walks a little farther, and all of a sudden another chukar flies up, and he shoots that one. You know, things are kinda strange here because, you know, chukars don't normally flush like that. They normally go out in a big covey.

Anyway, Don starts walking a little farther. Another chukar flies up, and he shoots that one, you know. He's really beginning to wonder now; walks a little farther. Pretty soon, the fourth chukar flies up and he shoots that one. So he's really curious now, so he gets down on his hands and knees, and he sneaks right up to the top of this little ridge, and he peeks over. And here the hunting dog is. He's got this covey of chukars, and he's run them in a rabbit hole, you see, and he's got his front paws over the rabbit hole, and he's letting the chukars fly out one at a time.

The Smartest Hunting Dog

Joann Low, a University of Oregon folklore student in 1974, recalled this story her dad used to tell. (RVMA, Low, 1974)

When my dad was a boy, he had a hunting dog that was so smart that all Dad had to do was put a drying board outside, and the dog would bring back an animal whose pelt would fit the board. If he wanted a rabbit, he put out a board the right size to dry a rabbit pelt on; if he wanted a muskrat, he put out a muskrat board, and so on.

Well, this dog became the wonder of the countryside, and people would come from miles around just to see and maybe pet him.

This went on for quite some time, but one day the dog did not come home at all. Well, Dad had quite a time figuring out what happened, 'til he happened to see his mother's ironing board leaning against the house—right where he usually put the pelt board.

Well, he didn't figure he'd ever see that dog again, knowing how proud he was. But one day, six or seven months later, here come the dog, dragging a coon skin coat, and a college kid right behind him, yelling that that darned dog had stole his coat.

Well, my dad had to give the coat back, and his dog never did hunt again. I guess he figured it weren't no use, if Dad was just going to hand the skin back to the critters he caught.

A Remarkable Shot

Recorded at Bill's Tavern in Cannon Beach, this hunting story belongs to a group of tall tales about "remarkable" or "slow" ammunition. Several may be found among the Hathaway Jones tales published by Stephen Dow Beckham. This particular tale was told by Victor Olson of Cannon Beach to Peter Lindsey. (RVMA, Lindsey, 1971)

Oh, I know about this here feller that went out huntin', and he drove up into the country. And he sees this deer walkin' along. And he got out his big old powerful magnum rifle. And he watched this deer for a little bit. And he got his sights set on it. And about the time he got his sights set on it, the deer jumped behind this big tree. And it made him madder than the dickens, and he whirled around with his rifle, and he shot it the other way! Shot it behind him. It was the last day of huntin' season, so he just emptied his rifle out, got back in his car and drove home.

So next huntin' season opened up, why, he went back up to this same spot. Here come a deer walking up there, and he loaded his rifle right quick, and he pointed it at it, and he went to pull the trigger. Just about the time he went to pull the trigger, the darn deer jumped behind a tree! So, he pulls his rifle back, and all at once the deer jumps straight in the air and dropped over dead! So he walked around behind the deer and looked at it. And that bullet that he'd fired the year before went around the world and come back and smacked that deer dead center.

Another Remarkable Shot

This tale was collected on May 21, 1971, from John Catlin, age 66, of Cannon Beach, by Peter Lindsey. It combines both the motifs of the remarkable shot and the wonderful hunt. (RVMA, Lindsey, 1971)

It's about the kid who was sent to school. He had to walk three miles to school every day, and he always carried a rifle, and he was given one shot. So comin' home—and he was supposed to bring home the meat for the family—so, coming home this afternoon, here was a deer and an elk right close together.

Well, that kind of excited him, so he took a shot at it. Well, the bullet hit a rock and split in two and killed them both. But the recoil knocked him back in the creek, and he came up with an eight-pound trout in his hip pocket.

A City Hunter

E. R. Jackman, in his chapter on "Mule Deer," in *The Oregon Desert,* points out that most hunters are courteous and good sportsmen and -women. It is the other two percent that leave ranch gates open, shoot holes in water tanks, and show little respect for wildlife or other hunters. The hunter in the following story is not specifically identified as a "Portland Hunter," but stories of such behavior are told among Central and Eastern Oregon ranchers whose lands are overrun with deer hunters each fall.—*The Oregon Desert* , pp. 240-241.

A few years ago a woman and her husband were hunting out of Burns. They went to a certain mountain where they knew the terrain. The husband said he'd go up the draw to the left if his wife would take the right draw. Each was to watch the ridge between, and they would meet around noon up above where the draws joined. It worked as planned. A fine buck came bounding over the hill and the wife dropped him with one shot. She tied her tag to the antlers and was dressing her deer when a big man with brand-new hunting clothes came up with an open knife, cut off her tag, threw it into the sage-brush, and tied on his own. The Burns woman, too astonished to argue at first, said, "What do you think you're doing with my deer?" The man said, "It's my deer now."

This lady from Burns was of sterner stuff than most. She said, "The hell it is, mister," and placed a shot carefully through his shoulder, below the bone. He began to yell, a car appeared on the road below, four companions came and led him away, the woman retrieved her tag, and went on cleaning the deer. She explained to her husband, "I didn't want to kill him, but I wanted to teach him never to do a trick like that again."

The Deer Hunter

This poem by Sunny Hancock and Lona Burkhart is in the tradition of Central and Eastern Oregon narratives about city hunters. The rancher's feelings are effectively conveyed through the poem's matter-of-fact tone and use of the uncomprehending hunter as narrator.—From Sunny Hancock and Lona Burkhart, all rights reserved, 1993.

Hello there, Mr. Rancher. Yep we're back, you know the reason—
In three more days they're gonna open up the huntin' season.
Sure I saw that big old sign that you got nailed up to that tree
That says "No Huntin' or Trespassin'," but I know you don't mean me.

We'll camp right here by this big spring by that old brandin' pen
And the next few days we'll just drink beer and sight our rifles in.
You say cows won't come in to drink with all us people here—
I didn't see no thirsty cows ahanging around last year.

Oh yeah, I think we learned a lesson, and we'll be more careful now.
You got a bit irate when Jody shot that brindle cow
But you really couldn't blame him; he was in an awful rush
And she sounded just like a big old buck acrashing through the brush.

I can call old Shep back better now, he has a lot more sense
Than last year when he ran that bunch of horses through the fence.
You sure have cleaned this place up nice; I really must confess—
When we pulled out of here last time we did leave quite a mess.

But we didn't think you'd mind too much, we did have other plans—
Besides, you must have made a killin' just from the rebate on the cans.
Yeah, we left the gates all open when we came in this afternoon
But shoot, there weren't no cows around 'em, and we're leavin' pretty soon.

We have to make a speed run back to town to get some brew
And to check the local bars out and maybe buy a jug or two.
In fact, we'll be goin' back and forth right regular, and we'll check
And if there's any cows around 'em, why we'll close 'em sure as heck.

Whatta' you mean by tellin' us that we can't camp in here?
All we want's some recreation and to maybe shoot a deer.
That's the damnedest thing I ever heard, and you with all this space—
You sound just like that bird that ran us off that other place.

You guys must think you own the world, but I'm gonna tell you true—
Most folks would be lots better off without the likes of you.
So those hunters did pack up and leave, but when they pulled their freight
They left three gut-shot dying cows beside an open gate.

Portland Hunters

The Eastern Oregon resentment of the annual invasion of westside deer and elk
hunters goes way back, and expresses itself in scornful anecdotes about "Portland
hunters" or "Burnsiders" like the following, recorded by George Venn in La Grande
from Christie Young and Forrest Warren, respectively.—From Venn Collection,
Eastern Oregon State College.

Hunting is very popular in Eastern Oregon. The one thing that isn't popular
is "Portland hunters."

Several years ago, a Portland hunter came over in this part of the country to
kill "the big bull elk." He brought a horse to do his hunting on. One day while
making a big hunt, the Portland man decided to get off his horse, tie it to a
tree, and walk for a while.

He made the hunt coming around in a circle. When he got close enough to
see his horse, he thought his prize bull elk was in sight. He fired, and his aim
was perfect. After walking cautiously up to it, he found his horse dead, still tied
to the tree.

Three years ago, a hunter was driving down a dirt road, only a mile or so from
his proposed camp site. This road was surrounded by bushes. As the hunter
drove down the road, with visions of big elk in his head, he heard his horses
kick around in his horse trailer a little. He thought nothing of it and kept
driving.

Finally reaching his campsite, he stopped to set up camp. He walked around
the back of the horse trailer and opened the doors. As soon as he opened them,
his horses rolled out on the ground—dead. He was appalled to find them both
shot through the neck. Suddenly a Portland hunter, dressed completely in red,
stepped out of the bushes. His face was as red as his outfit. He told the man
with the horses that all he could see were the two heads moving along, so he
shot for all he was worth. Apparently, he was a fair shot.

Coyote and Other Tricksters

If heroes embody "official" values in a society and stand for what is right and proper to their admirers, tricksters appeal to our self-seeking and irresponsible instincts; they are, by definition, not good citizens. Characters like Coyote and Fernando (in the Basque tradition) are wily, devious, and predictably unpredictable, always intent on fooling others but often ending up as their own worst victims. "Too clever by half," as we say! Part of the universal and cross-cultural appeal of a figure like Coyote is that when he turns up in a story (he is typically just "traveling around"), anything is possible; his energies and impulses regularly violate the rules of conventional morality and good sense. His exploits and come-uppances thus allow us to have our morality both ways: when he misbehaves, lies, tricks people, we can enjoy his freedom from moral restraints vicariously, and when he comes to grief (he is never killed), we can affirm our official moral position against such misbehavior. The considerable wisdom in trickster stories lies in the way such figures are, as we say, "all too human": their exploits may be morally outrageous, but their energies and impulses are inherent in all of us, not to be denied or ignored.

"Coyote and Animal Friends" by Audrey Myers from Great Basin petroglyphs.

Wasco Coyote Cycle

The following five stories, from the Wishram/Wasco community on both sides of the Columbia above The Dalles, illustrate Coyote's mixed career in Indian literary tradition as both a trickster and a mythic transformer of reality, creating the decidedly mixed, good-and-bad human condition we know today. These stories are part of a loose cycle narrating Coyote's journey up the Columbia, "fixing things up" with mythic finality according to his tricksterish nature, always moving on, never settling down until at last he *does* take a wife, loves and loses her to death, and in trying to bring her back forfeits, as Orpheus does in the Greek myth, the chance to set a mythic precedent for returning the dead to the land of the living.

—"Coyote Frees the Fish," "Coyote and the First Pregnancy," "Coyote Meets Tsagigla'lal," and "Coyote and Eagle Go to the Land of the Dead" from Curtis, *The North American Indian,* Vol. 8, pp. 107-109; 112-113; 145-146; 127-129, narrators unknown. "Coyote and the Mouthless Man" was narrated by Louis Simpson to Edward Sapir around 1907: Sapir, *Wishram Texts,* pp. 19-24.

Coyote Frees the Fish

Coyote heard about two women who had fish preserved in a pond. Then he went to them as they were collecting driftwood from the river. He turned himself into a piece of wood (trying to get them to pick him up). He drifted along. But they did not get hold of him. He went ashore, ran off way yonder up river, and transformed himself into a boy. He put himself into a cradle, threw himself into the river, and again drifted along.

The two women caught sight of him wailing. They thought: "Some people have capsized, and this child is drifting towards us." The younger one thought: "Let us get hold of it." But the older woman did not want to have the child. Now it was drifting along. The older one thought, "That is Coyote." Nevertheless the younger woman took the child and put it in a canoe.

The two women started home towards their house. The child was wailing, and they arrived home with it. They took off the cradle from it and looked closely at it. As it turned out, the child was a boy. The younger one said, "A boy is better than driftwood." And then she went and cut an eel and put its tail in his mouth. Then straightway he sucked at it and ate it all up. She gave him another eel, and again he sucked at it, (eating up) only half. Then he fell asleep, and half the eel was lying in his mouth. The two women said, "He is asleep; now let us go for some more wood."

And then they went far away. Coyote arose and saw them going far off. Then he made himself loose and seized their food. He roasted the fish on a spit; they were done and he ate. He caught sight of the fish, which were their food, in a lake. Then he examined (the lake) carefully, and discovered a spot where it would be easy (to make an outlet from it to the river). "Here I shall make the fish break out (from the lake), and then they shall go to the Great River" [*wi'mahl*—Columbia].

He made five digging-sticks, made them out of young oak. And then he put them down in that place. He started back home towards their house. Again, just as before, he put himself into the cradle. Again, there in his mouth lay the eel's tail. Again he fell asleep.

Now the two women arrived. "The boy is sleeping," they said, "very good is the boy, being a great sleeper." And then they retired for the night. Daylight came, the boy was sleeping. Again they went for wood. Again he saw them going far away. Then he got up and took their food. He roasted it on a spit and ate it all up. Then straightway he went to where his digging-sticks were.

He took hold of one of his digging-sticks. Then he stuck it into the ground; he pulled it out, and the earth was loosened up; his digging-stick broke. He took hold of another one and again stuck it into the ground. Then he loosened up the earth, and his digger was all broken to pieces. He took hold of another of his digging-sticks. Again, he stuck it into the ground; he loosened the earth all up, and his third digger was all broken to pieces. He took hold of the fourth one; again his digger broke. Now at last he took hold of the fifth, and stuck it into the ground; he loosened the earth all up, And then the fish slid over into the Great River.

Now then the older woman bethought herself. She said to her companion, "You said, 'The child is good.' I myself thought, 'That is Coyote.' Now this day Coyote has treated us two badly. I told you, 'Let us not take the child, that is Coyote.' Now we have become poor, Coyote has made us so." Then they went to their house, and Coyote met them there.

He said to them: "Now by what right, perchance, would you two keep the fish to yourselves? You two are birds, and I shall tell you something. Soon now people will come into this land. Listen!" And the people could be heard, *du'lulululu*, like thunder rumbling afar. "Now they will come into this land; those fish will be the people's food. Whenever a fish will be caught, you two will come. Your name will be Swallows. Now this day I have done with you; thus I shall call you 'Swallows.' When the people will come, they will catch fish; and then you two will come, and it will be said of you, 'The swallows have come, Coyote called them so.' Thus will the people say: 'From these two did Coyote take away their fish preserved in a pond; now they have come.'" Thus did Coyote call those two.

Coyote and the Mouthless Man

Again Coyote traveled up the river. In the water he saw the canoe of a certain person, a man. He saw how the man dived into the water. He came up out of the water, his hands holding one sturgeon on that side and one sturgeon on this; he put the sturgeons down in the canoe. Then Coyote saw him count them with his finger, pointing about in the canoe. He thought: "When he dives, I shall take hold of and steal from him one of his sturgeons; let us see what he'll do."

The person dived under water. And then Coyote swam towards his canoe. He seized one of his sturgeons. He went and took the person's sturgeon with him, and hid it in the bushes. And then that Coyote seated himself there and hid. Then the person came up out of the water into his canoe; he put his sturgeons down in the canoe, again one and one. And then he counted them; again he counted them. Quite silently he counted them; [one sturgeon was missing].

And then the person pointed his finger out, first up high, then a little lower, again a little lower still, finally lower still, on the ground. There he pointed, where Coyote was sitting! Silently he held his finger there. Coyote tried to move to one side, there again was the finger. No matter which way Coyote moved, there was that finger pointing at him, Coyote. Now where his finger was pointed, that person went straight up to Coyote. Straightway he went to meet Coyote. . . . He kept pointing at him; Coyote kept dodging from side to side, the person kept him well in eye.

Coyote looked at the person [as he came up]; he was strange in appearance. As it turned out, he had no mouth; he had only a nose and eyes and ears. He spoke to Coyote with his nose; but he could not hear him; just deep down in his nose could be heard: "*Dnn Dnn Dnn Dnn.*" In fact he was scolding Coyote in this way. Thus he said to him with his nose, "You are not good." Thus the person kept telling him; his heart was dark within him. Coyote thought: "Perhaps now this man desires the sturgeon; perhaps he is going to kill me. . . ."

And then the person went back to his canoe. Coyote made a fire when he had gone. He gathered some stones and heated them in the fire. And then they all became hot. He cut the sturgeon in two, cut it all up, and carefully made ready the stones. He laid the sturgeon out on the stones and steamed it; it was entirely done. And then he removed it and laid it down. Then the man who had no mouth came back; he met Coyote as he was eating.

And then [the person] took hold of that good well-done sturgeon. Then thought Coyote, "Wonder what he'll do with it!" [Coyote] looked at him; he took the good sturgeon. [The person] just sniffed at the sturgeon, then threw it away. And then Coyote thought, "It is not well." He went and brought the sturgeon back and brushed it clean. Now Coyote was thinking, "What is he going to do with it?" Once again the person took hold of it and did with it as before.

[Coyote] went up to him and looked at him closely. And then he thought, "I don't know what I shall do to make him a mouth." Secretly he took a flint and chipped it on one side; it became just like a sharp knife. And then he went up to the person with the flint secretly in hand and looked at him closely. In vain the man tried to dodge from side to side. Now Coyote put the flint down over his mouth. He sliced it open, and the person's blood flowed out. He breathed: "Haaaaa! Haaaaa!" Coyote said to him, "Go to the river and wash yourself."

When the person had come out of the water, he stopped and spoke to Coyote: "You do not seem to have steamed a large sturgeon." And then Coyote said, "Well, you would have killed me; you wanted the sturgeon for yourself. You got after me for the sturgeon."

Now the people [of the mouthless man's village] told one another: "There is a man whose mouth has been made for him." In truth, all the people of that same village were without mouths. And then they betook themselves to [Coyote]. He made mouths for all the people of that village. He called that village Nimishxa'ya [located below Castle Rock]. They said to him: "We will give you a woman." He said: "No! I shouldn't care for a woman; I'll not take one."

The First Pregnancy

So Coyote left Nimishxáya, and a little above that place he saw a man turning somersaults, landing on his head, and yelling loudly, as if it hurt him. Coyote was curious, and going to see what it all meant, he found that the man had his ankles tied, and between his legs was a bundle of firewood.

"What is the matter, friend?" he asked. "My wife is about to have a child," the man answered, "and I am carrying wood for the house."—"But that is no way to carry wood," said Coyote. He untied the man's legs, cut some hazel-brush, and began to twist it into a rope, which he attached to the bundle as a packstring. He swung the faggot on his back, passing the loop of the rope across his forehead.

"Take the lead, and I will carry this in for you," he said. So the man went ahead, and Coyote followed, bearing the bundle of fuel. "Here is my home," said the man after a while. Coyote threw down the load, and said, "That is the way to carry wood. Where is this woman who is to have a child?"

The man showed him a woman lying on a bed with a pile of robes wrapped around her hand. She did not seem to be pregnant, and Coyote unwrapped the hand, in a finger of which he saw a sliver embedded in a mass of pus. "Is this what is the matter?" he asked. "Yes," was the answer. "That is nothing; let me show you," said Coyote. He took a small sharp flake of bone, pricked the finger open, and pressed out the sliver.

"Now I will show you how to make a child," he said. He then did so.

Coyote remained a few days in that house, and the woman said she was soon to be a mother. In a short time the child was born. "That is your child," Coyote said to the man. "I give it to you."

Coyote Meets Tsagiglálal

A woman had a house where the village of Nixlúidix was later built [present-day Wishram, or Spedis]. She was chief of all who lived in this region. That was long ago, before Coyote came up the river and changed things, and people were not yet real people.

After a time Coyote in his travels came to this place and asked the inhabitants if they were living well or ill. They sent him to their chief, who lived up in the rocks, where she could look down on the village and know all that was going on.

Coyote climbed up to her home and asked: "What kind of living do you give these people? Do you treat them well, or are you one of those evil women?"—"I am teaching them how to live well and to build good houses," she said. "Soon the world is going to change," he told her, "and women will no longer be chiefs. You will be stopped from being a chief."

Then he changed her into a rock, with the command, "You shall stay here and watch over the people who live at this place, which shall be called Nixlúidix."

All the people know that Tsagiglálal sees all things, for whenever they are looking up at her those large eyes are watching them.

Coyote and Eagle Go to the Land of the Dead

Coyote had a wife and two children, and so had Eagle. Both families lived together. Eagle's wife and children died, and a few days later Coyote experienced the same misfortune. As Coyote wept, Eagle said, "Do not mourn: that will not bring your wife back. Make ready your moccasins, and we will go somewhere." So the two prepared for a long journey, and set out westward.

After four days they were close to the ocean; on the one side of a body of water they saw houses. Coyote called across, "Come with a boat!"—"Never mind; stop calling," said Eagle. He produced an elderberry stalk, made a flute, put the end into the water, and whistled. Soon they saw two persons come out of a house, walk to the water's edge, and enter a canoe. Said Eagle, "Do not look at those people when they land." The boat drew near, but a few yards from the shore it stopped, and Eagle told Coyote to close his eyes. He then took Coyote by the arm and leaped to the boat. The two persons paddled back, and when they stopped a short distance from the other side, Eagle again cautioned Coyote to close his eyes, and then leaped ashore with him.

They went to the village, where there were many houses, but no people were in sight. Everything was still as death. There was a very large underground house, into which they went. In it was an old woman [Frog] sitting with her face to the wall, and lying on the floor on the other side of the room was the moon. They sat down near the wall.

"Coyote," whispered Eagle, "watch that woman and see what she does when the sun goes down!" Just before the sun set they heard a voice outside calling, "Get up! Hurry! The sun is going down, and it will soon be night. Hurry! Hurry!" Coyote and Eagle still sat in a corner of the chamber watching the old woman.

People began to enter, many hundreds of them, men, women, and children. Coyote, as he watched, saw Eagle's wife and two daughters among them, and soon afterward his own family. When the room was filled, Nikshia'mchash, the old woman, cried, "Are all in?" Then she turned about, and from a squatting posture she jumped forward, then again and again, five times in all, until she alighted in a small pit beside the moon. This she raised and swallowed, and at once it was pitch dark. The people wandered about, hither and thither, crowding and jostling, unable to see. About daylight a voice from outside cried, "Nikshia'mchash, all get through!" The old woman then disgorged the moon, and laid it back in its place on the floor; all the people filed out, and the woman, Eagle, and Coyote were once more alone.

"Now, Coyote," said Eagle, "could you do that?"—"Yes, I can do that," he said. They went out, and Coyote at Eagle's direction made a box of boards, as large as he could carry, and put into it leaves from every kind of tree and blades from every kind of grass. "Well," said Eagle, "if you are sure you remember just how she did this, let us go in and kill her."

So they entered the house and killed her, and buried the body. Her dress they took off and put on Coyote, so that he looked just like her, and he sat down in her place. Eagle then told him to practice what he had seen, by turning around and jumping as the old woman had done. So Coyote turned about and jumped five times, but the last leap was a little short, yet he managed to slide into the hole. He put the moon into his mouth, but, try as he would, a thin edge still showed, and he covered it with his hands. Then he laid the moon back in its place and resumed his seat by the wall, waiting for sunset and the voice of the chief outside.

The day passed, the voice called, and the people entered. Coyote turned about and began to jump. Some [of the people] thought there was something strange about the manner of jumping, but others said it was really the old woman. When he came to the last jump and slipped into the pit, many cried out that this was not the old woman, but Coyote quickly lifted the moon and put it in his mouth, covering the edge with his hands.

When it was completely dark, Eagle placed the box in the doorway. Throughout the long night Coyote retained the moon in his mouth, until he was almost choking, but at last the voice of the chief was heard from the outside, and the dead began to file out. Everyone walked into the box, and Eagle quickly threw the cover over and tied it. The sound was like that of a great swarm of flies.

"Now, my brother, we are through," said Eagle. Coyote removed the dress and laid it down beside the moon, and Eagle threw the moon into the sky, where it remained. The two entered the canoe with the box, and paddled toward the east.

When they landed, Eagle carried the box. Near the end of the third night Coyote heard somebody else talking; there seemed to be many voices. He awakened his companion, and said, "There are many people coming." —"Do not worry," said Eagle, "it is all right." The following night Coyote heard the talking again, and, looking about, he discovered that the voices came from the box which Eagle had been carrying. He placed his ear against it, and after a while distinguished the voice of his wife. He smiled, and broke into laughter, but he said nothing to Eagle.

At the end of the fifth night and the beginning of their last day of traveling, Coyote said to his friend, "I will carry the box now; you have carried it a long way."—"No," replied Eagle, "I will take it; I am strong." —"Let me carry it," insisted Coyote, "suppose we come to where people live, and they should see the chief carrying the load. How would that look?" Still Eagle retained his hold on the box, but as they went along Coyote kept begging, and about noon, wearying of the subject, Eagle gave him the box.

So Coyote had the load, and every time he heard the voice of his wife he would laugh. After a while he contrived to fall behind, and when Eagle was out of sight around a hill he began to open the box, in order to release his wife. But no sooner was the cover lifted than it was thrown back violently, and the dead people rushed out into the air with such force that Coyote was thrown to the ground. They quickly disappeared in the west. Eagle saw the cloud of dead people rising in the air, and came hurrying back. He found one man left there, a cripple who had been unable to rise; he threw him into the air, and the dead man floated away swiftly.

"You see what you have done, with your curiosity and haste!" said Eagle. "If we had brought these dead all the way back, people would not die forever, but only for a season, like these plants whose leaves we have brought. Hereafter trees and grasses will die only in the winter, but in the spring will be green again. So it would have been with the people."—"Let us go back and catch them again," proposed Coyote; but Eagle objected: "They will not go to the same place, and we would not know how to find them; they will be where the moon is, up in the sky."

Coyote the Eye-Juggler

This is the Northern Paiute form of a very widespread story, probably a great favorite with children, about Coyote's insatiable curiosity and his talents for tricking his way out of, as well as into, difficulties. Like the Wishram "Coyote and the Mouthless Man," this tale is full of cues for comic gestures and grimaces by the storyteller, who is, of course, playing all the parts. For a Klamath form of the story, see M.A.R. Barker, *Klamath Texts*, pp. 13-15. The Paiute story was told to Isabel Kelly by Bige Archie in the 1930s near Burns (Kelly, "Northern Paiute Tales," pp. 418-419).

Coyote was walking along. He heard someone laughing. "Come in," they said. Wild Cat and some others were sitting there. I think Skunk was there too. Coyote asked them, "What shall I do?"—"Take out your eyes. Throw them in the air. Then hold your head back, and they will fall in again."

Coyote tried to take out his eyes. He took them both out and threw them up, but not very far. He held back his head, and the eyes fell right in the sockets. Everybody laughed.

Then Wild Cat tried it again. He threw his eyes way up in the air, and they came back. Everybody laughed and told Coyote to try it again. "Throw them way up in the air this time," they said. He did it. One had a stick in his hand. When Coyote's eyes were coming down, he knocked them to one side. Then everybody ran away. They took Coyote's eyes with them.

Coyote couldn't see a thing. He was all alone. He tried to follow but he couldn't find the way. He ran into the Sagebrushes, and he scolded them. They said, "We never move. You come right over us." Then he ran into the Rocks. "You're in my way all the time!" he told them. But the Rocks said, "We never move. You just run over us."

Coyote heard some Birds singing. He went over there and called them. The Birds came to him. "Will you give me your little eye so that I can see?" They gave him a little one so that he could see where he was going.

Coyote traveled until he came to a camp. An old woman was there and Coyote asked her, "Where is everybody?" She told him, "I have three daughters. They're out there dancing over Coyote's eyes."—"What do you do when your girls come back?" —"I tell them to get me water. That's the first thing I say," the old lady told him. Then Coyote asked, "How do you cook for them?"—"I cook *wa'da* for them."

Then Coyote took a rock. He hit the old woman on the head and hid her away. He took off her clothes and put them on. Then he lay down where she had been. The girls came back, and Coyote asked them for water the first thing. One ran to get water. Soon the girls said to him, "Everybody wants you over there, grandmother. They're going to dance over Coyote's eyes." —"How am I to go?"—"We can pack you on the back." One picked up Coyote and packed him. When she was tired, another packed him. The girls were pretty tired. Then Coyote said, "Let me go. I'll go myself." And then he went on alone. The girls were over a hill, and Coyote ran to gain time. When anyone was looking, he leaned on his stick and walked like an old woman.

Then he reached the place where they were dancing. "Let me have that Coyote's eye for a while. I want to dance with it," he said. They gave the eyes to him. He held them in his hand and danced. "I feel like flying away," he said. Then he ran, taking the eyes with him.

They all ran after him, but nobody could catch him. Fox tried to take the eyes from him. Coyote told him, "These are my own eyes," so Fox let him go.

Coyote put his eyes in a spring to soak. They were pretty dry. He soaked them and put them in their sockets. Then Coyote was all right again.

South Wind Loses His Eyes and Gets New Ones

This episode from the Tillamook trickster cycle of stories about South Wind as he wanders north up the Oregon Coast belongs to a very widespread set of stories about tricksters who get themselves trapped in stone or in a tree and must dismantle themselves to get out, usually losing their eyes to Crow in the process. (Compare the Paiute "Eye-Juggler" story, p. 121.) —Told in 1934 in English by Clara Pearson to Elizabeth Jacobs: in *Nehalem Tillamook Tales*, pp. 128-130.

South Wind walked along the beach until he got to some rocks. He was very cold. The sun was shining and he sat down on the sand. "Oh, that nice sunshine! I will sun myself. I wish a rock would come on this side of me so no wind would hit me."

He looked, there was a rock on that side of him. "I wish a rock would come on this other side so I would be in a cove." Soon he looked and there was a rock on that side; he was indeed in a cove. So he lay down there and slept. For some time he slept. He woke up, he was sweating. He opened his eyes, he was all in darkness. He did not know what to think of it. He felt around all over. He was all locked in, rocks were everywhere all around him. "Well, what is the matter? How am I going to get out?" Oh, he did not know.

"Well, I shall have to call something, a bird with a bill that will pick and pick. Maybe he can pick a hole." He called a little Woodpecker. She came. She pecked and pecked, she was unable to do very much. Then she broke her bill. She could not do any more. She flew away. He called Yellowhammer then. He called her, "Auntie, you come! I am in dreadful shape." She came. She pecked. Very soon she had made a large hole. Now he could see daylight. He looked up where she was pecking overhead. She was a woman. He could see her legs. He reached up and felt of her leg. She became angry, she flew away as if to say, "Confound you!" He called, "Oh, come back, auntie! I made a mistake. Come back!" But she would not come back, she would peck no more.

After a while he gave up trying to get her back. He took himself all apart and threw those pieces out of the hole. He removed his legs, his eyes, his arms, he threw everything out, then somehow that body crawled out. He put his arms back, he found his legs and joined them on, but his eyes were gone. Sea Gull and Raven were fond of eyes. They had come and eaten his eyes. He was blind then. He went along, he felt his way along. He thought, "I will have to follow the bank all the way, that is all I can do." Soon he felt some snowberries. He felt of them, "I think I know what they are." He put one in each socket in order to appear as if he had eyes. He went along again, feeling his way. Soon he felt the side of a house. "Well, I will keep feeling until I find the door." From the roof of the house a man spoke to him. "What are you measuring my house for?" South Wind said, "Oh, I have heard about this house for a long ways. I heard it was a wonderful house, such a large house. I wanted to see just how large. It is indeed a fine big house. What are you doing up on top of the house?" "Oh, I sit up here and look over the ocean, I can see all over the ocean. Come on up here!" "All right." He climbed up there and sat down.

Bald Eagle was the man on top of that house. He it was who said, "I can see all over, I can see everything." South Wind asked him, "Ha ! Partner ! Can you see clear across the ocean?" Bald Eagle said, "No." Then South Wind said, "I can see clear across. I can see men and women on the other side. I see women with big wooden bowls of berries. Can't you see them?" Bald Eagle said, "No, I cannot see that far. You have beaten me." "Well, I will tell you," said South Wind, "if you want to try on my eyes I will take them off and you can try them on. I will put on yours and then I will know just how far you can see." He also said, "Now, you will not be able to see with my eyes right at first." They exchanged eyes and South Wind quickly rolled off the house and ran away. Bald Eagle spoke to him. He was gone. Then Bald Eagle called to the people, "Catch that fellow! He was blind and he has run off with my eyes." They followed him, but he wished that they would not be able to run fast and they were unable to catch him, South Wind.

After a while Bald Eagle heard Snail up on the bank. He heard those Snails talking. Snails had very good eyes, but they could not travel fast. Eagle felt his way there, he found Snail, he took Snail's eyes and put them on. They were good sharp eyes. Eagle took Snail's voice as well, saying, "Snail, you will be nothing, having no eyes and no voice." Now Eagle was all right again. He had taken Snail's voice. The voice that eagles have now was once Snail's voice.

Coyote and the Strawberries

George Wasson, Coquelle folklorist and storyteller, observes that "this story's been told to me by most of my relatives from the Coos Bay area. I've heard my dad tell it. George B. Wasson. Aunt Daisy told it, his sister. Aunt Mary's the one who told it most often. And of course my brother Will also told the story to me. It's kind of a combination of those." For an account of the Wasson family's rich ongoing involvement in Indian and Anglo Oregon folklore, see J. Barre Toelken, *The Dynamics of Folklore*, pp. 158-171.—Personal communication to editors by George Wasson, 1992, all rights reserved.

Left to right: Susan Wasson Wolgamott, Bette Wasson Hockema, John Wasson, Wilfred C. Wasson, George B. Wasson, Jr. (ca. 1975)

Coyote was going down South Slough off Coos Bay, and he was going along when a hail storm came up. Big hailstones came down and started hitting him, pelting his body, and he was jumping around, saying, "Oh, that hurts! Oh! Oh!" And he had to get out of the hail storm, so over on the side of the trail there he found this big tree. I think it was a cedar tree. It had been burned, maybe even hit by lightning, which would make it a taboo tree to mess with, but anyway this big cedar tree that had a hole down in the bottom of it, a cavity had been burned to the bottom and partly hollow down there. So he rushed over, and he got down inside there, and he huddled up to get out of the hail storm. But it didn't quite protect him, so he used his magical powers, his *tamanawis*, and he commanded the tree to grow shut around him. So he said, "Tree, grow shut. Grow shut around me." And the tree did that. But he left a little hole he could see through, little hole he could look through, and he was looking through that hole and he could see outside, and he felt really proud of himself, saying how smart he was, how good he was. He had commanded that tree to grow shut.

Well, the hail storm passed by, and Coyote was sitting in there, and he decided, "Well, I guess it's time to get out of here now," so he used his power again, his *tamanawis*, and he said, "Grow open." Nothing happened. Then Coyote says again, "GROW OPEN." Still nothing happened. He thought, "Well, I'm not doing something right here," so he commanded the tree, "Grow open." And nothing happened, and on the fourth time, he still said, "Grow open." Nothing happened at all, and there was Coyote stuck inside of the tree. He must have been too proud of himself because his power wouldn't work, the tree wouldn't grow open. So he was looking out that little hole, and pretty soon he saw one of the Woodpecker Girls flying by, and he looked through the hole, and he called out through the hole, "Oh Miss Woodpecker!" She looked around, and she said, "Where's that coming from?" And he says, "Come over here, over here to this hole." And she flies over the tree, and she looks in there. And he says, "Yes, in here. Peck this hole bigger so I can get out." Well, she starts working away. She starts pecking on the hole, and she pecks on it and pecks on it, and it gets bigger and bigger. As the hole gets bigger, Coyote can see a little more of her, and he looks out and says, "She's pretty nice looking." He reaches out there, and he thinks, "I'm just going to stroke her tail feathers." And he reaches out and just starts to touch her on the tail feathers, and he grabs her, and she jumps back and says, "What are you doing?" He says, "Oh, oh, I didn't mean to do anything." He'd grabbed her by the tail feathers, grabbed her by the tail. "Oh, oh, I'm sorry. I didn't mean to do anything. I won't do that." And she starts work and says, "Okay. I'll work some more." She had started to fly away, and he said, "Oh, I won't do that again." And so she starts working away, pecking away, and the hole gets bigger, and she's inside pecking away, getting it bigger, working away. And he looks up. By that time he can see the front of her, and he says, "She has nice beautiful round breasts." He said, "Oh, she's got her head up in the air, she won't even notice me. I'll just reach up and just kind of, I'll just kind of stroke and just touch them a little bit." And he gets so excited, he grabs her, and she jumps back and flies away, says, "No more. I'm not going to help you."

Well you might know, there's a little woodpecker down the coast that has two marks on it: white marks across its tail and across its breast also. That's probably where they came from, Old Coyote messing with her when she was trying to peck the hole bigger.

So anyway, she flew away and left Coyote inside the tree, the hollow tree, and he's trying to figure out what he's going to do to get out. Then he has a bright idea: "Aha." So he reaches up behind his braid, behind his ear, in his braid, and he pulls out his clamshell knife, and he takes his clamshell knife, and he starts cutting himself up in little pieces. Reaches down to his foot, and he cuts out a piece and he pokes that out through the hole. Then he cuts off another piece and he pokes that out through the hole, and he just goes like mad. He starts cuttin' himself a little piece, poke, cut off a piece, poke it through the hole, cut off another piece, poke it through the hole. Working up his legs, all the way up his body, he cuts himself all up in little pieces, pokes 'em out through the hole, and then he's going to put himself together when he gets outside. But while he's doing this, he's cutting out his intestines, his guts, and he throws 'em out through the hole, but while he's doing this, here comes

Blue Jay flying along. Blue Jay flies along and looks down and says, "What's all that?" Looking around, down the bottom of that tree, all that interesting stuff, coming out of that hole over there, falling on the ground. Nobody's around any place. Blue Jay swoops down and grabs a string of intestines and flies away. Well, Coyote gets all finished, gets all poked out through the hole, gets outside, puts himself all back together [*sound of narrator patting hands together*]—back here, back there, everything back into place. He doesn't notice that Blue Jay has flown away with part of his intestines. And he just thinks he's just fine, so he's all put back together, and he goes on his way.

Walking on down, and he goes on down South Slough and comes upon where Coos Head is now, and he gets up on there, and here are strawberries all over. And Coyote says, "Oooh. Oh, look at that, nice strawberries." Well, you can tell that this is an unusual year because here's a hail storm when the strawberries are ripe out on the bluff out there, so unusual things are happening. And here's Coyote, "Oh, I love strawberries!" And he reaches down and starts picking strawberries. And he picks a strawberry and he eats it, and he picks another one and he eats it and says, "Oh, these are so good." He just keeps eating strawberries, picking and eating, picking and eating. Well, you know right away he's doing something wrong here because you're not supposed to pick strawberries and eat them yourself. You're supposed to take them back home to share with other people. So here's Coyote doing the wrong thing again. Picking and eating, picking and eating. But he just can't get full. He just can't—he tries eating faster. So he picks faster and eats faster, picks faster, pick and pick, and he just goes as fast as he can. He can't get full at all, when eventually he looks around behind him, and he sees a whole string of strawberries lying on the ground, and they come right up to his rectum, because that's when he discovers that Blue Jay flew away with the lower end of his intestines and flew away with his rectum. And he's just got a straight line right through, and the strawberries just go right in one end and out the other. And Coyote's looking, and he says, "I've got to stop that." So he got an idea. He said, "I'm going to have to plug it up." (Aunt Mary always said his "bunghole," plug up his "bunghole.") And so Coyote figured what's he going to do. So he looks around there and says, "This'll do." And he walks over, and here's this old rotten log, and he kicks on one of the knots sticking out of this old rotten log, knots sticking up, everything's rotted away. These knots are out there, and he kicks one off, and he grabs that, and he says, "Oh, I'll take that." And he takes it, and he shoves it up in his bunghole and jumps—"Ouch!" And he throws it down, "Oh, that hurts! That's rough, that hurts." And he says, "That won't do. I want something that's more smooth." And he looks over, and here's a rock down there. He says, "Well, I'll try that." So he picks up this rock, and he takes it, and he starts to shove it up, and, "Oh, that's cold." And it's too big and it falls right back out. "No, that won't do it. I've got to have some way to plug it up so I can keep strawberries inside of me." So he's thinking about it, and he looks down the trail there, and here's a wild carrot, a wild carrot growing down there. And he says, "Ah, that's just the right thing." You know it's just about so long, and it's tapered, and it's nice, soft and pliable, and that's just what he wants so he reaches down and picks it and very carefully turns it and pulls it up out of the ground. Yes, that's just right. He breaks off the stem and throws it away. But he's thinking, "You know, I ought to have something to make sure it stays in better." And right over on the side a little ways there's this great big fir tree that's been hit by lightning, and it's dripping pitch, pitch falling down there. So he takes this carrot—Well, you know something's wrong here also, 'cause he shouldn't mess around with a tree that's been hit by lightning. But here's this tree hit by lightning, and Coyote goes over and takes this carrot and rolls it around and around in the pitch, gets it all pitched up, and then he takes it and very carefully slides it up into his bunghole and pushes it up and takes some more pitch and packs it in place. Oh, he gets it all nice and glued up there and pats it real tight, and it's all sealed up. And he's really happy with himself.

So then he goes back to eating strawberries, and he's eating with both hands just as fast as he can go, eating and eating, more and more and more and more—eating strawberries until he gets so full he can hardly walk. His belly's just puffed way out, and by this time he's worked himself way down to the edge of the bluff. And he looks over there, and he can see a fire out there. He'd worked way out toward Bastendorf Beach. And he gets off out there, and he looks way out there, and he goes closer and closer, and he gets up on the edge of the dunes, and he looks out, and there are people out there with this fire on the beach. And he's thinking, "Oh, someone's cooking something." Well, you know, Coyote's such a glutton he's always ready to eat something more. And he calls out, "Halloooo." And the people look up. And it's the Seagull Boys out there, and they say, "Oh, hello, mother's brother." And he says, "What are you doing?" And they say, "We're playing 'Jump over the Fire.'" He says, "Oh, well I'm very good at that." "Well, come over and show us." So Coyote goes over there, and he goes along and he runs over by the fire. He's disappointed it's not food, but he comes down there, going to show off, and he runs up—here his belly's so big he can hardly walk—runs up there and he takes a little jump over the fire. And they say, "Oh, well, that was very good, but you really ought to jump over here where the flames are. That's where the contest is. Jump over the fire." "Oh, well, I can do that too." So Coyote circles back around, and he goes over, and he takes another run at it. He takes a run, and he jumps over, and he just barely gets over the fire, and he drags his tail right through the flames, and his tail suddenly explodes into fire. And he looks back there, and oh his tail is burning, and flames shooting up. And he starts batting at the flames, batting at his tail, and he's running in circles, and it gets too hot, and suddenly the pitch melts, and POP!—out goes the carrot. And Coyote's running in circles. Strawberries start spewing out. He's running in circles, batting at his tail, strawberries spewing out, and they're flying all over the Seagull Boys, just spewing out, covering everybody, strawberries everywhere. And the Seagull Boys are mad. They grab rocks and they start throwing rocks and sticks at Coyote.

And he runs and heads for the ocean as hard as he can go, runs and jumps out into the ocean, going to put his tail out. And he jumps out there, and what happens, but he jumps right out into the waves, and out in the waves is a big whale. And he jumps—right as the whale is coming up, he jumps right into the whale's mouth, and the whale swallows him. He goes clear down inside the whale's stomach. And everything's all quiet down in there. Coyote's down inside the whale's stomach. The tail is not burning any more; it's gone out. Coyote's feeling his way around: "How'd this happen? Where am I?" And he's wandering around in there, and BUMP, suddenly he hits his head on something. He reaches up, and there's the whale's heart, and Coyote bumps right into it. And he says, "Aha." And he has an idea, so he takes his clamshell knife again, and he says, "I'll get out of here." So he takes his clamshell knife and reaches up and cuts off the whale's heart. And the whale dies. There's Coyote, inside the whale, out in the ocean. The whale dies, and it floats up to the surface, and there's Coyote, standing up inside the whale, with his arms out, holding on. He can tell they're out in the big swells because the whale's going back and forth, real slow-like with the great big swells out there. Back and forth, back and forth. And pretty soon it gets a little rougher. They're going a little faster, and he can tell they're coming into the breakers on shore, and it gets faster and rolls some more, and the breakers are tossing him around, and he gets tossed around. Pretty soon there's a bump, and rolls over, and then everything's still. Aha, he knows then that they've washed up on the beach because the whale came ashore and washed up on the beach, and so Coyote is going to get out of there.

Once again he takes his clamshell knife, and he starts cutting between the ribs, through about that much blubber, about a foot thick or more of blubber. Coyote starts cutting, and he starts cutting, and cutting between the whale's ribs, trying to get a place to get out of there.

Well, the whale washed ashore right at Sunset Bay, and that's a very famous place where whales come ashore because there's another old story about a woman who went out in the ocean and married the sea otters, and she had them send a whale ashore every year. So whales are very important to the people, because they had been watching it. Now they didn't know Coyote was inside it. The whale comes ashore and washes in at Sunset Bay, and all the people are watching. They've all come down. All the people come down. This great gift from the ocean. And they're coming down to Sunset Bay, and the whale is on shore. And they're all waiting for the ceremonious occasion to cut up the whale and share it with everybody. And just as they all arrive, here comes Coyote. He cuts his way, finally cuts through between the ribs, last strike just as the people arrive, and here comes Coyote, squeezing out between the ribs, and he's just covered with oil and whale blubber, just covered like Crisco all over him, just really tight. His hair is all matted down, and he's real skinny, sliding out, and his tail's all burned off. Coyote's just squeezing his way out between the ribs, and everybody's mad. Well, the Seagull Boys are there too, and they haven't forgotten the strawberries yet at all. All the people are mad because Coyote's contaminated the whole thing, this great gift from the ocean for all the people. Coyote's contaminated it. Everybody starts throwing rocks. Seagull Boys throwing rocks. Everybody throwing rocks at Coyote. He can't see anything because of all this blubber in his eyes, and it's all blurry. But he can hear. Down south he knows where Big Creek is; he can hear it running in down there, and he takes off running as hard as he can down the beach. And all the people throwing rocks at him, and he runs and runs and goes way down the beach. And he goes way up to Big Creek, and he starts running up Big Creek, and he hears the Salmon Girls going up Big Creek, and they're out there paddling, paddling in the water. And he gets ahead of the people real fast, and he runs up and he says, "Oh Salmon Girls, oh come over here." All the people are still trying to catch up with him. He says, "Oh, you're so pretty. Come here, let me scratch your sides." And he reaches down and he's scratching their sides for them. He says, "Oh, you're so lovely. I could scratch better if you get up here in my lap." And so they let him. They get up in his lap, and Coyote's taking both hands and scratching both sides. Well, he's probably got other things on his mind, too, but he hears the people coming too soon. They're right on his tail. And he's scratching both sides so casually, rubbing their sides, and he gets right up to their heads, and he grabs their eyes, pulls their eyes out of their heads. He takes his own eyes out, which are all blurry and greasy, and he sticks them in the salmon's head. Because at that time salmon had bright shiny eyes, and Coyote had greasy eyes, and now he traded with them, so salmon now always have greasy eyes, and Coyote's got the bright shiny ones. And that's the end of that part of the story.

Fernando, a Basque Trickster

Fernando, the central character in a series of traditional Basque tales, is the village trickster. Many of the tales are humorous stories of Fernando's playing tricks on, getting the best of, or otherwise outwitting the village priest, the local authority figure. One scholar suggests that the original Fernando was Fernando Bengoetchea, also known as Fernando Amazketa, born in the village of Amezqueta in 1764. This Fernando was a shepherd and a *bertzolari*, a singer who improvises his own verses as he sings them, usually on a political theme. (Gallop, *The Book of the Basques.*) None of the contemporary tales, however, present Fernando as a historical figure.

The following Fernando tales were collected from Basques living in southeastern Oregon and Idaho, where many immigrated from four northern Spanish provinces of Alava, Guipúzcoa, Vizcaya and Navarra, between 1890 and 1920, to work in the sheep industry in Harney and Malheur counties. In the Basque provinces, the tales were told on the farms during long winter nights. Now the tales are told in the small towns of eastern Oregon at places where people visit, such as the grocery store or the gas station, or at home after a meal. Some of the tales have clearly been adapted to an American setting. Compare the two versions of "Fernando and the Platter of Meat." In the second version, the setting is a western small-town cafe, and the figure Fernando outwits is no longer a priest but a non-Basque who considers Fernando uneducated and ill mannered—a new "authority figure" in a social experience well known to new immigrants.

These tales are from the major sources of Oregon's Basque tales: Stanley L. Robe, "Basque Tales from Eastern Oregon," pp. 153-157; Sarah Baker Munro, *Basque-American Folklore in Eastern Oregon* and "Basque Folklore in Southeastern Oregon," pp. 159-175. The first two tales were collected by Robe in the summer of 1948 from John Madariaga of Burns, Oregon. Mr. Madariaga told the stories in Basque, and his wife, Bernadine, translated them into English. "Fernando and the Platter of Meat," (A) was recorded by Munro from D. U. in Arock in 1970 and (B) was collected in 1970 from J. E. of Meridian, Idaho, by Wendell Klein (Idaho Folklore Archives, Caldwell, Idaho). "Fernando's Sister Dies" was also collected by Munro from D.U. in Arock.

Fernando and the Priest's Pig

One time there was a fellow named Fernando and he had a large family. And a priest lived in the neighborhood and this priest had a pig and he asked Fernando if he would please go over and help him kill this pig. Fernando says: "Why sure, father. I'll be right over." And so he helps the priest kill the pig and they hung it up to dry.

About midnight Fernando rushes over to the priest's house and steals the pig. The priest in the meantime informs everybody that the pig was stolen and he goes over to Fernando's house and he says: "Somebody stole my pig."

"Oh, yes, sir, yes, sir," said Fernando to the priest. "That's what you'll have to tell them all. You just tell them all that somebody stole your pig."

So in the meantime the priest, getting no results, turned to the police. The police went all over town, not having had any luck. They didn't figure Fernando had stolen it but they thought they might go over to Fernando's place and search his place. So Fernando said to the police: "Sure, search all you want to. Come right on in." In the meantime Fernando had stuck the pig under the baby, under the baby in the crib. The baby being in the crib asleep, he thought he'd better stick a pin in the baby so the baby would cry and they wouldn't molest it to pick it up. And he said to them: "Do you want to search everywhere? It might be in the crib." They said: "Oh, no, no. We don't want to bother you and the poor little baby." So they left it be.

In the meantime Fernando had eaten all the pork except a very few pieces. And so he invited the priest to a feed at the last moment and he said to the priest: "Father, did you find your pig?" And the father says, "No, I haven't." Fernando says: "Oh, father! If you haven't found it until now you never will."

The Priest Invites Fernando to Dinner

Fernando and his wife quarreled one day and Fernando was chasing her with a big stick. And the father (the priest) noticed that Fernando was chasing her around and he yelled at Fernando: "Oh, stop!" He said: "Don't do that!" And so Fernando quit and it was just about noon. The father said: "Come on over." And so he went over to the father's house and the father said: "You sit down at my table and let's forget it. You can have something to eat with me."

So in the course of the meal they were saying grace, and the father said: "In the name of the Father, the Son, and the Holy Ghost." And Fernando repeated after the father: "In the name of the Father, the Holy Ghost." And the priest said: "Oh my, Fernando! What did you do with the Son?" Fernando says: "Oh, yes, yes, my son! Come on up, boy." So he got his boy to sit at the priest's table too.

And about that time they were sat down to eat he says to Fernando: "What would you have done if you'd caught your wife?" "Oh, I'd a fixed her all right," he said. "I'd a twisted her neck just like I'm going to twist this platter around." The reason he, Fernando, did that was that he noticed the platter was fuller on the priest's side than on his.

Fernando and the Platter of Meat

Version A

One time the priest was just sitting down to dinner when Fernando came. The priest couldn't turn him away so they sat down to eat. The priest had two pieces of meat on the platter—one large and one small one. He put the large one close to himself because he didn't think Fernando would be so crude as to reach across the table to the larger piece. They began talking about some neighbor and the priest asked him, "What would you do with someone like that?" Fernando said, "Well, I'd twist his neck just like this," and he turned the platter so the large piece of meat was on his side.

Version B

Two men, one a Basque, went to a cafe. Both men ordered steaks. When the waitress served the steaks, the Basque helped himself to the larger of the two steaks. The other man was very perturbed by this act and called the Basque uneducated and very ill mannered.

The Basque replied, "If you were in my place and had the choice, which steak would you have selected?"

The man said, "The small one, of course."

"Then," replied the Basque, "why are you unhappy? You got what you wanted, the small one."

Fernando's Sister Dies

Fernando had a sister, but she died. To get her to go to heaven, he had masses said every two or three weeks. The priest charged him two or three dollars for each one. Pretty soon Fernando ran out of funds. So Fernando went to see the priest. The priest said, "Well, you better have another mass. I think she's right on the brink."

Fernando was her only living relative since she wasn't married. Fernando said, "Well, you know she was an old maid."

The priest said, "No, she wasn't. She was married to God."

Fernando said, "Yes, well, you better have $100 worth of masses."

The priest asked, "Who's going to pay for it?"

Fernando said, "Just charge it to my brother-in-law."

At Work in Oregon

In a sense, the occupational literature of Oregon began in the nineteenth century with the arrival of Anglo "specialists," who brought their occupational dreams to the Promised Land—trappers after beaver; farmers from Missouri, Iowa, Illinois, Tennessee after bottomless virgin land; loggers from places east where the big trees were already cut; fishermen; miners, and so on. Not that the state's original Indian inhabitants didn't recognize and prize *skills* as such—prowess in hunting, for example, or in healing—but such recognition was not "occupational" in the Anglo sense of the word, and one rarely encounters in Indian stories the kind of professional lore and mystique that mark the tales that Oregon's loggers, for example, have been telling each other for well over one hundred years.

"Falling a Large Fir," photographer unknown.

Planting Rhymes

A farmer's crop is always subject to unforeseen and uncontrollable events: drought, floods, frost, bugs, and other pests. Today, the science of agriculture offers the farmer a host of techniques to control the crops, but traditional wisdom has also always provided a source of advice for insuring a bountiful harvest, whether it be advice about the best times of the moon to plant—advice still followed by many gardeners—or planting rhymes such as the following that not only instruct the sower to plant at least four seeds per hill but also acknowledge the farmer's place in the natural world. The first Oregon corn-planting rhyme was collected by Linda Bartron for the Randall V. Mills Folklore Archives (1970), and the second is a grain-planting rhyme that E. R. Jackman, in *The Oregon Desert*, notes has been "outlawed by DDT and other alphabetical combinations." Jackman writes that such "prodigality sufficed fifty years ago, but any present day farmer with such a philosophy is soon a regular customer at the county welfare office" (p. 206).

One for the raven,
One for the crow,
One to rot,
And one to grow.

One for the rodent
One for the crow
One for the worm
And two to mow.

Three Scythe Songs from Pioneer Oregon

The WPA folklore collection contains the following excerpt from *The Stagecoach* by George Estes: "The song of the good scythe sharpener was regular and never missed a beat. To its ringing bell-like notes could be fitted the following lines, which had a tune. The expert who could play the haying tune while whetting the scythe had passed one of the most important tests as a mower. When a farm hand applied for work in the meadows of the Umpqua Valley in the 1860s, the first examination he had to pass was whetting the scythe. If he missed a note in the haying tune there would be no employment for him on that farm. The farm boy practiced his scythe-whetting lesson many times before he could whet the blade so that his boy chum on the adjoining ranch would not laugh at him; for when whetted the ringing note could be heard for miles." Estes notes that the difference in the songs was solely in the manner of holding the blades.

Customary Scythe Song

Mow 'em, mow 'em,
Quick, quick, mow 'em,
Rake 'em, row 'em,
In the barn stow 'em.

Danger Song of the Scythe

Danger, danger,
Look for danger,
Run home, drive home
Watch the stranger.

Battle Song of the Scythe

Cut 'em, cut 'em,
Quick, quick, cut 'em,
Dig 'em, slash 'em,
Chop 'em, gut 'em.

John Alexander

According to the note that accompanies it in the 1940 WPA Oregon folklore collection, the text of "John Alexander" was "remembered by" Mr. Mason Y. Warner of Eugene and "known to him as early as the 1880s and sung in the upper Willamette Valley country." "John Alexander" is a version of "Springfield Mountain," considered the oldest native American ballad, composed in New England in 1761 about the untimely death of a Timothy Myrick from a rattlesnake bite. Other Oregon versions of the song include "Brownsville Mountain," sung by Orlo Flock of Powell Butte, Oregon, for Walter Bolton, Prineville, in 1969 (Flock and Warner were distant relatives); and "Rattlesnake Mountain," collected by Wayne Tabler while working on a Brownsville farm in 1946. These two versions can be found in Nash and Scofield, *The Well-Traveled Casket.*

'Twas in the early month of May
When John Alexander went to hoe hay.
Chorus: Ri diddle dink, E di de O
            Dinky dinkey di de O

He had hardly hoed around the field
When a great big rattlesnake bit him on the heel.
Chorus

He laid him down upon the ground
He rolled up his eyes and looked all around.
Chorus

Oh, Johnny dear why did you go
Down in the meadow for to hoe.
Chorus

Oh Molly dear I thot you knowed
It was dad's hay and had to be hoed.
Chorus

He raised his hoe with all his might
And hit that snake an awful swipe.
Chorus

The Big Combine

"The Big Combine" was recorded from working cowboy and folksinger Glenn Ohrlin, who remembered learning it in a Central Oregon bar in 1947. Ohrlin wrote that "It used to be featured during the night celebration at the Pendleton Round-Up. It has to do with the crew on a 32 horse combine harvesting grain in the hills around Pendleton. It was written about 1919 by Jock Coleman, a Scotchman and cowboy and harvest head . . . . Jock was known as the Poet Lariat of that region." The song is included on Ohrlin's album, *The Hell-Bound Train*. Folklorist Archie Green notes that the song is characteristic of the songs of the Industrial Workers of the World (I.W.W.), the "Wobblies," who attempted to organize timber, farm, and dock workers in the Northwest after World War I (*Rebel Voices: An I.W.W. Anthology*, ed. Joyce L. Kornbluh, pp. 249-250). The earliest account of "The Big Combine" appears in Charles W. Furlong's 1921 impressionistic account of the Pendleton Round-Up, *Let 'er Buck*, 1921, pp. 117-119, 125-133. According to Furlong, the song was composed while Jock worked on the big MacDonald Ranch near Pilot Rock. This version of the song is as it appears in Furlong.

(Tune: "Casey Jones")

Now come all you rounders, if you want to hear
The story of a bunch of stiffs a-harvesting here.
The greatest bunch of boys that ever came down the line,
Is the harvest crew a-working on this big combine.

There's travelin' men from Sweden in this good old crew,
From Bonnie Scotland, Oregon and Canada, too;
I've listened to their twaddle for a month or more,
I never met a bunch of stiffs like this before.

Chorus:
    Oh, you ought to see this bunch of harvest pippins
    You ought to see, they're surely something fine—
    Oh, you ought to see this bunch of harvest pippins,
    This bunch of harvest pippins on the old combine.

There's Oscar just from Sweden—he's stout as a mule,
Can jig and sew with any man or peddle the bull,
He's an independent worker of the world as well,
He loves the independence but he says the work is hell.

He's got no use of millionaires and wants ter see
Them blow up all the grafters in this land of liberty;
Swears he's goin' ter leave this world of graft and strife
And stay down in the jungles with the stew-can all his life.

Chorus:
    Oh! Casey Jones, he knew Oscar Nelson
    Casey Jones, he knew Oscar fine;
    Casey Jones, he knew Oscar Nelson
    When he chased him off of boxcars on the S.P. line.

Now the next one I'm to mention,—well, the next in line,
Is the lad a-punching horses on this big combine
The lad that tells the horses just what to do,
But the things he tells the horses I can't tell you.

It's Pete and Pat and Polly, you come out of the grain,
And Buster there you are again, you're over the chain,
Limp and Dude and Lady, you get in and pull,
And Paddy, you get over there, you damned old fool.

Chorus:

> Oh! you ought to see, you ought to see our skinner—
> You ought to see, he's surely something fine;
> You ought to see, you ought to see our skinner,
> He's a winner at his dinner at the old combine.

Now I'm the header-puncher, don't forget that's me—
I do more work, you bet, than all the other three,
A-workin' my arms and a-workin' my feet
A-picking up the barley and the golden wheat.

I got to push up the brake and turn on the wheel,
I got to watch the sickle and the draper and the reel,
And when I'd strike a badger hill and pull up a rock,
They holler, "Well, he's done it, the damn fool Jock."

Chorus:

> Oh! I'm that guy, I'm the header-puncher,
> I'm that guy though it isn't my line,
> I'm that guy, I'm the header-puncher,
> I'm the header-puncher on this old combine.

Dry-land Farming Lexicon

Compiled from Central and Eastern Oregon authorities, including Leslie Ramsey of Madras.

Combine: A complex harvesting machine, "combining" the functions of a header and a separator, originally pulled by horses or mules, and later by a tractor. Cutting capacity or "swath" ranges from 6 to 30 feet.
Hillside machine: A combine with a laterally hinged and counter-weighted header, to allow for cutting steep hillsides.
Self-propelled: A combine able to pull itself.
Header: The hinged front assembly of a combine, serving to cut and bunch the crop and feed it into the separator-assembly; adjustable as to the height of the grain.

Drapers: Wide heavy slatted canvas belts, fastened together with adjustable buckles and running over rollers, serving to convey the cut heads of grain from the header into the separator. If moistened by rain, would rapidly "draw up" and split unless loosened.

Riddles: Perforated screens sliding back and forth to further separate the kernels from the chaff.

Straw-walkers: A sequence of horizontally oscillating frames designed to slowly "walk" the straw out of the separator area (over metal fins or *fishbacks*) to the straw-dump.

Doghouse: the floored, often roofed work area on a large combine, where the *sewer* and *jigger* and *header-tender* (q.v.) worked.

Sack-sewer: The aristocrat and king-pin of old-style combining. Required the strength and skill to sew up 90 lbs. sacks of grain, in heavy crops as frequently as every 30 seconds or so, and heave each one onto the *sack-chute* to slide onto the ground. Used a modified sail-maker's needle and hemp sack twine. Farmers vied for the best sewers, and would bring them together for informal competitions for speed. A Central Oregon champion in the '40s was "Red," who could sew a sack ear to ear in four seconds flat.

Jigger: The sack-sewer's lackey; usually a teenager boy—kept empty sacks filling on the *receivers* or spouts and jigged them until they were full, then wrestled them over to the sewer.

Header-tender or *Header-puncher:* Faced forward and surveyed the field, so as to adjust the header to different levels of grain, usually by means of a spoked wheel as on a ship. Tense, critical work in a field of short grain and rocks.

Catskinner: the driver of the tractor which pulled the combine; originally, the driver of a Caterpillar or other track-laying tractor.

Smut: A fungus afflicting grains; prevented in seed-wheat by treatment with mercurous oxide (very dangerous). The presence of smut in a crop would make a cigarette taste sweet; if plentiful enough it could cause explosions in granaries.

Boot: The envelope out of which a stalk of wheat develops.

Stool, stooling: The development of more than one, and sometimes as many as twenty or more, stalks of wheat from one boot and one seed-grain: the basis of a bumper crop.

Rogueing: The pleasant task of walking through ripening fields at dusk to find and pull up tall stalks of rye, oats, and other unwanted grains.

Dead-furrow: Furrow at the exact center of a field, reached at the end of plowing the field in an inward spiral.

The Lane County Bachelor

The Donation Land Claims Act of 1850, which provided 320 acres of land to anyone who would "prove up" a claim, drew many settlers to Oregon. The experience did not always prove a success, as we learn in this song of "The Lane County Bachelor," which has been collected throughout the Northwest. This particular version was collected in 1987 by George Venn of La Grande from his cousins, Robin, Bill, and Daniel Boettcher of Alder, Washington.—Venn Collection, Eastern Oregon State College.

My name is Frank Foller, a bachelor I am
I'm keeping a batch on an elegant plan.
You'll find me out West in the county of Lane
a starving to death on a government claim.

Oh my house it is built on the national style—
the walls are erected according to Hoyle
the roof has no pitch but is level and plain
and I always get wet if it happens to rain.

Refrain:
So hurrah for Lane County, the land of the free
the home of the bedbug, the louse, and the flea.
There's nothing will make a man hard and profane
like starving to death on a government claim.

How happy I am when I crawl into bed
and the rattlesnake rattles his tail at my head.
The gay little centipede void of all fear
crawls over my pillow and into my ear.

And the nice little bedbug, so joyous and bright
he keeps me a scratchin' full half of the night.
The gay little flea with toes as sharp as a tack
plays "why don't you catch me" all over my back.

Refrain:
So hurrah for Lane County where blizzards arise
where winds never cease and the flea never dies
the sun is so hot that if in it you remain
it will burn you quite black on your government claim.

Now don't get discouraged, you poor hungry men,
we're all just as free as a pig in a pen
So just stick to your homestead and battle your fleas
and pray to your maker to send you a breeze.

Now a word to you claimholders who plan for to stay
You can chew your hardtack 'til you're toothless and gray
but as for me, I'll no longer remain
and starve like a dog on my government claim.

Refrain:
So farewell to Lane County, goodbye to the West
I'm a going back home to the gal I love best
I'll stop in Missouri and get me a wife
and live on corn dodger the rest of my life.

Oregon Cowboys and Buckaroos

The history of the Oregon cowboy is evident in the common term for cowboy in Southeast Oregon: *buckaroo*. It derives from the Spanish word, *vaquero*, and many of Oregon's earliest cowboys were in fact Mexican *vaqueros*. The *vaqueros* were brought north because of their expertise in handling cattle when the large California ranching operations extended their activities into Oregon in the late nineteenth century. (One of the tall tale masters included in the "Oregon's Folk Heroes" section, Tebo Ortego, was a *vaquero* on the P Ranch in the early part of this century.) Today many of the occupational terms used by Oregon's buckaroos are Spanish or of Spanish origin: *riata, McCarty (mecate), remuda, hondu, chaps, chinks, tapaderos, hackamore (jaquima), cavvy (caviata), bronc, bosal, latigo, romal,* and *rodeo.*

The buckaroo tradition is found in a region that includes southeastern Oregon, northern Nevada, northern California, and southwestern Idaho. It refers to a whole complex of folk speech and oral tradition—including poetry, custom, material culture, and respect for the role of individual skill in the control of animals. Mardi Wilson of the Mann Lake Ranch, Princeton, Oregon, offered a succinct definition of a buckaroo as "a man who can ride, rope out in the open, shoe a horse, and understands the behavior of cattle" (RVMA, March 1971). The following are traditional anecdotes from Oregon ranches, many from two rich sources of ranch lore: Herman Oliver's *Gold and Cattle Country* and E. R. Jackman and R. A. Long, *The Oregon Desert.*

How to Get Along

Reub Long of Fort Rock, when asked what sort of man a certain neighbor was, answered by a parable, just as Abe Lincoln often did. His reply was, "A long time ago when they were killing people over around Wagontire, a man from here worked there all summer. He came back in the fall and I supposed he would have all the dope. So I said, 'What did you find out at Wagontire?' This man had a deep voice and kindly manner." Here Reub dropped his voice to a deep rumble with the kindest tone, as though talking to a child. "He said, 'Reub, when I was a little boy, my papa told me how to git-along—out here—on the desert. Always ride a good horse—and breathe—through your nose.'" (Oliver, p. 182)

The Work Week on a Ranch

There aren't any 40-hour weeks on the cattle ranches. Reub Long says, "I always tell a new hand it don't take long to spend a night here; that in the morning he should reach down and feel of his clothes and if they are cold, he's overslept." (Oliver, p. 183)

Grant County Cattlemen

They tend to be reasonably generous with money, but niggardly with information. R. G. Johnson, former county agent here, told of his old uncle: R. G. was riding with the uncle one day, moving several hundred of the uncle's cattle down the road to another range. A stranger stopped them. This conversation followed:
Stranger: "Whose cattle are those?"
Uncle: "Feller up the ridge."
Stranger: "Where you taking them?"
Uncle: "Over the hump."
Stranger: "How many you got here?"
Uncle: "Quite a few." (Oliver, p. 181)

Buckaroo Geography

Cowboys were usually good at remembering terrain. If they got lost when out of sight of camp, they weren't much use to their outfit, so they noticed things, making maps in their minds. When two cowboys met and one tried to describe where he'd spotted a deer, or where a bunch of wild horses were grazing, or where a strange rider had been seen, both of them were soon off their horses. They smoothed off a place in the sand, drew in ridges and swales, and made a sand map. We called this "buckaroo geography." (Jackman and Long, p. 111)

Harney County Strawberries

In the early spring, dandelion, mustard, or pigweed greens were wilted with hot drippings from the salt pork and boiled eggs were sliced on top. I can't think of anything better after a winter running heavy to boiled beans, the "Harney County strawberries." (Jackman and Long, p. 60)

John Porter's Story about a Sheepman on His Range

One of John's stories relates to grass. As he tells it, "A feller told me a sheepman was up on our summer range and had eat out a couple sections of our best grass. So me and the hired man and my brother rode up there pretty hostile and sure enough, here he was with sheep all around him right on our range. The minute we came in sight he began yelling, 'I'm lost! I don't know where the trail is!' But we didn't pay any attention to that, 'cause that sort of an explanation just comes natural to a sheepman. So we rode up and I guess no white man ever took the abuse we gave him. One of us would use all the corral type words he could think of and when he stopped for breath, the next one would take off.

"He just stood there and took 'er 'cause he knew he was in the wrong. He was a big, red, hairy sort of feller. But then we made one of these here tactical errors, as the generals say. We figured we'd sort of took care of him, so we branched out and told him what we thought of all sheepmen in general. I guess he thought he didn't have to take that, so he said, 'Well, anyway, there ain't none of yuh has ever seen a picture of Jesus Christ in the Bible with a steer in his arms.'

"Mad? I was never so mad in my life. I wanted to say something, but couldn't think of a word to say. I looked to the other boys for help and they couldn't think of anything, so we just rode off. I've been sort of humiliated, I guess you'd call it, ever since. If I ever get money enough, I'm going to pay to have a special issue put out with that picture in 'er." (Oliver, p. 168)

Cowboy Vernacular

One of the best sources of cowboy folk speech is *Western Words: A Dictionary of the American West* by Ramon F. Adams. The following lexicon, from the WPA Oregon Folklore Collection, was compiled in 1940 by WPA writer, Charles O. Olsen, from his personal knowledge.

Colloquial names for a cowboy: *cow-waddie, rannie, cow-poke, tophand, cow-puncher, buckaroo, cow chaperone, hairpin, vaquero*

Names for whiskey: *querly, mule, bug juice, squirrel juice, poison, red-eye, booze, forty-rod, chain-lightning, barbwire booze, tanglefool, tequila, mescal*

Cattle ranch: *cow outfit, spread*

Strangers on the range: *galoot, coat, hombre, jasper, maverick, terrapin*

Miscellaneous: *blue around the gills* (scared to death or half-dead with fatigue); *hell-for-leather* (fast); *slick-ear* (animal without an ear brand); *loco* (crazy); *build a loop* (get lasso ready to throw); *point, swing and drag* (the front, middle, and rear of a trail herd)

Jesse Stahl

Jesse Stahl's Famous Ride

African-American cowboys and ranch hands played a more significant role in the history of the Far West than has been recognized until recently—and some went on to make their mark as rodeo performers. John Scharff, long-time manager of the Malheur Wildlife Refuge, told the following story about Jesse Stahl, a prize winner at several Pendleton Round-Ups, in a 1970 letter to Kenneth W. Porter.

I well remember Jesse Stahl who . . . was a legendary bronc rider during the 1920s and 1930s. The only thing that kept Jesse from getting into big money was the fact that he was a colored man. Jesse had a keen sense of humor and was liked and respected by everyone who knew him, and he always had a pleasant greeting for visitors. I recall one incident at John Day, sometime during the 1920s, when there was a horse there that hadn't been ridden successfully by any of the cowboys present and, as the show was over, and Jesse received second money, he put on an exhibition by riding this horse backwards with a suitcase in one hand . . . .

The Strawberry Roan

"The Strawberry Roan" is one of the most widely known cowboy songs in the United States and Canada. Originally written in 1914 by Curly Fletcher, a bronc rider who later became an actor in western movies, the song entered oral tradition and has been sung or recited since the 1920s by cowboys throughout the West. This version came from a woman from Madras, Oregon, who said that she first learned the song from her mother about 1925 (RVMA, Vonderheit, 1970). Curly Fletcher published many of his poems in a booklet, *Songs of the Sage*, which was recently reprinted with an introduction by Hal Cannon.

I was layin' round town just a spendin' my time
Out of a job and not makin' a dime.
When a feller steps up and says, "I suppose
That you're a bronc rider from the looks of your clothes."

"Well, you guesses me right. I'm a good one," I claim.
"Do you happen to have any bad ones to tame?"
He says, "I have one bad one to buck;
At throwin' good riders he's had lots of luck."

He says, "This old pony has never been rode,
And the boys that gets on him is bound to get throwed."
So I gets up all excited and I ask what he pays
To ride this old pony for a couple of days.

He offers a ten spot. I says, "I'm your man,
For the bronc never lived that I couldn't span.
The bronc never lived or never drew breath
That I couldn't ride 'til he starved plum to death."

He says, "Get your saddle; I'll give you a chance."
So we gets in the buckboard and drives to the ranch.
We stay until morning and right after chuck
We go out to see if this outlaw can buck.

Down in the horse corral standing alone,
This old *caballo*, Strawberry Roan.
His legs are all spavined; he's got pigeon toes,
Little pin eyes and a big Roman nose.

Little pin ears that crimped at the tips,
And a big "44" branded on his left hip.
He's U-necked and old with a long overjaw.
You can see with one eye he's a reg'lar outlaw.

I gets on the blinds; it sure was a fight.
Next comes the saddle, and I screwed her down tight.
I steps up on him and raises the blind
And ride in his middle to see him unwind.

He bowed his old neck and I guess he unwound,
He seemed to quit livin' down there on the ground.
He went up towards east; he came down towards west;
And to stay in his middle I'm doin' my best.

He sure is frog-walkin'; he heaves a big sigh.
He only needs wings to be on the fly.
He turns his old belly right up to the sun,
He sure is a sun-fishin' son of a gun.

He's about the worst bucker I've seen on the range.
He can turn on a nickel and give you the change,
And when he's a-buckin, he squeals like a shoat.
I'll tell you, no foolin', he shore got my goat.

I'll tell you, no foolin', this pony can step,
But I'm still in his middle and buildin' the rep.
With a phenomenal jump he goes up on high,
And it's me sittin' on nothin' way up in the sky.

I turned over twice and I came back to earth,
And I light into cussin' the day of his birth.
But I know this old pony I'm unable to ride;
Some of them left, they haven't all died.

But I'll bet my money that the man ain't alive
That can stay with Old Strawberry til he makes his high dive.

A Bear Tale

A common subject in cowboy poetry is the "wreck," an accident a cowboy has on
horseback. In this 1989 poem, Sunny Hancock, a rancher from Lakeview, Oregon,
offers us a rhymed version of a tall tale about a cowboy who ropes a bear and gets
into a real "wreck." For a Central Oregon tale about a cowboy who rides a bear, see
Jones, *Oregon Folklore*, p. 61.

I was up in the Sycan Black Hills Camp workin' for the old Z-cross.
This was my own piece of the country. I was cook and crew and boss.
The afternoon of that there year was comin' on as I recall,
Meanin' summer'd hit the Cap Rock and had slid right into fall.
The days were warm and pleasant, though the nights was kinda sharp,
But my nice snug little cabin kept the cold wind off my tarp.
Aspen leaves was turnin' yeller. Bees was buzzin' round the hive.
It was just that kinda day that it was great to be alive.

So I'm just jogging along that morning, looking out beneath my hat,
Thought I'd make a little circle down through Silver Dollar Flat,
Maybe tag some big slick yearling with the address of this farm
'Cause I sure did need to limber up my old stiff roping arm.
Now I'd been kinda traveling down this little open draw
When I came around a corner I'se amazed at what I saw.
I just pulled up there a-gawkin', and my eyes went plum agog.
There was a big old brindle he-bear diggin' ants out of a log.

Boy, my heart commenced to poundin', and I couldn't get no air.
I knew I'd never have a better chance to snag myself a bear.
I finally got a loop built as my horse began to dance.
Old dumb bruin, he ain't seen me, he's still busy diggin' ants.
I had my rope tied hard and solid, and I'd built that loop with care.
I let out a Cowboy War Whoop, and I built right to that bear.
Then the old beast heard me comin' and he headed for the trees
Weren't no moss a-growin' on him, and he shore did split the breeze.

But I rolled right up behind him 'n' like the Bible story told,
I cast my bread upon the water, and it came back seven fold.
So I pitched the slack right at him, then I turned my pony neat,
And I heard him grunt and hit the ground as I jerked him off his feet.

Now I headed for the timber just the way it should be done.
Hell, there wasn't nothin' to it, ropin' bears was lots of fun.
In the timber I got busy dodgin' limbs and brush and such,
And I ain't had time to check up on my cargo very much.

I'd start by breakin' him to lead, or at least that's what I hope.
Looked around, and here that bear come, just like this, right up my rope.
Things sure started lookin' different, so I tells him, O.K., Bruin,
I'll start payin' more attention to this little job I'm doin',
I'll just zig and zag and circle some, now you just follow me
'Cause I'm about to bash our brains out on some big old jack pine tree.
So I zigged and zagged and circled, tho' it seemed to no avail,
'Cause next time I checked, old Bruin's right behind my horse's tail.

About that time, why my old pony made a funny little jump,
And that old bear, he started climbin' up that rope across his rump.
I yelled and squalled and hollered, and I slapped him with my hat,
But I'll tell you he's plumb determined, guess he doesn't savvy "scat."
And nobody ever told me I was over blessed with brains
But it didn't take no Einstein with no extra high I. Q.
Nor no call from God to tell me what that bear was gonna do.
I know a coward's way out's a bad one in most anybody's book,
But he was almost in the saddle now, so that's the route I took.

I bailed off and checked it to him then a big rock broke my fall.
Old boy, I says, it looks to me like you just bought it all.
As they went crackin' through the timber, why I realized of course,
That I'd just lost a "damn good saddle" and the company'd lost a horse.
You took a plum good horse and saddle and just gave 'em to a bear.
Those thoughts and lots more like 'em was a-runnin' through my mind
As I went limpin' down the country tryin' to leave that wreck behind.

My clothes was kinda tattered, and I'd lost a lot of hide,
But my body wasn't hurtin' near as much as was my pride.
So I'm hoofin' down the mountain, mullin' over this here caper,
Sayin' things that—sorry folks, I just can't put down on paper—
When I hear a horse a-comin', and the sound began to swell
Back down the way I just had come from, and I wondered, "what the hell."
Then I see my horse a-comin', steppin' lively down the slope,
That old bear was in *my* saddle, had a loop built, swingin' my rope.

Mongo

This cowboy poem was composed in 1992 by Leon Flick, a cowboy who lives in Plush, Oregon. The setting is a fall cattle sale, and Flick describes the experience of trying to sell a less attractive calf in this poem that is rich with the occupational folk speech of the cattle industry—"lepy, bummer, dogie, dwarf." Although this is a poem by and for cowboys, the notion of trying to get by with something that is not quite acceptable is surely a universal experience to which many can respond. All rights reserved.

It's early in November,
and the calves are set to go.
And something rarely seen by man,
the trucks, not one no-show.
The steers are weighin' deep in five,
the heifers slightly lighter,
and the price I got was out of sight.
Things ain't looked much brighter.
The bunch is pre-conditioned, weaned,
none bawlin' for their mother.
And damned if they're not uniform.
They look like one another.
But standin' out amongst 'em
is one that's just not right.
His ears, well, they been froze off,
and his skin sure fits him tight.
His hair is dead, one eye is blue,
his jaw's a little lumpy.
You know the kind. Hard luck life.
He looks a little dumpy.
Lepy, bummer, dogie, dwarf,
whatever he might be.
Everybody knows one.
The kind you hate to see.
He lives on what the others leave.
He robs the best he can.
He'd get pushed away from a feedbunk
if he was alone there in the pen.

But you hope he'll go unnoticed.
You hope to slip him by.
Cuz you'd really like to get rid of him
cuz the booger just won't die.
He's cost you more in shots and pills
than he'd return if you sold him twice.
And though you treat him regular,
he just won't shed them lice.
But at last they're weighed and ready to load.
And the buyer, he's all bubbles.
And though he hasn't said a word,
you feel you still have troubles.
Then he takes on a fit of laughin'
till I thought that he might croak.
"That four-year-old you threw in there,
He's really quite a joke."
My face turns red, I try to smile.
Tears are so hard to keep in.
"You mean Mongo don't get to go?"
"This year?" "Again."

Reynaldo Rivera

Corrido del Difunto Nabor, Ballad of the Deceased Nabor

A *corrido* is a ballad that tells a story of a specific incident. Often the *corridista* (corrido composer) will write about a tragic or historical, local, or national event. Right after President Kennedy was killed, for example, several *corridos* about the event appeared. Traditionally, the *corrido* existed in oral form in the community and was not recorded, but as they have been passed down from one generation to the next, most traditional *corridos* have now been recorded. The most widely known *corridos* appeared at the time of the Mexican Revolution around 1910 and told the stories of battles and heroes of the revolution.

A true *corrido* is characterized by the inclusion of a date and place as well as the names of the principals involved in the event. This *Corrido del Difunto Nabor* was composed by Reynaldo Rivera of Hermiston, Oregon. Rivera grew up on a small ranch in Mexico and came to Oregon at the age of fifteen, yet he continues to serve as the *corridista* for his hometown of Pachuyaco, Nayarit. It was people back in Pachuyaco who knew him and his song writing and asked him to write a *corrido* about the death of Nabor Villarreal even though he was not there to witness the shooting.

Some further information may be helpful in understanding the events in the *corrido*. Nayarit is a Pacific coast state that borders Durango, an inland state to the northeast, and the Nayar is a mountain range in southern Mexico. San Juan Peyotan is a larger town near Pachuyaco where medical help would be available, and Tepic is the capitol city of Nayarit. The "twentieth of November" marks the date of the Revolution of 1910, often celebrated with a fiesta. The term *camioneta* in the fifth stanza commonly refers to a station wagon in U. S. Spanish, but in the Mexican lexicon it usually refers to a pickup truck.—Composed by Reynaldo Rivera, Hermiston; recorded on September 22, 1992, by Eva Castellanoz, Nyssa, for the Hermiston Hispanic Heritage Project; and translated by Norma E. Cantú, Washington, DC.

'Ño del ochenta y siete—
esto acaba de pasar—
Pachuyaco, Nayarit
ranchito del Nayar
murió Ezequiel de Durango
también Nabor Villarreal.

Veinte de noviembre por cierto
y era en una fiesta charra
cuando Cruz y Ezequiel
se echaron unas habladas—
los se quisieron tirar
porque parejo no andaban.

Como a las seis de la tarde—
ya el baile iba comenzando—
como ya se traían ganas
a balazos se agarraron
y en medio de tanta gente
a mucha la lastimaron.

De tantas balas perdidas
una a Nabor le tocó—
él sin ser hombre de pleito
fué el primero que murió.

Year of eighty-seven, it happened not
    long ago
That in Pachuyaco, Nayarit, a small ranch
    of the Nayar,
Ezequiel from Durango and also Nabor
    Villarreal died.

Twentieth of November, in fact, it was
    at a cowboy fiesta,
Where Cruz and Ezequiel exchanged
    words;
They wanted to shoot it out; they
    weren't seeing eye to eye.

Around six that afternoon, already the
    dance was starting,
And because they had it in for each
    other, the shoot-out started;
In the middle of so many people,
    many got hurt in the shooting.

Of so many stray bullets one was
    meant for Nabor;
He not being a fighting man was the
    first one to fall.

Dos camionetas se oían
que a San Juan iban llegando—
traían gente mal herida
también al de Durango—
y no alcanzó a llegar
su sangre ya lo iba ahogando.
	Two trucks could be heard as they
	   arrived in San Juan.
	They brought badly injured folks, and
	   also the one from Durango
	Who didn't make it; his own blood
	   was already choking him.

Con cuatro balas en el cuerpo
Cruz todavía tiene vida—
sería un milagro de Dios
o sabe Dios qué sería—
sería que no le tocaba
morirse ese día.
	With four bullets in his body, Cruz is
	   still holding on to life;
	May've been a miracle of God, or God
	   knows what it was;
	Could have been he just wasn't meant
	   to die that day.

Y adios Tepic, Nayarit
también sierra del Nayar—
murió Ezequiel de Durango
también Nabor Villarreal—
lo que a mí más me pesa
que la riña va a quedar.
	And good-bye to Tepic, Nayarit, also
	   to the mountains of Nayar
	Where Ezequiel from Durango, and
	   also Nabor Villarreal died;
	What saddens me the most is that the
	   feud isn't over.

Why a Cowboy Left Home

Death is a common theme in Anglo-American folksong, especially in the sentimental songs of the late nineteenth and early twentieth centuries. Thus, it is no surprise to find that many cowboy songs composed during this period when the occupation of the cowboy was at its height are sentimental narratives of death and violence. In this song, we learn that the reason "why a cowboy left home" lies in the young man's sad tale of a quarrel that turned violent and ended in his killing an acquaintance.

The song is also known as "The Cowboy's Home Sweet Home" and "The Wandering Cowboy." Cowboy folksinger Glen Ohrlin, who included a version of it in *The Hell-Bound Train*, pp. 159-160, noted that he had heard it in 1965 from a cowboy in Arkansas who reported learning it on the Miller brothers' 101 ranch in Oklahoma in 1931. According to Ohrlin, the song "must have had a wide following from Texas, where the Slaughter ranch is, to Oregon, for some versions have it on the French ranch, which was once a grazing empire in southern Oregon." This text from Oregon was submitted to *The Oregon Farmer's* "Old Songs" column of the magazine (n.d.) by Delta Hutchinson of Princeton, Oregon (Fife American Collection, Utah State University).

While lying out on the prairie,
At Frank Slaughter's ranch one night,
Our saddles for pillows,
Our campfires burning bright,
Oh, some were telling stories
And some were singing songs,
While others were [lazily] lightly smoking
Just to pass the hours along.

It was when we fell to talking
Of distant friends so dear,
A boy raised his head from his saddle
And brushed away a tear,
Said, "Mother owns a cottage
And far from it I've roamed
And I'd give my pony and saddle
Just to be at home, sweet home."

We asked him why he left it,
If it was so dear to him,
He raised himself on his saddle
And his eyes with tears grew dim.
He looked the rough crowd o'er,
Said, "Boys, I'll tell you the reason
That I'm compelled to roam.

"Oh, boys, it makes me shiver
When I think of that sad night
That Tom and I first quarreled
And I struck him with my knife.
And in my dreams I can still hear
Tom's voice as he fell to the ground
And said, 'Oh, Bob, old boy,
You'll be sorry when you see me lying dead.'

I dropped to the ground beside him,
A-trying to stop the blood
That was so softly flowing
From his side in a crimson flood.
Now, boys, you all know the reason
Why I'm compelled to roam,
Why, I'd give my pony and saddle
Just to be at home, sweet home."

The Ballad of Pete Orman

Before the advent of railroads in Central and Eastern Oregon in the first decade of this century, freight wagons rattled over the primitive roads of the region, hauling everything that the homesteaders and town builders needed, including barrels of whiskey; and along with their colorful language the muleskinning freight drivers were famous for their hard drinking, off the job and on. If they lacked their own supply on a haul from The Dalles south, legend has it that they would drill a tiny hole in the bung of a barrel and suck enough booze through a straw into a jar to last the trip. "The Ballad of Pete Orman" celebrates a late episode in the history of freighting (1910-15?), as indicated by Pete's reference to the Oregon Trunk Railway.—From Harold Benjamin, "Case Study in Folksong Making," pp. 27-30. According to Benjamin, the ballad was composed by a cowboy poet named Asher.

(Tune: "The Siskiyou Miners")

I'll tell all you skinners
   From John Day to Bend
That the road south of Shaniko
   Ain't got no end;
It's rut-holes and boulders,
   It's alkali dust,
But the jerk-liners gotta make
   Maupin or bust.

They rolled out Pete Orman
   A quarter past three.
He never had time
   To get over the spree
That he'd started at noon
   Only two days before;
When the call-boy came 'round
   Old Pete was right sore.

"Now what in hell
   Are they fussin' for me?"
He wanted to know,
   "Get out, let me be;
Last night my poor sidekick
   Was throwed in the can,
Today we ride jerk-line
   For no God-damned man!"

They rolled out Pete Orman,
   And bailed out McBee;
They set a stiff price
   With oats and grub free.
The boys had to take it,
   The contract was made—
They watered, fed, harnessed,
   And then hit the grade.

The weather was fine,
   They figured clear sailin'
To the Cow Canyon line;
   But while they was startin'
Up Shaniko Hill
   Orm tickled Old Tommy
With a porcupine quill.

"Put in the oats
   And shovel in the hay,
We're goin' to make it through
   If we can find a way;
We ain't quite as fast
   As the Oregon Trunk,
But we'll pull 'em into Bend
   If we are both drunk."

Loggers' Lore and Initiation Customs

Logging is much more than a job. For many Oregonians, it is a way of life, and the traditions and folklore of Oregon logging are rich and deep, some imported a century ago from the lumberjacks of the east, much developed regionally in the woods of the Northwest to reflect the specific nature of the work here. There are the age-old pranks played to initiate the new man on the job and stories and jokes, often expressing a pragmatic fatalism about the dangers, difficulties, or lack of monetary reward for the work. As the selection on "Bunkhouse Cussing" demonstrates, nowhere is the logger's eloquence and verbal dexterity more in evidence than in his swearing. Logging has one of the most expressive and extensive occupational lexicons in the United States, and an entire dictionary, *Woods Words*, was compiled by Oregon State Forester, Walter McCulloch.

Logging requires a great deal of cooperation among the members of a crew, and one time-honored way of forging bonds among individuals who work together is through traditional initiatory pranks played on any new members of a crew. These pranks plainly demonstrate to a new man how little he knows, thus keeping an eager novice from getting over confident and behaving in ways that might endanger his life or his crew. The following are stories of initiation pranks. The first two, published in *Oregon Folklore* (pp. 69-70), were recorded from Oregon loggers in the 1970s by university students. The third comes from the WPA Oregon Folklore Collection, from an interview with Charles Imus of Portland. Notes accompanying this story state that it "was first heard in the Michigan lumber camps and was carried 'on the hoof' to the Northwest woods."

A Bucket of Choker Holes

There isn't anything called a choker hole. Choker hole is just where you stick the choker underneath the log, you know. If there's a hole underneath the log then you—you run it [the choker] through there. Sometimes you get somebody going, and you say, "Well, we need some choker holes. Run down and get a choker hole—or a bucket o' choker holes."

And they'll run down to the landing and ask somebody for a bucket o' choker holes, and so they'll hand 'em a stick and say, "Go dig some." (RVMA, Jeri Johnston, 8/75)

The Axe Man's Test

Usually new men have to get some initiation from the older fellas. There's a whole variety of things they do. One of the common ones is the axe man's test, which—they'll catch you around the landing, which is where they load the trucks and haul the logs into, and [they'll] get a chopping block. When you're on break or something, one of the old timers'll get the axe and start chopping on the block, and he'll say, "Have you ever taken the axe man's test?" And most people don't know what the axe man's test is unless they've worked in the woods for a while. And what you got to do is hit the same spot on the chopping block four times in a row. And they'll show you how it's done, which all seems quite simple to you, and you wonder what the catch is to it, so you have to do it with your eyes closed.

So you close your eyes and take one swing and then take another, and you feel like you're coming pretty close to the same spot. And maybe on the third swing, they'll grab your gloves, or your hard hat, or your lunch bucket, or whatever's handy, and put it on top of the chopping block. And you come down and smash the hell out of it [*he laughs*] and everybody goes into hysterics. They usually talk about it and tease you about it for at least a couple weeks. (RVMA, Bill Agee, 6/1976)

The Swede and the Cant Hook

One time when I was working in a lumber camp, a young Swede came to work. Bein' purty young and not knowin' very much, he was plenty cocky. The bull puncher got a little tired of the young 'uns blowin' so he figgered he'd fix 'em up.

You know a lot of people don't know the difference between a cant hook and a peavy. The bull puncher figured this young Swede bein' a little dumb about things round the camp wouldn't know the difference. So the bull-puncher sent the young 'un after a cant-hook.

Sure enough! The Swede brought back a peavy. By ding! That bull puncher gave that young feller the finest piece of cussin' I ever heard one man give another. He started in on his ancestors and ended up with a jim dandy of a finish. I reckon I'd better not tell you what he said, you couldn't print it. [*The interviewer agrees it couldn't be printed.*]

The young feller took it all in, never said a word. When the bull-puncher finished, he just said, "By yimminy, I get one if it takes all day."

He kinda took the sting and fun outa the cussin' by bein so nice about it. It tweren't a case of bein' yellow—leastwise he didn't look scared a bit. I guess he was bound and determined to make good and no cussin' was gonna stop him.

Long toward evenin' I begin to get a little worried about the kid. I'd felt kinda sorry for him, and it was a cinch he was gonna be fired a spending a whole day lookin for a damn cant-hook.

Just before quitting time the feller wanders in with a damn old muley cow. "Fer God sakes," yelled the bull-puncher, "whatch doin' with that cow?"

The young feller with a real sober look said, "You wanted a cant-hook, and this is the only thing I can find that can't hook." After that the feller got along fine. (WPA Folklore Collection)

Walkaway

Rod Collins of Salem has written about a famous "packsack logger" who worked in Oregon in the 1930s. Collins notes: "Before the introduction of modern machinery made possible the rapid movement of men, machines and logs, before centralization and timber empires, every logger, in Oregon at least, fancied himself a gyppo and truly relished his independence as such. Perhaps the most independent were packsack loggers who traveled light and sometimes often. Carrying everything they owned in a packsack, they wandered from camp to camp, working a while for one outfit, moving on when they felt the urge to do so." Collins learned about "Walkaway" from his father, who had first heard stories of "Walkaway" in the early 1930s. (Collins, "Walkaway")

Walkaway was working "someplace" in Oregon as a teamster. A punk on the job asked him where he got the name Walkaway. (A punk was simply a young man who was starting in the woods. The term was not at all derogatory. A synonym might simply be "kid.")

"Here, hold these lines," Walkaway answered, and started down the trail. The woods boss came stomping up the skid trail about an hour later. The punk was still holding the reins of the team.

"Where's Walkaway?" the boss asked.

"That's what I'd like to know," the punk answered.

"What did you say to him?"

"I just asked him where he got his name."

"You son-of-a-bitch! He's walked off again."

A New Bride in Camp

Some logging camps accommodated married couples as well as single men, but camplife could be rather primitive. In 1969, Mrs. Claude Holman, North Bend, in an interview with her son, Dennis, recalled her experiences as a new bride in Oregon logging camps. Her account provides us with a woman's perspective on a way of life most often chronicled by men. Although Mrs. Holman's reminiscences would be classified as oral history rather than folk literature, they are rich in ethnographic detail of camp life.—From RVMA, Dennis Holman, May 1969.

Grande Ronde, Pope and Talbot company, was one camp your Dad worked in. It was along Salmon River. Your dad and his father was working together and living at the cookhouse, which had a bunkhouse, and the single men and ones that their wives didn't come too, lived in it. Your dad's mother stayed in Dallas where the kids were in school, so they lived in the bunkhouse. . . . Your dad's dad was supposed to tell the camp boss that one of the empty cabins (there were about ten there) was to be for us. They were shacks—one small room with a lean-to for a kitchen and an old cast iron bedstead and saggy springs and bulgy mattress and a heater they called airtight—it would get red hot in a few minutes and cool off just as fast so you couldn't keep even heat with it anyway. And if you shut the draft too tight it would hop up and down like it was blowing up.

We were married in Lebanon, and the camp where we were to go was about a hundred and fifty miles from Lebanon. We got there about midnight and went to this cabin that was supposed to have been reserved for us and went in, and here was a guy in the bed. Your dad cussed his dad—What in the hell was going on? Why hadn't he told them he was to have this place. He'd forgotten it, so we sat in the car the rest of the night 'til they got another place for us. The car was a Model A with one seat and a rumble seat. . . .

Also in the shacks were rough lumber and benches, and I'd brought a lace tablecloth and longstem goblets—to live in a place like that. You see, I didn't know what kind of a place I was going to. I had visions of something a little better. It took a few years before I used the lace tablecloth. I packed water and washed on a washboard. The first time I washed your dad's wool underwear I shrunk them to half the size. He said he put them on wet and would stretch them.

Of course, the newlyweds like us took a lot of kidding. The loggers and their wives all came to meet me. . . . I do remember one woman had the nicest place to live. . . . Her husband owned a logging truck, and he'd built a long-type of house with three rooms that he'd jack up and back the truck under it, almost like a trailerhouse. She had a piano and rugs on the floor. All I had then was that old bed and table and lumpy mattress. We did finally buy a few chairs to replace the benches, and we had to buy a cookstove because the one that was in the place had a firebox that was burnt through to the oven, so when you built a fire the coals fell in the oven.

The favorite book, of course, was Sears or Wards catalogs. The women just sat and shopped and wished—so we called them "wishbooks." The thing I wanted most was a closet instead of nails on the wall to hang my clothes on. So they had these cardboard ones that you ordered; they had to be put together—fold here and put a screw there. Well, I got it together okay, and it had a door that rolled on a spring like a blind. You had to pull it down and fasten it to a catch at the bottom. I pulled it down to fasten the catch at the bottom and was leaning down over it; the hook didn't catch, or it slipped, and the piece of wood flew up and hit me right between the eyes. The next morning I had two of the blackest eyes you ever saw. So your dad and I had a hard time convincing anyone we hadn't had a fight and I'd got the worst of it.

The other camp we moved to was up by a town called Elsie. When timber was cut there at Salmon River, the men went ahead with the equipment to cut timber and build a road. . . . Then they'd come back, and we'd pack our pots and pans. . . . I remember we had our old car packed solid when we were on the way to Elsie. I had a few plants I'd started, and by then I was about four or five months pregnant with Pauline. I had the plants on the floor and was squeezed in by the rest of the stuff. We'd gone a long way, and I was tired and wondering where the Godforsaken place was back in the mountains. We came around a turn, and here was a woman waving her arms for us to stop. There was no one around except her, no car or anything, about fifty miles from nowhere, too. Your dad asked her what she was doing there, and she wanted a ride to camp. Her old man and her had gotten in a fight, and he'd just stopped and pushed her out. Well, she half-sat on me the rest of the way, and by then I was ready to push her out too. Then they kissed and made up, but I never did like her.

The women gave me a big baby shower. . . . All the women gave me advice on what I should do while I was pregnant—get my vitamins and don't reach above my head to hang clothes or the cord would strangle the baby. . . . I craved watermelon when I was pregnant, and it was a long way to Astoria, the closest place to buy anything. You dad wouldn't let me drive out, and I was scared to 'cause the road was so narrow. . . . if you met a truck you couldn't get by, you'd have to back up to where the road was wide enough to let him by. I couldn't back a car up—I can tell you, out of necessity, I learned fast. But anyway, when some of the truckers went in with loads, if they found a place that had any watermelon, they'd bring me some. After I got about eight months pregnant, I was so far from a doctor, and your dad was afraid he couldn't get me to a hospital or a doctor—we left and never went back to live in a camp any more.

Paul Bunyan

The extent to which stories about Paul Bunyan flourished in the folklore repertoires of working woodsmen is uncertain. James Stevens, a sometimes logger and Northwest writer in the first half of the twentieth century, and one of the most ardent popularizers of Paul Bunyan, claims that the Paul Bunyan stories originated in the mid-nineteenth century among French Canadians. Stevens stated that he heard such stories first-hand from old-time French Canadian loggers and from lumbermen of Maine and the Upper Midwest who later concocted American adventures for Paul as lumber camp entertainment and stories for lumber trade publications. Through James Stevens's 1924 book, *Paul Bunyan,* among others, and through advertising and newspaper columns that featured adventures of the mighty lumberjack, Paul Bunyan quickly became a popular culture hero in America. Folklorist and historian Richard Dorson, in his 1959 study, *American Folklore,* explains that Paul Bunyan's widespread popularity and his significance in American life at this time was because Paul Bunyan represented the "American spirit," her bigness and power, in the United States during the decades of nationalism following World War I.

Of greatest interest to students of Oregon folklore is that one of the very few documented examples of Paul Bunyan stories in oral tradition comes from the diary kept by Edward O. Tabor, who as a young man worked in the camp of the Palmer Lumber Company at Palmer Junction, some fifty miles north of La Grande, in the summer of 1910. Tabor's associate at the time was Stith Thompson, then a teacher at Portland's Lincoln High School, who was later to become a well-known folklorist. In 1946, when arguments were flying about the origins of the Paul Bunyan tales, Thompson recalled the Bunyan tales he and Tabor had heard that summer of 1910 from a logger named Duffy. He contacted Tabor, then a Pittsburgh attorney, and they published an article in the *Journal of American Folklore* with quotes from the notebook Tabor had kept of his logging camp experiences. Although they provide clear proof that Paul Bunyan tales had some basis in Northwest lumber camp lore, Tabor's notes provide just the bare bones of the stories he heard:

> Paul Bunyan digging Puget Sound—first logger in the West. His big blue ox—fed bales of hay—men could drown in its tracks—winter of the blue snow. . . . Big camp—waiters on roller skates in the dining room—potato peels carried out by cartloads and fed to the blue ox—prune seeds shoveled out of the kitchen window. A garden rake was the curry comb for the blue ox. You had to climb a sycamore to get the hayseed out of his left ear. . . .

And Tabor writes:

> I remember one theme not mentioned above, namely, that when Paul decided to either move camp or haul big timber (trees 300 feet long), he would hitch the blue ox's tugs, which were elastic, to the camp or timber and then would get Babe (the blue ox) to take three or four steps forward, each step being about 20 rods, and he would stand still, with his breast and yoke forward, his feet planted in the ground, and he would wait a second or two until the elasticity in the tugs pulled the camp or the timber up to him, and then he would repeat this performance until the camp was moved. . . . The Puget Sound theme was very dramatic as I remember it. Paul had cleaned up all the lumber in the middle West and when he came to the Pacific coast he found the

trees so big and the work to be done so large and the facilities so small, that he decided to dig Puget Sound in order to have room enough to float his logs. He hitched Babe to this giant scoop or shovel, and in a day or two, he dug out Puget Sound and had enough water for the logs and the mill.

In the 1930s the Paul Bunyan legend expanded beyond its popularity in books and newspapers to pageants, dramas, carved statues at timber carnivals—and the 1939 World's Fairs—and local "Paul Bunyan's Day" in numerous timber towns throughout the nation. In 1934 in southwestern Oregon, the General Commmittee of the Marshfield Paul Bunyan Birthday Celebration authorized the publication of *The Book of Bunyan, Being the Exploits of Paul Bunyan and Babe, the Blue Ox, in Southwestern Oregon.* This is a collection of 37 Paul Bunyan yarns by men, women, and children of the Coos Bay area. Annotations next to some stories indicate that they were "Annanias Contest Prize Stories," winners in a liars' contest. While we have no evidence that any of these 1934 stories entered oral tradition in Oregon, we present several of them here as examples of how traditions are invented and how a well-known story cycle is regionalized by a southwestern Oregon logging community.

Paul Bunyan's Logging at Shoreacres

While Paul Bunyan and Babe, the blue ox, were logging around Shoreacres, Paul was puzzled as to where to put all the timber he was logging. One day while wading around in search of clams for his dinner he came upon a shallow place, three-quarters of a mile from land. Upon investigation he found it to be a sandbar. After he built his jetty there to hold his logs it formed what is now North Bay. You can still see some of the remains of his old jetty.

During his spare time from building the jetty, he taught Babe to bellow, so on foggy days he would have a way of calling the ships in to get his logs. Paul worked Babe so hard hauling out those logs that the ox became weary and restless and began bellowing continuously until the ship captains grew accustomed to the sound and would stay outside on foggy days.

If you should happen down that way now when the fog hangs over the bar you can still hear the echo of Babe's voice. (Mrs. L. W. Simmons, p. 6)

Paul's Great Auction

Paul Bunyan came to Coos Bay over the old Brewster Trail and when he landed on Isthmus Inlet he found plenty of feed for his faithful companion, Babe, the blue ox. Paul decided to wait there until spring and find a place to begin logging.

It was the winter of the blue snow, the coldest winter in Oregon, and the fog came in and froze so hard that when it raised it took all the timber with it for miles and left barren land which is now sand hills.

One day Babe disappeared and as Paul set out to find him, he came to the marsh where the Old Smith mill stands and there he saw a great form . . ., went over and found it to be Jack Stack viewing the remains of Babe. Paul asked Jack what he was doing there and Jack told him he was looking for a place to build a mill for C. A. Smith. Right then and there, Paul began to auction off Babe's parts. Jack bid on the shank bones for smokestacks, the ribs for rafters, the hide for belts, and the eyeballs for governor balls on the big engines; the tail for 6 peavies and 10 pike poles. The head was sold to the port commission and they anchored it at the mouth of the harbor where it can be heard bawling continually. The frozen intestines were sold to the water company for pipe lines, which was fine for a time, until they started to thaw out and caused a near riot, but it was stopped by the erection of a filter plant. Thus passed Babe, the blue ox. The writer has never heard whether the blue ox was a big steer or all bull, but this story is the only one in which facts are backed by evidence. (Si Steckles, p. 6)

The Sad Ending of Paul Bunyan's Blue Ox

Years and years ago Paul Bunyan came from east of the Coast Range Mountains seeking "Babe," his old blue ox. It was raining and the ground was soft, and every so often one of Paul's feet would sink down in the soft earth. (That is what made the lakes here in Southwestern Oregon.)

He found his beloved ox up at what is now the head of Coos River. The poor beast was very sick. Paul sat down beside him and cried. He cried so hard this tears made small trenches in the earth. The more he cried the deeper they got. (And that is what made Coos River and all the little inlets around Coos Bay.) The seagulls were very large in those days and they were sailing around waiting for the old blue ox to die so they could pick his bones. Paul got mad at the seagulls and threw rocks at them. Some of the rocks he threw landed down at Bandon and anyone can see them there on the beach today. The old blue ox died one day and Paul did not want the gulls to eat him, so he dug a big hole and put the ox in it and heaped the earth upon his grave—and that is what is called the Blue Ridge. (Mrs. C. H. Spooner, p. 9)

Bunkhouse Cussing

Charles Oluf Olsen, one of Oregon's WPA writers and folklore collectors, presents us with a testament to the logger's finely honed skill in one of the great traditional verbal arts—cussing— in this 1938 description of a hooktender from Coos County. (WPA Folklore Collection)

The best cussing I ever heard was done by one Jim O'Brian, a hooktender in Coos County, some twenty years ago. He and I had both quit camp because the bunkhouses were built on stilts and the hogs ran loose. The hogs had a habit of getting under the bunkhouses in the night and snoring loudly, or else rubbing their sides and backs against the uprights upon which the bunkhouses were built, making a sonorous, rasping, reverberating sound that absolutely forbade sleep; also of spreading fleas about camp, which in summer made life quite intolerable.

Well, Jim took the camp apart—vocally. He stopped at the edge of camp and looked back at it, then began cursing it, slowly, methodically, and thoroughly. He began with the boss, went to the timekeeper, the scaler, the cook, the filer, the strawbosses, down to the whistle punk and the bullcook. He spoke about each man's ancestry, peculiarities, desserts, and destination. He was lurid, matter-of-fact, obscene, profane, and indecent. But most of all picturesque. He never repeated himself as far as I recollect, though I was too lost in wonder and admiration to notice closely. When he had finally consigned the collective camp to sink into the ground in bubbling ooze and stinkweed to grow where it stood, he calmly asked me for a chew of snoose (Copenhagen) and we went on our seven-mile trail-hike to town.

I have seen a logger whittle a white stick and drive it into the bark of a log, so he might have something visual to swear at; I have seen a boss throw his hat on the ground and stamp on it, then climb a tree and dare Jesus Christ to come down and fight him; in the same mood I have seen a hooktender, with tears running down his cheeks from weariness and exasperation swear to God and all the known saints that he would pull that log in yet—if it was the goddam last skunk-blasted, blue-butted, cultus-mushed, belly-bound, conk-cursed job he ever did!

Selections from the Loggers' Lexicon

This is just a brief sampling of the working vocabulary of the timber industry, present and past, in the Northwest. Colorful and expressive, it provides us with some insight into the attitudes and traditions of Oregon's loggers. These entries are from *Woods Words: A Comprehensive Dictionary of Loggers Terms*, compiled by Walter F. McCulloch.

Calks: Short, heavy spikes in the soles and heels of woods shoes to give sure footing on logs.

Corks: The right way to say calks; means both the calks themselves and shoes with calks in them.

Dashboards: Farmers who work part-time in the woods; from the bib overalls which they wear instead of ordinary pants worn by loggers. A man wearing bib overalls in the western Oregon woods was known as a prune picker, that is, more a farmer than logger.

East side: East of the Cascade Mountains in Washington and Oregon.

Fog so thick the camp carpenter shingled half a mile of it off the end of the bunkhouse afore the sun comes up: A medium fog.

Fog so thick you could seine a salmon in it: A medium fog (there are seldom any real thick fogs in the West Coast woods—a genuine thick one has to be cut up in pieces like building blocks and laid to one side to make a passage through it.

Hooktender: A foreman in charge of the crew on a logging side. In early days he was the man in charge of skidding, and either hooked on the logs or told the teamsters what logs to hook on. Because he tended hook sometimes, the name has stuck. Known as the head hooker or hooker in some camps.

Jump a sock: A favorite bunkhouse operation; turning a sock over so that a hole worn in the heel comes out on top of the foot, and fresh material pulls around in back to make a new heel. Saves darning. A really experienced man could sometimes get three jumps out of one pair of socks.

Logger: (a) The owner of a logging outfit. (b) Any man who works in the operating area of a logging show, from woods boss down to whistle punk. (c) "He's a logger" is used to mean that a man is a good hand, as opposed to "Arkie" or "Oakie" meaning a green worker.

Logger's can opener: An ax.

Logger's small pox: This is the result of being stomped on by a man wearing calked boots.

Logging: All or any part of the job or turning trees into logs and delivering them to an unloading point; a West Coast term for the word lumbering as used in the eastern woods.

Long log country: The Douglas-fir region; southern British Columbia, Washington, and Oregon west of the Cascades, and northwest California.

Lumberjack: A genteel term used by fiction writers who should have said logger if they mean a man working in the western woods.

Measure: Loggers didn't measure things in the usual units familiar to city people. Big things were compared in size to Erickson's Bar [Portland, Oregon]; lengths were measured in ax handles; wide things were compared to the width of a fat schoolma'am; and small things were measured by plugs of Star tobacco.

North Sea Piano: A concertina played in the bunkhouse by a Scandinavian logger.

Number 17 collar and number 2 hat: A skookum man with no brains.

R'ar of snoose: A gob of snoose, as much as sticks to a crooked forefinger dug into a snoose can; this is usually tucked under the end of the tongue where it pushes out the lower lip, once a well-known trademark of the real logger.

Show: (a) A logging operation (cat show, high lead show, winter show, summer show, etc.). (b) The operating conditions which affect logging, as a poor show, a good show.

Side: A logging unit: the men and equipment needed to fall, buck, yard, and load any one unit of an operation. Known as cat side, high lead side, skidder side, etc.

Skidroad: (a) A road on which logs are skidded. At first they were dragged by bulls or horses across small cross skids laid on the road. Now the logs are skidded by donkey or cat, the skids have disappeared, and the term is usually shortened to road. The skidroad was in the heart of the old logging show and many words still in use date from the days of skidroad logging: hooktender, for example. (b) A street in the tougher parts of West Coast towns where loggers hang out. Careless reporters with dirt in their ears have written skidrow or skid row so often that this miserable, phoney term is accepted by the ignorant. There's no such damn thing as skidrow and there never was. The street of saloons, card rooms, flop houses, sporting houses, etc., is *the skidroad*. The present day use came from the famous skidroad built by Henry Yesler to skid logs from the woods to his mill on the Seattle waterfront in 1852. After it was no longer used for skidding this became just a road, and stores, saloons, and other establishments grew up alongside. Much of the old road remains today but is known by the more genteel name of Yesler Way. Let's hear no more about skidrow.

Swedish condition powder: Snoose.

Swede fiddle: A crosscut saw; particularly a bucking saw.

Tin pants: Heavy waterproof pants.

More Loggers' Jargon

Oregon Oddities, a newsletter published by the WPA Folklore Project, included a miscellany of the folklore gathered by the workers. The following are a few entries from volume seven (pp.1-3) on Oregon loggers' jargon.

When a Columbia River logger talks of *Big Eddy*, he is not discussing one of his friends or *sidekicks*, he is speaking of Portland's Third Avenue, known to loggers throughout the west as a rendezvous where fallers, buckers, high-climbers, donkey-punchers, rigging-slingers, and hook-tenders can find a kindred soul. That part of Third Avenue between West Burnside Street and the steel bridges was christened *Big Eddy* because of the way the river in the old days cast up flotsam and jetsam near the foot of West Burnside.

Although the plain but hearty fare of the Oregon lumber camp is noted for its wholesomeness and quantity, the loggers' pithy humor has developed a camp-table talk as pungent as white pine and as dry as a whining cross-cut saw.

In loggers' jargon, the camp cook is a *gut-robber* or a *meat-burner*. He is also called a *mulligan mixer*, a *kitchen king*, a *pie artist*, a *boiler*, a *slum-gullion fixer*, a *can opener*, a *stomach robber*, a *sizzler*, a *victual burner*, and a *stew-builder*. His chore-boy is a *bull-cook*, and his dish-washer a *pearl-diver*. But when a logger talks of the camp *butcher*, he is speaking of the camp surgeon.

Loggers do not flatter their cook, if one can believe the descriptive names of items on their menus. Thus, in logging camps, butter is *salve*, sugar is *sand*, and hotcakes are *monkey-blankets*.

When loggers say that their *bellies rise and fall with the tide*, they mean that hard times are upon them. This descriptive phrase, still heard in camps, became popular in the woods many years ago when times were so bad in the state of Washington that loggers claimed that they had to eat clams to keep alive.

A logger came into a restaurant about midnight and ordered a steak and potatoes. When the waitress brought him his meal, the potato ordered was a large baked potato with the jacket on. The logger gazed at it in amazement, and shouted: "Huh! That thing's neither barked, nor sniped, nor on the ride. Has the crew quit?"

The waitress looked at him disdainfully. "I want you to understand, big fellow, that we have manners here!"

"Thazzo?" growled the logger. "Well, bring me some of 'em. I'll try anything once."

The Wobbly Language

In their agitations for better pay and working conditions in the Oregon woods and elsewhere in the teens and early twenties, the Industrial Workers of the World (I.W.W., or "Wobblies") presented themselves to the world as a tight, secretive society, a kind of lodge of revolutionaries in fact, in which their very nickname was a mystery to the outside, at least—did it come from a Chinese member's inability to pronounce the group's initials, I.W.W.? The Wobblies evolved their own distinctive language, or *cant*, much of which has gotten into our Oregonian speech, as noted by Stewart Holbrook in *Wildmen, Wobblies, and Whistle Punks*, pp. 164-165.

Wobbly editors were quick to appreciate . . . terms used by the boys out at the "points of production." A worker who was not filled with revolutionary spirit was labeled a *scissorbill*. The Wobs wanted logging concerns to furnish employees with blankets and sheets, so the ancient practice of carrying one's own blankets from camp to camp was made ludicrous by *carrying a balloon*, with appropriate front-page cartoons. A *sab cat*—from *sabotage*—might be merely an organizer or he might be one well versed in the safest methods of wrecking machinery. A *hoosier* was a working stiff who didn't know his job; to *hoosier up* was to slow work purposely. *Pie in the sky* was a cynical reference to the bourgeois heaven. *Gyppo* was any sort of work done by contract and was much frowned upon. A town policeman was a *clown*. The prosecuting attorney was the *cutor*. The Wob press used *hijack*—"Hi, Jack!" a command to throw up the arms—long before it came into general usage. A *red card* was evidence of membership. A detective, company guard, or stool pigeon was a *fink*, by all odds the dirtiest word in the Wobbly thesaurus. There were many others, fully as pointed and all of them founded on sound etymological grounds and most of them containing humor . . . .

Fifty Thousand Lumberjacks

This I.W.W./Wobbly "marching song" seems to have originated in a 1917 strike of timber workers in Oregon, Washington, and Idaho that led to somewhat improved conditions in logging camps and mills. A version appears in the Wobblies' *Little Red Songbook* of 1917, to be sung to the tune of "The Portland Revolution"; this much angrier version was collected in the same year by Harold Barto in northern Idaho, and published by William Alderson in *California Folklore Quarterly,* pp. 375-376. The tune is "A Son of a Gamboleer."

Fifty thousand Lumberjacks
  Goin' out to work.
Fifty thousand honest men
  That never loaf or shirk,
Fifty thousand lumberjacks
  They sweat and swear and strain,
Get nothin' but a cussin'
  From the pushes and the brains.

Fifty thousand lumberjacks
  Goin' in to eat
Fifty thousand plates of slum
  Made from tainted meat,
Fifty thousand lumberjacks
  All settin' up a yell
To kill the bellyrobbers
  An' damn their souls to hell.

Fifty thousand lumberjacks
  Sleepin' in pole bunks,
Fifty thousand odors
  From dirty socks to skunks,
Fifty thousand lumberjacks
  Who snore and moan and groan
While fifty million graybacks
  Are pickin' at their bones.

Fifty thousand lumberjacks,
  Fifty thousand packs,
Fifty thousand dirty rolls
  Upon their dirty backs,
Fifty thousand lumberjacks
  Strike and strike like men:
For fifty years we packed our rolls,
  But never will again.

Ode to the Spotted Owl

The spotted owl has become the central symbol of the debate in the Pacific Northwest over continued logging of old-growth timber, the habitat of the spotted owl. This poem by Sunny Hancock, a Lakeview rancher who has also worked as a logger at times, uses the genre of traditional recitation to address the issue. It has been popular with audiences of loggers and others who work in the Northwest timber industry. (All rights reserved)

This old world is in a turmoil in 'most everybody's view
Seems like we all got different notions of the things we oughta do,
From balancin' the budget and the price of foreign aid
To that hole up in the ozone all those little spraycans made.
Unemployment's runnin' rampant; S & L's are goin' broke,
The peoples' jobs are disappearin' like a puff of engine smoke.
But one thing keeps me goin', though our problems aren't all solved,
Is that the dinosaurs became extinct before the EPA evolved.
Now what would have happened thirty million years ago today
At the annual convention of the caveman's EPA?
The chairman says, "Boys, listen here to what I'm tellin' you,
If we're to save this planet, here's some things we gotta do.
We've got to dam that river there and flood that great big flat
Because we've gotta have a bit more brontosauras habitat."
And from the front row came a voice that said, "Oh yes, we must comply.
This earth won't last a month if all our dinosaurs should die."
But from the rear there came another voice that said, "Doggone your livers.
You build a dam, and damn, there goes our wild and scenic rivers.
And all the caves these people keep, why they're a total mess.
Let's evict these slobs and tell 'em we've declared this wilderness."
Then Susie Cave Girl pipes right up and says, "But just look here,
At this big hole that's formin' in our upper atmosphere.
I have observed this all year long. We searched with my class.
It's caused by all those uncouth meganthropus passin' gas.
Let's build a fence and move 'em down where they can get more greens
And keep them plumb away from that patch of wild beans."
"Ah yes," said Billy Bonehead, "and let's tell those silly fools:
Quit makin' all those pretty rocks up into arrowheads and tools.

I think it's bloody awful, and now won't it be a shock
If your grandkids never ever get to stumble on a rock.
The rate they're goin' now, the only place you'll ever see 'em
Is the few small stones we'll gather up and put in some museum.
They must cut no more old growth trees for wood. We'd better have a care.
You thin 'em out, and those big birds spot our pot fields from the air.
And you think you got troubles, partner. Troubles you ain't got
Til you got a couple dozen Pterodactyls high on pot."

"Okay, then," said the chairman, "I want you all to hit the streets,
And you can browbeat all the workin' men and women that you meet.
And tell 'em all that if their sinful ways they don't abort,
We're goin' to merge with the Sierra Club and yard 'em into court."
So now the modern EPA is quick to holler, "Foul.
The timber industry is killing off our spotted owl.
It takes three thousand acres for this little beggar's nest.
I think we ought to let him propagate. Let's close the whole Northwest."
But the EPA might be surprised, 'cause this bird, if he must,
He'd be just like the coyote, and I'm sure that he'd adjust.
When he moved down into the second growth, this timid little guy,
Would find himself much closer to his mousy food supply.
And they'd be so handy for our little feathered cousin
That instead of havin' just one egg, he'd probably lay a dozen
So then in just a decade, why they'd be so blasted thick
That you could stand out on your patio and whomp 'em with a stick.
But then the EPA would surely set up such a howl,
They'd say, "We've gotta put a bounty on that blasted spotted owl.
We've gotta cut their numbers back, or what'll be the price.
That wretched little varmint is endangering our mice.
The appetite those buggers have would drive a man to drink.
Boys, the world won't last for thirty days if the mice become extinct."
But if there is one specie in this whole wide world around,
That for the good of humankind must be extinction-bound,
The one that most folks I know would put highest on their list
Is that large-mouthed, loose-lipped bird they call environmentalist.

Miners' Nicknames and Nomenclature

Collections of Oregon mining folklore show that the use of nicknames was a popular tradition among some miners. The nicknames usually refer to some aspect of the miner's character, and the story of "Walk Away Willy" has a direct counterpart in the logging camp story of "Walkaway" (see p. 159). The miners' nicknames and folk speech that follow are from collections of mining folklore made by University of Oregon students Chris Grissom, Candy Anderson, and Jean Staples in the 1970s for the Randall V. Mills Archives of Northwest Folklore.

Hardrock

Miners call other miners that are good at the trade "Hardrock." If he is a particularly good miner and they believe in him, they call him "Hardrock" because hardrock rings like steel, a true quality character. A soft ring is false, therefore you don't want to set foundations or timbers on it. (RVMA, Grissom and Anderson, 1970)

Two Week Tommy, Walk Away Willy, and Seldom Seen Charley

Some of the characters had reputations for moving around, and some of the names I happen to think of are one fellow who was called "Two Week Tommy," because his length of time was two weeks. And another fella was called "Walk Away Willy," because when the time came for him to leave, why he would just up and walk away. That was it; there was just no question about it, no arguing or anything. And then there was another fellow, and I'm not sure of the origin of his name, but it was—he was called "Seldom Seen Charley." But these are the kinda names that you met all the time. (RVMA, Staples, 1971)

Digsblaster

One of my bosses's names was "Digsblaster." They called him this because every night he stood at the opening of the tunnel and asked us as we finished for the day, "Did ya blast her?" Every day we either had to set a timber or drill a hole in the face and blast, on every shift. If you didn't do this, he would tap you on the shoulder, which meant go pick up your pay because you were fired. (RVMA, Grissom and Anderson, 1970)

Digmore

The name of my mine is the "Digmore." My men worked for six weeks, and one of them kept saying "we've go to dig more." A true miner never gives up; he is always seeking the mother lode. (RVMA, Grissom and Anderson, 1970)

Cousin Jacks

Miners from Cornwall, England, Cornishmen who had originally immigrated to California, moved north to Sumpter to work in the mines during the gold rush. They were known among the miners as "Cousin Jacks," and they had a lingo all their own. A Sumpter assayer recalls the instance of a "Cousin Jack" going into a shoe store and asking the clerk for "forth and back shoes." The Cornish miner wanted shoes to wear from home to the mine and back, a smart pair of shoes since the miners wanted to look like kings when they went to work. After they got there, they changed clothes in a "change house," and changed their shoes when they entered the tunnels. (RVMA, Grissom and Anderson, 1970)

Tommy Knockers

Tommy Knockers are little people that live in the mines. They are mischievous and do things like throwing rocks down on the miners' heads or digging holes under the timbers so that they cave in. Sometimes they even sneak up on an unsuspecting miner and blow his light out leaving him in darkness. Many a miner has laid down their tools and lunch boxes only to have them stolen. Because of the bad things that the Tommy Knockers do the old miners, especially, always leave something out of their lunches for them. The miners have to be careful not to leave their valuables around because the Tommy Knockers will take them, leaving something totally useless in its place. The Tommy Knockers live in Tommy Knocker nests made of rock eggs. These nests are usually located in high places where it is dark and so that they can spy on the miners without them knowing it. Sometimes if a miner is real quiet the Tommy Knockers can be heard laughing and talking among themselves.

Young miners were told that they had to leave a quarter on the timbers for the Tommy Knockers or it would be bad luck. The old fellows would come along and collect them. It was really a shakedown racket. See, you were considered to be in favor with the Tommy Knockers if they took it.

Sometimes if a true miner is in a mine that has been gutted long before and sits down and is quiet he often hears a timber creak or sand sift down. These noises come about when rotting timbers take on pressure; it's a good time to get out of the mine. I heard the Tommy Knockers one time and decided to get out of there. Another miner went in that wasn't a very good miner, and the mine caved in on him. (RVMA, Grissom and Anderson, 1970)

One of Sumpter's Well-Known Miners

A key figure in the local character anecdotes from the mining town of Sumpter in Northeastern Oregon was Ben, a section foreman who was known for his great strength. Many of the stories that circulate about Ben recount his exploits as a strongman, although at least one anecdote reveals that even a miner as big and powerful as Ben heeded the warnings of "Tommy Knockers." These stories are from the collection of mining folklore made by Chris Grissom and Candy Anderson in 1970 for the Randall V. Mills Archive of Northwest Folklore.

I knew old Ben. He was a section miner, a foreman who took care of the track. There was this here tunnel up on Bald Mountain that they thought might have some pretty good ore so they put up timbers. One day ol' Ben came trampin' down the hill with a 150 pound pack, all of his belongings. I asked him, "Ben, what's the matter? No ore?"

"Hell, yes, there's ore up there," he said, "but there's also Tommy Knockers.". . .

So I loaded ol' Ben in the Model T and brought him back to Sumpter. I wondered if ol' Ben was losin' his marbles, so I asked him if there really were such things.

"Hell yes. Two of 'em."

"Where are they? I've never seen one. Have you?"

"Well, one knocks over on this side of the tunnel in the drift of the base tunnel; the other one answers from the other place, as squeaky as a woman. So I'm not goin' back."

On the dredge, there is a short, steep winding stairway; these fellers was a tryin' to get this 550-pound bucket up there and were a-havin' quite a struggle. Ben said to them, "You fellers are weak." He picked up the bucket and put it on his shoulder and put it on the window at the top of the stairs.

Once ol' Ben wrestled a bear. It was a trained one so anyone could handle it. You got a big prize if you walked in and pinned the bear. Ben did just that. He just walked in and pinned it down. He just slammed it right onto the ground.

Ben came in one night, drunk. He made his brew so strong as to take the galvanizing off a boiler. He called it raisin wine. He said, "I'm the biggest, strongest man in town. Nobody can argue with me. Do you know what I can do? I can drink one whole pint of ninety-proof whiskey."

Well, he tipped it up and drank it down like water. He went down straight as a stove pipe and fell down the steps and cracked his head colder than hell. It took four men to pick him up. He came back to town the next day and didn't remember drinking the whiskey. He said in the future he wasn't going to put so many raisins in the brew.

The Ghosts of Chinese and Black Miners of Elk Creek

—Collected in June 1978 by Jeffrey Nicholson on Elk Creek, near its confluence with the middle fork of the John Day River, from "Macky," a reclusive old miner. —Venn Collection, Eastern Oregon State College.

During the late 1800s much prospecting was going on in Oregon. Much of the labor was low-paid Chinese and a few Black men. At a particular operation along this creek a company had the practice of enslaving the Blacks and not paying the Chinese much of the time. When any of the men became uncooperative they were killed and thrown in an old mine pit nearby. This was later covered by rock from the nearby mine. Today the picks and the shackles from the spirits of these laborers can be heard at night since the spirits are restless because of the injustices put upon them. The pile of rocks can still be seen today.

The Ballad of the Territorial Road

This song text, collected in the Willamette Valley in the 1940s, is about the experience of California miners traveling through Oregon en route to the Salmon River gold rush in Idaho in the 1860s. The hospitality accorded the "Californy bummer" by the Oregon "Long-Tommer" in this song is an early expression of a persistent Oregon attitude toward Californians. This song text is a variant of "A Trip to Salmon," written by returned miner Max Irwin, to be sung to the tune *Jordan Is a Hard Road to Travel* (Richard E. Lingenfelter et al., eds., *Songs of the American West*, pp. 108, 118-119). The text of "A Trip to Salmon," quoted from the *Portland [Oregon] Times*, was published in the *Los Angeles Star*, May 12, 1862. Notes accompanying "The Ballad of the Territorial Road" in the William L. Alderson Papers (Special Collections, University of Oregon Library) state that it was "gathered by Lester Thompson, 1940-41, in Lane County, Oregon." An identical text published in the *Oregon Historical Quarterly* (XLIII [1942], 149), came from University of Oregon English professor, Randall V. Mills, with a notation that "one of my students turned it up in the back-country."

The Umpqua country was the best ever found
for hills and rocks and fountains.
The Umpqua mud it stuck to our feet,
but we shook it all off on the Calapooia mountains.

Chorus:
Save your money, boys, to pay your way through,
two to one Salmon agin Caribou:
Save your money, boys, and don't get the fever,
for we'll all make a strike when we git to Salmon River.

The Umpqua country was the best ever found
for long tail frogs and alligators,
And when the hogs they root up the ground, the farmers
all come out and plant their potaters.

In the Long Tom country we all clumb a tree
to see the land of promise,
But clear to the north as far as we could see
there was nothing in sight but the river Long Thomas.

I asked a Long Tommer to lend me his hoss
and wait for his pay next summer,
But his wife railed out like lightin' flash,
"Git outa here, ya Californy bummer!"

Women Invade the Shipyards

Amy Kesselman's study of women ship-builders in the Kaiser Shipyards in Portland during World War II, *Fleeting Opportunities: Women Shipyard Workers in Portland and Vancouver* is based on revealing anecdotes, told forty years later by these female pioneers in a male work-force.

I worked in the clearance office and that's an office where the people that have either been laid off, quit, or fired come through. And I didn't like office work, I never did. So when they were coming through there and I found out how much money they were making, I decided that I would quit and go down and hire out as a helper. And I hired out as a helper and I went to work duplicating—now that's climbing up on plates, steel plates—and you have a hammer and a big heavy metal nail . . . and you had to hammer on little dots. And I didn't like that either and I said, "How do you get a job running a crane?" And he said, "Well, you have to talk to the man who hires for that . . . ." Well, evidently he told him about me, because the next day he came around and said, "I hear you'd like to run a crane." And I said, "I sure would." And he said, "Do you think you can do that?" I said, "Well, I don't know why not; other people are doing it." And the very next day he came after me. (Joanne Hudlicky, pp. 46-48)

I was working; I was what they called a *tack welder*. I was welding just the tack welds for the shipfitters and I was interested. I watched these guys on these drills and I just thought it would be interesting to operate one of those big drills. . . . When I asked to try out the drill, he looked at me kind of funny and he said, "Well, I've never had a woman driller on my crew." "Well, I think I can handle it." So he allowed me to try out. (Alice Erickson, pp. 46-47)

He really kicked up a storm when he found out he was going to have to hire women on the crew. They said he really threw a tantrum. Well, I couldn't imagine him throwing a tantrum till I saw him do it one day. He wore striped overalls and a striped cap, regular engineer's working outfit, and the time I saw him throw a tantrum he took that hat off, he threw it on the floor, he jumped up and down and he just turned the air blue. And that's what he did when he found out he was gonna have to have women on the crew down there because he wasn't raised that way. But we got along fine; he was no problem after we were down there. (Loena Ellis, p. 51)

So the boss came over and says, "Shorty, what are you doing working on that pipe?" He says, "You can do that tomorrow . . . the war is over. There's no hurry now. Nobody's working but you." And I said, "Well, I want to finish this pipe." I said, "This is the last pipe I'll ever weld." And he laughed and he said. "You're kidding, Shorty. You'll be here tomorrow." I said, "You wanna bet?" and he said, "Yeah, I'll bet." "Okay, name your bet." And he walked away and I went ahead and finished my pipe and that was the last pipe I ever welded. They laid me off the next day . . . the women in the pipe shop were all laid off. (Edna Hopkins, p. 110)

The Naming of Fishboats

As folklorist Horace Beck points out in *Folklore and the Sea,* "of all things that pertain to the building of a ship, the two most important events are the selection of her name, and the launching" (p. 18). Although the concepts that apply to the naming of ships have changed over the centuries and may vary from country to country or coast to coast, traditions relating to the naming of ships remain a prominent form of maritime folklore. Folklorist Janet C. Gilmore, in her study, *The World of the Oregon Fishboat: A Study in Maritime Folklife,* examines the boat-naming traditions of the commercial fishermen of Charleston on the southern Oregon coast. Gilmore reports that "with careful ceremony, each boat receives a name, and symbolically the breath of life, at its launching." She notes that "Charleston fishboats are fully personified by local custom" and often referred to "as female beings who have some measure of self-initiated behavior: 'that old girl's been so good to us for 31 years' . . . " (p. 109). The following passage from *The World of the Oregon Fishboat* (pp. 111-113) describes the boat-naming traditions of Charleston.

Charleston fishermen appear to select names for their boats according to coastal folk tradition. Thus, a good third of the local fishboats are named after women, mainly fishermen's wives, a custom that long-time fish plant manager Ruth Hallmark Day deplores:

> Oh, I waged a one-woman campaign for years to try to keep them from naming their boats for women. Hurricanes are great, but not naming their boats for women, for their wives. I like names like, oh, *Intrepid*, and *South Wind*, and *Rambler*, and even *Old Dry Rot* . . . I remember talking to a bunch of fishermen one day, and we were talking about boat names, and I said, "Well, our brand name I thought was such a pretty name, and I've never seen a boat named that, *The Wave King*, and I just thought that would be a beautiful name for a boat, and I didn't know why anybody didn't name it that instead of naming their boat for their wife. And this one fellow says, "Well, that is nice," he says, "I'll name my boat that." And it was the worst old junker in the fleet. It was just horrible looking, never painted, and in the back on the stern it had an old back seat of a car . . . that he sat on when he trolled, upholstery coming out of it. So I just dropped the subject, I never mentioned it again. I thought, boy, that'd be my luck.

Typically, the boat gets the woman's first name (*Anita, Joyce, Lilly, Almae, Karla, Cleora, Naomi,* . . .), or both her first and middle names (*Kelly Jo, Kathy Jo, Jana Jo, Shirley Lynn, Tammy Lynn, Christina Marie,* . . .), or her first name and the initial of her last name (*Wendy R, Pearl M, Zillah B, Ardis C, Georgia K,* . . .). Sometimes the boat is given two female names (*Ginny and Jill*) or a first or last name following Lady (*Lady Ann*), Miss (*Miss Everett, Miss Larene*), or Ms. (*Ms. Mills*).

A few boats, however, are named after particular men (*George, Edgar A, John Allen*), after particular places (*Pacific, Capistrano, Artic Sea II*) including stars and constellations (*Arcturus, Polaris, Pisces*), or after famous or legendary persons, places, or things often having some association with the sea (*Lincoln, Simon Peter, Odysseus, Barbary Coast, Arundel, Flying Cloud*). Some fishermen have combined two or more family names to come up with a name for their boats (*Faymar*), and some designate their boats only with the initials of someone's name (*RVA*), sometimes spelled out (*Cee Cee, Triple D*).

In short, most Charleston boat names (two-thirds of them) are proper nouns, primarily the names of women. The remaining minority (one-third) are overwhelmingly nouns, too, but common nouns. These nouns refer to classes of persons, places, or things that often possess certain characteristics that the fisherman imagines or wishes himself or his boat to have; not surprisingly, many reflect aspects of the fisherman's working environment. Of this group, about a third refers to classes of persons (*Ranger, Hustler, Dreamer, Vixen, Viking, Mermaid, Peasant, Pacific Belle*). Another third refers to classes of nonhuman, but mostly animate things such as fish, fowl, the sea, the heavens, and the elements (*Chickadee, Albatross, Eagle; Coho, Sockeye, Sea Trout, King Fish; Morning Star, Evening Star; Fog, Oregon Mist, Westerly, Pacific Breeze*). And another third refers to inanimate objects and abstract things (*Garnet, Brandywine, Mojo, Habitat, Conquest, Bounty, Ocean Pride, Renown, Legend, Moral, Quintessence, Wanderlust*).

Nouns and proper nouns aside, almost two-thirds of the local boat names refer to people, either to specific individuals, or to characters who possess particular qualities. Moreover, a boat's name, like a person's, is used repeatedly in the multiple legal and business transactions that attend the boat during its lifetime. At some of the local marine-related shops, a fisherman's account is kept in the name of his boat (probably so that shop owners can make easier claim against the fisherman's most valuable asset, should he fail to make good on long-unpaid debts). Also ordered according to boat name at local documentation offices and in government publications is certain information available to the public regarding each federally registered vessel. A change of boat name, further, requires legal procedures, and according to one person, must be announced in local newspapers, probably to notify would-be creditors.

Notably, however, a local fishing boat is known and discussed by name and not simply as so-and-so's boat. She has an identity of her own, irrespective of specific skippers and crew members. In fact, a skipper is likely to be identified by the boat he owns: "I don't know if you know Gordon or not, that has the *Metta Marie*." Similarly, crew members are often said to work on a specific boat rather than to work for a particular skipper: "Joe was a boat puller on the *Frank F* when we were buying shrimp" or "One of our sons used to fish on the *Lou-R*." (Perhaps to distinguish the boats from the humans after whom they are frequently named, in everyday parlance a boat's name is commonly preceded by "the." Thus, a boat named *Joyce* would be called "the *Joyce*." This practice is so much the rule that occasionally the officially registered name of a boat may include the "the.")

Fishermen's Folk Speech

When fishermen off the Oregon Coast say they are going "down the hill," they mean the boat is heading south from port, and "up the hill" indicates going north along the coastline. If they should see two red warning flags flying at the harbor mouth to warn of the approach of a storm, they might refer to them as "Maggie's drawers," while any obstruction that fouls or snags a fishing line is labeled a "rock bass." The following words and phrases are some of the occupational terms that were collected from commercial fishermen and charter boat operators in Coos Bay by Nancy Lorence (RVMA, Fall 1967).

Flopper stopper: Weighted flat surfaces (iron) hung from poles on boats (commercial only) put out in the water when the ocean is rough to stabilize the boat—look somewhat like airplane wings.

Girde: Either hand or powered—the winch that is used to pull in the metal line [to nets or seines]—keeps the line from getting tangled.

Sea sled: A weighted board attached to the middle of a drag net to keep the net down under water.

Iron mike: Automatic pilot—on commercial boats.

Mickey Mouse: Citizens band (vs. marine ship-to-shore radios); so called because it is only good for short distances.

Balls of tuna: Means the same as a school of tuna; "ball" is used because when a school of tuna is found, the boat goes around the school, usually in a circle of a quarter- to a half-mile in circumference. If a boat goes through the school the tuna, normally caught at the surface, go down.

Hump of tuna: A hump is 100 tuna; two humps are 200, etc.

Swivelneck: Term applied to the boatman, probably because he has to turn his head in all directions to see that people's lines are baited.

Shaker: Salmon too small to keep; must be shaken off the line; less than 20 inches.

Sneaker: An extra large breaker which breaks over the stern of a boat; it doesn't matter if the operator of the boat saw it coming and couldn't outrun it or if he didn't see it coming. Sneakers are most common when crossing the bar.

Lost Treasures

One of the storytelling traditions that the Euro-Americans brought with them to the Oregon Country centers on the finding of "lost treasure" —either raw gold or silver ore to be mined, or treasure already coveniently packaged as money, and hidden away or lost somewhere, waiting to be found. Not to put too heavy an emphasis on it, it is a tradition that links us to the earliest episodes in American history, in the age of Columbus and the gold-mad *conquistadors*. For the Indians of Oregon, for whom nothing really treasurable in nature was "lost" and who therefore didn't need stories about hidden wealth, the antics of early prospectors and treasure-seekers must have been puzzling and, at least at first, amusing. Talking to Isabel Kelly in Burns in the 1930s, a Northern Paiute elder named Sam Wata offered his own wry explanation of the natural origins of silver in his country—and of its bedazzling effect on whites: "The little streams of spring water are the places from which silver money comes. It comes from the Sun shining on the water. The first white man came to this land and saw that silver, but he lost himself and didn't get to it. Finally white people found this place, and they came this way looking for the silver." (Isabel Kelly, "Northern Paiute Tales," p. 438)

"Interior of Mine" by Jim Wood, Ashwood, Oregon.

The Neahkanie Mountain Treasure

The Neahkanie Treasure tradition is to coastal Oregon what the Lost Blue Bucket Mine legend is to Eastern Oregon—in each case a long-lived and persistent story about "misplaced" gold that is rich in historical implications and vividly set in a particular landscape. Unlike the unmapped site of the Blue Bucket Mine, of course, Neahkanie Mountain is a conspicuous landmark on the coast north of Tillamook, the sort of imposing natural feature that seems to draw tales of treasure and violence like a magnet. The following stories between them pretty much cover the main elements of the Neahkanie tradition in oral and written tradition; they exemplify how a story can vary from teller to teller. The best general account of Neahkanie lore, including stories of latter-day attempts to find the treasure that are almost as wild as the legends themselves, is by Ruby El Hult, "The Many Mysteries at Neahkanie," in *Lost Mines and Treasures of the Pacific Northwest* .

The Pirates at Neahkanie

When I was young, I remember my favorite bedtime story was about the pirates at Neahkanie. If I remember it correctly, it went something like this. Long ago, there was a queen's royal ship sailing home to England and it was full of jewels and gold. The ship was suddenly attacked by a ship of pirates. They were travelling along what is now known as the Oregon Coast. They quickly headed for shore and landed, trying to flee from the pirates. They were successful in burying the treasure but were captured. When the sailors refused to betray their mother country by telling of the whereabouts of the treasure, they were killed, one by one. And to this day the treasure remains buried and no one has been able to find it.

There is another part of the story that is familar to me, but I did not hear it in my bedtime story because my mother was probably afraid of frightening me. The segment that I didn't hear 'til later was that the sailors' ghosts still guard the treasure, and anyone who finds it will be haunted 'til death, which probably would come quickly. I think this is why no one from this area actively looks for the treasure. I think everyone in this area believes that there is a treasure but would just as soon leave well enough alone. Those archaeologists come here and say that there is no treasure but just the remnants of an ancient civilization. I think they're mistaken. (Recorded in March 1973 by Joanie Bayless, Randall V. Mills Archive, teller unknown.)

Buried Treasure from a Spanish Galleon

Around 1750 a Spanish galleon was sailing north from a South American port. They were thought to have gold. They were pursued by pirate ships and the primitive U.S. Navy. [?!] The galleon reached the coastline of what is now Oregon. They ran into a storm and were blown ashore at Cape Foulweather which is the shores of Mount Neahkanie. Sailors were able to get ashore, and I've heard that they struggled to bring ashore treasures. The Indians which inhabited this area attacked, and they were all killed.

Stories that have been handed down around here say that there is a map of the whereabouts of the buried treasure. There are no authentic reasons for this map as far as I can see, but the directions I've heard go something like this. Travel one mile east of the beach at Neahkanie to an enormous fir tree, then two hundred yards south to a big rock. . . .

I've heard these stories since I've lived in this area. Every native is familiar with the legend. At first I didn't believe them, but now I do. My children are as familiar with the tales as I am, although their tales involve more superstitions. . . .

I do actually believe that there is a treasure. I know the area well. Neahkanie is easy to see from the ocean, and there is a lot of truth to the facts that ships can be caught in the southerly drift off the coast. I would even be tempted to dig for the treasure, but for some reason I never have. I think it's because I would rather think about it, and I don't want to be disappointed. (Recorded by Joanie Bayless in March 1973 from a second unnamed informant: Randall V. Mills Archive.)

An Indian Account

When I first came here 51 years ago [in 1843]. . . there was beeswax among the Indians from the Salmon River on the south to the Columbia River on the north. They did not know what it was, using it for lights and leaky canvas. They said it came from a wreck near the mouth of the Nehalem River. . . .

In talking with the Indians from that place often they would tell us of the wreck, and of the vessel that brought up the gold and silver coin, and carried it up Necanny Mountain, and would refer us to some very old Indians, who never came to Clatsop. . . . Solomon H. Smith and myself concluded we would go down and buy the drugs [from an 1848 wreck at the mouth of the Nehalem River] and find out what we could from the old Indians about the wax and money vessels. . . . All they could tell us was that long before they were born, the wax vessel was lost on the spit, and another anchored near the shore, and some people brought a chest up on Necanny Mountain and carried sacks of money and put them in the chest and killed a man, and put him also in the chest. Afterward they marked a stone, or very large rock, rolled it on the chest, and went back to the ship and sailed away.

We took an Indian, went to the mountain to look for the coin, but found no sign of a marked rock, so concluded that it was only Indian tradition and not reliable. (John Hobson, account of 1894, in Ruby El Hult, *Lost Mines and Treasures*, pp. 16-17.)

The Treasure Ship

A ship dropped anchor as she approached land and sent a boat ashore with several men and a large chest or box. The box was taken up on the southwest face of the mountain above the road [the modern highway] and there buried. And some say a man was then killed, and buried with the chest. Then some characters were placed on a large stone, which was placed on the spot of burial, and the men then returned to the vessel, when she was put again to sea. . . . The treasure ship did not become a wreck. (Silas B. Smith, summary of Clatsop Indian accounts in "Early Wrecks on the Oregon Coast," excerpted in Hult, p. 17.)

A Portuguese Shipwreck

A ship came ashore in distress, in need of repairs, and was beached. A storm broke and smashed the ship. We people ran and hid on top of Neahkanie behind the rocks. The people in the boat had curly hair and in later years we called them Portuguese. We saw them lower with ropes a very heavy box. This box was lowered into a hole right on the beach beside the ship. It was too heavy to carry anywhere. When it was well down they covered the hole with rocks. No one was killed over the box. (Clatsop Indian account recorded by August Hildebrand of Astoria in 1926, Hult, p. 18. [Compare the Clatsop oral-history account of their first ship sighting in "First Contacts," p. 26.])

The Lost Blue Bucket Mine

There was certainly never a "mine," and even the memorable "blue bucket" that has given this celebrated story its title may be an invention—but the story of how children found some gold nuggets along the way of the calamitous Meek Cut-off wagon train of 1845 has become a staple part of Oregon's story about itself. Beyond the appeal of neglected gold *somewhere* between the High Desert and Crooked River, the versions of the Blue Bucket tradition catch our fancy with ironic images of treasure found—and disregarded—by small children while the grownups of a lost emigrant train are trying desperately to find their way to the durable treasure of the Willamette Valley. For a very thorough and readable account of the Meek Cut-off and its disasters, see Keith Clark and Lowell Tiller, *The Terrible Trail: The Meek Cutoff, 1845.* The first version given below is full of historical errors (the date of the wagon train, for example), but it typifies how the story lives on through reinvention in oral tradition.

Version 1

In approximately 1850 a wagon train from Missouri was en route to the Pacific Coast of Oregon. When they reached Juntura, Oregon, they had a feud over which route to take. They couldn't come to a compromise and as a result the train was split in three: one following the Columbia River, one going south along the Applegate Trail, and one going through the center of Oregon.

The train going through the center of Oregon ran out of water somewhere between Glass Mountain and Wagon Wheel Mountain, and made camp. Members of the train, even the children, spiraled out in search of water. Two brothers, their sister, and her boyfriend went north of the camp and found many animal bones within a small area. They thought there may have been a water hole that had dried up, and they began digging. The boys dug about ten feet into the earth and found a small spring. While they were digging, the girl sat at the top of the dirt pile playing in the dirt and found small golden nuggets. She thought they were pretty so she stuck them in her pocket. They had carried a small blue bucket with them and left it on a tree above the spring as a marker and went back to the train.

Other members of the train had found a larger spring by the time they had returned, and the children's spring was forgotten.

The train then went northwest to Bear Creek and up to the Astoria area [in fact, to The Dalles], where they reunited with the members of the original train. By this time they had discovered that the nuggets the girl was carrying were gold, but they [the brothers] had also heard of the abundant amount of gold in California and set out to make their fortune.

Several years later the brothers decided to come back to Oregon to find their Blue Bucket Mine. They found the general vicinity but were unable to find the exact area because of landslides. Up until this time there have been many searches for the mine, but none has been successful. (Recorded by Jan Frederick in 1970, teller unnamed, in Randall V. Mills Archive, first published in Suzi Jones, *Oregon Folklore*, pp. 35-36.)

Version 2

[My] mother, Mrs. L.W. Loughary (maiden name, Eliza Simpson) was a member of that ill-fated immigrant train which Stephen Meek led astray in 1845.

. . . She well remembers when the train was lost on the Meek "cut-off," and the irate disfavor under which Meek fell. She distinctly remembers how one of the older girls of the party picked up shining nuggets, carrying them in her apron and upon reaching the wagons, placed them in a blue bucket—a wooden bucket painted blue on the outside. They were not found in a stream, but taken from a mound of earth.

Those nuggets were examined by members of the train who were uncertain as to their quality or value.

The train came to a stream which my mother now thinks was Crooked River. The stream was too deep to ford; the oxen were forced to swim across. A rope crossing was improvised and by this means the belongings of the train were taken across the river.

By some mishap one wagon bed was capsized in the stream and all the contents were lost, including the blue bucket with the nuggets. . . . My mother knows, by experience, that the blue bucket mine is not a legend . . . . (Letter to the Editor, the *Oregonian*, Feb. 27, n.d., by Mrs. J. L. Hushner, in WPA Folklore Project.)

Version 3

In either the year 1846 or 1847 a man by the name of Steve Meek started to pilot a train of emigrants from Snake River to the Willamette Valley. Somewhere on the Malheur they had trouble with Meek and fearing that the emigrants might do him bodily harm he deserted them.

This emigrant train divided into three divisions: one section passed through Silvies Valley in southern Grant County and they turned back toward the Columbia River and crossed at Spanish Gulch, and there is no doubt in my mind that here is where they found the gold.

I learned this from personal acquaintance with some of the people who were with the train. James Officer, grandfather of the Officers now living in Grant County, was in the train. He said that gold was found on the waters of the John Day.

The Durbins and Herins were in that train. They settled near Salem and their descendants are prominent people in Marion County. The emigrants were from Missouri and did not know what gold was. Durbin took some of the nuggets home with him. After gold was discovered in California a man from Californa happened to stop at the Durbin home. The nuggets were shown to him. He said they were gold. When Mrs. Durbin learned that it was gold she said she could have picked up a blue bucket full of it. Noah Herin, a member of the train, lived near Woodburn in Marion County. He said that when they pulled out of the gulch where the gold was found they could see Mt. Hood.

I am a native of Oregon 67 years of age and had the acquaintance of a great many of the old pioneers. The Blue Bucket story is no myth. (George Irvin of Monument, in the *Blue Mountain Eagle*, April 25, 1919 [WPA Folklore Project].)

Version 4

Both my father, W.J. Herren, and my mother were members of the company that Steve Meek undertook to pilot from the crossing of Snake River to The Dalles in 1845.

Meek had trapped on the upper Deschutes at what was known as the Beaver Meadows two seasons, and claimed that he had been over the route from there to The Dalles and also from there to Boise and that he could take them over a much better route than the one over the Blue Mountains by way of the Grande Ronde Valley. He induced some 30 or 40 families [there were, in fact, 200 wagons] and their outfits to let him guide them over the route that he described, which was by way of the Malheur and Harney lakes and then across the mountains to the Deschutes and down on the west side of it to The Dalles.

But traveling over a mountainous country with a saddle horse proved to be quite different from traveling with heavily loaded wagons and ox-teams. They got along all right until they reached the foot of the mountains, where they found the country so rough and the hills so steep that they could not negotiate them. Meek tried to make it up several tributaries of the south Malheur, but each time had to turn back, which caused them to lose valuable time, and as their provisions were getting quite low they became very much exasperated at Meek and finally served him notice that unless he got them out of there within a certain length of time his life would not be worth very much. He became alarmed and skipped out and left them to their fate.

Several of the young men that had saddle horses scouted the country over and finally found a ridge that led to the summit of the mountain. They concluded that if they could once get their outfits up on this ridge they could make it over the mountains. By hitching ten and sometimes twelve yoke of oxen at one time to a wagon they finally succeeded in getting them up onto the divide.

There was no water on the divide so they had to make a dry camp. The captain of the company told all of the young people who had saddle horses to take buckets and go hunt for water. My father, who was then 23 years old, and his sister, who afterwards became the wife of William Wallace, took their old blue wooden buckets and started out to find water.

They finally found a dry creek bed which they followed until they found a place where a little water was seeping through the gravel, and while my father was digging for water his sister saw something bright and picked it up.

The account given me states that they found two good-sized lumps or nuggets, and that there were many fine particles in the gravel. He was quite sure that it was gold at the time, and when he arrived at camp he showed it to some of the older men, who told him that if it was gold it would be malleable. So one of them took a hammer and hammered both pieces out flat into a saucer-shaped disc.

He had a tool chest with a secret drawer in it. He hid the gold in the chest, therefore no one but the members of my family ever knew what become of it. I well remember the old tool chest and its secret drawer. . . .

My people have always hoped that some member of the family would eventually find the place where the gold was discovered, and many years ago my father gave me an old leather-bound memorandum book, with maps and diagrams showing the water courses and giving a general description of the country . . . . My father was among the first to mine on Feather River in California. He kept the gold found in the Blue Mountains and took it to California with him and bought provisions with it at Sacramento in 1849.

I once did some prospecting in the immediate vicinity of where the gold was found. I found some fine gold, but it was late in the fall and the ground froze so that I had to give it up. I intended to go back some time and try it over, but have never done so . . . .

The account given me stated that the place where the gold was found was nearly two miles from camp in a northerly direction, and that when they got back to camp they found that others had found water in plenty much nearer than where they obtained theirs, so none of them went back to the place and my father and his sister were undoubtedly the only members of the party that ever saw where it came from. (Letter to the Editor, the *Oregonian*, in March 4, n.d., by W.H. Herren of Heppner, from WPA Folklore Project.)

The Treasure at Columbia City

Judging from its ornate style, this tale is a "literary" retelling, but in outline, and in its narrative details—the mutiny, the quarrel of the greedy mutineers, the supernatural elements, the curse on the Spanish plunder—it seems to be based on a traditional "lost treasure" tale. Columbia City is just north of St. Helens, on the Columbia River; "Hez Copler's farm" has not been identified.—Charles M. Skinner, *Myths and Legends of Our Own Land*, pp. 292-293.

A Spanish bark, one day in 1841, put in for water off the spot where Columbia City, Oregon, now stands. She had a rough crew on board, and it had been necessary for her officers to watch the men closely from the time the latter discovered that she was carrying a costly cargo. Hardly had the anchor-chains run out before the sailors fell upon the captain, killed him, seized all of the value that they could gather, and took it to the shore.

What happened after that is not clear, but it is probable that in a quarrel, arising over the demands of each man to have most of the plunder, several were slain. Indians were troublesome, likewise, so that it was thought best to put most of the goods into the ground, and this was done on the tract known as Hez Copler's farm.

Hardly was the task completed before the Indians appeared in large numbers and set up their tepees, showing that they meant to remain. The mutineers rowed back to the ship, and, after vainly waiting for several days for a chance to go on shore again, sailed away.

Two years of wandering, fighting, and carousing ensued before the remnant of the crew returned to Oregon. The Indians were gone, and an earnest search was made for the money—but in vain. It was as if the ground had never been disturbed. The man who had supervised its burial was present until the mutineers went back to their boats, when it was discovered that he was mysteriously missing.

More than forty years after these events a meeting of Spiritualists was held in Columbia City, and a medium announced that she had received a revelation of the exact spot where the goods had been concealed. A company went to the place, and, after a search of several days, found, under a foot of soil, a quantity of broken stone. While throwing out these fragments one of the party fell dead. The spirit of the murdered captain had claimed him, the medium explained.

So great was the fright caused by this accident that the search was again abandoned until March 1890, when another party resumed the digging, and after taking out the remainder of the stone they came upon a number of human skeletons. During the examination of the relics—possibly the bones of mutineers who had been killed in the fight on shore—a man fell into a fit of raving madness, and again the search was abandoned, for it was now said that an immutable curse rests on the treasure.

Gold Found and Lost Near Canyon City

One of the recurring motifs of treasure stories is the theme of how a vein or outcropping of precious metal was found and then lost past finding, or found without recognition, and never relocated—as in these two matter-of-fact tales collected by Sandra Altman from Mr. J.J. Abbott, a retired editor from Canyon City (RVMA). The general location of these two lost discoveries is, of course, in the "Blue Bucket Mine" country.

In 1930 the Hines Lumber people were at work on their big sawmill at Burns. A highway crew was busy building the Canyon City-Burns route, and traffic was temporarily detoured to the west, toward Izee. The millwright for the new Hines mill spent the day at Burns and got a late start back to Canyon City. On his way back, he got to some point on Miller Mountain, when he got out of his car to rest. Before lying down, he tossed some pretty rocks into his car. Several weeks later he cleaned out his car, and a passerby looked at his rocks, then exclaimed, "Man, that's gold!" It was. The millwright could not remember where he had picked up the rocks.

Early in March 1915, Chuck McCorkle rented a horse and lit out for Miller Mountain, south of Canyon City. The snow was going off, the landscape dappled by patches of it all around. He sat down on a big quartz boulder to eat lunch. More by instinct than design, he broke off several pieces of the dirt-covered boulder and pocketed them. Days later he got them out, washed them, and found rich, gold-filled ore. He was not able to retrace his trail and could not locate the spot nor the boulder.

Jim Polk Leads a Gold Expedition

The late John Campbell of Madras liked to tell episodes from his boyhood
adventure in search of gold located, according to Indian lore, in the rugged
"Separation Creek" region west of the South Sister. The story, which like other
Oregon treasure stories features Indians, supernatural and uncanny elements, and a
curse, but in an unusual combination, has been "reassembled" by Jarold Ramsey
and given a historical and folkloric context in "John Campbell's Adventure and the
Ecology of Story," pp. 46-65.

One time—it was about 1906, so I was maybe 18—I went off with a neighbor, a widower named Frank Stangland and an old Wasco Indian named Jim
Polk, on a wild goose chase into the rough country west of the Sisters. Old Jim
had told us that he knew where some of his people had found gold nuggets on
"Quartz Creek," so right after harvest we took off on horseback to find it.

Jim showed us the old Indian trails on both sides of the Cascade crest, and
told us about the "Stick Indians" who lived up there, and could read your
mind as you passed through their country, and liked to lead you astray with
bird-songs if they could. One time, when Frank and I were about to shoot an
elk-calf for a little "camp meat" out of season, Jim told us not to—said the
Ranger down in McKenzie Bridge would somehow know about it and arrest
us. (Sure enough, when we stopped there for supplies on our way home, the
Ranger told us he was sure glad we hadn't killed that calf!)

We kept on south, and finally broke over the high saddle between the Middle
and North Sister—off to the west and south somewhere, according to Jim, was
Quartz Creek, and gold. But that night while we were in camp, a little early
snowstorm blew up, and the next morning, Jim announced that he was not
taking us any further. Said the storm had reminded him of something that
happened years before to some of his people when they were caught in this
country by an early blizzard while hunting. The snow trapped them in a basin,
and only a few survived—some people said because they ate human flesh. Bad
medicine, he said.

So, instead of going down into that country to look for the gold, we turned
around and came home. As we crossed over the Divide for the last time and
headed down toward the Agency, old Jim, he looked back up at where we'd
been, and said, "Good—the old ones didn't want us up there anyway."

Monsters,
Snakes,
Fabulous
Creatures

The twist of imagination that creates and continues stories about monsters and freaks of nature is apparently universal, and for the most part the monstrous creatures of Oregon Indian tradition and those of Euro-American folklore are close cousins, part of the "unnatural natural history" that as humans we seem to need to supplement the known animal kingdom. Indeed, Indian and Anglo traditions have borrowed from each other on this theme: our modern fascination with "Bigfoot" is accentuated by Native accounts of humanoid *sasquatches* lurking in high-timber country; and when the Nez Perces and the Kalapuyas encountered French-Canadian trappers early in the last century and from them heard French Provençal folk tales about seven-headed dragons, they felt right at home with such creatures and took them into their own repertories. In all folk traditions, monsters tend to be autocthonous creatures; that is, they come out of a particular place and identify it, as the Nez Perce Swallowing Monster literally identifies Nez Perce country (they say you can still see parts of him around Kamiah, Idaho) and as the Sidehill Gouger "signifies" the rugged hill country east of John Day.

"Indian Petroglyphs on rocks near The Dalles, Oregon." Photograph by B.C. Markham.

Coyote and the Swallowing Monster

Even in translation, in silent print, most Native American oral narratives convey a sense of *performability*, with dialogue and scenes and episodes ready-made for the voice and gestures of a skilled storyteller. "Coyote and the Swallowing Monster" is rich in such dramatic cues: the comically unequal sucking contest between Coyote and the Monster, to take just one example. Coyote's forgetfulness in leaving the Nez Perce out of his transformation of the Monster's corpse, and his ingenious correction of the error by giving the Nez Perce the bloody washwater, is typical of his career as Trickster and fixer-up of reality. With such a mythic sponsor, no wonder the world is other than perfect! —and yet for the Nez Perce there is much merit in being blessed by the Monster's blood.—Told by Wayi'latpu in Nez Perce Sahaptin to her son Archie Phinney, in Culdesac, Idaho, in 1929/30: Phinney, *Nez Perce Texts*, pp. 26-29.

Coyote was building a fish-ladder by tearing down the waterfall at Celilo, so that salmon could go upstream for people to catch. He was busily engaged at this when someone shouted to him. "Why are you bothering with that? All the people are gone; the monster has done for them."—"Well," said Coyote to himself, "then I'll stop doing this, because I was doing it for the people, and now I'll go along too."

From there he went along upstream, by the way of the Salmon River country. Going along he stepped on the leg of a meadowlark and broke it. The meadowlark in a temper shouted, "*limá, limá, limá,* what a chance of finding people you have, going along!" Coyote then asked, "My aunt! Please inform me, afterwards I will make you a leg of brush-wood." So the meadowlark told him, "Already all the people have been swallowed by the monster." Coyote then replied, "Yes, that is where I, too, am going."

From there he traveled on. Along the way he took a good bath, saying to himself, "Lest I make myself repulsive to his taste," and then he dressed himself all up, "Lest he will vomit me up or spit me out." There he tied himself with rope to three mountains. From there he came along up and over ridges. Suddenly, behold, he saw a great head. He quickly hid himself in the grass and gazed at it. Never before in his life had he seen anything like it; never such a large thing—away off somewhere melting into the horizon was its gigantic body.

Now then that Coyote shouted to him, "Oh Monster, we are going to inhale each other!" The big eyes of the monster roved around looking all over for Coyote but did not find him, because Coyote's body was painted with clay to achieve a perfect protective coloring in the grass. Coyote had on his back a pack consisting of five stone knives, some pure pitch, and a flint fire-making set. Presently Coyote shook the grass to and fro and shouted again, "Monster! We are going to inhale each other!" Suddenly the monster saw the swaying grass and replied, "Oh, you Coyote, you swallow me first, then; you inhale first." Now Coyote tried. Powerfully and noisily he drew in his breath and the great monster just swayed and quivered. Then Coyote said, "Now you inhale me, for already you have swallowed all the people, so swallow me too lest I become lonely."

Now the Monster inhaled like a mighty wind. He carried Coyote along just like that, but as Coyote went he left along the way great camas roots and great serviceberries, saying, "Here the people will find them and will be glad, for only a short time away is the coming of the human race." There he almost got caught on one of the ropes, but he quickly cut it with his knife. Thus he dashed right into the monster's mouth.

From there he walked along down the throat of the Monster. Along the way he saw bones scattered about and he thought to himself, "It is to be seen that many people have been dying." As he went along he saw some boys and he said to them, "Where is his heart? Come along and show me!" Then, as they were all going along, the bear rushed out furiously at him. "So!" Coyote said to him, "You make yourself ferocious only to me," and he kicked the bear on the nose. As they were going along the rattlesnake bristled at him in fury. "So! only towards me you are vicious—we are nothing but dung." Then he kicked the rattlesnake on the head and flattened it out for him. Going on he met the brown bear, who greeted him, "I see he [the Monster] selected you for the last."—"So! I'd like to see you save your people. . . ."

Thus all along the people hailed him and stopped him. He told the boys, "Pick up some wood." Here his . . . friend fox hailed him from the side, "He's such a dangerous fellow, the Monster, what are you going to do to him?"—"So!" replied Coyote. "You too hurry along and look for wood."

Presently Coyote arrived at the heart, and he cut slabs of fat and threw them to the people. "Imagine you being hungry under such conditions—grease your mouths with this." And now Coyote started a fire with his flint, and shortly smoke drifted up through the Monster's nose, ears, eyes, and anus. Now the Monster said, "Oh you Coyote, that's why I was afraid of you. Oh you Coyote, let me cast you out."

And Coyote replied, "Yes, and later let it be said, 'He who was cast out is officiating in the distribution of salmon.'"—"Well, then, go out through the nose." Coyote replied, "And will not they say the same?" And the Monster said, "Well, then, go out through the ears," to which Coyote replied, "And let it be said, 'Here is ear-wax officiating in the distribution of food.'"—"*Hn, hn, hn,* oh you Coyote! That is why I feared you; then go out through the anus," and Coyote replied, "And let people say, 'Feces are officiating in the distribution of food'."

There was his fire still burning near the heart and now the Monster began to writhe in pain and Coyote began cutting away on the heart, whereupon very shortly he broke the stone knife. Immediately he took another and in a short time this one broke also, and Coyote said to all the people, "Gather up all the bones and carry them to the eyes, ears, mouth, and anus; pile them up and when he falls dead kick all the bones outside." Then again with another knife he began cutting away at the heart. The third knife he broke and the fourth, leaving only one more. He told the people, "All right, get yourselves ready because as soon as he falls dead each one will go to the opening most convenient. Take the old women and old men close to the openings so that they may get out easily."

Now the heart hung by only a very small piece of muscle and Coyote was cutting away on it with his last stone knife. The Monster's heart was still barely hanging when his last knife broke, whereupon Coyote threw himself on the heart and hung on, just barely tearing it loose with his hands. In his death convulsions the Monster opened all the openings of his body and now the people kicked the bones outside and went on out. Coyote, too, went on out. Here now the Monster fell dead and now the anus began to close. But there was a muskrat still inside. Just as the anus closed he squeezed out, barely getting his body through, but alas! his tail was caught; he pulled, and it was bare when he pulled it out; all the tail-hair peeled right off. Coyote scolded him, "Now what were you doing; you had to think up something to do at the last moment. You're always behind in everything." Then he told the people, "Gather up all the bones and arrange them well." They did this, whereupon Coyote added, "Now we are going to carve the Monster."

Coyote then smeared blood on his hands, sprinkled this blood on the bones, and suddenly there came to life again all those who had died while inside the Monster. They carved the great Monster and now Coyote began dealing out portions of the body to various parts of the country all over the land; toward the sunrise, toward the sunset, toward the warmth, toward the cold, and by that act destining and forenaming the various peoples; Coeur d'Alene, Cayuse, Pend Oreilles, Flathead, Blackfeet, Crow, Sioux, et al. He consumed the entire body of the Monster in this distribution to various lands far and wide.

And now Fox came up and said to Coyote, "What is the meaning of this, Coyote? You have distributed all of the body to faraway lands but have given yourself nothing for this immediate territory."—"Well," snorted Coyote, "and did you tell me that before? Why didn't you tell me that a while ago before it was too late? I was engrossed to the exclusion of thinking. You should have told me that in the first place."

And he turned to the people and said, "Bring me water with which to wash my hands." They brought him water and he washed his hands and now with the bloody washwater he sprinkled the local regions, saying, "You [Nez Perce] may be little people but you will be powerful. Even though you will be little people because I have deprived you, nevertheless you will be very, very manly. Only a short time away is the coming of the human race."

Sea Serpent in the Illinois River

This account of a sea serpent "from the Diary of John Fry" is included in writer Arthur Dorn's collection of "Folklore of the Lower Rogue" for the WPA Oregon Folklore Project. John Fry (1861-1946) was raised in the Rogue River Canyon area of Southwestern Oregon. The son of an Indian woman and Abraham Fry who, along with his brother, James, had settled as miners along the lower Illinois in the late 1860s, John gained a local reputation as a storyteller. He was known for spinning his own yarns in addition to telling tales of the better known Rogue River *münchhausen*, Hathaway Jones (Stephen Dow Beckham, ed., *Tall Tales from Rogue River: The Yarns of Hathaway Jones*, pp. 18-19). John Fry's tale of a sea serpent who entered the Rogue and Illinois rivers during high water is evidence of his gifts as an inventive storyteller, and it is only one of many stories of sea and lake monsters to be found in Oregon.

Back during the winter of '81 the rivers were high most of the time for several weeks, due to torrential rains and little snow on the mountains. Fine cedar trees frequently came down the Illinois from Lawson Creek and other sections where they were dislodged by high winds and land slides. These logs were good for fence posts, pickets, split boards, and shakes, so John, helped by the other men of the family, made it a practice to salvage as many of them as possible. This was accomplished with many difficulties, except when the Rogue raised high enough to back up the Illinois, at which times there would be half a mile of almost still water up past the Fry ranch.

Both rivers could be seen from the Fry house where some member of the family was usually on watch with field glasses. One morning John had just finished half-soling his shoes and arming them with long needle-sharp calks when someone noticed a big log drifting around in the backwater of the Illinois. Immediately several of the menfolk hurried down to the river, manned their boat, and rowed out to the log.

They pulled the boat quite close when John, wishing to try out his new calks, leaped out of the boat onto the log. The sharp calks sank in, but the log, or what had appeared to be a log, gave a lurch and started upstream with a rush, throwing John into the river from which they managed to rescue him. Feeling a bit nervous, they decided to go to the house for the day. The creature was fully four feet thick, and they had seen at least one hundred feet of its body.

That night one of their cows disappeared, and the next night they lost a horse. Soon word came that stock was missing all along the river. One rancher had twelve big fat hogs in a pen and lost them all during one night, but he always suspicioned one of his neighbors. The following winter it came back, and one day when the sun happened to be shining, John saw it lying on a gravel bar. It was about two hundred feet long, and had long jaws full of big teeth. Being well out of the way, he took a shot at its head with his rifle, but the bullet ricocheted as if it had hit a rock, and the serpent merely raised up its head and looked around.

The next day a prospector who had been panning along the river bars disappeared, and the folk all around became uneasy. John said the serpent's body was a kind of brownish color, but its neck and head were blue with big red and yellow spots, while its eyes were the color of dull slate. Extending above the top of its head there was a horn about five feet long. It looked at John and stuck out its tongue just like ordinary snakes, only its tongue was fully ten feet long. As far as he could see it had no poison fangs, but his mind was more concerned about running than observing.

The next winter when the water was high it came up the river again. Or if it was not the same serpent it was one just like it. It became very bold and noisy. Its voice was something like a whistling buoy, only louder and more mournful, and it swallowed all stock which came near the river. The old timers held a pow wow. They had all taken shots at it without effect. While they were talking the thing was bellowing and splashing down in the river.

They discussed all sorts of plans, and at last an old fellow from Texas spoke up. He owned two old long horn oxen which he had driven across the plains from the states, one of which had horns eight feet long and sharp as dirks. He agreed to drive the old bull down where the serpent was making dreadful noises. He thought the old bull's horns would make the durned critter sick to the stomach, if they did not jab holes in its belly.

The moment the ox came out onto the bar seventy-five feet of snake struck and caught him. Swallowed him, too. All the rest of that night it threshed around and created a terrible din. When daylight came John slipped down through the brush where he could not be seen and took a peek at the varmint.

The serpent had its mouth open and was going through all manner of contortions. It had swallowed the old longhorn, but its horns were too long to go down its throat. A horn stuck out of each corner of the snake's mouth, which was only about eight or nine feet across, and the bull's head kept the serpent's mouth open. The old ox was still alive and bawling, and John felt very sorry for him.

That morning the sea serpent swam off down the river to the ocean, trying to either swallow the longhorn or spit him up, John was not sure which. And all the way to the sea the old bull kept bawling. The sea serpent has never been up the river since, and possibly it may be dead. One of the ox's horns was found on the beach near the mouth of the Rogue the following summer.

Several outside fishermen have from time to time reported seeing sea serpents near the Rogue River reef, and some think a colony of them live out there.

The Origin of Face Rock at Bandon

As told by Coquelle storyteller Susan Wasson Wolgamott, this story mythically accounts for a coastal landmark near Bandon, and features two widespread elements of Northwest Coast Indian culture: the practice of "potlatch" giveaways, and belief in an aquatic monster known as "See-atka" (sometimes spelled "Chetco"; see also "Tsiatko," p. 206).—Personal communication from Susan Wasson Wolgamott, 1992; all rights reserved.

Have you been down to Bandon? You know where Face Rock is? You've seen all the rocks out there? Many, many years ago, people had what they called potlatch. Potlatch was sort of a time when—lots of times you'd kind of show up other people—everything you have, you know, how much you have and everything, and you try to outdo other people, and really, up around the Columbia River, a lot of Indians could just destitute a person because everybody would have a potlatch and invite that same person to come, and he would have to give a potlatch back, and he'd have to give so many things away that he wouldn't have anything left.

There was a chief that lived over across the mountains, and his name was Siskiyou. And he'd invited the people along the coast of Oregon to potlatch, and it was such a big, fabulous potlatch we all said we don't have enough money, enough things, to give back, to give the kind of potlatch he did.

So four tribes went together, and they were going to have a big potlatch, all four of them together, and invite Siskiyou and his people. So they sent out the invitation, and they started in fishing, digging for clams, gathering mussels off the rocks and getting all ready for the potlatch.

And then one day a runner came in and said Siskiyou was coming, he was coming, all of his tribe and the people with him. So they started cooking. They had the big potlatch.

Siskiyou had a daughter named Iwanna and he was very fond of Iwanna. But out in the ocean is See-atka and he tried to get the people when they would get too far out in the ocean, and you had to be very careful of him. And everybody that lived along the ocean had a great deal of respect for the ocean, and they were very careful what they did.

But Iwanna came from across the mountains, and she didn't know anything about See-atka. So they had the potlatch, and everbody was eating, and she had with her little dog, and she had a little basket that was full of little raccoon babies that she had to play with. So she used to like to go down and run along the edge of the water and play, and they said, "Don't go out too far. He'll get you." But she didn't really have enough respect for the ocean.

So when everybody was feasting and having a good time she decided to go back down to the ocean, and the moon was shining and making a long streak down, and she thought it was so pretty, she took her little dog and her little basket of raccoons, and she went down to play. She put her little basket of baby raccoons down and she told her little dog to watch it, and she went out swimming. And first thing you know, See-atka tried to grab her. She had been told that his main power was in his eyes, so she didn't want to look at him. She looked away, and she looked up into the sky, and he kept trying to pull her out and get her to look into his eyes so he could capture her, but she just looked up at the sky.

Well, pretty soon the people noticed that she was gone, and they started searching for her. Well, her little dog tried to come out and catch her, and See-atka took him and threw him and the coons and they landed up on the beach. And if you go down there today, you'll see there she is in the rock—turned to rock looking up at sky. There you see the rock, that's her little dog, and the little baby coons in the basket are there. You go out and you see them at Bandon, down by the jetty, south of the jetty. Anyway, that's where Face Rock came from.

At'unaqa and the Forest Fire

Told by Hiram Smith in Wasco Chinookan to Dell Hymes at Warm Springs in 1956 and translated in measured verse according to Hymes's discovery that Chinookan oral literature is organized poetically (see also pp. 34 and 258), this eerie little story locates its hybrid monster realistically in a particular time (turn of this century) and place (upper Clackamas River). The *At'unaqa* is strictly a west-side-of-the-mountains monster; killing her has very modern consequences: a forest-fire that, as Hiram Smith notes drily, "the state of Oregon put out a lot of money" to extinguish!—Hymes, *"In Vain I Tried to Tell You": Essays in Native American Ethnopoetics*, pp. 188-189.

A long time ago,
      maybe fifty years ago,
            it attacked them.
They were staying on the Clackamas river;
      one fellow climbed a pine tree,
            then she saw them.
He pulled his arrows out,
      he shot her maybe three or four times:
            nothing to her,
            she bled through her mouth.
This thing looked like a coyote on the head,
      short ears;
            teeth like a wild hog's tusks,
            long white front claws,
               long hind legs,
               short front legs.
He *tried* to do everything to her,
      then he got afraid:
            only two arrows left.
Then he took one,
      he lit I don't know what,
            he put it on this arrow,
               then he shot the (arrow),
                  then it started to burn.
Again he did the same with one (arrow),
      then this (thing) went down into a canyon,
      there it burned.

This thing is what they call *At'unaqa*.
    Then it really started to burn.
        Then a lot of white men ran up,
           they put it out;
                the state of Oregon put out a lot of money.
There's nothing of that sort to be seen on our [eastern] side of the mountains.
Only on the other side could things of that sort be seen.
    A long time ago,
        maybe as much as fifty or sixty years ago,
           this thing was seen.

Bigfoots Galore

Tales of huge, hairy humanoid creatures have carried right on in the Northwest from Indian tradition to modern Anglo storytelling, and together constitute one of our region's distinctive contributions to American folklore. From George Gibbs's 1865 summary of native sasquatch beliefs and Clara Pearson's Tillamook "Wild Man" narratives to contemporary "sightings" near Estacada or Idanha, the elements of Bigfoot lore are remarkably constant. (For historical and scientific commentary, see Peter Byrne, *The Search for Bigfoot* and Grover Krantz, *Big Footprints.*)

Reports on the Sasquatch in the 1860s

One other race of beings I have classed separately, as they in particular are supposed to infest the earth, and do not appear to have been properly *Elip Tilikum* ["First People" in Chinook Jargon]. They are *Tsiatko* .... The belief in these beings is apparently universal among the different tribes, though there is a great discrepancy in their accounts of them.

By some, the *Tsiatko* are described as of gigantic size, their feet eighteen inches long and shaped like a bear's. They wear no clothes, but the body is covered with hair like that of a dog, only not so thick. Others describe them as of natural size and resembling men, except that they gibber and chatter, one *Tsiatko* making noise enough to represent a dozen persons. They are said to live in the mountain, in holes under ground, and to smell badly. They come down chiefly in the fishing season, at which time the Indians are excessively afraid of them. At the report of *Tsiatko* they all run for their houses, fire their guns and shout. They are visible only at night, at which time they approach the houses, steal salmon, carry off young girls and smother children. Their voices are like those of the owl, and they possess the power of charming, so that those hearing them become demented, or fall down in a swoon.

A Klickitat informed me that he believed they were not *Elip Tilikum*, or of the demon race, but came afterward, and that part of them are still men and dwell beyond the mountains where they hunt and are very hospitable, while the others steal at night. They are sometimes seen spearing fish themselves. Dr. Tolmie states that an Indian woman, married to a Canadian, who lived at Fort Vancouver, some twenty years ago, told a story of having been taken prisoner by the *Tsiatkos* and carried into the woods between the fort and the mill.

Lash-high and Swatiloh, a couple of Nisqually Indians, once pretended to have wounded a *Tsiatko* and tracked him by his blood for some distance. They also said that near where he was shot at a piece of mountain sheep blanket was found. Another Indian told Judge Ford that he had shot at and wounded one while carrying off a young girl and all the next day tracked him by his blood. At the approach of night he espied him sleeping against a tree, but the *Tsiatko* started and ran and he found it impossible to follow him. (George Gibbs, "Account of Indian Mythology in Oregon and Washington Territories [1865]," pp. 313-314.)

Wild Man Helps Himself to Elk Meat

The Tillamooks had an extensive array of stories about encounters with Sasquatch-like Wild Men and Wild Women. The Wild Women, probably related to the terrifying *Tsonoqua* child-eating monsters of North Coast cultures, were especially dangerous; their male counterparts seem to have been more easygoing, and killing one gave the killer a special spirit power, as in this story.—Told by Clara Pearson to Mrs. Elizabeth Jacobs, *Nehalem Tillamook Tales*, pp. 164-165.

There must have been a whole tribe of Wild Men because there were always some around.

A Nehalem man was not married. He would go hunting and permit the married people to have the meat he got. One summer he killed an elk, and he saved the blood. He took the elk's bladder and filled it with the blood. He made a camp near there. He placed that bladder of blood near his feet, lay down, and went to sleep. Wild Man came and helped himself to the elk meat. The man awoke. He was too warm, he was sweating. "Goodness! What is the matter?" he asked himself, looking about. It was like daylight, there was such a great fire burning there. Wild Man had placed large pieces of bark between the man and the fire so the man would not get too hot while he slept. You see, he treated that fellow well. When he spoke to him, Wild Man called the man "My nephew."

The man awoke to see Wild Man, that extremely large man, sitting by the fire. He had the fat ribs and front of that elk on a stick, roasting them by the fire. He said, "This is how I am getting to be. I am getting to be always on the bum, these days. I travel all over, I cannot find any elk. I took your elk, dear nephew, I took your elk meat." That man stretched himself, he had forgotten about that bag of blood. He kicked it with his feet, causing it to make a noise. Wild Man looked around; he said, "It sounds as if a storm were coming." (A Wild Man does not like to travel when it is storming.) When the man discovered that Wild Man was afraid of that noise, he kept kicking that bladder of blood. He said, "Yes, a storm is coming." Wild Man asked, "My dear nephew, would you tell me the best place to run to?" That man showed Wild Man a high bluff. "Over in that direction is a good place to run," he told him. Wild Man started out running. Soon the man heard him fall over that bluff.

The man did not go back to sleep any more that night. In the morning he went to look. There Wild Man lay, far down at the foot of the bluff. He went around by a better route and climbed down to see the body. He took Wild Man's quiver, he left Wild Man lying there. Then he became afraid, so he made ready and returned from the woods taking as much meat as he could carry. He would not permit anyone to bring in the rest of the elk. He said, "Wild Man found me. He jumped over the bluff." He too found all kinds of bones in that quiver. They must have been lucky pieces because elk would come down from the mountain for him, and only he could get sea lions on the rocks. That is a real happening.

Bigfoot, Our Contemporary

Oregon's latter-day contributions to the Bigfoot/Sasquatch tradition have been substantial, widespread (centering on Colton, the Upper Santiam drainage, the Coast Range east of Reedsport, and the Klamath Wilderness), and ongoing: there is even a "Bigfoot Research Project" operating out of the village of Mt. Hood.

Some girls down the Sixes River . . . was takin' out a church group, I believe it was a church group, it's been a long time. Anyway, they were camped out . . . [on] a big sandy bar out there alongside of this river and they were throwin' rocks . . . bigfoot was throwin' rocks at them and some of the rocks was upwards of 50 pounds, yet they was throwin' them clear across this river and that was probably another 50 yards. Well the girls, plus all the kids, encountered this situation three or four nights in a row and the girls went back again and all this took place in September. This was, I think, in '71 or '72. They could hear it and see it, I mean what man's gonna throw 50-pound rocks 50 yards? . . . But they were sleeping in a wagon-wheel type, you know, where everybody . . . had their feet in towards the fire. I don't know the distance they were from the fire, but bigfoot was placin' rocks right around them just exactly like he knew where he wanted every rock to go. And the girl said that, you know, she lost her concern after the fact that he was so accurate. He placed the rocks exactly where he wanted . . . he could have hit any one of them at any time, but he didn't . . . .

There were these cutters, they were workin' the El Dorado outfit . . . . They, ah, was up there cuttin' in the Olallie Forest which is about another 15 miles past Blue River. While they were up there cuttin', well they stopped for lunch 'n' happened to see a bigfoot . . . 'n' it, it scared the livin' hell out of them. Buckets and saws went in all directions, 'n', ah, they took off and I guess they were down in the canyon probably a mile and they just beat it right on out of there. They didn't even stop to pick up nothin', they just . . . and they didn't go back either. And you know, a man 45 years old isn't going to make this thing up. Sometimes you'd suspect this off of teenagers or your young kids. They're tired of an environment and just everyday things, so they create a situation, you know . . . if there's one squirrel there's five. But a man of this age, you know, he don't create nothin'. (Tony Romo, July 20, 1974, Dot's Cafe, Leaburg [RVMA, Heikes and McMullen, 1974].)

Four months ago [1974] they had a sighting down in Florence . . . . A schoolboy had reported seeing a creature within the Florence city limits. There's about a mile-long strip of brush that runs between Quince Street and the Siuslaw River, and the boy had been walking along the street on his way to school one morning, and had heard some noises in this patch of brush and turned to look and claimed that he saw bigfoot standing there watching him. (Mike Jay, July 18, 1974 [RVMA, Heikes and McMullen, 1974].)

We talked to at one time a lady who lives in Portland now who claims to have been brought up near Dallas, Oregon, and as a tiny girl, like about 10 or 11 years old, she claims to have actually observed the birth of one of these things. She saw one out in the woods and she, she being a girl was relatively unafraid and she just watched this creature and . . . she just simply observed the birth of a bigfoot baby and I think that it brought it over to the creek and washed it off. (Jack Sullivan, Colton [RVMA, Paul Axtell, 1973].)

There's a lot of stories about loggers seeing the bigfoot. I heard of guys logging up on Mt. Hood, up near the timberline; they were living out of this big strong cabin on the mountain and one day while they were out logging, away from the cabin, one of the guys spotted the bigfoot and shot and wounded him. They tried to follow as the bigfoot ran off but they lost him. That night when they were back at the cabin, there was all of a sudden a noise outside that set the dogs barking. The bigfoot burst in the door. He was on two feet with an angry ape face. He knocked the door down, broke up the furniture and killed one of the dogs. The men took off out the back door as he burst in. He was inside only a short time when he turned and ran out the way he came. (Anonymous [RVMA, Helen Rockey, 1974].)

The Man Who Lived with Thunder Bird

Much more amiable Native monsters are Thunder Bird and his wife, in Tillamook oral tradition. The Tillamooks were related linguistically and culturally to the Salish peoples of northern Puget Sound and Vancouver Island, and the Thunder Bird of this story is a cousin to the great thunder birds of Salish mythology and totem-pole art. The vividness with which the narrator skillfully works out the physical disproportion between the gigantic Thunder Birds and their human "grandson" is comparable to Swift's treatment of Gulliver's stay amongst the kindly Brobdignagian giants in *Gulliver's Travels.* —Told by Mrs. Clara Pearson to Elizabeth Jacobs, in *Nehalem Tillamook Tales,* pp. 167-171.

A man lived at Tillamook. In the wintertime he went far up small streams to spear steelhead. When he went fishing he wore a waterproof cape. It was fastened at the waist with a belt. He wore a spruce-root rain hat. It was held on tightly by an inner cedar-bark band. One day he put on his cape and his rain hat and started out. It was a bad day, hailing, and there was lightning. When the hail stopped he would go along and look for fish. He did not get any. Soon again there was thunder and lightning. He became angry, he said, "Confound it! That Thunder!" He cursed him. "I cannot get any fish," he said. "You

[Thunder] might just as well come along and take me with you." Then how it hailed! He stood under a tree for shelter. Now he saw a man, a huge man. The big man said, "You wanted me to come. I have come to take you home with me." He seized the man, he took off that cape, he hung all of the man's clothing on that fish pole, he put the spruce-root hat on the top, and stood the fish pole there against the tree. Thunder said, "I will take you home now. You will not remain long with me, I will bring you back within two days." The man thought, "Oh, that will not be bad. Two days are nothing." Thunder told him, "I will keep you under my wings. Do not ever open your eyes. Never try to peek out. I could not help it, if you were to open your eyes, I would drop you, I would be unable to save you." "All right," the man said. He obeyed because he was not just a young man, he was married and had two children.

Then they started. He heard the rushing sound Thunder made going. Presently Thunder said, "Be careful now, we are on a bad spot here, this is a windy spot." After a while Thunder arrived home with him. He told the man, "We are home now." The man looked. Thunder's home was on the ground just like any other place. He went in the house. There was a very big old woman. She was his wife, Thunder Bird's wife. They called the man, "Our grandchild." He looked like a child to them because they were so many times his size.

Every day Thunder Bird would say, "I am going out fishing." When he returned home he brought a whale. That was his fish. They had a big board in the house. Thunder would lay the whale on that and cut it into what was supposed to be small pieces. "There, grandchild, you go ahead and eat." The man could not even lift that knife, it was so big and heavy. So he made himself a knife that he could handle. Thunder said, "Bring it here. Bring me that little knife that you made." Thunder held it. "Oh, how can you see to make that little thing?" he asked. The knife slipped under Thunder's fingernail. He had to get a stick and dig it out from there. "Ah, you make very fine things!" he told the man. Those pieces of whale which were just a mouthful for Thunder or his wife made a whole meal for the man. He could cut it up with the knife he had made himself. "Ah, our grandchild is such a small eater," Thunder and his wife would say. They watched him carefully as if he were really a child. "Do not run around near the bank, you might fall over." "Do not go far away, you might become lost." They were always warning him in that manner.

After a while the man became sick of having nothing but whale meat. He thought, "I wonder what may be in this water over here? I am going to sneak away." He went over by the bank. He saw quantities of fish. (Thunder had never bothered with them because they were too small to interest him.) The man made a fish pole for himself. From whale bones he made a spear. Old Woman Thunder asked him, "What are you making?" He answered, "I am making a fish pole and I am making a spear. I am going to spear fish." She said, "Bring that thing you are making here." He took it to her. "Oh, you are so cute! How can you manage to make things so tiny? My goodness! You who are so little know so much about building things." (Nevertheless he was almost an old man.)

Already his two days were past. Thunder was out fishing. The man thought, "My! It is past two days already. Thunder said I would stay only two days. Oh! I would like to get home." The old woman said to him, "Why grandchild! Have you become homesick? You have not remained very long with us." Then the old woman told him, "Your grandpa will take you home inside of two days. That is two of your years." He answered, "Oh! That is a long time." "No, that is not very long, grandchild. For just two days we would like to have you with us." He went out then to spear fish. He was tired of whale meat.

He speared a great many fish, perhaps twenty. "My, that is a lot!" he said to himself. He fixed a string, he strung those fish on it, he dragged them home. He called out, "Oh! Grandma! I speared all these fish out here." She came outside. "Why, how can you hit those little fish?" Then she took out her big clam shell in which she drank her soup. She put those twenty fish in that soup shell, she was going to boil them for him. After a while that water was boiling. She would take a stick and stir those fish around, so they all would be cooked. They were cooked. Then she took a small board. She asked him, "How many do you want?" "One," he told her. "Oh, that grandchild! My! How can you be satisfied with one? It's not a mouthful!" Then she brought the clam shell, she put one fish on the board. "There you are," she said, "go ahead and eat." She put that clam shell to her mouth and with a stick she lifted those fish into her mouth, one at a time. They were just a taste for her, each fish was barely a taste. That one fish that the man had, lasted him all day however. "Well, they are good!" she admitted. "But Thunder would never bother with such little ones."

They thought he was so cute. He was so small and yet he did all sorts of entertaining things, he built so many objects. One mouthful of whale meat lasted him for so many meals. How did he live on so little?

One day while Thunder was gone, the old woman asked her grandchild, "Would you mind looking around in my head to see if you find any head lice? I feel rather lousy." When she sat down, it was all the man could do by standing on his tiptoes to look up into her head. "Oh, my goodness ! She has water dogs in her hair. Maybe they are her head lice," he thought. He said, "Yes, you do have something on your head." He did not want to handle them, he was afraid of them. Indeed they were her head lice. She told him, "You pick them off and lay them in my hand." He picked them up by the tail, he laid them in her hand. She said, "My! You can pick up tiny things! I can scarcely see them." As he laid them in her hand, she would put her hand to her mouth and crack those water dogs with her teeth. "Ah! My head lice! They are extremely small," she said.

One day the man was observing Thunder's wife. He thought, "Oh! Is she not a huge woman? And my grandpa, is he not a large man? My goodness! How high they must reach when grandpa gets on top of her! When they copulate, oh! It must be extremely high up." Presently she looked at him. "Yes, yes, grandchild!" she said. "We are very large indeed. When we copulate, when grandpa lies on me, we reach quite high. We must have big, wide covers to cover ourselves." Then he was ashamed. "After this," he promised himself, "I will not think any such foolish things." (She knew what was his mind without his saying anything.)

Then at last his two years were past. His grandfather came home. Thunder said, "Well, your two days are up now. I will take you home." He was so pleased. Thunder told him, "I brought one fish for you to take home with you, so you can have it to eat when you get home. You cannot have it right at your house. I will just let it lie on the beach and you can tell all your friends to go and pack some home. It will belong to you, but you may let your friends have some of it." Then the man went and kissed his grandmother goodbye, and Thunder was ready to take him home. Again he told him, "You must not look around. Just keep your eyes closed and hang on." He brought him back to the same place where he had picked him up. He set him down by that tree. He told him, "Your whale will be there. Go get it immediately when you reach home. It is on the beach. That is for you."

The man began to wonder, "I wonder if I will find my wife. Perhaps she has forgotten me already. Maybe she has married again." He went towards home. He hated to walk into the house. He saw his little children; they were almost grown up. Those two children had their hair cut short in mourning style. He called them, "Come here, I want to talk to you." They came to him. "Is your mother home?" "Yes," they answered, "she is at the house." "Who is living there?" "Oh, uncle and aunt, they are living with us." He asked, "Anyone besides them?" "No, just them and mother and us." "Has she a husband, your mother?" "No, our father was killed. He went out fishing and never came back. He is dead." He told them, "That was I. I was not dead. Tell your mother to come out and meet me." The children ran into the house. The older one said, "Mother, we saw father out there, outdoors." "How can you talk that way ? Father has been dead two years." She reproved them. "He wants you to come out and meet him. He is out there," they insisted. She just knew that could not be true but she went. She went out. Well! There he was indeed. She went to him, she said, "Why! We thought you were dead." "No," he explained, "but I could not return when I wanted to. Something took me and kept me and has just now brought me home. I will tell you about it later on." Then he advised his wife, "You go on into the house and I will follow later. Clean that house." "That house is clean," she answered. She went in and fixed her bed for him. Then he came in and went to bed.

He was going to sing. His brother ran and told all the people, "He has come back. He is going to sing for now. He says everyone shall go down on the beach tomorrow for a whale. He says the whale is from him, he brought it with him." It was summertime and whales had never before drifted ashore in summertime. Only in winter had they ever come to the beach. For that reason people disbelieved. They thought when they saw it, "He must be more than just a common person. He is more powerful. He can do almost anything because he has been up above." When they were getting their pieces of whale he told all the people, "Do not ever eat that back fin. That is the best part, that big, fat part. You bring that back fin home and burn it in the fire. Give all the people portions of the rest of the whale. Whenever I want another whale I can ask for it." His brother did all that he told him. Then that man sang for seven or eight days and people came from all over to see him, to see that he was indeed alive.

That is a real happening.

The Woman Who Swallowed a Snake

From Colonial times onward, snakes seem to have occupied a special place in American folklore, from the rattler who bit the young man on the heel in "Springfield Mountain," the oldest native American ballad (represented in this anthology by an Oregon variant, "John Alexander"), to the deadly snake bite pivotal in the legend of the "Three Murderer Sons," to the popular jump rope rhyme in which "Cinderella, dressed in yella" made a mistake and "kissed a snake," to modern urban legends of snakes found in the sleeves of imported fur coats purchased in various American discount stores.

Oregon has its share of snake stories, including tales of the annual winter migration of the snakes and frogs from the Klamath Falls area to the base of Mt. Shasta (*Oregonian*, November 3, 1935). However, one of the strangest Oregon snake stories, collected for the WPA Oregon Folklore Project, was reported in *The Dalles Times Mountaineer*, December 14, 1889. It was taken from a letter written by a lady in Wasco County to her friend in Caldwell, Idaho. The correspondent describes an unusual birth that took place at Tygh Valley: " Where the child's fingers and toes ought to have been there were rattlesnakes' heads; and there was a small snake grew from the top of its head and hung down in its face. The head of the snake was the child's nose and whenever the baby moved the snake on its face would rise up, run out its tongue, and hiss. The baby only lived five hours, but the snake part lived five hours longer."

Another remarkable snake story from the WPA project files was copied from the March 31, 1876 *Corvallis Gazette*. The *Gazette* attributes this story to the *Vancouver Independent*. In this tale, a woman who has been, perhaps inappropriately, drinking from a spring in the dark, swallows a snake, which stays with her for months until St. Patrick's Day—a holiday commemorating the saint known for driving the snakes out of Ireland.

The *Vancouver Independent* of the 25th inst. relates a most wonderful "snake story," which culminated in that city on St. Patrick's Day. Mrs. Sarah Linderner, of that city, formerly of Camp Bidwell, Cal., about one year since, in taking a drink of water from a spring, or hole in the ground, in the dark, swallowed something which wiggled in her throat and was apparently about the size of a horse hair. She came to Vancouver last September, and has, for several months, been troubled by his snakeship, which, at times, would bite her stomach very severely, and made life a burden. We will let the *Independent* tell the story as follows:

The poor woman was kept almost constantly eating and dosing for the benefit of his snakeship, and it may easily be imagined that her life was one round of unmitigated horror. Despairing of a cure, she wrote to Dr. Jaynes of California, who sent her a prescription, which was simply to starve herself and drink nothing but brandy. Friday morning of last week, after having suffered fearfully the day previous, she began the new regimen; building up a hot fire, she dosed heavily with the liquor and reclined on the floor, with her face close to the fire. Along in the afternoon she became deadly sick at the stomach and vomited violently. After several severe retchings, she felt the snake coming up; its head was so near her mouth as to impede her breathing, when, rising to her feet in her agony, and leaning her head against the mantelpiece, directly over the fire, she thrust her fingers down her throat, stretching it to its widest tension, and the SNAKE GLIDED FROM HER MOUTH and fell into the hot coals of the fire below and was burned up. At this moment there was no one present but a little girl 12 years old and she did not dare to take the animal from the fire and the woman fainted away. The snake is decribed as closely resembling a common garter snake and was about 16 inches in length. It thrust its tongue from its mouth as it came forth and squirmed in a lively manner when it fell into the fire. One or two of the neighbors were called in and they say the coil of the snake was plainly visible in its entire shape upon the coals of the fire. The woman who has pined away from 180 pounds to a living skeleton feels a wonderful sense of relief and declares "that St. Patrick and the good God have been very merciful" to her.

The Girl Who Swallowed a Pearl

This first-person narrative was told by Victor Olsen of Cannon Beach in 1965. Described as a man who spends many hours in the leisurely pursuit of fish and in collecting disintegrating automobiles to be pieced back together, Olsen was reported to have "a sizable following among the youth of the village, who join him in fishing the sea and listening as he recounts absurd tales." Peter Lindsey of Cannon Beach heard this tale from Olsen one day in the spring of 1965 while they were fishing together from the base of Haystack Rock. Lindsey sets the scene as follows: "Mr. Olsen had been prying mussels from the rocks to be used as bait for fishing and succeeded in extricating a sizable imperfect pearl from the fleshy part of one of the mussels. The girl accompanying us promptly expressed a desire to own this find, and at this point Mr. Olsen began presenting this tale which he claimed to have participated in at a time some few years past" (RVMA, Lindsey, 1969).

"I remember," he said, "a time a couple of years ago when I was fishing down by Pacific City. A bunch of fellows and I were fishing then, just like we are here today, and I was slicing open mussels for bait. I found a few big pearls. A gal came along and wanted a pearl to take home for jewelry, so I gave it to her. She had no pockets in her pedal-pushers, just like you don't (at this point he was speaking to the girl with me) so she stuck the pearl in her mouth so she wouldn't lose it as she walked from the slippery rocks to the beach. About half way off of the rocks she slipped and *swallowed* the damn thing. She was real sorry to lose it like that, but figured it wouldn't hurt her any, and she could just crap it out of her system.

"Well, about five months later her belly began to ache and swell up. Her family figured she had gotten knocked-up by some fellow, but they wouldn't take her to a doctor because they were ashamed of the whole damn business. They sent her off to a home to live while she had the baby. Well, about 2 months later the poor girl died. When they took an autopsy on her and cut her belly open, they found a half-grown *octopus* inside!

"That girl hadn't swallowed a pearl from a mussel at all; she'd swallowed a damn octopus egg."

At this point Mr. Olsen, with exceedingly straight face, proceeded to expound on the merits of seeing medical authorities whenever faced with pain, and offered to carry the pearl we'd found that day off of the rocks in his pocket.

Spirits
Corpses
Haunted Places

O regon's non-Native, immigrant populations have brought ghost stories with them from many traditions, and this cultural relocation process continues today, as illustrated here, for example, by Hispanic *La Llorona* stories. As for Indian ghost and haunted-place stories, they are no less deliciously frightening for coming out of a religious tradition that is neither Western nor Eastern. In Native terms, what we call the "supernatural" is continuous with the "natural"; the world is full of spirit-power to be reckoned with and sought after, sometimes visible, often concentrated in particular locations—mountains, rivers, lakes. People's souls are capable of out-of-body travel, under conditions of trance or illness; after death, souls journey to a distant limbo-world where the circumstances of mortal life are restricted and inverted: the dead sleep during the day and come out only at night, and so on. The souls of the dead can linger or come back to haunt the living; conversely, as in the Western "Orpheus" tradition, grieving mortals can attempt to bring the spirits of loved ones back from the land of the dead, but in the nature of things they never quite succeed in doing so.

Detail from Petroglyph by Hansen Studios. Cast stone document from The Dalles Dam Reservoir area, Crawfords Point.

Lulu Lang

Lulu'laidi

Like the Wishram "Orpheus" story (pp. 118-121), the narrative of Lulu'laidi gives imaginative form to the universal human wish to somehow bring loved ones back from death—and in doing so mediates for us between that powerful wish and our knowledge that death, when it comes, is permanent and unappealable, at least in this life. Orpheus stories aim to reconcile us to the permanence of death by showing how the Orphic quester is, finally, all too human, mortally fallible, and thus humanly incapable of bringing his heroic quest to a successful conclusion. One of the striking things about "Lulu'laidi" is that it is not fallibility and lack of self-control in the husband that brings the quest to grief, it is the heedless *community*'s fault that the dead woman's spirit is frightened back to *nolis gaeni* just as she reaches her earthly home.

Lulu Lang, a master Klamath storyteller, probably translated this story out of her native-language repertory as she performed it in English. In Theodore Stern's sensitive transcription, the text is rich in Klamath details and conventions. Important actions happen in sequences of *fives* (the Klamath sacred number), which Mrs. Lang exploits in building up tension and excitement; likewise, she frequently draws out certain words for special emphasis ("she went clo . . . ser to her"). All in all, such a text conveys to us, even in print, something of the dramatic power of Native storytelling.
—Told by Mrs. Lulu Lang to Theodore Stern in 1951, and used with Prof. Stern's permission. Copyright 1994; all rights reserved.

Once there was a lot of people living at the mouth of this Williamson River. So, this Lulu'laidi, she was grea . . . t singer. And she had husband. Whenever people would get together and when they sing songs and she would be the loudest singer all the time; and she was pretty woman, too. And so, she took sick, and finally after quite a while, somehow she died. And her spirit-soul went toward West, toward *nolis gaeni* [the spirit place].

And so, her man started to get ready, and he followed her. Whenever night came, he would camp, and his wife's spirit would be taking pity on him and would be setting up on limb there all night, waiting for him. She didn't like to leave him behind. And so, next morning he got up early and started again. And

he traveled *all* day, tired, never eating anything, all scratched up, looking pitiful. Then night would come up on him again. Then there he would camp
again, and this spirit-wife would be *same* way, would be up there someplace,
taking pity on him, don't want to leave him behind. Then he would start up
early in the morning again. Then he would be going *all* day. Then night would
come up on him again. And again he would stop overnight, pretty tired and
worried over his wife's leaving him. Then he would get up early next morning
again. Then he would start out again next morning to follow her. And so, this
woman in spirit, she was taking *awful* pity on him because he was looking so
pitiful, tired, and worn-out traveling. So that night came over on him again.
Then again he stop overnight and his spirit-wife, Lulu'laidi, would be sitting
up in tree above him. She didn't like to leave him. And so, next morning, again
he got up *early*, weary, tired, and worn-out. He struck out again, he traveled
a . . . ll day. And so, then night come on him again. And there he stop overnight again, take rest—he was pretty badly worn-out. Then he started out
again, *early* morning; and finally in evening he got to *nolis gaeni*.

And so, when he got there, Lulu'laidi, his wife, was there already. And so,
he stayed there, and those people, daytime they was all quiet, them *skoks* [ghosts].
And so, that evening, all these dead people come back to just like live people,
they going to have [a] time. Then start to singing. And he could hear her voice
just like he hear her voice when she was living on earth. Oh, and he recognize
her voice. And so, he said to himself, "Oh, that's her!" —Lulu'laidi, his wife.
And so, next morning they was all just like sleep again.

And he figured around, he don't know what to do, and he study about it
pretty nearly all day, thinking what to do and what can he do, and what he's
going to try to do. And so, evening come, and he was there, and when darkness come, people began to walking around this way and that way, just like
they were waking up. So they got together again that night. Then they start
their songs up again. And he would hear her voice just the same as he would
hear her voice on earth. Singing *loud*, loud above *all* of them. And he said
[*narrator: gentle voice*], "Well, there she is. She's there." And next morning
come, and sometime that day he happened to come across this Kemuk'amps's
daughter—she was living over there in *nolis gaeni*. And he went to her and he
started to talk to her. And he told her about what happened. And so, he said to
her, "Can you get that soul back for me some way? Can you do something for
me?" (It was great loss to him that Lulu'laidi, great singer and all, it was a great
loss to him.) And Kemuk'amps's daughter said [*narrator: reflective voice*], "Well,
I'll see, I see if I can get get close enough to her." (Spirits, you can't touch it,
you can't get close to it.)

And so, that night again they got together. And this Kemuk'amps's daughter, he got one of these 'nai [basket] and a seed gatherer. Those dead people start to singing. And this Kemuk'amps's daughter, she heard Lulu'laidi's voice among them, and so does her husband. And this Kemuk'amps's daughter, she tried to get close to her, and she couldn't make it. She couldn't make it.

So next night again, she's going to try it again. And she come li . . . ttle bit close to her when they were singing. So she couldn't get chance to get her. (Kemuk'amps's daughter wasn't spirit, she just happened to be living there, *nolis gaeni*.)

And so, the next night again they got together again, they come to be people—daytime there was nobody to be seen. And now, they start up their meeting again, and so old Kemuk'amps's daughter, [she] got this *'nai* again and seed gatherer, and she went clo . . . ser to her. She was singing lou . . . d and had goo . . .d voice, Lulu'laidi. And [she] come close to her—and she couldn't make it.

And so, next morning come and everybody disappear—gone. All go back to ghosts. And then, that night again, this man, this Lulu'laidi's husband, commenced to see people walking around again, going this way and that way—all directions. Then a . . . ll at once, they got together again. And they start to sing again. And this Lulu'laidi's husband, he hear her voice singing, and he feel glad just to hear her singing, even though he was almost worried to death about losing her. And so, this Kemuk'amps's daughter, [she] got his *'nai* again and that seed fanner. So, [she] went around to them again and [she] got li . . . ttle bit closer, by ca . . . reful movements. And so, [she] come pretty close to getting her that time.

And so, daylight come, and everybody's gone—nobody to be seen. So that man, Lulu'laidi's husband, he just wandered around, almost worry himself to death. And so, then night come again, and he was glad, because he could hear her voice. And so, darkness come again and he could see them walking as persons in all directions. Then, pretty soon they a . . . ll get together in crowd. And so, they start to sing, and he could hear her voice as she was singing above all of them. And this Lulu'laidi's husband, he said, "She's there. That's her voice." And so, now this Kemuk'amps's daughter, she worked around so that now [she's] going to do something. Then [she] got got his *'nai* and that seed fanner. Then she come in right close to them and by quick action she did the trick. She took the seed fanner and she whipped that soul into that *'nai*. And she covered the *'nai* up, quick as she can—she sealed it up tight. And now he got her back

And then next day, Kemuk'amps's daughter, she told this man, "Now," [she] said, "when you take this *'nai* back and this soul sealed tight, when you stop overnight on the way, if she try to talk to you, do . . . n't answer, don't answer. You be sure do . . . n't answer when she try to talk to you." And he said, "All right!" She said to him, "She'll bother you e . . . very night when you stop. She'll try to talk to you, try to make you speak and answer her, but do . . . n't answer. Don't speak."

And so, he strike out, started to come back home with his wife's spirit in that 'nai sealed up tight. So he come a . . . ll day. Night overtook him. So he took off the pack off his back—that 'nai—and set it down on the ground. So, after he went to bed, Lulu'laidi, she said, "My husband!" She started to talk to her husband. And so, he pretty near speak. But a thought came into him not to answer, because Kemuk'amps's daughter advise him to no . . . t say anything to her and not answer her.

So, next morning again he got up early, almost worn out, tired. And he put the pack on his back and he started out again. Traveled a . . . ll day, walk. And he walked, tired and worn-out. Then night came on him again. And he stop overnight right there, took his pack off and set it down and went to lay down. Then again that night, she told him, "My husband, my husband!" He didn't answer. Then she talk to him, try to make him speak, try to get him to answer when she call him. And she kept *after* him, *after* him. But he never answered. He never say anything.

So, he woke up early, in the morning, ragged and tired. So, he got ready and he pick up that 'nai put it on his back and he started out again. And so, he walked a . . . ll day. He tried to come *fast* as he could so that he could get home. And so, night come on him again. And so, he start to camp again. He took his pack off and set it down on ground. Then he start to lay down alongside it, go to bed. And when it got so dark, she commenced to talk to him. And she talked, kept on talking to him, asking him questions. He never answered, he *never* answer.

So, next morning he got up early and he strike out again and he come as fast as he could, even [though] he was all worn out, tired. So, night overtook him again. And he took his pack off and he set it down on ground. And he lay down alongside of it. That's where he go to bed. And so, soon as darkness come, she said, Lulu'laidi said, "My husband!" She said, "My husband!" She spoke suddenly, so that he might answer. But he didn't answer. Then she commenced to talk to him *everything* that they were talking when they were both living together. She ask him questions, call upon him and tell him things. Try to make him say something. But he *never* speak, *never* answer her.

So, next morning he struck out. He started early. So, he come just as fast as he could come, even though he was a . . . ll worn out, tired. And night overtook him. So, he set this pack down on ground and started camping again.

And this man, he lay there and listened by that pack. He was listening. So, she commenced to call on him, tried to tell him something. Tried to make him answer. But she couldn't. That man stick to the advice of that Kemuk'amps's daughter. And Lulu'laidi cou . . . ldn't make him speak and cou . . . . ldn't make him answer all those nights they were on road traveling.

And so, he struck out a little bit earlier in the morning. So, he started fast, and he got back across the lake, towards Pelican Bay. He got back there and he hollered over for someone to come and get him. And that he had got back and that [he] was Lulu'laidi's husband. And so, people hear of it. They begin to get excited, because she dies and her soul went to *nolis gaeni*. Somehow, they guessed that something happened. And there was one or two canoes got ready. And there was people stirring around, getting ready to get into canoe to come over to get him. And this man saw them moving like that and he hollered over, he said, "No, just one person! One canoe got to come after me—not too many!" And he kept hollering over for them to not come—only one, and one canoe.

So the people didn't mind him. There was two, three canoes and two or three in each canoe started to come over after him. And he still hollered over, "No, no! only one, only one person, one canoe!" So these people didn't mind him; they kept coming.

And so, they got over there, close to shore, and this Lulu'laidi, she start to flew out of that *'nai* and went back. Went back. And that man, he pretty near drop over and fainted. He told them [*narrator: calm, reproachful tone*], "Now, you people ought to know and listen to me, what I told you to do." And he said it then [*same tone*], "You see what you people done to me?"

And so, he got ready again, going to follow his wife again. He struck out to the west to that *nolis gaeni*. And he stop over-night. So, his spirit-wife sat up in the tree, took pity on her husband, saw him tired, worried, broken-down, almost a goner.

And next morning he started out again. She didn't leave him. So, night come on him again. And he lay down, stop overnight again—tired, worried, almost a goner.

Then next morning he struck out again. The she stayed close to him in the air, taking pity on him that he was looking so pitiful, tired, broken-down, worn-out. And he was going, he was going, still going *and*, somehow, when he stopped to camp that night, he died—worried, tired, worn-out. He died.

And then, his spirit-soul went right up to his wife, and they both strike out for West, *nolis gaeni*, going both in spirit now. And when they got to *nolis gaeni*, they started to settle down and live there with the rest of the people.

At gadani hak. [And that ends the story.]

The Ghosts at Mosquito Flats

All over Oregon, settlers have supposed (without factual foundation) that hillocks or mounds in their territory are "prehistoric Indian graves." In this tradition from Harney County, they're not only "Indian mounds," they're haunted. —Collected by Carol Peterson from George Hibbard in Burns on July 22, 1972 (RVMA, Peterson, 8/72).

There's another story my father used to tell me when I was a boy. You know where the Lone Pine Road is? Well, it's about 16 miles out of town toward the Five Mile Dam. They call that area out there Mosquito Flats because all over the valley floor there are little raised dirt mounds that look like bumps, about two or three feet high. The old timers claim they're Indian mounds. And they said, the old timers, that if you went out there late in the evening and sat down on them and listened real close you could hear the ghosts of the old Indian braves and chiefs that were buried there calling back from their graves: "Nothing at all. Nothing at all . . . ."

The Stick Indians

Belief in the Stick Indians, a race of small, furtive, mischievous beings said to haunt the deep woods and lakes of the High Cascades and other mountainous areas, is still current in the Native communities of the Northwest. ("Stick" probably derives from the all-purpose Chinook Jargon word for anything related to wood or timber, as in *stick-skin* for "tree-bark," but it might also derive from a Chinookan word for spirit: *stiyakha*.) The Stick Indians are thought to be telepathic, and capable of imitating bird-calls and human sounds in order to distract unwary visitors to their country and get them lost. Occasionally, however, as in the Nez Perce story below, they are helpful to humans. The Stick Indians are not ghosts, but apparently are spirits who were never born into human life.—This account was given by Mrs. Dave Isaac (Nez Perce) to Dell Skeels in the 1940s. (Skeels, *Style in the Unwritten Literature of the Nez Perce Indians*, p. 272.)

About an Indian family, just an old couple. It was toward fall, Indian summer, and everybody was hunting, out hunting deer and elk, and this old lady said, "I wish we were camping on the Seven Devils. I wish we were there. We'd surely get some meat or somebody'd help us get some."

And that night they slept early, and one of these Stick Indians, the vanishing kind of Indians, saw this poor man and his wife were wishing for venison. "We'll help them. They'll be surprised." So these Stick Indians put them to sleep. So they packed their stuff, took their camp and all to just the place they wished for. The next morning they got up. They had skinned deer and deer meat right out on their doorway, and so the old man said, "It was one of the Stick Indians that helped us." So he told his wife not to think anything out of the way. "We might have a way going back."

In about a week they had all the dried meat they wanted. They were satisfied. She ran out of Indian trunks [tote-bags] and had to use green hides, but she said at night, "I think I want to be back where we started." And so that night they [the Stick Indians] moved them again, and the [other] Indians wondered where they had disappeared and which way they went, and they found they were back, and they were glad they were back, and they all knew what took them.

Old Man Donovan's Wake

Charles Imus, who described himself as English and Irish, was born in Roxberry, Kansas, in 1879 and moved to Portland, Oregon, in 1900. Imus had worked as a farm worker, logger, livery stable keeper, stage coach driver, dance hall manager, and jack-of-all-trades when he was interviewed for the WPA Oregon Folklore Project by William C. Haight on February 24, 1939. Haight conducted the interview in Imus's small apartment in an unpainted, weather-beaten, two-story building in southwest Portland. He described Imus as follows:

> Light blue eyes shaded by light eyebrows accentuate the informant's smooth features. His face is expressive; the movements of his eyebrows punctuate his speech. A faded, ragged, brown tie, against a once bright green shirt supplied a concession and mark of distinction to the occasion. His suit was a peculiar color of blue, nearly green. He wore light brown shoes and dark socks that were held up by large safety pins.

After fairly lengthy conversation about his childhood and his experiences logging with oxen and driving a stage coach from North Yamhill to Tillamook, Imus tells the interviewer a number of "ghost stories," including the following story about the wake of Old Man Donovan, the father of one of his classmates. The story reveals the narrator's anti-Catholic sentiments; the colloquial style in which it presented is probably the WPA interviewer's attempt to give it the flavor of the spoken word.

Are ya religious? If you are I won't tell the story. All right. I ain't got nothin' against Catholics; I don't figger you can blame 'em for bein' Catholics. I don't understand much about what they're aimin' for, and I don't like much the way they aim for whatever they're aimin' for. This old man Donovan I'm goin' to tell ya about was a Catholic. Because he wuz a Catholic it resulted in makin' most of his life mighty miserable, aside from makin' him awful dingblasted mad.

Old man Donovan had two kids, Harry and Joe. Joe and me would fight every day I went to school; mainly, what I went to school for, I reckon. One day I went to school and Joe wasn't there. Right away, I figgered somethin' pretty important musta happened or else Joe'd be there. Sure 'nuff! Later in the day we heard old man Donovan had died. Soon's the teacher heard that the old feller was gone, she dismissed school. Seems like they sort of needed some people to help around up at Donovan's, so the teacher asked my side-kick, Bill, and me to go up there. Seein' as how my old man loaned the widow the money to send for the priest to come and pray Donovan out of purgatory, I guess the teacher thought I'd be a good one to send.

The priest did his job all right. They laid Donovan out on a board that was supported by two chairs, threw a sheet over him and put the candles at his head and feet. After the priest left, Bill and me were delegated to sit in the kitchen and watch the corpse, which wuz in adjoining room. In the other room the widow and every Irishman and German within forty miles was a-holdin' the wake. Plenty of good liquor they were drinkin'. I remember seein' two demijohns sittin' on the table when somebody opened the door.

The house wuz on a hill and built out of shakes. The wind could sure make a howl when it tore into those shakes. The wind, coupled with the wailing of the wakers, made it sort of eerie settin' in the kitchen. Bill wuz plenty scairt anyhow. This wuz the first time he'd ever been around a corpse. All of a sudden Bill and me heard the doggonedest sound I'd ever heard. I decided the cat must have got into the corpse someway. God! I thought that wuz terrible. Here those people wuz dependin' on Bill and me to guard the corpse, and we'd let the cat into the body. I told Bill to pick up the metal-plated lamp and follow me. We went in there and could see the sheet goin' up and down, up and down, with the most peculiar noise I ever heard a-comin' out of that corpse. Bill was a shakin' so that lamp sounded like a rattle. Bill takes a good look and says, "By God, I'm gettin' out of here." He shoves the lamp in my hand and runs . . . for home.

I goes over and lifts up the sheet. By that time some of the wakers heard the noise and come in to see what it wuz all about. By golly, old Donovan was alive! They picked him up, put warm blankets and hot water bottles around him. He got well and lived for 17 years.

Funny part about it wuz the fact that the priest wouldn't let him or his family go to church no more. The priest said he was a sinner and God had refused to take him, so he had to come back to earth. Anyway, he'd been prayed out of purgatory and there wuzn't anything could be done about it. Old man Donovan was the maddest man you ever saw. Poor bugger, he wuzn't no more of a sinner than anybody else. He died when he stepped in front of a freight train 17 years after this all happened.

The Corpse and the Pickles

This legend was told to the WPA Oregon Folklore Project interviewer, Sara Wrenn, by Mrs. Mary Fisher of Portland, Oregon, in April 1939. It reminds us that we ought not to assume we know what another person wants, and what seems inevitable is not always so. This story and the previous one about Old Man Donovan are Oregon examples of a type of folk tale known to folklore scholars as "The Seemingly Dead Revives." (Aarne-Thompson, *The Types of the Folktale.*)

This is a true story. I ought to know because the woman was my father's sister and my aunt, though it all happened before I was born.

Aunt Jane had been sick for a long while. For days and days she had laid in a state of half-coma, without either eating or drinking. Once in awhile she would give a faint whisper about something she wanted. It sounded like pickles but that, of course, was preposterous. Anyway, to give her pickles was unthinkable; though death seemed inevitable, to give Aunt Jane pickles would, in the opinion of her grief-stricken family, be nothing less than plain murder.

Finally, sinking into complete unconsciousness, Aunt Jane passed away. As was the custom before the days of undertakers and morticians, friends came to "sit up" with the remains. In an adjoining room, while the watchers, sad and respectful, were murmuring reminiscences of the deceased, they were startled by the crash of crockery. Rushing into the kitchen, from which the sound came, they found Aunt Jane, still wrapped in her white shroud, pulling down pantry jars in a frantic hunt for pickles. Upon finding these, she ate them eagerly. She lived for many years thereafter to tell about the occasion.

Petrified Bodies West and East

Tales of the petrification of corpses are found throughout Oregon. They seem especially numerous east of the Cascades. (Cf. Black Harris's tale of the "Putrefied Forest," p. 70.)

The Petrifaction of Mrs. Confer

This happened in the days of Chinese contract laborers, when Chinese coolies did most of the grubbing toward clearing the land, as well as the grading of the railroad beds. When the survey was run for the old narrow gauge down here [Lake Oswego], it was found that the survey run right through an old burial place. There was two graves there, the grave of Mrs. Confer, whose husband filed on the land originally, and the grave of their hired man. I don't remember his name. Well, of course it was necessary to remove the bodies. We took up that of the hired man first. For some reason, I don't recall just why, the boxes was left in the ground. When we came to Mrs. Confer's body we had trouble. We just couldn't lift it. Somebody said mebbe the coffin was full of water, so we bored holes in it, and sure enough there was some water. We let it run out, but still we couldn't lift the coffin, so we sent for help. It took six men to lift that coffin on the two trestles, so someone thought we ought to open the coffin and we did. We found the body was completely petrified, all except where the tip of the nose was gone, and the ends of the great toes. Seems like the water about there, and all around here for that matter, has a lot of mineral in it, and as high as the water went in the coffin the body petrified. Not only that, but the lines of the shroud were petrified, and the gold pin at her neck was embedded in the petrified body. We estimated the body weighed 600 pounds. (Collected by Sarah B. Wrenn from A. J. Howell of Lake Oswego on March 10, 1939 [WPA Folklore Project].)

The Petrified Girl of Hay Creek

In 1920 an undertaker, F. H. Watts, came to the Hay Creek Cemetery with a Mrs. McPherson to move the body of her daughter to The Dalles to be reburied by the side of her father. The young lady had been buried at Hay Creek for six years and great difficulty was experienced in digging, for the soil is similar to that found in the Burns Cemetery, very hard to dig, but pulverizing when exposed to air. The outside box and coffin had completely rotted away. This made digging more difficult, and as Watts carefully lifted the body he was astonished to find it petrified. It was a new experience, so with interest he noted the darker hue the skin had taken on, resembling leather. He considered this the only perfect work of sculpture he had ever seen.

The trip to The Dalles was a nightmare of fear, lest the body break. The body of stone was wrapped in a blanket and placed in the back of a pickup on a board. As he bounced over the rough roads he could hear the body rattle and he was sure that the fingers and toes would be broken off, but when he reached The Dalles he was relieved to find his fears were groundless. (Recorded by Mrs. Tom [Evada] Power, in *Jefferson County Reminiscences*, p. 33.)

A Stone Man at Ashwood

Several years back, Mr. Mosley told of a large petrified man they plowed up while living on their homestead in the Ashwood country. He was a nuisance—too heavy to load, too dead to walk, and too large to roll out of the way. In the ensuing years, just when they were getting used to him, he started breaking up. The Mosleys were too busy coaxing a living from the inhospitable ground to take trips of a scientific nature by horse and wagon to either of Oregon's universities. Treasures are lost in simple ways. The stone man was probably worth a fortune. (Recorded by Russell Baehr, *Oregon Outback*, p. 16.)

Haunted Skookum Lake

This story, told in 1939 to WPA interviewer Sara B. Wrenn by A. J. Howell of Lake Oswego, provides a rational explanation for the weirdness of Skookum Lake in contrast to the Indian story which follows. For other A. J. Howell stories in this volume, see "The Petrification of Mrs. Confer," and "Goose Hunting Near McMinnville and Fishing at Meadow Lake." All are from the WPA Oregon Folklore Project, Oregon State Library.

Out on the summit o' the Coast Range mountains, between McMinnville and Tillamook, there was a lake that in 1874 they used to call Skookum Lake. I think it has another name now. Anyway, it was Skookum Lake then, an' everybody said it was haunted. The Indians was scared to death to go near the place. They jest wouldn't go near it, that's all; and some of the whites was jest as bad. They said there was the most terrible noises came from there you ever heard, jest like this: some of them was, "Oo-oo-*uh!*" The first all drawn out like, an' the last, the "uh" quick an' sharp, "Oo-oo-*uh!*"—like you'd been kicked in the middle. There was other sounds, kind of awful screechin's.

Well, a young feller an' I, we decided we'd go an' find out what all these noises was. It was in the spring, a nice, bright, warm day, an' we took a light camp outfit, an' off we went to the mountains. It was still light when we got to the lake, an' we set up camp, but not very close to the water. All the time we kep' perty still, jest as still as we could. It was terrible still an' quiet all about— kinda solemn like.

An' then, all at once, we heard it. "Oo-oo-*uh!* Oo-oo-*uh!*" It kept up, that noise did, till dusk, an' we couldn't see a thing. We was gettin' kinda nervous ourselves, but there wasn't anything to do but stay out the night. We'd killed an elk that afternoon, an' we had a good supper of elk steak, an' jest as we was eatin' there come the most dang-dingest crash—jest like a car-load of lumber fallin' down a mountain-side. By this time we was both about ready to pull up stakes, but we decided to stick it out, an' then we heard the awfullest screech, endin' in a long wailin' sound, jest like a woman screamin', an' it wasn't once, it came over an' over again. I tell you there wasn't much sleepin' we did that night, an' we was up at daybreak.

While we was eatin' breakfast that first sound came again, "Oo-oo-*uh!* Oo-oo-*uh!*" We hadn't heard that noise all night—not since dark. We decided it came from the water all right. We hurried to the edge of the lake. Jus' as we got there, we heard it again. An' then saw somethin'—an object. We saw somethin' go down, an' we heard that sound, an' then somethin' went up. All jest like a flash. An' *then* we saw what 'twas. What do you suppose? It was fish-hawks was livin' high, an' ev'ry time they swooped down to the water for a rat [muskrat] they'd give that funny cry, as they hit the water.

Well, we felt perty brave then, so the next thing was to find out about what the crashin' was. We knew it didn't come from the lake, but 'twas some place near, in the forest somewheres. We tramped all around, lookin', an' at last we found it. A great big ol' dead tree, where the bark had come loose, an' we jest happened to be there, when that bark decided to slide down, an' there it was, all piled up about that big ol' tree. Mebbe you guessed what that awful screechin' was we heard. No? Well, you see, that elk we killed—we only took the steaks, an' there was that nice fat carcass, hangin' on the tree where we left it, an' there isn't anything a catamount [mountain lion] likes better'n a nice, fat, young elk, an' so he was givin' us a serenade about it.

Amhuluk, the Skookum of the Lake

In Oregon Indian tradition, the state's terrain is dotted—especially in the hills and mountains—with *skookum* places, *skookum* being the Jargon word for "power" or "spirit." Before Crater Lake was "discovered" by Anglo prospectors in 1853, it was well known to Indians of the region as a powerful spirit-site, to be visited only by shamans and spirit-questers. The Kalapuya story of Amhuluk exists in several versions, each with its own "haunted lake" location in Washington or Yamhill County—in this version, the site is apparently Wapato Lake, near Gaston. Compare this Native haunted place story with the rationalized Anglo tale that precedes it.— From Albert Gatschet, "Oregonian Folklore," pp. 141-142.

Amhuluk found himself a place on Forked Mountain; he stopped there and has lived there ever since. Every living being seen by him is drowned there; all the trees there stand upside down in his stagnant water. His legs have no hair on them, his horns are spotted and huge. He keeps several kinds of dogs with him.

Three children were busy digging for *adsadsh-root*, when Amhuluk came out of the ground nearby. The children said, "Let us take his beautiful spotted horns, to make digging-tools out of them!" But Amhuluk came up fast and lifted two of the children on his horns; the oldest child managed to escape. Wherever Amhuluk set his feet the ground was sinking. When the boy reached home he said to his father, "Something dreadful has come near us, and has taken away my brother and sister!" Then he went to sleep, and his parents noticed that his body was spotted all over.

Immediately the father started out for Forked Mountain. He found the tracks of the boy who had escaped and followed them, skirting the mountain. There he saw the bodies of his children emerging from the muddy pool. Then they disappeared for a while, and then reappeared on the opposite slope of the mountain. This happened five times, and finally the father reached the exact spot where the children had been drowned. There was a pool of water, with a mist over it, and in the mist he saw his children lifted up high on the horns of Amhuluk. With his hands he signalled to them, and the children replied: *"Didei, didei, didei,* we are changed, we are changed, we are changed!"

The father began to mourn, and stayed on the shore all night. The next day the mist came up again, and again the children rose up on the horns of Amhuluk. The father made signals again, and the children answered, *"Didei, didei, didei."* He made a lodge on the shore and stayed in it five days, and every day the children appeared to him as before. When they stopped appearing, the father went back to his family. His oldest son had died. The father said, "Amhuluk has taken the children. I have seen them; they are at the Forked Mountain. I have seen them upon the horns of the monster; many trees were in the water, the crowns down below, the trunks looking upward."

The Creaking Mantel

Jenny Alexander, age 19, of Jacksonville, Oregon, told this story to her friend, Leslie Clason, who was collecting stories for her folklore class at the University of Oregon in the spring of 1984. This narrative and the one that follows, "The Rocking Cradle," are local legends that were often told to Jenny by her grandmother, a native of the Rogue Valley, as Jenny was growing up.—From Leslie Clason, RVMA, May 1984.

Oh yes, the story of the creaking mantel, one of my grandmother's famous ones. This occurred in an old dairy along the Rogue and, if I remember right, my grandparents were invited to a housewarming party that was held by some friends of theirs that had just built one of those modern-style, large ranch houses. And they had just moved out to this old country farm. And since this was a pretty big occurrence, this building of this new house, they had invited most of the people of the valley to come an' see their house. Since it was pretty chilly outside all the guests gathered around the large fireplace in the middle of the room, and everyone was talking and havin' a good time, but as it neared midnight, and the clock began to chime, the room fell silent. [*pause*] Because they were hearing strange cre-e-e-aking [*narrator's voice creaks*] and gro-o-o-aning [*narrator's voice groans*] an' that was coming from within the room. They couldn't figure out where it was coming from, but they finally kind of located it. It seemed to be coming from the wooden mantel on the fireplace that they were around. Between all this cre-e-e-aking [*voice creaks*] and gro-o-o-aning [*voice groans*], they heard stomping and whinneying of horses—all this commotion—everyone was just *amazed*. They couldn't believe what was happening right there before their eyes.

And so my grandmother, a few weeks later, she called them, and the family wanted to know if they had found out anything about what had happened— was it some kind of practical joke or had she found out anything about this. The hostess told her that she had went back and did some investigating of the property and had found out that the mantelpiece that they had put on their fireplace had once been a part of a central beam of an old barn that had stood on the property and had been torn down before they built the house. Apparently many years ago, on that same date as the house-warming party, a man had been hanged [*pause*] and this occurred at midnight [*pause*] from the barn's central beam. And this was done by a gang of outlaws who then fled and the ghost of the man could still be heard on the anniversary of his death just creaking and groaning as he swung from the beams, the rafters.

The Rocking Cradle

Like the previous story, this one was recorded from Jenny Alexander, Jacksonville, in 1984. Jenny learned these "ghost stories" from her grandmother who, according to Jenny, witnessed the mysteriously creaking mantel and rocking cradle at homes in Jacksonville.—From Leslie Clason, RVMA, May 1984.

She [Grandmother] especially liked the ghost stories. She told me one which was quite interesting; she called it her "Rocking Cradle" story. And this oc-curred out along the Applegate, the river that runs past town. There was a family that lived there—I think it was, they were called the Stevens, I believe, and my grandparents went to go visit them one day. And they were all sitting in their living room talking and all of a sudden this old cradle that was sitting beside the fireplace began rocking and it was creaking as it moved. My grand-mother, of course, was *amazed*. She couldn't figure out *why* the cradle was moving by itself—there was no one there rocking it. And the lady of the house, she went on to explain that the cradle rocks by itself quite often and that the house had been in her family for generations. And after each family had left, they just left the cradle in its place sitting by the fire. It was not moved. And, for as long as she could remember, the cradle rocked by itself. There was no explanation for this.

She went on to explain to my grandmother that there was a old family leg-end behind all of this that had been passed down to explain why the cradle rocked. She said many, many years ago when the house was first built, newly built, apparently there had been a fault in one of the walls in the room, and one day the oldest daughter—she was, oh, about ten years old—she was sitting by the fire and rocking the baby in his cradle. And there had been a lot of rain that year and she started feeling some shaking, and she realized what was happen-ing, that there was a mudslide and so she immediately covered the baby, just threw herself across the cradle to protect the baby just in time before the wall caved in. The girl *was* killed, but the baby was saved because she had thrown herself over him. And the family said that this rocking is caused by the ghost of the girl who comes back to sit by the fire and watch her little brother. And this is the only reason that they could give for this mysterious rocking.

Well, my grandmother not accepting this—this is just too far out for her, she went outside the house and searched all around and inside the house, covered all the areas, and she couldn't find any logical or so-called "scientific" reason for why this would happen. And, just like the other story I was telling you, this house is still there.

La Llorona, The Crying Woman

Legends of the Crying Woman, *La Llorona*, are current throughout Mexico and in Mexican-American communities in the United States. In some cases, these legends are localized; someone in the area has seen or heard the crying woman as she wanders about crying for her children—whose deaths she may have caused. The crying woman tale is very old. According to some scholars, it is a Mexican tale that has existed since Aztec times and is related to stories of an Aztec goddess who appears dressed in white and carrying a cradle. The goddess abandons the cradle, and the Aztec women who look into it find only an arrowhead that is shaped like a sacrificial knife. Later the goddess is seen wandering at night, crying and weeping, then disappearing into a lake or river (Dorson, *Buying the Wind*, 436-38).

These *La Llorona* tales were collected in Eugene in 1973 by Alicia Rodriguez for the Randall V. Mills Folklore Archives. A study of such stories from southern Oregon can be found in Pamela Jones, "There Was a Woman: *La Llorona* in Oregon," pp. 195-211.

There was a señora who had three sons and no husband. She then fell in love with another man but he didn't want her unless she got rid of her sons. She then drowned them in a river. When she went back her lover no longer loved her. Now she walks back and forth on the river bank crying for her sons. (Gloria Talavera Florez)

In Mexico there lived this woman who had three kids, all of them boys. While her husband was away working she had an affair with another man. He didn't want her because she had her family already, but she happened to be madly in love with her lover, so for him she drowned the three boys and went to his house to tell him the good news. He didn't live where he told her he lived so she couldn't find him. Now she no longer has a family and she cries every night by the river in hopes that she can find them. (Esteven Estrella)

At the age of ten Angie was with a group of girls going home from the house of another girlfriend. It had become dark. Angie's brother and a group of young men were following a quarter of a mile behind them. Everyone was walking. They were by an arroyo when Angie's little sister and another young lady saw someone following them. They thought it was her brother and friends so they stopped and waited for the person to move, and they saw a bulky figure standing behind a bush. They started walking again pretending they didn't see what they saw. They continued down the road and turned around suddenly and saw *La Llorona* standing in the middle of the road, opening her arms . . . wide, and then the girls started screaming. Someone picked up a rock and threw it at her, then everyone else started doing the same. Then she said, "*No pendejas, si soy yo!*" ["No you crazy girls, it is I!"] Then everybody started running, followed by *La Llorona* (there was no leg motion in her gown as she was running). When [Angie's] brother and friends heard it they were stuck in the arroyo because the banks were very steep. The girls ran to the house. *La Llorona* stoped at the *canova* [overhead] because water stops all evil or supernatural beings. The boys came up to the house only steps after and said they saw no one. (Angelina Beatrice Valdez de Romero)

El Troquero y la Joven, The Trucker and the Young Girl

This *corrido* is a version in song of the widespread legend of "the vanishing hitchhiker." This story of a roadside ghost has a long history in legends of the supernatural. Early twentieth-century American accounts involve horse-drawn vehicles, but automobiles start appearing in stories collected in the 1930s, according to Jan H. Brunvand, who has researched this and other urban legends exhaustively (*The Vanishing Hitchhiker: American Urban Legends and Their Meanings*). For another Oregon version of the legend, see "Lavender," the next story in this volume.

"*El Troquero y la Joven*" was recorded from T. J. Jimenez of Nyssa, Oregon, one of several *corridistas* (*corrido* composers) in the Snake River Valley region of Eastern Oregon and Idaho. In addition to his own compositions, Jimenez sings ballads of others such as this one, which was recorded by Robert McCarl and Eva Castellanoz at Nyssa, February 14, 1991, as part of a Hispanic Folk Arts Survey. Transcription and translation are by Eva Castellanoz and Newell Morgan (*Living Treasures: Hispanic Artisans and Traditionalists of the Snake River Valley*). For another example of a *corrido*, see "*Corrido del Difunto Nabor*" in the section, "At Work in Oregon," p. 152.

Señores, pido permiso pa' cantar este corrido lo que le pasó a un troquero en la sierra de Saltillo.	Gentlemen, I ask your permission, In order to sing this song, This is what happened to a trucker In the sierra of Saltillo.
Al cruzar la guardarraya de Coahuila y Nuevo León, a una muy hermosa joven el troquero levantó.	Just across the border Of Coahuila and Nuevo León, A very beautiful young woman This trucker picked up.
Le preguntó por su nombre y que rumbo llevaba. —Vengo a ver a mi familia ella espera mi llegada.	He asked for her name And where she was going, "I'm coming to see my family; They are waiting for me."
—Acércate aquí a mi lado para [dar]te una acariciada. Cuando venga de regreso, te levanto de pasada.	"Come closer, here to my side, So I can caress you. When I return this way, I'll pick you up on the way by."
—¿Ves aquella' lucecitas que se devisan allá? Es el rancho de mis padres; yo allí me voy a bajar.	"Do you see those little lights, Those that can be seen over yonder? It's the ranch of my parents; I'm getting out over there."
A los tres o cuatro días el troquero regresó. Se detuvo en aquel rancho y por ella preguntó.	In three or four days The trucker returned. He stopped at that ranch, And he asked for her.

—Pase, señor, para adentro;
déjeme explicarle yo.
A esa joven que usted busca,
hace un año que murió.

"Come right in, sir.
Let me explain to you.
That young woman you are looking for,
She died a year ago.

Hace un año en esta fecha
en esas curvas chocó.
Se alcanzó a salir
del carro y un ratito caminó.

A year ago about this time
In those curves, she crashed.
She managed to get out;
She walked a little ways from the car.

Desde entonces se aparace,
pero ya sin esperanza,
haciendo siempre el esfuerzo
de llegar aquí a su casa.

Since then she appears
But without hope
Always trying
To return her to her home."

Ya con ésta me despido.
Esta es una historia cierta
lo que le pasó a un troquero
que le dio *ride* a una muerta.

Now with this I say good-bye.
This is a true story
About what happened to a trucker
Who gave a ride to a dead woman.

Lavender

"Lavender" is an *urban legend*, a modern American folk narrative set in the recent past. Like older legends such as those about buried treasure or outlaws, urban legends are "told seriously, circulate largely by word of mouth, are generally anonymous, and vary constantly in particular details from one telling to another, while always preserving a central core of traditional elements of 'motifs'" (Jan Harold Brunvand, *The Vanishing Hitchhiker: American Urban Legends and Their Meanings*, p. xii). While such legends are believed to be true by their tellers and are marked by specific—usually local—times and places, the events they portray can seldom be documented, and their truth lies more in the emotional truths they represent, the social values or anxieties they reflect. The "Lovers' Lane" legends in the "Family Matters" section of this volume are other examples of popular urban legends. "Lavender" was collected in 1986 from Bonnie Ables.—Venn Collection, Eastern Oregon State College..

Two men were on their way to the Saturday night dance a few years ago, when they saw a young woman walking down the Mission Highway, near Pendleton. They stopped to ask the woman if she would like a ride. The woman, dressed in a long, flowing, lavender evening gown, got into the beaten-up old Ford pickup with the men. The men asked the woman what her name was, and she replied, "Lavender." Then one of the men asked Lavender if she would like to go to the dance with them. She agreed to go to the dance, and they talked as they rode down the road, on their way to the Vert Auditorium, where the dance was being held.

The threesome had a lovely time that night—dancing, talking, joking, and laughing. After the dance, they dropped Lavender off by the gate in front of an eerie-looking, two-story, run-down old house. They said their goodbyes, and the two men went on their way. The next weekend, the two men stopped by the old house to see if Lavender would like to go to another dance. They stepped up to the door and knocked. An elderly lady answered the door, and they asked if Lavender was in. She invited the men in. Then, she walked over to a desk near a hallway and picked up a picture of a woman. She brought the picture over to the men and asked if this was the woman they were looking for.

The men examined the picture, and one of them replied, "Yes, we picked her up along the highway last weekend and took her to the dance in town."

Then, the other man said, "We would like to take her with us this weekend, also."

Then the elderly lady laid the picture down and informed the men that the lady they were looking for had died ten years ago. She took the men out the back door, where there was a large grave. On the grave was a lavender dress—which the men recognized as the one Lavender had been wearing the weekend before. On the tombstone was inscribed, "Lavender May Holmes." Puzzled, the two men said they would have to be going; then, they left.

Since then, there have been other reports of a woman wearing a lovely evening dress, standing along the Mission Highway.

Family Matters

I n this section, stories, rhymes, and songs from a variety of cultural settings in Oregon reflect their differences and similarities on the vital topic of growing up and getting along in a family.

The differences here—as to the use of oral traditions to *educate* children, for example—are fascinating; but taken together these pieces remind us that, whatever its format, the family unit counts as a primary folk-group in all cultures, and that family life is a dominant theme in folklore everywhere. How could it be otherwise? In a very real sense, folklore begins and renews itself in childhood. (See Philippe Aries, *Centuries of Childhood*.)

"Girls' Backyard Tea Party" by Timothy L. Graves. c. 1900, Oakland, Oregon.

Baby-land

In traditional Tillamook culture, it was understood that babies come from another country, and until they learn their parents' language must be talked to diplomatically in their own tongue! —Mrs. Clara Pearson, to Elizabeth Jacobs, Garibaldi, 1934: *Nehalem Tillamook Tales*, pp. xxvi-xxvii.

Babies come here from a land of their own. It's somewhere in this country, only grown-ups cannot see it. Babies live there on sandy beaches, around a big blue lake. They have their own language, their houses, and they marry just like big people. They're just like big people, only they run naked. When one of them decides he'll come to this land for a change, oh, they don't like it, and they all throw mud on him. If he's a married baby, his baby wife will probably come here too, but always to a different mother. They never get themselves born as twins or relatives of any kind, because they want to marry again here, when they are grown. They speak their baby language and they remember about Baby-land, until they learn the language here. Then they forget, and that's a sign that they're sure to stay here now.

[*According to Mrs. Pearson, each Tillamook village had a "baby-diplomat"— her term—who knew the Baby-language and would speak to sickly or cranky infants as follows:*] "Now see here! No one asked you to come here. You came of your own accord. Your parents love you, now that you're here. They would be heartbroken if you left. You have no right to do such a thing as long as they treat you well." [*In the case of a young couple's first-born child, the baby-diplomat might say:*] "You must realize that your parents are young. You are their first child. There are lots of things they don't know about taking care of you. But they treat you pretty well, and they'll do better as time goes on."

Babes in the Woods

This sentimental song has been popular in the English-language folksong tradition for more than three centuries and is widely known in America. Genevieve Jones of Ontario, Oregon, recalled that in the 1920s, as a very young child growing up in Midvale, Idaho, she would listen to her mother sing this song as she did the ironing. The many versions of this song that have been collected vary little in either text or tune. This one was recorded from Clarice Mae Judkins by Barre Toelken in the 1960s in Eugene, Oregon.

Oh, do you remember a long time ago,
When two little babes, their names I don't know,
They wandered away one bright summer day,
And were lost in the woods, I heard people say.

And when it was night, so sad was their plight,
The moon had gone down, the stars gave no light.
They sobbed and they sighed and they bitterly cried,
And those two little babies lay down and died.

And when they were dead, a robin so red
Brought strawberry leaves and over them spread,
And all the day long they sang their sweet song
Over those two little babes lost in the woods.

Joobering

Juba is the generic name of a whole family of Black folk-dances, originating in Africa, and popularized in the first half of the nineteenth century in American minstrel shows. Juba dancers usually provided their own complicated rhythmic accompaniment by stomping, hand clapping, and patting themselves.

Dancing Juba has exerted a broad influence on American popular dance, including the Charleston—and in at least one Central Oregon pioneer family, the Helfrich-McCoin-Mendenhall clan, an odd derivation known as *joobering* continues as a children's game. How an African dance evolved into a plantation entertainment of slaves and then into a staple of nineteenth-century vaudeville, and then made its way into the heritage of a Euro-American frontier family is a real puzzle—and also an excellent example of the unpredictable dynamism of folklore.

The *jooberer*, seated, stands a child between his/her legs, and, grasping the child's legs below the knees, jerks them up and down as if running, while chanting verses like these. At the end of the last verse, the child is flipped up by the legs into the jooberer's lap, with a shout of "Whoopee!"

Joober up and joober down
    Joober all around the town,
Joober this and joober that
    Joober killed an alley [or the yaller] cat,
Joober here and joober there
    Joober, joober everywhere!

Counting-Out Rhymes

Children's folklore usually circulates by word of mouth among children without the knowledge of—or instruction from—adults. Rhymes play a major role in children's lore and may be employed as taunts or insults ("Liar, liar, pants on fire . . ."); as comebacks ("Sticks and stones'll break my bones . . ."); to jump rope ("Cinderella dressed in yella . . ."); and in pre-game ceremonies to choose the one who will be "It" by "counting out" ("Eeny meeny, miney, moe . . ."). In their book, *One Potato, Two Potato: The Folklore of American Children*, Mary and Herbert Knapp have noted the antiquity and widespread distribution of counting out rhymes:

> Children who count out are repeating a ceremony that is hundreds of years old, and found in many different countries. In the 1880s, Henry Carrington Bolton collected 873 counting-out rhymes in English, German, Platt-Deutsch, Swedish, Dutch, French, Italian, Spanish, Portuguese, Bulgarian, Greek, Romany, Marathi (a language of western India), Basque, Arabic, Turkish, Armenian, Malagasy, Japanese, Hawaiian, and Penobscot (an American Indian language) (pp. 21-22).

We learn from the Knapps and from Iona and Peter Opie's classic study of British children's lore published in 1959, *The Lore and Language of Schoolchildren*, that counting-out rhymes collected in the late twentieth century are nearly identical to those collected a century earlier. The first of the rhymes below was collected from Julia Weimers, Portland, by Peter Lindsey (RVMA, 1970). This rhyme is, of course, the source for the title of Oregon author Ken Kesey's novel, *One Flew over the Cuckoo's Nest*. The other two rhymes, "as recited by Mrs. Mary Neet, Fall Creek, Oregon, and remembered by Mr. Mason Y. Warner, Eugene, Oregon," were collected for the WPA Oregon Folklore Project.

Intry, mintry, cootry, corn,
Appleseed and apple thorn,
Wire, briar, limberlock,
Three geese in a flock,
One flew east,
One flew west,
And one flew over the cuckoo's nest.

O, U, T, spells out goes he!

Zo, zi, zu, zink;
Chitter, lilly, black trout;
Gibby, ganey — you're out.

Anny, manny, miney, moe;
Basel, louney, bonny, stine;
Air, wair, crown;
Fe, fi, fo finn.

A Clackamas Girls' Game

The description of this charming Clackamas Chinook game was narrated by Mrs. Victoria Howard to Melville Jacobs around 1930: *Texts in Chinook Jargon*, p. 12.

My mother told me how they used to play a game long ago. They would go get flowers, they would break off just the flowers, and they would tie them to a long rope. Then of as many of them as were there, one would stand a little apart. One of them hung the flowers on her, they placed them all over her, until her body was just covered with flowers. Then they danced.

One of these young girls would go to where that one was standing, and the one who was standing there would say, "Well, come! I see you are playing. What is the matter with your nose? It does not seem to be right. What is the matter with your eyes? One side is small. What is the matter with your head? It's crooked. What is the matter with your mouth? It is sort of twisted. Now you laugh! Look at me! Don't make your eyes crooked." Until at last if the young woman would laugh at the one who did the talking, when she had not yet reached her, then she might laugh. "Now I have beaten you. Come now!"

Klamath String Figures

Play with string figures is one of the most widespread human pastimes, and probably one of the oldest. Many string-play forms are associated with and actually illustrate *stories*, like these examples from the Klamath Indians, recorded by Leslie Spier in *Klamath Ethnography*, pp. 84-85.

String figures or cat's cradles . . . are for amusement. Yet if played in winter the months will grow longer. Their number is legion. I was told a few: "the stolen baby," "*Tca'kiak*," "sunrise," "owl's nest," "sick coyote's knees," "the girl who fetches water," "a bundle of arrows," "the abandoned boy who grows," and "two coyotes who run from each other." The interesting feature of these figures is that they depict moving scenes; thus sick coyote sticks up his knees; the girl goes to fetch water crying *omdia, omdia*, "water, water," until she spies an Indian when she cries *maklaks*, "human," and flees to the other hand to begin again. . . .

The figure of the stolen baby is called *swensowa'tkeas*, "taking from the cradle." Put each hand through the loop so that it lies on the back of each wrist. Lift the radial string with each little finger from the ulnar side and the ulnar string from the radial side with each thumb, so as to form a loop on these four fingers (fig. 8a). Insert each index finger under the intersection on the opposite palm. Using the lips, lift the loop from the back of each wrist so that it rests in front of all the fingers (fig. 8b). With each index catch the strings at A and pull them through the loops on each index while allowing the latter to slip off the dorsal side of the index. This forms a horizontal rectangle at the center which represents the cradle. This is narrowed by bunching the fingers of

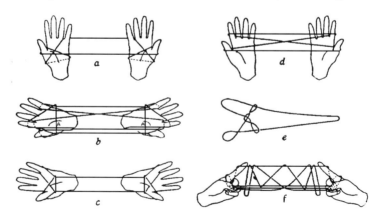

Fig. 8. String figures

each hand. A little stick is thrust through this with the lips; this is the baby. Let slip the loops from each index finger. Pull the hands apart and the stick will fly toward one of them (fig. 8c). The hands represent two Old Women spirits (*wile'akak*), fighting over the baby; the one who gets the stick wins.

A second figure forms *Tca'kiak*, Little Boy spirit. The loop is placed over the right thumb and the left thumb and index finger. Hold both strings against the palm with the three other fingers of the left hand. Insert the right index under the loop over the left thumb and index from the dorsal proximal side (i.e from the direction of the wrist). Release the strings held by the other fingers of the left hand. This gives figure 8d. The final figure showing *Tca'kiak* is given by figure 8e. The third figure, "sunrise," (*sa'basdini'gi*), is shown in figure 8f. Pulling the hands apart makes the middle loop stand as a triangular figure, representing the appearance of a mountain peak gradually emerging against the dawn.

Old Mr. Fox

"Old Mr. Fox" is a favorite folksong in the Wasson Hockema family of Pistol River, Oregon. Bess Finley Wasson Hockema, who came to Oregon from Texas in 1911, always sang this song to her own children and now sings it to her grandchildren and great-grandchildren. Bess explains that her mother, Genarah Beckham Finley, originally from Arkansas, sang the song to the accompaniment of her concertina, and although now it is often sung unaccompanied, the singers still pause at the end of the first two lines of each stanza, just where Genarah always paused to draw more air into the concertina bellows.—Personal communication, Bess Finley Wasson Hockema, 1994.

Old Mister Fox on a moonshiny night,
Stood on his hind feet just about right; [*pause*]
I'll have some meat for my supper tonight
Before I leave this town-e-o,
Before I leave this town-e-o.

He marched up to the farmer's gate,
There he spied an old black drake; [*pause*]
"Mister Drake, Mister Drake come and go with me—
I'm the finest old fellow in this town-e-o,
The finest old fellow in this town-e-o."

Mister Drake stood still and he replied,
"No, Mister Fox, I will not go; [*pause*]
If you never eat meat 'til you eat me, oh,
You'll never eat meat in this town-e-o,
Never eat meat in this town-e-o."

Old Mister Fox he took his track back,
Picked up the gray goose by her back; [*pause*]
Her wings went flip flop over his back
And her legs hung dingle dingle down-e-o,
Her legs hung dingle dingle down-e-o.

Old Mrs. Flip Flop lyin' in the bed
Raised up the window and poked out her head; [*pause*]
"Old man, old man, the gray goose is gone,
For don't you hear her goin' crank crank-e-o?
Don't you hear her goin' crank crank-e-o ?"

Old man raised up in a mighty, mighty rage,
Wiped out his mouth and it full of sage, [*pause*]
"Old woman, old woman, just let them go
I'll make mighty music come-a-hime-e-o
Make mighty music come-a-hime-e-o."

He marched on 'til he came to his den;
There were the young ones, nine or ten, [*pause*]
The old ones eating up all the meat
And the young ones gnawing on the bone-e-os,
The young ones gnawing on the bone-e-os.

"Daddy, oh daddy, when you goin' agin?"
"Hope to the dingle dingle never ta go agin"
"Why?" [*in falsetto by youngsters*]
"Oh, don't you hear the music come-a-hime-e-o?
Don't you hear the music come-a-hime-e-o?
Don't you hear the music come-a-hime-e-o?"

Little Raccoon and His Grandmother

In traditional Indian family life, one's grandparents are supposed to be venerated and obeyed. In a Modoc myth, "Once while Dove was engrossed in playing a game he was told that his grandmother had died and that he must mourn. He replied that there would be plenty of time to mourn later, and continued playing. He has been mourning ever since." (Told by Evaline Sconchin to Verne Ray: Ray, *Primitive Pragmatists: The Modoc Indians of Northern California,* p. 253.) In the following Wasco-Warm Springs version of a very widespread story, the misfortunes of Little Raccoon and his grandma have instructive value: children ought to obey their elders and seek good reputations; parents and grandparents must not spoil the children in their household.—Narrated by Mrs. Alice Florendo to Jarold Ramsey at Warm Springs in 1971; revised from text originally published in Ramsey, *Coyote Was Going There,* pp. 58-60.

Little Raccoon lived with his grandmother; he was her *k'itch* [paternal grandson], and she spoiled him. They were gathering acorns over the mountains, and one day she asked Raccoon what he wanted to eat for dinner. "Would you like some wapato?" she asked, and Raccoon answered, "No, I'm tired of wapato." "Some jerky, then?"—"No, I'm tired of jerky."—"How about some dried fish-eyes?"—"I don't like dried fish-eyes!" So Raccoon's grandmother grew angry and told him to just go out and find his own dinner. "But stay out of the acorns!" she told him.

Well, after a while Raccoon came to the five pits where his grandmother was storing her winter's acorns. "I'm so hungry!" he said to himself, and after awhile he said, "Grandmother surely won't miss just one acorn." So he reached into the pit, under the dirt covering, and took out one acorn to eat—and then another, and then another, until pretty soon the pit was empty! "Now what shall I do?" he said. "Grandmother will be very angry." So he thought he would crap once for every acorn in the pit, but eating acorns had given him diarrhea, and what he left was a smelly mess—which he covered up. But he was still very hungry, and he went on to the second pit. "Well, maybe I'll just take one more acorn," he said, but after awhile that pit was empty too, and so he filled it up, as before, with his dung. Well, Raccoon just seemed to get hungrier and hungrier, and before long he had eaten every acorn in each of the five pits, and filled each one with his dung.

After awhile his grandmother went out to get some acorns for their supper. But when she reached into the first pit all she felt was Raccoon's smelly mess!

"Somebody has been messing around here!" she said. So she went on to the second pit and reached in, and felt the same thing—and so on through all five pits. She was getting angrier and angrier. "I'll bet it was that Little Raccoon!" she yelled, and when she found him by the fire she grabbed a fire-stick [braided willow wands to carry live coals in] and whipped him from his nose to his tail. This is why raccoons have those stripes across their backs.

Little Raccoon ran away then; he thought he would go live with some friends in a village nearby. But when he arrived there everybody came out and jeered at him: "Ha ha, here comes that Little Raccoon; he stole all his grandmother's acorns and replaced them with his dung!" So Raccoon felt silly and went on to another village, but there again all the people ran out and ridiculed him, "Ha ha, here's that Little Raccoon, we've heard how you pilfered your grandmother's acorns and left her only dung!" He was ashamed, and went on to three more villages, but every time he arrived the people would come out and make fun of him. So Raccoon learned how stories about the mean things you do travel ahead of you, and he went off by himself into the woods.

Now about this time his old grandmother began to feel badly about whipping her little *k'itch;* she felt sorry for him. So she set out to find him, but when she came to the first village, they told her that Raccoon had gone on to the next village, and so on, until she had visited all five villages without finding him. She was feeling pretty bad. Now Raccoon was up in a serviceberry bush, eating berries, and he heard his grandmother coming up the hill, crying, "Oh my little *k'itch,* my little Raccoon, where are you, where are you?" Raccoon yelled, "Here I am, Grandmother, just eating serviceberries." Pretty soon she came up, nearly blind from crying so much, and she said, "My *k'itch,* I'm so hungry, throw me some berries."

Now that his grandmother had found him, that Raccoon was feeling mischievous again, so he threw a whole handful of berries, leaves, and twigs right down her throat, and she began to choke. "Kak-kak," she cried, "my *k'itch.* I'm choking; here, take my basket-hat and get me some water!" So that Raccoon climbed down, took the hat, and ran to a creek and filled it up, but he was feeling mean again so he poked a hole in the hat and by the time he got back he had only a little water. "Kak-kak!" cried the grandmother, "get me some more water!" So Raccoon went to fetch her water again, but he poked another hole, and brought even less water this time. He was obeying her, but not really. Each time he went he poked another hole into the hat and brought back a little less, and a little less, until the fifth time, when the grandmother could hardly talk, he brought her only one drop of water. And just as he handed her the basket-hat this time, she cried "Kak-kak-kak" once more—and turned into a blue-jay and flew off, scolding the way blue-jays do. Little Raccoon just sat down and cried; it was all his fault.

Wild Woman Ate Children

Although Indian oral literatures are calculated to entertain listeners of all ages (a typical winter-evening storytelling session included everybody), in many stories a special emphasis falls on the education of children about the moral way of the tribe. In this Tillamook learning story, a female bogey, one of a race of "Wild Women," is invoked to dramatize the consequences (potentially serious in a subsistence economy) of disobedient eating between meals. —Told by Mrs. Clara Pearson to Elizabeth Jacobs, *Nehalem Tillamook Tales,* pp. 158-161.

People were living at Flower Pot, right near Bayocean. They had one daughter just in her basket cap [at puberty] and several other children who were small, none of them more than eight or nine years old. The maiden had a little baby brother to take care of. The people told those children the Indian rule, "Children must not eat when they are alone when there are no grown people present." That older girl remembered that. But the smaller children, they often became hungry.

One day the children were all together in one of the houses. They were hungry, they said, "Our grown people have been gone too long. We are going to eat, we are hungry." They proceeded to eat. They broke off pieces of dried salmon eggs and ate them. They were all very fond of them, in those days. They passed the older girl a piece of those salmon eggs. She took it, but she would not eat it, she just held it in her hand. Those younger children ate, sitting by the fire they were keeping. The maiden carried her baby brother on her back. She walked about with him to keep him from crying. He himself was too small to eat dried salmon eggs.

Presently someone opened the door and came in. It was a woman the children had never seen before. She tossed about ten sharpened red huckleberry stakes into the house. She carried a basket of dry wood, rotten wood, with her. The older girl thought, "My! It looks to me as if she is that Wild Woman [*ha'lgu*] whom the older people speak of. They say that she acts this way. She uses those sharpened sticks for cooking little children." That woman built a roaring fire with that rotten wood. She seized each child and smelled its mouth. Those that had been eating salmon eggs she caused to be numb so they could not run out doors. That older girl was unable to run as well. The woman smelled of each child's mouth. She went to that maiden, noticed that she had not eaten any salmon eggs. She smelled of that little baby's mouth, he had not eaten any. Then she began.

She took away that older girl's voice so that she could not speak. In the same manner the baby was unable to cry. She took her stakes and inserted one in the anus of each child who had eaten salmon eggs. She put them around the fire to cook.

In the meantime the grown people were all clam-digging. It was not yet dark. They chanced to look toward the house. One said, "What can be happening? It looks as if that house is burning up. The whole house is smoking. We must go home, the children might get burned, they have not enough sense to run out if the house were on fire." They came home. Wild Woman saw those people coming. The children were not yet cooked enough to be eaten. She hastened away from there, she ran into the woods.

The grown people came in. There was that older girl walking about, unable to speak. There were those children staked around the fire, roasting. The people knew at once who had done that, they knew. That maiden could not talk to tell them anything. The next day the people put those children away [in burial canoes]. The father who had lost more children than anyone else said, "You people pack all of your things and leave." He said this to his wife as well. They did not want to go far away, they all went down to the sandspit to stay. There were houses there because it was a summer place for drying clams. They moved there.

That father said, "I will remain here, I will allow her to come to cook me." He knew her, he had her power, Wild Woman's. His wife did not like that, but he said, "Oh, I do not care. I want her to cook me. Do not leave any food of any sort except one piece of dried salmon eggs. She is more jealous of them than of anything else I can eat."

The man was there alone. He sharpened his knife as sharp as a razor. He gathered quantities of wood, kept a bright fire, and went without eating for four days. In the evening of the fourth day he ate those salmon eggs. Soon he heard a noise at the door. He knew that she was coming. She opened the door, she threw in a very large stake of red huckleberry bush, sharpened on both ends. She entered. She brought in that dry rotten wood. He sat up, watched her build up the fire. While she was doing that he got ready with his knife, he ran at her, grabbed her by the hair, he stuck his knife in her eyes. That was the only place she was soft. Those Wild Women are solid all over. Their flesh is not like a person's flesh, one cannot thrust a knife into them. He put her eyes out. He had a club in readiness. She was blind now, so he seized that club and clubbed her. She died. He put her in that great fire she had built. Then he tore the house down and made a larger fire.

Those others who had left had been watching every day. Now they said, "Well, that house appears to be burning." They wept, "He must be killed then." That Wild Woman was full of oil. The sky turned as red as if it too were burning. Then it turned black, pitch dark, though it was not yet night. At last when Wild Woman was nearly burned the man went down to the beach, got into the canoe he had kept there, and paddled down. He arrived at the place where his people were. He said, "I killed her when she was preparing to cook me. I put her eyes out, I mashed her after that, and I burned her."

No one has ever lived in that place since. Everyone is afraid of that place. After Wild Woman was dead that older girl could speak again. She described what Wild Woman had done, how she had smelled the children's mouths and cooked only those who had been eating. In the olden days [myth age] Wild Woman ate only lizards and poisonous things. But later on she ate children.

That is a kind of real happening. This story was told to children to keep them from eating when their parents were away.

Bloody Fingers

Ghost stories are a staple of children's folklore and are often performed at slumber parties or on camping trips. The performance of ghost stories is often highly dramatic as narrators attempt to provide a scary experience for their audiences. This tale, collected in 1971 from eleven-year-old Muffin Rheinburger, was told in a "quavering, low, gravelly voice." (RVMA, Joel Marrant, 1971)

It was a really windy night, and the hotel, this hotel—they say it was haunted. One room of it was haunted, and that was the only room vacant. And this man went into this hotel, and he sat down and waited for the clerk. And the clerk came, and he said, "May I help you?" And the man says, "Yes, I'd like a hotel room." So the clerk says, "There's only one left, and it's the haunted one." And the man goes, "Oh, I don't believe in that haunts thing; I'll take the room. How much is it?" "You can have it for free if you want it." "Okay."

So he goes upstairs, and he washed his face, and he's watching TV for a while, and then he decided to go to bed because it was twelve o'clock. So he went to bed, and after a while he heard: "Blo-o-o-o-dy fing-g-g-gers, blo-o-o-o-dy fing-g-g-gers." And he was looking all around the house, and he got so scared that he jumped out the window and killed hisself.

So the next night—it was the same kind of night—all bleary and windy and rainy and stormy, and lightning out, and a little boy rushed into the room with his parents, and they were waiting for the man [hotel clerk], and the man came and said, "May I help you?" And he said, "Yes, we'd like a hotel room." And he says, "The only one left is the haunted hotel room." And so he says, "Okay, we'll take it." And the family went to bed, and that night they heard: "Blo-o-o-o-dy fing-g-g-gers, blo-o-o-o-dy fing-g-g-gers!" So they all killed theirself.

And then, it was another stormy night—just like the other two, and the nurse came in. And she said, "I'd like a hotel room, please." And the man said, "The only one left is the haunted room." And so she said, "Oh, I'll take it. I don't believe in haunt any way." So she took the room, and she went up. She put down her nurse kit and her robe. And she went to bed, and she heard, "Blo-o-o-o-dy fing-g-g-gers, blo-o-o-o-dy fing-g-g-gers!" And she said, "Well, if they're so bloody, why don't you put a band-aid over them." The end.

The Golden Arm

"The Golden Arm" is a classic ghost story. It's widely known and has been recorded in many variants. Like "Bloody Fingers," it is a favorite to tell in the night-time settings of campfires and slumber parties, to scare young listeners when darkness and the absence of adults creates a heightened sense of vulnerability. Few children grow up without hearing this story. This text was collected in 1971 from Barbara Shirk, a junior high school teacher in Eugene (RVMA, Cindy Shirk, 1971). For a different and much longer version of "The Golden Arm," see *Oregon Folklore*, p. 66-67.

Once upon a time there was a man, and rather late in life he married a woman who in her youth had lost an arm. And she was rich and so had replaced it with a golden arm. After several years of married life the wife became very ill. She knew she was about to die so she called for her husband. She said to him, "Darling, I know I'm about to die and I have only one last request: that is that I be buried with my golden arm." And her husband, of course, agreed to her wish.

Several days thereafter she died, and according to her last wish the husband had her buried with her golden arm. And he went home from the funeral, and after several days without his wife, he began to think: "Why should she have the golden arm? She's dead and doesn't need it, and I could use some money to live on. The allowance she left me wasn't much. I could always use more money." But he put the thought out of his head. And after a few more days, the thought occurred to him again: "Why should she have the golden arm? I could really use the money more. She doesn't need it." But he put it out of his head again.

But then after a few more days he thought of it again, and this time the thought wouldn't go away. And so at the very dead of night, he went down to the graveyard and dug up her grave and took the golden arm out of her coffin, reburied the coffin, put the golden arm under his coat and hurried home.

He entered the house, put the golden arm in the closet of his bedroom and got ready to go to bed. He hadn't been asleep for very long when something awakened him. It sounded almost like the wind whistling, but there seemed to be words attached. "Who's got my golden arm?" He thought he just must have been having a bad dream or that the night was playing tricks on him. So he went back to sleep.

A little while later he awakened again. This time the voice was more distinct, clear. It seemed to be coming from the street outside his house. "Who's got my golden arm?" He ran downstairs and made sure that the front door was bolted securely. And then he listened again, and from the front porch he heard a voice: "Who's got my golden arm?" He ran upstairs and he shut and locked the bedroom door, and he heard a voice from the living room saying, "Who's got my golden arm?" So he pushed a chest of drawers in front of the door, and he heard a voice from the stairs say, "Who's got my golden arm?" He ran and jumped in bed and pulled the covers up over his head. And he heard a voice from outside his bedroom say, "Who's got my golden arm?" He became a little bit curious, so very carefully he peeked up over the edge of the covers, and he heard a voice say, "YOU'VE GOT IT!"

The Boyfriend's Death

Teen-age anxieties about dating and sex may be reflected in several well-known urban legends about terrible events that are supposed to have happened to young couples out parked in secluded spots. These legends are usually believed to be true; they depict events that are to have happened in the favorite local parking area or, as in the case of the legend that follows, relate an event that happened to someone local—"one of the guys that went to my school." However, as this narrator also says, he can't attest to the truth of this story "because it's been related second-hand." Related as true incidents, urban legends are characteristically grounded in specific local details, but they are almost always told at one remove—a friend of a friend—so that verification is more difficult. And, in fact, folklorists who have attempted to track down the sources of urban legends find that they can rarely verify them.

One of the best known lovers' lane legends is "The Hook," in which the parked couple turns on the car radio and hears a news bulletin warning listeners about a sex maniac who has just escaped from a local mental institution. The escapee can be identified by the hook on his left arm. Frightened, the girl insists the boy drive her home, which he grudgingly does. The story ends when they arrive at the girl's house and the boy walks around the car to open the door for the girl and discovers a hook hanging from the door handle. "The Boyfriend's Death" has a more gruesome ending.—Collected from Ron Dunagan, Eugene, by Cindy Shirk (RVMA, 8/1971).

I can't attest to the truth of this story because it's been related second-hand. One of the guys that went to my school took out one of the girls that went to my school. They went out for a typical date—dinner, dancing. So they'd had a pretty good time so they decided to go out and park. Good thing to do on a nice moonlit night. They were out there listening to the radio and other things, and it started getting foggy. Doesn't bother most people. Then they started hearing funny sounds. People moaning it sounded like. Must be the wind. Then they heard other funny sounds like people were being killed and things like this—groans and moaning and mad panting. "What are those?" "I don't know," he says, "I'll go check." So he gets out and shuts the door. Can't hear anything. And then more moaning and then a scream. "What is it? What is it? Who's there?" She can't hear anything any more. Then all of a sudden she hears a scraping sound on the roof. "What's that? Who's there?" "Scrape, scrape." That's all she can hear. Nothing but scraping on the roof. Finally, she's just so terrified that she just can't take it any longer, and she passes out.

All of a sudden she hears a sound outside, and she wakes up, and there's a policeman with a flashlight. So she opens the door, and he says, "Now, Miss," he says, "you can get out of the car, but," he says, "don't look back at it." So she got out and started to walk away, and she thought, "Why can't I look back?" She looked back, and there it was: her boyfriend hanging by his neck and his feet were scraping back and forth on the roof.

The Three Murderer Sons

This legend was told by prospector, Al Renfro, of City Creek, Oregon, to George W. Braddock on April 24, 1976. It is set in a specific Oregon location, and the narrator explains that he heard the story because he almost married the daughter of one of the three sons. The legend does follow the narrative pattern of many traditional European and American tales in that there are three sons and the climax of the story occurs when it's the third son's turn to act.—From RVMA, George W. Braddock, May 1976.

Now this guy lived up above Canton Creek, had himself a little homestead up there and a real fine wife. Well, sir, she bore him three of the meanest sons-of-bitches you ever laid eyes on. They were lazy and shiftless drunk most of the time, too, you know. Wouldn't do a God-damned thing to help out their Mom or Pop. Well, sir, one day the old man went into Roseburg and bought himself a pair of the finest walkin' boots money can buy. He hardly got them broke in where they was just fine when one day while he was coming home a rattler struck him in his left leg right above the ankle. That snake was so powerful its fangs went right through the boot and into his leg—you know that snake was an old one and the older they get the stronger the poison gets—killed him almost instantly, I suspect, least-wise he was dead when his sons found him. They didn't even care that he was dead; they took to fightin' over who was going to take what—They stripped the old man and just threw his body in the river for the fish, being too lazy to even bury him right. Well, sir, a fight started right then and there and over those Spanish boots. Finally they drew lots and the middle son won. He didn't waste a minute's time pullin' them on either. So off they goes to spend the money they had stole off their dead father. They hadn't gone half a mile when the one who had won the boots started to hang behind—and it weren't a mile till they looked back and he was dead. The other two looked him over real close trying to figure out what had killed him—there weren't a mark on the boy but he was dead as can be. Didn't make a lot of difference to them though—they stripped him just like the father and dumped him in the river and took to fighting over them boots again. This time they flipped a coin and the oldest boy won. He pulled the boots on like before and off they went. Well, but this time it was getting to be late and night was coming on so they decided to make camp. They had just started to get set up when the boy that had the boots says he ain't feeling so good and lays down—weren't a minute later his brother turns around and he is just as dead as can be. That boy dropped down on his face and he started to pray like he had never prayed before 'cause he was convinced that the Lord was punishing them for the way they had treated their kin. And he said how sorry he was and that if the Lord would spare him his life he would walk the straight and narrow always. Well, he stayed right there on his face for a long time waiting to see if he was going to die or not an' all the time going on about being good from now on. . . . After a while he set up and it was all dark and getting cold so he started a fire and laid his brother out on the ground so he could get him ready for burying. When he got around to pullin' off the boots that's when he saw it—stuck in the side of the Spanish boot, just above the ankle was a fang from that rattlesnake that had got broke off when he struck the old man. And you know that boy stayed good to his word too—he even went on home and took care of his mother till she died, married and raised himself a right fine family—hell, I damn near married his daughter, that's how I heard the story about the fang.

Seal and Her Younger Brother Lived There

Since Dell Hymes retranslated and reinterpreted it along ethnopoetic lines in the 1960s, this little masterpiece of domestic horror from Mrs. Victoria Howard's Clackamas Chinook repertory has become the most widely known and discussed item in traditional Oregon Indian literature—see Hymes's work in *"In Vain I Tried to Tell You": Essays in Native American Ethnopoetics*, pp. 274-308.

As Hymes was the first to reveal, the story uses the intrusion of the sinister "wife" (probably a trickster in disguise) into this household to dramatize a conflict between "being smart" and "being proper": Seal's brother, the head of the household, is murdered because Seal ignores her daughter's disturbing observations about the "wife," in order to maintain propriety. Coming from at least three generations of female Clackamas narrators, the story may well reflect a special woman's perspective in the Contact Era, when the old Native norms of social propriety and conduct were breaking up. For a very different formulation of this plot and of the "smart/proper" conflict, see the Coos hero-tale, "The Revenge against the Sky People," p. 67.

They lived there, Seal, her daughter, her younger brother.
After some time, now a woman got to Seal's younger brother.
They lived there.
> They would "go outside" in the evening.
The girl would say,
> she would tell her mother:
> "Mother! something is different about my uncle's wife.
> "It sounds like a man when she 'goes out'."
"Shush! your uncle's wife!"
A long long time they lived there like that.
> In the evening they would each "go out."
Now she would tell her:
> "Mother! something is different about my uncle's wife.
> "When she 'goes out' it sounds like a man."

"Shush!"

Her uncle, his wife, would "lie down" up above on the bed.
Pretty soon the other two would lie down close to the fire,
> they would lie down beside each other.
Some time during the night, something comes on to her face.
She shook her mother,
> she told her:
> "Mother! something comes on to my face."
> "Hmmmm. Shush. Your uncle, they are 'going'."
Pretty soon now again, she heard something escaping.
She told her:
> "Mother! Something is going *t'úq t'úq*.
> "I hear something."
"Shush. Your uncle, they are 'going'."
The girl got up,
> she fixed the fire,
> > she lit pitch,
> > > she looked where the two were:
> > > > Ah! Ah! blood!
She raised her light to it, thus
> her uncle is on his bed,
> > his neck cut,
> > > he is dead.
> > > > She screamed.

She told her mother:
  "I told you,
   'Something is dripping.'
   "You told me,
    'Shush, they are "going".'
   "I had told you,
    'Something is different about my uncle's wife.
    'She would "go out"
     with a sound just like a man she would urinate.'
   "You would tell me,
    'Shush!'
She wept.
Seal said:
  "Younger brother! My younger brother!
  "They are valuable standing there.
  "My younger brother!"
She kept saying that.
As for that girl, she wept.
She said:
  "I tried in vain to tell you,
   'Not like a woman,
   'With a sound just like a man she would urinate,
    my uncle's wife.'
  "You told me,
   'Shush!'
  "Oh oh my uncle!"
  "Oh my uncle!"
She wept, that girl.

Now, I remember only that far.

The Legend of the Magpies

Since World War II, and especially since the Korean War, South Koreans have come to Oregon in numbers, like other Oregon immigrants bringing with them both the will to adapt and assimilate and the will to conserve old-country family-borne traditions. The following legend was recorded by Valerie Kang of Gresham from her grandmother, Sung Hark Lee Kang, in 1972 (RVMA). Magpies play a significant role in Korean folklore and are frequently pictured in Korean folk art. Sociable birds that nest near peoples' homes in Korea, they are believed to be bearers of good tidings.

On July seventh, by the lunar calender, magpies lose their feathers on top of their heads because they formed a bridge so that Kyun Woo and Chin Nyo can meet over the Heavenly River. Although the night of July seventh is not a holiday or celebration, everyone recalls the legend of these two lovers, the Star of the East (girl) and the Star of the West. Chin Nyo was the dutiful daughter of the King of the Heavens, In Goom Nim. A devoted daughter, she wove beautiful silk cloth for his garments. However, after marrying Kyun Woo who lived across the Heavenly River, she stopped weaving cloth for her father. Angered by what he thought was his daughter's negligence, In Goom Nim asked his daughter to come home for a visit. After she came home, he scolded her and forbade her to return home to her husband. She loved her husband dearly and pleaded with her father until he finally allowed her to meet her beloved once a year on July seventh. Once a year the magpies form a bridge over the Heavenly River so that the two lovers can meet and on that night the two stars meet in the heavens and thereafter the magpie loses his feathers on top of his head. This story is always repeated on July seventh and there is hardly a person in Korea who has not heard it.

The Girl Who Married a Sea Otter

Transcribed from a telling by Susan Wasson Wolgamott, this Coquelle tale embodies a persistent theme of Native stories from the Oregon coast: social interactions between the people of the land and those of the sea. Sunset is a small coastal community near Sunset Bay, in Coos County.—Personal communication from Susan Wasson Wolgamott, 1992, all rights reserved.

Over at Sunset, you know how the little creek goes up Sunset and goes up to the park where you can camp. Well, lots of times the Indians camped along that. There was a chief there whose wife was dead, and he had five sons and one daughter, and she was a very, very sweet girl. Everybody liked her. She took care of her father and her brothers.

So one morning, really early in the morning when it was still rather foggy, she went down to the creek to get water, and she looked and here she saw come swimming up the creek a sea otter. He came up and he got out on land and turned into a very handsome young man. And she was quite surprised to see him. And he said that he had been watching her; he wanted her to go back down in the bottom of the ocean with him and be his wife. She said, "Why, I couldn't do that. I'd drown. I can't live in the ocean." He said, "Oh just come. Take my hand and we'll jump into the creek." So she took his hand. They jumped into the creek, and they both turned into sea otters, and they went swimming down the creek and way out into the ocean, down to the bottom of the ocean where his father was the chief of the sea otters.

She lived there with him for quite a while, and then she got rather sad, and they asked what was wrong. And she said she missed her father and her brothers. She wanted to go back and see her family, and so the chief of the sea otters said, all right, she could go back and visit them. So she and her husband went back, and they went swimming down there, and they got through Sunset and they started swimming up the creek, and the people saw them and they shot arrows at them. So they dived under a little place under the bank where there was a little cave back in there, and they hid there all day until it was dark. And then when it got dark, they crawled out and they got up on land and turned back into her and this handsome young man.

So they walked up to the village where the people were camped and they told them that they were the sea otters that they had been shooting at that day. Well, the people said that they would never, ever harm a sea otter again then. Well, they stayed there for several days, and then they decided they would go back. So they gathered up all the arrows that had been shot at them down in the creek, and they took them back with them down and gave them to the chief of the sea otters and told him that this was a present for him from her family. Well, the chief of the sea otters was very happy to get those arrows so he said, "I want you to go back and you tell your people that they are to leave the ocean, leave the coast, leave the sand, the beach, everything. They are to go way, way back up on a hill, on a very high place, and they are to stay there until after—this big storm is coming, and they are to stay until after the storm is over, or they will all be washed away, and they would all be drowned."

So they went back and told them. And he said, "Now after the storm is all over and they come back down to the beach there will be a present for them from me on the beach." So they went back and they told them, and the people all left. They picked up everything, and they went way up in a high place.

And the storm came. It was a terrible storm. After the storm was over, they came back and all of the houses were washed away that they'd been living in there. They went down on the beach, and there was a big whale on the beach. Oh and the people were so happy to get this, and they cut it up and used the whale.

So ever after that none of the people along the south coast of Oregon ever would harm a sea otter, and every year they put a bundle of arrows in the water for the chief of the sea otters, and every so often he threw a whale upon the beach.

Split-His-Own-Head

Another story from Mrs. Pearson's rich Tillamook repertory centers comically on the misadventures of a naive adolescent boy who understands idiomatic expressions literally and thus is always embarrassing himself—much like the "Sillies" in European folklore.—Told by Mrs. Clara Pearson to Elizabeth Jacobs, *Nehalem Tillamook Tales,* pp. 118-120.

Split-His-Own-Head was living with his older sister. They had no mother or father. One day she told him, "Oh, I am tired. I am getting so tired of it. I go on foot all the time to dig yetska roots. Why do you not make a canoe for me? Even one of rotten wood would be better than walking all the time." "Ha!" he said. "Your brother certainly can do that. Nothing will stop me from making a canoe." He made a canoe for her. That canoe was quickly finished. It was very fine looking. She made preparations to go digging roots. She threw her root digger into the canoe. That stick went right through the bottom of that canoe because the canoe was made of rotten wood. She became angry. She came back in the house. "Oh, goodness, you made a canoe of rotten wood." "Well, sister, you told me to do that." "Oh, I did not really mean rotten wood. I just said it that way because I meant why on earth can you not make a canoe for me."

She started out on foot then to go for roots. Before she left she said, "You must make a canoe out of a good cedar log." "Oh, indeed, nothing will stop me." When she came home he had it already finished, another canoe made from a good cedar log.

One day she said, "My digging stick is becoming worthless. Go split that head end [of yours]." He understood her to say, "Go split your face." She should have said, "Go split the head end of a spruce limb." "All right," he told her, "I can do that." He went. Presently he returned with his head all wrapped up. She noticed, "Your head is all wrapped up. What for?" He replied, "Oh, I nearly died. You told me to go split my face." She scolded, "No! I told you to hunt up spruce limbs, split one, and make a root digger for me." "Why, you did not tell me that, sister. You told me to split my face." She told him, "You should have known that I did not mean that." He went, obtained a spruce limb, brought it home, he made a root digger for her. That was all right then, he had done it right.

One morning she sent him, "You go along. Some people are going to buy whale meat, you go with them. In some manner you can fasten yourself in the stern of the canoe. If the boat is crowded you can hang on to the stern." "All right, sister." She gave him some dentalia. "Maybe you can take these money beads, and remember, throw your money beads on any old woman's privates." [By that expression the native would understand, "Buy whale meat from anyone who gives you a good trade. Do not just trade with some special one."]

They went in that canoe. Those people were paddling along. They noticed that the stern of the canoe seemed to drag. They looked, there he was in the water, hanging on to the canoe. They said, "Oh, I suppose your sister told you to do that. Get into the canoe." He got in. When they got there where that whale was, Split-His-Own-Head did not attempt to buy any. He just stood about watching the old women. One went outdoors, he followed her. He watched her squat down, he sneaked up close to her and threw those money beads between her legs. "Why did you throw your money where I would urinate on it?" she asked. He replied, "I came to buy whale meat." "Oh, I suppose your sister told you to do it that way." After that he bought whale meat and they all went home.

His sister gave him a dried salmon, saying, "We are nearly out of dried salmon now." She did not tell him not to eat it all at once. But she said, "Today you will throw rocks at the sun all day." [By that was meant, "Do not eat it all at once, save some for your supper."] He was gone all day. In the evening he returned, saying, "Goodness, I am all sore and lame." "Why?" she asked. "Where are you sore?" "My arm is almost worn out from throwing rocks at the sun all day, like you said." She told him, "You are very foolish. I did not tell you to throw rocks, I told you to save some fish for supper because we have not very much left to eat."

Again some people were preparing to go buy whale meat. She told him, "You can sit on a mat or blanket on the floor of the canoe." He answered, "I can certainly do that." People got in the canoe, they sat down to paddle. They sat on him, they did not see him because he was under those ferns that were in the canoe to sit on. He became tired. He grunted and attempted to change position. The people said, "Why, it feels as if someone were underneath us." They looked, there he was. "Oh get up! Sit up and help paddle! I suppose your sister told you to do that!" "Yes, she told me," the little fool answered. They arrived at that [market] place. They all purchased some whale meat and returned home.

Later on his sister said to him, "You are getting grown now, you should hunt a woman for yourself. You are old enough to get married. Any old thing, a dead person is perhaps better than no wife at all." "Huh! I can do that all right, sister." He went to look for a wife. He returned late at night. His sister was already in bed and did not see him. Presently she heard him say, "Oh! My wife is sticking me with her scratcher." His sister thought, "Why, he must have found a maiden bathing after her first menstruation." Daylight came. The sister arose and built the fire. Split-His-Own-Head got up, he had no wife. "Where is your wife?" his sister asked. "In bed." "Is she not going to get up?" He told her, "No. You told me to obtain a dead person for a wife. That is a dead woman I went and got." She said to him, "Now you take that dead body and put it right back where you found it." He took it back. Then she said to him, "I told you to get a live person. I meant to marry a live person, no matter if she were old." "All right, sister." He took that body and went.

That evening he brought home an old, old woman with a walking cane, nearly blind, who could scarcely stand. His sister objected, "Why, that old woman might drop dead any minute! What are you going to do with her? An old woman ready to die! You go take her home." He made preparations to take the old woman home. His sister emphasized, "Young! Young! A young girl, a youngster, that is what you want to get for yourself." "All right, sister, I can do that." He went. He waited till late at night. Then he went and stole a woman's baby. He arrived home with it during the night. Soon that baby cried. He got up and tossed that cradle, "Oh, my wife! My wife! Keep still, my wife!" His sister thought, "Perhaps he has gotten a widow with a baby." She asked him, "Have you a woman with a baby?" "No, sister. This baby herself is my wife!" "Oh, goodness! You take that baby right back where you got it." He arose, dressed, took that baby back to her mother.

Then his sister knew she must explain carefully. She said, "I told you a young woman, a young girl, not an old woman, not a baby." "All right," he said. He went. He found a young woman in her basket cap. He brought her home. He had done all right then.

That is ended.

The Two Brothers

When Owen Gould told this Nez Perce story to Dell Skeels in the late 1940s, he noted that it was "a story of real people, not animals," and although the circumstances are fantastic, the theme of one brother betraying another is not. What's striking here is that after he is abandoned by his wicked sibling, the virtuous younger brother is accepted by the eagle family and eventually receives their spirit power. The story offers some interesting parallels with Shakespeare's drama of betrayal and forgiveness, *The Tempest*. —In Dell Skeels, *Style in the Unwritten Literature of the Nez Perce Indians*, pp. 212-217.

There were two brothers. The youngest was married. So they decided they would move out from the group that they were camped with and they packed their belongings, he and his brother and his brother's wife, and they went far up the river to hunt game. There they made their camp. The reason was so they could hunt a short distance from camp and get their game. One day the two brothers went up the river together and they came to a high cliff. There they spied an eagle's nest, and they wondered how they could get there to get the little eagles, and they went around and around the cliffs but they couldn't find a way to get to the nest where the little eagles were. So the older brother said to the young brother, "I know how one of us can get down to that nest and get these little eagles out from the nest. We'll peel long willows and get the bark and we'll braid three barks together. It will be strong enough to hold one of us and we'll make it long enough so it will reach to the bottom of that cliff where the eagle's nest is."

So they both agreed and they started to peel willow bark and braid it to-gether until it was long enough to reach down to the branch where the eagle's nest was. The older brother said to his young brother, "You are much lighter than I. You climb down on this willow bark rope and I'll stay up here and when you give me signals with this willow bark braided rope by giving me jerks, then I'll know that you are ready to come up."

The young brother agreed and said, "I'll go down." So the young brother started climbing down until he reached the bench where the eagle's nest was. Four young baby eagles were in the nest, and he sat by them and he started to pet them until he could get ahold of them, and he had a little sack made of cedar bark, and he put those little eagles in that sack of cedar bark.

When he went to give the signal to his older brother above him the older brother let go of the rope and it fell clear down to where he was. The older brother shouted, "I'm sorry. I missed my hold and it slipped out of my hand. I'll go down to the camp and get a rawhide rope which we have at the camp."

And the younger brother said, "Well, hurry back," because the older father and mother eagles were getting pretty fierce with him. They almost grabbed him with their claws and he was scared to be there too long. He had to put the little eagles back into their nest so the eagles would calm down and not try to attack him.

The younger brother waited and waited. Night passed and another day passed, the second night passed. He began to get hungry and thirsty. There was no way to get down or get off that bench where he was and he stayed there days and days, night after night.

When his older brother came to the camp where he promised he would go after rawhide rope, instead of getting the rope and taking it back to rescue him, he said to his sister-in-law, "My brother has vanished away into the cliff, fallen hundreds of feet to his death. I have no way I can get him out from where he lit so I just covered him up as best I could and left him." And he took her as his wife. The following morning he told her to pack up. "We are going home where we came from. There's no reason for us to stay here because this place is haunted and we might have bad luck also." So they moved back home where they came from.

The young brother was up there still waiting. He had been so long with the eagles that the eagles paid no more attention to him. He became one of the eagles' family. The father and mother would bring to the little ones, rabbit, grouse, little fawn and other game which they could catch. This young brother would join in with the baby eagles and take some meat. He would spread it on the rocks to dry and eat it when it got dry enough to eat, and he survived that way until the eagles were big enough so that he tied each one of the four of them together onto a rock so they could not fly away from him. He figured his only salvation was when the young eagles got big enough to fly he would tie them together and lie between that four. They would fly and land safely. He watched them very closely and he was always on the alert so they wouldn't get away from him.

So one morning he examined them, pushed them around and he decided they were strong enough to fly across the canyon. And he tied the four young eagles together through the body and set them on the edge of the cliff and said to himself, "I'm going to take a chance. I'm going to die here anyhow. If I fall it will be the same, if these birds won't carry me up."

So he pushed these young eagles off from the edge of the cliff and he lay crosswise on the four birds. He had them tied so they could use their wings freely, and he said, "Well, here it goes." And he pushed the four young eagles off the cliff, and they flew across the canyon, down, but they lit safely on the other side of the canyon, and he said to the young eagles, "We are now going to part and I'm going to free all you four that I have kept all this time." So he untied them and he let them fly one by one and they flew back to their nest where they had grown up and he watched them as they flew back there. They sat on the edge of the cliff. He hated to leave them because he had lived with them for many months.

He was so weak that he could hardly walk. Anyhow he tried and walked down to the old camp where they had been camped and when he came to his old camp he fell asleep. He was tired. In his dream the father and mother eagle came to him and talked to him. "We are very thankful that you did not harm our children and we have considered you as one of us. Now you are going back to your homeland. We are going to give you our power and spirit. Hereafter you're going to be as one of us since we have provided for our children and you through these months, and you're going to have the same power and spirit as we have, and you will be a good hunter, and you will get your game anywhere you hunt." So he woke up, sat right up and looked around, nobody in sight and he said to himself, "I must have been dreaming."

So he got up. He felt very strong. All his strength seemed to come back to him. So he started down the trail in the direction where he thought the people were. When he came near to the place where people were staying, again he fainted when he came into sight of the people. So they went and met him and carried him to the nearest lodge. There they laid him and they called a medicine doctor and went and worked on him. Again he was well and he told his whole story to them, what all had happened, why he was away so long.

And one of the members of that home said to him, "Your wife is now married to your brother. They came back and told their story that you had got into an accident, that you had fallen from the cliff to your death and they had buried you because they had no way of taking you out and bringing you home and that was their side of the story. There is their home. That is where they are now staying."

He answered them and said, "I love my brother. I have nothing against him or towards his wife. If they're happy let them stay together. I have no hard feelings against either one of them because I am alive after what I have struggled through and I am glad that I am back among my own people, which I have longed for. I'll be friends with everybody." And so he lived thereafter among his own people.

The Earring Story

This family legend was recorded from third-generation Oregonian, Mrs. Clyde B. Huntley, Portland, on February 13, 1939, for the WPA Oregon Folklore Project (Interviewer: Sara B. Wrenn). Mrs. Huntley was the great-granddaughter of Samuel Kimbrough Barlow, pioneer road builder and developer of the Barlow Road.

What has come down in our family as the "Earring Story" should probably be called the Twin Story. My grandmother, whose maiden name in full was Martha Ann Partlow, had a twin sister, Mary. They were born in Virginia, and they were so exactly alike that, for identification purposes, great-grandmother put earrings of different design on them at a very early age. Here, tied in the scrapbook, is one of the earrings that grandmother wore from the time she became a young lady. It is one of the earrings, too, that took part in the incident I am relating. You see, she had this pair on in this daguerreotype. Eventually Great-aunt Mary married a Colonel White, and moved with her husband to Fort Worth, Texas, after which, it is said, grandmother pined and grew so puny that Great-aunt Mary sent for her to join her in her new home. Now, this isn't a part of the story, but, in case you are ever bitten by a Black Widow spider, you may find it interesting. Grandmother had barely reached Fort Worth when she was bitten by a spider, and she swelled and suffered so they despaired of her life. Then the negroes took her in hand.

They buried her in mud up to her neck, and it cured her, or at least she recovered. While grandmother was at Fort Worth she met and married a young lieutenant, named Tull. They were transferred to Missouri, where they heard much about and became interested in Oregon, but within seven months grandmother's husband died, and her first child was born fatherless. Sometime later she met a Doctor William Allen, from Kentucky. He was a widower, with three young children. He, too, it seems, wanted to come to Oregon, and eventually they arrived here, but it appears nobody was sick in the Oregon country, and, to make a living, he turned to teaching dancing. Then very suddenly, he died from a heart attack. Grandmother had two children by him, so his death left her practically penniless with six children to support. There was one thing grandmother knew about, and that was good food. I forgot to mention that two of the old family servants, Peter and Ol' Rose, had joined her. So they were on her hands too.

Canemah, at that time, was a point where all the Willamette River boats discharged both supplies and passengers. It was a fairly lively little place, and here my grandmother, with the help of her two servants, put on big suppers for dances and other gala affairs. Meantime grandmother's twin, Great-aunt Mary, and her husband had come to Oregon. Great-aunt Mary was much concerned about her twin. While grandmother was doing very well for herself, her six children and her two servants, Great-aunt Mary looked on the enterprise with little favor. Grandmother was still a young and comely woman and great-aunt Mary thought she should be picking out a husband from the many prosperous and otherwise eligible men about. Among these was a young man by the name of William Barlow. Great-aunt Mary selected him as her future brother-in-law. He was not only personable, but he was a money maker. He owned a lot of land, for all of which he paid cash; never, strange as it may seem, filing on government land. But grandmother was shy, despite the fact that she was twice a widow, and no widow is supposed to be bashful. Nevertheless, grandmother was unequal to the plan suggested by her twin; she declared she couldn't "make up" to any man, and that was that. Great-aunt Mary went into action. There was to be a big dance at Canemah one night, and grandmother was going to give the usual supper. She had been in Oregon City where Great-aunt Mary lived. William Barlow, it was learned, was going to Canemah also. This was a Providence-sent opportunity, in Great-aunt Mary's opinion. If grandmother wouldn't make the best of it, she would. She prevailed on grandmother to exchange earrings with her, and off she went on the same boat with the handsome young farmer. She contrived an introduction, and flirted with him to such effect that she won his interest and affection on the spot — a combination that she shortly turned over, with a second exchange of earrings, to the widowed sister and her six orphans. And all of them, with the children that came along later, lived happily ever after.

The First Family

At the conclusion of most versions of the Northern Paiute creation myth comes this poignant episode of family strife; dispersal, creating the different human races; and (symbolically, after death) reconciliation. When the Paiute leader Truckee met the first whites to enter Nevada in the 1840s, he welcomed them as long-lost kinsmen according to this myth (see the account by his granddaughter, Sarah Winnemucca, in her *Life among the Piutes,* pp. 6-7.) —Told in English to Isabel Kelly by Bige Archie: Kelly, "Northern Paiute Tales," p. 370.

Pretty soon they [the first couple] had one boy. The next time they had a girl. Then they had another boy and then another girl. They had four of them. They were always playing somewhere outside. One boy and one girl and the other boy and the other girl played together. They were pretty rough. The boys fought with each other, and the girls fought too. The girls cried a lot.

The father said, "Don't fight. You fight too much. You make me angry." The father sat down. He had a girl and a boy on each side of him. He had a short stick, and he pricked them on the legs until he made the blood come out. Then he kicked them away from him. He sent them in opposite directions. "Go somewhere and fight," he told them. Each pair went in a different direction. Once in a while they built a fire and then moved on again.

The next morning the man told his wife, "Stay here. I want to go away. Follow me when you die." This is what he told her. Then he went away, and the woman followed. Pretty soon he came to the ocean. He got up on it just like it was ice. That woman came along and tried and tried, but she couldn't get up. She just cried around there close to the water. The man kept on going for a long time. Pretty soon he was out of sight.

Then that woman died. Pretty soon she found that man. They stayed together again. He had water there and they bathed. Pretty soon their children died too, and they came over there. That's how the Indians started.

Husbands
Wives
Lovers

As the saying goes, the selections in this chapter hardly need a thematic introduction. The interplay of the sexes, sometimes a tender *pas de deux* (or at least a do-si-do), sometimes a deadly duel, permeates and energizes folk literature just as it does written literature, but generally with less sentimentality, and more directness of feeling. "There was a lady lived in York/Fell in love with her father's clerk," begins the old Anglo-American ballad *The Greenwood Side*, and given such leading clues, who can turn away? In all of these selections from Oregonian oral tradition, the motives of love and sexual attraction and difference intersect (as they do in our lives) with other interests: in social standing and wealth, in spousal authority (Chaucer's Wife of Bath calls it *maistrie*) and so on. All novelists and storytellers know the principle: bring the sexes together, and "the plot thickens."

"McCully Wedding Party." Photographer unknown. June 1892.

Ang Toy and Farm Pei

This story was told by Lai Pou Sae Lee, a member of the Mien community in Portland since 1979. Originally from Laos, she left with her family in the mid-1970s, spending four years in a refugee camp in Thailand before she came to the United States and settled in Portland. Stories like this one were originally told as family entertainment in the evenings and are widely known. Other sacred stories are not generally known and are the province of shamans or other leaders. This story was recorded in an interview in 1981 or 1982 by Jodi Lorimer and was translated by Lai Pou's son, Ay Choy Sae Lee, with assistance from his wife, Farm Yuen.
—Personal communication from Jodi Lorimer and Steve Siporin.

Once upon a time there was a beautiful and wise girl named Ang Toy. She wanted more than anything to go to school but girls were not accepted in the schools. Ang Toy had a magic bowl that, when you covered something with the bowl, what you had covered would cease to grow. When you uncovered it, it would resume growing. She put the magic bowl over her breasts to keep them small, dressed in men's clothing and walked to school.

On her way she met a handsome boy named Farm Pei. Farm Pei thought he had never seen such a pretty young boy and began to tease Ang Toy and call her a girl. This made Ang Toy flush with anger and embarrassment and she told him angrily, "I am not a girl. I am a boy, like you."

Soon they were friends. They sat together in the shade of a big tree and rested from their walk. Farm Pei asked where Ang Toy was going and she replied "I am going to school in the city." "So am I!" he replied. "Let's travel together. Who is the older, he shall walk in front." The Mien people are very respectful of age and position and many social customs reflect this. Farm Pei was two years older than Ang Toy so he led the way to the city.

They had been at school now for three years and they were inseparable friends. They shared everything, pens, books, and most secrets. But Ang Toy never told Farm Pei her biggest secret and he never knew that she was a girl.

One hot day Ang Toy went alone to the river to bathe and, thinking she was alone, she took off all her clothes to swim. A schoolmate of hers named Ma Cha, happened by and recognized her from school and was astonished to discover she was a beautiful girl. He decided he wanted to marry her and ran home to ask his parents to arrange a wedding for him.

His family was very powerful and rich and Ang Toy's parents were delighted to make such a good match for their daughter. They wrote her a letter to tell her they had arranged her engagement and she must come home.

She was very sad about leaving school but even sadder about leaving Farm Pei. She wrote him a letter and explained to him at last that she was a girl. But she wrote it in backwards script so that only its reflection could be read. Then she put it where he would find it after she was gone. She went to find Farm Pei and told him she had to go home but she didn't say why. She asked him to please say good-bye to their teacher for her and she prepared to leave.

Farm Pei was very sad and offered to walk home with her so he could spend just a little more time with his friend. When they had walked for a long time, they came to a bridge over a river. They stood together on the bridge and looked down into the water. Ang Toy said, "Do you see those two fish swimming side by side? Can you tell which one is male and which one is female?"

Farm Pei said no, he couldn't tell. They looked both the same to him. Ang Toy said, "People can be like that too."

They walked on and came to another river where they saw two ducks swimming in the water. Ang Toy asked him again if he could tell which was male and which was female. But Farm Pei shook his head. "No, they look the same to me." Not long after that they arrived at her village and said good-bye. Ang Toy went to her parents' house and Farm Pei walked sadly back to school.

Farm Pei was very lonely when he got back to school. Then he found the note Ang Toy had left for him but he didn't understand it. He took it to the teacher and asked him how to read it. The wise teacher looked at the backward script and said, "Get a bowl of water and hold your letter over it and you will be able to read what it says." Farm Pei didn't understand at first but he tried it and finally he was able to read what Ang Toy had wanted him to know. All the questions she had asked him on the walk home to her village made sense to him now.

Farm Pei was even sadder now. He knew Ang Toy was a young woman and he knew he loved her. He couldn't stay at school any longer without Ang Toy. He left at once to go to her village and find her. When Ang Toy returned to her parents' home they made her take the magic bowl off her breasts so that they began to grow as they should and she would not be able to lie to them any more about being a boy. She put on women's clothes too and suddenly, where there had been a boy, stood a beautiful young woman. Farm Pei arrived in her village and saw this same lovely woman and asked her where he could find Ang Toy. He didn't recognize her as a woman. Ang Toy said, "This is her village and I will take you to her but first you must come and have some tea." When they were in her home and she had made him comfortable with a cup of tea she said, "I am Ang Toy. I am a woman now." Farm Pei couldn't believe it. He couldn't believe her transformation, how different she looked, and how beautiful she was. So she showed him the books they had shared at school and recalled stories of the time they had spent together. Sadly, she also told him the reason she had to leave school, that she was to marry their schoolmate, Ma Cha.

All of this was too much sadness for Farm Pei to bear. He had to get away. He went home to his own village and was despondent for days. He refused food and became thinner and thinner. His mother was very worried about him. As she took away his food again, untouched, she asked him what was wrong. Why was he so sad? Why didn't he eat? Farm Pei finally told his mother the story of Ang Toy, that he loved her and that he would marry no one else. His mother was very sympathetic. She sent a messenger to Ang Toy's parents and asked them to let their daughter marry her son but they refused. They had already given their word to Ma Cha, and, besides, his family was powerful and wealthy. But while the messenger was at Ang Toy's house awaiting her parents' answer, she asked him to take a letter to Farm Pei in secret. She tore a piece of cloth from her jacket and, biting her finger, she used her blood as ink. With tears on her cheeks she wrote that, although they could not be married in this life, they would be husband and wife in the afterlife.

The messenger hurried back to Farm Pei's village, bearing his bad news. He gave Farm Pei the letter written with Ang Toy's own blood and he sat very quietly for a very long time. At last he put the letter in his mouth and pushed it far down his throat so that it strangled him and he died. They buried him on the mountainside near the high road and put a marker on the grave that told everyone that poor Farm Pei was buried there.

Not many days after they had laid Farm Pei in his grave Ang Toy, dressed as a bride, was being carried in a palanquin to the home of Ma Cha for the wedding. On the way they passed by the sad grave of Farm Pei and to her horror Ang Toy read the name on the marker and knew her lover had died. She begged to be let down so she could go to the grave but her family forbade it. She cried and wailed and made such a noise that they had no choice but to let her go. With tears staining her pretty face she ran to the graveside. Ang Toy stamped with her small feet on the grave and called out, "Farm Pei! Farm Pei! If you love me you will let me in. Take me with you!" The ground rumbled and split open and Ang Toy, smiling and radiant, dressed like a bride, jumped into the hole and the earth closed over her.

The wedding party was crazy with confusion and grief. A messenger ran to tell Ma Cha what had happened but he didn't believe it. He was furious and thought someone was playing a cruel joke on him. He ran to Farm Pei's grave where the distraught family was gathered wailing in misery. He threw himself on the grave and began digging. He dug and dug and found a piece of Ang Toy's long jacket. He dug deeper, anxious now that what they said was true. He dug once more and out of the dirt and empty clothes flew two beautiful butterflies. They fluttered together, wings touching, circling higher and higher until they were lost in the sky.

The Honorable Milt

The moral of this amusing Clackamas "wish-fulfillment" story seems to be the need to be wary about one's wishing, especially on sexual matters. The emphasis on the "milt-man's" whiteness (along with his utter wimpiness) suggests that Anglo males are being satirized from a Native woman's perspective—see Mrs. Howard's "postscript" at the end of the selection.—Told in Clackamas Chinook by Mrs. Victoria Howard to Melville Jacobs in Oregon City around 1930: Jacobs, *Clackamas Chinook Texts,* Part 2, pp. 348-350, 560. The widow's song and the story's title have been retranslated by Dell Hymes.

Victoria Howard

People were living there. They were continuously smoke-drying salmon and various things. There was one widow. They [fishermen] would come, they would come ashore there. Now she would be going about at that place. Right after they threw them [their catch of fish] ashore, she would get one or two to take with her. She smoke-dried them. [In consequence] her house was full of food. In the winter they [other villagers] would get hungry, and they would buy various things from her. That is how she had many valuables.

I do not know how long a time, and then she got one [large and fat] salmon, she butchered it well, she took out its milt. She thought, "Dear, oh dear. It is nice. I shall not eat it." She wished, "Oh that you become a person." I do not know where she put it.

I do not know how long a time afterward, and then some person was sleeping beside her. She thought, "Oh my! I wonder where the person came from to me." She lay there for a while. Then she thought, "Perhaps he is not from here. Perhaps the person got to here from a long distance away." Presently as she was thinking about it, he then said to her, "What is your heart making you know [What are you thinking about]? You yourself said to me, 'I wish that you would become a person.'" She reflected. "Oh yes," she thought. "It just has to be that milt." She looked at him in the morning. "Goodness. A fine-looking man, he is light of skin." Now they remained there, I don't know how long a time they lived there.

Then some other woman began to steal him away from her. After quite some time then she [the other woman] took him away from her. She continued to live there. When she [the other woman] saw her, she would say, she would tell him, "Oh dear me. Your poor, poor [former] wife! Look at her!"

He would reply to her, "Leave her alone!" After quite some time then she laughed at her all the more. They [villagers] said to her (the deserted wife), "Dear, oh dear. Why does your co-wife laugh at and mock you all the time?" She said, "Oh let it be!"

Now time after time when they [the married couple] were sitting there, she [the deserted wife] passed by them [two], she [the second wife] nudged her husband, she said to him, "Look at your [former] wife! Oh dear! The poor, poor woman!" He replied to her, "Leave her alone!" She laughed at her all the more. She [the deserted first wife] went along, she went back to them [the married couple], and now she danced in front of them. She said [in the words of her song]:

"The honorable Milt!
    I supposed him for myself.
The honorable Milt!
    I supposed him for myself."

She [the second wife] nudged him again [and again mocked his first wife by saying], "Oh dear oh dear! that poor poor wife of yours." He continued to say, "Do leave her alone." The fifth time [when she had sung the song five times] she extended her spirit-power regalia [toward the couple]. The woman [the second wife] turned and looked, only milt lay beside her. She [the second wife] arose, she went away. That first woman took the milt, she threw it at her, [saying] "This thing here is your husband!" She [the second wife] went back home, she reached her house, and there she remained, she stayed there. And that is what she continued to do.

Now I recall only that much of it.

Mrs. Howard's recollection of her mother-in-law's joke about Milt illustrates how allusions to well-known stories could serve the purpose of humor and satire in everyday life:

Our house (was) near the road.
    Someone will pass by us.
        She will look at them.
Now she will laugh and laugh,
    she will say:
        "Dear oh dear . . .
        "A light one!
        "Maybe it's milt!"
Now she will sing,
    this is what she will say"
        "The Honorable Milt!
        "I supposed him for myself."

Niggedy Naggedy

This song was sung by Orlo Flock, Powell Butte, for Walter Bolton in 1969 (RVMA, Bolton, 1969). It is also known as "Nickety Nackety," "Risselty Rosselty," or in its longer ballad versions as "The Wee Cooper of Fife" or "The Wife Wrapt in Wether's Skin." It was recorded as early as 1810 in the United States. In Oregon, a version sometimes called "The Rassle Song" was collected in 1940 from Mason Warner, Eugene, as part of the WPA Oregon Folklore Project. Warner reported that he had learned the song from John Cain, a farmhand in the upper Willamette Valley in the late 1870s and 1880s.

Oh I married me a wife in the month of June
Niggedy naggedy now now now
Carried her home by the light of the moon
Niggedy naggedy hey John Daggedy
Willady wallady crustofy quality
Niggedy naggedy now now now

She churned her butter in Daddy's old boot
Niggedy naggedy now now now
For a dasher she used her foot
Niggedy naggedy hey John Daggedy
Willady wallady crustofy quality
Niggedy naggedy now now now

She combed her hair but once a moon
Niggedy naggedy now now now
And then she'd beat me with the broom
Niggedy naggedy hey John Daggedy
Willady wallady crustofy quality
Niggedy naggedy now now now

The saddle and bridle did lay on the shelf
Niggedy naggedy now now now
If you want more singin' just do it yourself
Niggedy naggedy hey John Daggedy
Willady wallady crustofy quality
Niggedy naggedy now now now

There Was an Old Woman in Trenton

Like "Niggedy, Naggedy," another song from Orlo Flock, this is about the travails of married life. In this case, the wife attempts to get rid of her husband so she can run off with another man. It is similar to "Johnny Sands," an English broadside from the 1850s that was popularized in America in the mid-nineteenth century by traveling troupes of singers.—Sung by Orlo Flock, Powell Butte, Oregon (RVMA, Walter Bolton, 1969).

There was an old woman in Trenton,
In Trenton she did dwell.
She loved her husband dearly,
But another man twice as well.
Chorus: With a rum-sig-thithery-ump-see-day.

She went to a doctor
To see if she could find
By any means at all
That would put her old man blind.
Chorus

He told her to get six marrow bones,
And make him suck them all
And that would make her old man
So he couldn't see at all.
Chorus
She went and got six marrow bones
And made him suck them all.
Says he, "My dear beloved wife,
I can't see you at all."
Chorus

Says he, "I'd go and drown myself
if I could find the way."
Says she, "I'd better go along
for fear you'll go astray."
Chorus

She went down to the river,
For to push him in.
He stepped a little to one side
And headlong she went in.

Chorus

The old man got tender-hearted
For fear she'd try to swim.
He went and got a big long pole
And pushed her further in.
Chorus

Now she began to cry
And she began to bawl.
Says he, "My dear beloved wife,
I can't see you at all."
Chorus

And when he thought she had enough
He took her by the hand
That put her out of the notion
Of getting another man.
Chorus

"That's How She Got Him on the Train"

Mrs. Verdell Rutherford's anecdote about how her mother "persuaded" her father to move from Oklahoma to Oregon in 1913 typifies the kind of family story that through repeated tellings becomes a family tradition.—Told to Stephen Martin in Portland, April 14, 1993.

It was her [my mother's] idea to move West. A tornado struck the house before I was born, and [it] turned the house around, and that's when she decided that she was coming as far west as she could come without going into the ocean. That's when she started planning and saving her pennies and what not.

My dad didn't want to come 'cause all his family was living there [in Oklahoma], and what would he—what would she want to come way out west for? She had been reading in magazines about Oregon and the homesteading and what not, not knowing at the time there was restricted covenant as far as Negroes were concerned, you know.

So she said the fare was thirty-five dollars, that's what the train fare was. (Our children used to ask us did we come in a covered wagon. I said, "No, the train was running when we came in 1913.") And she had already sold the house and the buggy. The man was waiting at the train station when papa took us down, and she told him, "You might as well come on and go with us because I've sold —the man is here to get the buggy and the horse, and you've got no place." And that's how she got him on the train, and that's how they came West.

The Quarrel at Kirk Canyon

A bad marriage comes to its tragic end in this Klamath story set in post-Myth Era times. The villainous husband can abuse his wife and neighbors, and get away with it, but his quarrel with the owl (which in Klamath lore speaks Klamath) leads to swift retribution. Kirk Canyon is located north of Klamath Falls, along the Williamson River. After Mrs. Marie Norris told this story to Roger Weaver, she added this footnote: "[This] legend I named myself, for I do not know the true title. I have never seen this legend in print before, although it may have been. I heard this story only from my mother and aunts. The story is not told in the exact manner which my elders used, but the details are the same. I do not think that I nor others like me will ever capture the magic of storytelling that our elders possessed." —Told in English by Marie Norris to Roger Weaver in the 1970s, and used here by permission of Weaver; all rights reserved.

In the long ago days a band of the Klamath Lake people were on their way to the Klamath Marsh to pick the *wocus* needed for the long season of the heavy snows. They walked as they had no other means of travel, for this was the time before the horse was known to the Indians. Among the band was a couple who were in the fall time of their years.

The woman was good and was liked by all those who knew her. Her man was the exact opposite, very cranky and hateful to all his people. Finding any reason to quarrel with those who came near him, he was, needless to say, shunned by almost all of the people. Neither was he good to his woman, the reason for his bitterness being that they were childless. There had been children born to them in the springtime of their years, but all had been taken to the land of the dead in the very early days of their young lives.

The band had walked all day and all were weary so they stopped for the night at the age-old stopping place on the [edge] of the very deep Kirk Canyon. There they made the evening meal, and after visiting a short while they all went to their beds which had been made out in the open (some under the stars) while others chose to sleep under the huge pine trees. All knowing they would rise at an early time, soon they were fast asleep. The man and his woman made their sleeping place under a tree away from the others, as he wished to be near no one.

Just as they had crawled into their beds, an owl sitting in the tree above them began to hoot. The man, seeing a chance to quarrel, hollered out *ka-puks-gi* (shut up), but the owl kept on with his hooting. The woman warned the man, "Don't quarrel; you know the owl is a bad one. He may try to hurt you." The man would not listen to his woman; he and the owl quarreled far into the night while the woman slept.

Early the next morning, the Indians were up making their morning meal. The woman went over where her man was still lying and called out, "Get up, we will soon start for the Marsh. I told you last night to sleep, not quarrel. Now get up." There was no answer from him. He sat up and as he turned toward her she cried out, for her man had no eyes. Where the eyes had once been there were only deep holes. She knew that while her man had slept the angry owl had flown down and pecked out his eyes.

Out of his mind because of this, the man jumped up and started to chase his woman, following her in every direction that she ran. Although he was sightless, he could follow her by the sound of the small bells that she had sewn on the apron she wore. As she ran she jerked off the apron and threw it over the bluffs of the canyon. The man, still following the sound of the bells, leaped into the deep canyon after it and there he met his death.

The Clever Wife

This is one of many stories known by Lai Pou Sae Lee, a member of Portland's Mien community. Like another of Lai Pou's stories in this volume, "Ang Toy and Farm Pei," it is told as family entertainment. It was recorded in Portland in 1981-82 by Jodi Lorimer. The translation is by Lai Pou's son, Ay Choy Sae Lee, with assistance from his wife, Farm Yuen. Readers may want to compare this story with the Tillamook story, "Split-His-Own-Head," in the "Family Matters" section. —Personal communication from Jodi Lorimer and Steve Siporin.

Once there was a very clever woman who was married to a very stupid man. Even after they had been married for three years he had done nothing at home. He never worked. Not because he was lazy but because he was too dumb to do anything. Finally his wife said, "Why don't you go make us a trap to catch a deer or something for food?" But he said, "How? I don't know how. I am too dumb." She replied, "You must try to learn. I cannot do everything for us all the time. My father is going to the forest today to set a trap. You go with him and he will show you how."

"But what do I do?" he asked, stunned to think he should do anything.

Impatiently she told him, "You just do exactly what your father-in-law does. Now go!"

The father-in-law knew how stupid his son-in-law was and didn't want to have to teach him anything. He would have to try very hard not to get impatient with him. So, mindful of his temper, the father led his son-in-law off into the forest.

When they had found a good place the father-in-law pointed up the hillside. "I'll make my trap up there. You make yours a little farther down," and he began to dig a hole to lay the trap in. The stupid son went to where he thought he would build his trap and began digging too, imitating everything his father-in-law did.

A short time later the father-in-law stopped digging and began to rub his eye. He walked over to his son, opening his eye very wide and said, "Will you help me? I have some dirt in my eye."

But the son thought this was part of trap-building too and he too opened his eyes very wide and started blinking wildly. The father-in-law was so angry with this idiot son that he slapped him. But the son, remembering what his wife had said, thought he was imitating him and slapped him back.

The father-in-law was in a towering rage by now. He knew his son-in-law was dumb, but not *that* dumb. He spun on his heel and went home, swearing never to have anything more to do with this blockhead and leaving his bewildered son-in-law to find his own way home.

The clever wife finally despaired of her husband's ever learning to make a trap so she made the traps from then on. But, she thought, he can't get into too much trouble if he goes to check on the traps to see if we have caught anything. So she sent him to the forest one day to do just that.

When he arrived at the trap he saw a deer caught there. But he thought it was one of his father's calves that had wandered into the trap and he turned it loose. When he got home his wife asked him if there had been anything in the trap and he answered, "No, only one of father's little cows so I let it go." His wife, knowing how dumb he could be, asked him how many horns it had. He put his hands on top of his head with the fingers pointing up in the air and wiggling and said, "Oh, it had many many horns!" Then she knew they had lost a deer and she was furious with him. "After this," she told him, "anything that gets caught in the trap is food for us. Don't let it go! Kill it and bring it home to me to cook."

Some days later she sent him out again to check the trap. Now, sometimes people are out hunting or just walking and they get caught in traps by mistake. A poor woman had done just that. She sat in the trap crying and crying because she couldn't get free. The husband saw her there and thought, "Now here is a woman in my trap. But my wife says anything in the trap is food, so . . ." He killed her, threw her over his shoulder and took her home.

His wife saw him coming home with a body over his shoulder and she was terrified at what he may have done. When he told his wife that the woman was in the trap and so he had brought her home to be cooked for dinner, his poor wife was frantic. "What will we do now? You have killed her! Oh what will I do with this imbecile husband?" she moaned. They buried the woman in the garden so no one would know.

The next time the trap had to be checked she knew she couldn't trust him to go alone so she went with him. There was a big buck waiting for them there. They butchered it and brought it home and the wife was very relieved that nothing more had gone wrong.

Now, whenever the Mien people kill a deer or other large game, they always share it with their neighbors. It is very bad manners to eat a whole deer yourself. But, because the Mien people are a very courteous people, when the meat is offered to them they will first refuse it and say, "No, no, there isn't enough to share with us. You must keep it and eat it yourself." Then, of course, good manners demand that you insist that they take some and they will, to be courteous, good neighbors.

The wife cooked the deer and, setting some aside for them, she put the rest in a bowl and told him to take it around to the neighbors.

He took the bowl to the first house and, of course, they said, "There isn't nearly enough to share. Why don't you keep it and eat it yourself." So he sat down right there and ate and ate and ate. Then he went to the next family and offered them some meat but the same thing happened. And he ate and ate and ate some more. It was a very big village with many families living there so he did this all day. At last he came waddling home that afternoon holding the bowl still full of meat in one hand and his stomach with the other. His wife said to him, "You still have a lot of meat left. Why don't you go to our neighbors again and give the rest away?"

But he just lay down and groaned, "No, no, I can't eat another bite!"

"*You* eat?" she said. "You're not supposed to eat it, the neighbors are!"

"But they all refuse and tell me to eat. So I eat. But I can't eat anymore. I won't want to eat for a week now." He continued to groan and moan and hold his stomach.

The wife just shook her head and sighed a heavy sigh. Then she picked up the bowl and went to her neighbors' houses, one by one.

Once more she thought she would let him check the trap and there was another big buck caught there. But the husband thought the deer was a tree that had fallen down and the horns were the branches. When he got home he told his wife there was nothing in the trap but a fallen tree. At first she thought he may be right and went about her business. But then she remembered that there were no trees near the trap to fall on it. So she went back with him and there was the buck. But she determined he wasn't going to eat the whole thing himself this time and make them look like fools in the village. She asked him to go get some water from the river while she cut up the deer and she cut a big piece of hollow bamboo for him to carry the water in. But she cut both ends off so that when he poured the water in one end, it ran out the other. So, he turned the piece around and poured more water in, which, of course, ran out the other end. In this fashion he spent the better part of the morning, pouring water in one end only to have it run out the other.

Meanwhile, she butchered the deer and put all the good meat in her bag. Then she dug some roots nearby that, when they are cut open they are very red and look like raw meat. These, along with the bad cuts of meat, she put in his bag and made it very heavy for him to carry. Then she went home, leaving him at the river pouring water back and forth through the bamboo tube.

It began to get dark and he was getting hungry when he realized his wife had gone home. He picked up the heavy bag she had packed for him and started after her. On the way he came to the river and all the frogs were croaking loudly. He thought, "Well it's dinner time, they are probably hungry like me." So he reached in his bag and threw a piece of meat to them that splashed when it hit the water. The noise frightened the frogs and they were all quiet for a short while. Then, one by one, they all began to croak again until their song was deafening. "They must be very hungry," he thought, and threw them a piece of the red-colored root. Again they all became quiet. The third time they set to croaking he threw in the lung of the deer which floated on the water. "There. That should be enough," he said. "There is so much meat in the river now that it's starting to pile up." And on he went till he got home.

By this time his wife could hardly stand the sight of him. He had been too stupid for too long for her to tolerate it any more. She cooked the meat for herself and it was delicious. But she cooked the root, which has a terrible taste, for her husband. She sat, smiling to herself with satisfaction and eating her savory venison while he gagged on the horrible-tasting root—but he ate it all the same.

Coyote Falls in Love and Creates Crater Lake

Susan Wasson Wolgamott's telling from her family's Coquelle tradition of a widespread Indian story about Coyote grandly in love—the Klamath, for example, have a similar tale: see "Coyote in Love with a Star," in Ramsey, *Coyote Was Going There*, pp. 210-211. —From Susan Wasson Wolgamott, personal communication, 1992; all rights reserved.

How many of you have been to Crater Lake? You've all heard of Coyote. Way, way back, long, long, long ago at the very beginning of things, Coyote was living out in the central part of the state, and every night he watched the stars come up, and there was one little star that Coyote thought was so beautiful. It was a blue star. And he thought she was so beautiful. Coyote fell in love with that star, and he would look up at her and watch her.

Well, he got to watching, and he could see that she seemed to come up over this one mountain. It was so close to that mountain that he thought, "If I could get to the top of that mountain, maybe I could reach her." So Coyote started running at night, and he would run toward that mountain and he would watch it. Then in the daytime he would rest, and then when nighttime came again he would look toward that mountain, and he would run to that mountain.

Finally he got there, and he started climbing the mountain. He rested, and climbed and climbed and climbed and waited, and finally he saw it was getting dark, so he waited for the star. Sure enough, here came this blue star. He was clear on the very tiptop of the mountain, and he saw this star coming and he stood there and he said, "Little star, I love you so much. Won't you be my wife?" And the star looked down and said, "Why would I want to be your wife?" He said, "Oh please," and he reached up and he jumped up and he grabbed her. And he got up, up in the sky, and he thought, "Oh, I'm going to fall, I'm going to fall."

And so finally she said, "Oh, come on, you silly coyote," and she reached down and she grabbed ahold of his paws and she held on to them until they got way up in the sky, and she said, "You foolish coyote, to do a thing like that." And she took him and she threw him down right on top of the mountain because she didn't want anyone ever to be able to reach up and get her again. And Coyote hit the top of the mountain so hard and the whole top of the mountain exploded. And he lay there and he cried, and he cried, and cried and cried, he hurt so badly. And he looked at his hands—his paws were all blue where he had been holding on to this little blue star, and he cried so much that his tears filled up the top of this hole in the mountain, and that's why Crater Lake is blue.

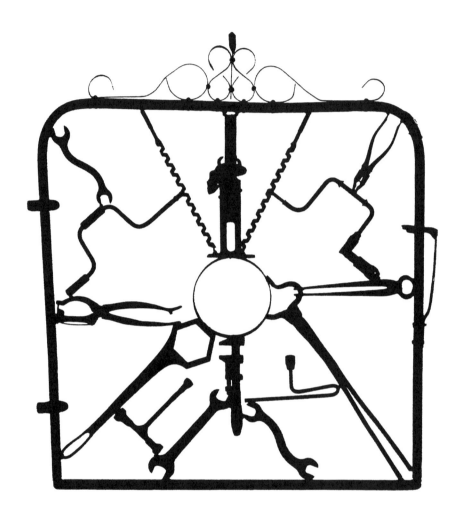

New Old Stories

When very different cultures impinge upon each other, as they have in Oregon steadily since the mid-nineteenth century, the process of sorting each other out and adjusting (anthropologists speak of *acculturation*) usually proceeds on an imaginative, storytelling level as well as on social, political, and economic levels. People of different cultures tell stories about each other, as if trying out each other's strangeness in the imagination (safer to do so there than face-to-face); they also self-consciously *borrow* stories from each other and adapt them to their own conventional understandings, as the Native peoples of Oregon and elsewhere did with the Biblical narratives they heard (initially in Chinook Jargon) from missionaries, and as (belatedly) Oregon's non-Indian population is beginning to do with the state's Indian and other ethnic literary heritages.

And for all cultures undergoing rapid changes, but especially for groups like Native Americans who have suffered much disruption and dislocation, there is likewise a powerful impulse to assert cultural vitality and continuity by adapting traditional stories and forms of speech to the new realities . . . tales about Coyote outwitting anthropologists, for example; old-style cowboy ballads about dubious modern uses for old barns. Hence, "New Old Stories," reminding us that if folklore and oral literatures look to the traditional past, they also engage our imaginations in the ever-changing present, helping us to understand it.

"Rosebrook Gate" by Rod Rosebrook. Iron, 1979.

Christianity in Chinook Jargon

As a kind of esperanto or "universal language," Chinook Jargon (see p. 32) served many purposes during the first generations of Indian/white contact in Oregon, including the purposes of evangelism. Here are two instances of "old wine in new bottles."——From *Dictionary of the Chinook Jargon*, p. 42.

The Lord's Prayer in Jargon

Nesika papa klaksta mitlite kopa saghalie
Our Father who stayeth in the above

kloshe kopa nesika tumtum mika nem;
good in our hearts (be) thy name

kloshe mika tyee kopa konaway tilicum;
good thou chief among all people

kloshe mika tumtum kopa illahie, kahkwa kopa saghalie.
good thy will upon earth as in the above.

Potlatch konaway sun nesika muckamuck,
Give every day our food.

Spose nesika mamook masachie wake nesika solleks,
If we do ill (be) not thou very angry

pe spose klaska masachie, kopa nesika wake nesika
and if any one evil towards us, not we

solleks kopa klaska. Mahsh siah kopa nesika konaway masachie.
angry towards them. Send away far from us all evil.

Kloshe kahkwa.
Amen (lit. "That is right")

Old Man Daniel

—To the tune of "Father Abraham": from J. Barre Toelken, "Northwest Traditional Ballads: A Collector's Dilemma," pp. 12-13.

Caw altaklosh Old Man Daniel [repeated three times]
Where, where, is Old Man Daniel?
Saa yaa sahali kopaklosh illahee.
Way over in the promised land.

Alki naskika klatawaw nanitch,
Bye and bye we'll go see him,
Saa yaa sahali kopaklosh illahee.
Way over in the promised land.

Munata'lkni, or the Devil

When the Indians of Oregon and elsewhere in the West first heard stories from the Christian Bible, as told by missionaries in Chinook Jargon, they retained what pleased or interested them, or seemed compatible with their own oral traditions, adapting details and motives as they saw fit. In this Klamath "appropriation" of the story of Adam and Eve, God becomes the Klamath Trickster and Transformer K'mukamtch, and Satan becomes a thievish Klamath shaman. Traditional Klamath winter houses were underground, hence the references here to "knocking at the top of the house."—Recorded in summary form by Albert Gatschet in the 1880s: Gatschet, *The Klamath Indians*, pp. xciii-iv.

When K'mukamtch created this world, he made one man, and one woman intended to be the man's sister. The creator placed them in a garden (*ha'shuash*) studded with trees producing sweet fruits, and built a house for them. The adjoining stable contained domestic animals for their use. All this was upon the prairie watered by Wood River.

Man and Woman were both blind, and had to remain so until the fruits would be ripe. K'mukamtch told them he would visit them on a Sunday and would knock at the top of their house. Should anybody knock at the door, the knocks would be those of Munata'lkni and they must not open.

Munata'lkni came and knocked at the door, informing them that the fruits were ripe and that he brought them all kinds of berries. The woman said to the man, "Open the door, K'mukamtch is here!" But the man said, "Don't open; it is not K'mukamtch who stands at the door!" The woman opened; Munata'lkni put one sweet berry in her mouth and she tasted it. He was wearing a long head-dress of feathers tied to the top of his hair, his emblem as a conjurer, and this string of feathers was so long as to touch the ground. He then stole all the fruits in the garden and went with them to his underground abode.

Then K'mukamtch, who had observed all this from a distance, arrived and knocked at the top of the house. This time it was the man who opened. When asked what had become of the fruits, he excused himself by stating that Munata'lkni had taken all of them. This put K'mukamtch into such a rage that he threw the woman out of the house and whipped her to death. Then he cut open the eyelids of both, which previously had been fastened together, and the man said: "I can see the sun."

K'mukamtch then instructed the man how to make his livelihood by using the bow and arrow, and how to manufacture sinew-strings and obsidian arrowheads. Upon this he brought the man's sister into life again and both went into the mountains to hunt, for they had nothing to eat. Ever after this K'mukamtch remained angry with them.

White Men Are Snakes

In this Northern Paiute reinvention of Genesis 1-2, the refiguring of Biblical details is clearly scathingly ironic, all the more so when one realizes that in the nineteenth century the derogatory Anglo label for Paiutes and other Shoshoneans was "the Snakes." For the intruders to "ask these Indians where they had come from" is of course the last straw of presumptuous arrogance. —Narrated by "Piudy": Isabel Kelly, "Northern Paiute Tales," p. 437.

Almost everything was Coyote's way. The Indians planted the apple. When he planted it, he said for all the Indians to come and eat. When he told them that, all the people came.

The white man was a rattlesnake then, and he was on that tree. The white people have eyes just like the rattlesnake. When the Indians tried to come to eat the apples, that snake took everything away from the Indian, because they were snakes. If that snake hadn't been on the tree, everything would have belonged to the Indian. Just because they were snakes and came here, the white people took everything away. They asked these Indians where they had come from. That's why they took everything and told the Indians to go way out in the mountains and live.

Laptissa'n and the Seven-Headed Monster

Adaptations of French folktales about "Le Petit Jean" (Little Jack) have been recorded in the oral repertories of Indian groups all over North America, attesting to the influence of French-Canadian trappers and traders, and illustrating how acculturation can work on an *imaginative* level, new story materials being played with and assimilated into traditional narrative forms. Of such "Indianized" European stories, none is more widespread than the adventure of Le Petit Jean and "La bete-a-sept-tetes" (see J. Ramsey, "Ti-Jean and the Seven-Headed Dragon: Instances of Native American Assimilation of European Folklore," *The Native in Literature,* pp. 206-224.)

This abbreviated Nez Perce version (probably a summary) was recorded by Herbert Spinden around the turn of the century: "Myths of the Nez Perce Indians," pp. 200-201. The Kalapuyas of the Willamette Valley told a much more fully elaborated version: see Ramsey, ed. *Coyote Was Going There,* pp. 112-117.

In the early days there was a chief who owned all kinds of property. He found the seven-headed monster running with his horses and cattle. This kept on for several years, and the monster grew bigger and bigger. The chief thought it gave him a big name to have such an animal running with his stock, so he did not molest it.

Finally the monster began to kill off the stock. Then the chief wanted to kill the monster, but he did not know just how to go about it. Then the chief thought to himself, "Tomorrow I shall take half this band of Indians, and we shall go and kill the monster."

So they went out to kill it; but when they came in sight of the monster, and fired at it, the monster attacked in turn, and began killing the Indians. It killed all those who had gone out against it, except the chief himself. After this, the chief was afraid to attack a second time, and resigned himself to the loss of his stock. Then the monster stopped killing off stock, and took to killing off Indians. It attacked the people in the village, and the chief made every effort to find a man who would win out over the monster.

Now there was a poor man in this band named Laptiss'an [Le Petit Jean]. This Laptiss'an told the chief that he would kill the monster if only the chief would furnish him a mule. So the chief gave him the mule, and Laptiss'an went out. He did not know exactly what to do, but he began by riding round and round the monster on the mule. Finally he rode around so many times, that the monster grew weary of watching, and fell asleep. Then Laptiss'an got down off the mule, and cut the throat of the monster where the seven heads were joined into one neck.

Coyote and the Anthropologist

Coyote the trickster continues to serve the Indian people of Oregon and elsewhere at the end of the twentieth century as a figure of fun, vicarious release, and ironic defense against the encroachments of Anglo society. Native writers and artists like Simon Ortiz and Harry Fonseca show Old Man Coyote at large and making it in modern cities; in this widely shared joke, he "scores" on an anthropologist searching for "coyote stories."—Told by Larry Calica to Barre Toelken in the 1970s at Warm Springs, and included by Toelken in his "Foreword" to Barry Lopez, *Giving Birth to Thunder, Sleeping with His Daughter: Coyote Builds North America*, pp. xi-xii.

On the Warm Springs Indian Reservation in central Oregon, some people tell a story about a wandering anthropologist who came across a coyote caught in a trap.

"Please let me out of this trap; if you do, I'll give you lots of money," the coyote said.

"Well, I'm not sure. Will you tell me a story, too?" asked the professor.

"Sure I will; I'll tell you a real, true story, a real long one for your books."

So the anthropologist sprung the trap, collected a big handful of bills from the coyote, and then set up his tape machine. The coyote sat, rubbing his sore legs, and told a long story that lasted until the tape ran out. Then he ran off.

The anthropologist went home and told his wife about what had happened, but she wouldn't believe him. When he reached in his pocket to show her the money, all he came out with was a handful of fur and dirt.

And when he went to play his tape for the other professors, all that was in the machine was a pile of coyote droppings.

A Prophecy about Coyote and the People of the Lake

Gordon Bettles, Cultural Heritage Specialist of the Klamath Tribe, recently composed this remarkable oration on the status and future of his people. If it deals with modern circumstances (libraries, museums, and universities; the ecological crisis; the dislocations of Indian life and culture), it does so in traditional Native forms—old-style oratory, prophecy, and of course, stories about Coyote as a sometimes-helpful transformer, thus reaffirming the vitality of these literary forms. —Gordon Bettles, 1991, by permission of the author; all rights reserved.

Once, *euksikkni*, the People of the Lake, were beset by very hard times. Indeed! The elders would cry, "How pitiful we live now, not like our ancestors, even those who passed on not a little while before us!"

A new race of people had come to make easier the way of life but brought troubles with them. Disease, warfare, and doubt troubled the People of the Lake.

Soon, prayers to *blaydalkni*, He Who Lives Above, who long ago would be called upon by the *euksikkni*, and their elders, now would no longer be answered.

The language of the Tribe and the ways of the land became distant to most of the people. Sweet things to eat and the rapid ways of moving replaced the way that the elders used to enjoy teaching. Indeed, elders became complacent because they couldn't find anyone to listen.

Bones became weak, muscles became a part of the body that began to work against the body!

Now, mighty eyes in the sky rummaged throughout the surface of the world. There were no secrets among the Tribe.

A person could be heard without being there. Ways of teaching the young was done, not from memory, but by slashes and dots on material or on moving and shining eyes. The elders, forced by punishment, became quiet, unused, and irrelevant teachers.

The new people, resting in their rich lodges, became large chiefs, not caring for all, just themselves. All that they could learn from the People of the Lake they took and placed in caves of knowledge, always keeping the doors locked. They wrote in secret fashions so that no one would know these ways.

Soon, they ran out of wood for the fires and had made many untrusting slaves. They became aware, finally, that they would soon have no air to breathe and no water to drink!

Once in a while, the new race would ask Tribal Elders, "What will make our life easier again?" Elders would answer but no one understood what they had said except for a few *euksikkni* that had remained faithful.

Blaydalkni, moved by the plight of his people, let knowing become free. He created knowledge, known as university, or "the way of things" to let loose their hairs. They would gather the way of things and become part of things and then teach the way of things once again. *Blaydalkni* opened Coyote's eyes and showed him the secret of night seeing so he could walk through the caves of knowledge. To Coyote he also gave discernment to understand the secret writings to learn the ways of the old ones.

Now, Coyote would slay the "Quiet Kill" monster of disease by sending out the hairs on his fur. Grizzly Bear would defeat the disease of intimidation and the Great Blue Heron would answer, once again, the prayers of the young men.

Now, I say to you! We still live in the time of legends! Heed, listen! Every voice you hear, you may hear for the last time!

The Coyote, the Bear, and the Moon

This Basque story, recorded in Burns in 1948 by Stanley Robe from John Madariaga, is remarkable for incorporating the Indian trickster, Coyote, into a widespread European folktale formula, that of the "Silly" who confuses the moon's reflection in the water for a cheese. Presumably Mr. Madariaga, a native of Guernica, brought the tale along with him from Spain, and then adapted it to local, eastern Oregon realities. —Stanley Robe, "Basque Tales from Eastern Oregon," p.155.

Once upon a time there was a bear and he was hungry and he couldn't find anything to eat so he went and he met a coyote. He said to the coyote, "I'm going to eat you." The coyote said, "Ooooh, not just yet. Let's go over to the lake and drink some water first."

The moon was reflected beautifully in the lake, so the coyote said to the bear, "You see that big cheese in the lake?" The bear said, "Yes." It was a fine-looking cheese. So he said, "In order to get that cheese you will have to drink the water in the lake." The bear agreed to do as the coyote said, so he drank the water and he drank some more and he drank some more. Finally he said to the coyote, "When will I get to the bottom so I can get that cheese?"

The coyote said, "Any minute now." So he drank some more and in the meantime he was so full of water he fell down. The coyote trotted off, saying, "That is fine. Now you are so full of water you won't have to eat me."

The Sycan Barn

Sunny Hancock, a gifted poet and a working cowboy in South-central Oregon, remarks that, "I wrote this poem back in the late '60s. I was workin' for the ZX, and one of the owners realized that an old barn we had up in Sycan [Sycan Marsh country, along the central boundary of Klamath and Lake counties] was made out of hand-hewn timbers, no nails in it except in the siding and the roofing, and the rest of it was put together just by wooden pegs. He decided he'd take it down and move it down to the headquarters ranch and make him a big beautiful house out of it. And when they was tearin' this barn down, I wrote this poem." By permission of the author; all rights reserved.

Sunny Hancock

What was that you said, Old Timer?
There's something wrong with this old place?
The landscape just don't seem to fit in?
I see the question on your face.

No, the willows ain't no bigger.
But you got it! Comes the dawn!
Big ol' hole in the horizon,
That old shake-roofed barn is gone.

Yep, they tore it down last summer,
Tack room, blacksmith shop and mow—
Hauled 'er off the rim to Paisley,
It's a high class mansion now.

Sure, I guess you think I'm crazy,
Sounds like tales from Mother Goose.
No, I didn't have no nightmare,
I ain't been drinkin' cactus juice.

No, they didn't take the siding.
Left it piled up by the corral.
Sure does make the place look junky,
Scattered nails from here to hell.

Took one out of a horse's foot this morning,
He'll be lame a month or two.
Maybe have to chicken-feed him,
Chances are he'll make it through.

Yeah, they're gonna build another'n
Outta poles the last I hear.
Just a saddle shed or somethin'
And a grain room, that's the word.

Yeah, that barn saw lots of history.
A hundred years or more, I s'pose.
Buckin' horses, wild buckaroos
But that's just the way she goes.

Us old boys here sure do miss 'er.
I hear 'em cuss and stomp their feet.
When they saddle up them humpy ponies
And knock the snow off the saddle seat.

When you shod a horse in summer,
Led him back into a stall.
While you nailed some iron on 'im
Away from the horseflies, bugs and all.

Then sometimes in the evenings
Down around the barn and corral
Maybe someone had a bottle.
Lord, the lies them boys would tell.

Now them big old hand-hewn timbers
Have been hauled off down the ridge,
And built into a fancy playhouse
Where ladies sit and play at bridge.

There's a swimmin' pool behind it,
Hardwood floors without a scar,
And a game room and a sauna,
And a high-toned rustic bar.

Lookin' out across the valley
Out toward the Coglan Rim,
Standing statuesque and lonely,
Built to satisfy a whim.

I'll say one thing sure and certain,
That ladies' club would get a shock,
The tales they'd hear would singe their eyebrows
If that old barn would start to talk.

Well, the whole durn country's changin'
Highways everywhere you go,
Ranges fenced up into pastures,
Cowboys gone like the buffalo.

What was that you said, Old Timer?
We're just relics of the past.
The country's cluttered up with people,
Cowboys' days are done at last.

They follow trails we blazed and conquered,
Starve us out and leave us broke,
Pollute our ranges with their garbage,
Foul our air with smog and smoke.

Won't do for us to get religion
And walk the straight and narrow way.
They don't let cowboys into heaven.
We'd lead the proper folks astray.

Oh well, there ain't no need to worry
'Bout where we'll go from where we're at.
Nor to sweat and stew and bother,
Father Time takes care of that.

Well say, old pard, no need to hurry.
Have a chew—here, take the plug.
I surely have enjoyed the visit.
There's one more drink in this here jug.

If you're back this way, stop in and see us,
Plan to stay a night or two.
It's seldom when we get to visit
With old time folks the likes of you.

You drive careful when you hit the freeway.
That weekend traffic's sure a fright.
You sure you folks won't stay for supper?
No? Well, OK then, goodnight.

Buckskin

Elizabeth Woody's hilarious and loving account of the classic "Indian Car" deftly incorporates many details of Native popular culture—not only modern ones relating to life today on the "Urban Rez," but others extending far back into Northwest Indian tradition. Like the innumerable Plains songs in honor of somebody's "One-eyed Ford," Woody's celebration of old Buckskin as a "bona fide, temperamental, restless War Horse" looks back, ironically but affirmatively, to the days when herds of Indian horses, appaloosas and cayuses and buckskins, ran free in Indian territory.—By permission of the author, copyright 1992; all rights reserved.

Buckskin was a yellowish-tan behemoth, a '76 Galaxy 500 automobile. The family loved her. We still talk about the beast with affection. At best, she carried us all up the deeply rutted, dirt road on the mountainside to Lester's remote cabin, with ease. No dragging on bottom, the springs agile and strong. At worst, her transmission linkages popped out of place once during a manic Seattle rush hour traffic crisis. When this happened, Leslie would have to coast to a stop, jump out, hoist the hood, reach into the engine, balance on her solar plexus, skirt and legs up in the air, and pop the mechanism into its socket, check the hanger wires, then run like crazy back into the driver's seat. She was named "Buckskin" not to honor our Native American heritage, but because she was a bona fide, temperamental, restless War Horse, an Indian car. In that legacy, she had to earn her name.

She was faithful, with a face that only a mother could love, big enough to haul four 30-gallon garbage cans, and on occasion two or three generations of Palmers. The Palmers are big, no matter the age or gender. I am a good example of our size, six foot four, long black hair and round. A mountain of womanhood, I have heard from my admirers, but back to my love story. This is a love story between a family and a car. Brief, true, and bittersweet, like all those sad occurrences when people meet their match and circumstances wrench them apart. Buckskin was a "spirit" car.

When one of us was blue, like Leslie, or SugarMom, or Tone, or Gladys, better known as Happy Butt, we would plan a trip to a Pow Wow or celebration, load up all the camping gear, dance outfits, cans of oil, in the massive space in the trunk, gas up and go. Nothing but a song and prayer, and the injinuitee of our collective genius, the product of the school of "Make-Do." You see, when we first acquired Buckskin, we had been carless for years. Tone said, "Yeah, she's going to be a collector's item, one of these days. She's a tank. A good old-fashioned American Gas-hog. God love her! Now we can go anywhere!"

Of course, he was the first to groan when her parts started to wear out and drop off. That is basically how she earned her name. Like any mechanic's staple, bread and butter, her parts wore out, or dropped off at inappropriate times. Tone and I were driving down "Sideburns," the nickname we had for Burnside, during another typical Northwest squall, and Buckskin flipped off her wiper, driver's side. Tone hollered and looked to me, as I clutched my seat. "Now what?"

"Pull over, Tone. We can't drive without a wiper, 'less you want to stick your head out," which was our previous solution in cars. So, we pulled over. Tone picked up the wiper, and tied it on. We weren't savvy to all of Buckskin's ways then, so we didn't have any coat-hangers in the car. I had a buckskin tie holding my hair, so I offered it to Tone. He rigged up a tie for the wiper. When we related the incident to SugarMom, who was angry, waiting in the rain for us, downtown, she exclaimed, in merriment, "Buckskin!!! Yeah, that's a good name for her. What a gal." Her mood changed to the better by the event.

So Buckskin became a character, well known, and all on her own. We learned how far she would go on the gas gauge's E. We lovingly cleaned her carburettor so she wouldn't stall. The kids squealed in delight as she backfired, resounding in the streets like a shotgun. We offered everyone who needed a ride, a ride they would never forget. She could go with ease down the freeway to Celilo Village at 80, no problem, nondescript, maybe even invisible to the Smokies, State Patrol. She even had a sister car at Ace Wrecking yards to donate parts to her in financial emergencies. One of our many Indian mechanics said, "The way her vinyl top is ripped off, it looks like Buckskin has a giant skid mark on top. HA HA HA!" Since he was laughing at her, and not with her, we dropped him off our list of mechanics. Eventually, he just left town.

Of course she became a celebrity. The most important trip was the trip that did her in. She came through for us, even though her front end was going out. We needed to go to Lewiston, Idaho, to rescue Leslie from out-of-state justice. We drove carefully, made it in time to hear the Police Chief testify to Leslie's actions that led to her arrest. It was hard not to burst into outrage as he exaggerated a description of Leslie, screaming a karate yell, leaping ten feet to kick the officer in the groin, and finally slash him with her house keys. Of course Leslie was acquitted and we rode home, triumphant, in Buckskin, laughingly teasing Leslie, calling her "Leslie Lee," after Bruce.

Buckskin was with us, "all the way," as they say on the rez. A true-blood, so it hurt when we realized that we couldn't keep her any longer. Too much of our energies were tied up in willing her to keep running, so we could keep on with our rescue missions when one of our clan would get into trouble. We had to trade her off at Chevy Town. SugarMom cried. Leslie reported a resurrected Buckskin to us, her whereabouts, in which direction she was heading. Always, we could tell it was her by the Indian head decal on her backside. It was like an identifiable tattoo of a past lover's name. It did take years to forget her faithfulness, in spite of her temper, backfires, and flat tires.

We have a Toyota now, "White Buckskin," '89. You have to count the clicks in the automatic transmission to get in gear, and tell the passengers, as fast as you can, "Don't roll the window down any further than half, because the door pops open," and they could roll out. The "ejector seat," we call it. If you don't like your date, you can ask them to roll down their window and then turn sharply to the left. When SugarMom brought her home, Tone said, "God, those Japanese sure know how to make good American cars. God love 'em!" Happy Butt said, "Oh, geez, SugarMom, you bought a 'pop-together-car'." White Buckskin is an Indian car, though. We haven't had to tie her up, yet. A few more years and she will be broken in, just the way we like it.

How It All Began

In point of historical fact, the first literatures of Oregon were the oral traditions of myth and song cherished—for how many thousands of years?—by the state's Native peoples; and our first literary artists were the skilled performers of those traditional repertories, in Klamath and Nez Perce Sahaptin and Wasco Chinookan and at least twenty other distinctive, richly expressive languages. Much has been lost from this imaginative heritage, both knowledge of the languages themselves, and understanding of how the repertories "worked" for their tribal audiences as literature. But much remains and continues (including the creative energies of young Oregon Indian *writers*); and it seems right to conclude this gathering of the state's folk literature, the stories we tell, with a classical Indian myth. We lose much, obviously, in reading such a story in printed English rather than experiencing it in performance in its first language. But the text is an unusually full and sensitive transcription of its original, and therefore conveys something of the wonder and authority of a story about the beginnings, and therefore the future, of the world we know as "Oregon."

"Petroglyphs." Photograph by B. Gifford.

The Tututni Genesis

The Tututnis, or "Joshuas," were an Athapaskan-speaking people whose main settlements were north and south of the mouth of the Rogue River, near the present-day town of Gold Beach. Very little survives of Tututni culture or language: the imaginative richness and fullness of elaborated detail of this myth of creation suggests that in losing such a heritage we have lost something of great value. Notice how, at the end, the narrative emphasizes conservation of tribal resources, and (like the Paiute creation myth, p. 271) accounts for the diversity of Native tribes. To the Tututnis, it all began with the visit of The Giver and his companion to create *their* homeland at the mouth of the Rogue. As with comparable narratives from other Native groups (cf. the Klamath myth, pp. 2-3) the terms of creation are generous: human life, if not perfect, will be open, bountiful, and socially and spiritually accessible. (A summarized version of this myth was recorded in Chinook Jargon in 1884 on the Siletz Reservation by J. Owen Dorsey, "Indians of the Siletz Reservation," pp. 58-61.)

For a vivid account of life among the Tututnis after the whites came, see John H. Adams, "Awful Hard Time When I'm Baby" in *Many Faces,* Oregon Literature Series, pp. 134-137.

—Narrated by Charlie Depoe: Leo J. Frachtenberg and Livingston Farrand, "Shasta and Athapascan Myths from Oregon," pp. 224-228.

In the beginning there was no land. There was nothing but the sky, some fog, and water. The water was still; there were no breakers. A sweat-house stood on the water, and in it there lived two men—The Giver and his companion. The Giver's companion had tobacco. He usually stayed outside watching, while The Giver remained in the sweat-house.

One day it seemed to the watcher as if daylight were coming. He went inside and told The Giver that he saw something strange coming. Soon there appeared something that looked like land, and on it two trees were growing. The man kept on looking, and soon was able to distinguish that the object that was approaching was white land. Then the ocean began to move, bringing the land nearer. Its eastern portion was dark. The western part kept on moving until it struck the sweat-house, where it stopped. It began to stretch to the north and to the south. The land was white like snow. There was no grass on it. It expanded like waves of the ocean. Then the fog began to disappear, and the watcher could look far away.

He went into the sweat-house, and asked, "Giver, are you ready?" and The Giver said, "Is the land solid?"—"Not quite," replied the man. Then The Giver took some tobacco and began to smoke. He blew the smoke on the land, and the land became motionless. Only two trees were growing at that time, redwood to the south, and ash to the north. Five times The Giver smoked, while discussing with his companion various means of creating the world and the people. Then night came, and after that daylight appeared again. Four days The Giver worked; and trees began to bud, and fell like drops of water upon the ground. Grass came up, and leaves appeared on the trees. The Giver walked around the piece of land that had stopped near his sweat-house, commanding the ocean to withdraw and to be calm.

Then The Giver made five cakes of mud. Of the first cake he made a stone, and dropped it into the water, telling it to make a noise and to expand, as soon as it hit bottom. After a long while he heard a faint noise, and knew then that the water was very deep. He waited some time before dropping a second cake. This time he heard the noise sooner, and he knew that the land was coming nearer to the surface. After he had dropped the third cake, the land reached almost to the surface of the water. So he went into the sweat-house and opened a new sack of tobacco. Soon his companion shouted from outside, "It looks as if breakers are coming!" The Giver was glad, because he knew that the land was coming up from the bottom of the ocean. After the sixth wave the water receded, and The Giver scattered tobacco all over. Sand appeared. More breakers came in, receding farther and farther and farther westward. Thus the land and the world were created. To the west, to the north, and to the south there was tide-water; to the east the land was dry. The new land was soft, and looked like sand. The Giver stepped on it and said, "I am going to see if the great land has come," and as he stepped, the land grew hard.

Then The Giver looked at the sand, and saw a man's tracks. They seemed to have come from the north, disappearing in the water in the south. He wondered what that could mean, and was very much worried. He went back to his first piece of land, and told the water to overflow the land he had created out of the five cakes of mud. Some time afterward he ordered the water to recede, and looked again. This time he saw the tracks coming from the west, and returning to the water on the north side. He was puzzled, and ordered the water to cover up his new land once more. Five times he repeated this process. At last he became discouraged, and said, "This is going to make trouble in the future!" and since then there has always been trouble in the world.

Then The Giver began to wonder how he could make people. First he took some grass, mixed it with mud, and rubbed it in his hands. Then he ordered a house to appear, gave the two mud figures to his companion, and told him to put them into the house. After four days two dogs—a male and a bitch—appeared. They watched the dogs, and twelve days later the bitch gave birth to pups. The Giver then made food for the dogs. All kinds of dogs were born in that litter of pups. They were all howling. After a while The Giver went to work again. He took some white sand from the new land, and made two figures in the same way as before. He gave the figures to his companion, and ordered a new house for them. Then he warned the dogs not to go to the new house, as it was intended for the new people. After thirteen days The Giver heard a great hissing, and a big snake came out of the house, followed by a female snake and many small snakes. The Giver felt bad when he saw this, and went to his companion, telling him that this trouble was due to the tracks that had first appeared in the world. Soon the land became full of snakes, which, not having seen The Giver, wondered how everything had come about. The world was inhabited by dogs and snakes only.

One day The Giver wished three baskets to appear, gave them to his companion, and told him to fill them partly with fresh water and partly with salt water. Then he put ten of the biggest snakes into the baskets, crushed them, and threw them into the ocean. Two bad snakes got away from him, and all snake-animals that live today come from these snakes. The Giver said to these two snakes, "You two will live and surround the world like a belt, so that it won't break!" Then he crushed five bad dogs in the same way, made a great ditch with his finger, and threw the dogs into the ditch. These dogs became water monsters, all animals that raise their heads above the water and smell, and then disappear quickly under the water, came from these five dogs.

Pretty soon The Giver began to think again, "How can I make people? I have failed twice!" Now, for the first time his companion spoke. He said, "Let me smoke tonight, and see if the people will not come out of the smoke." For three days he smoked, at the end of which a house appeared with smoke coming out of it. The man told The Giver, "There is a house!" After a while a beautiful woman came out of the house, carrying a water-basket. Then The Giver was glad, and said, "Now we shall have no more trouble in creating people." The woman did not see The Giver and his companion, as they were watching her. After nine days the woman became sad, and wondered who her father and relatives were. She had plenty of food.

One day The Giver said to his companion, "Stay here and take this woman for your wife! You shall have children and be the father of all the people. I am leaving this world. Everything on it shall belong to you." And the man answered, "It is well; but, perchance, I too may have troubles." Then The Giver asked him, "How are you going to be troubled?" So the man said, "Do you make this woman sleep, so that I can go to her without her seeing me." The woman found life in the house very easy. Whenever she wished for anything it appeared at once. About noon she felt sleepy for the first time. When night came, she prepared her bed and lay down. As soon as she was sound asleep, the man went in to her. She was not aware of this, but dreamed that a handsome man was with her. This was an entirely new dream to her. At daybreak she woke up and looked into the blanket. No one was there, although she was sure that someone had been with her. She wished to know who had been with her that night. So next evening she prepared her bed again, hoping that the same thing would happen; but no one came to her. She did the same every night without any one coming near her.

Soon the woman became pregnant. The Giver and his companion were still on the land, watching her; but she could not see them, because they were invisible to her. After a while, the child was born. It was a boy. He grew very fast. The young woman made a cradle for him. After six months the boy could talk. The woman still wanted to know who the father of her child was. So one day she wrapped the child in blankets, and said, "I will neglect the boy and let him cry, and, perchance, his father may come. I will go and look at the country."

She started south, carrying the baby on her back. She traveled for ten years, seeing no one and never looking at the child. After a long time she could hear only a faint sound coming from behind. Nothing remained of the boy but skin and bones. Finally she stopped at Salomä [a camas prairie far up the Coquille River] and here for the first time she took the child from her back and looked at it. Its eyes were sunken and hollow; the boy was a mere skeleton. The woman felt bad and began to cry. She took the boy out of the cradle and went to the river to bathe. After she had put on her clothes, she felt of the child's heart. It was still beating!

The boy urinated, and was dirty all over. His body was covered with maggots, and he had acquired various diseases. The woman took him to the water and washed his body. She had no milk with which to feed him; so she sang a medicine song, and milk came to her. She gave the breast to the child, but it was too weak to suck; hence she had to feed it gradually. As the days went by the boy grew stronger. After three days his eyes were better. Then they went back to their house, where they found plenty of food. The boy grew soon into a strong and handsome young man, and was helping his mother with her work. One day he asked her, "Mother, where is your husband?" and she replied, "I only dreamed of my husband." Then she told him all that had happened before he was born, and the boy said, "Oh! Maybe my father may turn up some day."

Then The Giver said to his companion, "The woman is home now." That night the woman longed for her husband. She had been dreaming all the time that he was a handsome man, and that her boy looked just like him. At dusk it seemed to her as if someone were coming. Her heart began to beat. Soon she heard footsteps. The door opened and her boy exclaimed, "Oh, my father has come!" She looked and saw the man in her dreams. At first she was ashamed and bashful. The man told her all that had happened before, and claimed her as his wife.

One day The Giver told the man that all the world had been made for him. Then he instructed him how to act at all times and under all conditions. He also admonished him to have more children, and the man had sixteen children. The first one was a boy, then came a girl, then another boy, and so on. Half of his children went to live north of the Rogue River, while the other half settled down south of the river. The Giver told the man that hereafter he would obtain everything by wishing. Then he straightened out the world, made it flat, and placed the waters. He also created all sorts of animals, and cautioned the man not to cut down more trees or kill more animals than he needed. And after all this had been done, he bade him farewell and went up to the sky, "You and your wife and children shall speak different languages. You shall be the progenitors of all the different tribes."

Bibliography

This bibliography lists all collections, books, and articles cited or consulted by the editors in the course of preparing this anthology. Hence, in addition to documenting our research, it can serve as a starting point for other projects in the oral traditions of Oregon and the Northwest, along with other general collections and studies listed below—notably Nash and Scofield's *The Well-Travelled Casket;* Erik Bromberg's "Frontier Humor: Plain and Fancy"; Suzi Jones's *Oregon Folklore* and *Webfooters and Bunchgrassers: Folk Art of the Oregon Country;* Jarold Ramsey's *Coyote Was Going There* and "Resource Guide for the Study of Native Americans"; and Zucker, Hummel, and Hogfoss's *Oregon Indians.* There is at present no comprehensive bibliography of Oregon folklore and oral literature.

Archives and Special Collections

William L. Alderson Papers, Special Collections, University of Oregon Library, Eugene, Oregon

Boas Collection, American Philosophical Library, Philadelphia, Pennsylvania

Fife Folklore Archives, Utah State University, Logan, Utah

Harney County History Project, Harney County Historical Society, Burns, Oregon

McKay Family Papers, Pendleton Public Library, Pendleton, Oregon

Oregon Historical Society Archives and Special Collections

Randall V. Mills Archives of Northwest Folklore, University of Oregon, Eugene, Oregon

Venn Collection, Eastern Oregon State College, La Grande

Works Projects Administration (WPA), Oregon Folklore Project, Oregon State Library, Salem, Oregon

Books and Articles

Aarne, Anti, and Tith Thompson. *The Types of the Folktale: A Classification and Bibliography.* Folklore Fellows Communications No. 180, Helsinki, 1961.

Abrahams, Roger, and George Foss. *Anglo-American Folksong Style.* Englewood Cliffs, NJ: Prentice-Hall, 1968.

Adams, Ramon F. *Western Words: A Dictionary of the American West.* Norman: University of Oklahoma Press, 1968.

Alderson, William. "Fifty Thousand Lumberjacks." *California Folklore Quarterly,* Vol. 4 (Oct. 1942), 375-376.

Aries, Philippe. *Centuries of Childhood: A Social History of Family Life,* trans. Robert Baldick. New York: Vintage Books, 1962.

Baehr, Russell. *Oregon Outback.* Bend: Maverick Publications, 1988.

Barker, M.A.R. *Klamath Texts.* University of California Publications in Linguistics, Vol. 30 (1963).

Beck, Horace. *Folklore and the Sea.* Middleton, CT: The Marine Historical Association, 1973, reprinted 1985.

Beckham, Stephen Dow. *The Indians of Western Oregon.* Coos Bay: Arago Books, 1977.

———. *Requiem for a People: The Rogue Indians and the Frontiersmen.* Norman: University of Oklahoma Press, 1971.

———. *Tall Tales from Rogue River, The Yarns of Hathaway Jones.* Bloomington: Indiana University Press, 1974. Reprinted by Oregon State University Press, 1991.

Benjamin, Harold. "Case Study in Folksong Making." *Tennessee Folklore Bulletin,* XIX (1953), 28-30.

Bingham, Edwin, and Glen Love, eds. *Northwest Perspectives.* Seattle: University of Washington Press, 1979.

Boas, Franz. *Chinook Texts.* U.S. Bureau of American Ethnology, Vol. 20 (1894).

———, ed. *Kathlamet Texts.* Bureau of American Ethnology, Bulletin 27, Washington, DC, 1901.

———. *Texts in Chinook Jargon.* University of Washington Publications in Anthropology, Vol. 7, No. 1 (1936).

The Book of Bunyan, Being the Exploits of Paul Bunyan and Babe the Blue Ox, in Southwestern Oregon. Coos Bay, 1934.

Botkin, Benjamin. *Treasury of American Folklore.* New York: Crown Publishers, 1944.

———. *A Treasury of Southern Folklore.* New York: Crown, 1949.

Bright, Verne. "Black Harris, Mountain Man, Teller of Tales." *Oregon Historical Quarterly,* 52, 1 (1951), 3-20.

Brogan, Phil. *East of the Cascades.* Portland: Binford and Mort, 1964.

Bromberg, Erik. "Frontier Humor: Plain and Fancy," *Oregon Historical Quarterly,* Vol LXI, No. 3 (Sept. 1960), 261-342.

Brunvand, Jan Harold. *The Study of American Folklore.* New York: W.W. Norton, 1968.

———. *The Vanishing Hitchhiker: American Urban Legends and Their Meanings.* New York: W.W. Norton, 1981.

Buan, Carolyn, and Richard Lewis, eds. *The First Oregonians.* Portland: Oregon Council for the Humanities, 1991.

Buchanan, J.A. "A Brave Pioneer Girl," *Pacific Monthly,* Vol. 6 (1901), 162.

Byrne, Peter. *The Search for Bigfoot.* New York: Simon and Schuster, 1976.

Chan, Jeffrey Paul, Frank Chin, Lawson Fusao Inada, and Shawn Wong, eds. *The Big Aiiieeeee! Chinese-American and Japanese-American History in Literature.* Washington: Howard University Press, 1982.

Clare, Warren. "The Slide-Rock Bolter, Splinter Cats, and Paulski Bunyanovitch." *Idaho Yesterdays*

Clark, Ella E. *Indian Legends of the Pacific Northwest*. Berkeley: University of California Press, 1953.

Clark, Keith, and Donna Clark, eds. *Daring Donald McKay*. Portland: Oregon Historical Society, 1971.

———, and Lowell Tiller. *The Terrible Trail: The Meek Cutoff, 1845*. Caldwell: Caxton Printers, 1966.

Collins, Rod. "Walkaway," *Northwest Folklore*, Vol. II, i (1967), 18.

Curtin, Jeremiah. *The Memoirs of Jeremiah Curtin*. Wisconsin Biography Series, Vol. 2, Madison, 1940.

———. *Modoc Myths*. Boston: Little Brown, 1912.

———. "Wasco Tales and Myths," in *Wishram Texts*, ed. Edward Sapir. Publications of the American Ethnological Society,Vol. 2 (1909).

Curtis, Edward. *The North American Indian*. Norwood: The Plimpton Press, Vol. 8 (1911), Vol. 13 (1924).

Davis, H. L. *Kettle of Fire*. New York: William Morrow, 1959.

A Dictionary of the Chinook Jargon or Indian Trade Language. Seattle: Shorey Book Store, 1971.

Dorsey, J. Owen. "Indians of the Siletz Reservation," *American Anthropologist*, 2 (1889), 55-60.

Dorson, Richard. *American Folklore*. Chicago: University of Chicago Press, 1959.

———. *Buying the Wind: Regional Folklore in the United States*. Chicago and London: University of Chicago Press, 1964.

Fletcher, Curley. *Songs of the Sage*. Introduction by Hal Cannon. Layton, Utah: Gibbs M. Smith, 1985.

Flick, Leon. *Home for a Buckaroo*. Shallowwater, TX: Adobe Records, 1992.

Forest Log. Corvallis: School of Forestry, Oregon Agricultural College, 1934.

Frachtenberg, Leo J. *Alsea Myths and Texts*. U.S. Bureau of American Ethnology, Bull. No. 67 (1920).

———. *Coos Texts*. Columbia University Contributions to Anthropology, Vol. 1 (1913).

———, and Livingston Farrand. "Shasta and Athapascan Myths from Oregon." *Journal of American Folklore*, Vol. 23 (1911), 207-242.

French, Giles. *Cattle Country of Pete French*. Portland: Binford and Mort, 1972.

Furlong, Charles. *Let 'er Buck*. New York: G.P. Putnam's Sons, 1921.

Gallop, Rodney. *The Book of the Basques*. London: Macmillan, 1930.

Gatschet, Albert. *The Klamath Indians*. Contributions to North American Ethnology, Vol. I (1890-91).

———. "Oregonian Folklore." *Journal of American Folklore*, Vol. 4 (1891), 139-143.

Geer, T.T. *Fifty Years in Oregon*. New York: Neale Publishing Co., 1912.

Gibbs, George. "Account of Indian Mythology in Oregon and Washington Territory," ed. Ella E. Clark. *Oregon Historical Quarterly* 57 (1956), 133 ff.

Gilmore, Janet C. *The World of the Oregon Fishboat: A Study in Maritime Folklife*. Ann Arbor: UMI Research Press, 1986.

Hafen, LeRoy, ed. *The Mountain Men and the Fur Trade of the Far West*. Vol. IV. Glendale: A.C. Clark, 1966.

Haines, Francis. "Goldilocks on the Oregon Trail," *Idaho Yesterdays,* Vol. 9, No. 4 (Winter 1965-66), 26-30.

Hancock, Sunny. *Cowboy Poetry: New and Used* (audio cassette). HC60: Box 3310, Lakeview, OR.

Hanley, Mike, and Ellis Lucia. *Owyhee Trails: The West's Forgotten Corner.* Caldwell: Caxton Printers, 1975.

Harrison, Russell M. "Folksongs from Oregon." *Western Folklore* XI, 3 (July 1952), 174-184.

Hawes, Bess Lomax. *Step it Down: Games, Plays, Songs, and Stories from the Afro-American Heritage.* New York: Harper and Row, 1984.

Hays, M. *The Land that Kept Its Promise.* Lincoln County Historical Society Publications No. 14 (1976).

Helm, Mike. *Oregon's Ghosts and Monsters.* Eugene: Rainy Day Press, 1983.

Holbrook, Stewart. *Wildmen, Wobblies, and Whistlepunks,* ed. Brian Booth. Corvallis: Oregon State University Press, 1993.

Hult, Ruby El. *Lost Mines and Treasures of the Pacific Northwest.* Portland: Binford and Mort, 1957.

Hurley, Gerald. "Buried Treasure Tales in America." *Western Folklore,* X (1951), 197-216.

Hymes, Dell. "Folklore's Nature and the Sun's Myth." *Journal of American Folklore,* 88 (1975), 345-369.

———. *"In Vain I Tried to Tell You": Essays in Native American Ethnopoetics.* Philadelphia: University of Pennsylvania Press, 1981.

———. "Languages and Their Uses," in Buan and Lewis, eds. *The First Oregonians.* Portland: Oregon Council for the Humanities, 1991, pp. 37-38.

Jackman, E.R., and Reuban Long. *The Oregon Desert.* Caldwell: Caxton Printers, 1977.

Jacobs, Elizabeth, and Melville Jacobs, eds. *Nehalem Tillamook Tales,* reprinted with intro. by Jarold Ramsey. Corvallis: Oregon State University Press, 1990.

Jacobs, Melville. *Clackamas Chinook Texts.* Bloomington: Indiana University Research Center in Anthropology, Folklore, and Linguistics, Vol. 1 (1958), Vol. 2 (1959).

———. *The Content and Style of an Oral Literature.* New York: Wenner-Gren Foundation, 1959.

———. *Coos Ethnologic and Narrative Texts.* University of Washington Publications in Anthropology, Vol. 8, No. 2 (1940).

———. "The Fate of Indian Oral Literatures in Oregon." *Northwest Review,* 3 (Summer, 1962), 90-99.

———. *The People Are Coming Soon.* Seattle: University of Washington Press, 1960.

———. *Texts in Chinook Jargon.* University of Washington Publications in Anthropology, Vol. 7, 1 (1936).

Jansen, William H. *Abraham "Oregon" Smith: Pioneer, Folk Hero, and Tale-teller.* New York: Arno Press, 1977.

Jefferson County Reminiscences, ed. by "Many Hands." Portland: Binford and Mort, 1957.

Jones, Pamela. "There Was a Woman: *La Llorona* in Oregon." *Western Folklore,* 47 (July 1988), 195-211.

Jones, Suzi, ed. *Central Oregon Folklife Festival*. Salem: Oregon Arts Commission, 1978.

———, ed. *North Coast Folklife Festival*. Salem: Oregon Arts Commission, 1977.

———, ed. *Oregon Folklore*. Eugene: Randall V. Mills Archive of Northwest Folklore, University of Oregon, 1977.

———, ed. *Umpqua Folklife*. Salem: Oregon Arts Commission, 1979.

———, ed. *Webfoots and Bunchgrassers: Folk Art of the Oregon Country*. Salem: Oregon Arts Commission, 1980.

Kelly, Isabel. "Ethnography of the Surprise Valley Paiutes." University of California Publications in American Anthropology, Archaeology, and Ethnology, Vol. 31 (1932), 67-209.

———. "Northern Paiute Tales." *Journal of American Folklore,* 51 (1938), 367-437.

Kennedy, G.W. *The Pioneer Campfire*. Portland: Marsh Printing Co., 1913.

Kesselman, Amy. *Fleeting Opportunities: Women Shipyard Workers in Portland and Vancouver*. Albany: State University of New York Press, 1990.

Kessler, Lauren. "Spacious Dreams: A Japanese Family Comes to the Pacific Northwest." *Oregon Historical Quarterly*, Vol. 94, nos. 2-3 (Summer-Fall 1993), 163 ff.

Knapp, Mary, and Herbert Knapp. *One Potato, Two Potato: The Folklore of American Children*. New York: W.W. Norton, 1976.

Kornbluh, Joyce, ed. *Rebel Voices: An I.W.W. Anthology*. Chicago: Charles H. Kerr, 1987.

Krantz, Grover. *Big Footprints*. New York: Johnson Books, 1992.

Lingenfelter, Richard E., et al., eds. *Songs of the American West*. Berkeley and Los Angeles: University of California Press, 1968.

The Little Red Songbook. Chicago: Industrial Workers of the World, 1917.

Lockley, Fred. *Conversations with Bullwhackers, Muleskinners, etc.* Ed.Mike Helm. Eugene: Rainy Day Press, 1981.

———. *Conversations with Pioneer Women*. Ed. Mike Helm. Eugene: Rainy Day Press, 1981.

Lowenstein, Steven. *The Jews of Oregon, 1850-1950*. Portland: Jewish Historical Society, 1987.

Lyman, H.S. "Items from the Nez Perces." *Oregon Historical Quarterly*, Vol. II (1901), 295-296.

———. "Reminiscences of Louis Labonte." *Oregon Historical Quarterly*, Vol. 1 (1900), 167-188.

Mackey, Harold. *The Kalapuyas: A Sourcebook on the Indians of the Willamette Valley*. Salem: Mission Mill Museum Association, 1971.

McArthur, Lewis. *Oregon Geographic Names*, 4th ed. Portland: Binford and Mort, 1974.

McCulloch, Walter F. *Woods Words*. Portland: Oregon Historical Society and Champoeg Press, 1958.

McLagan, Elizabeth. *A Peculiar Paradise: A History of Blacks in Oregon 1788-1940*. Portland: The Georgian Press, 1980.

McPherson, Kathryn. "Hathaway Jones, the Rogue's Paul Bunyan," in *Oregon's South Coast*. Coos Bay: World Publishing Co., 1960.

Mills, Hazel E. "The Constant Webfoot." *Western Folklore,* XI, 3 (July 1952), 153-164.

Mills, Randall V. "Oregon Speechways." *American Speech* (1950), 81-90.

Mullin, Susan. "Oregon's Huckleberry Finn: A Munchhausen Enters Tradition." *Northwest Folklore* II, i (1967), 19-25.

Munro, Sarah Baker. "Basque Folklore in Southeastern Oregon." *Oregon Historical Quarterly,* 76 (1975), 153-174.

———. *Basque-American Folklore in Southeastern Oregon.* M.A. thesis in folklore, University of California, Berkeley, 1972.

Nash, Tom, and Twilo Scofield, eds. *The Well-Traveled Casket: A Collection of Oregon Folklife.* Salt Lake City: University of Utah Press, 1992.

Nelson, Ray. *Memoirs of an Oregon Moonshiner.* Caldwell: Caxton Printers, 1980.

Ohrlin, Glenn. *The Hell-Bound Train.* University of Illinois: Campus Folksong Club Records CFC 301, n.d.

Oliver, Herman. *Gold and Cattle Country.* Ed. E.R. Jackman. Binford and Mort, 1961.

Opie, Iona, and Peter Opie. *The Lore and Language of Schoolchildren.* London and New York: Oxford University Press, 1959.

Oregon Writers Program (WPA). "Tall Tales and Legends," in *Oregon: End of the Trail.* Portland: Binford and Mort, 1940, pp.81-85.

The Original Tracks: 1983 Portland Foxfire Project. Portland, OR: Portland Public Schools, 1984.

Pearce, Helen. "Folk-sayings in a Pioneer Family in Western Oregon." *California Folklore Journal,* 5, 3 (1946), 229-242.

Peterson, Emil R., and Alfred Powers, eds. *A Century of Coos and Curry: History of Southwest Oregon.* Portland: Binford and Mort, 1952.

Phinney, Archie. *Nez Perce Texts.* Columbia University Contributions to Anthropology, Vol. 25 (1934).

Ramsey, Jarold, ed. *Coyote Was Going There: Indian Literature of the Oregon Country.* Seattle: University of Washington Press, 1977.

———. "John Campbell's Adventure and the Ecology of Story." *Northwest Review,* XXIX, 2 (1991), 46-65.

———. "Resource Bibliography for the Study of Native Americans." *Oregon English Journal,* XIV, 1 (Spring 1992), 62-67.

———. *Reading the Fire: Essays in the Traditional Indian Literatures of the Far West.* Lincoln: University of Nebraska, 1983.

———. "Ti-Jean and the Seven-headed Dragon: Instances of Native American Assimilation of European Folklore." In *The Native in Literature,* ed. King, Calvert, and Hoy. Oakville: ECW Press, 1987, pp. 206-224.

Ray, Verne. *Primitive Pragmatists: The Modocs of Northern California.* Seattle: University of Washington Press, 1963.

Rea, Lori, ed. *Living Treasures: Hispanic Artisans and Traditionalists of the Snake River Valley.* Nampa, ID: Hispanic Folk Arts Survey Committee, 1991.

Riddle, Claude. *In the Happy Hills.* Roseburg: M-M Printers, 1954.

Robe, Stanley. "Basque Tales from Eastern Oregon." *Western Folklore,* 12 (1953), 153-157.

Ruxton, George Frederick. *Life in the Far West.* New York: Harper and Bros., 1849.

Sam, Wong, et al. *English-Chinese Phrase Book*. San Francisco: Wells, Fargo, 1875.

Sapir, Edward. *Takelma Texts.* Anthropological Publications of the University of Pennsylvania, 2 (1909).

Skeels, Dell. *Style in the Unwritten Literature of the Nez Perce Indians*. Unpubl. Ph.D. dissertation, University of Washington, 2 vols., 1949.

Skinner, Charles M. *Myths and Legends of Our Own Land,* Vol. II. Philadelphia and London: J.B. Lippincott, 1896, 1926.

Smith, Helen Krebs, ed. *With Her Own Wings: Historical Sketches, Reminiscences, and Anecdotes of Pioneer Women*. Portland: Beattie and Co., 1948.

Smith, Silas. "Early Wrecks on the Oregon Coast." *Oregon Native Son,* Vol. I (1899), 37-49.

Southeast Asians and Their Memories: Southeast Asian Foxfire Project 1981. Portland, OR: Multnomah County School District, 1981.

Spier, Leslie. *Klamath Ethnography*. University of California Publications in American Anthropology, Archaeology, and Ethnology, Vol. 30 (1930).

———, and Edward Sapir. *Wishram Ethnography*. University of Washington Publications in Anthropology, Vol. 3, No. 3 (May 1930).

Spinden, Herbert. "Myths of the Nez Perce Indians." *Journal of American Folklore,* 21 (1908), 156-201.

Stern, Theodore. *The Klamath Tribe*. Seattle: University of Washington Press, 1965.

———. "Some Sources of Variability in Klamath Mythology." *Journal of American Folklore,* 69 (1956), 1-9, 135-136, 377-386.

Stevens, James. *Paul Bunyan*. New York: Ballantine Books, 1975.

Swadesh, Morris. "Cayuse Interlinear Texts." Film 373.1, Reel 48, Franz Boas Collection, American Philosophical Society Library, Philadelphia.

Talkington, Henry L. *Heroes and Heroic Deeds of the Pacific Northwest*. Vol. I, "The Pioneers." Caldwell: Caxton Printers, 1929.

Thompson, Stith, and Edward O. Tabor. "Paul Bunyan in 1910." *Journal of American Folklore,* 59 (1946), 134-135.

Toelken, J. Barre. *The Dynamics of Folklore*. Boston: Houghton Mifflin, 1979.

———. "Foreword" to Barry Lopez, *Giving Birth to Thunder, Sleeping with His Daughter: Coyote Builds North America*. Kansas City: Sheed Andrews and McNeel, 1976.

———. "Northwest Traditional Ballads: A Collector's Dilemma," in Bingham, Edwin, and Glen Love, eds., *Northwest Perspectives*. Seattle: University of Washington Press, 1979.

Thomas, E.H. *Chinook, A History and Dictionary*. Portland: Binford and Mort, 1937.

Victor, Frances. *All Over Oregon and Washington*. San Francisco, 1872.

Williams, William Carlos. "Kenneth Burke," in *Selected Essays of William Carlos Williams*. New York: Random House, 1954, pp. 132-133.

Winnemucca, Sarah. *Life among the Piutes*. Boston and New York: G.P. Putnams Sons, 1883.

Zeitlin, Steven J., Amy Kotkin, and Holly Cutting Baker. *A Celebration of American Family Folklore*. New York: Pantheon Books, 1982.

Zucker, Jeff, Kay Hummel, and Bob Hogfoss. *Oregon Indians: Culture, History, and Current Affairs*. Portland: Western Imprints, 1983.

Genres of Folk Literature

This glossary is a list of some of the most common types of folk literature found in this volume. It is by no means exhaustive, and readers who would like fuller definitions and discussions of the genres of folk literature and folklore might wish to consult some general folklore texts such as Jan Brunvand, *The Study of American Folklore*, Eliot Oring, ed., *Folk Groups and Folklore Genres: An Introduction*, Stith Thompson, *The Folktale*, or Barre Toelken, *The Dynamics of Folklore*. Local examples organized by genre may be found in Suzi Jones, *Oregon Folklore*.

Ballad—A folksong that tells a story, a narrative folksong. See, for example, "The Ballad of Archie Brown," p. 96.

Corrido—A well-known type of Mexican folksong that is narrative, often an account of local historical events or persons. See, for example, "*Corrido del Difunto Nabor*," p. 152.

Folk tale—A traditional story that is a fictional prose narrative, often told for entertainment but may also convey a message or a moral; includes fairy tales. Folk tales are the "short stories" of folk literature. See, for example, "Ang Toy and Farm Pei," p. 274, or "The Golden Arm," p. 254.

Etiological tale—An explanatory tale that purports to explain the origins or characteristics of various things, especially animals, plants, and geographical features. Many folklorists point out that the moral lessons of these stories are their most important function and that their "explanations" are seldom meant to be taken literally.

Folk poetry—Traditional poems or rhymes that circulate by word of mouth, such as jumprope rhymes, counting-out rhymes, and the longer, more complex recitations such as those in this volume by Sunny Hancock.

Legend—A narrative told as a historical account and regarded as true by the teller. Legends are usually secular with the events of the narrative situated in a specific time and place.

Myth—Myths are sacred narratives, often peopled with sacred beings and set in a "mythic" time that predates the historic period. See, for example, "Tututni Genesis," p. 304, or "The Sun's Myth," p. 34. Note: to call a narrative a *myth* does not mean that the story is false; it refers, rather, to the religious, or sacred, character of the narrative.

Tall tale—Sometimes referred to as *lies, yarns, windies,* or *whoppers,* tall tales are humorous stories that involve some sort of exaggeration but are usually told with a straight face to the naive listener. See, for example, "A Remarkable Shot," or any of the tales by B.F. Finn, Hathaway Jones, Tebo Ortego, or Abraham "Oregon" Smith.

Copyright Acknowledgments

Every effort has been made to find the legal copyright holders of the materials reproduced in this book and to secure permission for use herein. If we have overlooked a copyright holder who should be acknowledged, we have done so inadvertently or because our best efforts to do so have failed. Thus all of the previously reprinted and copyrighted materials included here are included in good faith. If anyone can bring to our attention failures to secure permission and acknowledge copyright, we shall be happy to correct such oversights in a subsequent edition.

A number of texts are from student folklore collections, deposited with the Randall V. Mills Archive of Northwest Folklore, Department of English, University of Oregon. Upon advice of the archivist, we have attempted to contact all collectors who requested notification of use on their signed release cards, as well as those whose collections were not accompanied by release cards. In all cases, the collectors and narrators are credited in the notes accompanying each entry.

Texts

American Folklore Society, for the following materials in *The Journal of American Folklore*: Dell Hymes, "Folklore's Nature and the Sun's Myth," 88 (1975), 360-367; Isabel Kelly, "Northern Paiute Tales," 51 (1938), 368, 418-419 and 437; Stith Thompson and Edward O. Tabor, "Paul Bunyan in 1910," 59 (1946), 134-135. Reproduced by permission of the American Folklore Society. Not for further reproduction.

Arno Press and William H. Jansen, for passages from *Abraham "Oregon" Smith: Pioneer, Folk Hero, and Tale Teller*, pp. 224, 292-293, 293-294, 296-297.

Beattie and Co. for "Aaron Meier and and the Darning Needle Story," *With Her Own Wings: Historical Sketches, Reminiscences, and Anecdotes of Pioneer Women*, ed. Helen Krebs Smith, pp. 117-120.

Binford and Mort Publishing, for passages from Ruby El Hult, *Lost Mines and Treasures of the Pacific Northwest*, pp. 16-18 and for portions of the "Treasure Map" by James Tower, endpapers; and for *Jefferson County Reminiscences*, p. 33; and for passages from Herman Oliver, *Gold and Cattle Country*, ed. E.R. Jackman, p. 168 and pp. 181-183.

The Book of Bunyan, Being the Exploits of Paul Bunyan and Babe, the Blue Ox, in Southwest Oregon. Coos Bay, 1934.

California Folklore Society for the following material in *Western Folklore*: Russell Harrison, "Folksongs from Oregon," Vol. XI (1952), 174, and Stanley Robe, "Basque Tales from Eastern Oregon," Vol. XII (1953), 153-157; and for the following from *The California Folklore Quarterly*: Helen Pearce, "Folk-sayings in a Pioneer Family in Western Oregon," Vol. 5 (1946), 229-242, and William Alderson, "50,000 Lumberjacks," Vol. 4 (1942), 356-357.

The Caxton Printers, Ltd. for selections from E. Jackman and Reuban Long, *The Oregon Desert*, pp. 62, 111, 182, 347-348, 385; and for Jack Dalton's story in

ART

"Coyote and Animal Friends" by Audrey Myers from Great Basin petroglyphs on page 112. From Ramsey, *Coyote Was Going There*.

"Falling a Large Fir," photographer unknown, on page 134. Reproduced courtesy of Oregon Historical Society, negative number OrHi6017.

"Interior of Mine" by Jim Wood on page 184. Ashwood, Oregon. Reproduced courtesy of Oregon Historical Society, negative number OrHi 90388.

"Indian Petroglyphs on rocks near The Dalles, Oregon" on page 196. Photograph by B.C. Markham. Reproduced courtesy of Oregon Historical Society, negative number OrHi 48962.

Detail from Petroglyph by Hansen Studios on page 218. Cast stone document from The Dalles Dam Reservoir area, Crawfords Point. Reproduced by permission of Hansen Studios.

"Girls' Backyard Tea Party" by Timothy L. Graves on page 240. c. 1900. Oakland, Oregon. From the Beckham Collection. Reproduced courtesy of Douglas County Museum.

"Klamath String Figures" on page 246. From Spier, Leslie, *Klamath Ethnography*, University of California Publications in American Archaeology and Ethnography, 30. Berkeley, CA; University of California Press, 1930. Reproduced by permission.

"McCully Wedding Party" on page 272. Photographer unknown. June 1892. Reproduced courtesy of Oregon Historical Society, negative number 1756022.

"Rosebrook Gate" by Rod Rosebrook on page 288. Iron, 1979. Courtesy of Randall Mills Archive, University of Oregon.

"Petroglyphs" on page 302. Photograph by B. Gifford. Reproduced courtesy of Oregon Historical Society, negative number Or 2567.

AUTHOR PHOTOGRAPHS

The Oregon Council of Teachers of English and the Oregon State University Press would like to thank the following for providing photographs of authors and for permission to use them: Orlo Flock, photograph by Michael Mathers, Central Oregon Folklife Festival; Reub Long from *The Oregon Desert*, ed. E.R. Jackman and R. Long; Charles Cultee from *Chinook Texts*, ed. Franz Boas; Fish Hawk from *Coyote Was Going There*, ed. Jarold Ramsey; Moses "Black" Harris in the painting entitled "Trappers" by Alfred Jacob Miller, reproduced by permission of Walters Art Gallery, Baltimore, Maryland; Tebo Ortego, courtesy of Harney County Historical Society; Lou Southworth courtesy of OSU Horner Museum with thanks to Lucy Skjelstad; Jack Dalton and his wife from *Owyhee Trails* by M. Hanley and E. Lucia; Wasson family, photograph by Clydia Nahwooksy, ca. 1975; Reynaldo Rivera, photograph by Eva Castellanoz, 1992, Oregon Folk Arts Program; Lulu Lang, photograph taken in 1956 by Theodore Stern from *Handbook of North American Indians*, National Museum of Natural History, Smithsonian Institute; Victoria Howard from *The People Are Coming Soon: Analysis of Clackamas Chinook Myths and Tales*, ed. Melville Jacobs; Sunny Hancock, photograph by Kevin Fuller, 1989, Western Folklife Center;

The following photographs of authors were provided courtesy of the Oregon Historical Society: Jesse Stahl, negative 12526, file 855-A; Aaron Meier, negative 010219; Donald McKay, negative OrHi655, file 701.

Index

THE BLUE NILE REVEALED

Lost and Found Series

*Classic Travel
Writing*

THE BLUE NILE REVEALED

The Story of the Great Abbai Expedition
1968

RICHARD SNAILHAM

Signal Books
Oxford
2005

This edition published in 2005 by
Signal Books Limited
36 Minster Road
Oxford
OX4 1LY
www.signalbooks.co.uk

First published in 1970
© Richard Snailham, 1970
Foreword © John Blashford-Snell, 2005

A catalogue record for this book is available from the British Library

ISBN 1-902669-93-2 Cloth
ISBN 1-902669-94-0 Paper

Cover Design: Baseline Arts
Type Design and Imaging: Devdan Sen
Cover Image: Richard Snailham

Printed in Malaysia

CONTENTS

FOREWORD

LIKE most great challenges The Great Abbai or Blue Nile Expedition was a milestone in the lives of many who took part.

Looking back on it I still remember numerous funny and frightening moments. There were also times of stress, fear and sadness. However, without doubt the eventual success of the project was due to teamwork. The expedition achieved excellent scientific results, made important archaeological discoveries and led to the development of inflatable boats capable of navigating rapid-strewn rivers that had hitherto been considered unnavigable. The exploration of many of the world's wildest rivers became possible as a result.

Most of us who took part were relatively inexperienced and had to learn the hard way and in order to maintain the pool of expertise we formed The Scientific Exploration Society, which continues to flourish. The enormous support of His Imperial Majesty Haile Selassie and the British Army made it all possible but we were also fortunate in being backed by many kind sponsors in Britain and Ethiopia.

Although it was 36 years ago, I can still see Richard scribbling away in his notebook by the flickering light of a candle beside the river, and this book is a tribute to his skill and diligence in recording the events of this dramatic venture. It is fitting that his book should be republished as we prepare to revisit the legendary river and follow up some of the earlier scientific work.

John Blashford-Snell
2004

ACKNOWLEDGEMENTS

I should like to acknowledge my gratitude to the following for giving me permission to use their photographic material: John Anstey, Editor of the *Daily Telegraph Magazine*, Chris Bonington, Patrick Morris, "Johnny" Johnson, Nigel Sale, Gavin Pike, Roger Chapman, John Fletcher, Gage Williams, Hilary King, John Blower, The Ministry of Defence.

In Memory of

CORPORAL IAN MACLEOD, BLACK WATCH

1941-1968

PREFACE

THE Great Abbai Expedition of 1968 was planned as a scientific expedition; but it carried out its scientific enquiries in a remote and dangerous region, and this made its eventual achievement a triumph of personal survival in the face of severe natural and human hazards as well as a useful contribution to science.

Almost seventy people, British and Ethiopian, were involved for nine weeks in a survey of the deep gorge of the Ethiopian Blue Nile, or Great Abbai. For most of its length this river is swift-flowing and punctuated by falls and cataracts; its gorge is almost entirely uninhabited; certain corners of it had never been penetrated by Europeans before, and these areas were infested by robber bands beyond the control of the central government in Addis Ababa. All these factors posed problems; there were a few disasters, and many near-disasters. And they had to be overcome before the scientific tasks could be resumed.

The leader of the Expedition, Captain John Blashford-Snell, R.E., had asked me at an early stage to act as Treasurer of the whole undertaking. Soon I also became Chief Nilographer—reading up everything on the river that I could find, and writing prospectuses and appeals. It was also foreseen that a book could result from the Expedition's adventures, and here it is—not really an "official history", however, but much more a personal view. I have aimed at a fair and truthful interpretation of events, but I could not, of course, be everywhere at once. Where I was not a first-hand witness, I have relied on the evidence of diaries, tape-recordings and photographs—and I am specially grateful to John Blashford-Snell, Roger Chapman,[1] Chris Edwards, Alastair Newman, Nigel Sale and Kay Thompson for the use of these. I depended greatly on the tolerance and helpfulness of all members, both during the expedition and subsequently, when their good memories have repeatedly come to my rescue. I hope they will find that, in return, I have done them justice—*all* of them. They come to quite a formidable number, but I have introduced them as gradually as possible over the course of the whole book.

I am particularly indebted to William McElwee, who painstakingly read the first draft of the book and enabled me to remove some of the worst infelicities of style and syntax. Miss Robina Ricketts and Mrs.

Jones's team of typists at the R.M.C.S., Shrivenham, together produced the final typescript, and for this I thank them. Lieut.-Col. Philip Shepherd, at the R.M.C.S., and Capt. John Wilsey, at the R.M.A. Sandhurst, did a great deal to help me. The Expedition, of course, recognises its debt to a multitude of people and organisations, and makes its acknowledgements separately in the "Final Report".

A word about place names: I have used the terms Great Abbai—or, simply, Abbai—and Blue Nile, or Nile, indiscriminately throughout, although it should be remembered that the name Abbai is a useful limiting factor because it refers only to the *Ethiopian* section of the Blue Nile: our expedition was concerned only with this, the classic, daunting, virtually unknown part of the river. In the case of most other names, I have avoided the italianised forms which appear on many of the older maps, and used instead a more English orthography, i.e. not Scioa, but Shoa. The spelling of the English version of Amharic words, however, is at the moment entirely arbitrary (Danghila? Dangila? Dangla?).

Yateley, Hants.
June, 1969

[1] John Blashford-Snell, for his leadership, and Roger Chapman, for his courage, were both awarded the M.B.E. in the Summer of 1969.

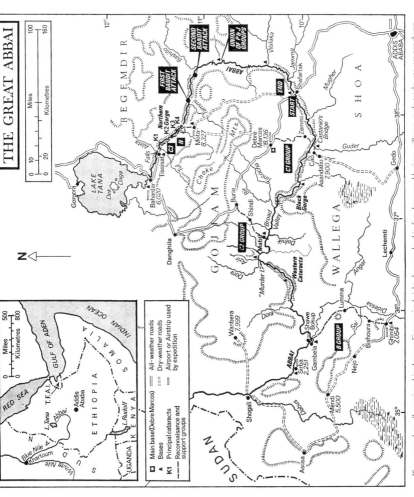

THE GREAT ABBAI

Places named are all mentioned in the text. Figures give height above sea level in feet. Innumerable rivers, villagers, mule-tracks, etc. are not shown

Chapter One
THE GREAT ABBAI

FOUR boats are moving down the broad, brown river. They seem to be made of metal and are green-coloured. They are in line ahead. The river current brings them swiftly downstream and the steady throb of engines is heard. Behind a brown canvas "dodger", the heads and shoulders of seven or eight seated figures are visible in each boat. Most of them are wearing some sort of drab uniform. One of them in the leading boat is wearing a large white helmet. He raises an arm imperiously to the left. The boat swings round in a tight arc towards a shingle beach; the others follow, alternately slipping sideways downstream and then fighting the strong current with engines roaring. Soon they are in quieter waters near the bank, and in reverse order, facing upstream. A man in the leading boat rises, clutching a rifle, stands precariously and then leaps ashore. With a crunch of shingle three more follow from the other boats, run up the steep bank with weapons at the hip and disappear into tall grasses. Soon some of them reappear briefly on a higher bank, standing and peering about them.

Meanwhile others have jumped ashore bearing grapnels on long ropes which are being knotted round rocks and tree roots. Slowly all disembark, bearing tins and plastic bags, and gather in small groups opposite their boats. One stands unconcernedly by the river and adds his quota to what is by now a sewer for three provinces. Others stroll about, stretching, talking and laughing. A fish eagle sits undisturbed on the further shore. Soon smoke rises from a fire or two, and eventually the clink of tins indicates that drinks are being brewed and food eaten. Thirty-two members of the Great Abbai Expedition, 1968, have just started what is to be the first virtually complete navigation and exploration of the Ethiopian Blue Nile.

* * *

Earlier in the year, on a Spring afternoon, some forty members of the Expedition were gathered in a lecture theatre at the Royal Military College of Science at Shrivenham. They were being addressed by its leader, Captain John Blashford-Snell, R.E. In 1964 and 1966 he had led expeditions from the Royal Military Academy Sandhurst, to Ethiopia. On the second occasion they were granted an audience by His Imperial Majesty, Haile Selassie I, who was kind enough to say that he would like to see them return to his country with some further scientific purpose. His Department for the Conservation of Wild Life also suggested more specifically that the gorge of the Blue Nile, or Great Abbai as it is known in Ethiopia, and the basins of some of its tributaries, would make a good subject for scientific survey, and John agreed. Although we were primarily a scientific expedition, therefore, the river we were to survey had never been fully navigated: there was indeed a stretch of about two hundred miles which had never seen boat or white man, and only a handful of navigators had covered the other three hundred miles.

For this task John Blashford-Snell had selected a team of servicemen and civilians: broadly, the servicemen were to get the civilian experts into the area, help them in their work, and extricate them safely with specimens, skins and other finds. The main body of this team was to leave Gatwick on July 30th by air and join a dozen or so others, English and Ethiopian, who were already out there. After a day or so of liaison in Addis Ababa, the team was to move to Debre Marcos, the provincial capital of Gojjam, where the Base Camp would be set up, and from which numerous air recces would be carried out in the light plane which the Army was sending out to us from England. The first part of the gorge survey, called Phase 1, would begin on August 2nd at Shafartak, where the only road from Addis Ababa to Gojjam bridges the Nile. Six weeks were to be spent on the exploration and survey of the Abbai region west of this bridge. This was to be the work of Group A, consisting of thirty-two people travelling downstream in four Army Assault Boats. Simultaneously, Group B— about eight people, moving on foot with mules—were to carry out a game survey of the Angar-Didessa basin, eventually joining Group A on the Abbai, near Sirba. Both groups would then be withdrawn, by some means or other, to Ghimbi and Addis Ababa. This might involve a hundred-mile trek over the mountains. The various groups would then reassemble at Debre Marcos, and after recuperation proceed by road to

Bahardar, where Phase 2 would begin, on September 16ᵗʰ, with the descent of the northern parts of the river by nine men in three inflatable rubber dinghies, backed at several points on the western bank by a considerable support party. In two weeks it was hoped that they would have paddled their way through to the Abbai bridge at Shafartak. The survey would be complete.

A youthful love of weapons and explosives led John Blashford-Snell *via* Sandhurst to a Commission in the Royal Engineers. He is a big man, broad of shoulder, heavily boned. He wears a military moustache, well-cut suits, and, on frequent festive occasions, hired theatrical costumes representing such great generals as William the Conqueror, Oliver Cromwell or Marcus Vipsanius Agrippa. He throws his feet out as he strides along with a cream labrador at his heels, and he drives, entirely suitably, a heavy, fast, low-slung Bristol. There is a warm humanity about him, which his stern exterior sometimes conceals; and he harbours no race consciousness, which is fortunate in a man devoted to exploring Africa. (How much better James Bruce fared in this respect, than that despiser of the black man, Sir Richard Burton!) John has an engaging Victorian quality about him which suggests that he would have been far happier sapping and mining the Redan at Sebastopol, than he is today with sophisticated, electronic gadgetry, which is all too long-range to be much fun. Queen Victoria asked Lieut.-General Sir Robert Napier to lead a punitive expedition against the Emperor Theodore of Abyssinia in 1867. This is the sort of call that John would have relished. Instead, it is Theodore's successor who invites him to his country to lead a scientific expedition pitted against a largely inanimate enemy—the fury of an untamed river, with its possible threats, animal and human. Glamorous punitive expeditions are not sent any more; the British Army increasingly develops a peaceful role. To overcome the Blue Nile and open it to British and Ethiopian scientists is a good modern substitute, John would argue, for the assault on Theodore's camp on the heights of Magdala.

From the beginning a strong team had been steadily assembled. John's second-in-command was Nigel Sale, a stocky, serious Captain in the Royal Green Jackets. Nigel led Group B on their pioneer march from Ghimbi across the Didessa basin to the Abbai, and proved to be a very tough character. He was a useful rock climber and commanded the support party on the lip of the northern gorge in Phase 2. He kept his red hair and freckles well covered from the sun and the peaked cap with a képi gave him the appearance of a latter-day Livingstone.

The key man on Phase 1 was Jim Masters, the Chief Engineer. Jim, a quiet, forty-year-old Somerset man, was to be responsible for the passage of the four Assault Boats from the Abbai bridge to Sirba, and was in general charge of a strong team who were to cope with all our practical engineering problems. He was also in a group led by Roger Chapman, to whom fell perhaps the greatest responsibility for life and limb. Roger was asked to organise the White Water Team, who were to attempt the unnavigated northern stretches of the river in rubber dinghies. A tough, intense Yorkshireman and a dedicated and energetic soldier, he approached this task with exacting thoroughness and probably encountered more problems, human and natural, than any but John himself.

The scientific team was led by Patrick Morris, an extremely capable, inventive, young zoologist. He had been on John's 1966 Expedition to Ethiopia, when the two had sparred amicably over the conflicting requirements of soldiers and scientists. In 1968, the same relationship was maintained—founded on mutual respect, but crackling with superficial gunfire. Patrick's efficient, acidulous manner kept everyone on their toes.

These were some of the leading figures in our expedition. During the spring and summer of 1968 their interest was more and more fixed on the river with which they were to be so totally involved. Research was focussed predominantly on the Blue Nile itself. All the available books were read, previous navigators corresponded with, and maps consulted. An aerial reconnaissance by John Blashford-Snell in March, 1968, brought back a number of photographs of the dry season river and a taped commentary. Slowly a geographical picture of the Blue Nile was built up and the history of the various attempts at its navigation studied.

The Blue Nile gorge in north-west Ethiopia runs from Lake Tana south and then west for about five hundred miles until it comes out in the open plains near the Sudanese frontier. The traditional source of the river is at Gish in the district of Sakala, some seventy miles south of and 3,500 feet above Lake Tana. To locate this source—*Quaerere caput Nili*—had been the hope of many great captains and geographers of the classical age: Herodotus, Cyrus and Cambyses of Persia, Alexander the

Great, Julius Caesar, Nero. The first European actually to find it was Fr. Pedro Paez, a Portuguese Jesuit missionary, who was taken there by the Emperor Susenyos in 1618. The first Briton to make his way to the source was that courageous Scot, James Bruce of Kinnaird. After many frustrations at the court of the Emperor Takla Haimanot II in Gondar, he was able to reach Gish, of which the Emperor had made him Governor, in November, 1770. With his Greek companion Strates, he stood on the damp hummocks by the spring and drank toasts to King George III, the Empress Catherine of Russia (for Strates' sake), and to Margaret Murray, the girl he had left behind him. In a little swamp, 9,000 feet above sea level and surrounded by mountains, the waters of the little Abbai well up from the "coy fountains" and start to tumble northwards to Lake Tana. At the point where the road from Danghila to Bahardar bridges the Little Abbai, it is a considerable river in the wet season. As we approached it, we saw it was a tossing, brown torrent, which would have been an interesting navigational exercise in itself.

When its waters reach Lake Tana they are thought to move in a semicircular course through the placid expanse of the lake before flowing out near Bahardar in the broad stream which is the Great Abbai proper. It would be difficult to improve on Alan Moorehead's[1] graphic description of the Blue Nile as it debouches from Lake Tana and starts on its 2,750 mile journey to the Mediterranean. The first twenty miles of this are as dangerous as any: savage cataracts interrupt the smooth, even flow a few miles south of Bahardar. Major Cheesman[2] had some idea of this, for he speaks of "unending rapids" and seems to have tried to take an iron canoe on the river at this point. As one motors along the straight road from Bahardar to Tissisat—never more than a mile from the river and often only a hundred yards or so—an occasional, muffled booming on the left is the only indication of its presence. Strangely, there is very little audible warning of one of Africa's greatest wonders, which lies just ahead. Approached from the north, it is marked only by a thin puff of white cloud hanging above it. As it draws near the Tissisat Falls, the river snakes for eighteen miles around the feet of low, scrub-covered hills to the east, until its string of rapids culminates in a mile-long lagoon, which broadens from 400 to 600 yards in width.

Tissisat, "the smoke of fire", is one of Ethiopia's most wonderful natural features. Here the Abbai plunges over a basalt lip into the narrow gorge of the River Alata, running at right-angles to it across its

5

front. Tree-clad islands on the lip break up the falls into four parts. In three cases, the water plunges 150 feet directly into the boiling surge at the foot; in the other, it cascades on to a broad step, only to spout out again in a second arc. A veil of water droplets drifts up from the low bank opposite the falls, where clumps of reeds wave back and forth in a perpetual breeze.

Jerome Lobo, another Portuguese Jesuit, has described a visit to Tissisat, one dry season between 1624 and 1633. Like Cheesman in 1926, he was able to walk on a shelf and sit watching rainbows through the falls themselves. James Bruce, in May, 1770, witnessed a fuller flood of water and called it "one of the most magnificent, stupendous sights in the creation".

It was at Tissisat that the only previous attempt to sail down the first twenty miles of the Great Abbai was virtually abandoned. The Sutton Expedition of March, 1968, backed by the *Sunday Mirror* and aided by a group of manufacturers of whisky, cigarettes, etc., used three French Zodiac inflatable dinghies; but they had chosen the dry season and rocks soon ripped the bottoms out of them. This team of five men and two girls was preceded by a considerable fanfare of publicity in the Ethiopian press, but was racked by personal dissensions and split up before reaching the falls.

After plunging over Tissisat, the Abbai, turning to its right, curls under the high cliff at the top of which now stands the fine modern Yugoslav-built hydro-electric station. After half a mile of steep-sided gorge, the river becomes narrower than at any time since its origins in Sakala. It churns through a deep, 20-foot-wide fissure in the rocks, which is bridged by a seventeenth-century structure of the Emperor Fasiladas' time. In the dry season the chasm is only half-filled; in the wet, the river may brim over it and pour through five subsidiary approach arches.

Downstream of this bridge, known as Agam Dildi or the First Portuguese Bridge, the river soon snakes out of sight in a turmoil of brown and white water, hemmed in by permanently wetted walls of volcanic rock. It was 500 yards below this that the only earlier attempt to navigate this section was begun. In 1966 two Swedes, Arne Rubin[3] and Carl-Gustav Forsmark,[4] put their two-man Klepper canoe into the water. They took many a tumble but managed to ride out fifteen miles of the river before Forsmark was almost drowned in a whirlpool. They had by this time lost a critical amount of vital kit, and so decided to come out of the gorge and walk to Mota.

Contrary to popular belief—and our own imaginings before the expedition—the river below Tissisat does not run all the way for 190 miles between slab-sided, vertical cliffs. After just a few miles it opens out to low, grassy banks, and the occasional sandy beach where cattle come down to water, and in September it is a full, fast flood, broken only every five miles or so by a serious cataract. From the river there is the odd glimpse of a field, with the dark figure of a ground hornbill strutting on it, but most often the banks are lined with osiers and shrouded behind by thick trees inhabited by noisy baboons. Above the highest branches rise scrub-covered hills, on the top of which is a narrow tableland rimmed by lines of cliffs—already the river is cutting a gorge within a gorge, and this process is to be repeated until at its deepest it runs a mile below the plateau edge, whose southern rim may be seen from the northern only as a hazy, blue line some fifteen or twenty miles away.

Between the First Portuguese Bridge and the Second—about twenty-seven miles in a south-easterly direction—there are, of course, numerous sheer, basalt cliffs, and the river is often hemmed in and invisible from the nearest path—if there is such a thing. For most of its length there is no easy way of proceeding along the banks of the Abbai; it is always quicker, and certainly more dramatic, to take to the water. Below the Second Bridge it is much the same, until the extraordinary Northern Gorge is entered: here are a profusion of sheer faces, bedding planes, natural arches, tall monoliths; and this gradually fades into a more denuded, lunar landscape. Then, below the Bashillo River entrance, the gorge assumes even more majestic proportions. Looking up, one can see layer upon layer of scrubby scree-slopes, cliffs and terraces, until, perhaps 3,000 or 4,000 feet above and in the distance, the setting sun picks out a lofty, red sandstone butte.

And so, as will be shown, the river, now a very broad flood indeed, continues in a very similar way to the modern Abbai bridge and beyond. A flat, alluvial plain terminates in a narrow, rocky gorge, which in turn opens out into a broad valley followed by a further gorge. This is virtually uninhabited country. So, through some 470 miles and a fall from Lake Tana of 4,500 feet, to the Sudan.

Five attempts to navigate the Blue Nile have begun at the Abbai bridge or below it, of which four are well recorded. They differ from one another in almost every respect and make a fascinating story. As early as 1903, in the reign of the Emperor Menelik, a wealthy American big-game hunter, W. N. McMillan, tried first of all to take boats downriver towards the Sudan, where he hoped to meet a Norwegian colleague, B. H. Jessen, coming upstream from Khartoum. It was a big undertaking, and *Figaro* sent Monsieur De Bois to cover it. Unhappily, the Expedition got off to a poor start, for the gentleman from the Press was castrated and murdered in Danakil country.

However, in June, 1903, McMillan had his three steel boats carried in sections from Addis Ababa down to the confluence of the Mugher River and the Abbai, about thirty-five miles downstream from the site of the present Abbai bridge. The river level in June would still be quite low, but McMillan was hopeful.

"For the first few miles," Jessen[5] writes, "everything went well, but then a bad cataract, curving into an S-shape around rocky points, was encountered, and here the Expedition came to grief. One boat upset and the other sank, thus depriving the Expedition of all their stores and most of their ammunition, making it of course impossible to proceed further." Very short of food they walked back to the capital.

Meanwhile Jessen, in the launch *Adis Abeba*, was steaming manfully upriver towards the Ethiopian frontier at Bumbodi. He made the first low-water ascent of the cataracts at Roseires and Famakka, before turning back when he heard news of McMillan's retreat. Later, in April, 1905, Jessen made a heroic march with Sudanese bearers up the northern bank of the Abbai to Zakas Ford, or even further, before climbing out to Burie.

Thereafter nothing moved on the river, save native *jendies*,[6] for half a century, although it was traced out and, where possible, inspected from the northern bank by the indefatigable Major Cheesman in his long marches of the years 1926-33.

The first aeroplane to overfly the gorge used it in November 1930 as a navigational aid on the way from Addis Ababa to Khartoum. It was carrying film of the Coronation of Haile Selassie (hitherto Regent) as "Negus Neghest", or "King of the Kings" of Ethiopia.

In 1954, Herbert Rittlinger and his wife Mary, German naturists, went with a few friends on a canoeing and sun-worshipping holiday in the Red Sea. From there they moved to Lake Tana and, almost as an afterthought, attempted the Blue Nile. They put the canoes in at the Abbai bridge and covered thirty-five miles to the Mugher River. Here Frau Rittlinger was disconcerted to have the forepart of her canoe badly damaged by an attacking crocodile, and at this confluence, where McMillan had put his boats in, the Germans pulled out. Herbert Rittlinger tells the story in *Schwarzes Abenteuer*,[7] and his wife remains the only woman to have navigated the river below the Abbai bridge.

Dr. A. Amoudruz led a party of six men, French and Swiss, from the Canoe Club de Genève in January, 1962. They planned to pass from the Abbai bridge to the Sudan in two large rubber Canadian canoes with quite a high freeboard. They had considerable success, even though they chose to go in the dry season: by dint of repeatedly roping their canoes down the more treacherous sections they got them through to Sirba and beyond in under a week. Here tragedy struck: a band of roaming *shifta*—a form of highwayman peculiar to East Africa—fell upon them in the middle of the night near Shogali. Two of the Expedition were shot and killed as they lay in their sleeping bags by their canoes. The other four abandoned everything, got away downriver in the darkness, and eventually walked out towards Asosa.[8] History was to do its best to repeat itself in the case of our Expedition, but there were one or two merciful differences.

Next followed an escapade of high fantasy, of which the facts, unfortunately, are sketchy. In 1964, a twenty-year-old Austrian sculptor (Gerhard Heinrich? or Heinrich Gerhard?) is believed to have walked from Egypt into Ethiopia and to have constructed in Addis Ababa a raft, 8 feet by 5 feet, supported on two petrol drums. He left from the Abbai bridge in December, with the platform of the raft already below the water surface. Surviving on fish, he was borne on a river perhaps swollen by the "small rains" through a series of rapids. When he heard the thunder of a cataract beyond Melka Yekatel he wanted to scout it out; but the crocodiles were too thick on the bank for him to land, and so he stood, arms cruciform, and plunged on. His raft was wrecked in a 10-foot chute, and he scrambled ashore with all else lost. He walked painfully back to the Guder River mouth, the nineteen miles taking him six days. Here he was found in an uninhabited hut by a village chief[9] who, thinking him at first to be an escaped convict, nonetheless virtually carried him to the plateau.

We come, finally, to the greatest of them all—Arne Rubin. This tough Swede, at the age of forty-seven, canoed alone from the Abbai bridge to Khartoum in nine days. A burly economist, who had worked for the United Nations in the Sudan, he chose to make his epic journey in September, 1965, at the height of the wet season. Many crocodiles made individual attacks on his canoe; he generally drove them off with three or four blows of his paddle, though one he struck with an empty Coca-Cola bottle. Idly filming another at the Didessa mouth, he delayed too long and it perforated his bows. After riding countless rapids in earlier gorges, he was finally capsized by one of the very last ones just short of Sirba, and lost a cine-camera, maps, notebooks, pens and the like. As a single-handed achievement by a skilled canoeist, Rubin's journey [10] surely rates very highly indeed. He was often in our minds as our flotilla of four fully-equipped boats motored, somehow inexorably, down the same channel.

For all of the foregoing enterprises the journey itself was enough—to survive, to make the passage, and live. We were proposing to attempt something more than this—a full investigation was to be conducted by a team of scientists whilst we passed through the gorge. We were badly let down by the Mineral Survey section of the United Nations Development Project. (It had been planned that four geologists were to come with us, but we arrived in Addis Ababa to find that none was available[11]); however, we had with us an archaeologist, two doctors, and five zoologists. The emphasis was on the collection of small animals and fish, but important archaeological work and medical research was also carried out. A further difference—ours was to prove the first successful descent of the Blue Nile with engines; this power was invaluable to the researchers for it enabled us, where necessary, to turn our descent into an ascent.

NOTES:

[1] Alan Moorehead, *The Blue Nile*, Hamish Hamilton, 1962.
[2] Major R. E. Cheesman, *Lake Tana and the Blue Nile*, Frank Cass, 1968.
[3] See pp.9-10.
[4] See n., p.17.
[5] B. H. Jessen, *W. N. McMillan's Expedition and Big-Game Hunting in Southern Sudan, Abyssinia and East Africa*, Marchant Singer, 1906
[6] Skins or bundles of reeds tied together, on which local people cross the river, half swimming, with their shammas and other possessions stacked at the dry end.
[7] H. Rittlinger, *Schwarzes Abenteuer*, F. A. Brockhaus, Wiesbaden, 1955.
[8] Jean Laporte, *La Tragédie du Nil Bleu*, "Camping Voyages", Paris, April, 1962.
[9] See Chapter 7, p.17.
[10] Arne Rubin, *Ensam med Blå Nilen*, Forum, 1966.
[11] Dr. P. Martin Kaye was subsequently most helpful in lending us transport for use in the Ghimhi area.

Chapter Two
CHISELDON TO DEBRE MARCOS

WHEN John Blashford-Snell became a student at the Royal Military College of Science at Shrivenham in September, 1967, his plans for the Great Abbai Expedition were already well advanced. Whilst he had been Adjutant for the Third Division of the Royal Engineers at Tidworth, his Commanding Officer, Major-General Anthony Deane-Drummond, had offered men and materials for the Expedition, which later proved invaluable. Fortunately, the energetic and peppery Commandant of the R.M.C.S., Major-General Napier Crookenden, also supported John and took the Expedition under his wing as a thoroughgoing R.M.C.S. venture.

John Blashford-Snell and Nigel Sale—Expedition Leader and Second-in-Command—point to a plaster model of the gorge during a briefing at Chiseldon. John Fletcher, Spencer Lane-Jones and Ian Carruthers look on.

The complex and sophisticated technical plant at Shrivenham offered obvious possibilities. In a matter of weeks the principal unknown factor—the flotation capability of boats in the face of cataracts—could be examined scientifically. In the Fluids Laboratory a simulated section of the Great Abbai was constructed complete with adjustable cataract. Interesting wave patterns could be created and the pressure of water passing down the sluice varied. With this equipment, tests could be made with plastic model boats of differing hull shapes; the likely behaviour of the boats with various payloads, variously distributed, could be found out.

Having selected the best type of craft for the job, in this case the standard Army Assault Boat, there remained the problem of conveying four of these bulky items to Ethiopia; and they were only a part of 34,000 lb of freight and passengers that had somehow to be carried from Britain to the Blue Nile gorge.

The R.A.F. had lifted the 1966 Expedition by charter flight to Aden and back, and in an Argosy from Aden to Addis Ababa and back, at low cost, and had cut the travel bill substantially. But whilst we could hope that negotiations for similar help would again be successful, we had to make much more certain travel plans a long time before our date of departure. Through Mitchell Cotts, our agents, a Canadian-built CL 44 of Transglobe Airways was chartered to take the Expedition stores and personnel on July 30th from Gatwick to Addis Ababa, and another to fetch us back again on October 2nd. The two double journeys were to cost £11,300—a sum which we could not easily afford, and, indeed, did not at that time possess. So we were especially interested in the possible availability of an R.A.F. training flight, which, even if it materialised for the outward run only, would have saved us £5,000 or so of mainly private money. As it turned out, the R.A.F. could not help and so we gave Transglobe two of their last assignments.[1]

Since thirty-six of the members of the Expedition were services personnel (thirty-four Army, two Royal Navy), a great opportunity for tough training and rare experience was offered to the Armed Forces. The Ministry of Defence recognised this by giving an Adventure Training Grant of the statutory maximum of £12 per head. Furthermore, many individual regiments and corps to which our members belonged gave us a grant. Service support in other respects was, of course, colossal—the *sine qua non* of the Expedition: Army

Spencer Lane-Jones and John Blashford-Snell watch tests on various types of boat in a simulated Nile cataract specially built at the Fluids Laboratory of the Royal Military College of Science, Shrivenham.

rations, radio sets, Assault Boats, engineering tackle and a mass of other *matériel*.

Every member of the Expedition, service and civilian, made a private contribution. Those from Britain paid £85; members joining at Addis Ababa paid £10. A considerable number of companies and individual well-wishers made contributions and, despite the bleak economic climate, continued to do so long after the Expedition had returned successful. It took almost a year, however, to pay off all our final debts.

In my role as Treasurer, I had more paper work to do before and after the Expedition than ever I had on it; away from Addis Ababa we were soon in regions largely ignorant of His Imperial Majesty's coinage and bank-notes, where barter prevailed, or the shadowy influence of the Maria Theresa Dollar. There were no large markets between Debre

Marcos and Ghimbi, so little normal spending was possible. Beads and trinkets and rounds of our weaker .22 ammunition were the only currency of any use to most of us for the seven weeks in which we lived from what we had brought with us and—meagrely—off the land. Expenses in the field were slight compared with the bills that mounted up at home before we left.

Meanwhile John Blashford-Snell had converted his Army quarter in a disused camp near Swindon into the Expedition Headquarters. The Wiltshire lanes were soon marked with bold signs to direct the hesitant visitor, and Chiseldon was a place to which members went with increasing frequency. A Chief Clerk, Lance-Corporal Henry, was installed in the Expedition nerve centre, a caravan, from which over four thousand letters were sent out before the office was packed up to be carried in brief-cases to Ethiopia. Postmen grumbled about "that 'ere Blashford-Snell", who not only lived inconveniently deep in the country, but also had a daunting daily delivery of mail.

In these months the sponsorship of the *Daily Telegraph Magazine* was secured, to add the weight of the Press to that of the Army. Its charming and helpful Editor, John Anstey, did much to smooth the Expedition's path at home and abroad.

Small groups of members went off from time to time on various kinds of special training. Christian Bonington, Nigel Sale, Roger Chapman and I went to the Cheddar Gorge, where we knew we could find rock as sheer and challenging as anything that we believed we might have to climb in the Blue Nile gorge. This we later found to be so, for in almost all cases it was possible to avoid the vertical faces and pick an easier scramble route. However, to show that we could do it, we abseiled dizzily over a limestone crag 400 feet directly above the car park, and jumared back up again like monkeys on sticks. Those who expected to be driving mules on overland re-supply columns went to Aldershot; here they did training in the loading, leading and general management of animals, and a bit of "practical" in which horses were used in lieu of mules.

A much greater number of us went for watermanship training to North Wales. We could have found conditions more like the Nile, perhaps, in some cascading Norwegian river, or in the Durance in the French Alps, but the extra time and money involved precluded it. In fact, nothing that we could have done by way of training in Europe would have prepared us even remotely for the shock of the Abbai, with its extraordinary volume combined with alarming velocity. Nevertheless the Dee and the Conway at least gave us a chance to get used to the wetsuits, to conduct experiments with lifelines, and to capsize the dinghies to see if we could get back into them again.

The Assault Boats were tested out equally thoroughly on the upper reaches of the Severn; but despite our growing confidence in the equipment that we had chosen, tried and modified, there was still the imponderable nature of the River Nile: nothing but the attempt itself would really prove if everything could stand up to it. A number of people shared our apprehensions. Some, including Tom Stacey of the ill-fated *Sunday Mirror* Expedition of March, 1968, told us that we were mad to attempt the Northern Gorge in September. This section, we were all inwardly beginning to realise, was the crux of our whole journey. However, others, including Carl-Gustav Forsmark[2] were more optimistic: "I know that you can do it," he was to tell us in Addis Ababa, and his opinion was the more valuable since he had actually canoed down parts of the Northern Gorge.

After a Final Briefing at Shrivenham, everyone concentrated on finishing off their personal preparations: rucksacks were tried on, ponchos strung up in gardens, drastic crewcuts acquired, and the daily anti-malarial Paludrin tablets started. Medical preparations of other kinds had been going on for some time. We were to be immunised against Poliomyelitis, Cholera, Tetanus, Smallpox, Yellow Fever, Diphtheria, Typhus and Infective Hepatitis (Bilharzia, another anticipated scourge, could not be medically forestalled). So as not to "mix the drinks" this extensive course had been begun for most of us in May, and by late July we were reporting as automatically as addicts for our regular perforation.

❋ ❋ ❋

After six or seven hours the roar of four engines was becoming wearisome. Crosswords had been done, drinks drunk, air stewardesses chatted up, and sleep now enveloped most of us. Suddenly there was a commotion at the front of the plane, where a group of people stood by the mountain of baggage that filled most of the fuselage.

"God, not a Cuban hi-jacker!" I thought.

"There it is!" someone shouted.

Excited fingers were being pointed through windows, and faces and camera lenses pressed to them. There, 18,000 feet below us, was the dark, sinuous Blue Nile—somewhere on the scrub-covered borderlands of Ethiopia and the Sudan.

Soon Captain Vernon brought us in to Haile Selassie I International Airport at Addis Ababa. It was a drizzly, cold, early morning and the damp, tussocky grass, the sheep safely grazing, the distant rise of the Entotto Hills, all suggested some windswept Scottish airfield rather than one in Latitude 9° N. But, of course, we were about 8,000 feet above sea level and it was July 30th, still very much the rainy season.

"Warmer in good old Glasgow," said Alec Murray as we climbed into a borrowed Land-Rover. Soon we were bowling off down the prestigious avenue of dual carriage-way that leads across open fields to this sprawling capital, that is such a mixture of ancient and modern. As if to prove the point, a train of donkeys laden with brushwood was being driven by a bare-footed woman past the newly completed triumphal arch that spans the road, and towards the vast, stone, sejant lion, the symbolic Lion of Judah that marks the entrance to the city.

I do not know whose whimsical notion it was to quarter us all in a Theological College. But the well-laid scheme to put us in Sabah Hall at the University had gone a-gley, the way these things will, and the foul language, as we lurched about the next day in this Ethiopian Wycliffe Hall with great loads of stores, stubbing toes and cutting fingers, was not at all like that of the shy ordinands who normally flit about the disinfected corridors. Nor was the first night in Ethiopia, for some, spent wholly appropriately for sojourners in this seat of ancient Christian learning.

We had intended only a day of high-speed liaison in Addis Ababa before we moved off to Gojjam to establish our Main Base at Debre Marcos. However, there were delays, particularly in Customs clearance, which, as is shown later, had not been pre-arranged by the British Embassy because of the late grant of political clearance, and the column of lorries and buses did not get under way until two days later, Friday, August 2nd.

All this day was spent in crossing the delightful plateau of Shoa, then the more tedious uplands of Gojjam. In between, however, came the awe-inspiring transit of the Blue Nile Gorge at Shafartak. From rim to rim must have been about twelve miles, and as the bus engaged a noisy third gear, we knew we were in for a long descent. Down and down we wound, over stone bluffs, round hairpin bends and across broad, sloping terraces where fields of maize grew, and gangs of roadmenders lived in portable tin shacks. At one moment there was a thrilling, Italianate viaduct, which snaked out into space momentarily, and then brought us back to *terra firma* again; only fairly *firma,* it seemed, for gabions filled with great stones lined the upper sides of the road to prevent landslides.

The humidity of the gorge was perceptibly increasing. As we dropped down, step by giant step, the world seemed smaller, more closed in: cultivation ceased, and the heat became intense, compared with the windy uplands we had just left. Finally, we rounded the last hairpin, and there was the Great Abbai below us, a rich brown, fast-moving stream about three or four hundred feet across. This was to be our element for the next eight weeks; this was the great natural barrier with which we were to try conclusions. Above us was a belt of blue sky, between the close horizons that were habitually to overshadow us.

Arching over the Nile, to our left, was the beautiful, light, concrete bridge that was to be both start and finishing line for us. This majestic structure, only twenty or so years old, carries the only road across the river from the Shoan plateau—Gojjam's umbilical cord. The bus slowed as we approached the frontier post, and then changed down again to cross this solid piece of engineering with unnecessary care. At the far side hovered a posse of Gojjam police, whom we disconcerted further by stopping by their hut to take a hurried picnic lunch in the suffocating heat.

This African Grand Canyon is certainly a divider of worlds: the Abbai had isolated Gojjam from the main influences of Ethiopian history, and it provides an excellent and rare example of a river making a good frontier. When Gondar was the Imperial capital there were countless wars with the Galla-dominated peoples south of Lake Tana; it was in one of these petty civil scraps that James Bruce was caught up in 1770. When the Shoan dynasty assumed control of the Empire in the nineteenth century, a line of independent Gojjami Rases, culminating in Ras Hailu in this century, adopted a particularist and even a secessionist policy from time to time.

This separateness has a distinct social expression. Many traditions circulate which ascribe magical powers to the Gojjamese people, and their Amharic and Tigrean neighbours are still said to be in fear of them. Tadesse Wolde Gossa, our young friend from the 1966 Expedition, was a striking example of this. He is a slender, good-looking Amhara boy of seventeen, who has now just begun a training course for science teachers at the University of Addis Ababa, and is interested also in history and geography. As the buses ground slowly up out of the gorge we came every now and then upon groups of Gojjamese peasants, walking up the road with gourds of water, or driving flocks of goats before them. Tadesse seemed to shrink further and further into the upturned neck of his anorak.

"Do you know that there are cannibals here, Sir?" he said.

General disbelief was indicated by John Wilsey and me.

"Yes, Sir," he insisted.

He went on to explain that there are certain Gojjamese who are called *boodda*, and could be of either sex.

"When they look at you, they do you harm. You do not know it, but there is some power from here," he said, tapping his head. "I believe they are not good people these *boodda*. They do evil things: some of them are cannibals and others do magics."

This was astonishing. Here was an intelligent, westernised and quite well-informed student, now at the Princess Bede Mariam Laboratory School, doing 12th grade work, talking sincerely of cannibalism. He seemed to have believed entirely what his parents had told him; and he said he was not alone in this belief—all other Ethiopians share this fear of the Gojjamese, he said. It is held that they can transmit evil influence by their gaze and that, as Tadesse said, "they can make troubles for you."

"What do you call the wind from the body that stinks?"

"A fart."

"Yes. They make you do these things, and it is not good in Ethiopia."

"It is not good in England, either," I added.

"Oh, they are very evil. They make your penis that it will not come up and they cause many troubles. If a man is drinking and he lifts his cup to his lips and a *boodda* looks at him, the drink will become a very terrible thing."

Tadesse, slumped in his seat, seemed to be genuinely afraid to be entering Gojjam and kept his eyes turned inboard. This sort of fear seems to be the substance of one of the stories that Byron de Prorok tells in the fantastic book *Dead Men Do Tell Tales*. His "men that sleep with hyenas" may well be husbands of the *boodda* women who behave, Ethiopians allege, in a way tantamount to cannibalism. In the evening, the *boodda* woman will give her husband a magic potion with his food, Tadesse said, and when he lapses into sleep, she places on his chest the stone which is used for grinding corn. Then she peels off her hair from her scalp and goes into the darkness outside the house, where there is a heap of ashes from the hearth. Now unclothed, she rolls in the ashes and from her body sprout hairs, so that in a few moments she becomes a hyena. In this new guise she can stalk about, attacking and eating unsuspecting humans, until the time comes for her to return home, when she becomes a woman again, lifts the stone from her husband's chest and wakens him up with another draught.

It seemed impossible to shake Tadesse's belief in this horrific superstition.

"Once a man was eating," he went on. "A *boodda* looks at him through the window, and he takes the meat out of his mouth with his fingers and puts it under his foot. And when the *boodda* is gone and he takes up the meat again, the bottom of his foot is all worms."

As we bowled along over the dull Gojjam plateau-lands, John Wilsey and I did not quite know what to make of it all. Did our Amhara friends really believe that these thin, bent men in outlandish hats, frantically beating their cattle out of the bus's path, were possessors of the evil eye? Did they think the flocks of womenfolk, scuttling like sheep up the grassy bank as the klaxon sounded, could transform themselves at night into ravening hyenas?

❉ ❉ ❉

Our camp at Debre Marcos was sited in the only really suitable place near the town, though it was not in itself very promising, being exposed and damp-looking. We were to be on gently sloping ground by the side of a mud road running parallel to the airstrip—we had an Army Air Corps Beaver, a handy single-engined monoplane, and it could taxi right up to the roadside. However, the journey by Land-Rover to the town, whose corrugated-iron roofs were visible amongst the thick clumps of eucalyptus that crowned the ridge to our south, involved a dog-leg of about two miles. Inevitably, we had to pitch tents on thinly-grassed earth, which, although sloping, drained badly and after the first thunderstorm turned into a veritable Passchendaele.

Within two hours the six vast American marquees were erected and the unloading and sorting of stores could begin. By evening, before a perplexed and fascinated throng of small boys, a zareba of thorn brush had been cut and laid around the perimeter. To maintain these token defences, a small detachment of bewildered young policemen had been sent from the nearby barracks, and were also putting up tents.

A scratch supper was concocted individually, and such rations as we had managed to extract from Customs were stacked in the Cookhouse tent. Soon, "Buck" Taylor, our quiet and imperturbable Quartermaster, had amassed sufficient kit for some to be issued to us and as evening quickly descended we drew camp beds and mosquito nets. Captain Taylor, a patient, fair-haired Cornishman, went to bed in a Stores tent crammed, like Fagin's den, with a rich assortment of Expedition gear.

There was more gear still in the Headquarters tent, which housed, apart from John Blashford-Snell and his more important aides, the considerable mass of signals equipment—a C11 set, for direct communication with Bulford in Wiltshire, and various smaller sets, A13s, A16s, etc., for our radio links with the British Embassy in Addis Ababa, with the Beaver, and with the parties soon to be out in the field and on the river. Soon, enormous aerials were hoisted up—one almost as tall, though not so beautiful, as the nearby eucalyptus saplings—and an intricate web of supporting wires pegged in.

The other three marquees were given over to personnel—roughly apportioned between the scientists, with their drums of evil-smelling chemicals, the soldiery, constantly coming and going for days on end on various exhausting missions, and the airmen, who returned to Debre Marcos nightly, with their private and more permanent world. From these rude and hasty beginnings a quite sophisticated camp was to spring up over the ensuing two months. Storm trenches were dug round the edges of the tents and at strategic places near the cookhouse; a commodious latrine was built; poles were erected at the main entrance, from which fluttered British and Ethiopian flags;

refinements such as a volley-ball court and an overhead shower were made; and some garden furniture, carpentered by the inmates of Debre Marcos jail, was later purchased to add comfort to our *al fresco* meals.

Major Alan Calder and Lieutenant Richard Grevatte-Ball, our two pilots, with Sergeants Davies and Tomaney, who maintained their plane, lived in the Base Camp virtually the whole time. Mrs. Kay Thompson was there, too, keeping a close eye on the rations and ensuring that fresh and varied food was available for "base wallahs" and members in transit. She was helped in her other Public Relations work by Barbara Wells, whose first care was for the reception and proper handling of all our zoological specimens: they had to be recorded, prepared, preserved, labelled and stored away, as the various re-supply teams brought them back from the river. Barbara was also in charge of mailing special envelopes to philatelists: each evening she, Richard Grevatte-Ball and the others would set to work putting Ethiopian stamps on some of the 3,500 specially designed envelopes. Once, the incessant rain got among the stamps and E$51 worth stuck together; at the end, the set franked at Mota were never recovered. In view of the unstable political situation there, it is not to be wondered at.

Mota was, in some ways, the Ethiopian Rennes: as the Bretons resisted Charles de Gaulle, so the Gojjamese peasantry of this remote north-western town were up in arms at the time we arrived in the province—but not, in their case, against His Imperial Majesty so much as against his Governor-General, Dejazmatch Tsahaye Inku Selassie, who had tried to impose a new system of tax assessment on the region, involving the accurate measurement of the land—a sort of small-scale Domesday Survey.

At all events, although evidence about its motives was sketchy, a miniature civil war actually seemed to be in progress. Ethiopian Air Force planes and helicopters flew about, and wounded soldiers were said to be coming in to a Debre Marcos Hospital. The protest was such that the Governor-General had been relieved of his command on the very day we arrived, and an interregnum began, presided over by Kenyazmatch Hailu Shebeshe, with whom the Expedition had to negotiate for mules, *laissez-passers*, etc.

John was very happy about his first dealings with this caretaker government. A long interview had produced promises of mules; an individual letter, heavily stamped and sealed, was drafted to the headman of each village on the routes of our northern re-supply teams; police were summoned immediately by telephone.

"Even as we speak," said John, "little men with cleft sticks are bowing their way in to clutch the Kenyazmatch's ankles and receive their sealed orders. Soon they will be trotting away over the fields to distant villages, and at first light anxious chiefs will be marshalling our mules..."

The truth was slightly less impressive, but at least it was an encouraging start.

NOTES:

[1] The R.A.F. were later able to provide two Hercules transports for which we were most grateful. They flew to Addis Ababa a week after the arrival of the CL 44, bringing five Army Land-Rovers, two trailers and petrol.

[2] A Swedish safari organiser now resident in Ethiopia, and successful navigator, with Arne Rubin, of fifteen miles of the Northern Gorge below the Tissisat Falls.

Chapter Three
TERRIBLY CAMP

AS the sun came up over the dawn cloud-line, two people were already on the wet grass outside the Cookhouse tent, wrestling with a dangerous, petrol-fired contrivance called a hydroburner. Presently, Lance-Corporal Henry, inside the tent, gave instructions from the depths of his sleeping-bag, and a little later tins of sausages and beans had been dropped into boiling water and thin, lumpy, unpromising porridge was bubbling near-by. A local youth came in through a gap in the zareba bearing a basket of bread rolls, of which we bought thirty-six. The two cooks this morning were Chris Edwards and David Bromhead—"the long and the short of it" as they were known to the Junior Infantrymen's Battalion at Shorncliffe. Chris, a smiling curly-headed giant, was an Army Rugby Footballer whose powerful physique was later to be important to his own survival in white water; while his friend David, from Grahamstown, Cape Province, had the slight build of a stable lad. Since being commissioned in the British Army he had abandoned the twangy tones of the "Sayeth Efrican" for the U-est of accents. This was his third Ethiopian expedition and in all of them his exact knowledge of fauna and his marksmanship had been valuable.

With breakfast over, we began another day of busy preparation. The moment of the great diaspora was approaching—when parties would leave for various places, and Base Camp would be reduced to a nucleus of ten or so. As the sun dried the grass, the six Avon Redshank dinghies were spread out on it, and Roger Chapman and Chris Edwards got on with the numerous modifications which had to be made. These dinghies, chosen for the really tough white water work, were 12 feet long and 5 feet wide. Their walls were a continuous inflatable sausage, divided into two compartments; their flat undersides were made of specially strengthened neoprene. To help maintain buoyancy in the event of a tear we had evolved the ingenious plan of introducing football bladders into the walls. Roger was now fitting special valves in the two compartments, so that 24 bladders could be squeezed in, blown up, and knotted, in each dinghy. When this had been done an ordinary valve allowed each compartment to be further blown up to the required rigidity.

Across each dinghy were two detachable neoprene bolsters to act as thwarts. Chris Bonington had had the brilliant notion of cutting into them along their length, and fitting a specially strong, water-tight zip fastener. In this way, the White-Watermen could use these thwarts as very valuable storage space for dry clothes, sleeping gear, food, cameras, cigarettes and so on; they, likewise, could be fully blown up to stiffen the whole dinghy.

Extra pockets for odds and ends had been stuck on in numerous places, and lifelines had been attached from strongpoint to strongpoint along the waterline. These had been fitted with rubber hosing for a more comfortable grip, especially during portage. This corner of the camp looked, and smelt, a bit like a chandler's shop, as toggle loops were patiently stitched on, floorboards sawn to shape, and paddles tipped with a toughening band of Araldite[1] and then painted.

✳ ✳ ✳

"This looks like the 'avgas', at last," said Alan Calder, now in his orange flying suit.

A lorry, loaded with drums, came lurching along the mud road. Lack of aviation fuel had kept the Beaver grounded since its arrival a day or two before. Now a programme of vital reconnaissance flights over the area could begin.

Alan Calder, like a number of other members of this expedition, belied his appearance. A youthful, almost waif-like air, and a laconic, quizzical manner, masked one of the Army's most experienced pilots. As the only soldier among twenty-five R.A.F. men, he had won the Aerobatics Competition between instructors at Little Rissington, and though, oddly, a Sapper, he now runs the instruction of Beaver pilots for the School of Army Aviation at Middle Wallop. His colleague from the same place, Richard Grevatte-Ball, was a big, breezy Lieutenant, cheerful and fast talking.

These two pilots, although born in Worthing, had not met until their flight with the Beaver to Addis Ababa began—a flight pleasantly routed from England through some of the more sybaritic

Mediterranean haunts, although later filled with alarming incident in Egypt and the Sudan. Once at Debre Marcos, they operated in conditions of great variety; but it was their convolutions in the bottom of the gorge that will be remembered, whether one was in the plane, or watching, open-mouthed, on the river bank. In their nine weeks of very considerable activity, "Teeny-Weeny Airways", as they were known, won the respect and admiration of us all.

Alan was ready, fresh and immaculate, for the first reconnaissance of the day. Coming towards him across the mud were John Blashford-Snell, Martin Romilly and Gage Williams—going to look at the route via Burie to the river, which his re-supply column must take in a few days' time. Gage, a polished, quick-thinking Old Etonian from Cornwall, was a keen hunter, with an Ethiopian expedition already behind him.

Alan was a bit worried about flying time. He had been allotted 160 hours by the Ministry of Defence. He explained to John Blashford-Snell that it had taken 35 hours to reach Addis Ababa, and so, setting aside the 35 it would take to get back, he had only 90 for use in Ethiopia. John, who had drawn up a considerable programme of reconnaissance and aerial re-supply, leant on his walking-stick and listened, his lower jaw moving slowly from side to side. He then emphasised that he had to fly over all of the river at least once, taking the leaders of mule columns with him over the regions they had to cover; and they would all have to hope that there were no unexpected calls on the Beaver's time later on. So they all set off, John moving magisterially towards the entrance, the sun glinting on the Sapper badge that he wore on the front of his white topee. Approaching the line of small, grubby boys who stood in permanent enfilade on the roadway outside, he assumed his most fearsome expression and raised his stick before him. Like the waters of the Red Sea, the line parted and rolled back, the boys giggling and clutching their elder brothers in mock terror. Martin Romilly, the Information Officer, staggered after, with brief-case, binoculars, polaroid camera and several awkward rolls of maps.

The ground just inside the camp entrance was becoming a vehicle park for various forms of transport. Our own Land-Rovers were yet to arrive by R.A.F. Hercules, but the Ethiopian Tourist Organisation had lent us two, and its live-wire Director-General, H. E. Hapte Selassie, had organised three enormous Ethiopian Army lorries to bring out from Addis Ababa the bulk of our remaining stores, including the four Assault Boats. They had driven in in the course of the previous morning, with David Bromhead, Ian Carruthers and Claude Charnotet, our Deputy Director of Photography.

Baron Claude Charnotet d'Autrey Les Grey was a forty-two-year-old cameraman from Paris, who had worked for the Dutch magazine *Avenue*. He had roamed the southern tracts of Ethiopia a previous summer (when John Blashford-Snell and I had first met him), specialising in the photography of crocodiles, and now had the air of a seasoned campaigner. As *raconteur-en-chef* to the Expedition his only rival was our voluble Welsh vet, Keith Morgan-Jones. Claude's style was a blend of French and American—but he could tell jokes against both.

Behind the Stores tent Keith Morgan-Jones, Gage Williams, Chris Edwards and Peter Hampson were attending to the mule saddles and harnesses. Chris was smoothing off the sharp edges of a girth with a knife, to avoid causing the animals unnecessary discomfort; Peter was rubbing over the leather work with saddle grease. Keith Morgan-Jones, who was superintending all this, is an enormous man: "11¾ lb at birth, and steady progress ever since," as he has it. He is a highly qualified vet., who has had a very varied career. At Ghimbi, where he spent a lot of his time, his looming bulk was always impressive among the slighter townsfolk—although he lost two stone during the expedition, flying home at a mere eighteen stone.

Near-by, Jim Masters and his Assault Boat helmsmen were making modifications to their craft. The Shell lorry that had brought the aviation fuel would in a day or two carry all four boats, nested, back to Shafartak ready for their launching. Joe Ruston, another fresh-faced Old Etonian of considerable intelligence and wit, was one of our three naval members. He was to helm *Kitchener*, the leading boat, with the skill of a sailor and the *élan* of a twenty-two-year-old. In some contrast was Alec Murray, an experienced, canny Scot, almost twice Joe's age: an R.S.M. with twenty-five years' service in the Black Watch and R.E. Staff Sergeant "Hank" Mansley, R.E., droll and imperturbable, looked after *Wingate*. The fourth helmsman at work on the boats was a further sapper Staff Sergeant, twenty-nine-year-old John Huckstep—a lively, talkative ex-Dartford Grammar School boy, who was to bring up the rear in our small fleet, at the tiller of *Sandford*. We were to be totally dependent on these four for a safe passage between a succession of

Scyllas and Charybdises from Shafartak to Sirba, and their coolness and expertise were never to let us down.

We were to have had with us two or three liaison officers from the Ethiopian Army. John had specifically asked for officers whom he knew and liked, but these, like the geologists, failed for some reason to arrive. However, and perhaps more appropriately, we were sent a Lieutenant (J.G.) from the Ethiopian Navy, through the good offices of the head of that service, H.I.H. Prince Desta. So it was that the gentlemanly and soft-spoken Telahoun Makonnen was moved at short notice from the Naval Base in sweltering Massawa to the cool of Debre Marcos. "Tilly", slight and slender, with his large, peaked cap worn just fractionally crooked, proved to be quietly effective and was a friend of us all.

During the long afternoon, members of the first two re-supply teams were getting their kit ready. Lt. Garth Brocksopp, Royal Irish Rangers, was to be with Lt. Gavin Pike, 14th/20th King's Hussars, and Lt. Ian Carruthers, Royal Signals, on the first of these. They were to travel in the Assault Boats from the Abbai bridge at Shafartak to the first Forward Base at the mouth of the Guder River. Then they were to walk out of the gorge, carrying zoological specimens, a parachute used in the first air-drop, mail and exposed film, and return with it all to Debre Marcos. The second column, under Gage Williams, consisted of Chris Edwards, Barry Cooke, Mike Henry, Peter Hampson, Claude Charnotet and Mesfin Abebe, a young Assistant Game Warden from the Wild Life Conservation Department. These seven were to set off a few days later on an overland journey with mules, from Burie to the north bank of the Abbai below the village of Mabil. Five of them were then to return to Base Camp with the same sort of burdens as the first column, but with empty fuel jerrycans and an unwanted engine in addition.

For both these groups weight of personal kit was a vital factor—and especially for Garth Brocksopp's first party, who had to climb out of the gorge over country too difficult for mules. As the inevitable afternoon storm bucketed down outside, packing went on inside with a care and forethought usually only found among honeymoon couples working to an airline's baggage ceiling.

The following day these re-supply parties, together with Nigel Sale's Group B, attended a four-hour briefing in the H.Q. tent, at which the tricky question of rendezvous was hammered out—where and when the overland columns would meet the boats, in an unknown terrain and with maps that could not reliably be used in conjunction with compasses. The question of possible rescue was explored, too. Radio contacts were obviously essential. Corporals Tony Davidson and David Fisher would open up from Main Base on A13 and A16 sets three times a day—at 7 a.m., 12 noon and 6 p.m. If nothing was heard by a re-supply party, then messages could be relayed by the Beaver. John Wilsey, commanding the Base Camp and co-ordinating all overland movements, undertook to try to be on the air at noon each day. In an emergency, the drill was that if a group had not been heard from for twenty-four hours, then a rescue flight would be made over their last known position.

There was briefing, too, from Lt.-Col. Roger West, the Senior Medical Officer, on the care of people, and from Keith Morgan-Jones on the care of mules. The animals would have to be injected every five days against Nagana[2]; in the case of people, wet, sore, blistered feet might be the biggest problem, but cuts, burns and snake-bites had to be considered, too. Roger West explained the use of the survival kits he and Nigel Marsh had packed up. Nigel, his deputy, was our third naval member, a Surgeon Sub-Lieutenant newly qualified at Edinburgh University. One of them tended to be out with a party, whilst the other remained at Base Camp, though this was not rigidly adhered to. At Debre Marcos, there were great boxes of medicaments surrounding their field consulting-room—one end of a marquee. Here they fought an unending battle against mud, damp and infection. Their almost continuous stream of grubby patients, with varying forms of rot, internal upset, and minor cuts and abrasions, have every cause to be grateful to them.

One morning—it was Sunday, August 4th—the first radio link with Britain was established. We marked the virtual completion of the Base Camp by erecting flagpoles and running up the two national flags at our entrance; a short Morning Service was held by John among the eucalyptus saplings by the camp; the sun shone brightly and it was a pretty joyful sort of morning. Even the mud paths began to congeal a little.

Later, the Shell lorry carried off to Shafartak the four Assault Boats and the advance river party, squatting perilously on top with all their kit. Jim Masters was in the cab, looking like a prolific gypsy chief with his motley family. They were to conduct certain trials before the main river party arrived with John Blashford-Snell two days later. August 6th duly found John's party climbing into Land-Rovers and leaving behind them a sadly depleted Base Camp. With them went our two cameramen, to film the boats at the memorable moment of departure from the Abbai bridge.

The 16mm colour film was to be a valuable end-product of the Expedition. With Claude in this important work was our Director of Photography, "Johnny" Johnson, an experienced film-maker and ornithologist, who had been with John Blashford-Snell in 1964, when he had shot the film of the 1st Sandhurst Ethiopian Expedition. "Johnny", forty-nine, had made many previous expeditions to study wild life, especially in the Sahara, and had contributed films and recordings to the B.B.C. Other occasional cameramen were Nigel Sale, who led Group B, and Alastair Newman, a young Science lecturer at the R.M.A. Sandhurst, who shot a good deal of film below the Northern Gorge.

The first Land-Rover was driven by John Blashford-Snell. Kay Thompson was in front, and Chris Bonington, Claude and Tadesse were with me in the back. Soon the Gojjam countryside was passing featurelessly by, and there were three hours of it to pass. Eventually we stopped for a drink at a roadhouse in Dejen and then, leaving its last wooden cabin behind, we slipped over the edge of the plateau and began the long, winding drop to the gorge bottom, and the great challenge of the river that it contained.

I turned to Tadesse, whom some of us had previously met when the 1966 Expedition had camped near his home town in Gemu Gofa, and said, "Well, this will be a fine experience to tell the other lads back home in Arba Minch!"

He sat there, grinning nervously.

"Are you afraid, Tadesse?" Chris Bonington asked.

"*Everybody* is afraid," he said.

Moments later everybody was distinctly afraid, for John Blashford-Snell, hunched in the driver's seat and reminiscing merrily, took a fast corner as we were beginning to plunge down the final, tortuous stretches. The Land-Rover lurched sickeningly first one way then the other, and we very nearly made a dramatic, unscheduled descent into the gorge by a previously unexplored route.

"Sorry about that," said John, "damn thing just jumped out of gear."

In minutes we were on the broad beach of stones just upstream of Shafartak Bridge, where Jim's advance party had already held successful trials in the Assault Boats. Everything was ready for the morrow.

Four Assault Boats were brought by lorry to the Nile at the Shafartak Bridge, where our journey began.

NOTES:

[1]   An immensely strong glue.

[2]   Nagana: A trypanosomal disease similar to human Sleeping Sickness, and carried in the same way by tsetse flies.

Chapter Four
INTO THE BLACK GORGE

CHRIS BONINGTON often used to expatiate on the many differences he found between conquering a mountain and a river: one came naturally to him, the other was new and rather alarming. About the only similarity, we felt, as we stood looking west from the bridge at Shafartak, was that most mountains begin with easy approach slopes, and we had picked a starting point on the Abbai with a comparably undemanding opening. Downstream from the bridge there were for several miles no navigational problems in the rainy season. Over a dozen people had set out from here in different craft and had gone varying distances in safety. Only seven, however, had survived the rigours of the whole gorge and reached the plains on the western edge of the Empire, and two of these had been subsequently killed by *shifta*; only one—Arne Rubin—had got through to the Sudan relatively un-scathed. But behind us, upstream, was water that nobody had so far navigated completely, and it would not have been wise to have attempted this first. In fact, the unnavigated parts, east and north of the Abbai bridge, had not been included in our projected survey until fairly late in our planning.

We therefore proposed to begin our survey in the middle of the Ethiopian section of the Blue Nile, at Shafartak (variously called Dejen, the Abbai bridge, or "Abbai Dildi") and to proceed downstream (Phase 1) to a village called Sirba, about seventy-five miles from the Sudanese frontier. Thence we were to return by some means, even at this stage still uncertain, to Debre Marcos, and then go to the beginning of the Great Abbai at Bahardar, where we would again start to work downstream (Phase 2) to Shafartak. We intended, in fact, to go from M to Z and then from A to L—confusing for the reader, but safer for us. A survey of the Little Abbai, held by some to be the true beginning of the Blue Nile, never formed part of our plans.

To go down the river from Shafartak to Sirba Group A had been formed, consisting of thirty-two men, to be carried in four Army Assault Boats. John Blashford-Snell was to lead this group personally, with Roger Chapman as his second-in-command.

The rest of the passenger list can be seen in tabular form:

KITCHENER
Capt. John Blashford-Snell
  (Leader)
Lt. Jim Masters
  (Chief Engineer)
Lt. Martin Romilly
  (Info. Officer & i/c boat)
"Johnny" Johnson
  (1st cameraman)
Patrick Morris
  (Senior Scientist)
Lt. Barry Cooke[1]
  (Signaller)
Cpl. Peter O'Mahony[2]
  (Signaller)
Lt. Ian Carruthers[3]
  (Re-supply)
J/Sgt. Chris Whitwell
  (P.A.)
Sub-Lt. Joe Ruston, R.N.
  (Helm)

WINGATE
Lt. Spencer Lane-Jones
  (i/c boat)
Alastair Newman
  (Met.)
Colin Chapman
  (Croc. Survey)
Malcolm Largen
  (Zoologist)
Cpl. Ian Macleod
  (Recce)
Chris Bonington[4]
  (Press)
Lt. Garth Brocksopp[3]
  (Re-supply)
S/Sgt. "Hank" Mansley
  (Helm)

CHEESMAN
Lt. (J.G.) Telahoun Makonnen
  (i/c boat)
Richard Snailham
  (£sd)
Derek Yalden
  (Zoologist)
Hilary King
  (Zoologist)
Assefa G. Yohannis[1]
  (Water Resources)
Tadesse Wolde Gossa
  (Interpreter)
A Policeman[3]
WO 1 Alec Murray
  (Helm)

SANDFORD
Capt. Roger Chapman
  (i/c boat)
John Fletcher
  (Boatfitter)
Surg. Sub-Lt. Nigel Marsh
  (M.O.)
Claude Charnotet[1]
  (2nd cameraman)
Mansel Spratling
  (Archaeologist)
Lt. Gavin Pike[3]
  (Re-supply)
Assefa G. Yohannis[5]
  (Water Resources)
Cpl. Peter O'Mahony[1]
  (Signaller)
S/Sgt. John Huckstep
  (Helm)

[1] Joined at Mabil. [2] To Mabil, then to Sandford. [3] Left at River Guder. [4] Joined at River Guder. [5] To Mabil, then to Cheesman.
(John Blower, Nigel Sale, Rex Matthews, Alem Berhanu and Tigre joined various boats on the last leg from the Didessa River junction to Sirba.)

Responsibility for the boats and all practical engineering questions connected with the river was given to Jim Masters, who had a team of three sappers, a naval officer, and a civilian to help him. Pat Morris was the Senior Scientist, and with him were the four zoologists, the archaeologists and the M.O. The work of this scientific element was, of course, the foremost consideration, so long as it was compatible with the general safety of the group as a whole. It was hoped to give them three to six days of clear survey work in at least three places on the river's banks, with briefer stops in between. This was in fact what happened.

The Army Assault Boats were 17 feet 6 inches long, 6 feet 6 inches wide, and weighed 400 lb, so the crew could if necessary manhandle them, empty, over obstacles. As we saw from the terrain later, this would have been very difficult, and I was personally relieved that it was never actually required of us. Getting them from the lorry into the Abbai at Shafartak was exhausting enough. They came from Debre Marcos, nested one inside the other on the back of the hired lorry. Jim Masters and his team had as their first engineering task the job of roping them down one by one from the road near the Gojjam frontier post, over the rocky sides of the gorge to the river.

These craft were made of metal alloy, were double-hulled for extra strength and safety, and were standard Army Issue Assault Boats. The space between the two hulls was filled with Polyurethane foam, so that we could not sink even if holed. They looked a bit like pointed shoe boxes and proved to be exactly right for the job. Jim had modified them in various ways, of course: a canvas sheet, or "dodger", was lashed across the top of the boat at the bow end, to stop us being swamped with water and to provide some protection for our kit from the breaking waves and spray. This was strengthened by a curved metal strut fixed from gunwale to gunwale. The crew were afforded some protection by long, wooden splashboards, which had the effect of raising the sides by a foot or so.

The weight of water crashing on the "dodgers" frequently tore the canvas and bent the metal struts, and running repairs went on all the way to Sirba. Extra buoyancy was provided by a number of inflated, canvas "sausages", called "roll-a-boats", which were attached at the waterline at various places on the hull, according to the whim of each helmsman.

Each boat depended for its power on a massive 40 horsepower

outboard engine, which was firmly bolted on to the metal transom. These weighed 120 lb and would therefore have posed problems had portage been necessary. They gave excellent service on the run to Sirba, and our only difficulties with them came when they were getting tired at the end of the Expedition; John Wilsey gave them some very hard running upstream and two burnt out. Nor do I think one can blame the manufacturers when one engine failed to survive being dropped by parachute, on the only occasion that a parachute failed to open.

On the downstream run, where they were more gently used, the engines gave little trouble. When a rock, shingle or floating drift-wood was struck, the shearpin would break as it was designed to do, and our helmsmen became adept at replacing these under pressure, often whilst spinning at ten or twelve knots in a confined reach of water between two cataracts. John Huckstep in *Sandford* went from Shafartak to Sirba without breaking his shearpin once.

The boats themselves were pretty sparsely furnished—in fact unfurnished. We sat on whatever kit presented itself—usually the flat-topped, wooden zoological boxes, or failing them, the tops of jerrycans. Personal kit in rucksacks was stowed forward, but each boat also carried heterogeneous articles for general use: drums of rope, spare fuel, weapons, lamps, medical boxes, photographic gear, and various mysterious, unwieldy items of zoological stores. As the journey progressed, collected specimens multiplied in number and one might find on one's sleeping bag a grinning crocodile head, or a rigid, leathery turtle, done up into the sort of dripping parcel that the GPO refuses to accept.

The boats were named after distinguished Britons who have recently had to do with the Blue Nile, usually in some military context. Herbert, Lord Kitchener, had entered the Royal Engineers in 1871 and so was an obvious choice of the strong sapper contingent amongst us. He had also, of course, been Sirdar of the Egyptian army and in 1898 overcame the dervishes of El Khalifa at Omdurman, not far from the confluence of the Blue and White Niles at Khartoum.[6]

That strange, unorthodox officer, Lieutenant-Colonel Orde Wingate, later of Chindit fame, had led the Emperor Haile Selassie back from exile at the head of "Gideon Force" in 1941. In so doing he fought numerous engagements against the Italians on the Gojjam plateau, and crossed the Great Abbai on his way in to Addis Ababa.

Brigadier Daniel Sandford, who had lived in Ethiopia since 1928, and who still does, led the military mission which went into the country from the Sudan a month after Italy's entry into the war, to assess the strength of possible Ethiopian support for a British liberating force in Gojjam. He reported favourably and was soon joined by Lieutenant-Colonel Wingate and the Emperor, to whom he became personal adviser. He now owns an estate which overlooks the valley of the Mugher, one of the larger southern tributaries of the Great Abbai.

Major R. E. Cheesman was connected most intimately of all with the Great Abbai. He was H.M. Consul in North-West Abyssinia—based at Danghila—from 1925 to 1934. Whilst there he made several journeys by foot and mule, which established more or less exactly the course of the Blue Nile from Lake Tana to the point at which B. H. Jessen had left the river on his way in from the Sudan. Cheesman's book, *Lake Tana and the Blue Nile*, painfully written for a second time after his first manuscript had been stolen with his car, was the first description of much unexplored country in southern and eastern Gojjam.

John Blashford-Snell, standing stolidly at ease under a great, spreading tree on the sloping bank of the Abbai, began the final briefing. He had already lost the attention of the zoologists who, sitting like inattentive children at the back of the class, were busy throwing powerful beams of light up into the branches where bats were flitting to and fro. It was a beautiful night: there were no mosquitoes (contrary to our earlier fears), only the gentle susurration of the swift river beyond us in the dusk. Everybody was still, and against the sky in the half light we looked like a group of sculpted figures in a municipal park. No noise, apart from John, the river, and an occasional eructation from someone who had finished his curry too hurriedly. He said that the river level was high enough at the moment, but that he wanted more rain to keep it up. Departure the following morning would be at 8.30, so reveille would be at 6 a.m. Forward Base 1 would be established in the evening at the entrance of the River Guder, and there would then be five days of scientific research.

John went on to outline the chain of command as described above. I was pleased to find that my only duty seemed to be to look after a water pump. The fact that I lost touch with it on the second day might suggest that I had a pretty easy time on this phase, but there turned out to be, in fact, other duties.

With the experience of Dr. A. Amoudruz's Franco-Swiss expedition very much in mind, we set guards scrupulously throughout every night. This habit undoubtedly saved the lives of a number of us later. From 10 p.m., usually, to 6 a.m., there would be two people on guard, each doing a two-hour spell. One of them would go and rouse another colleague at the end of every hour. John stressed that all of us in Group A should co-operate fully with the scientists in their work. The guard should be prepared to help the zoologists at night in whatever way they could; perhaps in bat catching, or by carrying out a crocodile count. In point of fact the zoologists were so exhausted by the work of specimen collecting by day that the late evenings were given over to the organisation and treatment of the day's bag. This they usually preferred to do themselves, before they crept, reeking of formalin, into their tents often in the small hours. Sensibly, they were themselves excused guard duties. However, the guard was also to keep busy checking the boats every ten minutes, looking for water in them and testing the fore and aft mooring lines. The level of the river was so capricious that all these precautions were constantly necessary. Otherwise, the guard would generally patrol the camp area, armed with a shotgun and three rounds, pausing every so often to sit for a while and crank the handle of the power generator for the radio set.

John then went on to instruct the group in some boat drills. Life-jackets must be worn at all times. Everybody in a boat must sit, save for two—the helmsman at the engine and a guide, who was to stand forward and keep a sharp eye out for obstructions close under the bows that the helmsman might not be able to see. In a rough passage he could also give directions by hand signals.

Each boat was to have a Boat Commander, who was to control the affairs of that boat's crew whilst on land, but on the river it was firmly stressed that the helmsman was the skipper and his orders must be obeyed. The only exception to this was in respect of weapons: they were always the concern of the Boat Commander, who alone could give the order to fire whilst on the river, and that to a specific person only. He was also to see that weapons came into the boat "made safe", i.e. with chamber empty, but magazines loaded.

In the event of a capsize, everyone should struggle to stay with the boat, rather than swim for the bank. If a man went overboard the boats would put about, throttling up their engines, and one of them would try to drag him in over the side.

John then proceeded to outline the three possible types of hazard—natural, human and animal, and suggested how we might deal with them. The worst natural danger was flooding, then perhaps landslips. However attractive as camp sites, beaches must be avoided, for heavy rain on the plateau above us caused the river to rise suddenly. We were to have dramatic confirmation of this when at Forward Base 1 the water level rose 15 feet in the course of one night, driving everybody gradually up the hillside, and then before dawn fell just as rapidly to its former level.

It was difficult to outline a drill for human dangers, John said. There might well be *shifta* in the gorge, especially towards the Sudanese end. We must maintain alertness at all times, and always carry weapons, even in camp. At night there would be a Guard Commander (one of the Boat Commanders) who could be awoken in the event of trouble. The guard, of course, was to fire if the victim of an attack, but otherwise only on the Guard Commander's order. We would keep a light burning in the camp, but—and here we were applying the lesson of the Amoudruz shooting—not one placed so as to illumine any sleeping figures on whom *shifta* could draw a bead.

The main animal menace was, of course, the crocodile, and the main danger point, the water's edge. Before disembarking into shallows it was prudent to hit the water with a boathook, John said, and anybody going down for a wash or anything should heave a few rocks in first, and if possible get someone else to cover them with a gun. These were maximum precautions which gradually became relaxed as the danger from crocodiles seemed to recede. No doubt if someone had been seized by the leg, like the unfortunate American Peace Corps worker at Gambela, we should have been more meticulous.

A landing drill was devised, with two or four armed people clearing every beach to the left and right; but the Nile crocodile we found to be initially a discreet reptile, who preferred to slip off his sandbank into the enveloping murk of the river long before we ever landed. It was made clear that there was to be no needless slaughter of crocodiles; we were to let them go for the water first—avoiding placing ourselves between it and them—and to forbear firing, even if they came within two or three feet of the boats. Indeed, throughout the whole expedition we only killed one—on the final day and for zoologists' use—and only once was a boat menaced by a crocodile: this was when *Sandford* moved in on one at the request of the photographers, and the creature attempted to grab a mouthful of aluminium. An ominous "clunk" was heard, which must have dislodged one or two of its incisors.

Hippopotami, even more timid unless roused, would be less of a threat. The only danger here, unless a boat happened to pass over one as it surfaced, might come from a confrontation on land. They make elaborate "runs", and even slides, in the tall elephant grasses. Although the ground here would be superbly flattened, we were advised not to camp in the vicinity of such "runs", as hippo emerge from the river after dark and stomp along them. We doubted if a ton and a half of hippo would be much deterred by a few strings and a sheet or two of flimsy tentage slung across his nocturnal promenade.

John finished by telling us how we might deal *in extremis* with these two sorts of menace, and then gave the immediate orders for the night. We then crept onto various damp and uncomfortable ledges for our last night's sleep on the fringes of civilisation. For Roger Chapman and me it was a night full of menace of the human kind: John, who had not had time to put up his own *basha*, crawled under ours; he stretched himself alongside but above us on the sharp slope, and spent most of the night rolling down it. We were periodically squashed into the ground by the Great Abbai himself, as he was becoming known, or else enveloped in his bear-like embrace. Dawn found us dishevelled, bruised and grumpy.

We packed up and loaded the boats. The engines opened up at 8.40 a.m. and at 9·15 we slipped away from the rocky beach, leaving behind a waving crowd of well-wishers—policemen, cameramen, other Expedition members. *Kitchener* led off, followed by *Wingate*, with *Cheesman* third. *Sandford,* which had been ceremonially christened the previous day by the Brigadier's grandson, brought up the rear. The boats had been fully tested and the departure was slick and uneventful. We passed at about eight knots below the looming span of the Shafartak bridge. After all the months of preparation, we were under way.

At first the river meandered unsensationally between wooded slopes and red sandstone bluffs. From time to time a tributary came in

For mile after mile the Abbai runs between steep scree banks covered with elephant grass.

at one side or another, and occasionally the channel was divided by an island. Painted storks and grey heron stood about, and once a little leopard looked at us from a sandy beach. After an hour a cry of "Azzo!" went up from the Ethiopian contingent, and we followed their pointing fingers to sight our first crocodile.

An Ethiopian policeman told me that the Gojjamese know this part of the river as Ghion. Now the second chapter of Genesis tells us that "the name of the second river is Gihon: the same is it that compasseth the whole land of Ethiopia". Jerome Lobo, writing in the seventeenth century, is sceptical of suggestions that this could refer to the Blue Nile, on the grounds that the River Gihon could hardly rise in the terrestrial Paradise—which he places in Arabia—and later "spring up and appear in a place perhaps the highest in the World". It remains strange, however, that some Ethiopians should today still know it by this ancient name.

It was cool, cloudy and breezy with only patches of blue visible. The river seemed to flow quite fast at the edges, whilst in the deeper middle it bubbled up like thin porridge. We stopped for lunch on a shingle bank just above the entry of the River Mugher, where the Rittlingers gave up in 1956 and where in 1903 W. N. McMillan began.

Afterwards we ran through flat alluvial plain for a while, where there were several surprised people and the smoke of burning fires. Soon the scrub-covered slopes returned, rising now from 60° to 75°. We were entering the Black Gorge. Here the rocks on the banks were mainly a blue-black colour, though there were some outcrops of pink stone protruding into and narrowing the stream. The river was now faster flowing and only thirty yards wide; wherever it widened slightly there were severe whirlpools, which tried perceptibly to suck down the Assault Boats, but without success. It was in one of the narrow passages that we encountered our first cataract. The normal seethe and suck of the river rose to a clearly audible roar; the brown ribbon on which we were carried surged down, just perceptibly, to a lower level, and at the bottom, the churning crest of a large wave fell back on itself.

"My God, look at *Kitchener!*" someone shouted.

She had disappeared from the view of the three following boats. Then we saw her, sitting on her stern like a West African cocoa boat butting out through the Guinea surf. She rode over it safely, and equally

Kitchener, *Wingate*, *Cheesman* and *Sandford* leave the bridge at Shafartak on
the first day.

the succeeding lesser waves, and we all followed, cheered by this hopeful example.

For short spells both banks were vertical stone cliffs. Floating with us down the river, like riderless horses in a steeplechase, were great logs of wood. "What's wrong with *Kitchener*?" shouted Hilary. It looked as if she had struck one of these. Whilst Joe Ruston bent over the engine the boat spun along uncontrollably. *Wingate*, following up, threw a line over, but the repair was finished before a tow became necessary.

As we all sped on down this narrow cleft, we came suddenly upon one of the rare and most interesting artificial landmarks in the whole course of the river, Signor Castanio's "bridge". Round about 1903 the Emperor Menelik decided to improve communications between Shoa, the province in which Addis Ababa stands, and Gojjam, beyond the Abbai. There were several fords then used by merchants to cross the river, but no bridges south of the second Portuguese Bridge. So Signor Castanio, an Italian engineer, was commissioned to build one and selected a site at Tateso, about 500 yards upstream of the Guder River junction. Here, at a point where the river narrows conveniently, but between alarmingly steep approaches from above, he planned to construct a single span of iron about 280 feet long from one abutment of dressed granite to another. A road was begun on the plateau to link Gindabret with Zemmi and open up southern Gojjam to the influence of the capital. But Gojjam, as already mentioned, has always exhibited separatist tendencies and a bridge over the Abbai could mean greater centralised control. Ras Mangasha and other Gojjami notables, therefore, viewed the whole concept with suspicion and their attitude throughout was obstructionist.

However, the bridge was a non-starter for other reasons. Signor Castanio ordered and paid for the ironwork from a firm in Milan, and went off on the ten-day mule journey from Addis Ababa to the river to superintend the building of the abutments. The iron sections arrived at Djibouti but failed to turn up in Addis Ababa. The Franco-Ethiopian Railway at this time only reached Dire Dawa; camel caravans carried goods thence on a slow and hazardous journey to Menelik's capital. Undeterred, Castanio put in a second order, which he also paid for. This, too, was mysteriously spirited away on its way across the Danakil desert. All *ferenji* responsible for aid programmes in Ethiopia need a great fund of patience, but at this point Signor Castanio's became exhausted. He had, nevertheless, built two magnificent granite structures meanwhile, and they still stand, without bridge or approach roads, in this most unlikely spot. Major Cheesman found them in 1930, and he and his wife crossed the Abbai in 1933 on a flying pontoon, which Castanio, still struggling on in the service of Ethiopia thirty years after, had just rigged up close by.

The four boats approached the great granite walls in good order, negotiating cataracts and extricating themselves from whirlpools in a way which was almost becoming routine. As we passed between them, there was a good deal of photography going on, and this may have discomposed some people, especially navigators, and slowed our reactions for what was to follow. Suddenly, we were aware in *Cheesman* that *Wingate* was drifting rather than motoring: paddles were being hastily plucked from their string attachments on the gunwales and dug into the stream. Earlier in the day, whilst changing helmsmen, *Wingate* had suffered engine failure when the fuel line had been trodden on; but this time it was a little more serious—another piece of floating driftwood had been struck and the shearpin had gone, and it could not have happened in a much worse place.

"Come on all of you, get paddling!" shouted Spencer Lane-Jones, while "Hank" Mansley worked feverishly to replace the pin; but the effect was imperceptible as the stream grew faster in the narrowing river. *Wingate*, which had a loaded dinghy attached, spun slowly round as *Cheesman* drew near and caught a rope thrown from the endangered boat. Unfortunately there were no cleats on these craft to which a line could be quickly made fast. "Tilly" held on with his hands, but as *Cheesman* turned upstream and her propeller bit into the brown waters, the weight of the other two boats, like a gigantic sea-anchor, became intolerable. However, he managed to take a turn round something and *Cheesman*'s engine did what it could to propel the three loaded boats against the skimming stream.

This would have been drama enough if we had been on a clear reach, but the accident had occurred just before the Guder River junction appeared. We had hoped to place Forward Base 1 a little way up this more placid tributary, near an Ethiopian Water Resources Department camp. Because of the steep, tree-clad sides, we had little warning of the proximity of the Guder. Although *Kitchener* had turned in good time to get clear of the Abbai stream, *Cheesman* and *Wingate*, locked together, with Alec Murray urging the highest possible revs from his engine, slipped slowly but surely backward. It soon became clear that we were trapped by the stream and that the waters of the quiet Guder were unattainable. *Sandford*, too, had been taken unawares by the swift appearance of the tributary mouth, had turned too late and, even alone, was unable to combat the current successfully. *Kitchener*, the flagship, lay poised at the confluence and watched the rest of its fleet scattered and struggling. Eventually, *Cheesman* had to cast off *Wingate's* rope as it looked as if to continue towing might bring destruction on both of them, but she too could not make separate headway. "Hank" Mansley, working coolly in this crisis, got his engine going and nosed his boat into a small rock-girt cove about 600 yards below the Guder mouth. *Cheesman* and *Sandford* selected a slightly larger sandy enclave and beached there. *Kitchener* perforce joined them, and later *Wingate* was warped upriver by hand to reunite the four. All of this had occupied only three or four minutes. A quiet mooring had been lost, but mercifully no more than that.

This was the only camp site of the six or seven that we made on our way to Sirba that was imposed on us by circumstances, and it turned out not too badly. The boats were sheltered in the lee of rocks and there was just enough room on a sloping grass bank for the thirty of us to measure our lengths in fair comfort.

Patterns of camp life as we came to know them began to develop first of all here. The Boat Commanders would agree between themselves upon "boat areas", and then their crews would stagger up and down from boats to areas carrying the necessary camp kit. Some boats preferred to combine all their tents and ponchos and make a vast marquee, like a Bedouin establishment in the desert; others, more markedly individual, would put up an estate of desirable detached residences, each covering its own occupant in his hammock or bedroll from the inevitable evening storm. Boats usually devised some sort of division of labour: one man would clear the area of grass and scrub with a machete, another would forage about for straight lengths of sapling for use as tent poles, whilst a third would make a fire and perhaps a brew of tea. The tents and *bashas* would then be put up and supper prepared.

Our rations were distributed by boats, and in some cases cooking was done communally by boats on a rota basis; others preferred to cook

A 24-hour one man army ration pack.

in smaller groups still. We started off with an issue of one 24-hour Army Ration pack per man per day. Later, for reasons that are made clear elsewhere, this had to be cut to two per three days and even less. Even when cut, this was generally ample as far as calories were concerned; for although nobody systematically ate all 2 lb. 8 oz. of food in his pack every day, we probably devoured enough to take in most of the 3,600 calories available. What was lacking as the three weeks unfolded was variety. The 24-hour packs were supposed to be of three kinds —A, B, and C; but the actual difference between them was negligible. So we were all eating almost exactly the same things every day, in some cases for over four weeks. All three packs contained enough tea, sugar and instant milk to make the essential three pints per day on which we so much depended in the heat of the gorge. Dehydration of the body seemed to occur even without exertion, and a quick brew was normal in every natural break in the programme. The packs also contained an oatmeal block, very good to eat as a biscuit, or else to boil up into a form of porridge. There were also plain biscuits, a tube of margarine, but no jam. In lieu, one supposes, was a small cylindrical tin of sweet, distinctive, Army cheese—not specially popular except with the catfish, who succumbed readily to it, and with other fauna whose traps were heavily baited with it. Lunch, day in day out, week in week out, seemed inescapably to be a tin of sardines. Those of us who, like myself, existed on 24-hour rations rather than the more variegated tinned Compo ration for all of the eight weeks spent in the field, bar about four or five days, came to regard the humble Portuguese sardine with a loathing from which we have probably not even yet recovered. Eaten with plain biscuit and margarine, it was equally invariably topped off with a Mars bar, which, if fresh and dry, was always popular, even if sometimes a little cloying in the African heat. There was coffee, salt and vitamin tablets in every pack, and the only element of variety came finally in two respects—1. Menu "A" included a bar of chocolate, but Menu "B" had boiled sweets; and 2. Packs contained a block of Accelerated Freeze-Dried meat—in one case beef, in another pork (both with a sachet of pre-cooked rice), and in the third pack a combined curry bar and rice, which was by far the most popular. All the budding Robert Carriers amongst us had brought little jars of extra curry powder, or garlic, Oxo cubes, drums of cinnamon, red and white pepper. These spices that enlivened our dull meats were prized by us as they had never been since the sixteenth century.

It was an evergreen hope that we might be able to live off the country. Regular shooting for the pot had been planned, and copious supplies of cartridges for our two 12-bores had been brought. At dawn and dusk intrepid hunters went out from the camp to all points of the compass; some even sat out all night, uncomfortably lodged in trees near to water. Not one four-legged animal was bagged in the gorge throughout the three weeks. The most that ever reached the cooking pot were two or three birds—a guinea fowl, a francolin or the odd stunted pigeon. We seemed to be in a green desert.

The successful shot usually shared the kill, if large enough, with his own boat, but our fresh meat intake was pitifully small. Assefa once prepared most meticulously a tiny dove shot by Barry Cooke. It was delightfully boiled in a sauce of black pepper, paprika, margarine and vegetables. My menu for lunch that day was positively regal:

> *Gin and Lemonade Powder*
> *Colombe à l'Éthiopienne*
> *Mars Bar*
> *Café*

Catfish steaks proved quite palatable despite the unpleasant look of the fish. Meat from a crocodile's tail also once or twice produced a lunch that was agreeably different. Our only vegetables came from Debre Marcos market by the occasional air drop; a plentiful supply of sweets also came, like manna, from heaven. In a largely uninhabited gorge there could, of course, be no local source of food supplies. When a number of us marched up to the plateau at Mabil, the traditional kid was killed and we dined that night on goat's meat. Otherwise, the Shankilla villages in the western reaches of the river produced only the occasional stringy hen or perhaps a handful of minuscule eggs.

In river exploration water is never much of a problem. Each boat had its jerrycan, which we tried to keep filled with clear water from one of the many streams that tumble into the Abbai. There was usually some source within a few hundred yards of each camp. The more ingenious capitalised on the frequent rain storms and placed plastic mugs and mess tins around the fringes of their tents. If need be, one could make a passable brew of tea from Abbai water itself. This would have to be boiled and then poured off very carefully so as to leave the considerable sediment at the bottom of the tin. It was only possible to get actual drinking water from the Ahbai by hanging up the admirable Millbank bags and collecting their steady drips. They had to be regularly scrubbed out, of course, but still worked better than the Berkefeld pumps, which were clogged too soon by the rich and earthy Nile. Sterilisation tablets were at first carefully applied to water bottles, but, like our crocodile drills, this routine lapsed as time went on, and no one seemed to suffer. I think we felt that we had all been inoculated so much that we could have safely drunk from the Cloaca Maxima itself. We were kept liberally provisioned from the air with whisky and gin, though the breakage rate in supply drops without parachute increased as the expedition wore on. In the last week one's only hope of a taste of whisky was to eat a handful of broken cheese biscuits that had been well impregnated with it after some awful smash.

In our more permanently established camps we generally cooked over open wood fires: the banks were generously supplied with driftwood and dry kindling. For the quick brew at lunchtime we had regular issues of hexamine, a solid white fuel looking like Kendal Mint Cake, which we burnt in special folding metal cookers the size of a fat paperback.

From the River Guder downstream the Great Abbai seemed to have four distinct aspects: there were a further forty miles of cataracts in the Black Gorge, followed by the Broad Valley, which was about sixty miles long. Then came another thirty miles of rapids and sheer cliffs, which we called the Western Cataracts, and finally about fifty miles of increasingly easier water before Sirba was reached. In the course of this whole journey we made five camps, which we occupied for anything from two to seven days.

We preferred where possible to turn into the shelter of a tributary to make camp, so after leaving the Guder we negotiated a very lively thirty miles of river before stopping on a broad sandbank at the mouth of the Fincha River. This journey involved the passage of two belts of cataracts known to us as C1 and C2. In these there were several hundred yards of severely choppy water and brown waves sometimes seven or eight feet high. These were often disposed across the river in a V-shape, with the point downstream. Generally, too, they would end in a line of "hydraulics", in which the wave breaks back on itself at the bottom of a slope of water. In these conditions it was best for the Assault Boat to head for the middle of the V at full throttle and turn at the last minute to one side or the other to meet the rolling wave head on. Shipping a fair amount of water, the boat would rear up and then climb over the top, the propeller occasionally spinning wildly clear of the water. Then there would be the inevitable trough into which the boat would plunge, taking in more water. Quite often we could not maintain our selected course but were drawn into the worst of the waves by the pull of the river. But this was generally safer than the risk of striking a rock at the sides of the cataract.

Expedition members relax amongst the Assault Boats at the Fincha River.

After the cataract there would be the whirlpools: great areas of circling water with a centre like an inverted shield-boss, sometimes a metre deep. These would exert a tremendous pull on the sterns of the boats, and it usually took all of our 40 h.p. to get clear of them. We imagined the deep bed of the river to be made up of sinks which imparted a rotation to the water as a plughole will; possibly with captive boulders in them, like the stones which erode great cauldron-shaped cavities in submerged rocks. At all events, the cataract was always followed by an area of seething, shifting water, which was moving cyclically up and down, like a pan of simmering consommé.

Strong counter-currents at the edges of the river actually flowed upstream, and these, if not too strong, were often a help when coming in to a mooring.

Shoulder after shoulder of green-clad hill sloped down repetitively at angles of 60° or 70°. There were no signs of life, animal or human, though the bird population was rich and varied—in this stretch, sand-martins, pied wagtails, fish eagles. The only insect nuisances were horse flies and the occasional tsetse fly, though further down river a small, biting grass fly infested the boats and caused much irritation. Mosquitoes were happily still absent.

We reached the Fincha River with mounting confidence. Some of the worst features of the Black Gorge had been successfully passed; the Assault Boats had behaved splendidly; the helmsmen had quickly picked up the required techniques. In *Cheesman* Hilary King had coolly changed the film in his camera in between cataracts, whilst Tadesse baled. Parts of the journey had been uneventful enough for me to fall asleep on two occasions. We were frequently soaked by waves, but almost as quickly dried out in the warm sun.

It was our intention to leave the camp at the Fincha mouth on the following morning, but during the night, despite half an hour's rain, the river level had fallen six feet. What had been a modest beach when we landed was now a great platform of black sand on which the Assault Boats lay stranded like whales, with the Abbai swirling past several feet lower than their dry sterns. This sort of change in river level was the key to all our movements in Phase 1: John had decided on the evidence of a previous air reconnaissance, and of the two days we had so far spent in the Black Gorge, that the best conditions for safe progress over rocks were when the depth of water in mid-stream was 10 metres, as recorded by the gauge at the Guder River Water Resources Camp. We therefore resolved not to negotiate difficult sections of the river unless the water level was at least that. It ought not to be more than 12 metres, however, for another air recce at a time when the Guder gauge read 14.8 metres reported gigantic waves and terrible turbulence as the excessive volume of water was forced through the narrow gorge. When we had reached the Guder, therefore, we had found out the then depth of the Abbai from the gauge, and had established a point on the opposite bank that marked the 10-metre line. When the river was at that point or just above it, we knew we could safely go.

How could we be sure that we always knew where this optimum level was in relation to the river further downstream? We observed that the level did not seem to alter significantly by day as we were sailing on it—after all, we were motoring down only slightly faster than the river's own water speed, and were therefore keeping pace with the same general belt of water all the time. If you walk slowly down a moving escalator in the London Underground, whilst the advertisements may flash upwards quite swiftly, your feet pass over a belt of only about a dozen steps on the way to the bottom. Whenever we stopped, a marker pole was put in the sand at water level: we felt we could safely say that this was "10 metres at the Guder" level, and observation would show next morning how safe it was to proceed. It was in the gorges that these fluctuations had to be most carefully noted. Where the river was narrow, sometimes as narrow as 25 yards, the fall in level could be colossal, and rocks and ledges brought treacherously near the surface. In the Broad Valley, on the other hand, where the river could be as much as 100 yards wide and quite placid, such falls were barely perceptible and did not much increase the dangers of rocks.

Our move from the Fincha to the Broad Valley provided another day of excitement. The river was still fairly low and the waves consequently frequent, short, and choppy. Quite soon we were swept into C3, the last series of cataracts in the Black Gorge; the usual two hundred yards or so of severely broken water in which the river level visibly dropped. *Kitchener* swooped down and was lost to sight by the other boats. Then we saw it lifted up as it smashed through the first brown wall, and then as it subsided into broken water beyond, waves pummelled it from all sides and it was nearly pooped—the stern was the only place we had not rigged splash-boards. At moments like this, it was often difficult to tell which way the river was flowing. *Kitchener* lurched and wallowed and all we could see of it was a large white Wolseley helmet. Perhaps the boat would capsize and this symbol of imperial power would be all that survived, floating down to Khartoum, a reminder of the palmy days when All was Sir Garnet. But no; presently we saw the boat shake itself clear of the water and at the bows the dripping figure of Jim Masters clutching a damp cigarette stub. After the first wave he had complained to the crew that it had "washed my bleeding fag away", whereupon another wall of water had inundated the lot of them. The other boats followed with much the same result.

A sudden fall in river level often made launching difficult.

Soon we emerged for a while into gentler country. As the immediate cliffs fell away, the very top of the gorge could be seen ahead of us, for the first time since Shafartak. Somewhere near Wamet, where the French explorer Antoine d'Abbadie crossed the river on his surveying expedition a hundred years ago, we saw our first hippo. Almost immediately we were caught up in a very rough cataract in which it was *Cheesman's* turn to come unstuck. We followed the first two boats through, but shipped a terrific sea of water over the side, which quarter-filled the boat and knocked helmsman Alec Murray off his feet. We drifted freely for a few agonising seconds and turned completely round. Fortunately, Alec was unhurt, and was soon able to steer us into an area of back eddies where immediate baling could begin. We got away, eventually, and shortly stopped again for a rather damp lunch, at a point where the first signs of distant hillside cultivation and columns of blue smoke betokened the presence once again of farmers. I dried out after spending a morning almost permanently wet.

This now began to look like the Broad Valley, but we had no precise idea where we were, for the maps that we were obliged to use were too inaccurate. Some were based on Major Cheesman's surveys, adjusted to d'Abbadie's triangulation of 1869, and printed about 1940. Others were the result of Italian surveys and sketch-maps of the years 1937-41, grafted on to Cheesman's information and published by the War Office in 1946 and 1947 with whatever additional information had been gleaned during the Liberation. There are, of course, in various Top Secret places, superb American air photographs of the whole of Ethiopia, with which the U.S. Mapping Mission is producing for the first time really reliable maps of the Empire. Martin Romilly got a brief glimpse of some in London and made a few hurried notes to supplement Cheesman and the Italians, but to all intents and purposes we blundered blindly and ignorantly down the river, comforted only by the fact that we must inevitably come out at the Sudanese end. The Beaver had once flown up the Mugher mistaking it for the Abbai, but we felt that we probably would not make such errors going downstream. The problem was not one of direction but location. In fact, Spencer Lane-Jones took a series of very good "star-fixes" at night in every river-bank camp site. These gave him a latitude and longitude accurate to about fifty yards. The trouble was that when related to any of our maps they revealed that we were actually halfway up some mountain-side.

On the move it was very perplexing. Tributaries came in where they should not, and refused to turn up when they should. Mountains were quite unidentifiable and we passed over fords in the full flood of the rainy season without realising it. There were no other recognisable features. The convolutions through which the river went bore no relation to the flattened wiggle on the map.

We were now trying to find the famous ford at Mabil, crossed by a Mr. Doughty-Wyllie in April 1912, and visited by Cheesman in 1927. Here we were to meet Gage Williams, who had been leading a re-supply team with mules from Debre Marcos *via* Burie to the river below the village of Mabil. "Williams' Light Horse", trotting across the plateau, pennants flying, might have only just reached the rim of the gorge, and it would be likely in that case that we would overshoot them. Indeed, we did. They saw the flotilla of four tiny boats when they were still quite high on the plateau. They fired off a round, but it was not heard.

The flotilla approaches Mabil.

In the event, the boats chose to stop, for this and other reasons, about two miles below the ford, so contact was later established without too much difficulty.

We had to select a fairly open piece of land in the Broad Valley so that we could stop and receive our second air-drop of supplies. An air-drop at the Guder River mouth had been the first occasion that either Alan Calder or Richard Grevatte-Ball had attempted this most difficult manoeuvre along the floor of the gorge, and although they had pulled it off without loss, the reception committee on the ground, then as now, had some hazardous moments and learnt a few lessons. We now tied up by the reed-covered north bank as the Beaver again appeared, quite high. It circled low, made two trial runs and then dropped a canister of mail in the river, which was retrieved by Joe Ruston in *Kitchener*. This was to be an entirely "free drop", without parachutes, mainly of yard-long cartons of ration packs.

"Keep your eyes on the Beaver at all times. Look up! Look up!", shouted John through the loudhailer to the crowd of thirty or so who were scattered along the grassy river edge. The plane roared over and dropped three boxes quite near a large group. It wheeled away and climbed over the nearest range of hills to reappear, dipping down now to about thirty-five feet above river level. It headed straight for my position on the bank by *Cheesman*. A stick of three large boxes was pushed out of its side by unseen hands. They came hurtling through the air directly towards me, close together. There was no time to move. I was thoroughly strafed. On their brief drop to the earth they barely had time to spread apart at all. One carton plummeted into the river, one hit the bank in front of me, and the third smashed into *Cheesman's* "dodger", collapsing it, and splintering the splashboard. Two more runs were a bit less lethal: one put more food into the tall grasses, another dropped sandbags and a wooden box, which split open, sending squares of hexamine cartwheeling across the mud and into the river. This was more dangerous than anything yet experienced on the Nile, and I thought what a strange and ridiculous epitaph I might have had—

The Army Air Corps Beaver, ably piloted by either Alan Calder or Richard Grevatte-Ball, dropped food and fuel to us even in the deepest recesses of the gorge.

"Struck by a box of Compo on the banks of the Blue Nile, August 13th, 1968".

After completing the first successful powered transit of the Black Gorge we settled down to six and a half days of zoological collecting and exploration in the area of Mabil Ford and the Dolnik River. After one night in an *ad hoc* site near the dropping zone, we moved 500 yards upstream to make a more sophisticated camp in a cool, shady, riverside wood. From this place we radiated daily on our respective tasks. "Johnny" Johnson sweated to the top of the hill behind the camp, where he would sit counting carmine bee-eaters and listening to the provocative whistle of the red-winged starling. John Huckstep and Alec Murray went off fishing, and brought back some large catfish and a creature not quite terrapin, not quite turtle, called *trionyx*. Roger Chapman, Mansel Spratling, Tadesse and I went inland far up the scree-covered ridges behind the camp, almost to the final plateau, on a totally fruitless hunt for snakes. As we turned over boulders among the thin elephant grasses, we found no wild life of the kind we wanted, but it was a paradise for the entomologist. We were plagued at every stop by grass flies, and the only respite was to prop oneself in the branches of a tree and eat a precarious lunch gazing out towards the ribbon of the distant Abbai. The zoologists sought out a large cave two and a half hours' march from the camp, where they found hordes of bats of various species: they caught about fifty, mainly sheath-tailed, and also brought back some excellent honey—an Ethiopian thrust his arm into a hole to pull out the comb, and withdrew it covered in stings which his friend then calmly plucked from the skin. Hilary King, who had already distinguished himself by taking alive a spitting cobra the day before, was nearly lost when he fell twenty feet from a ledge by the cave: happily he landed on sand. Colin Chapman, on his way back to camp, trod on a four-foot-long monitor lizard, and had the zoologist's presence of mind to bend down and pick it up; it was a most photogenic specimen, and certainly earned its ultimate freedom. One day, almost the entire group made a weekend excursion to Mabil, but the story of this frustrating adventure will be told later.

NOTES

[1-5] See p.34.
[6] His biography by Philip Magnus describes him as "a terrific Imperialist" which would therefore further commend his name to our leader.

Chapter Five
OUR MAN IN ADDIS

IT has been said that the Trafalgar campaign was guided to success as much by the untiring vigilance of Lord Barham at the Admiralty in Whitehall as by the brilliance of Nelson on board H.M.S. *Victory*. Every overseas undertaking, service or civilian, has to have its firm base, its link with politicians, contractors, diplomats. An expedition of our size could not just go off into the unknown and hope that all would be well behind it. We needed a Senior Military Officer in Addis Ababa to sort out supply and communications problems, and possible unforeseen emergencies once the expedition was in the field. The man to whom this unenviable lot fell was Lieutenant-Colonel Philip Shepherd, a fresh, youthful Gunner from the Directing Staff at Shrivenham. Although upset by the death of his father during the course of the Expedition—which involved his return for a week to Britain, and weakened by an attack of sand fly fever, which sent him for another week into an Addis Ababa hospital, he did prodigies on our behalf and without him the Expedition would not have been the success it was.

His role was all the more vital because, although our relations with the Ethiopians were good, there are certain conditions prevailing in the country—though not, I am sure, unique to it—which make the conduct of affairs tedious and frustrating: demands for paper authorisation, the insistence on signatures and rubber stamps, the difficulties of actually tracking down Ethiopian officials, and so on. Coping with all these problems is a vital but time-consuming matter which we could not expect anybody else to undertake—least of all the staff of the British Embassy.

Herein lay another difficulty. Our relations with the British Embassy were not good. In 1966 the Sandhurst Ethiopian Expedition took place when there was no British Ambassador. Sir John Russell had left and was soon to go to Rio de Janeiro, so this expedition fell under the aegis of Mr. Robert Swann, the Chargé d'Affaires, who looked after it pretty well and sent it home with a splendid party at the Embassy for the Sandhurst Officer Cadets. Relations were only superficially warm, however, and between John Blashford-Snell, who led that expedition, and the Defence Attaché, Lt.-Col. Christmas, they were, to say the least, strained. Between John and Robert Swann, an extremely conscientious servant of the Crown and correct in every punctilio of diplomatic procedure, there was a distinct clash of personalities, which emerged as early as 1966. It is difficult to feel lukewarm about John; he leaves behind him a trail of friends and enemies. He is burly, aggressively masculine, superbly self-assured, dogged, determined, and just not Robert Swann's type. This antipathy to John, shared by others in the Embassy in 1966, spread to antipathy to whatever John touched, which in their view was sure to involve them in a fair bit of extra work. There was a clear feeling in September of that year that whatever else happened the shadow of Blashford-Snell was not again to disturb the unruffled calm of the British Embassy in Addis Ababa. Imagine the dismay, then, when it was learned that he was to lead an even bigger expedition to Ethiopia in the Summer of 1968. From the time of its very first germination there was a concerted effort by the Embassy to terminate the whole thing in embryo, and the Great Abbai Expedition was nearly never born.

The Ministry of Defence, which naturally favoured an Army-backed venture of this kind in Ethiopia, found itself—via the Foreign Office—in conflict with the Embassy over this, and the result of a reconnaissance in the Spring of 1968 was that the diplomats only accepted the idea of the Expedition in principle if there was to be a liaison officer attached in some way to the Embassy to iron out Expedition problems: a sane and practical decision, in fact, which led to the dispatch of Philip Shepherd.

Although it was requested as early as May 1968 that political clearance for our work should be sought from the Ethiopian Government, the securing of it does not seem to have been pressed home with any vigour by our Embassy, though there were difficulties later on from the Ethiopian side. We were once more without an Ambassador: Sir Thomas Bromley was on leave, as was the new Defence Attaché, Lt.-Col. Desmond Vigors. Robert Swann again held the fort. The Embassy entertained hopes that the Expedition might be thwarted by a refusal of clearance, and until about a week before we were due to arrive there was a distinct possibility of it. This was why there was so much preparatory work left undone when Philip Shepherd arrived out there. These hopes of a cancellation were encouraged by political unrest in Gojjam—the province in which we were to be based—which flared up in July. This became an ideal pretext on which the whole carefully planned Expedition might at the eleventh hour be refused diplomatic clearance. In fact, when the Gojjam situation seemed to be in hand, clearance was given by the Ethiopian Government, but only on July 26th; and, as had been planned long before, Philip Shepherd flew out on the following day and the rest of us two days after.

Despite it all being such a near run thing, the main body of forty-three of us nevertheless descended on the country. The Embassy, not liking it at all, had to regard us as a *fait accompli*. Robert Swann, whose concern anyway was primarily for British interests rather than British nationals, did not need to be so directly involved. In fact, although we gave him no burden of extra work this time, he maintained a persistent interest in our affairs. His extra work resulted from the Biafra crisis: there were constant meetings at Africa Hall between the Nigerian and Biafran delegates to try to end their war, and in the nine weeks that we were in Ethiopia more signals passed between the Embassy and the Foreign Office than had done in the previous two years.

Responsibility for British nationals was, of course, the affair of our Consul in Addis Ababa, Mr. Thomas Mitchell. Few of us saw anything of him. This was, indeed, understandable, as we had few problems involving people; but when things did go wrong, Philip Shepherd found it more effective in every case to take the necessary action himself.

✳ ✳ ✳

Right from the start Philip was involved in some extraordinary undertakings. His problems and perplexities began the moment he walked off the tarmac at the International Airport, where he was to spend so much time in later wranglings. He telephoned the British Embassy and talked to Warrant Officer Stead. His arrival, despite a warning signal from the Ministry of Defence giving flight times, was clearly a surprise. The Warrant Officer was sorry that as it was only 2.30 p.m. and the Embassy did not resume work until 3 p.m. he would not be able to come and pick up the Colonel until then. So Philip had half an hour in which he was able to discover that the Airport authorities were quite unaware of the proposed arrival, two days hence, of the Transglobe charter flight booked months before by Mitchell Cotts. Because we were coming in a CL 44—a *rara avis* amongst aircraft—an airport official had written "not understood" across the telegram, and in that way consigned us all to limbo. He also found that no arrangements had been made by our Embassy for Customs clearance for the Expedition stores, a matter which the Ethiopians said normally takes three weeks. A freight list of items to be imported had been sent out to the Embassy as early as June, 1968, but clearly they had banked too heavily on a political refusal and nothing had been done about it. So the long wrangle of clearing ourselves through Customs, as we had experienced it in 1966, would unfold again; and the Expedition would suffer the same delays.

For about a week after our arrival part of our stores, mainly food, was kept back by Ethiopian Customs, whilst discussions went on as to whether we should pay duty on it. It was then agreed that it could be released if we undertook in writing to pay any duty that might later be levied. H. E. Colonel Solomon, the Vice-Minister of Finance, himself outlined this arrangement in a letter dictated to Robert Swann, which was duly typed out on Her Britannic Majesty's Embassy notepaper and sent down to the Deputy Director of the Customs Department at the Airport, who said to Philip Shepherd:

"This letter seems very badly worded and most ambiguous."

"Well, in fact, it has been drafted by your own Minister," said Philip.

"And another thing, it needs a further signature."

"Well, will it be all right if I sign it, or any of these people here?"

"Yes," the Customs man said. "You can sign it."

So Philip Shepherd wrote underneath, "This letter is null and void," and signed it. The letter now was quite acceptable and the food was released.

This encounter was a picnic compared to the problems that ensued when two R.A.F. Hercules transports flew in a day or two later with the final instalment of our stores. These were items that we had not been able to bring with us in the Transglobe CL 44. They were mainly boxes of food, and were flown over packed in a Land-Rover and two trailers.

The Inspector of Customs asked the pilot for the manifest, which included the item "Trailer, Sankey (Compo)".

"What is this 'Compo'?" asked the Inspector.

"Oh, it's a different type of trailer," said Philip. "We have all kinds of trailers in the British Army and Sankey Compo is one of the types of trailer we have." This seemed to satisfy him and he did not look in the two Land-Rovers, one empty, one full of food, nor the first trailer. But the canopy of the second trailer did not quite reach the metal side because of the load of cartons, and on one of them the Inspector read, "Compo—24-hour Ration Packs". The next day our drivers took away the four empty Land-Rovers and one trailer, but we had to leave the fifth Land-Rover and a trailer stacked high with Compo rations on the airport tarmac under firm police guard.

Now the fun really began. Philip Shepherd first of all tried to get the rations out of the grasp of the Customs by enlisting the aid of the Haile Selassie I University, who have the privilege of being able to import certain things free of duty. After all, we had one of their lecturers and a student with us on the Expedition, and our scientific results were first and foremost to be made available to the University.

Professor Whipple, the dynamic Acting Dean of the Science Faculty, was most cooperative. He drafted a letter on the afternoon of Friday, August 9th, to Colonel Solomon, the Vice-Minister of Finance who controlled the Customs Department, outlining our work and asking for our stores to be regarded as coming within the University "arrangement" and to be released free of duty as a matter of urgency. The urgency was real enough, for the river party at this point had suffered much loss of food through dampness and were shortly to go on half rations.

It was next necessary for Philip to have this letter signed by the University President, Kassa Wolde Mariam. But his Personal Assistant said over the telephone that he was not in his office, nor, regrettably, did she know where he was. The President's wife was equally unable to help, except to say that her husband was to attend a cocktail party at the Ghion Hotel at 6 p.m., as a prelude to a conference on Agricultural Studies in Central Africa. So Philip changed into a suit, clipped the vital letter to a millboard, went to the Ghion, and at 6 p.m. was hanging about on the steps with a pen in his hand.

No President Kassa. Other guests were downing drinks merrily.

Philip phoned Kassa's wife again.

"He's at a cocktail party at the Ghion."

"I fear he's not: I am here, he is not."

At 6.45 p.m. the guests moved into the conference room. Philip followed.

"Who is going to speak?" he asked of a delegate.

"President Kassa."

At this point Professor Whipple entered, and said in great surprise, "Good God! Haven't you got that letter signed yet? All right, we will get him," and they moved out on to the steps again. At 6.50 p.m. a chauffeur-driven car arrived, pennant flapping. President Kassa got out and bounded up the steps; two figures converged on either side of him.

"Would you mind signing this letter before you go in?"

"What is it all about?" Kassa said.

At this moment two other figures loomed up, the sponsors of the conference, and abducted the President and began to hustle him up the steps. A mêlée ensued: the sponsors, the Professor and the Colonel wrestled for possession of the University President, who was forced back down the steps, hair ruffled. As they all walked down the aisle, Philip said: "It's to try to get the food released for the Great Abbai Expedition."

Kassa said: "What, please, is the Great Abbai Expedition? I've never heard of it."

"I can assure you, Sir, it's quite all right," said Professor Whipple. "You're not signing your life away, and in point of fact, you're doing a lot of good."

They reached the rostrum. The puzzled eyes of a roomful of delegates had followed this strange procession. At the rostrum the President took the letter and signed it. Philip and the Professor grabbed it and fled.

The following morning at 9.30 a.m. Philip triumphantly presented the letter to Colonel Solomon.

"This is the letter you required, Colonel, for the release of our food."

"Yes," replied Colonel Solomon, "this letter is very good; the only trouble is it hasn't got the University seal on it."

Philip knew that this seal was kept in the office of President Kassa's Personal Assistant; his eagle eye had spotted it on a previous visit. It looked as if the only thing to do was to go immediately and get the stamp put on it, He drove into the University grounds; everything was ominously quiet; just a few guards loafing around.

"University shut today, Sir," said his driver, "Saturday morning." All the doors were bolted. The driver engaged the guards with cigarettes whilst Philip examined the windows. There was one open on the ground floor. He climbed through it and dropped down—into the boiler house. For a moment Philip wondered what a Colonel in the British Army was doing breaking into boiler houses on a Saturday morning in Addis Ababa.

He ran upstairs, found the P.A.'s office, next to the President's. There was the seal in the drawer. He banged it down onto the letter and envelope, put everything back tidily and ran down to the boiler house. Out of the window, suit dusted down, he sprang into the car and was off. As he drove away he thanked the guards for being so helpful, and returned to the office of Colonel Solomon.

Philip handed over the letter and the Vice-Minister examined it. Slowly he looked up and said: "You realise, don't you, that these privileges don't apply to consumable items like food; they only apply to things like bunsen burners and scientific equipment. Therefore, I cannot authorise the release of this food."

It took a further two weeks before the food was freed, finally on the intervention of the Emperor himself, and in obtaining it Philip Shepherd was told by the airport authorities that he had made 147 telephone calls from the Director's office.

* * *

At a later stage he was able to get his own back on the intransigent Customs authorities. We had resolved to mark our gratitude to H.I.M. the Emperor with a gift, and we had the happy inspiration of giving him a mate for his chihuahua dog, Lulu. Accordingly, a chihuahua bitch was bought in Shropshire and flown to Addis Ababa. Philip had to arrange for its passage through Customs.

"Are there any difficulties in importing a live animal, i.e. one dog, into Ethiopia, and how long will it take?" he asked an official.

"Yes, there are several formalities to comply with, and these usually take from five to seven days."

"Good God!" said Philip, "As much as that? Can't I get it through in one day?"

The Audience, at which the gift was to be made, was imminent.

"No, Sir. One day, that's completely out of the question. Anyway, why do you want to know this?" asked the official.

"It isn't I, in fact, who wishes to know; it's the Emperor really, because he's having a dog sent out from England, and he just wondered how long it would take. And now I can tell him that it may take up to seven days. Thank you so much for your help," said Philip, putting the receiver down.

He walked into the adjoining office at the Embassy and said to Warrant Officer Hartley, "If the telephone goes in the next two or three minutes and it happens to be the Customs, tell them I am not in." He had barely finished explaining why when the telephone rang.

"British Embassy," said Mr. Hartley. "No, I'm very sorry, Colonel Shepherd has just left."

For twenty-four hours men from the Customs Department combed Addis Ababa for Philip, and eventually a nervous and perspiring high official caught up with him.

"About that dog," he said, "there'll be no delay at all; it'll be quite all right to bring it in straight away."

So on the appointed day Betteena of Benrue, renamed Lulette, was borne before His Imperial Majesty on a satin cushion.

The Emperor's considerable personal control of his country even affects the attitudes of diplomats from outside. One day in the first week of the Expedition, when Philip was living with the Mitchells, who had moved into the Defence Attaché's house whilst their own was being renovated, he failed to turn up at his usual hour for lunch. The Consul and the Chargé d'Affaires were on the telephone and Philip's absence was commented upon.

"Oh, he's probably run up against officialdom somewhere, and gone off to see the Emperor about it," said Robert Swann.

Almost immediately the Embassy received a telephone call from the Imperial Palace and the presence of the British Chargé d'Affaires was requested at 2.30 p.m.

"Merciful Heavens!" thought Robert Swann, "it must be that fellow Shepherd again." And he left his soup and rushed into the Chancery to look for the files on the Great Abbai Expedition. These he read hurriedly, even doing some last-minute homework as he drove in the Embassy car to the Palace. When he reached the presence he was disconcerted, and perhaps relieved, to discover that the Emperor merely wished to try to enlist the support of the British Government in the United Nations over Biafra.

✳ ✳ ✳

The great problem of our impounded rations was the one that exercised Philip Shepherd most, however. All kinds of approaches were tried in an attempt to speed up their release. It was particularly the contingent at Base Camp who were becoming desperately short of food. They lived entirely on tinned Compo, and it was this that was still held at the airport. John Wilsey, an infantryman with the dark good looks of a slightly bird-like Gregory Peck, was in command at Debre Marcos, and carrying out reconnaissance flights and generally supervising the re-supply teams moving overland towards the river at various points. He received a signal from Addis Ababa on Monday, August 12th, which said that Philip Shepherd, whose father had died, had left suddenly by air for Britain. John was asked to go to Addis Ababa and collect the outstanding rations. When he drove in with Kay Thompson and "Buck" Taylor on the following Wednesday he believed (naïvely) that it was just a question of collecting the food—Philip had had no time to brief him on what had been done so far, and how little had been actually accomplished. Accordingly, he went to the Customs shed at the airport and was calmly attaching his Land-Rover to the trailerful of rations, when two armed policemen came up and steered him forcefully to the Director's office.

Now began a series of negotiations which almost duplicated Philip's travail of the week before. John knew nothing of the University President's letter and its failure to move Colonel Solomon, and set about again trying to free our food under the auspices of the University's duty-free privileges. He was told at one point of the prolonged dispute that was going on over our rations, and that only the Prime Minister could authorise their release. So John went to call on the Prime Minister only to find that the P.M.'s Personal Assistant did not know where he was. So the Deputy Prime Minister saw him and advised the procurement of a letter from President Kassa at the

University. The President, no doubt puzzled at a request for a second one, said he would write a letter the next day, but when John went to collect it, the President's Personal Assistant said that although Kassa had been to the Palace, the letter was no good. Nevertheless, John took it to the Prime Minister's office, where a very helpful Private Secretary said that it would in fact do the trick if President Kassa would sign it and present it at the Palace next day at 9.30 a.m. for Imperial approval. John tried to run the elusive Kassa to earth, but was only able to explain this arrangement to his wife. The following morning, John telephoned his home to confirm that he had left for the Palace, only to discover that the President was still asleep; he would see John in his office at 10 a.m. Then followed a highly charged, crucial interview. John, who had now seen a week slip by and who knew Base Camp were in dire straits, spoke out peremptorily to the President, who was by now clearly getting tired of the whole affair.

"You say you did not go to the Palace because the letter is no good, despite what the Prime Minister said. You realise, I hope, that there are now a number of people almost starving in Debre Marcos?"

"What do you expect me to do about it?"

John reminded him of the Bilharzia research, of the zoological survey, of the specimens for the University Museum.

"You are the key to the whole thing. You sponsored us; if you now don't want us to accomplish any of this, well, we'll call it all off, and the Expedition can be abandoned."

The President, a big representative of a proud race, drew himself to his full height. His Private Secretary, sensing danger, whispered,

"You have said too much; I think you had better go now. Come back at twelve o'clock."

John did, and he was amazed to be told the rations could now be collected. President Kassa, stung by the criticism, had driven to the Palace and got Imperial sanction for their release. He now sent a letter to Colonel Solomon, the Vice-Minister of Finance, who in turn wrote to the Director of the airport Customs Department authorising the clearance of our food, providing a full inventory was made.

Whilst John had been so busy—driving 1,000 miles in his Land-Rover in Addis Ababa alone—the Customs Department had come up with a compromise, and now demanded £300 for these rations. This seemed illogical to us since they had allowed in our first instalment duty free three weeks before, as well as similar rations in 1966. The Ethiopian Tourist Organisation, under the extremely capable and helpful Hapte Selassie, were naturally concerned to retain our goodwill, and although themselves a Government-controlled department, offered to pay half of this sum. Robert Swann, "because of the pressure of other Embassy business", could not do more than keep an eye on John's efforts, but he advised against the payment of this money as creating a dangerous precedent: we might have had an even larger bill for the larger first consignment that had been let through. John Blashford-Snell was naturally incensed and also advised that we refuse to pay. Furthermore, he proposed to invoke the power of the Press, and drafted a report— "EXPEDITION STARVING IN MID-ABBAI"—for publication in the *Daily Telegraph* if the release of food was not in the meantime obtained. In the event, it was; but before we could get our hands on the boxes the airport Customs had to have their inventory.

There were 199 boxes of Compo rations. Nobody would have minded opening one or two, but it seemed as if the zealous functionaries at the airport were intending steadily to open the lot. Philip and John were to have a wearisome evening. The game began at about 6 p.m. The copper wires on the first box were snipped and Philip read out the contents: "4 tins of sugar, 3 tins of steak and kidney pudding, 2 tins of matches and sweets, 4 tins of evaporated milk" and so on, in the greatest detail. It is hard to say whether it was deliberate filibustering by the thwarted Customs, but when they saw that there were packets of lavatory paper in the boxes, they demanded to know how many sheets each packet contained. Philip found that there were 146 in his box, but there was general dismay when they opened up the second box and John was still counting his sheets at 158. The Chief Inspector of Customs said ominously: "You have evidently been lying. The contents of these boxes are not the same."

A recount was ordered and Philip and John, like eager tellers on General Election night, fingered their way through the piles of thin sheets. Midway, John could bear it no longer.

"Do you realise," he shouted, "that this man is a Colonel and commands a thousand men in battle, and here you have him counting sheets of lavatory paper?"

"And what are you in battle?" the Inspector blandly replied.

"I am a Captain," said John. "I command a hundred men in battle, and you make me check that my Colonel can count properly!"

"Come on," said Philip to John, "let's get on, and for Christ's sake make it a round one hundred and fifty." And so it was.

When they had counted all the contents of a carton the laborious business began of multiplying it all by 199. Nobody thought of multiplying it by 200 and subtracting 1. Minute after minute the slow calculation went on, all by long multiplication with all the attendant errors and erasures. Exasperation on our side of the counter was mounting. Philip wondered what had happened to that 200th box which would have made it all so much easier.

Doubts were then expressed by the Ethiopians about the contents of the tins themselves.

"Watet ba korkoro?" They shook their heads dubiously. "How do we know it's milk in these tins?"

John Wilsey, enraged, stabbed a tin with his knife and a thin stream of white milk shot up over the dark suit of the nearest doubter. It was a pregnant moment, and one at which a tin of tea might well have been opened and a conciliatory kettle boiled. However, the matches and sweets were next to arouse suspicion: you cannot have these things in *tins*. Furthermore, the sweets sounded very much like bullets. So another tin was opened and a boiled sweet to every warehouseman lessened the tension slightly. But only briefly.

The long night in the Customs shed wore tediously on. The Chief Inspector now moved to three adjacent cartons and snipped them open. It was nearly 9 p.m.

"You're not going to open the whole lot of boxes now, are you?" cried Philip. The Inspector nodded.

"I trust you are going to bind them up again when you've examined them?" Philip went on.

"No," the Inspector answered, "that is entirely the importer's responsibility."

"But in many cases these boxes are going to be parachuted into the Nile gorge."

"I can't help that; we do this to all incoming packages. All these other cases will be opened." He gestured to the stacks of goods from all nations which were piled up around them.

A demon suddenly seized Philip.

"Do you mind if I borrow those snippers for a moment?"

He grabbed them and instantly began to cut open every package within reach. Wires and hands flew apart and a varied assortment of imports fell to the floor—pots and pans, ladies' skirts, door hinges, screwdrivers.

Two policemen came up and hustled him into the office of the Director of Customs, who said,

"Do you mind telling me what you are doing?"

"I was just helping you out," said Philip disingenuously. "I understand all these things have to be opened, and we are not getting on very fast with ours, so I thought I'd do something useful. Your men are going to open all one hundred and ninety-nine boxes of rations. Don't you think that if they were to open just twelve, say, they would see that they were all identical?"

After a moment the Director agreed. John and Philip went to fetch twelve boxes. Now the mortifying fact is that not all boxes of Compo rations *are* identical—we had six different types, S, T, U, V, W and X, each with slight variations. If the Customs were to notice these variations, then assuredly every box would be opened and its contents counted and the whole rigmarole would take at least a week. Two S's had already been opened, so, making a great pretence of doing a random selection, John and Philip picked out all the other S's they could find. For an agonising moment it looked as if they did not have twelve of this kind, but in the end the number was made up, their sheets of lavatory paper were made to tally, and at about 9.30 p.m. the Customs were satisfied. A Land-Rover was backed up and John Wilsey set off on the long haul to Debre Marcos with his "duty-free" cargo of sausages and beans and other goodies.

Involvement with Ethiopian officialdom can be likened to some sort of macabre variant of tennis, with elaborate, illogical rules and the Emperor up on the umpire's ladder. It may be that the Ethiopians privately enjoy enmeshing the westerner in this sort of game, for they love to protract it far beyond the patience of their opponents. The ball is lobbed from court to court with nightmarish deliberateness, either side waiting for the other's impetuous smash into the bottom of the net.

As John and Philip discovered, some sort of gamesmanship is necessary to terminate the meaningless rallies that developed. A good example of what can happen when the game is played strictly according to the rules occurred when Chris Bonington gave Philip a package of thirty cassettes of exposed film to be sent by air to the *Daily Telegraph*.

"No trouble at all, Sir," said the man in the Air Freight Department. "It will go this evening. What does the package contain?"

"Exposed film."

"Ah, well, you will have to step next door to get the Customs' stamp on it."

Philip complied and the same questions and answers ensued.

"Oh, I see. Well, you have to have it sealed with our official seal. Just go into the warehouse, please."

Here they bound the package with wire and affixed a small lead seal, for which Philip paid twenty-five cents.

Back in the Air Freight Department he proffered the sealed package. "Yes, it is sealed now, Sir, but you haven't got the Customs' stamp on it."

In Customs once again.

"We can't put the stamp on it because this has to be cleared by the Ministry of Information."

Three quarters of an hour had now elapsed and Philip called it a day. Next morning, with Kay Thompson, who wanted to look at the intricacies of Ethiopian red tape, he went to the Ministry of Information. Here there was a considerable delay whilst they waited for some official to return to the virtually empty offices. Ultimately an enormous form was produced requiring details of the contents of each film. Philip, not certain of the exact subjects, made a guess at what they were: 1-14 crocodiles; 15-25, hippo; 26-38, boats on river, etc., but the official would not accept this simplification: he wanted every line filled in—all the 36 exposures of each of the 30 cassettes. This meant that Philip's imagination had to extend to 1,080 items, and the morning moved on into afternoon as his pen scratched away at the bogus details. At the foot of the form it asked:

"Do the pictures taken, if printed, tend to the improvement of Anglo-Ethiopian relations?"

Philip wrote, "Yes, certainly; but the completion of this form does not."

However, the official ultimately applied his rubber stamp. A letter had to be drafted, typed and stamped in an adjoining office, yet another in another office, and finally a photostat copy of the form obtained and paid for; it looked as if, with the working day almost over, the requirements of officialdom had been met. And for once, it was so. At the airport the package went off. But the next day Chris Bonington sent in another similar box of film.

Philip, however, thought this one would be easy as he had so recently obtained the letter of authority for the last lot. But the airport Customs were adamant: that only applied to the one package. The whole performance at the Ministry of Information had to be gone through again. At this point Philip lost his equilibrium.

"This is preposterous. You fellows really are blithering idiots!"

"May I have that in writing?" said the Customs official gravely.

"Certainly. Bring me some paper."

Paper was furnished. Philip wrote his pithy comment and signing it, thrust it towards the man. He then took the package, walked over to the airport and gave it to a friendly *Vogue* photographer about to take a plane to London after an assignment with lions and model girls in the Embassy gardens. Bonington's film reached the *Daily Telegraph* the same day.

✳ ✳ ✳

The last job that Philip undertook was the sale of our five Army Land-Rovers and two trailers. The Ministry of Defence had authorised us to do this, and had set a reserve price on them which we were to repay. There had been efforts in our last days in Addis Ababa to dispose of them, but none was conclusive. Three days after the main body of us had left for Britain, Philip held an auction in the grounds of the Embassy at 10 a.m. Throughout the previous week there had been numerous telephone calls from would-be purchasers and much interest shown in these desirable vehicles, which are so well-suited to Ethiopian road conditions. But at 10 a.m. Philip was the only person there.

"Don't worry," said Sir Thomas Bromley, the British Ambassador, who had returned to Ethiopia the day our main party left, and who was most charming and most interested in the Expedition's work. "Give them forty-eight hours; they'll turn up!"

Presently, Philip strolled down to the gates and discovered that the Sudanese guard, as wary as most of us of second-hand car dealers, had been dutifully turning them all away. However, Philip explained what was happening and by 12.30 p.m. there were over thirty potential buyers assembled, Ethiopian and foreign. From the bonnet of a Land-Rover he concluded a perfectly normal auction and by 2 p.m. all had been sold. As he jumped down, an Ethiopian strolled up.

"That Land-Rover I bought," he said. "It doesn't go."

Philip said: "No, I've got the ignition key in my pocket."

"Can I have it, please?" asked the Ethiopian.

"Can I have the money, please?" countered Philip.

"Would it be all right if I pay you tomorrow?"

"Yes, no problem at all; but you get the key tomorrow."

"Can I have the key now and pay you tomorrow?"

"No, I'm afraid that's not on. I only let these vehicles go for cash."

The only thing Philip received from any of the purchasers of the seven items was a post-dated cheque for January 1st 1970, which he felt justified in tearing up. None of them had any ready money.

That afternoon he was struck by fever and was taken by Lt.-Colonel and Mrs. Vigors into hospital. From his sick-bed, in due course, the long drawn-out sale went on. When his temperature had subsided an Ethiopian was let into the ward.

"I wonder, Sir, have you by any chance sold all the Land-Rovers?"

"No," said Philip, "I think I've got one left."

"Is there any chance of seeing it?"

"Oh, no! The man I sold it to is coming with the money this afternoon, and that will be all of them gone."

Philip plucked a grape and slowly peeled it.

"If I give you money now," the Ethiopian said, "could I take it?"

"Yes, I suppose so," said Philip.

The man pulled out a wad of hundred dollar bills and counted several out onto the sheet. Philip felt under his pillow, where there were five ignition keys. He pulled one out and, glancing at the number, gave it to the man, and then took the wad of grubby notes and put them under the pillow. When his customer had gone, he struggled out of bed and made his way slowly past Sister's office to a telephone. He got through to Mr. Hartley at the Embassy and asked him to push into hiding the trailers and all the Land-Rovers except for one, which was in due course collected and driven away.

In this way, day by day, Philip sold all the other vehicles. One man made him regret his stratagem when he said, "You know, it's a pity you've sold all the other Land-Rovers, because I would have bought the lot!" Another came back to the hospital looking very crestfallen, but bearing by way of a bargaining counter a superb pineapple.

"About my Land-Rover," he began tentatively. "It's the wheels."

"What's the matter?" asked Philip, accepting the pineapple. "Don't they go round?"

"Oh, yes! But they're full of sand."

The Expedition, short of money to buy new inner tubes, had had to fall back on this old device to keep the vehicle on the road. But we had gone away and forgotten all about it. A trail of sand had aroused the poor chap's suspicion and so Philip said that if he went off and bought two new inner tubes and produced the receipts, he would be reimbursed; but, as was so often the case, he never came back. No doubt there is still a Land-Rover giving a particularly hard ride and discharging a thin trickle of sand on Addis Ababa streets.

✳ ✳ ✳

On another occasion, too, Philip had won the Ethiopian game with a passing shot down the backhand which was never returned. According to our passports, which were locked up for safe keeping in the British Embassy, we should all have renewed our visas after thirty days in Ethiopia. When we had been down the river for five weeks or so, Philip had a telephone call from the Immigration Office in Harar Road enquiring why some forty-three people had neither left the country nor had their visas properly renewed.

"I'm afraid it has been quite impossible to renew them because they're away on an expedition," said Philip.

"It doesn't make any difference, this expedition," the voice replied. "They must come to Harar Road immediately with two photographs and have their visas extended."

"Look, I don't think this is going to be easy," said Philip. "Would it not be possible for one of your men to come out to the expedition, and you can check them and stamp them then and there?"

In the end it was agreed that Philip was to make all the arrangements for an official to visit us in the field. After forming some completely imaginary plans, he telephoned back two days later.

"I've fixed everything up," he said. "If your official could kindly report to the Military Airport at ten a.m. tomorrow he will be picked up by a Beaver aircraft and flown to an area on the Great Abbai one hundred and eighty miles from Shafartak. He will then parachute to a point on the river bank which, I can assure you, the main boat party are due to reach by tomorrow evening. I have warned the Expedition leader by radio that an Immigration official will be visiting him in this way, and he says he will have everything ready."

There was a lengthy silence. Then the voice said that perhaps it was after all not possible to stamp the passports just now. But he added that it would also not be possible for us to leave the country at the end of the Expedition. Somehow, when the time came, amidst much noise, form-filling, order and counter-order, we did get away—with the same sort of inevitability with which we had arrived.

Chapter Six
CRUISING DOWN THE RIVER

ON August 20th, whilst Russian tanks were rumbling into Czecho-slovakia, the twenty-nine of us now on the river, oblivious of greater world events, were preparing, after a morning air-drop, to move further west. We motored off into a region of placid, broad waters, rich jungle and dramatic, distant mountainscapes.

More and more people appeared on the banks. At the sound of our engines excited Shankilla would emerge from fields of tall maize and stare astonished at the four boats. Reassuring shouts and waves from us—"*Garridá, Atámaré,*" whatever they may mean—brought waves and chatter from them. Many stood with raised arms and bowed to the ground a number of times just in case we were of any importance. Assefa passed on to them through a loudhailer greetings from their Emperor. Some ran along the marges of their plantations encouraging us to stop, but the speed of our engines in the swiftly moving stream soon outstripped them.

On either side there was a wide, alluvial plain, dotted with blue columns of smoke from burning tree-roots, and ahead of us the prominent massif of Mount Gum. Along the edges of the river was a thick forest in whose branches swung noisy baboons and beautiful black and white colobus monkeys. It was a time for photography, reading, meditation, dozing.

In the late afternoon we met a few whirlpools, and the hills ahead seemed to loom up closer to the river. We passed the mouths of the Welmet, the Zinghini and the Dim, although a firm identification of these rivers was not made at the time. Slipping down between islands, it was quite easy to miss an important tributary whose entrance might be shrouded by trees or hidden by sandbars. The unchanging and featureless terrain was no real help either. Set down on the Thames somewhere between Cricklade and Canvey Island, one could fairly accurately hazard a guess as to where one was; on the Blue Nile this is really not possible.

As if to show that it was still capable of confounding us, the Nile then presented a quite steep cataract, somewhere near the mouth of the Azir River. We negotiated it easily and swung round to pitch camp along a long sandy beach beyond it.

There is still some debate as to which is the best time of year to navigate the Great Abbai. Probably no single answer will prove right for the whole length of the river with its different problems. We felt that we had so far proved that Arne Rubin's view was the more sound: the greater flood of water in the wet season carries boats more safely over rocks and robs cataracts of much of their lethal power. Though for the northern reaches, above Shafartak, the declining waters of the period immediately following the official rainy season (June-September) seemed best. Jean Laporte, who safely canoed from Shafartak to beyond Sirba, argues for a dry season approach, but to do it he had to make many strenuous portages, and to "rope down" his canoes in many places, which was time-consuming. We made the whole transit without any need for manpower or engineering support of this kind.

Our two days near the Azir produced much of the spirit of a holiday camp: we swam, sunbathed, washed clothes, fished and gently maintained the boats. John Blashford-Snell stretched his great bulk in the shade of the Command Tent and turned his mind for the first time to Phase 2. Mansel Spratling, deprived of any archaeology, built large sandcastles on the beach. Hunters were out at dawn and dusk, and, although Jim and Roger put up a wart-hog, returned virtually empty-handed. Cameras clicked and whirred as the Assault Boats took small parties across river and bounced back, lightly laden, through the cataract: it was now a thing to sport with, to add a bit of zest to dull ferrying.

Next day after a quick lunch we left, and at speeds of between seven and eight knots approached a maze of islands without sighting any evidence of Zakas Ford or the mouth of the River Dora. One large island, which we left to starboard, was clearly the "Murder Island" of B. H. Jessen's fateful journey of 1905. Here his twenty-year-old Sudanese servant had been killed. After marching with mules 300 km along the river bank from the Sudanese frontier to Zakas Ford, just upstream of "Murder Island", Jessen had left the river, Cheesman says, and walked out to see Ras Mangasha at Burie (Jessen's own map shows him pressing on to the River Fatam). However, since the river below Zakas Ford had thus been traced, Cheesman, in 1927, called off his survey of the river at this point and made inland to Wanbera.

Between thickly populated banks we proceeded on a south-westerly course. The river seemed broad and brimming full as if it was dammed or confined in some way further down. In a sense it is, for it must pass through the narrow defile of the Western Cataracts. Here we would encounter rapids reminiscent of the Black Gorge. At that moment, however, it was placid; six hippo snorted in the stream on our left and another crocodile made for the water like a sprightly old lady running for a bus.

Boats vied with each other in getting close to crocodiles for photographs. In all ways there was developing a rivalry between our four boats which grew from a growing awareness of their differing identities and a sense almost of a "boat personality". After over a fortnight together a certain *esprit de bateau* was natural enough: *Kitchener* seemed somewhat aloof—diverse characters, most with important responsibilities and thus in the Command boat. *Wingate* contained perhaps the toughest, closest-knit crowd; all its members were highly independent, and yet together. *Cheesman* never emerged as distinctly as the others, and remained mainly a happy, somewhat accident-prone bunch of Ethiopians and zoologists. *Sandford* were exuberant, consciously communal, apt to tear off all their clothes and rush around naked in the rain, happy as Sandford boys. Communal living had its disadvantages for them, though: it was not until August 28th that they managed to cook a supper which didn't come to the boil just in time for the nightly Orders Group meeting.

We had now reached the looming banks, with their occasional slabs of cliff, of the Western Cataracts. Sure enough, there were cataracts ahead: the river discernibly dropped like an undulating fairway, except that the usual hydraulic waves and severely broken water lay in the trough. The boats took it well, as we now knew they would. Chris Whitwell in *Kitchener* slept through it all, as he had through most of the cataracts recently. Where the river, trending now south-westwards, went into an S-bend, there was a vast cliff high in the hills to our right. Under the shadow of this we came into a tree-lined beach and made our fifth camp.

Cheesman was allotted the left-hand end, and cut a terrace site laboriously out of the soft bankside. There were a number of enormous hanging lianas attached to tree branches above, and from the terrace, one could do a passable imitation of Tarzan on these, until the rubbery strands broke off, sending one sprawling among rock and thornbush.

Sandford filled the right-hand berth, amongst a number of large boulders. Their normal practice was for John Huckstep to put up a large tent, while John Fletcher refuelled and attended to the engines; Roger, Nigel, Claude and Peter O'Mahony decanted the kit from the boat and helped to fix the tent. Mansel Spratling was to get the fire going and brew the tea. On this occasion, with the camp rigged and the kit stowed away, they all turned, expecting to see the fire and bubbling water and Mansel tossing tea-bags in; but instead they saw only his torn, blue bathing shorts, as he bent, head down, over the chosen hearth area and scrabbled at the earth like a frantic Jack Russell.

"Look at this!" he shouted. He held up three or four sherds of dark pottery with a clear pattern etched on them. "Just where I was going to make the fire!"

Soon the area was being closely gone over by the others with trowel, knife or finger, and stone-cutting tools and fragments of pot were accumulating in polythene bags. In a wide crack between two great boulders someone found the broken parts of an almost entire pot the size of a soccer ball. The whole area must at full flood be under the river, so the finding of yet other fragments at the same level further upstream was specially odd. Perhaps it was all from a bank settlement that had been undercut by the rising water and had collapsed onto the rocks; the soil would be washed away, leaving only stone and pottery. Accordingly, Mansel next day concentrated on the earth bank and the heap of spoil immediately below it.

He dug and sifted all day, with a steady turnover of volunteers to assist him. By nightfall there was still a great deal to do. We were due to leave in the morning, and so, with the aid of the Tilley lamp, Mansel went on and, in the end, excavated throughout the night. In the morning we found a gaunt-looking, dark-eyed figure, black with earth and tattered, like some pre-Shaftesbury child-miner, sitting surrounded by bags full of possible treasures.

"Got yourself some nice artefacts, then, Mansel?" asked John Huckstep, using Mansel's favourite jargon word.

He was too tired to answer; nor did he show much emotion when it was announced that, since the water level had fallen a metre in the night, we would not after all be leaving that day.

Mansel explained later that he seemed to have found an extensive river settlement, which might be a quarter of a million years old, although much of the pottery was akin to La Tène work of the pre-Roman Iron Age in Western Europe. Again it was similar to much pottery produced in Ethiopia today, so dating was going to be difficult, unless some organic material such as bone or wood was turned up, which could help to give an accurate radio-carbon dating.[1]

Whilst Spencer Lane-Jones was surveying the whole dig, we received later that morning a further air-drop of supplies—this time including some tins of ten-man Compo rations, lately released by the reluctant Customs. After days of sardines and rice, we could now enjoy the luxury of Army sausage and beans. A few circular loaves of bread were also dropped; these were cut up with Euclidian accuracy and we all enjoyed one segment of bread, butter and apricot jam. A supper of Irish stew, followed by coffee and evaporated milk, mitigated the miseries of "Hank", Hilary and John Huckstep, who had been led by Roger at a fast pace for four and a half hours to the vast cliff face above us, and four and a half hours down again, to find nothing but a bag of Fools' Gold.

✳ ✳ ✳

We left this camp at the unprecedented hour of 7.30 a.m. on the morning of Sunday, August 25th. The water had risen considerably and was now reckoned high enough to carry us over the remaining rocks in the Western Cataracts. With fluffs of cloud hanging in the valley, the four boats turned into the current and, when all engines were functioning soundly, swung round and peeled off downstream like fighter planes. Though we were still in a gorge there were some quite wide reaches where the surface was pocked with rings, like water going down the kitchen plug-hole after a very grubby wash. We encountered many rocky islets and the occasional groyne of rock projecting into the stream. These might have been dangerous but good helmsmanship and the sluicing effect of the waters carried us past them.

After a fifty-minute break for tea on a mudbank, we moved on into a stretch of increasing narrowness with sheer cliffs on both sides, and then the river opened again to a region of rocky islands. Just as we felt we must be getting close to the Didessa River entrance a succession of three or four massive cataracts loomed up. *Cheesman* and *Sandford* were inundated by two vast waves in the first one, and were almost immediately swamped again in the second before baling had made any impression. *Kitchener* struck a rock—the only occasion that this happened on this phase—and drifted powerless for half a mile. *Wingate* took her in tow just above the third cataract. The shearpin was replaced, but then Ian Macleod could not undo the towrope. Ultimately, with Jim Masters sprawled perilously on the canvas "dodger" as the two boats drifted down, the rope was cut. Further cataracts were shot and we all emerged drenched. This was the last severe test, in fact; the hills about us were moderating and the sky opening out.

"I would say we must be coming up on the Didessa very soon," said John in *Kitchener*.

"Don't think so," said Martin Romilly, the Information Officer. "By my reckoning we're not at all near it yet."

Even as he spoke the line of trees on our left came to an end and the mouth of a very considerable tributary was revealed.

"The Didessa!" we shouted, and motored across the broad confluence to a large tree-clad island which lay in the middle.

"Sir, how do you know it is the Didessa?" asked Tadesse Wolde.

"Well, it's so big, it's obvious—it's about as big as the Abbai itself," I said.

"Oh, Sir, don't say like that! It is not good. The Abbai will be angry with us!"

We tied up on the island after motoring for nearly four hours.

It was about a hundred metres across, flat and roughly triangular, and it made an ideal base for almost four days. Covered in thick vegetation, it was very much a wild-life sanctuary: in the morning, fish eagles; in the evening, the haunting whistle of the red-winged starling; and later at night, the deep hoomphing of hippopotami as they wandered round about the camp site. Luckily, the shy river horses seemed to keep their distance from us, and were never seen by day.

One of our first tasks here was to rig up a "flying ferry" from the island, across an arm of the Didessa, to the nearest mainland. This was the work of the engineer section under Jim Masters' direction, and it fascinated the other members as much as the local population, who had gathered in wonderment on the far bank. A long nylon rope was stretched taut across the hundred yards or so of swift-moving water, and an Assault Boat, attached by a twenty-yard line to a pulley wheel, moved across it with equal ease either way, and without power. This manoeuvre was performed in much the same way that a yacht can tack against the wind, and only needed a slight shift of the attached rope at the end of each crossing. Hunting trips to the south bank of the Abbai and visits to the Shankilla village of Gambela were now made easier.

✳ ✳ ✳

At lunch-time on the second day there was a notable encounter: Group B, led by Nigel Sale, had marched for thirteen days over a terrible seventy-five miles of country parallel to the Didessa, from the township of Ghimbi to the Abbai. Bearing enormous loads, Nigel, with John Blower and Alem Berhanu of the Ethiopian Wild Life Conservation Department, and the burly Rex Matthews, and Tigre Bishoura, a Shankilla chief's son, were accorded a warm welcome and began a brief but well-earned rest. They had carried out a useful reconnaissance for possible game, and had been the first white party to make this overland journey down the Didessa.

Early on the fourth day, Nigel was considered to have rested sufficiently and was off again. This time he was to lead an advance party in one Assault Boat to Sirba, about twenty-five miles down the Abbai, and our terminal point. The problem of how to extricate from Sirba over thirty people and their kit, together with the four Assault Boats, was one which had been exercising not only John, but Philip Shepherd in Addis Ababa. At first, there seemed to be no answer to the problem of the boats; but then we had heard from the Ministry of Defence that they were not expendable and must be recovered in some way. Perplexed, Philip had discussed H.M. Government's concern for them with Colonel Don Finney of the U.S. Mapping Mission in Addis Ababa, who, with characteristic American generosity, had undertaken to try to lift them out with a Mapping Mission helicopter. If this plan failed, Philip had secured permission for a skeleton party to fly the United Nations flag from the boats and proceed in them over the frontier to Khartoum!

So Nigel and the crew of *Wingate* were to go on ahead and create a landing pad for the helicopter on the banks of the Abbai somewhere near Sirba. Even this presented its difficulties because Sirba was a large village in undulating country over two miles south of the river, and there would be no indication on the Abbai when they were at the nearest point to it. After finding it, however, and cutting out a landing area, they were to move inland to Sirba and investigate the state of the airstrip constructed by the Lutheran Mission for their occasional visits to the village. Finally, they were to arrange with the chief for the provision of a platoon of porters to carry all our impedimenta on the following day from the river, over the rough path, through the scrub to the airstrip. It was to be from this airstrip that all personnel and kit would be lifted out by Beaver plane or Huey helicopter to Ghimbi or Debre Marcos.

This superb plan replaced one in which a handful of selected members vitally needed for the preparation of Phase 2 were to be flown out by Beaver, and the rest, in the absence of a helicopter, were to have to march with their kit in seven days the seventy-five miles or so of scrub-covered hill country between Sirba and Ghimbi. Those of us in this latter category, who in fact went out by helicopter, glanced down at the barely penetrable jungle with an immense sense of relief, and praised God for Uncle Sam and the Special Relationship.

At the Didessa Junction the days passed pleasantly in visits to neighbouring Shankilla villages. The nights, however, were less agreeable. I had placed my air-bed on the flat earth under Alec's stretched sheet of polythene. One evening, as I lay reading just before last light, I was aware of an ominous subsidence—elbow and haunch were touching the ground. Furthermore, I seemed unusually restless and itchy. I leant up on one elbow and pulled back the inflated pillow. On the ground, and adhering to the air-bed's underside, was a myriad tiny red ants tumbling over each other, and all within the rectangular outline of my bed. Dense clusters of them seemed to be concentrating on the air-bed at various points where they had eaten through the canvas and laid bare the rubber. There was nothing to be done; it was almost dark, and as only half a dozen or so had bothered to penetrate my sleeping bag, I re-inflated the air-bed and fell asleep.

Next day, I asked our senior zoologist to disinfest the area with a lethal dose of formalin. It seemed to have some effect, although the red ants held onto life with great tenacity. I took them down to the Didessa to drown the remainder, and some were still hanging on and twitching gamely when I hung the air-bed up to dry. Pat Morris's "final solution" had more effect on the human species, in fact. The formalin made such a choking smell that the *Cheesman* area was uninhabitable for hours after.

The following night about 10 p.m. a rushing wind blew up warm and boisterous for half an hour, with thunder and sheet lightning, followed by very heavy rain. Alec and I had constructed our shelter like a gardener's cloche, and so were not prepared for a storm which came at us virtually horizontally. Great drops fell, some being blown through the "tent", over our recumbent forms and out the other end. Soon our sleeping bags were spattered with mud and shrieks of hysterical laughter came from the darkness as this freak downpour caught us all in various ways unprepared. Just as the damp was beginning to penetrate my Army issue bag, I felt the familiar subsidence of the night before. Hauling up the top of my air-bed, I revealed the same rectangle of seething ants. Formalin enough to kill a baboon, as Pat had said, had made no impact on this indestructible colony, and had, indeed, been a sort of fertiliser to them. Whilst I still lay on relatively dry ground, to one side of the foot of my air-bed was a large, gathering pool of about an inch of rainwater. I dragged my bed over into the middle of the pool and clambered into it again. It seemed to clamp the ardour of the ants somewhat, but the air-bed was never the same again.

The *Kitchener* crew was well protected from the storm in a bushy hollow, but the *Sandford* crew were thoroughly exposed. They had constructed an angled shelter which lay directly open to the oncoming elements. Their roof filled like a sail. Like storm-wracked mariners, they hung on to spars and rigging to prevent the whole thing from taking off. There was laughter and argument as pools of water spread. The canvas flapped angrily, and the howling wind for the most part drowned Nigel Marsh's naval execrations and the snoring of Claude Charnotet, who slept peacefully through it all.

The journey from the Didessa to Sirba on the next morning had a wonderful, dreamlike quality. Fears of fuel shortage on this final run-in caused us to try drifting without engines. The river was wide and sluggish and the three boats seemed to hang motionless on the bright water like junks in a Chinese painting. Spinning slowly round, one boat would unaccountably overtake another as we sat silent and slightly dizzy and admired the circling panorama.

It was an interlude between two periods of some danger; those of us, like "Hank", who were not to be in the White Water team, naturally had a sense of anticlimax. Alastair, Ian and Chris Bonington looked ahead thoughtfully. For them it was more likely to be the beginning of the drama: they were three of the nine that had been chosen by Roger Chapman for his White Water Team (Group WW) to attempt the notoriously hazardous northern reaches of the river.

"Didn't seem too difficult, really, Phase 1," said Spencer Lane-Jones.

"Piece of cake," said Alastair.

As we coasted idly along to Sirba. Phase 1 seemed easy in retrospect. It had been entirely within our capabilities. There was only one section of turbulence this particular morning, where a bar of rock projected and narrowed the river; the sound and fury of the Black Gorge were already receding in our memories. It was thrilling, however, to recall some of the worst of the cataracts, to remember how the boat had coursed swiftly, borne like a twig in a game of Poohsticks, towards the curling hydraulic wave; how with an audible bang it had struck it and risen up over it, as water spilled over and off the sodden brown "dodger"; how we had wallowed into a trough and risen abruptly again as waves struck each side of the boat madly. We remembered the twinges of doubt as the boats were swept to a sharp bend. It would have been difficult, if not impossible, to stop in the narrower stretches of gorge. The enormous, deceptive power of the whirlpools came back to mind, whirlpools which momentarily took possession of the boats and held them stationary. It was amusing to remember those Spring days in North Wales when we tested the boats in conditions as near to those on the Nile as we could easily find. How puny and trivial the Severn seemed in comparison to the broad flood on which we were now carried!

After entering what seemed like a wide sea, we started the engines and motored into a narrower passage, dotted with great rocks—one like a toad, another like the bows of an approaching tugboat. Soon the broad tableland of Wanbera loomed up in the distance, but immediately around us the land levelled out to an unaccustomed flatness with a scattering of low knolls only. Looking behind, we saw the Ethiopian plateau, pierced by the gorge—the view that must have given pause to Jessen as he marched up the northern bank in 1905. As we passed first one, then another large, reed-clad island, the nearby land assumed an almost East Anglian quality. We marshalled the boats in an arrowhead formation, and they were still dwarfed by the breadth of the stream. Suddenly a red smoke-bomb exploded by a tree on our left. There, somewhat ahead, was *Wingate*, tethered. We reciprocated with ministars[2] and distress flares—no distress here, but joy: we were at Sirba.

NOTES:

[1] See Chapter 18, pp.242-3.
[2] Red, green and white stars, giving out 7-8,000 candlepower for about 5 seconds, could be shot two hundred feet or so from a small spring-loaded hand flare shaped like a propelling pencil. They are made by Pains-Wessex Ltd., and were very useful in Phase 2.

Chapter Seven
GOING ASHORE

SWEAT was dripping from my face as I stumbled amongst the sharp boulders, dragging one leaden foot after another. We had been marching for three hours, keeping rigorously to a pattern of fifty minutes' slog followed by ten minutes' rest. It had been climbing all the way. Near the end of the morning some of us were finding this a little inflexible.

We were *en route* from our first Forward Base on the river to the southern edge of the plateau. We were seven in all, to start with. Roger Chapman, superbly fit, was leading us, preceded only by Ato Mamo, our guide. We had picked up this tiny, wizened figure at the Water Resources Camp at the confluence of the Guder with the Abbai. He had already walked the nine or ten miles from his village down to the gorge bottom that morning and now he was guiding us back. Chief of the village of Charra, he was a thin-faced, close-cropped old man with a ready smile, but crooked, tarnished teeth. On his forehead was a prominent bump where there was a piece of shrapnel from an Italian shell that he had tried to melt down three years before. His thin legs were clad in blue jeans, tucked into black Wellington boots and the rest of him was covered, at all states of the weather, in a black PVC cape and a sou'wester, worn back to front.

Next was Nigel Marsh, the A Group Doctor, carrying his satchel with its bright red cross, like the Pardoner with his box of "pigges bones", but with much more honourable motives. One aspect of our scientific research was into the prevalence of Schistosomiasis—or Bilharzia. Nigel wanted specimens of human excreta and urine for the University in Addis Ababa. He also planned to do what he could to relieve suffering. Mansel Spratling struggled along with his ill-fitting rucksack, hoping to do some archaeology, and I brought up the rear with Tadesse and Ato Berhanu, the amiable and helpful manager of the Water Resources Camp, who spoke English and Gallinya.

It was part of the Expedition's work to explore the sides of the gorge and the land fringing its rim, and so John Blashford-Snell had despatched Roger and his team to march out for two days from the Guder River mouth up onto the plateau of North-East Wallega to investigate the villages of Charra and Cao and a possible Italian fort at Asandabo. Other parties were to cover the uplands east of the Guder and the lower reaches of the Guder itself.

We had set off up the Abbai in a slow-moving armada of three Assault Boats. With engines at full throttle they had hung virtually motionless in the fierce stream. Only by slipping to the sides of the river could we gain on the black rocks at its edge as the brown water swirled past. Eventually we had edged under the wire measuring gauge, which spans the Abbai here, and into the quiet, crocodile-ridden Guder. At the Camp we had disembarked and set off on the first, stiff ascent through elephant grass and thornbush. An hour later, we had reached a shoulder of flat land on which lay a deserted village that we had investigated the day before. On B. H. Jessen's map of 1906 it appears as "village", but it had begun to decline a century ago when the tsetse fly first struck its cattle. Fields and walls were still visible and the stone cairns of the dead, but little else.

We had passed over wild, undulating country where Ato Mamo at 6 a.m. that morning had seen lion, but now nothing stirred before us as the sun rose in the sky. Extremely stony paths and stream-beds cut our boots. It is doubtful if a barefoot Ethiopian, or a shod *ferenji* for that matter, would have had much warning of a lion on these paths. Every step has to be picked with care, and on the march there cannot be much observation of the country around. The traveller's head is permanently bent down on the watch for the great stones that lie in the way.

For a further hour there had been no water, no people, no animals. Then brown patches of cultivated land had come into sight—the village of Charra, nestling on the underslopes of the final cliff escarpment. We had toiled on along the ancient path, past great isolated monoliths. Soon the whoops and cries of distant Galla could be heard, and presently we wound our way up between steep fields, whose cultivators stopped work to stare at the strange, sweating column, with their chief striding along at its head. After a brief rest, we staggered on away from them, now in dark, winding lanes among the scattered *tukuls*. In a moment we came to a small village green, dominated by a large fig tree. Here, a few yards from a comforting spring, we collapsed.

Roger turned to Ato Berhanu.

"When he's recovered, Nigel, our Doctor, will hold a surgery. At about 2 p.m.; the *hakim* will look at sick people then. Can you please tell Ato Mamo that?"

Ato Berhanu turned it all into Gallinya.

"O.K. Yes, O.K.," said Ato Mamo, smiling evilly. This is the only English he knows. In a few words he told his flock and there was an immediate quickening of interest.

For half an hour we brewed tea, rested and ate lunch—much to the enjoyment of a large crowd—soon the entire village—who gathered round us. They stared steadily and laughed a lot, and I took the opportunity of staring back to discover what the average Galla peasant looks like.

He has large, slightly spatulate, bare feet. He has virtually no toe-nails, or at most a disfigured nail on his big toe—the result of years of rough walking and constant damp. If he is old he may have open sores in cracks between the toes, and his feet and ankles may be swollen. He is of slight build and has quite short, thin legs, hardened, flaking and rather greyish. His long shorts have been patched copiously and many of the patches are ripped, showing portions of dark, hairy leg. Perhaps secured by one vital safety pin, they hang shapelessly, looking dirty and uncomfortable. Over the upper part of the body is folded the ubiquitous *shamma*, a toga-like garment, once white, but in the poorest villages a dingy grey-brown sheet, constantly twitched and re-twitched over the shoulder or held over the mouth and nose in his thin, cold hands. From the corner of his mouth may protrude a length of twig; this is *mafarka,* the natural Ethiopian tooth cleaner, snapped off from a shrub which is used commercially in the manufacture of at least one toothpaste. The Galla is unlikely to be smoking: cigarettes and pipes are rare. His head is generally uncovered, unless covered by a great broad-brimmed straw. If he is of some substance, he may wear a pair of old cream jodhpurs instead of shorts; on his feet, Wellington boots or sandals; on his head, a plastic topee. In the past, the Indian influence has been strong and pervasive. Umbrellas, also, are carried by the well-to-do, and by priests, who generally wear white turbans.

The long grubby dress of the women is similar in colouring, often revealing neck and shoulders and held together by the prized safety pin. The hair might be trained in a multiplicity of intricate patterns, and the townswomen often cover it in a net of bright cyclamen or canary-coloured nylon. Round the neck of the Galla women are small, coloured beads, or a silver cross beaten from a Maria Theresa dollar. Shoes, socks and underwear are only worn in the larger towns.

Children wear the least possible. A single filthy old shirt is often enough. Boys inherit tattered shorts as they grow older. Their hair, like that of the very old of both sexes, is general shaved—though not completely in the case of most children: a tuft of black, frontal curls is a standard cut often seen. Ethiopian children, especially Amhara, are good-looking and high-spirited, but the Galla village youngsters were sometimes undernourished, with thin limbs and pot bellies. It was to this sort of problem that Nigel Marsh now had to turn.

The villagers of Charra seemed, in general, quite healthy. However, there was soon a large crowd pressing round him as he spread out his pitifully limited wares under the fig tree. It was obvious that treatment by a *hakim*—the first, I imagine, ever to practise in Charra—was an experience also to be enjoyed by the healthy, and quite soon crowd control was necessary. There were clearly a number of *malades imaginaires* in the throng, but it was difficult for Nigel, communicating painstakingly *via* Ato Berhanu, ever to be really sure that one of them was a malingerer. To those who could not be more specific than to indicate a headache, Roger Chapman dished out an aspirin as some sort of palliative. One old woman with a worried frown came round three times, tapping her temple with a forefinger and shrugging helplessly—and she got her three aspirins.

Genuine illness, of course, there was in plenty: malaria, venereal diseases, liver complaints, open sores, avitaminosis, scabies, a whole host of eye disorders, and various results of dietary deficiency, such as elephantiasis. None of these things could be cured or very much relieved in one treatment. We wondered afterwards how much useful advice got through to them, and was acted on; their diet would go on consisting mainly of maize and *injera* (see page 96), anyway. However, ointments and plasters were applied and pills distributed, and there may have been some psychological benefit, too. We saw men standing about hours after with a magic dab of anti-histamine cream cradled carefully in their palms.

One of the strange aspects of this and other attempts that Nigel made to heal or comfort sick villagers was that they never seemed to be particularly grateful for what he did. Surgery was always apt to become a mêlée as they struggled for his attentions. When his supplies were exhausted, those who had not been treated seemed distinctly aggrieved. Once at Mabil, a man whom he had treated three days before for gonorrhoea refused to carry Nigel's rucksack up to the village for less than three dollars. Though medical treatment at Charra must have been extremely infrequent, if not unknown, before this, it was received churlishly as if it was only their due. Yet the nearest alternative was a hospital at Debre Marcos, a four or five days' march away, involving a crossing of the Nile. And treatment there by the Bulgar and his wife who run it would cost money. Perhaps this is why their sixty beds could seem to be adequate for a catchment population of half a million.

Whatever hypochondria there was amongst his villagers, and however graceless they were, Ato Mamo himself was a shining example to them. When Nigel removed the shrapnel from his head under local anaesthetic, he bore the operation with fortitude and his thankfulness was obvious. Indeed, there were, too, some of his people who reciprocated by helping us with our Bilharzia research: Nigel's graphic instructions were translated, little bottles and phials were given out, and they went away to carry out the incredible behest of the white man.

Nigel Marsh and Ian Macleod take the piece of shrapnel from Ato Mamo's forehead. He had once unwisely tried to melt down an old Italian shell he had ploughed up.

When he had collected the results, which he put carefully into his otherwise emptied Red Cross satchel, he and Tadesse, with Ato Berhanu, set off back to the river. Roger Chapman, Mansel and I got ready to continue our march with Ato Mamo to the top of the cliff. One little piece of courtesy cheered us on our way. I was just pulling on a damp and quite nauseous sock when an old man, with a squint of Ben Turpin ferocity, bowed down low before me and, raising my right ankle slightly, kissed my foot. I was not sure how to receive this generous tribute from a wrinkled fifty-year-old and so smiled at him and shook his hand. "Tilly" spoiled it rather by telling me later, "Oh, that is traditional, especially if they think you are an older person."

After 4.30 p.m. the four of us left Charra for the topmost plateau, Ato Mamo clomping along at the head in his Wellington boots. Soon we came to the cliff bottom and there followed a long, meandering ascent up a narrow, tree-shrouded path floored with large boulders; about 1,000 feet was climbed up this dank lane before we emerged two hours later on the dewy grasslands at the top. If it had not been for three young men whom Ato Mamo enlisted as porters, and a break for ten cents' worth of *muz*, or sweet bananas, which were carried up from the village, two of us would have been quite distressed. By dusk, however, as we pitched a tent before an immense panorama, we were able to say that we had climbed from the gorge floor to the highest uplands, at a height of 7,900 feet, in one exhausting day. As Ato Mamo, warily at first, spooned up his mess tin of curried rice, the sun set in the direction of the Sudan and the gorge below us was filled with puffs of grey cloud.

The next day was spent wholly in investigating the sprawling settled area of Cao and Asandabo on the edge of the plateau. The interest it provided was almost entirely human and hardly at all architectural, as our hopes of an extant Italian fort were to be unfulfilled. The people seemed very interested in us and were most welcoming. White men were not unknown here, but rare: Cao is very much at the end of the line, the furthest point on a long road north from Gedo. It is rather ambiguously called "Cow Market" on Jessen's map.

After a bitterly cold night—a sharp contrast to the bottom of the gorge—Ato Mamo, quite properly, was to lead us first to the house of the Balambaras of Cao—the chief of the settlement. After a long march along the cliff edge in the chill of a damp, misty morning, we approached some *tukuls* clustered around a large, open green. Dark shapes glanced shyly out at us from doorways. Ato Mamo seemed well known to them all. He was something of a local hero as we had discovered. Earlier on the previous day he had pulled a crumpled letter from a pocket. It was in Amharic and German. Ato Berhanu had explained that four years ago a young man who was trying to go down the Nile on a raft was wrecked below the Guder River mouth. It was Ato Mamo who had found him half-drowned in a deserted hut and had virtually carried him the dozen miles or so up to safety in Cao. This, we believed, was the young Austrian sculptor whose raft had become waterlogged and finally smashed in a severe rapid at Melka Yekatel in 1964. Ato Mamo still treasured the letter from Europe thanking him and praising his humanity and determination.

The Balambaras' house was recognisably the seat of the Lord of the Manor: a cube of wood and mud, topped by the ubiquitous corrugated iron, flanked by eucalyptus trees and a number of subsidiary round *tukuls*. We paused outside while the occupants were told of our approach. The Balambaras was out, but his two sons came to welcome us—Aberra Duferra in "western" dress, short Wellington boots over nylon socks, belted khaki shorts and shirt, and Kassa Duferra in sandals and *shamma*—the former a student at Ambo, the latter managing his father's estate. They ushered us into a narrow space to the right of the door surrounded by wooden rails, a kind of verandah. Three home-made chairs were produced and a stool for Ato Mamo, who began to explain the purpose of our visit. This was easy since Aberra Duferra knew some English, and he quickly took the little bottles and phials away to be filled. Meanwhile, Roger Chapman put the fruits of a fortnight's Army Medical Course to some use on the growing crowd of sick and wounded. Again, however, among the simple cuts and sores there were liver disorders, Leishmaniasis, malaria and so on. He took care to explain that in almost all cases he could not cure, but only ease, the trouble.

Presently we were summoned inside into a dark, fly-ridden interior. The Duferras were clearly of some substance, for there was a metal Army bed in the room and a gallery of small, formalised photo-portraits stuck irregularly on the mud walls. There was no light, except from the doorway, and in the next room a group of women squatted round a smoky, central fire. A wooden bowl was brought in and water in a gourd, which a boy poured over each of our hands in turn. Then on a circular table between us was placed, inevitably, Ethiopia's national dish, her *only* dish, it is fair to say—*injera* and *wat*.

For some of us on the Expedition this dish always presented a social stumbling-block; others ate it and enjoyed it, even when it was covered in *ber-ber* sauce. Although London has a large number of national restaurants from Polynesian to Polish, I do not feel that an Ethiopian Restaurant there would ever hold its place with a menu which contained virtually one dish only, and that one an acquired taste of a very bizarre kind. Every day the well-to-do Ethiopian eats *injera* and *wat*, sometimes several times. Hot or cold, it is breakfast, lunch, tea and supper. The *injera* is a flaccid, grey substance, looking like some synthetic foam rubber, which comes in large sheets, or folded like a heavy napkin. Made from *teff*, or *Eragrostis abyssinica*, a kind of millet, it is laid before him on a special, circular, basketwork table. Then bowls of hot, spiced meats in a highly-seasoned sauce are spread upon it. This is the *wat*. One has to pluck pieces from the *injera*, as one might tear up a disintegrating old bath mat, and seize chunks of *wat* in the fingers with it. The *wat* can be made from chicken, mutton or beef, but in whatever way the Ethiopian gastronome might enliven it with clots of sour cream, or follow it up with slices of raw beef, the basic *injera* and *wat* is as unvarying as the afternoon thunderstorms in August. I do not see the Londoner tucking into this with much enthusiasm, even in trendy N.W. 11.

Gingerly I started on it. All eyes watched us. Luckily, Roger and Mansel seemed to quite like the stuff. "Mmmm!" I said, nodding and widening my eyes, and reached out and tore off another large portion. I brought it to my mouth, glanced quickly round, and then, in a manner reminiscent of darkest school days, quickly palmed it into a trouser pocket. The most welcome offering a few moments later was a glass of fresh milk, followed by another glass. This lowered the temperature of the roof of the mouth, scorified by the *ber-ber* sauce, to something nearer 98.4°. As soon as was decently possible, I rose from the table and gave the Balambaras' wife one of the strings of beads that John Blashford-Snell had thoughtfully brought from England. We had a large bag of broken, unfashionable necklaces and earrings, discards from the jewel boxes of numerous elderly relatives—and all of them went down very well with chiefs' wives, many of whom wore precious little besides. Mrs. Mamo, down in Charra, was already sporting a string of hideous paste that we had bestowed on her on the way up. So breakfast passed, our second that day, and was followed by the return of our bottles and phials suitably filled.

Afterwards a large entourage moved out with us and across the fields towards the Italian fort. After so long a walk it proved disappointing for almost all trace of it had disappeared. It had occupied a commanding position over the Carsa valley and had presumably been built between 1936 and 1941. Two or three large gun emplacements remained, some stone flooring and fragments of metal and glass. No walls still stood: presumably all had been cannibalised for other buildings. We investigated a twenty-foot tunnel in the face of the escarpment for an alleged "doorway", but it contained only large, black spiders, two of which we collected in an old Three Nuns tin. We ambled across the fort, said by one old Ethiopian to have once housed a thousand men, until we came to the point where the River Carsa pours off the tableland into the valley beyond. The following day in the boats we were to pass its junction with the Abbai.

✳ ✳ ✳

Then the homeward trek began. Before reaching the village we deviated to a group of *tukuls* over some fields to the right of us. Here lay a very sick woman, we were told. The long procession, three of us with what was now a long train of curious villagers, filed silently between fields of maize and *teff*. Five lean and suspicious hounds of no predominant breed lay sprawled in the dust outside a *tukul*; goats, lambs and chickens picked their way about amongst them. Inside the massive wooden portals all was darkness. Most of our entourage pressed in with us. In what looked like a miniature four-poster squatted the patient. An even older, shaven-headed woman, shrunk and wizened in her dirty shift, leaned against an interior post. She coughed bronchially and pressed a corner of her sleeve to a suppurating eye.

It was difficult to see how any human being could stay healthy long in such stench, smoke and darkness; but a little child skipped about happily and fetched a gourd of clear water for Roger to administer a palliative. From her moans and wheezes and after a few interpreted questions it seemed that the woman on the bed had tuberculosis. Perhaps it was a monstrous deception to give her two aspirin tablets in a cup of water, and yet at the time it was the only humane gesture that we could make. Later we advised that in this clear, highland atmosphere, it would be more beneficial if, on the right days, she were brought out to sit in the air and sunshine in the corner of a field.

✻ ✻ ✻

In the centre of Cao there occurred a sudden, torrential, half-hour rainstorm. We sheltered in a shop and examined the poverty of its contents. I bought a *tej*¹ bottle for fifty cents. Biro pencils were ten cents each, cheaper than in England. Later Roger discovered why: they were used. The rain battered on the corrugated iron and from the doorway we could fill our drinking mugs with raindrops in two and a half minutes. Soon it abated and we went off to look at the Coptic Christian church, St. George's. The old church had been burnt down the previous year and the new structure, almost finished, stood on its circular mound in the usual grove of eucalyptus, two hundred yards from the village green, gleaming with new corrugated iron and fresh wattle-and-daub walls. No priests yet inhabited the cabins which ringed the inside edge of the outer enclosure, but the Balambaras, who had just joined us, was clearly proud of the reconstruction.

To see us off from the village green was a group of men including one of those picturesque characters in which Ethiopia abounds: an old man, swathed in a white *shamma*, and under his shiny, plastic topee, a profusion of iron-grey curls and, quite rare, a full, flowing grey beard.

"*Barba grande* " he exclaimed, proudly twirling his whiskers and patting my stubbly cheek. Anyone over forty is likely to break out in pidgin Italian in Ethiopia.

"*La mia barba e più grande che la vostra!* " he shrieked, vastly amused. His cronies gathered round what was obviously the fount of village wit.

"*Ogni cosa ha il suo tempo,*" I countered—"everything matures in time"—and we each stood there tugging at the other's beard and laughing. Ato Kebeda, as he was called, told us a lot about the Italian occupation, and about his long life and many children. His wild eyes

Ato Kebeda, "the fount of village wit", surrounded by some of the other elders of Cao.

radiated a puckish sense of fun, and he spoke in a mixture of Amharic and Italian. "You have much knowledge, but I am seventy and have wisdom," he said. After much handshaking and a solemn photograph—a camera will invariably reduce the merriest Ethiopian to a stiff, unsmiling statue—we began to march off.

"*Viva la Libertà!*" he shouted, raising his topee, "*E buon viaggio!*"

"*Così fan tutte!*" Mansel shouted back hopefully.

Over the wet fields we sloshed, behind Ato Mamo, headed now for the deep river gorge far away. We stumbled down the steep path to Charra and camped on the village green that had been the surgery the day before. Soon Roger was busy again, applying plasters and giving out the final tablets. Supper was taken before a crowd of forty or so.

"A poor house tonight," I said.

"Yes. Well, it's the television that's killing it," said Mansel.

Unfortunately the last moments of supper were marred by a village dispute. We believe it arose from some sort of challenge to Ato Mamo's authority, possibly in connection with people pressing too close upon us. At any rate, he laid down the mess tin of curried beef we had given him, his face flushed with anger, and rounded upon a young man nearby. Later, as the argument flickered on in the darkness outside our tent, he came in to squat with us, and was later joined by his young son and his wife, resplendent in her beads. She had brought a bowl of *injera* and so we all dipped into it with varying degrees of enthusiasm. Later still, Ato Mamo summoned the village scribe and wrote a letter of complaint to the Balambaras of Cao about the insubordination he had suffered. Soon his wife left, but he and his son, forsaking their *tukul*, curled up on the grass to guard us with an old carbine.

At about 6.15 a.m. a stately figure walked slowly across the green and mounted a large rock. From the folds of his *shamma* he took a horn and blew a muted, monotonous reveille. Despite hopes of a stealthy departure, there were soon a dozen or so silent, dark faces watching us dress and make tea. They came like courtiers to Louis XIV's levée, and stood or squatted on their haunches, enthralled at the ease with which we made fire from little white fragments.

Eventually, we packed up and marched away. In three hours we were stumbling back down the last terrace into the oven-like heat that hangs over the Abbai at midday, and into the Forward Base Camp at the Guder River, which John Blashford-Snell had already struck.

Amidst the bustle that preceded embarkation we sensed a tension in the air. During the night there had been an alarming rise of fifteen feet in the river level. Just before dawn, however, it had all fallen away again and was still falling. John Blashford-Snell was most anxious to leave as soon as we had returned. Half an hour before we came in, three figures had appeared on the far bank opposite the camp. Binoculars had revealed them as Chris Bonington and two guides, and they were brought over in an Assault Boat. When movements were being planned at Base Camp in Debre Marcos, Chris Bonington had intended to walk to Mabil with a re-supply team and join the boats there, but after they had sailed from Shafartak he had decided that to get the best Press coverage he must join them as soon as possible. Anticipating that our departure time from the Guder might have to be advanced, John had firmly vetoed this over the radio, but Chris had set off all the same.

After a courageous forced march of thirty-five rough miles in two days, he had reached the river.

But it was sobering for us to realise that if Ato Mamo had not paused on the outskirts of Charra for about an hour whilst his wife fetched his pot of breakfast *injera* and he ate it, we might have arrived at the river early enough for us all to have gone from the Guder camp before Chris could reach it. As it was, he was fortunate enough to strike the river at exactly the right point; but if we had sailed he could not have crossed the river and would have had to retrace his steps to Debre Marcos.

NOTES:

[1]   *Tej*: A tasty and potent drink, akin to mead; made of honey and water, and fermented with the leaves and bitter roots of the *saddo* (*Rhamnus saddo*) or *gesho* (*Rhamnus pauciflorus*) trees.

Chapter Eight
INTO SHANKILLA COUNTRY

MABIL is a settlement 2,000 feet below the actual plateau, some four or five miles north of the Abbai, and it probably grew in importance because the river immediately below it is easily fordable in the dry season, and traders coming from Wallega to Gojjam would find the track up from Melka Mabil[1] to Gumar, once a flourishing slave market, much more manageable by loaded mules than any other nearby route out of the gorge.

No fewer than twenty of the river party were to take part in the next climb up this track onto the plateau. Nobody seemed to have a clear picture of Mabil, but our imagination raised it to the status of a flourishing market and orders for things were hopefully placed by those who preferred to stay in the camp. The prospect of beer and perhaps Italian food was pleasing; the gorge was becoming a bit claustrophobic and most of us were keen to escape for twenty-four hours or so.

One of our re-supply columns led by Gage Williams had just passed through Burie, Telele, Gumar and Mabil on the way to the ford, and two of its members had stayed up in Mabil itself. It was not so surprising then that a day or two after our arrival downstream of Melka Mabil we received a visit from three or four local dignitaries. At their head came Ato Bekele Negash, Chief of Mabil, and he was hailed by John Blashford-Snell as an important District Governor. Important he looked, tall and grizzled, with khaki army trousers, an impressive Sam Browne and a pistol in a leather holster. We had contrived a sort of garden seat from the trappings of a pack-mule and placed it by a fire in the centre of our encampment. Over it was fixed Spencer's large surveyor's umbrella. Ato Bekele and his three aides were much impressed and took their places. They were introduced to a number of us, including, of course, "Tilly".

"This is Lieutenant Telahoun Makonnen of the Imperial Ethiopian Navy."

"Navy?" said Ato Bekele, "Navy? What is that?"

"We go in boats on the sea," said "Tilly".

"What is this 'sea'?" one of them asked, perplexed.

"A Great Water," said "Tilly", waving his arm in the general direction of the Red Sea, "greater than the Abbai."

"Oh! You mean Lake Tana," said Ato Bekele, nodding understandingly.

They drank their tea thirstily and expressed much interest in the Expedition. The chief had presented the traditional gift of a live, white kid goat to the re-supply column and he invited us all up to Mabil to help to eat it. There would be feasting, singing and dancing. Rosy visions of a soft break in the ordinary riverside routine appeared before us.

We accepted this, and, in return, invited him for a ride in an Assault Boat. It was almost incredible to Ato Bekele that he should pass over the dreaded Abbai in a watercraft. He was soon able to overcome his first apprehensions, and began laughing. The boat wheeled and planed and demonstrated its mastery over the river. The chief was so pleased that he took up his rifle and loosed off a round, which passed narrowly over Gage Williams' right shoulder. When they all returned to the camp, the chief said that he would call his people together and tell them of the Great Abbai Expedition, and of its great leader, in the house of whose god-parents the Emperor himself, he had been told, had lodged whilst in exile in England. With many friendly farewells they left.

✳ ✳ ✳

Two days later the great excursion began. Our camp was over two miles below the ford where the track began, but we were too large a party for the boats to take all of us upstream as fuel conservation was so important, so, whilst some rode in state, nine of us had to walk along the north bank.

And so, with the melodious, almost human, notes of the boo-boo shrike in our ears, we stumbled and squirmed up the scrub-covered edges of the river, whilst two boatloads of outgoing stores and the few select idlers churned slowly past us.

On the bank at the now submerged ford was a crowd of mixed Amhara and Shankilla porters who had come down with their mules and donkeys from Mabil: a motley crowd in shirts, shorts, *shammas* and animal skins, some with old army jackets, and most carrying spears. Their presence had been prearranged, for not only was Nigel Marsh taking up a load of medical supplies to treat the Mabil sick, but, of course, one of the main functions of the re-supply column was to carry out of the gorge preserved zoological specimens and unwanted stores, such as empty fuel cans and parachutes. Gage Williams was beginning his arduous four-day overland journey back to Main Base at Debre Marcos.

Soon after we landed, a scene of unexampled confusion broke out. Here were loads enough, and here were donkeys and mules, assembled for this purpose. None need be overloaded, none unemployed. And yet the cacophony of argument and bickering that slowly grew, made us wonder whether the porters intended to carry our gear at all, and some of us set off independently. Repetitive arguments over money dragged on and our three Amharic-speaking members showed amazing patience in the face of such obstructionism. Clearly, Ato Bekele's address to his people about the greatness of the Great Abbai Expedition had fallen on stony ground.

Eventually some sort of agreement was made with those of us who stayed the course, and the porters, squabbling and bawling at each other over bits of rattan, and occasionally brought up short by an exasperated order, sorted out the various loads and strapped them on their long-suffering animals. Finally, at noon—exactly the wrong time of day—the whole column was ready to march up the four or five miles or so of stony track to Mabil.

The sun was merciless, and shade from the thin, seasonal vegetation was patchy. Each of us plodded on, fighting the pain of his own discomfort and exhaustion. The path on the ridge wound on and up relentlessly, as we each passed others slumped against trees, oblivious of the settling flies. As I rounded a corner, I was alarmed to find, blocking the path, the body of John Blashford-Snell, stretched out prostrate on the ground.

"Ah! There you are," he said, struggling to his feet and dusting himself down, "just having a breather!"

We were now spread out over a mile or two, and I think that traffic had been so light that he had been able to go to sleep.

Roger Chapman apparently arrived first with the leading muleteers, and the rest of the column, weary and dehydrated, some with packs, some without, staggered into Mabil in ones and twos. What sort of Mecca did we find? What promised town with shops and busy lanes?

Soon I saw cultivated fields and the edge of the settlement: then the burnt-out church on the hill, marked on some maps as a Mission Station and once in the care of a Roman Catholic priest; finally, round a further bend, was Mabil itself—a grubby cluster of five flea-bitten *tukuls*, standing among patches of maize, and over the hill, beyond this Amhara hamlet, a similar sprinkling of Shankilla *tukuls*—only a few people, listless and unwelcoming, flies, dogs, no shops, no shade, and worst of all, no water. The spring on which these people depended was a ten-minute walk away, at the bottom of a narrow, reed-filled valley, and a tiny dribble of rather warm water was all it produced. Our disappointment was profound. Although the two who had been camped here for three or four days had made friends and found it pleasant enough, the river party found only the breathtaking view over the gorge some solace for the poverty of Mabil.

However, the goat was there, tied by a hind leg to a tuft of grass, and seemingly aware of its fate from the noise it made. Soon two villagers slit its throat before us and silenced its anguished bleats. We constructed a temporary camp among some maize on a little hill. John went into conference with Ato Bekele, and many others went off to try their hand at amateur anthropology among the Shankilla, the first negroes we had come across in Ethiopia.

We found them, by contrast, most friendly, and hospitable in a manner tinged with a becoming shyness. Many photographs were taken, especially of a few fascinating young girls, bare-breasted and beaded, who were anointing each other's tightly-curled hair with a rich, greasy, brown ochre. They wore what amounted to the bottom half of a bikini, with a tasselled fringe, numerous brass bracelets beaten from old cartridge cases, and their blue-black bodies were hatched all over with markings in white ash, as if in readiness for a mammoth noughts and crosses session. However much the toothless old ladies hovered around, laughing and chattering like sparrows, it was their granddaughters who were the centre of attention.

As darkness fell, the boiled goat was produced on its bed of *injera*, borne up to us with all the ceremony accorded to the Boar's Head at a Cutlers' Feast. By the light of two candles set in the grass, twenty of us in a large circle picked at and munched it, whilst Corporal Henry, who had been entirely accepted by the community, amused the children with repeated renderings of "Old Macdonald Had a Farm" and other ballads.

After a good round of traditional English songs, we called on the villagers to give us some of theirs as we all sat together round a blazing fire. A farmer called Banzo was the life and soul of the party and led a few women and children in a song and dance or two, though with some reluctance; eventually he cast a slight blight on the proceedings by demanding *santims* for their efforts.

At all events, John thanked the chief's wife with a necklace and distributed colourful baubles to all the other dancers. The idea of giving out beads to natives may be viewed by some progressives with abhorrence, as a patronising piece of Victorianism; but it was practically demonstrated that they gave immense pleasure to these relatively simple people, and in any case we did not have any IUDs or sacks of fertiliser with us.

Next morning there was a repetition of the previous day's scene on the river bank. Some of us arose rather grumpily, having found overnight that a parachute is not waterproof; but our dispositions were sunny in comparison with some of the gathering muleteers. Haggling, choleric outbursts, and frustrations ensued. Should the donkeymen be paid before they left, or at Gumar? If you pay before, you risk a defection; if you pay at the end, you risk an increased demand above the agreed price. It is, perhaps, safest to work on the "deposit down, balance at end" principle, if it can be properly explained. Furthermore, Ato Bekele, who had been keen to show our zoologists some interesting caves in his area, was now prevaricating and withholding his guides—on the specious grounds that he was unwilling to reveal to *ferenji* the whereabouts of this useful retreat, in case his people had once again, as in 1936-41, to shelter there from an enemy. In the event, we suborned two of his men as guides and made a great killing of bats in these caves on the following days. Gradually our tireless interpreters got some sense across and loads were strapped on. Gage Williams got away to Gumar at 11 a.m.—"a course record", he claimed.

The rest of us, who wanted some porterage for our packs and photographic equipment on the way down to Melka Mabil, had less luck. Ato Bekele, who was no District Governor, apparently, but merely

Atbia Dagna of Mabil, or a sort of Sheriff, dispensing petty justice, was turning sour on us. He asked three dollars and ten rounds of .22 ammunition for half a dozen men and boys, and when we accepted this, he raised it to four dollars.

Once again, the sun stood almost vertical at noon, before we set off back down the track. Gage's party had not left without some embarrassment over jerrycans, of which there should have been twenty, but only eighteen had been found. Eventually, one was flushed out of a *tukul*, but we left without the other—a priceless replacement for the local gourd—and also a water bottle, a shirt, and a personal acquisition by Ato Bekele to complete his sheriff image—a second leather pistol holster.

✣ ✣ ✣

The Emperor Haile Selassie I's style and title is King of Kings, Elect of God, Conquering Lion of the Tribe of Judah. One of the Kings of which he is King lives today in Asosa, in the far west of the Empire, near the Sudanese frontier: this is the King of the Shankilla, who exerts a loose control over the lower reaches of the Great Abbai on whose banks the jet-black, often blue-black, Shankilla live.

These people have a tradition of subjection to the proud mountain Amhara, and for centuries, until quite recently, were habitually enslaved by them. "Shankilla" means, simply, "black man" in Amharic, and can still be used pejoratively by one Amhara chaffing another, slightly darker-skinned.

We came across these long-suffering and hospitable people in four places: at Mabil—already touched upon; at Gambela, south of the Abbai about a mile west of the Didessa confluence; at Shawe Bokup, north of the Abbai and opposite Gambela; and at Sirba. They lived in a scattering of *tukuls* often some distance from their maize plantations. Gambela and Shawe Bokup were small villages, Sirba very much larger and more regularly planned. No roads reached any of them, and the nearest town with school, hospital and dry-weather road, was Mendi, about forty miles away to the south. It was a day's march away for the villagers, or two days with donkeys. Sirba had its airstrip and was visited for two or three days twice annually by a Swedish mission with medical supplies. Two young men, Tadesse and Balo, stay behind and teach, but were on holiday when we arrived. The population of the area was roughly half Christian, half Moslem, and Arabic was understood in places, as well as Shankillinya.

When we reached Sirba there was a crowd of between thirty and forty men and boys on the bank. Nigel Sale and the local chief had done well. There the porters were, squatting on their haunches in shirts and shorts, spears and rifles pointing upwards. The chief, a listless, sloe-eyed man, was given the customary joy-ride in the Assault Boat, but did not seem much impressed. When he returned to the bank we tried to encourage him to organise his men into some sort of a queue to begin the porterage. Unfortunately, the first load was a large, green, trunk-like box of zoological materials. A spindly-legged Shankilla bent down and pulled at the handles. He promptly keeled over onto his head and then, with a gesture of infinite suffering, indicated that his frail constitution was not up to this sort of thing. The chief lazily bent down and tried to lift one end. He straightened up and shook his head sadly. He said something quietly in his own language. Ashenna, a bright ten-year-old by his side, who had been a boarder at the school in Mendi, put it into Amharinya. Tadesse Wolde gave us the verdict: "He says these things are not to be carried by human beings." Laboriously we demonstrated that two men could easily lift the box, but he was adamant. In desperation, Martin Romilly stepped forward. "Look!" he said, "it's not as heavy as all that," and he bent down and raised the box to his chest single-handed. But these men were clearly not going to be shamed into action, and the chief refused to pressure them. Tigre Bishoura, himself a Shankilla, said, "These people on this side of the river are a little bit lazy." In fact, it is no part of the life of a Shankilla to lift heavy things. He may occasionally work in the fields, but the carrying of bundles of kindling wood or of gourds of water is essentially women's work. Men spend the day sitting in the shade under the eaves of their *tukuls*, arguing, spitting, taking snuff, whilst the women suckle the children, make string, or, kneeling on the floor, grind millet between two stones, their pendulous breasts swinging to and fro. It was said that when the Swedes arrive by plane twice a year, the local people refuse to carry their medical stores to the Mission House.

Eventually, Derek Yalden and Hilary King, burdened with their own rucksacks, picked up the zoological box themselves and set off to the airstrip. I looked for signs of amazement or self-consciousness

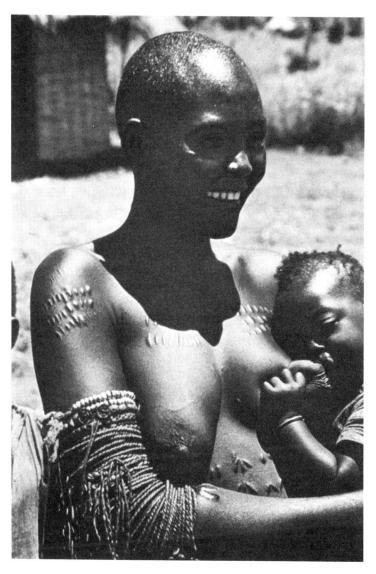

As we moved west towards the Sudan we came to regions inhabited by the Shankilla.

among the reluctant porters, but as they stood and stared I could see only a slightly insolent torpor in their expressions. Repeated efforts to induce individuals to help with lighter loads produced only an abrupt negative—the unmistakable Shankilla word for "No!" is "Ba!", short and sharp. We had old, slightly dented jerrycans, which they would have loved, and sheets of canvas, wooden boarding—all sorts of inducements; but they would not risk damaging their status in the eyes of the village by coming forward to carry things and, in fact, negotiations soon collapsed and they drifted slowly home, with their arms in W-formation, gripping the spears or rifles that they slung across their shoulders like a yoke.

As the days went by, we found that the solution lay not in these indolent men, nor in their over-worked womenfolk, but in the children. For empty tins, for sardines, for sweets, an army of small boys would make light of a heap of stores. But on this auspicious evening our high spirits were damped by the prospect of humping all the expedition kit, as well as our own, over these two and a half miles of undulating track. Most of us made two or three journeys that night and a further one or two between 5.30 and 8.30 the next morning.

While they were unwilling to do any deals involving physical exertion, they were quick to take up the chance of sale or barter. At Shawe Bokup we had bought a bottle of undrinkable *araki* for fifty cents and ten cigarettes, and at Gambela two eggs had cost ten cents (4d.); but it was clear that they did not much care for the green dollar bills that we had passed in exchange for the attractive snuff boxes, covered in monitor lizard or crocodile skin. Much pointing to the Amharic script and cries of "Ityopia" and "Haile Selassie" had failed to convince them of the worth of the paper money. Even *santims* were despised, and the only coin recognised by the Shankilla was the *shillinga*, the silver fifty-cent piece, rare in Addis Ababa, and very like our own shilling or five New Pence.

Far more sought after as currency was ammunition, and we soon worked to a scale of values based upon rounds of surplus .22: one round purchased six maize cobs; a snuff box could be had for three rounds, or a chicken for four. At Gambela a round would fetch fifty cents or one *shillinga* (1s. 8d.), though at Sirba the market hardened a little and it took five rounds to acquire four *shillingas*.[2] Many of us had only a few short hours in Shankilla country before flying away up to the plateau again. So, like middle-aged ladies dropped briefly by their cruise liner at Sorrento, we conducted a certain amount of frantic haggling for souvenirs, and prices at first were high. With the Ethiopian dollar then standing at 3s. 4d., we bought their small sheath knives, worn rather awkwardly on the left upper arm, for between ten shillings and seventeen shillings. Three-legged stools, carved from a single log section, cost around thirteen shillings for the most part, though at the end of our stay Doc West picked one up for 1s. 8d. For those of us who lingered on in Sirba, a goat, for immediate consumption, was sold for 16s. 8d, and a few cooking tins. Much of our time was spent in the slow processes of the market place, and although our patience was often on the point of wilting, Tadesse kept the protracted dealings going and was reviled by the men of the village for doggedly keeping up the price of ammunition to the bitter end.

One of the most open-handed of Shankilla chiefs was Ato Chejigu of Shawe Bokup. He and his five wives lived in a spacious *tukul* set in its own palisaded yard. The *tukul* consisted of two concentric rings of posts, pierced by two staggered doorways. Goats and chickens picked their way in and out, mainly in the narrow space between the two rings. Inside there were four or five massive wooden pillars supporting the dark thatch above. Across the back was stretched a partition of sackcloth, over which from time to time peeped a shy wife. Stools, gourds and large iron dishes lay scattered about. Two or three wives, their black bodies glistening in the firelight, squatted by a stone hearth, making coffee. The feet of naked children pattered on the hard mud floor.

Ato Chejigu invited five of us in, and stools were set round. A few old men were already seated there smoking. "Tilly" had difficulty in understanding their Amharic and so we fell back on well-tried ploys: Peter O'Mahony combed forward a luxuriant shock of hair and, waving his arms about and crying "Ambessa! Ambessa!", did a passable imitation of a lion. This broke the ice, after which I kept them interested by methodically filling a pipe. A wife brought a glowing ember from the fire, held in a coiled leaf, and after producing a pall of blue smoke, I handed the pipe to Ato Chejigu, who puffed approvingly for a few moments before passing it on to three or four rather apprehensive cronies. I subsequently tried a large, water-cooled pipe of theirs, but I found the tobacco dry and coarse and the mouthpiece, which was like the neck of a sherry bottle, difficult to draw on.

When these innocent exchanges began to flag, Ato Chejigu called for coffee. We rinsed our hands ceremonially as water was poured over them into a bowl. Presently a kettle of coffee was taken to the chief, who rose and, muttering some formula to himself, spilled a little of it over the central post and then again over the feet of the doorposts. Then tiny cups, flower-patterned and handleless, were filled with the black fluid and given round. With pleasurable anticipation I raised mine to my lips. We were all thirsty, and I still had the nasty tang of home-grown tobacco in my mouth. I took a sip—to find that it was heavily salted. This, apparently, is done to bring out the coffee flavour, but it seemed to me to kill the taste.

Next, "Tilly" told us, he was going to offer us beer. Fleetingly, a glorious vision of a clear pint of cold keg bitter passed through my mind. The reality, of course, was a toothglass full of thick *talla*, a crude and unfiltered brew, looking like Ovaltine and full of pieces of grit. Though everyone put on a brave face the taste was revolting. There seemed to be no respite from noxious drinks, for Ato Chejigu, in his determination to please, now produced an old lemonade bottle filled with *araki*, a fiery liquor reminiscent of turpentine, which we drank from small glasses. Every time we managed to empty one, it was refilled by an assiduous wife. There was much hilarity among the younger men of his household and the *tukul* now reached the noise level of the average western cocktail party.

I gave earrings to the chief's wives, and some sachets of instant coffee, and cigarettes. He reciprocated with a scrawny brown hen. Goodwill abounded.

Before we marched back to the river, the chief and his wives lined up like a tennis team for a farewell photograph. They were a gay spectacle. The Shankilla woman wears a short skirt generally slung low under a protuberant, frequently pregnant, abdomen. Bound round five or six inches of her upper arms are coils of brown twine with pendant tassels. On one side a small knife in a decorated sheath is attached. Round her neck are long strands of red, yellow and white beads, and she wears bracelets and anklets made of brass loops. She may have a nose-ring, and will invariably have two incised aluminium earrings shaped like French horns. Very often a sleeping baby will be strapped on her back. Perhaps the most unusual feature is the marking of her body: on shoulder blades, above her breasts and on the shoulder muscle itself, are rows of small cicatrices, painfully made by rubbing salt or earth into small cuts. One laughing mother in Gambela risked being carried off as British Government property, for her stomach was covered in this way with symbols like the old War Department arrows.

✳ ✳ ✳

But it was at Sirba that we made the closest study of the Shankilla, for we lived for a week on the fringes of their village. As I was Air Quartermaster at the landing strip, and had to supervise the flight out of all kit and personnel, I was enabled to stay there longer than anyone else. Four times a day for two days the Beaver would be brought skilfully onto the sloping airstrip by either Alan Calder or Richard Grevatte-Ball; it would roar off again at full throttle, downhill over the bumpy grass with its payload of about 800 lb. It circled round, buzzed low over our little camp, sending crowds of Shankilla spectators shrieking into the bushes, and turned away for Ghimbi or Debre Marcos.

On the second day the U.S. Mapping Mission helicopter duly arrived, and, after making one run to Ghimbi with seven men and their kit, returned for the Assault Boats. As we were wondering if it would, as suggested, lift all four boats nested one inside another, we saw the Huey rise up over the distant riverbank with two separate boats dangling below it, like the traditional stork bearing new-born twins. Apparently, moving at speeds as low as 20 mph., it expended its fuel more quickly than was reckoned and had to park the boats in the wilderness and go on to Ghimbi to fill its tanks.

Unhappily, there was no more fuel available in Ghimbi and there now began a chapter of misfortunes which led to some of us being marooned in Sirba for eight days. First of all, the next day was a Sunday and the day after was an Ethiopian holiday, so it seemed unlikely that a lorry-load of fuel for the helicopter could be moved from Addis Ababa to Ghimbi before the middle of the following week. However, the Beaver came in just once again to evacuate John Fletcher and Chris Bonington, needed for Phase 2, and "Johnny" Johnson, and Mansel Spratling, who was by now in rather poor physical condition. It brought in Lt.-Colonel Roger West and radio operator David Fisher to join Colin Chapman, Tadesse and me as the residual Sirba garrison.

Our first day was spent in moving camp, with the aid of a squad of village boys enlisted by Tadesse, from the Abbai to an idyllic woodland glade on the edge of the village of Sirba and by the banks of the modest Sirba River, where a natural swimming pool afforded some relief after a longish portage. Then we heard—just after we had bought a goat for the larder—that the helicopter would, in fact, arrive the next day, a day early. So we moved the next morning in good time to the hot airstrip, only to learn on the first radio schedule that the helicopter would, after all, be delayed twenty-four hours because of continued fuel difficulties: Keith Morgan-Jones, in Addis Ababa, had secured the fuel and eventually got a lorry from the Ministry of Mines. Now Keith is a big man, and when he opened the lorry door it came off in his hand. However, it was by no means Keith's doing when the first drum of helicopter fuel that was lifted onto the back of the lorry fell through the floorboards. It was disconcerting for him to find, too, that the steering wheel came off the top of the steering column. Closer inspection, which revealed that bald portions of the tyres were covered with patches of cardboard fixed on somehow with tacks, suggested that perhaps some other lorry ought to be acquired. Thus, the helicopter flight was further delayed.

A safer lorry was provided by the good offices, once more, of the Mapping Mission, but highway regulations precluded the driver taking it in one day further than Lechemti. On the following morning, he rose so late that he did not get the fuel to Ghimbi in time for any useful flight to be made that day… And so the drama slowly unfolded.

As we lay in the perforated shade of the trees by the landing strip, the air was filled with the whine and buzz of innumerable insects. The pace of life slackened, and despite a daily swim in the Sirba we grew scruffier. Our only violent activity was an occasional rush, Robinson Crusoe style, to the top of a nearby hillock at the imagined sound of a helicopter.

Later in the day we lit the excellent Volcano kettle and soon sparks and blue smoke were roaring out of its mouth. We lay on our bedrolls and enjoyed the cool of evening and a mug of sweet tea. As Colin slowly cranked the handle of the A13 set, the flat, Lancastrian voice of Corporal David Fisher was intoning the ever-changing, ever the same, incantations of the Royal Signals:

"Hallo, Charlie One. Hallo, Charlie One. This 'ere's Sulphur One. This 'ere's Sulphur One. Radio Chekhova…"

❉ ❉ ❉

The days of waiting may have been tedious, but our evenings were beguiled by the distant and seductive throbbing of native drums, which, siren-like, drew us into Sirba on one or two occasions. It began in the late afternoon as a single, slow drumbeat. As the brief dusk fell, a raucous pipe and a tin trumpet were added; a syncopated rhythm slowly developed, beaten out by a crowd of youths gathered round two great drums that lay on the ground in the centre of the village.

One evening, Roger West, David Fisher and I joined them. Some of the boys I recognised, and, grinning broadly, they went on hammering the drum, while others round them, heads nodding in concentration, blew out their weird polyphony. I noticed also in the crowd a beautiful young girl who had said "Hai! Hai!" and given me a piece of cucumber as I had strolled through the village a few evenings previously. She came dancing slowly up towards me, a spear in her right hand, her feet shuffling in time with the drum; her head and shoulders were still, her firm breasts bobbing slightly, as she came closer and then backed away again. Every so often she gave out shrill squeaks, "Hai! Hai!", alternating with a very provocative "Ts! Ts! Ts!" and a flashing white smile. I followed her movements with a contemporary western gyration that seemed somehow to fit quite well into this African scene.

The monotonous drum beat suddenly broke off: but when it resumed, she first moved to Roger and then to David, who each in turn jigged up and down to the amusement and applause of a growing crowd. Now it was a regular band playing, and a cacophonous but subtle sound, rather like a change in bell-ringing, was in progress. Under the bright moon, little Miss Cucumber continued her erotic approaches, her breasts dancing and her eyes flashing. Suddenly a Shankilla youth threw his arms about her, as if to show how it should be done, and with his hands on the small of her back, worked himself up and down in front of her unresponding body. After a few moments of this frank play, he stopped and motioned me to take over, which, casting off English reserve, I did. However, it was all rather disturbingly public, so I was not dismayed when she planted her spear in the ground near my left foot and we continued dancing at the earlier distance.

When a villager kills a leopard, we were told, they dance every night for a month. This must have occurred, for the following evening at the onset of darkness, drumming and then singing started again. This was a larger, more formal affair, with some forty or fifty people dancing around two great drums to a monotonous but tuneful chant, and the accompaniment of trumpet, tin whistle and sistrum. A single "caller" pranced round the drums, giving a solo lead to the chorus. Around him was a great circle of men with spears and rifles, advancing and retreating. Standing behind them was a larger, broken circle of small boys and women, undulating and stamping and moving forwards and backwards as the theme unfolded. The moon was their light, and their Chief, Ashenna senior, invited Colin and me to sit by him and watch. After a time, long wooden poles were inserted into two leather loops on the drums, and young women, inevitably, hoisted them on their shoulders, and the whole troupe, like a carnival procession, was moved to another quarter of the village, drums still thumping in transit. Colin and I strolled with it, fascinated.

Under the great white disc of the moon the black outlines of *tukuls* stood out sharply, and within them dim fires burning and the low voices of the elderly as they stretched on their hard beds. Occasionally a donkey strolled across the patch, and in the distance there was the horrible cry of a hyena. This, we felt, was nearer to the real Africa.

※ ※ ※

Two days later we learnt that the helicopter, now refuelled, had left Ghimbi and had found the boats abandoned in the hills five days before. Nothing in them had been touched. One of them, *Sandford*, was picked up and carried safely to Ghimbi. The Americans returned for the other, and were flying with it ten minutes away from the landing strip when "a malfunction in the lifting apparatus developed". Philip Shepherd looked through the "hell-hole" as the pilot cried, "There she goes! Bombs away!" and saw the Assault Boat plummeting down 700 feet into the jungle.

NOTES:

1 *Melka* = ford
2 A black market traffic in ammunition is conducted in these regions on a vast scale and is, of course, illegal: our sales were private and not under the aegis of the Expedition. They were confined to the weaker sort of .22.

Chapter Nine
A Treadmill in a Turkish Bath

THE most abiding memory of the Great Abbai Expedition for a number of its members will not be of plunging down a river through curling waves of water, but of slogging mechanically up an endless path, through waving elephant grasses, with about 70 lb of impedimenta slung from raw, sweat-soaked shoulders. This valiant contingent must be given its due recognition. With it must be included those who patiently cajoled unwilling mules and donkeys to share some of the problems of porterage with them, and those who flew numerous long sorties over unvarying miles of plateau and down into the hazardous gorge.

If we include in the tally the Ethiopian policemen who were attached to us, the Expedition numbered about seventy people. Of these, only about half were actively employed on the river for any considerable time. The dog wagged a long and useful tail. Many members fulfilled a vital role which kept them in Land-Rovers, in the Beaver, or on their two carefully powdered feet, rather than in boats.

These roles were manifold. At various times some of us had to undertake reconnaissances from the air or on foot; to deliver supplies to the boat party, again by air or on foot, with the occasional services of mules or donkeys; to carry material from the boats out of the gorge, by foot, mule or donkey; make game surveys of certain regions; and to act as a bank-side escort to boat parties, especially in white water areas. The duties of these members presented a set of very different problems to the groups concerned—among them, navigation, animal care, native relations, natural obstacles, climatic conditions, communication difficulties, and by no means least, sheer physical fatigue.

A great quantity of food and fuel was required for the thirty-two-man Group A to survive on the river for three weeks, and for four 40 hp engines to propel them some 280 miles. It was clear that such extra weight could not be carried from Shafartak to Sirba—for the first few days the Assault Boats would have been up to their gunwales, if indeed they had not foundered. The problem was complicated by the fact that as we progressed, our gradual loss of weight would be redressed by increases in the form of zoological and medical specimens.

So John had drawn up plans for a twofold solution: first, there would be overland parties, men and mules, who would bring supplies into the gorge and recover specimens and other surplus items from it. These would be brought by Land-Rover to the nearest points served by roads, where animals would be hired for the march to the river and back. Second, a string of points down the course of the Abbai was plotted at which the Beaver could parachute or drop consignments of food and fuel.

The preparations for the first two of the overland parties have been described in Chapter 3. The first, led by Garth Brocksopp, was not required to march out to the river; room was found in the Assault Boats for the five of them—Garth, Gavin Pike, Ian Carruthers and their two policemen—and they went with the river party as far as the mouth of the Guder. After two days there, they set off for Debre Marcos with about 75 lb per man—their own kit, rations and radio, plus a parachute used in the first air drop, exposed film, and our initial gorge specimens. They had so much gear, that in crossing the river Alec Murray's boat had to make two runs against the Abbai current.

The first day's climb out of the oven-like gorge was a severe strain. No one was properly acclimatised yet and Ian Carruthers felt it especially keenly. "It wasn't muscle exhaustion that was the problem," he said, "but the lack of oxygen supplied to the brain. At one point my pulse rate was between 160 and 172, and on one steep stage I was having occasional blackouts. One had to stop after twenty or thirty paces and have a good breather and a drink of water." And there was another problem: the paths went up ridges, where there were no streams. Dehydration, now, as frequently later, was a big factor in our lives. The water bottle, and the need to recharge it at every opportunity, assumed the importance of the syringe of insulin to the diabetic. Had it not been for some local people who were coming down to the river in the hope of medical attention, Garth's party would not have got themselves and their enormous packs up to Zemmi. "It was like being on a treadmill in a Turkish Bath," said Gavin.

At Zemmi the headman made the usual Ethiopian demand for some paper authorisation to explain the presence in his village of three *ferenji*. Garth's two policemen tried to appease him, but with no success. *Ferenji* are a liability to headmen. Whilst all the traditional offers of hospitality must still be made, *ferenji*, like paupers in sixteenth-century England, must be bundled off as quickly as possible to the next parish. They might be robbed or shot, and are the responsibility of the local chief whilst in his territory. So in country districts we tended to get moved on like buskers or arrested "in the interests of our own safety". Furthermore, a traveller in Ethiopia must have his documents. Without sheaves of Amharic covered in the purple ink of two or three rubber stamps, he is as conspicuous and vulnerable as a City business man waiting for the 8.10 on Godalming station with bowler hat, umbrella, but no trousers. Garth, however, had a trick up his sleeve. To meet just such an emergency as this, we had had fifty photostat copies made of an old document of mine, with printed superscription, lines of painfully hand-written Amharic and a large purple device at its foot. The fact that it proclaimed that the bearer (in all fifty cases) was one Richard Snailham, who had had his passport stolen in 1966, made no difference at all to the illiterate headman, who went away satisfied, nodding sagely.

Next day, Garth's party procured two donkeys and in the remainder of their thirty-five-mile march met with many of the normal experiences of the Ethiopian plateau—torrential late afternoon storms, guides for whom the destination was always "just over the next hill", pitifully diseased children, nocturnal visits from over-attentive hyenas, and even a blind abbot to show them round his Coptic church.

The second overland party to set off was led by Gage Williams; they had a somewhat easier time on their three-day march to Mabil. Dropped by Land-Rovers at Telele, they immediately fell in with an intensely pro-British Sub-district Governor, Ato Worku Morga. His father had been an officer in Brigadier Sandford's Habash[1] Guerrillas during the liberation, and the Brigadier had recently introduced Ato Worku to the Emperor and had been instrumental in getting him his local governorship. The name Sandford and his Habash patriots still worked magically in these parts.

Major H. W. Watkins, who served with this force, recounts an illuminating incident in which they were involved:

"In the River Omo region we stopped to watch an action between Patriots and Italians. The Emperor was seated in a camp chair with his entourage around him, while I stood some yards away. The Italians had an artillery piece going and without warning (most unkind) pushed one over at us. It was going to be very close, and I went to ground in a very smart and soldier-like fashion. The shell burst in the air about fifty yards behind, but dead on line. To my intense humiliation I looked round to find that I was the only one to have taken any notice at all: the Emperor was still seated and his party had stood fast. The Italians pushed about a dozen our way, same range, same line, and I also stood and pretended a nonchalance I was far from feeling, until Brigadier Sandford persuaded the Emperor to move."

When Gage had told Ato Worku that we had named one of our boats *Sandford*, he could do no wrong. The governor's house was placed at his group's disposal, ten horses (five pack animals, five to ride) were brought, and when Ato Worku toasted the group in *tej*, Gage replied with brandy—"English *tej*" he described it, with an inaccuracy that must have made Claude Charnotet wince. For breakfast they ate thirty eggs scrambled, and shortly afterwards rode off, surrounded by crowds of townsfolk, before whom, unfortunately, Corporal Henry's horse chose to bolt, throwing him unceremoniously into the road. They made an easy passage over wet country to Shindi, and the following day to Gumar, a former slave market, where a central fig tree still exhibits the rings to which the shackles of the Shankilla were once fastened. Here Gage's party stood on the lip of the gorge. The next day they moved on down a knife-edged ridge to Mabil, where they eventually joined up with the river party. On the way back to Debre Marcos a short cut took them across the fast-flowing River Fatam and Gage unfortunately lost some expensive kit.

* * *

By far the most impressive of these overland journeys was the achievement of Nigel Sale's Group B, four members of which marched seventy-five difficult miles from Ghimbi to the Didessa-Abbai confluence in thirteen days.

This was not a re-supply party, but a game survey focused on the basin of the Didessa River, to see if it was suitable country for a future National Park. The Didessa, the Abbai's biggest tributary, is a considerable river which rises in the south-western plateau, near Gore, and flows north. Not far from Ghimbi it is already 200 yards wide in the wet season. Unlike other southern tributaries of the Abbai further upstream, it cuts no gorge in its lower reaches. Rather, it flows broad and fast through forest and scrub, and there had been many reports of the presence of elephant and buffalo in the area.

To carry out this survey, Nigel had with him John Blower, Senior Game Warden in the Department for the Conservation of Wild Life, and Alem Berhanu, a cheerful and capable young Assistant Game Warden in this Department. For such a journey pack animals were obviously needed, and it was also hoped that mules, led in this way to the Abbai, would help the river party to extricate their stores from Sirba and carry the heavier items back to the wet weather road-head near Ghimbi. Animal transport, of course, was Keith Morgan-Jones' province, and he had brought with him an impressive amount of saddlery and numbers of universal carriers, which the Army then kept in the event of mules being once again called to the colours. The fifth and sixth members of the group were David Bromhead, zoologist, and Rex Matthews, radio operator.

At Ghimbi, where they assembled, they were given invaluable aid by Mr. Andersen, who runs the Seventh Day Adventist Mission. Not only was the group lodged at the Mission House, but its pack animals were corralled there. The Governor at Lechemti had not been forewarned of our plans and was not especially helpful in the matter of mules. It was soon found that mule owners were decidedly unwilling to hire out their animals for journeys into the Abbai basin: even though Keith explained graphically that he had the perfect prophylactic, they still feared the effects of "malaria". Furthermore, mule purchases seemed out of the question—prices varied from $150 to $300. Keith inspected a few that were on offer, one vicious, club-footed specimen kicking him as he did so. Well-practised in animal management, Keith kicked it back.

In the end, they had recourse to donkeys. These, too, although not for hire, could be bought for between $35 and $40, and in quick time the Expedition acquired eleven. The substantial mule saddles enveloped them totally, but on August 13th, with a *Shambel*,[2] appropriately, at their head, the cavalcade got under way down the main street of Ghimbi. Townsfolk lined the route for this unprecedented treat and we did not let them down: donkeys trotted off at tangents, loads hit the dust faster than Hollywood Indians, and the vast figure of ringmaster Keith Morgan-Jones presided rather uncertainly over the whole show from the rear.

From Ghimbi to Bikalal, a prominent hill feature, Group B were still in highland country, between 7,000 and 8,000 feet, picking their way northwards over green, rolling countryside dotted with eucalyptus groves and tin-roofed shacks. With each member supervising two donkeys, and their loads redistributed in accordance with size, they made better progress; but there were frequent mud-filled streambeds to be crossed, where loads had to be painfully removed and replaced. It took two days to cover ten miles, and Ghimbi was still in sight. The game surveyors expected, and saw, few signs of wild life in this fertile region heavily populated by Galla farmers.

At Bikalal the whole Didessa basin was spread before them, and they began to drop down into Shankilla country. They collected a guide to the village of Bishoura, to meet the Shankilla chief of that name who presided over it, and he led them slithering down stony hillsides and along narrow paths, now under a canopy of bamboo and tall grasses. Towards the bottom, he told them that the donkeys could not actually reach Bishoura's village, but that the last two hours must be covered by the group alone. Although the country was now more suitable for them, there was still no evidence of the larger forms of wild life; perhaps they would occur in the flatter scrub-lands nearer the Didessa and the Abbai. Tall grasses obstructed their view, but there were still plenty of clues; the only spoor found, however, were of bush-buck, duiker, pig and sometimes leopard. Olive baboons were plentiful and occasionally the tracks of hyena, jackal, mongoose and porcupine were seen—but none of the classic bigger game.

After covering, with the greatest difficulty, only fifteen miles in five days, and with more obstacles forecast, a reappraisal seemed necessary: either the full survey of the basin would have to be abandoned and the whole group return to Ghimbi, or they must split, allowing some to proceed on foot to Sirba, whilst others went back with the donkeys. Three days were spent, just short of Bishoura's village, securing clearance by radio for a change of plan and investigating the country immediately ahead. In the event, Nigel Sale, John Blower, Rex Matthews and Alem Berhanu prepared to march on to the Abbai with vastly increased personal loads; David Bromhead and Keith Morgan-Jones, whose heels had been giving trouble, set off back up to the plateau.

At Bishoura's village Nigel persuaded the chief's son, Tigre Bishoura, to accompany them to Sirba, on the promise of a flight out there to Ghimbi. Tigre wore bright blue shorts, T-shirt and baseball cap, and carried a transistor radio everywhere. He is one of many examples in present day Ethiopia of the local boy who has made good up to a point: speaking Amharinya and English as well as his local Shankilla tongue, he had acquired at the Mission School in Ghimbi a veneer of westernisation which must have left him socially rather confused. Like all small towns, Ghimbi has its quota of young men of the new semi-educated élite, dark-suited, cigarette-smoking, with sunglasses and pointed shoes. They hold court in the smarter bars, drinking bottled beer or Ethiopian-type Chianti, and chatting to the sallow, moon-faced beauties who hover behind the counter in such places, not only an adornment but also an occasional source of extra profit to the management. From this environment Tigre, clutching his transistor, would trudge home for the holidays to a cluster of dark *tukuls*. Here, bare-footed, bare-breasted villagers sit in an atmosphere of almost perpetual torpor, with flies gathered on their many open sores, quaffing beakers of sour *talla*, while dogs lope hungrily about. Like Richard Hoggart's working-class "Scholarship Boy", Tigre doubtless has problems of adjustment, and his cheerless manner is perhaps the result of partial rejection by his own village.

Nigel, with his team of three, after drinking *talla* and eating corncobs with Bishoura, set off northwards. They crossed the shoulder-deep Sai and the next day reached the broad, fast-flowing Didessa itself. The going, along its western bank, was terrible—swamp and thick elephant grasses twice the height of a man. So they regained higher ground and came to the village of Lumma. Here they were involved in a human drama of a particularly beastly and tragic kind. One villager, aiming his rifle at a jackal, had shot another villager. The bullet had passed through the left leg, leaving neat entry and exit holes, and through the scrotum, and had entered the right leg, causing terrible haemorrhage. The mess was grim, and obviously required immediate surgery. Nigel knew an air-drop of supplies was due, and medical advice was requested by radio. The following day, the Beaver flew over with Doc West alongside the pilot. Rations were dropped and Roger gave what medical help he could from fifty feet up. As the victim lay in a field covered by a portable *tukul*, the previous day's bandages were cut off, morphine and penicillin administered, and antiseptic cream smeared on dressings and applied. The bullet holes in the left leg were covered with small plasters. Nothing else could be done. His father was told to have him carried immediately to the Mission Hospital at Ghimbi, and Nigel learned later that he had died on the way.

For three days after this episode, Nigel and his men trudged on steadily, leaving Jalo, a sharp-toothed volcanic plug, to their left. They now decided not to head for Sirba, as planned, but for the nearer Didessa-Abbai confluence, where Group A were likely to be until August 28th. John Blashford-Snell had intimated that there was room for the five of them in the lightened Assault Boats.

The country here was savannah woodland with Shankilla settlements every few miles and footpaths between them. Still there was a remarkable absence of game. John Blower concluded that elephant and buffalo must once have abounded here, but that the recent wider spread of weapons and ammunition among the Shankilla may have helped to drive game to the basins of the Angar and Dabus near by, which are reputed to be well-stocked. So a useful game survey produced a virtually nil return. Nigel's party strode down to the Abbai on August 26th and were lifted by Assault Boat to Group A's island camp. It had been a singular physical achievement.

❊ ❊ ❊

Keith Morgan-Jones and David Bromhead reached Ghimbi successfully with their donkey train. Keith had looked after his charges well—they had had their shots of Berenil every five days, and emerged from the gorge, to the great surprise of the men of Ghimbi, with no trace of sickness and in the donkey equivalent of the pink of health. He was thus able to dispose of them at a reasonable price. He and David Bromhead then joined forces with Group C2—Garth Brocksopp, Gavin Pike and Ian Carruthers—who had reached Ghimbi a few days before. Despite the gradual shift of the Expedition's centre northwards to Bahardar, Ghimbi remained the hub of intense activity for a further two weeks or so.

Garth Brocksopp's group were to have followed up their first march out of the river gorge by a much more severe re-supply journey from Lechemti northwards to the Abbai. As this involved crossing the River Angar and about twenty other rivers, all then in spate, this journey was ruled impossible—even for the great Brocksopp. So with an eye on Group A's possible evacuation from Sirba by land, Garth was sent on a reconnaissance of the road from Ghimbi (where the maps say it ends in the wet season) north-westwards to Nejo and Mendi. Once again Mr. Andersen at the Seventh Day Adventist Mission was wonderfully hospitable: not only were C2 housed at the Mission School, as Group B had been, but when Garth's Land-Rover—which had lost its first gear—failed to defeat the mud on the way to Nejo, Mr. Andersen drove them there himself in his Toyota Cruiser.

The Police at Nejo were suspicious of the outlandish *ferenji* party and detained them. After several 'phone calls to the Governor at Ghimbi, who had shown no interest in the Expedition and therefore was not very helpful, Mr. Andersen was asked to stand surety for his passengers, which he did. They all drove back to Ghimbi and reached the Mission at 2 a.m. The clear result was that the road beyond Ghimbi was in no shape yet for heavy vehicles without chained tyres, and Group A must choose between flying or walking from Sirba to Ghimbi.

Group C2 now got clearance from John Blashford-Snell to stay on at the Mission School, and carried out a great deal of zoological collecting work, which even Pat Morris, with his stringent standards and slight regard for the military in general, has described as a "valuable effort". Garth, Gavin and David are experienced "military zoologists" and they conducted regular night-shoots in their Land-Rover, during which they bagged specimens of serval cat, bushbuck, varieties of mongoose, civet cat and even hyena, which caused a good deal of local interest—great superstition attaches to the hyena, especially, as has been noted, in Gojjam. Night and morning traps were set and cleared, and processions of small boys came daily to the schoolhouse bearing rats, mice, lizards, bats and snakes in various mangled states. Unlike Gerald Durrell in the Cameroons, we required our "beef" dead, but there was often little care taken in the administration of the deathblow and many specimens, mainly snakes, were ruined. During the day, the group

Alan Calder and Richard Grevatte-Ball check the engine of their Beaver by the airstrip at our Main Base.

meticulously cleaned and prepared skins and skulls from the previous night's bag.

When the evacuation from Sirba began, they had, of course, to drop their scalpels and assist with the unloading of the Beaver and the Mapping Mission helicopter at the airstrip. They helped, too, with the despatch of people and their kit in a shuttle service of assorted vehicles to Addis Ababa. On September 5th they themselves went, leaving Ghimbi in Land-Rover and the U.S. helicopter—the "sick bird" that had just damaged its own underbelly and dropped an Assault Boat.

It was on one of these journeys from Ghimbi that an alarming incident occurred, involving Assefa and Hilary King, one of our zoologists. They were taking a punctured tyre to Lechemti and, together with three drunk Ethiopians, had cadged a lift on a lorry. Assefa had travelled downriver with us from Shafartak to Sirba. Dark, simian, and

127

whiskery, he wore an almost permanent grin and had a friendly, relaxed manner, which verged at times on the *dolce far niente*. Now he was in the cab next to the driver and Hilary was in the back with the drunken trio. The lorry turned off the road to a small village, stopped, and the Ethiopians climbed down. Soon they came back and the lorry rumbled off into the deep country. Presently the three produced guns from their *shammas*, pointed them at Hilary and set up an excited jabbering. The lorry stopped again. They motioned to Hilary to get down and then began to demand his money with menaces. They had seen him produce a 10-dollar bill when he and Assefa had been discussing the costs of the tyre repair. Fortunately, Assefa intervened forcefully and after a long and noisy argument he was able to satisfy the *talla*-sodden gunmen with three 12-bore cartridges.

✳ ✳ ✳

Mota, in the foothills of the Choke Mountains, was, like Ghimbi, an important focal point for us. A highland town of much the same character—groves of eucalyptus shading corrugated iron roofs and muddy lanes—it depended on its airstrip even more than Ghimbi, for there was no approach by road—we either had to fly there or walk there along damp mule trails.

The first of our Expedition in this area, the precursors of Phase 2, was Group C3, pruned now to a total of four and led by Gage Williams. Their job was to reconnoitre the west bank of the Abbai from Tissisat to the 2nd Portuguese Bridge, and then to walk out to Mota.

They were carried to Tissisat in a Land-Rover—Gage, Chris Edwards, Mike Henry and Mesfin Abebe—and the first three days were hard, satisfying, uneventful: no mules to trammel them, the lightest possible packs—six days' rations and little else, the fitful services of boy porters. Each night they seemed to find a clear, tinkling stream by which to camp. The local population was, by turns, terrified and warmly hospitable: one man came four miles from his village to bring them the traditional *injera*, *wat* and *talla*; others tightened their *shammas* round them and fled.

On the third morning, having for the first time kept no guard during the night, they woke to find themselves surrounded by about a dozen armed men. The warriors had brought eggs and milk, however, so the morning opened peaceably enough; but when Gage prepared to move, the chief of them, Ato Shiferra, made it plain that he would not allow it. First he wanted to see their paper authorisation for the journey. It was a disturbed area, he said to Mesfin, and he was detaining them for their own good. When he discovered they had no credentials, he demanded a letter from them indemnifying him from all responsibility should *shifta* later attack them. All this was very awkward for Gage. Ato Shiferra, however, treated them with great consideration and their "capture" was, in fact, a pleasant interlude. He had his own motives for what he proposed: unpopular, new Government tax laws had caused a number of villages to reject their "Establishment" chiefs and install popularly elected ones—Ato Shiferra was one of these. His tenure was obviously rickety and he desperately wanted a formal letter addressed to him, Chief of Zanat (or somewhere thereabouts), to strengthen his own position.

Gage informed Main Base by radio and John Wilsey enlisted the help of the Chief of Police at Debre Marcos. Instructions to release Gage's party were given in Amharic and Ato Shiferra clasped the headphone uncertainly to an ear. At the end he turned his sad, Old Testament face to Chris Edwards as if to say, "Who, in the name of Abba Salama, was that?" Arrangements were being made for the despatch of a suitable letter by Beaver air mail, when two friends of Ato Shiferra's were found in Debre Marcos. John Wilsey brought them to the radio in time for the next call and the grizzled, old chief, recognising one of their voices, was persuaded to let the four of them go.

They subsequently met a number of friendly chiefs—one of whom still treasured the signature of Arne Rubin, the Swedish canoeist who walked out of this area with Carl-Gustav Forsmark in 1966. They were well escorted to the River Abaya, swam over it a good deal upstream of the point later used by Roger Chapman's column with such tragic results,[3] and reached the 2nd Portuguese Bridge and thence Mota in good order.

David Bromhead with Group I, coming into Mota later by air, ran into much the same sort of trouble. He was to provide a bank support party for the White Water Team at K4, a series of fierce cataracts just above the Portuguese Bridge. When he reached the area and prepared to camp for a few days, he was warned off by the surrounding chiefs, who said that his group of four was too small to be safe. He had to withdraw to Mota, until he could be reinforced by the Command Group. Whilst there, he very efficiently assembled a train of eighteen mules on which were loaded, under Mesfin's watchful gaze, all the stores for the new group (Group P) that was to move off shortly down the unknown river below the Portuguese Bridge. Shortly after, John Blashford-Snell arrived with his Group C and, suitably mounted on two sturdy riding mules, he and "Johnny" Johnson rode off down the twelve miles to the gorge, with the pack animals and a foot party of five, leaving the sick Rex Matthews in Mota to operate a radio relay station.[4]

It was during this time that Corporal Henry first really came into his own. In a village near the Abaya he began to style himself as a prince in his own country, and by this means secured preferential treatment for the day—the most comfortable stool (if there was anything to choose between them), the largest *talla* beaker. Later, tiring of the attentions accorded to royalty, he set himself up as a doctor. For a while this was all in line with our policy: we had certain surplus medical stores which could be administered to the local populace. Soon, however, the tribesmen near the Portuguese Bridge became wearisome in their demands. Henry's diagnoses became more cursory and his therapy brisker; furthermore, he began to run out of spare drugs. An importunate villager, who kept returning with the same headache, had a water sterilisation tablet sellotaped to his forehead; another one with some invisible eye complaint had his head almost completely swathed in bandages—which were plentiful. One of the more unpleasant chiefs there complained bitterly of a sore foot; nothing appeared to be wrong with it, so *Hakim* Henry put a Horlicks tablet between each toe and told him to hop back on one leg to his village three miles away up the gorge side. Hippocrates may have turned in his grave, but it ensured peace in the troubled camp for some little while. However, the local people continued to give us a difficult time and Henry showed great restraint in not completely pacifying the district with his bottle of 250 Cascara tablets.

Nigel Sale, with the remnants of Group N, also ended up at Mota, lodged for the night in the picturesquely thatched, bamboo airport lounge there. He had had a long and interesting series of tasks, which had brought him from Bahardar down the western bank of the Abbai. Most of his group's work was interwoven with that of the White Water

Team. At the cataracts in the Northern Gorge they gave both warning and support. Some of his party joined Group P for the further journey down river below the Portuguese Bridge; others—after a painful brush with some wild bees, in which Nigel and Gage Williams were quite severely stung—marched with him into and out of the grim Abaya gorge and up a further 5,000 feet to Mota.

Most of these complex movements by the land parties, involving quite frequent modifications of plan, would not have been possible without radio communications. The release of Gage's party from "arrest", Nigel's dismissal of his donkeys, the summoning of medical aid for the villager with bullet-torn genitals—all depended on the various sets we had brought and the skill of their operators. Most groups in the field had A13 or A16 sets, although the Racal Squadcal TRA906s were widely appreciated, especially on Phase 2, as were the lightweight SARBE Radio Beacons for very short distance work. The Main Base housed the larger C11 set for direct communication with Bulford in Wiltshire. Whilst we had signals specialists with us, who were, of course, excellent, much responsibility fell on others, like John Wilsey, Joe Ruston and Rex Matthews, and often at quite critical times.

At Debre Marcos Corporals Tony Davidson and David Fisher, were constantly communicating with Bulford, or with Philip Shepherd at the British Embassy in Addis Ababa, with the Beaver, or with one or other of their four or five outstations in river gorge or on mountain top. Barry Cooke or Ian Carruthers struggled long and hard each day with one of Chris Bonington's Press Reports for the *Daily Telegraph*. Its three hundred words would have to be sent twice for the sake of accuracy, and in Morse Code this might take them up to three hours.

The Beaver was often a good relay station for transmission to difficult corners of the gorge, and was a key part of our communications network. Its key role as an instrument of reconnaissance and of re-supply to river parties will have already become evident. "Teeny-Weeny Airways" flew bodies and kit here and there; they dropped fuel, food, drink, mail, outboard engines, messages; they carried out searches. Alan Calder would fly in at Sirba at about 2,500 feet above sea level, and would later be struggling in the thin air over the shoulders of

Sometimes parachutes were used, otherwise stores were dropped free. At the Dankoro River, John Wilsey (bottom left) recovers items that were badly shattered on the rocks.

Mount Choke at about 12,500 feet. He was even shot at once by angry tribesmen in the wild country below the Portuguese Bridge.

* * *

As dependent as all of us on signals and air support was John Wilsey's Group J in their successful prosecution of one of the final tasks of the Expedition. An Assault Boat was put into the Abbai at Shafartak on September 17th and John and his crew of three began their arduous upstream journey. This first recorded ascent on the Abbai was undertaken so as to meet John Blashford-Snell and his Group P coming down river with two Redshank dinghies and two Recce Boats. Group J were aiming to reach the Bashillo River junction, where they would provide extra motive power and the reassurance of some metal protection against the numerous crocodiles of that region.

In three days they had reached the Walaka River and were heading due north. But excessive use of their engine at full throttle had blown a sparking plug, and John had asked for another engine to be dropped by parachute. They had been able to motor on, since he had prudently brought a spare engine with him; but this, too, was weakening and so to lighten its load they began to make caches of surplus stores on the bank-side. Cutting the load from 2,000 lb to 1,750 lb helped "Ticky" Wright to nurse the engine, and at two to three knots John Huckstep at the helm pushed on above the Shita River. Here, Telahoun Makonnen, the fourth member, reported the locals to be timid but friendly.

The fifth day was pure tragedy. The Beaver, with another 40 hp engine, came over, and cans of fuel were successfully parachuted down. But the next consignment plummeted straight into the Abbai, the 'chute having failed to open. It contained not only the new engine, but all the rations and mail for the group. They stood open-mouthed and empty-bellied—to keep the boat's weight down they had only carried three and a half days' rations per man.

In the event it was the *Daily Telegraph* that provided. Money was advanced so that an Ethiopian Air Lines helicopter could be hired and another engine brought out from Addis Ababa. This, with some welcome food supplies, was accomplished the following day at 3 p.m., which says a lot for our administration in the rear. That evening, with morale boosted, Group J were halted by a particularly shallow cataract just south of the Dankoro River, which they were unable to take at a rush as they had done with others.

Next morning another decanting of heavy stores had just been completed when Group P appeared round the corner. The link-up was accomplished. In one sort of boat or another we had covered the whole length of the Great Abbai, and the final support team had effected a rendezvous and completed its work.

On the last day of the Expedition I saw in the Ras bar in Addis Ababa an amply built man whose clothes hung about him somewhat loosely. I was about to enquire who it was, when I recognised him as Keith Morgan-Jones. I had not seen him since Day 6 of the Expedition, eight weeks before. On an undertaking like ours with so many separate, supporting groups some members saw scarcely anything of some others. And yet our whole relationship was close-knit, for day by day on the river we learned by radio of the progress of those who were toiling on the treadmill—either on their way towards us, or retracing their weary steps to the plateau.

NOTES:

1 Christian highlanders: hence "Abyssinia", the former name of Ethiopia.
2 *Shambel* = Captain; in this case, a local guide.
3 See Chapter 13.
4 The fate of these groups converging on the Portuguese Bridge is shown in Chapter 14.

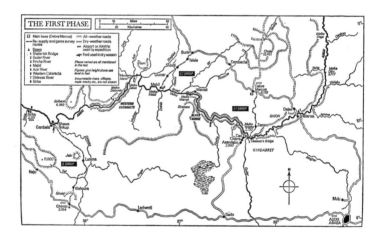

Chapter Ten
NINE MEN IN THREE BOATS

PHASE 2 began to command attention more and more as Phase 1 drew near its end. From the Azir River onwards John was beginning to make his plans for it, and Roger Chapman, whom he had long before appointed leader of the river party, was first consulted in the Western Cataracts. Here the White Water Team was first formed by Roger, though not yet announced. Roger had almost complete freedom of choice over his personnel and thought long and deeply about it. He had to pick eight companions who would all be able to lend some individual talent to this most hazardous enterprise and yet together make up a homogeneous team. There was inevitably much speculation and some lobbying for places; the White Water Team began already to gather an air of mystique and selection to it seemed to some to be the final accolade. People had various claims: many of us had been for two or three training sessions on the Dee and Conway; some had taken care to bring their own wet-suits; others hoped that fitness and firmness of purpose would be enough. Roger kept tantalisingly quiet about it all until he felt that he had the balance absolutely right.

His White Water Team were to be mainly concerned with the Northern Gorge—from the Tissisat Falls to the 2nd Portuguese Bridge near Mota. However, John Wilsey, who had been carrying out reconnaissance flights over this gorge, had lately also made one over the first few miles of the river, from Lake Tana to Tissisat. This unsensational section formed no part of our programme at this stage. John reported it to be fairly easy and had asked John Blashford-Snell if he might do it in a couple of Redshanks with some of the Base Camp party. This turned out to be a bit like Bonington being told by a maître d'hotel in Grindelwald that he would like to take the kitchen lads and waitresses up the first 3,000 feet of the Eiger one morning. Moreover, Roger thought it unwise to commit two Redshanks to inexperienced hands and that, if time could be spared, it would be a good "warm up" stretch for the White Water Team before tackling the fearsome

A Redshank negotiating a cataract between Lane Tana and the Tissisat Falls.

Northern Gorge. John Blashford-Snell had agreed and allotted him four days for this purpose. In the event, it took over a week and was far more than a "warm up". However, it now looked for the first time as if the whole of the Blue Nile, from its virtual source to Sirba, would come within our compass, and a "conquest" of all of it might be possible.

Roger announced his team at the Didessa Junction on August 28th. Jim Masters, our dependable and popular Chief Engineer, was to be his second-in-command in *Hope*. With Jim would be John Fletcher, the wizard with the repair kit, who had staked much on this expedition and had devoted himself particularly to white water problems as well as his beloved engines; and John Huckstep, quite unperturbed at this stage by the alleged dangers ahead. Roger had with him in *Faith* Peter O'Mahony and Alastair Newman, both with experience in one of the toughest regiments in the British Army. Peter, Signaller to the White Water Team, was not quite sure whether he was going to be exactly in his right clement. Not in any doubt whatever was Alastair Newman—short, dark, almost Napoleonic—who had also staked much on the whole venture. A nuclear physicist at Sandhurst, with a love for practical soldiering which he seems to satisfy even in a Britain at peace, he was immensely confident and did not disguise his impatience to get amongst the danger.

The distinguished mountaineer, Christian Bonington, now more of a climber-photographer and writer, was to travel in *Charity* and to record his impressions with pen and camera for The *Daily Telegraph Magazine*. With him was Chris Edwards, and the wiry Corporal Ian Macleod, a most popular Glaswegian and a tough, resourceful soldier, yet sometimes with the owlish look of a scholar about him.

It seemed an impressive team, indeed, and was to move in three of the Avon Redshanks as shown:

Faith	*Hope*	*Charity*
Alastair	John	Ian
NEWMAN (29)	FLETCHER (31)	MACLEOD (27)
Roger	Jim	Chris
CHAPMAN (30)	MASTERS (40)	EDWARDS (26)
Peter	John	Christian
O'MAHONY (26)	HUCKSTEP (28)	BONINGTON (34)

Chris Edwards, the only one of the nine not also on Phase 1, lay writing his diary near the Portuguese Bridge, whilst on a reconnaissance to Mota: "On the lunchtime radio call I learnt that England had won the Fifth Test, and also that I was in the White Water Team for the final phase—great news!" The other eight were among the first to be flown out of Sirba, and soon almost all the team was back at Debre Marcos, getting on with the final preparations under Roger's direction. The boats had been very largely made ready in the opening days at Base Camp, but there were still refinements—nets to be fixed in the bows to hold kit in the event of a capsize, wet-suits to be tailored to fit each individual, new-painted paddles—red, green and, for the helmsmen, white—to be sandpapered down to a comfortable grip.

One day Roger flew off on a reconnaissance of the Tana-Tissisat stretch; on another he and his team concentrated on safety drills.

"Now, I've asked you to change into your full kit," he said, standing on the grass outside the Cookhouse tent, "because we've got to get used to it, and furthermore we must practise our capsize drills as realistically as possible."

John Fletcher and John Huckstep prepare the transom of one of the Assault Boats at
Debre Marcos.

The eight stood in a half circle, hands on hips and eyes down,
whilst "Johnny" Johnson prowled about with his camera. They were
clad in full, black, neoprene wet-suits, now inscribed with various
arcane forms of identification in white paint—"POM", "BIG CHRIS",
"PRESS" etc. White plastic canoeing helmets, perforated like colanders,
were strapped on their heads, and on their feet plimsolls or light boots.
Smart blue lifejackets were buckled on, and here and there a sinister
dagger was strapped round a bulging calf muscle. All were sweating
steadily in the afternoon sun.

"What I want three of you to do is to get into this dinghy and then
roll out of it on to this grass. Then we'll turn it over and you can
simulate the drill for righting it and getting inboard again."

Alastair Newman and Chris Bonington looked at each other in the
way that two men, strangers to one another, will look when they see a
woman driver commit some highway solecism. "You have to be joking,"
said Alastair.

They rolled about on the grass while the cameras whirred, and
then, as if in the river, they reached up and grabbed the special
handstraps that he had had sewn on the undersides of the boats. With
a pull the dinghy canted up on its side and then, as the crew scuttled

from under it, plopped back again on the ground. After this, the drill was that the outside two men were to hoist the centre one up into the boat, and he would then help to haul in the others, giving occasional attention to the helm.

It was all rather difficult to do convincingly on land, but surprisingly easy, and effective, in the buoyancy of the surging river. Training that day concluded with a few climbing tips from Chris Bonington, hung about like a Papuan headhunter with slings, lifelines, bright new jumars, and daisy-chains of karabiners. Again, practice on a eucalyptus was poor substitute for the gorge, but the reality would be present soon enough.

Of course, the White Water Team were not simply to be shot off into outer space like an Apollo crew. Whilst this training was going on John Blashford-Snell was in his Headquarters tent organising an interlocking support network every bit as complex and comprehensive as that which had buttressed the Phase 1 navigators.

Expedition personnel were divided up into no less than eleven separate groups, and John, with the legerdemain of a juggler, controlled and plotted each of their movements for the ensuing three weeks.

In simplified form, the White Water Team (Group WW) were to embark at Bahardar on September 8th. On the 11th they would portage their dinghies round Tissisat (one would be lowered down the falls by the Engineer Group for the sake of continuity), and on the 14th it was hoped they would reach the 2nd Portuguese Bridge. They would have been supported all the way along the western bank by Nigel Sale's Group N, and nearer the bridge by David Bromhead's Group I from Mota. At the Portuguese Bridge there would be a certain amount of reorganisation of groups and their personnel: from Groups WW, N and I, and the Command Group (which would fly into Mota), a new group would be formed—Group P—which, with two powered, inflatable Recce Boats as gunboats and a fourth Redshank, would proceed downriver to the Shafartak Bridge. On the way, it would meet John Wilsey's Group J coming upstream in an Assault Boat.

"We've had to reappraise our arrangements," said John Blashford-Snell, "as far as Phase 2 is concerned." It was a quiet, tense Orders Group meeting in the Cookhouse tent.

"As you may know by now, Hawkeye[1] has revealed that there are far more crocodiles above the Big Bridge than I had previously indicated. Pat Morris thinks it may be because of the increased volume and force of the water in the lower reaches. Anyhow, they're there, and we need some sort of escort to protect the vulnerable Redshanks. This is one reason why I'm bringing in the Recce Boats at the Portuguese Bridge and asking John Wilsey to make the first ascent of the Great Abbai in an armed Assault Boat which will come up from Shafartak to meet us…"

When I had got back to Debre Marcos from Sirba, after working myself out of the job of Airport Manager there and spending four days drowsing under an acacia, I had noticed a faintly conspiratorial air about the Base Camp: groups of members sat about in furtive discussion, then an argument would break out and voices rise querulously in the night. This was the first indication apart from the occasional personal rift between individuals, that not all was harmonious in our views of Expedition policy.

After that final meeting a knot of members was gathered round two camp beds.

"Look," said Chris Edwards, "what's the point of breaking up the White Water Team at the Portuguese Bridge? A whole lot of new people are going to come in at a place where the river's still bloody dangerous."

"Maybe," said Martin Romilly, "but the White Water Team was always intended to end there. Roger recognises this. And anyway, the new crocodile situation demands some form of protection. We can't just send the three Redshanks on down with neither bank support nor armed river escort, can we?"

Chris Bonington broke in stridently, "It's sheer folly to kick out people who will have become really hardened on the way down from Tana, and it's far more dangerous than your crocodiles to replace them with inexperienced people and bring in a fourth Redshank and a couple of Recce Boats."

"'Hank' says the Recce Boats are all perished anyway, and won't last ten minutes," said Alastair.

"Obviously," said Martin, "no-one wants a team broken up needlessly, but I reckon you're thinking of keeping the team intact more than of the proper, safe coverage of the river."

"Oh, balls!" they chorused.

"Look," said Chris Edwards, "you can't put a chap like 'Johnny' Johnson and his expensive cameras into a Recce Boat and send him off into the cataracts with no chance of getting out before Shafartak."

"Maybe we won't send him. How do we know until we actually see the river?" rejoined Martin. "It's supposed to ease off at Mota, and that might be the case."

"Well, you're the Information Officer," said Alastair.

The White Water Team had had a full week of preparation at Base Camp and by now it was beginning to seem a tedious interlude. With so much time to dispose of, discussion could easily merge into intrigue. Perhaps I was lucky to have come straight from Shankilla country, with only eighteen hours to turn round in before joining the move to Bahardar.

Packing of personal kit, however, occupied the last hours. It had been fined down to "the absolute minimum" several times, but always some vital additional item came to mind and necessitated a repacking. Kay Thompson gave out some "goodies" from the ration stores, and most people found room for a half bottle of scotch—kindly given by the Distillers' Company. Lance Corporal Mike Henry and Junior Sergeant Chris Whitwell had been toiling away in the Headquarters tent, duplicating copies of the programme for the next three weeks. Martin Romilly issued these, together with the specially waterproofed maps of the area, for what they were worth. "Buck" Taylor began the confusing business of issuing weapons and ammunition: most of us were to carry .455 Smith and Wesson revolvers, whilst some had .303 sporting rifles, converted from S.M.L.E.s in Britain. There were also .22 B.S.A. rifles, 12-bore shotguns and two heavy calibre rifles of 9.3mm and .375 in. Keeping guns and ammunition dry on Phase 2 was to prove an impossibility, but it did not affect their use in moments of need. More difficult was actually finding the right weapon for a target at the given moment as the river soon reduced our initial tidiness to considerable disorder.

Along the rail on the southern side of the long, low span of the bridge were ranged about 120 people. The bridge, which had been opened by His Imperial Majesty in 1960, carried the road out of Bahardar over the Abbai and north-west towards Gondar and Eritrea. It linked Gojjam and Begemdir and was the only road bridge over the Blue Nile until

Shafartak was reached, after the 190 taxing miles of river that was to be Phase 2. The crowd was made up mainly of interested Bahardar townsfolk and a few visiting Europeans: oddly, not a single pressman for this, the great beginning—or rather, the great resumption.

The three Redshanks had been brought down from Land-Rover and trailer to a grassy bank and the members of the White Water Team, irrepressibly buoyant now that their work was finally to begin, strode about in the warm sunshine making everything ready. To the local populace, they must have seemed outlandish in their black rubber dress with its various bizarre additions: now they wore revolvers in leather holsters and had nylon lifelines attached at the belt by coloured rubber bands; spare rubber bands adorned some wrists, and others, who had discarded their neoprene jackets in the warmth, revealed leather necklaces, with a pendant watch, tin-opener, or mysterious amulet.

The previous day they had driven from Debre Marcos with Group N in four Land-Rovers, through Burie and Danghila to Bahardar. They had camped in the pouring rain at a Water Resources Depot by Lake Tana, where Roger hoped that a good corporate spirit would be fostered. The rest of us had shown less Spartan self-denial and had booked in at the Ras Hotel. Here was the bungaloid hotel plan usual in Ethiopia, but dazzlingly modern. Attractively perched on the edge of Lake Tana, it offered the first hot bath for five weeks, a chalet room and a bed with sheets—for 23s. 4d. per night, at the special rate we struck with its most obliging manager. There was a bar and restaurant, where minestrone, fish from the lake, wienerschnitzel, and crème caramel could be enjoyed for £1. I thought of the *corps d'élite* in sodden tents; one might envy them their approaching glory, but it was pleasant after Phase 1 to sit once more on a bar stool and have a glass of beer poured by a white-jacketed waiter.

In the morning John Wilsey and I drove through Bahardar, destined to be Ethiopia's second city, to the river. Surprisingly, it has a network of dual carriageways and roundabouts, though filled for the most part only by strolling pedestrians and donkeys. They have been building for the future and Bahardar's moment is not yet come. Like Addis Ababa, it is a mixture of squalid cabins and ultra-modern structures—the work of Russians, West Germans and other benefactors. Well placed for Lake Tana, with its islands and monasteries, and the Tissisat Falls, it clearly has an eye out for tourism,

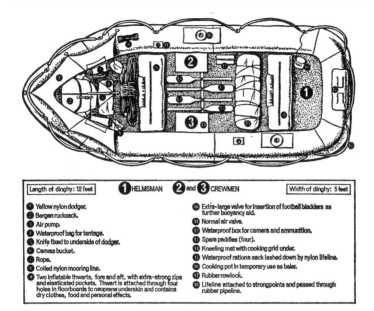

| Length of dinghy: 12 feet | ❶ HELMSMAN | ❷ and ❸ CREWMEN | Width of dinghy: 5 feet |

❶ Yellow nylon dodger.
❷ Bergen rucksack.
❸ Air pump.
❹ Waterproof bag for tentage.
❺ Knife fixed to underside of dodger.
❻ Canvas bucket.
❼ Rope.
❽ Coiled nylon mooring line.
❾ Two inflatable thwarts, fore and aft, with extra-strong zips and elasticated pockets. Thwart is attached through four holes in floorboards to neoprene underskin and contains dry clothes, food and personal effects.

❿ Extra-large valve for insertion of football bladders as further buoyancy aid.
⓫ Normal air valve.
⓬ Waterproof box for camera and ammunition.
⓭ Spare paddles (four).
⓮ Kneeling mat with cooking grid under.
⓯ Waterproof rations sack lashed down by nylon lifeline.
⓰ Cooking pot in temporary use as baler.
⓱ Rubber rowlock.
⓲ Lifeline attached to strongpoints and passed through rubber pipeline.

and already the Blue Nile Springs Hotel, with its economy class hotel rooms at 10s., vies with the Ras. Soon John and I were at the bridge.

The three dinghies made a brave sight as they got away with their happy crews about 9.30 a.m.

"Good luck and God speed!" cried John Blashford-Snell, raising his topee, as they paddled slowly off on the broad, sunlit stream. For over an hour they moved over the placid surface watching the weaver birds flitting amongst the papyrus reeds, and only surprised by the sudden, unscheduled appearance of a hippopotamus. A suppressed excitement filled them all.

The day before, Roger Chapman had made a second air reconnaissance of the river below Tana, this time with Jim, Chris Bonington and Ian. They had come back considerably chastened —it was to be no easy run. Not only were there long stretches of turbulent white water, sometimes between two to three miles at a time, barely relieved by smoother passages, but the ever-broadening river was dotted with a mass of wooded islands breaking its course into several channels, which would make navigation difficult and support from the bank in places impossible. Roger that night had stressed the forthcoming dangers for the benefit of the others, and had painstakingly reiterated all his previous instructions. It had been a tense occasion, followed by a long, edgy discussion. Some of the team were beginning to resent this close cosseting, which they felt to be over-fussy and unnecessary. The events of the next few days showed how necessary it was, but it was more, perhaps, in the manner of its putting across that his exhortation was irksome to some of them.

Impatience was forgotten, however, when in the distance a formidable booming was heard. *Faith*, in the lead, saw a mist of water droplets where the level river fell away into the first cataract. The line of trees on the bank seemed to drop down some twenty or thirty feet. The three dinghies pulled in to the right bank and the cataract was inspected on foot. For a hundred yards or so the river cascaded down through a series of swooping hydraulic waves up to ten feet in height. It was all very frightening.

Roger decided that this first challenge had to be met; they had to prove to themselves the waterworthiness of the Redshanks and, indeed, their own courage. He checked the arrangements for calling up the other boats on the light SARBE radio beacons that each carried, and then he, Alastair and Peter pushed off.

The bank party—a fragment of Group N—had managed to find this cataract and were stationed on the rocks below it. Even Claude was there with his cinecamera, and was enabled, with Gage Williams' help, to shoot some of the finest action sequences of the whole expedition. John Blashford-Snell and "Johnny" Johnson droned overhead in the Beaver. All eyes were on the tiny dinghy and the boiling chaos it was about to enter.

Paddling hard to keep the nose butting into and over the waves, they were swept swiftly down. Disappearing frequently from sight, they always reappeared, swamped but still paddling. Alastair just had time to turn a glistening face and smile at Roger. When they were almost through, a giant wave lifted the dinghy, twisting it to the left. Instantly, the bows buckled up over them and Peter and Alastair were thrown out; Roger was somersaulted backwards over the stern and into the raging water. They all surfaced near by, each still holding his paddle which was attached to a strongpoint in the dinghy. Alastair was first to clamber in, raising his clenched fists in a boxer's salute. Soon Roger and Peter had each grabbed a lifeline and they all drifted to the edge and climbed ashore on the black rocks on the right bank. One lifejacket was burst but they had lost nothing, and Alastair was able shortly afterwards to use a cinecamera which had been for some time immersed.

Hope and *Charity* insisted on following, although over the SARBE radio Roger had at first urged them to carry the dinghies round. Captains Masters and Edwards took a lead from Lord Nelson—"I really do not hear the signal," they had agreed. *Hope* rode the cataract without incident. Then came *Charity*, with the added tension of actors who don't come on until Act 3 and who have been watching nervously in the wings. Chris Edwards wrote: "...and we were suddenly in the seething waves—sensation of being bounced like a rubber ball—huge wall of brown water immediately in front of us—we can't get through that— the boat is skewing sideways—water everywhere—the brown wall has gone—rushing down into a hydraulic—no control of the boat—body and mind completely numbed by the excitement—Oh, Christ! I am being thrown out—no, just tossed up into the air as the rear end kicks up—Chris and Ian still there—and suddenly we know we are through it…" The tension burst like a bubble, and on the rocks afterwards there was talk and laughter. All agreed it was a most magnificent experience, and on a practical plane it gave them a yardstick by which to measure future cataracts.

After a joyous lunch—albeit sardines and Mars bars—they set off for the waterfall some three or four miles distant, their target for the day. The river was now much more broken in rapids, though they were not of the ferocity of the first one. When the waterfall was reached they pulled in to the right—"Keep to the right! Keep to the right!", this was to be the first article in our Tana-to-Tissisat Highway Code—and searched for a way of by-passing it. John Huckstep and Chris Edwards found a shallow, rocky channel of fast-flowing water down which the dinghies could be lowered. They then proceeded, sometimes paddling through the reeds and under a canopy of enveloping brush, sometimes leaping out and hauling the dinghies through the tangles. It was exhausting work but the ominous boom of the fall on their left reminded them that it was worthwhile.

In fading light they tethered the boats, grabbed armfuls of kit and waded inland through swamps until soon they were on hard, dry ground. Here a camp was made and Ian Macleod walked further inland to the parallel Tana-Tissisat road, where a prearranged Expedition Land-Rover was patrolling.

"What an absolutely fantastic day!" said Chris Bonington.

NOTES:

1   "Hawkeye": Army jargon for Army Air Corps.

Chapter Eleven
DEATHS AND NEAR-DEATHS

WHILE Group WW were enjoying their watery baptism, it was a day of death on the roads. "Hank" Mansley, coming up from Debre Marcos in a Land-Rover with the Engineer Group, killed a dog, and Joe Ruston struck a donkey near Danghila. It got up and walked away, but police told Joe as he stopped for lunch that it had subsequently died and they tried to get him to pay for it.

Accidents of this kind are very common in Ethiopia, where there are constant streams of loosely superintended animals often on both sides of the road at once, but on this particular day Malcolm Largen struck and killed a man. The Tana-Tissisat road, about eighteen miles of virtually single track with a surface of loose gravel, is a busy thoroughfare by Ethiopian standards. Villagers from the plains west of the Abbai use it to reach Bahardar with its new market. The Expedition Land-Rovers, with Group N now based at the Tissisat Hydro-Electric Station and the zoologists camped in a field a few miles south of Bahardar, were frequently buzzing up and down amidst swarms of people and animals.

Malcolm was in the University Land-Rover, which he had borrowed for the zoologists' use. With Barbara Wells, Hilary King and Pat Morris, he was following another Land-Rover when a lone woodcutter, having jumped off the road to avoid the first vehicle, ran immediately back onto it again and then suddenly across it. Malcolm bowled him over; he went under the vehicle and was killed instantly. His bundle of wood hit and smashed the windscreen.

Pat Morris got a lift back to Bahardar in a passing car and was joined there by John Wilsey. Together they went to the Police Chief with whom John was on excellent terms. Strangely, the police were reluctant to get involved, for fear of angry mobs. However, they were persuaded to arm themselves and come. There were, in fact, no ugly crowds at the scene of the accident; the victim was obviously a man of no local importance. John Wilsey laid the corpse in the back of his

Land-Rover and drove it to the morgue in Bahardar. With an arm dangling brokenly and nose full of flies, it was already just a bundle of bones in a dirty *shamma*. Death in Ethiopia comes frequently and often publicly. What might in the western world have been long, complex obsequies were starkly simplified here. Evidently this was just a lone pauper, since no relatives came to claim him, which, said the police, made things considerably easier. It all depended on the social status of the deceased, and we seemed to have run down a man from the lowest stratum of the peasantry. There would be a brief court hearing the next day and no further formalities. Nothing better illustrated how expendable certain sorts of human life still are in Ethiopia.

Death, this time intentional and allowable, occurred further still down the road. John Blashford-Snell and a considerable entourage were blundering about in swampy fields trying to reach the river's edge, where it was hoped the White Water Team might be observed and filmed again. Such is the nature of the terrain here that it was quite impossible to get to the bank. Though we waded up to the chest in water-logged paddy fields, clumps of trees still cut us off from the roaring river. Suddenly there was a loud crack: Kifele Deredje had shot an enormous black and white spur-winged goose, which plummeted heavily into the wet grass. The son of Dejazmatch Deredje Makonnen, the new and most co-operative Governor-General of Gojjam, Kifele had come in his father's Land-Rover, with a cousin and an elaborate tent and accoutrements, to spend a few days with the Expedition in the field. Rather inappropriately clad in smart mackintosh, narrow trousers and winkle-pickers, he was happily splashing about with us in the mud with a 12-bore, trying to bag something for the pot.

❉ ❉ ❉

Next morning, exactly at nine, the Command Group Land-Rover waiting on the Tana-Tissisat road saw a red ministar arc up through the mist above the river. The White Water Team were ready and about to move off on their second leg. It was to end with the evening sky lit by red ministars with an altogether more serious significance.

Progress was made at first on the lines of the previous afternoon— the dinghies were lowered, hauled, and lifted down narrow channels, over rocks, through arching undergrowth, and all the time to the right of the great waterfall system. Care had to be exercised not to thrust the rubber skins of the dinghies against the clumps of thornbush which grew amongst the trees on the rocky islets.

"I hope there are no crocodiles in this lot," said Peter O'Mahony with a nervous laugh, as Roger and Alastair, up to their waists in water, cut a way with machetes to ease the boats through. But there was plenty of evidence later that crocodiles abounded. In the dim light Chris Bonington and John Fletcher took pictures of the others pushing and pulling, while Alastair shot several feet of film with a hand-held cinecamera.

The stream, four or five feet deep for the most part, gurgled on down this warren of waterways, splitting and reuniting in a bewildering manner: "Keep to the right! Keep to the right!" was the cry. Suddenly the channel broadened, there was a sharp bend to the left between two islands, and the water ran more strongly. Open blue sky replaced the dark ceiling of trees and foliage; they were back in the main river.

They paddled on down increasingly rough water, until Roger halted his flotilla at the familiar brim of a cataract: white spume was being thrown up and the noise of the water grew deafening. An inspection on foot showed that huge black rocks—fatal to rubber dinghies—dotted the course of the cataract, but also that a chute of brown water ran down the right hand side. Roger decided to try to control the descent at the bottom by means of ropes. This was an answer to the abiding problem in our mode of travel—how to stop. Each crew in turn would take its dinghy down the brown chute and the others, now a bank party, would throw out a line and haul them in to the edge. This was a rather hazardous system, for it depended on three things all happening successfully: (i) the crew in transit must keep on the right side of the cataract; (ii) the line must be accurately thrown to the fast-moving dinghy (no time to coil in and toss again); and (iii) someone in the boat must catch and secure the line quickly.

Chris Bonington belayed a rope to a tree and Jim stood calmly ready to throw the coiled end. *Faith* came swooping down the chute and the rope snaked out. It looked as if it would fall prematurely, but the dinghy was carried swiftly underneath it and Peter and Alastair made it fast. The bank party pulled her in like a great fish, and baling began for the *n*th time. There was a moment of fear as the rope, thrown inaccurately by Chris Edwards, missed *Hope*, which was swept towards the next series of cataracts, but John Huckstep ultimately gathered it and *Hope* joined *Faith* and *Charity* in the haven.

After this time-consuming manoeuvre they rode out another nasty cataract, and then there was a comparatively peaceful run for a mile or so down a river sluicing along now at a steady five or six knots. Chris Bonington, occupied with photography, dived repeatedly into the watertight ammunition boxes in which he kept his store of cameras. His dinghy was thus in the hands of Ian Macleod and Chris Edwards, who noticed that they were squatting in a rapidly deepening swill of water—*Charity* had been holed on the last cataract, and so Chris began to bale as they skimmed along.

Inevitably, they came upon another cataract. The routine of stopping, inspecting and making decisions was beginning to impose a strain on Roger. Then for all of them came the moment when they had to screw their courage to the sticking-place and plunge over the lip of the rapid into the wild cascade. Most of them felt like young children picked up by an over-zealous father in the back garden and whirled around by an arm and a leg—they did not know whether they were enjoying it, or whether to cry out for it to stop.

Faith took this cataract, with its fearsome central hydraulic, and arrived safely in the reeds; *Charity* came after, with Chris Edwards leaning his big body out over the stern and thrusting his paddle this way and that in an effort to control the course of the dinghy. They disappeared, and then emerged, filled with water, and struggled clumsily to the bank, almost all steerage way gone.

Hope followed, wallowing deep and then rising yards high over the wave's crest. A sudden blow struck them and Jim Masters and John Huckstep were flipped out. John Fletcher stayed inboard, laughing excitedly. The other two were sucked down to the bottom of the river by the churning waters and held under. Both pulled the knob to release the CO_2 into their inflatable lifejackets and soon surfaced, ashen-faced and spluttering, and John Fletcher hauled them in. It had been a nasty moment for both of them.

Roger wisely permitted an hour and a half's break whilst they recuperated, and the L-shaped gash in *Charity's* underside was patched and the glue allowed to dry. Jim, his jaws working mechanically on biscuits and sardines, sat apart and stared dully at the river.

"What I think we'll do now," said Roger, after he had been on a brief downstream reconnaissance, "is rope the boats down this next stretch—it looks pretty nasty."

"I wouldn't say it was any worse than what we've done," interposed Alastair.

"Maybe. But remember," said Roger, "we've already had a pretty long day…"

"But we haven't covered a very great distance, Roger," Chris Edwards said; "nothing like the twelve kilometres we're supposed to do."

"Well, I don't think we ought to be too bound by self-imposed targets. Safety comes first."

"I agree," said Jim.

"Jim," went on Roger, "I would be very grateful if you would assist me with your engineering know-how on this business of roping down. I reckon this time we should let the boats down empty in some way…"

And so a scheme was arrived at whereby the boats were to be lowered singly with a line at bow and stern. Alastair turned away and kicked a stone into the water. The two Chrises and Ian Macleod exchanged glances; a great fellow-feeling was springing up among the crew of *Charity*, the only dinghy not yet to have been capsized. They were brimming with confidence and eager to get to grips with the Abbai again.

So the "roping down" began. By 4 p.m. they had not covered much more than a mile.

General impatience was evident as they approached the top of another of the many geological steps in the twenty miles from Tana to Tissisat. As with almost all of them, it was difficult to see the actual course of the rapid even from within a few yards of the edge. So Chris Edwards bent down and Roger climbed up and stood on his shoulders; slowly Chris straightened up.

"I still can't see," said Roger, carefully poised, "but I think it'll go. It looks better if we aim over to the left of that big rock and make for the left bank."

"O.K.," he said, when they got back to the others, who were waiting upstream in the boats. "This'll be the last one today. Same formation. Same procedure. Paddle like hell to the left-hand side."

Roger dropped into the stern and Peter and Alastair dug away vigorously at the water. But they could not defeat the enormous strength of the current and were carried down to the right of the big rock. They disappeared from sight over the rim of the cataract.

✳ ✳ ✳

At just about this moment seven members of the Expedition—John Blashford-Snell, Martin, Nigel Sale, John Wilsey, "Johnny" Johnson, Claude and I—were being entertained to tea by Mrs. Tony Crewe-Gee, whose husband is the Manager of the Hydro-Electric Station at Tissisat. Inevitably, much of the talk was of the last attempt to navigate the waters above the Falls—the Sutton Expedition of March, 1968. Five men and two girls had set off from Bahardar in three Zodiacs. Their kit was stowed amidships in large chests, and it soon became apparent that they were drawing too much water to clear the rocks in the dry-season river. After a series of accidents, they began to jettison even quite expensive things in a desperate attempt to remain afloat—for they had no lifejackets, no protective helmets or special clothing.

"They had everything they didn't want, and nothing that they did," Mrs. Crewe-Gee said.

Halfway to Tissisat four of them mutinied; the other three wanted to go on with tarpaulins over the ripped bottoms and the lightened kit on top. When they reached Tissisat they were almost starving—their staple diet had been Complan—very dull fare indeed. The Manager's wife fed them, and one of them stayed with her for two or three weeks, trying unsuccessfully to get permission to go on. They had had brushes with the local Governor at Bahardar, and he still acted somewhat biliously towards intending Nile navigators when we arrived six months later.

It was very pleasant to be sitting in a garden in the sun, drinking tea from a cup and saucer. Cakes and biscuits went round and our gratitude to the Crewe-Gees was boundless. Their home was a little suburban oasis, and outside—mud, flies and the surging river. Tony Crewe-Gee, a big, slow-speaking East Anglian, with considerable African experience, took us to his power station to see the remains of the two Zodiacs that he had inherited from the Sutton Expedition. We looked down from the white railings a hundred feet or more, into the gorge proper and the waters of the Abbai below Tissisat. This was the great problem, on which White Water and N Groups would combine their efforts.

For the moment, however, Group N strolled in the sun and drank Coca-Cola in the Electric Club beneath portraits of Haile Selassie I and Queen Elizabeth II. The group was camped on the only available flat, dry ground—a nearby cattle pound, strewn with cow-pats. They were waiting for the Redshanks to reach Tissisat, when their support duties would begin. The Engineer Group, under "Hank" Mansley, who were to fix an aerial ropeway over Tissisat, down which a dinghy would later be lowered, were camped below Group N, near the 1st Portuguese Bridge, or Agam Dildi, about 500 yards downstream from the power station.

As the afternoon drew on, John Blashford-Snell knew it was time to go. A Land-Rover had to be patrolling the road at 5 p.m. so as to regain contact with the White Water Team in their new position. Dusk was quickly falling as John Blashford-Snell, Claude and John Wilsey, were cruising slowly north. Suddenly, an oncoming private car flashed its headlights and stopped. Out fell John Huckstep whom they had obviously picked up just along the road. He ran over to John Blashford-Snell's vehicle and collapsed on the bonnet. His matted hair was sticky with sweat and his face drawn with exhaustion.

"There's been a terrible accident, John," he began, fighting for breath. "We all came over an appalling cataract, and *Charity* capsized and we've lost the three crew. Ian Macleod went past us riding on top of the upturned dinghy and the other two haven't been seen at all."

Claude was left on the road to mark the exact point, John Wilsey ran with John Huckstep over the fields to the river, and John Blashford-Snell drove back fast to Tissisat to set an emergency operation in motion. Groups N and E were alerted, and soon Land-Rovers were roaring urgently up the road again. Even the zoologists were called out in this moment of distress. "Hank" Mansley's Engineer Group were asked to fix a taut rope across the Abbai some distance above Tissisat, to prevent Ian or the others being swept over the Falls. This job taxed "Hank's" ingenuity considerably, for it was dark and moonless. Group N were deployed by Nigel Sale along the river bank some miles up, where it was thought that the lost crew might fetch up. They spent some time blundering about with torches endeavouring to find a way through the dense scrub and actually reach the river. The likelihood of any of them emerging near body or boat was, of course, minimal. But *something* had to be done at such a time, however futile.

The typical V-formation of an Abbai cataract: at a slight narrowing of the river there is also a fall in level, followed by hydraulic waves breaking back on themselves, strong eddies and whirlpools.

✳ ✳ ✳

What had happened to Group WW, and particularly to the crew of *Charity* after their first capsize? As the first dinghy approached the brink of the cataract Roger and his two companions saw to their horror that they were being drawn helplessly into a long chute culminating, after a considerable drop in height, in a frenzy of white waves. Somehow they survived it, and paddling hard they managed to pull over to the left bank and came to rest in some trees. They tried to talk to the others over the SARBE radio, but nothing was heard. So after long deliberation—during which time John Huckstep, waiting apprehensively above, became convinced that all must be up with them—Roger fired a green ministar into the air, the signal for the go-ahead.

Hope's crew responded, but they too were swept to the right, striking a rock and holing the boat. It soon filled with water and they were carried downstream willy-nilly, fighting hard to get to the side. They were pitched over a second series of rapids and, exhausted, ultimately seized a mooring in some bushes about 500 yards below *Faith*, but on the right hand bank.

Roger made ready to follow them, but as luck would have it *Charity* appeared at that moment on the lip of the cataract, having managed to get onto the left hand side of the stream. They were moving very fast indeed. Chris Edwards' last clear thought for some time was, "God, it isn't a cataract, it's a bloody waterfall!" Coursing over the curved brim, they were dashed against a submerged rock and the dinghy tipped over, throwing all three of them down the fall. After a sickening pause, Roger saw three white helmets bob up near the overturned dinghy, but at intervals they disappeared in the churning welter. He fixed his lifeline to the tethered *Faith* and thrust out, swimming into the fast-moving water, though still a good way below the waterfall.

After what seemed an interminable delay during which the white helmets were repeatedly lost to sight for long spells, one of them moved away from the falls. Under it Chris Edwards, his face contorted, was swimming feebly as he was borne along on the current. Roger tried to reach him, but Chris was carried past, hysterically crying "Help!" Alistair and Peter watched aghast as he was swept downstream towards the next set of rapids. Amazingly he stopped, lodged on the very edge, his head and shoulders clear of the water and facing down river.

Minutes after, Ian Macleod, who had similarly been lost to sight for long spells, was seen climbing on top of the upturned *Charity*. He had a paddle, and slowly the dinghy moved away from the turmoil at the foot of the fall and was carried away downstream to the right. Jim Masters and the crew of *Hope* saw him come bucking down towards them and quite close. He was squatting on his haunches and paddling gamely. Jim hurled a rope but it fell short and Ian was swept on his rubber platform towards the next hazard—a waterfall whose terrible booming seemed to presage disaster.

"Lie down! Lie down!" they all shouted to him, but he disappeared over the falls, still sitting up.

For Chris Bonington the ordeal had been much the same. He had been drawn down several times by the undertow of the waterfall and had imagined himself on the edge of drowning. He had already lost a son in this way, and through his mind flashed thoughts of his wife Wendy, to whom he is devoted. No doubt he wondered, too, if he would ever again feel the rough assurance of a gritstone handhold, or ever stand, safe on a good belay, and stare across an Alpine valley as No. 2 climbed slowly up.

Swimming with difficulty—his wet-suit trousers had been torn down and were now gripping his ankles—he managed to reach an exposed rock a little way below the falls. From here he could see Chris Edwards caught in the faster middle of the stream and now moving away down river. He also saw Ian Macleod climb onto *Charity*, and he made an effort to swim over; but after a couple of strokes *Charity* was gripped by the current and carried away. So Chris Bonington turned down river towards *Faith* and eventually reached the line which Roger was swimming out with, and he was hauled in to join Alastair and Peter.

The attention of all four was now concentrated on Chris Edwards, pinned helpless and exhausted to his rock on the very edge of the cataract. His first disquieting experience had been to discover that when he was drawn down under the water by the falls, he could not rise again even though he swam strongly. After a lengthy submersion, however, he was vomited up by the whirling waters and believed himself safe, but he only had time for a gulp or two of air before he was dragged down again under the waves. This cycle recurred three or four times and in a state of considerable panic he realised that he was not going to be able to get clear of the whirlpool. During each immersion he was spun round and tumbled about like clothes in a washing machine. Fumbling frantically for the release knob, he filled his life-jacket and for the first time was stabilised in an upright position. His head broke the surface again, and there was *Charity*, trapped still in the same pool. With one hand he grabbed a lifeline. Here was reassurance indeed, and an end to the nightmare. But, seconds later it was snatched from his fingers, and this time as the whirlpool drew him under the fall, he felt the blow of tons of water thudding down on top of him, and he swallowed a good deal of it. Again and again the terrifying revolutions threw him up and drew him down.

At last, he was washed to the edge of the pool and found himself floating, panic-stricken and drained of energy, clear of the tumult. There were the white helmets of Chris and Ian, and there *Charity*. He tried limply to swim; but he was caught in the main stream and, like Chris Bonington, his wet-suit trousers were ripped down to below his knees. Then to his left he saw Roger breasting the water towards him. Roger stretched out his arm. It was a sickeningly close thing—but Chris could not be reached and was swept past. Now he was aware of another serious danger: he was moving towards the top of the next cataract. The water grew shallower and his bare knees knocked against submerged boulders. The sharp, volcanic rock lacerated his legs and took chunks out of his fingers as he clawed at them in an effort to stop himself. For some fifty yards he bounced along in this agonising way, until at the very edge of the rapids his leg struck a large rock under water which he was able to grasp with his hands and at last check his progress. For five minutes his body shook and his breathing was erratic. His strength was almost sapped, but the glimpse of salvation that this rock offered enabled him to summon up enough energy to hang on; and hang on he did, for thirty long minutes.

He could barely move, for water was breaking strongly over his back. To hold his position he had to push hard away from the rock and into the flow of water. He scarcely dare lift one hand off, although he did succeed in taking out his knife and sawing blindly under water at the tangle of neoprene trousering around his ankles. After ten minutes he had, to his great relief, cut it right away.

Every now and then he glanced over his left shoulder. Surely to God they would come and help him soon? Roger, Peter, Alastair and Chris Bonington with *Faith* were, in fact, moving downstream in a methodical and careful way, until finally the four men and their boat were at the nearest point of river bank to him—about 200 feet away.

"Help!" cried Chris, waveringly. "Help!"

"Hold on, Chris, just hold on! We are almost with you!" shouted Roger.

To distract his gaze from the hideous spill of water just in front, Chris stared hard at the "V34" marked in black ink on his life-jacket. "V34. Neat, regular lettering," he thought. "Someone stamped that on in some nice, dry ordnance factory in dear old England. What's the 'V' for? Why '34'? They'll have different codes for all the different pieces, I suppose. Dear old England: you'll get back there, my boy, don't worry. Look at that kingfisher hovering over the cataract. If only *homo sapiens* could do that. Super black and white colouring. Wonder what sort it is?

'Johnny' would know. He'll be all right: striding along in his gaiters on some dry path, with his notebook at the ready. Those are weaver birds down there amongst the waving papyrus—I know those. Noisy little devils. Can't hear them now though because of the din of this water. Oh! God! My arms are going numb. How long can I hold on here? I must think of something else to think of."

He glanced again over his shoulder and here were Roger and Alastair coming towards him in *Faith*. Up in a tree Chris Bonington and Peter were paying the boat out slowly on a 150-foot line. Just two minutes more, and then he would be in the dinghy. He managed a rather pained smile. Then, about thirty feet above him, they stopped. They had come to the end of the line. Roger was paddling furiously in an effort to keep the dinghy out in the stream above Chris: the current was forcing it all the time to swing in to the left-hand bank. Alastair threw a nylon lifeline to him, but it did not uncurl well and dropped far short. Roger could not hold the boat in the stream any longer, and they drifted in to the left as Peter and Chris Bonington began slowly and painfully to haul them in.

This was the unkindest cut of all, thought Chris. A black despair momentarily gripped him; they had failed. He was angry, afraid, hysterical, as he saw the boat slowly receding. However, he grimly resolved to go on living and hoping just as long as they went on trying to rescue him. Soon they came out from the bank, paddling hard, the line that held them whipping up droplets of water as it tautened. Again they got to within thirty feet and then stopped. This time Alastair tied three nylon ribbons together, lashed a paddle on the end, and threw it out. The line was now long enough to reach Chris and the paddle floated down to him. He reached out to take it, as a pilgrim would the Holy Grail.

He lashed the line round his waist, but then found himself totally unable to move: mentally and physically he was pinioned. He was filled with a real dread of the rushing water, and now feared to give up his sanctuary rock. Furthermore, when he did try to move, he found that a foot had become wedged in a crevice and he had too little strength to wrench it free. Seeing this, Alastair, with great courage, clipped himself onto the long ribbon with a karabiner and hopped overboard into the thigh-deep waters. With infinite slowness he moved towards Chris and finally took his hand. With macabre thoughts of underwater amputations in his mind, he helped him, by taking the tension off his lifeline, to ease his foot free.

"I don't think I can make it, Alastair."

"Of course you can. I'll hold you up and give you balance."

"No, I think I'd go under and if I did Roger probably couldn't hold me."

"O.K. I'll go back and help him pull."

Alastair made his way gingerly back, and he and Roger pulled in on the lifeline as Chris, like a sleepwalker, stumbled slowly towards them. Eventually he made it and rolled into the boat and lay in the bottom, his heart brimming with a sense of immense relief. Peter and Chris Bonington, under the trees, strained and heaved as they pulled the fully laden dinghy up against the current.

Although Chris had been saved from this harrowing experience all was not yet over. Five men had to cross the river in a leaking boat and negotiate at least one cataract to reach the crew of *Hope* on the opposite bank. The sun had declined to about 10° above the horizon whilst the rescue had been taking place. So as soon as First Aid had been applied to Chris's bleeding legs, they set off with some urgency, paddling hard across the stream. They grounded frequently, ripping the boat's underskin, but with nerves now numbed they leapt mechanically into the water to shove her off. At one time Chris Bonington was swept away, but calmly waited until *Faith* caught up with him. Soon, in the gathering dusk, they found Jim Masters searching for them, and with him Ian Macleod, last seen sitting on the bottom of an upturned dinghy as it disappeared into a rapid.

It had turned out to be a waterfall of twelve to fifteen feet, and as he plunged over it vertically the dinghy had struck a confusion of waves at its foot and folded upwards into a U-shape, trapping Ian inside it. He had been seen to reappear several yards downstream, still paddling vainly for the edge. He tried to snatch at passing branches but they were rotten and broke off. Eventually a handful held him and he prepared to pull himself onto the shore in some way, but his lifeline had become entangled round the paddle, which he had thrust under two of the straps on the underside of the dinghy, and the boat dragged him away. He freed his lifeline, grabbed at more branches, but again the boat spun off, this time leaving him suspended from a tree like a weaver bird. He struggled to the right-hand bank and made his way upstream to Jim and John Fletcher. It was characteristic of him that after a lone ordeal that would have been quite enough for any ordinary man, he should set off up the bank again with Jim Masters to look for his other friends.

As the eight of them were reunited on the bank—John Huckstep had been sent in earlier to the road—a heavy thunderstorm broke. And with the darkness, the rain and the cold came a sense of failure, only tempered by the fact that, although *Charity* had gone, no lives had been lost. It was only the end of the second day of the phase, but it was to prove a definite turning point in the expedition, and the most memorable day in the lives of at least nine of its members.

Chapter Twelve
NEVER A HAPPY PHASE

THE bitter-sweet outcome of the day's adventures was relayed from road to river and from one search party to another by our modern equivalent of the Armada beacons system: in the night sky green ministars soared up and then the news came over the SARBE radio which each group carried—"All White Water Team safe. Only *Charity* missing". There was general jubilation amongst Groups N and E. While some had been thrashing about hopelessly along the river bank in inky blackness, others had been posted on the lower platform at the Hydro-Electric station and told to watch for dinghy and crew in the swirling water below the Tissisat Falls. Only slightly less depressing was the task of some of the Engineer Group, who had to rig a net at the first Portuguese Bridge at a point where the whole Nile is compressed into a twenty-foot-wide chasm. This was to be a sort of Long-Stop with which to catch anything that might be carried so far down. The ferocity of the topmost waves there, however, made dangling and fixing any kind of net quite impossible.

Roger Chapman, Alastair, Peter and John Fletcher were encamped near their landing place of the previous night. The rest of Group WW had been withdrawn to the Ras Hotel at Bahardar to receive medical attention and recuperate. Next morning Roger's residual team from the North and Group N from the South began the search for *Charity*. All one fruitless day they poked about in swamp and thicket by the river's edge. The Beaver had been asked to help and was on its way from Debre Marcos. The aptly-named Hawkeye[1] soon found the dinghy caught among reeds about one and a half miles downstream of the incident, and marked it by dropping a flare. A watchful land support party on the road took a compass bearing on the flare, and marched in on it to the river.

A gently flowing stream some forty yards wide soon confronted them. Chris Bonington crossed it with a line, and the rest swam after. Nobody spoke of crocodiles although it was ideal water for them.

The Tissisat Falls — here the Great Abbai drops for the first time into its gorge.

Damp undergrowth grew thickly beneath the interlaced branches. There were yet more streams and rivulets to plunge through before Garth Brocksopp, shinning up a tree, shouted out, "I'm sure I see a patch of yellow across there!" Chris Bonington swam again with a rope, and there among water grasses he found *Charity*, with her yellow nylon dodger intact. Nothing was lost from her, except Chris's own rucksack—and even this was later recovered a little further downstream. Amazingly, the films and cameras in the waterproof tins were unspoiled, despite almost two days' immersion.

Charity was lugged back to rejoin the other two dinghies in a new Group WW Base Camp, which was established near an Abbai tributary in a fly-ridden field roughly halfway from Tana to Tissisat. Here, just beside the road, the concrete floor of a demolished building afforded a flat surface on which the patient John Fletcher could repair the boats.

Meanwhile, Roger West and Nigel Marsh were busy repairing the members of the White Water Team themselves in the rooms of the Ras Hotel at Bahardar. Chris Edwards was their first concern, but Ian Macleod was also badly cut about and shaken. John Huckstep and Peter O'Mahony had not been entirely fit since leaving Bahardar, and Chris Bonington suffered delayed shock and was under close observation. There was also "Hank" Mansley, who had a bout of 'flu at this stage, and Rex Matthews, who had been unwell since the start of the expedition.

For a full week, as it turned out, the Ras and the Blue Nile Springs Hotels were occupied by droves of Expedition members. By day the hotel would empty, except for sick and wounded, but by night the rooms, restaurant and bar would be alive with bizarre figures: The archaeological team (Group S), permanent residents at the Ras, full of talk of newly discovered fortresses and their crenellated gatehouses; a few of Groups N and E, who did not often make the eighteen-mile journey up from Tissisat, enjoying their Melottis; Group WW, track-suited and in some cases bandaged, engaged in animated discussion of the wisdom of this course and the folly of that.

Roger Chapman and his Group WW were almost all, of course, badly shaken by the events of Monday, September 9th. This perhaps helps to explain the bitter differences of opinion that rent the expedition in the succeeding two or three days at the Ras. Clearly the group were going to have to be extensively reorganised in some way.

Tension in the White Water Team began to show even at Bahardar: Roger Chapman (left), Alastair Newman, Chris Edwards.

Although, with *Charity*'s recovery, there were no grave losses of equipment to prevent further progress, it was soon obvious that a number of team substitutes would be necessary.

Chris Bonington had been active in the search for *Charity*, but in the anti-climax afterwards the shock of his experience in the last waterfall overcame him. Appalled at the dangers he had been facing, and their possible results for his family, he went to Roger and told him that he did not want to go on. John Huckstep made it known that he had had enough: he had lost a lot of his earlier enthusiasm for working with Roger, and, besides, he was uneasy about his health. Peter O'Mahony, not exactly a volunteer, had been drafted in as a signaller. Unwell too, he now indicated that he would prefer to go on helping the team from the bank. Chris Edwards and Ian Macleod recovered their equanimity, but were badly mauled physically. Whilst Ian, however, was fairly soon passed fit, Doc West told Chris "No more water!" as his legs and hands were going to take some time to heal.

This left Roger with Ian, John Fletcher, Jim and Alastair—not enough to man even two dinghies. John and Jim, although stunned and weary like the others, had developed a strong sense of loyalty to Roger and the Expedition, and intended doggedly to go on. Alastair showed an icy nervelessness throughout, and alone seemed quite unaffected by the events.

The accident naturally invited a review of the whole phase. Could we afford to continue? I was first reserve, and so I left Group N to replace John Huckstep. Two dinghies at least could now go on. But could they go on as if nothing had happened? We had already used up the four days that had been allotted to the Tana-Tissisat stretch. It seemed to some, perhaps, more realistic to cut losses and jump into the Northern Gorge so that this more important length of river might be properly and safely covered, and time still be available for a useful survey of the unknown water below Mota.

This suggestion was greeted as defeatist and caused a great furore. Many of us argued that, after all, we had a unique chance to navigate the whole of this hitherto unbeaten river and it must not be allowed to slip.

"What's the point of risking our necks going down all these cataracts," asked Chris Edwards, "if we're going to skip the last half of the run to Tissisat?"

"Frankly," said Chris Bonington, "from the story point of view it'll be a bloody fiasco if we don't cover the whole thing."

By this time the White Water Team was dividing into two groups, which can be loosely categorised as Hawks and Doves. The Hawks were becoming obsessed with the importance of covering, even at some risk, every possible inch of river, and with the same nucleus of people; the Doves, on the other hand, felt that the first requirement was survival, that speed, and therefore completeness, might have to be sacrificed, and that the Expedition—even in this more dangerous phase—should still pursue its scientific aim.

The principal Hawks were probably the two Chrises and Alastair, with John Wilsey as *éminence grise* in the background. They argued that a refurbished White Water Team should quickly resume its work. Chris Bonington was beset by private doubts as to whether or not he personally should go on (after all, Jim Masters and John Fletcher were family men, too), but there was no question in his mind, as he paced about the Ras, that from the press and publicity angle delay by the Expedition would be fatal. Chris Edwards, chafing at his own disabilities, was a dedicated Hawk. When Roger Chapman later went off for three days on a reconnaissance of the river below Tissisat, there was such impatience and suspicion among the Hawks that John Wilsey was actively canvassed to take over the command of Group WW. John Blashford-Snell, of course, would hear none of it and by and large he stood aloof. And John Wilsey knew anyway that he had shortly to lead Group J in their ascent from Shafartak.

The Dovecote was presided over by Roger Chapman, with quiet support from John Fletcher and Jim Masters. The importance of caution was uppermost in their minds; no "World First" was worth the taking of blatant risks. Progress, daily mileage, continuity—all were secondary criteria to safety. Never again must cataracts be embarked on blindly, and therefore time spent by Roger on bank reconnaissances— even if it limited our coverage of the river—was of the utmost value.

There was a complementary "third world" of members who did not want to get drawn into either faction—but it was difficult to remain neutral. It was also difficult at first for them to see what it was that the Hawks were opposed to. There had been no overt plan to abandon any part of Phase 2, although Roger, obviously aware of his responsibility for the lives of his group, had become more cautious. The Doves were ready to go ahead at any moment, though prudently, and on the third day after the disasters at the last cataract, progress down the river was resumed.

Suspicions of Roger's motives had been fanned the day before this by the circulation of a bit of highly controversial intelligence: it was said that he proposed to drop Alastair from the White Water Team. This was unthinkable to the Hawks. Relations had now virtually broken down between Roger and Alastair: Roger despaired, in spite of many careful, courteous overtures, of ever establishing any real *rapport* with the hard, unsentimental Alastair; Alastair, for his part, was now prepared to dismiss Roger as an unadventurous, over-fussy leader. Fundamentally, it was a clear clash of temperaments, though their attitudes were found equally among other Hawks and Doves: John Wilsey thought Roger was vacillating, and John Fletcher and Jim Masters found Alastair aggressive, and both now jibbed at the prospect of working with him in the same boat.

The report was that Colin Chapman, our twenty-four-year-old crocodile expert at the moment with Group N, would go into the first

The reconstituted White Water Team rest before pushing off again three miles below the Tissisat Falls. Left to right: Macleod, Fletcher, Snailham, Roger Chapman, Masters, Newman.

Redshank with Roger and Ian, whilst Jim, John Fletcher and I would crew the second. This news was received by Hawks with amazement and anger.

"Here's this chap," said Chris Bonington, "who saved Chris Edwards' life only four days ago, being kicked out because he wants to get on with the job."

"So he did. But Chris, wouldn't any one of us in his position have done the same?" asked John Fletcher.

"Look, mate, how many times have you been close to death?"

"If he is being kicked out," went on John, across the dinner table, "it's not just that. Perhaps it's because he's too impetuous, too foolhardy—he represents a sort of danger in himself..."

"Christ, man, we all know it's a bloody dangerous river; but we'll never overcome it without people like Alastair. What expedition ever got anywhere that didn't have a good proportion of hard men in it?"

"But Alastair will go down *any* cataract," countered John, "and most of us are not prepared to do that any more. If it's to be Colin Chapman, well, he seems a tough enough character, and balanced, and we all get on with him."

Alastair had only two days' more practical experience of white water work than Colin, but, of course, they were two quite extraordinary days. Colin was ready to join, and, in his modest way, very keen. But a strong "Newman-must-stay" movement mobilised during the evening, and Chris Bonington, who had now reversed his own decision to stay out and was determined to rejoin Group WW, was Alastair's chief advocate. Alastair himself was, as he said, "choked off" by the rumour. To have been relegated to a support group would have been a living death for him at this time. His single purpose now was to be amongst the few who would cover all the parts of the river navigated by the Expedition.

It was Chris Bonington who was the spearhead of the White Water Team's cause, of Alastair's, and of his own. Assertive and independent, he had crossed swords with John Blashford-Snell a few times already. This had usually arisen over one of Chris's changes of plan; he had rather confusing "windvane" tendencies, and John found nothing more disruptive of careful military planning than to have Chris argue strongly against a course of action which he had a few days earlier strongly favoured. He certainly gave free rein to his feelings during these three highly-charged days at the Ras. Lightning flickered over Lake Tana and tropical rain lashed down on the hotel lawn; in the dining-room the atmosphere was just as electric.

"We've got to make sure for the story that Roger goes down that river, all of it," Chris said. "The story's a damned important part of this whole Expedition; you feel this, surely, Richard?"

"He'll go down pretty well all of it," John Fletcher butted in. "He just doesn't want to kill us doing the impossible bits."

"What distance are they going to be? We've got to get some continuity in this; there mustn't be any loopholes."

"I suppose we'll do what we have time for," John said. "We're starting again tomorrow, more or less at the point that we pulled out. We want to try to reach Tissisat while Roger's away on his recce. I reckon we owe it to him to finish off that bit."

"I just don't know about Roger," Chris mused, "he seems to be going soft."

Chris was by now Roger's most outspoken critic, but even he persisted in trying to paper over the cracks.

"I like him, and I respect him," he went on, "I think he's a good man, but…"

Next morning, before Roger set off on his three-day reconnaissance, Chris tried unsuccessfully to get himself reinstated in Group WW by asking Roger to add a third Redshank and pull two more men from the long-suffering Nigel Sale's Group N. But Roger, with four "casualties" in his team, had determined to go on with only two dinghies (this saved much time from Tissisat onwards), and to paddle with him he wanted in one of them, Ian Macleod and me; in the other, Jim Masters, John Fletcher and—after all the recriminations—Alastair Newman.

That things quietened down was probably because of factors beyond the White Water Team. They were, after all, only part of a larger organisation operating in the Lake Tana area. Zoologists made important additions to their collection, archaeologists carried on unaffected by these personal storms, Group N prepared for the march down the western edge of the gorge, and, in distant Mota, David Bromhead and his Group I were getting ready to move to the 2nd Portuguese Bridge.

News from this bridge perturbed John Blashford-Snell far more than the petty squabbles in the Ras bar. David Bromhead had run into difficulties with local villagers, and had signalled that he had had to move away from the gorge. Also, there were other niggling matters—such as the fact that most of the inner tubes in our Land-Rover tyres seemed to be perishing simultaneously, and no new ones were available in Bahardar. However, when the strife in Roger's team began to affect the workings of the whole expedition, it had to be resolved. John Blashford-Snell was masterminding about eight groups at this time, and liked to delegate as much control as possible to their leaders. So it was reluctantly that he now intervened to exert a moderating influence on Group WW.

Roger had attributed the nervous tension in the shattered White Water Team to a fear of what the river held in store. So he had left on a three-day reconnaissance of the Abbai below Tissisat. Unreliable assessments made from the air, coupled with the difficulty his dinghies had had in coming to a stop, convinced Roger and John Blashford-Snell that for the reputedly more hazardous water in the Northern Gorge we simply had to know beforehand the configuration of the river and the location of its main cataracts with much more accuracy. He had set off from his Base Camp on a staggering forced march with Gage Williams, Peter O'Mahony, and—for a mile or so—Assefa, which took them some twelve or thirteen miles down the heavily overgrown right-hand bank.

As they do not yet appear on any maps, we gave codenames to the cataracts they found. Three miles south of Tissisat a 500-yard stretch of severe rapids was called K1, and Roger began his bankside march below this. Fifteen miles from Tissisat was K2, another fearsome and unnavigable feature, which we already knew about. But between them, Roger found K1 Alpha and K1 Bravo, which we did not know about; later, in the dinghies, we went down K1 Charlie, which Roger did not know about!

Meanwhile, a party of six, of which I was now one, began on Thursday, September 12th, the completion of the river above Tissisat. *Hope* and *Faith* were used for this stretch, but not in convoy. As we could only afford two days, we decided to proceed in relay—*Hope* beginning more or less where we had quit the river on Monday, and aiming for a prominent spur which pushed the river in a westward bend towards the road; *Faith* putting into the water at the spur and aiming for some point safely above the Falls.

My own baptism in *Faith*, under Jim Masters' command, was a quiet one: heavy rain, a quite untypically placid, steel-grey river, wooded islands loud with the calls of the brilliant avifauna. There was only one ugly moment, in which John Fletcher nearly lost his life. We had gingerly approached the edge of a very long series of rapids, and had found a fast stream flowing off to the right almost on its lip. To reach the relative safety of this stream involved passing the boat round projecting, tree-clad rocks, and this we did with John Fletcher sitting in the dinghy and letting himself out on a line. However, we underestimated the immense force of the water against a fixed object, and soon, as he held himself perilously four or five yards down the cataract, the river spilled over the bulwarks and flooded the boat. John was groping on the floorboards for a coiled rope he had left ready to throw to Jim, but it was some time before he found it in the swirling waters. He was once or twice almost submerged, but managed after a few moments to wade ashore with the rope.

Foolishly, we had not been prepared for this sort of upset and lost

The three dinghies shoot cataracts above the Tissisat Falls.

three helmets, three spare paddles and a foot pump, though the last was fortunately recovered the next day. The rest of Thursday, and Friday the 13th, which ominously followed, were safe and unsensational. We by-passed about 600 yards of cataracts and falls, stumbling about in gurgling streams and pulling the dinghy over rocks and under branches—only to emerge into the main stream immediately above a waterfall. We felt like prisoners of war who had tunnelled our way from the barrack block and come up just short of the wire. So the afternoon was spent in laborious portages to try to get back to the calmer water above Tissisat. The other crew, with *Hope*, also made long portages, some of which were over flooded fields adjacent to the river—a ploy which seemed to be within the rules.

Meanwhile, the Engineer Group under "Hank" Mansley had erected an aerial ropeway over the Tissisat Falls. It was hoped to photograph a Redshank being lowered over the Falls and down to the rocks on the opposite side of the gorge. A dinghy, attached to the rope, floated downstream to the brink, but instead of lifting clear and running free down the rope, it was sucked into the Falls themselves and disappeared as if it were a leaf carried into a street drain. The rope had passed over Alpha Falls, which is the section of Tissisat nearest to the power station and the one made up of two steps. Subsequently, Peter Hampson saw the Redshank in the pool at the bottom of the first step, and it was recovered, not too badly damaged.

Another ropeway was rigged up a day or two later when on Sunday, September 15th, the new White Water Team had marched away from civilisation to begin our survey of the river below Tissisat. It spanned the first of the right-hand tributaries that we had to cross, the River Tul. An extraordinary cavalcade had set off from the power station across soggy fields, with the team and their supporters painfully carrying the two Redshanks and all their kit, but attended by a crowd of fascinated, though unhelpful locals. Eventually, the lure of rounds of ammunition was too much, and they succumbed to the blandishments of Gavin Pike. Soon the dinghies, each borne on eight fuzzy heads, were moving briskly across the wet plain. Martin Romilly was marshalling this labour force, and with cries of "One, two, three, *Ishi!*" he even coaxed them two or three times into a run.

The River Tul is an incredible gash in the surface of the plain, only ten or twelve feet wide, but a good forty feet to the water, a brown, churning thread in an eroded, vertical-sided chasm. A native bridge of four thin branches offered a somewhat precarious way over; hence the need for a ropeway on which to sling dinghies and kit safely across.

Once over, we carried on through tussocky grasslands to the Abbai. I found myself left with a Redshank and six or seven rather feeble little men whom Martin had hired. In height, they only came to the level of my shoulder, and so whilst they bore the dinghy easily on their heads, I stumbled along, my neck bent sharply forward, seeing nothing. One of them, shorter than the others, was also wilier: he walked along the whole way with his head not quite touching the dinghy bottom, and at the end collected his rounds as solemnly as a judge.

We came to the Abbai by a dry stream bed just below K1. Here we organised and prepared for an early departure the following morning. Our supporting party began their walk back to Tissisat and we set up our tents under the trees. After supper, we turned in.

"Well, this is where it all really begins for me," I said a little apprehensively to Roger, as I lay in a sleeping bag smoking a final pipe. "I suppose you feel you've had half a lifetime on the white water already?"

"Debre Marcos is a hell of a long way away," he said.

"Addis is further," I reflected idly, "and London—that's in another galaxy."

Smartly at 8 a.m. Roger, Ian and I, in our wet-suits, pushed *Faith* out over the stones, and Jim, John and Alastair came after with *Charity*, now back in commission. We hopped in and paddled off into a current of twelve knots or so. The river, three miles below the Falls, was surprisingly open; fields lay along both banks, though the water's edge was fringed with thick trees and bushes. There were a few sporting passages, but it was generally a straightforward run for the first hour. At one point, sheer, basalt cliffs loomed on either side, and on top of one, Chris Bonington crouched with Assefa and clicked away as we spun down underneath him. While we paused in this brief gorge, there were sudden, strange cries and two naked Ethiopians came coursing past on *jendies*. These are bundles of reeds on which the local people cross the Abbai; they roll up their *shammas* and other possessions and stack them at the dry end, and then they leap into the river and, grasping the other end, kick their way over with powerful leg strokes, all the while ululating and slapping the water to scare away crocodiles. With a current of this speed, they probably passed down river for half a mile in the course of getting across it.

Presently we came upon a large red panel hung on the right-hand bushes, and then a red flare curved up—Gavin Pike was here to warn us of our approach to K1 Alpha. We pulled into a dry river bed and then began the laborious portage of our two boats and kit around this dangerous set of cataracts. With all six of us putting a shoulder under each fully-laden boat in turn, it took us two hours to complete the double haul over half a mile of bumpy meadow. Roger and I marched in front supporting the bows, where ropes, tins, rucksacks and front thwarts were stowed, on our braced necks and arms. Every part of the body was involved, and I imagined at one stage that I was being driven into the soft ground like a tent peg. I honestly believe these two hours presented the severest physical strain I have ever had.

After a few moments' break we moved on, glancing back at the tumbling falls we had circumvented. The river was rougher now and as it seemed likely that there were more hazards ahead, I was asked to be "the eyes of the fleet": Roger had to remain squatting at the helm; Ian normally wore glasses and, furthermore, the scars on his knees made repeated bendings in the wet-suit very painful. So, from time to time, as we creamed along, I stood and scanned the distant river line for the tell-tale signs of a cataract—smooth approach water, the occasional tossed spume, but above all, the perceptible fall in the tree-line on either side.

As we sped on, it all seemed so regrettably transitory. Passing a colourful colony of weaver birds, I felt I wanted to arrest everything for a moment or two. I recalled an accelerated film of the railway journey from London to Brighton which I had seen. It lasted about four minutes. The abiding impression was of parallel silver lines snaking ahead, a blur of sleepers, and the frequent dark bridges winging over. This sort of thing might be all we should remember of the Blue Nile— an endless brown ribbon, curving along between tree-clad banks. Memory would encompass the 500 miles of the Abbai in about four minutes; in our subsequent lectures, this sort of time would be allotted to "The River".

Soon I heard a distant booming and our course appeared to veer sharply to the right.

"Is this K1 Bravo, Roger?" I asked.

"Well, if it is, it should be manned. Any sign of Chris Edwards or Peter Hampson?"

"Not yet. I think we should creep up on this cat and surprise it."

So, with a hand signal to *Charity*, we slipped circumspectly up the right-hand bank towards the brink. Luckily it was perfectly possible to drag our boats about thirty yards across some open rocks, and put them in a pool just below the five-foot falls we had now reached. This we did, pausing for lunch in the sunshine. Chris Bonington and Gavin soon arrived after their brisk bank-side march, and took pictures of our re-entry into the turbulent foot of the fall.

It was a lively getaway, and the river remained exhilarating, with a succession of inclined planes, each with lines of waves at the bottom, like a heavy swell at sea. We were ineluctably drawn into these waves, but rode them well. The sides of the gorge, still forested, drew in steeply above us and the frequency of rapids increased. We were still some two miles from K2 when we approached a cataract that seemed a little longer than most. *Faith* had to draw closer than was prudent to see where the river went at its end. By the time I was able to say that it seemed to curl to the right, we were inescapably drawn into the cataract's magnetic field. Before plunging into the white, we signalled to the others to stop, but they were also too close to do much about it. *Faith* encountered a series of big waves and rode them all well, until about halfway down we saw an enormous swooping trough, followed by a large, inverted V of white. We subsided almost vertically into it and rode up, slightly sideways, over the creaming wall. Then all was confusion: Ian and I felt ourselves lifted clear of the floorboards, and we grabbed first a lifeline and then each other. Water spilled over the gunwales and we were inundated. Slowly we moved into lesser waves, and eventually away from the cataract. We paddled hard for the right bank, but as a drowned boat loses almost all steerage there was little response.

Now we were faced with two great whirlpools, each the size of the centre ring of a soccer pitch. We paddled furiously, but we could not escape that awful feeling of sinking. The water in the boats was already up to our groins as we knelt, but still more lopped over the sides. With agonising slowness, we edged clear and the river carried us gradually away, not to the right, but to the left, where immediately there was fast, choppy water. Now it felt as if we were paddling a canal barge: the load of water made our mass almost immovable.

Charity had taken a worse battering still. Jim, having gone into the great wave sideways, shipped a boatful of water straight away. They wallowed for some time through the successive bands of waves and then made a landfall on the right.

Ian and I in turn grabbed at vegetation as *Faith* spun down the edge of the stream. If we had secured a firm hold we would have been jerked from the boat, such was the speed of the river. Finally, we succeeded in braking and came to rest against thick clumps of osiers, where baling, which I had begun in midstream with minimal effect, could really start.

Roger fired a green flare to bring *Charity* alongside us then we all slipped down to moor under a canopy of trees on a convenient black beach. "I suppose we call that one K1 Charlie," I said. The mood in *Charity* was as black as the beach: the clear feeling was that we should not have attempted the cataract.

"You'd better not take us blind down a K1 Delta," said John Fletcher bitterly.

Nervous tension seemed fairly general; Alistair alone was composed—even bored, he claimed. "We're breaking our own rules, you know," said Jim. He sat hunched in the dinghy, smoking, and looking very worried.

"I tell you," said John, "if we do any more of that kind of thing, I'm coming out at K2."

The experiences of the second day out of Bahardar had left the older hands feeling apprehensive. The tireless Roger, concerned to soothe these ruffled nerves, set off on one of the many lone reconnaissances that he made that day, and the next 400 yards of river was plotted. Apparently, we were now rounding a spur that he had been forced by the terrain to cut over on his original recce—hence the surprise cataract. After a few more cigarettes—kept lovingly by John and Jim in a dry polythene jar—*Faith* led off downstream.

"Funny, isn't it?" said Ian. "We're three bachelors here, and in *Charity* they're all married blokes!"

We drifted cautiously along the right bank, looking all the while for signs of K2. There were rough passages, but nothing severe, and at 4 p.m. we pulled in to camp on an island in the narrow course of a tributary, the River Yete.

After curry, Roger and Jim set off to walk to K2. The support party there were expecting us by nightfall and it was only fair to tell them that we had stopped slightly short of them. Returning in darkness, our two helmsmen had a punishing struggle through thornbush. Luckily, they saw one of the many red ministars I fired up, and came in exhausted to our camp on a compass bearing.

It was as well that, tired as we had been, we had stopped to camp by the cool, pellucid Yete: for early next morning, when we pushed down to the Abbai, we emerged immediately into huge waves. The river was beginning to run very fast—though the gorge was, in fact, opening out—and soon we saw a broad red panel displayed. Although we kept as far as we could to the right bank, the swollen river was flowing amongst bushes and trees which forced us out into the stream, and we coursed along past the red flag at between twelve and fourteen knots, quite unable to stop. Some distance ahead we saw two members of Group N. They were Colin Chapman and Joe Ruston, standing on a rocky outcrop ready to receive our rope. But just up-river of them and about fifteen yards out from the edge of this now broadening river was a group of three or four partly exposed rocks; and they were in the direct line of our drift. "Easy," we thought, "just paddle inside them and throw the prepared rope to Colin and Joe." This was Roger's immediate order. Ian and I dug feverishly into the fast current, and made virtually no impression. The black rocks seemed to move up on us with force and inevitability. Futilely, I stabbed out a paddle to fend off, but *Faith* in a flash was wrapped round the first rock. The starboard edge was submerged, the floorboards smashed and bent back like the roof of a house. Water poured in, and sluiced out under the dodger, endangering our loose wet-suit jackets.

We all three leapt swiftly on to the rocks and tugged at the stricken boat, but it was immovable. The immense water pressure forced it against the rock, and once again we had a demonstration of the vast power of the Abbai current. Resourcefully, Ian threw a rope to Joe and Colin and attached his end to the Redshank. A shift in the river flow enabled us suddenly to slide it up over the rocks, but in so doing some of our kit was washed out. Soon it was emptied of most water and hauled in to shore. The rope was thrown back to us and tied to our rocks. Ian and I in turn clipped ourselves on with karabiners and pulled ourselves hand over hand through the torrent to safety. Roger then tied the rope to himself and swam over.

After this chastening experience, we portaged the dinghies— *Charity* had moored up without incident—to a large bay which the river has formed just above K2. The cataract itself was an alarming sight—an apparently endless, thirty-yard-wide cleft in the volcanic rock, through which the entire Nile tumbles and boils. At one point there is a great vortex where it hits a projecting wall and turns sharply right before straightening up again. The noise drowned all talk.

NOTES:

1   Richard Grevatte-Ball, pilot.

Chapter Thirteen
To the Dark Abyss

EVEN the most determined White Water enthusiasts were convinced that K2 and the visible length of water beyond it represented a check to our progress down the river. So we fell back on an arrangement that had been discussed earlier.

We knew that after K2 came a number of narrow passages where a maelstrom of water churned tortuously between sheer black walls—places which the local people called, perhaps, the Amharic equivalent of "The Devil's Cauldron". We knew them from previous air reconnaissances and had named them more prosaically, K3, K4. No doubt, as with K1, closer inspection would have revealed other intermediate obstacles which we would have called K3 Alpha, K3 Bravo and so on. It would have been tedious and exhausting to attempt close portages of each individual obstacle, so we had decided to launch the two Redshanks empty, somewhere below K2, and let them sweep alone down this terrible ten to twelve-mile stretch of river. In this way some measure of continuity would be maintained and we would not have such a back-breaking portage. John Blashford-Snell's Group I, newly arrived at the Portuguese Bridge, were to attempt to recover the dinghies, with results which will be shown later.

In the meantime, while Nigel Sale, with Gage Williams, Peter O'Mahony and Peter Hampson, were to stay behind for a couple of days to launch the boats, the amphibious White Water Team would join with some of their supporting Group N and march overland to the Portuguese Bridge.

Despite our relinquishment of the boats it was a back-breaking portage: we carried overland not only our personal kit, but several lengths of climbing rope, photographic equipment, three full inflatable thwarts, weapons, medical gear, cooking pots and all the other impedimenta that had been attached to the dinghies. The long march began, from Cusquam over the River Yezzat, the first of many tributaries that cut their way down from the foothills of Choke to the

Abbai. Some of us were carrying packs with 60 to 70 lb of gear; others had lighter but more awkward loads. Only Jim Masters and Chris Edwards were fortunate enough part of the time to engage the services of porters. Guided by Chris, who had carried out a reconnaissance in this area a week or two before, we made our way further inland along established local paths. Finally, near exhaustion point, we stopped by the edge of a clear stream, the River Yidabla, just below the village of Zanat.

Rows of tents and *bashas* appeared, baths were taken in the stream and suppers were cooked. Soon we were visited by a distinguished but wild-looking chief, in white *shamma* with broad red edge, old khaki tam-o'-shanter, and with the customary ancient rifle. This was Ato Shiferra, from a neighbouring village. When Chris Edwards had earlier strayed into his territory, Ato Shiferra had "arrested" him. But the matter had been cleared up, they had parted friends, and the old chief, hearing that his sometime prisoner was back again, had come with a basket of sweet bananas. And he offered to be our guide on the following day.

"*Enkolal?*" said an old man standing by my *basha* as I rose. A grubby hand held out four tiny eggs. "*Sinteno?*" I asked, and after a few moments of haggling a price was agreed. Omelettes for breakfast, and coffee. The camp hummed with egg salesmen. Ato Shiferra had obviously made it clear that we were *persona grata* now. He even came with some more bananas.

From this excellent place we eventually moved away up to Zanat and then followed the contour line round a series of projecting spurs. Soon the brown Abbai was glimpsed way below in the gorge. Roger Chapman, at the head of the column with Ato Shiferra, drove us hard all day. We kept up a pattern of fifty minutes march, ten minutes rest, and there were many anguished glances at wristwatches as the sun climbed up in the sky. Our mouths were too dry for much conversation, and what there was became somewhat soured.

The column became extended and was often strung out along both sides of a re-entrant. The tiny figure of Alastair Newman, carrying heavy cine equipment struggled along in the rear. Last man, in fact, was Assefa, but he was never really with the column as he preferred his own pace and liked to sit under a tree occasionally and chat to the locals.

We crossed the River Yamogat, a mere trickle, and round the next spur caught glimpses of the tumult of K3 far below on our left. Hard by a village the path divided and we decided, fatally, to take the left-hand course. Ato Shiferra had a long conference with a tall, spindly-legged man who met us on the way. They seemed to be pointing to our ropes, and this must have influenced their choice of direction, for we were approaching the River Abaya, which would pose more of a problem, we realised, than any of the smaller streams we had so far crossed.

The Abaya is a considerable river in its own right and has cut a deep gorge down through the volcanic rock as it makes its way from the west to join the Abbai. We now stood overlooking a wedge-shaped tract of fertile land which pointed towards this confluence. There were no bridges over the Abaya, but farther inland was a relatively easy fording point, while due south-east and ahead of us was another one, more difficult. It was probably the ropes that made Ato Shiferra and his old friend choose the latter.

There were several young boys around us now, as we stood between low stone walls surrounding fields of *teff*, the crop from which *injera* is made. In some fields men with whips lashed at slow-moving oxen as they dragged single-shafted wooden ploughs that would have been familiar to Iron Age Britons. I suddenly had a notion that I would like to try this, so as we stood about, talking and resting while the conference proceeded, I walked into a field and motioned to a ploughman that I would like to relieve him for a minute or two. He grinned complaisantly and stood aside. I took the plough in one hand, the whip in the other, and let out a passable imitation of a wild, Amharic cry. The ox lurched forward, I let fly with the whip but it was way off target. Unaccountably, the ox seemed to be swinging round to the left. "Hey!" I shouted, forgetting all my little Amharic, "Straighten up!" but the ox blundered on round and a new furrow began to run across all the others. I heard laughter behind me. The only person not enjoying this lamentable exhibition was the ploughman, who had lost his grin, and who now ran forward and seized back his whip. I was glad to leave him to his ancient and confoundingly difficult art.

Soon we moved on across the fields and presently came to the grim gorge of the Abaya. Its convex edge was clad in trees and prevented a view of the river. Porters refused all inducements to go on and threw off their loads mulishly. As mine had only been carrying for about 150 yards, resumption was not too painful. John Fletcher and I, last of the column now, staggered on down, grumbling to each other. Gradually we came to a sharper edge, and about 250 feet down caught a glimpse of moving water. A brown sinuous coil spills between great blue-black rocks, short straight stretches interspersed with tumbling falls and hydraulics. On either side is a considerable, if uneven, ledge of continuous rock. We picked our way down steadily, like mountain goats, periodically forced to descend the rock face hand over foot, our loads poised dangerously or tossed down ahead of us to rest on some scrub-covered ledge. Ultimately we reached a broad platform, and a traverse down on the rock, gripping convenient tree-roots, brought us to a point which Ato Shiferra and the old man told us was the normal crossing place. We were all dog-tired and threw our packs down gratefully.

Roger and Jim Masters appraised the situation. Between the two level ledges on either side was a gulf of about 40 feet of swirling brown water.

This sort of thing was no problem at all for a man of Jim's engineering experience. "You see that large boulder over on that side?" he said in his rich Somerset burr. "Someone will have to swim over with a rope and tie it round it. Then we must fix our end as high as we can up this cliff, and slide the kit down it."

"That makes good sense," said Roger.

Alastair Newman had heard this and offered to swim over first. He took a line round his waist, selected a suitable crossing point and climbed over the lip of the ledge in his pink bathing shorts. He plunged in and was carried instantly downstream, but at the same time he cut through the water with a strong crawl. He circled in to a good exit point and just succeeded in grabbing a firm rockhold. He climbed out, undid his bowline and began to belay the rope to the large boulder. Another was thrown over to him and the beginnings of an aerial ropeway were constructed whilst the rest of us moved the baggage up to a convenient point at a higher level.

Chris Bonington had been examining the rock behind us and he had found it very insecure. One piton would not hold and there were no boulders or natural projections, so he drove into the cliff wall two pitons quite wide apart, and tied a line between them. To the middle of this line the aerial ropeway was attached.

Now there was obviously a lot of haulage to be done on the other side. Only Alastair was over and there were eleven of us on our side. Roger had said he would require another person to cross and help. I offered to go, but Roger was preoccupied and non-committal. Minutes later Jim Masters made the same offer, but Ian Macleod said, "It's all right, Jim, I'll go." Roger had to decide. Jim was over ten years older than Ian, but Ian had had some gland trouble resulting from his leg injuries of nine days before. However, it seemed he had largely recovered from this and he had carried a good load all day without trouble. It was not known how good either of them were as swimmers. Jim's expertise would be more useful to Roger on this side when it came to getting personnel over later.

"O.K., Ian. Thanks," said Roger.

Although there was already one rope made fast across the river, it had not yet been tested by kit. Ian decided to follow Alastair's example and swim over on a line. He stood in his black T-shirt with OMO chalked on it, and his olive-green trousers, taking some last drags at a cigarette while Jim put a bowline round him with one end of the rope which Alastair had already received, the other end being tied to the great boulder on the far side. The rope from the boulder passed round a projecting knob of rock on our side of the river and thus up to Ian's waist. He had, therefore, about eighty feet of rope to draw out from our bank.

He flicked his cigarette into the water, climbed down a ledge some ten yards further downstream than Alastair had done, and dropped in. He was quickly carried away, but was swimming strongly on his side. His course was a shallow arc, but it was clear about three-quarters of the way across that he was not going to reach Alastair's exit point. As he swam, the river drew him away downstream. The bank immediately opposite was a rough, unscalable overhang. All of us were watching interestedly now. We guessed he would get out at a shallow ledge some thirty or forty feet further down, if the rope would allow it.

Suddenly it went taut. Ian's head jerked up, then disappeared for a second or two. He reappeared, spouting water. Jim dashed forward and grasped the angle of rope that passed round the projecting knob of stone. We would lose direct control of Ian's movements, but casting the rope off would give the necessary extra footage for him to reach the bank. Jim lifted it free and released it. Ian drifted down further, now only seven or eight feet from the far side and just upstream of the convenient ledge; but he did not appear to be swimming so well. Everyone had dropped what they were doing and had started running down the rocks, including Alastair, who had gone to be ready to help Ian out of the water. The line, now out almost at its full 120 feet, tautened again. A wave was seen to cut over Ian's head and shoulders and he submerged once more. "We must enable him to swim these last two or three yards," was the thought in everyone's mind. Alastair rushed back to the knot and scrabbled at it furiously, but the tension on it was, of course, immense. He bent to tear at it with his teeth. The nylon was stretched like elastic and the effort was useless.

Ian, meanwhile, was for long seconds dragged down by the weight of the rope attached under his arms. A grey face occasionally reappeared. We were still set on the plan of giving him additional swimming room, though, on later reflection, he was no longer in a condition to swim.

"Cut the rope!" some of us cried.

"Here's a knife!" shouted Garth Brocksopp, and detaching it he hurled his pocket knife over the river to Alastair.

"Someone will have to go in and get him," said Colin Chapman.

Roger, who had been watching, tense and white-faced, now leapt bravely into the river in swimming shorts and army boots. He swam across to Ian and grabbed him just as Alastair finally managed to cut the rope. Roger seized him by the encircling nylon and the two bodies were carried swiftly towards a cataract. Ian's face was now mottled, his eyes bulging and red, and he was vomiting water. Roger shouted to him, "Keep fighting, Ian, keep fighting!" but he was fighting only for air and his limbs made no movement in the water. The frenzied crowd on the northern bank rushed downstream with ropes and life-jackets. A shot rang out, presumably discharged accidentally or else in his excitement by one of the half-dozen Ethiopians who were running down with us.

Roger had his left arm crooked under Ian's chin to try to keep it clear of the river, which was now bearing them down at about seven or eight knots. With his right arm he tried to swim for the edge, but progress was minimal and they were now approaching the cataract. As they entered it, both went under water and Roger grabbed Ian with his two hands while they were spun and twirled by the river. Swallowing water copiously, Roger suddenly cannoned with great force into a rock and, shooting out his right arm, clasped it. This was on the very lip of a waterfall below the cataract. Although Roger's arm was clear of the water, his head and Ian's were still submerged. Clawing at the rock with his fingers, he managed to lift his own face clear. His left hand held the nylon knot and Ian's back was towards him. He hoped to be able gradually to draw him closer in.

He expected Ian to be extended horizontally by the current, but suddenly his body was tugged irresistibly downwards. Perhaps the severed rope had now passed underneath and its weight, drawn by the sluicing Abaya waters, pulled Ian down. This sudden force broke Roger's grip on the rope and Ian was lost.

"At this moment," said Roger afterwards, "it was a matter of personal survival and I had to fight my way up the rock face to get out of the water. I was spewing up water and I was very shaken." Alastair arrived, took him by the shoulder and after some minutes said, "Let's go back," and they climbed slowly over rocks towards the great boulder.

Ian's body was not seen again. The nine of us now on the northern bank ran hopelessly along the broken ledge, traversing the rough volcanic rock at speeds we would not normally consider, glancing all the time at the brown foam, looking for a hand or a head that might show that this incredibly tough little S.A.S.[1] Corporal was still in the struggle: but this mean and forbidding river had in two minutes snatched away a life that we had previously considered to be a charmed one—a life that had survived being borne over raging waterfalls below Lake Tana on an upside-down Redshank, and had previously survived who knows how many untold hazards in Cyprus, Borneo and Aden. And it had all happened with terrifying swiftness, probably in less time than it takes to read about it. Soon we came to a point where the ledge terminated in a sheer cliff wall. Here our impotence was complete. Our minds were an uncomprehending blank before the completeness of the tragedy.

Back at the ropeway, Jim Masters, drawn and shaken, was getting on with the engineering problem in hand, the safe transportation of everything to the south bank. Chris Bonington, his lip quivering with emotion, Garth Brocksopp, Colin Chapman and I, undertook a downstream search which, by scaling the northern sides of the gorge, avoided the impassable cliff. A hundred yards below it the river curled into a spout of water that no human frame could possibly survive. In silence we picked our way sadly back over the shattered blue-black rocks to complete the crossing before dark.

Alastair and Roger were working hard hauling kit down the rope slide, Roger brusquely shouting out orders to keep people moving. When it was done, Alastair slipped away to attempt a quick private search for his great friend. Meanwhile, Roger and Jim Masters had rigged a second rope across, and Jim was the first to go over on it, followed by Gavin Pike and Chris Bonington, their bodies secured in a bight in one rope and clipped by a karabiner on to the other. While the rest of us waited to cross, Roger and Chris went off to follow the southern edge of the Abaya to its confluence with the Nile—a last forlorn attempt to trace Ian's body. Ato Shiferra and his friends, who might normally have expected gifts and warm thanks at this point, were sadly neglected. They felt the tragedy, too; Ato Shiferra, his knees drawn up to his face, his hands clutching the sides of his head, rocked backwards and forwards and moaned. Soon, with muted farewells, they dwindled off on their way back up the cliff.

We camped close at hand on the southern bank by two vast boulders, black and water-smoothed, like monstrous globules of caviare. That night we all lay on the grey sand, shrouded in ponchos or tents that we had been too distressed to erect properly, the rain pattering steadily on all the wakeful forms. Though always likely on an expedition of this kind, the swift and futile loss of such a well-liked member reduced most of us to a deep misery. Only one or two clearly showed it, but for all of us the dark gorge of the Abaya, with a vulture circling in the dusk above, became a very terrible place to be.

We tried to think it out all over again: there were several points at which Ian might have been saved—first of all, and assuming that someone *had* to go across the river at this moment, he could have risked crossing by the existing rope, hand over hand, with a lifeline. Painful, but perhaps safer, provided the pitons held. This he chose not to do. Secondly, if the ten men on the north bank had remained in touch with part of the rope they could always have pulled him in. All were agreed when the rope was cast off, however, that he must be given the chance to swim to the bank. Thirdly, if Alastair had moved down the bank with the line in his left hand he might have been able on his own to draw Ian to the side, and possibly even haul him out to administer the kiss of life: but the cries in his ears were all "Cut the rope!" so he did. Throughout

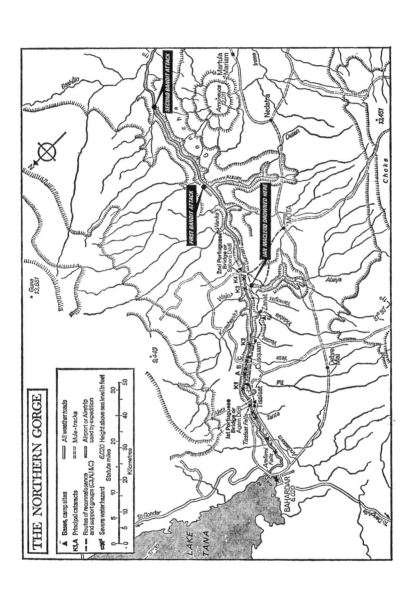

THE NORTHERN GORGE

Legend:

- ▲ Bases, camp sites
- K1,A
- === Principal cataracts
- All weather roads
- === Mule-tracks
- --- Routes of reconnaissance and support groups (C3,N.I & C)
- ⊁ Severe water hazard
- Airport or Airstrip used by expedition
- 6,020 Height above sea level in feet

Statute miles 0 5 10 20 30 40 50
Kilometres 0 5 10 20 30 40 50

SECOND BANDIT ATTACK

FIRST BANDIT ATTACK

IAN MACLEOD DROWNED HERE

Basillo

• Guna 13,881

2nd Portuguese Bridge or Sabera Dildi

9,449

Kunebach?

Wojo?

Merka

Guren

Gunal

K3 K4

K2

K1 A B C

Tississat
Tississat Falls

1st Portuguese Bridge or Agam Dildi

Tanta

Fanta

Tul

Yetu

Tississat?

Zanat

Abaya

Yeza

Yarnbar

Yezan

Tarnowei

MOTA

Debre Wal

To Gondar

LAKE TANA

Andumi Falls

BAHARDAR 6,020

Wossenan

To Dangila

Desen

Nedatra

Martula Mariam

Ampucuca 12,011 Mariam

Jnese

Choke

13,451

• 37° 30'

the night everyone was thinking over the events of the afternoon: how it might never have been necessary for Ian to have swum over at all: how it might all have been ordered differently: how a more effective rescue could have been carried out—and each of us came to a stop before the numbing fact that the whole sequence was irreversible.

NOTES:

[1] Special Air Service

Chapter Fourteen
POLITICS ON THE
PORTUGUESE BRIDGE

WE were relaxing on a grassy bank after a slow, tedious climb out of the floor of the Abaya gorge. No one now remained except Garth Brocksopp and Alastair Newman, who were at this moment just beginning to carve a memorial for Ian Macleod on the great, black boulder. The cliff side, though covered in tree and scrub, had been well-nigh vertical and in places we had had to haul up our heavy loads on ropes. Now we were in the valley of a stream which trickled rather drily towards the lip of the Abaya cliff and the hot morning sun was bringing out some colourful and extraordinary insect life.

"I'm sure we're heading in the wrong direction for the Portuguese Bridge," said Gavin Pike.

"Well, never mind," said Jim, "we've more or less got to follow up this stream bed."

Assefa suddenly gave vent to a piercing whoop. In the distance came a faint answering cry: the Ethiopian direction-finding system was coming into play. Soon we descried a figure on the skyline high above us. Unfortunately, the distance was too great for Assefa to conduct a meaningful exchange about our course and it petered out after the usual extensive string of greetings.

"O.K.," said Jim with infinite weariness, "saddle up!" We assisted each other into our harness and plodded off, first through long grasses, then over broken, ploughed land and finally up the steep sides of cotton fields, Assefa leading, then Jim Masters, Colin Chapman, Gavin Pike, John Fletcher and me.

Presently we reached a village where enquiries confirmed the route we were taking. As we left it and struck up the shoulder of a hill we heard the roaring of a familiar aircraft engine in a valley near by: the Beaver was carrying out the final search for Ian's body—a fruitless ritual, but one that we all acknowledged must be performed. We staggered on, the silence only broken by the unmelodious clinking of John Fletcher's pack, which was festooned with kettles and tins. Another village, incredibly smelly; another valley. We now seemed to have rounded a corner into the gorge of the Abbai itself. Like Hillary and Tenzing on the last assault, our pauses for rest became more and more frequent. We ate our inevitable lunch of sardines and Mars bars by a stream bed, then the six of us struggled on up a cruelly steep mud path. Another village, full of snarling mongrels; another valley.

As we filed through the leafy shade of another stream bed, there came one of those sounds so improbable in this context that it was some time before I looked round: "Can I carry your bag, my dear?" said a rich, West Country voice. I turned, and Corporal Henry came bounding over the path, his face red, sweating and wreathed in smiles. He had come out from the Bridge to receive us, but had taken an alternative route, missed us, and so caught us up from behind.

Nods and smiles all round; then Corporal Henry took over the lead to guide us in and told us the story of the dinghies.

It had been arranged that the two Redshanks that had come down with the new White Water Team from K1 were to be put into the water by Nigel Sale's party immediately below K2. They were to be launched *empty* and at a given time early in the morning of Thursday, September 19th, and with an interval between them. Later that morning they were to be retrieved by John Blashford-Snell and his party, now installed a few miles further downstream at the Portuguese Bridge. John had rigged a flying ferry below the bridge: a rope was fixed across the river diagonally and just clear of the water. Attached to it by a block and line was a third Redshank. From a certain hour in the morning a watch was to be kept upstream and at the first sighting of the two dinghies an alarm was to be given and the ferry instantly manned. Manoeuvring across the river slowly the "flying" Redshank was to pick up first one floating sister, then the other.

This excellent plan unfortunately went awry. The two dinghies— *Faith* and *Charity*—first of all became lodged on rocks soon after the launch. When they were freed by Group N, they were released *together*. They came earlier than expected: the guard at the Portuguese Bridge was not in position. They were, however, seen by chance by David Bromhead and a hasty attempt to retrieve them was made. Flinging aside their breakfast, some of Group P ran down to the ferry and got clear of the bank in it. The two empty dinghies came bearing down upon them, one capsized, the other the right way up but filled with water. Here again the boundless momentum of a waterlogged boat was experienced. Hands reached for the lifelines of the first dinghy; the ferry line stretched, backs strained, knuckles whitened. The pressure was immense.

"For Christ's sake, hold her!" cried John Blashford-Snell, the palms of his hands already raw with rope-burns. But the river began to surge over the side of the ferry and the salvage party were themselves awash. Soon the ferry line would part and all would be swept down on the flood. To their dismay they had to let the first Redshank go, and abandon it again to the river. To complete their sense of mortification, it was observed that while this struggle had been going on the second Redshank had drifted by untouched.

So *Faith* and *Charity* were lost. Or were they? Perhaps John Wilsey's party, coming up river from Shafartak, might ensnare them? But, of course, it was a fifty-fifty chance that they would pass by at night. Or they might lodge again on some rock or shingle bank. If not, they would float unimpeded into the Sudan.

Speculating in this way, we came to the edge of the cliff down which the path twisted to the Abbai itself, hidden from us until now in its last, deep gorge. There, suddenly, was the river, and, spanning it, this unlikely structure—Sabera Dildi, or the second Portuguese Bridge. Built originally by the Portuguese in the seventeenth century, it had two arches over the river and three increasingly smaller ones on each side. There were two quite impressive approach ramps, with low walls. But we felt the siting of the bridge was bizarre, for both Gojjam and Begemdir banks rise up almost sheer above the bridge, and there is nowhere for the approach ramps to go; they end abruptly at the foot of a daunting rock scramble of some three hundred feet to the cliff top.

The bridge must have collapsed at some earlier stage, for the Emperor Menelik in 1908 ordered its reconstruction. This was very thorough, and the stone used differs markedly from the original. Menelik added an imposing gateway on the Gojjam side, on which there is a cement panel commemorative of this work. At low water the bridge looms high over a deep cleft, like some Victorian railway viaduct, but in the rainy season the river swirls high round its ancient legs.

More recently it had suffered another grave blow. In the late 1930s the Ethiopian Resistance were trying to stop Italians in Begemdir from joining up with those in Gojjam. Fitaurari Tamrit with a band of forty men dug up the central arch. Unfortunately, whilst they were digging it, it collapsed into the Abbai, and the Fitaurari and his forty men were drowned. The Italians shot a further five or six men in Mota as a reprisal.

Since then the bridge has never been permanently repaired. It is made usable by a rickety structure of logs, saplings and gravel, which snakes from one stone lip to the other. Periodically it is weakened by the action of rain and river, and nearby villagers underpin it with more logs and branches. For all that, it was good once again to see something actually *built*: there cannot be any other bricks and mortar on or near the river between Tissisat and Shafartak.

We turned off down a tortuous, precipitous path, and soon emerged at the bottom and dropped our loads. There was a large dump of equipment and a cluster of *bashas* on the Gojjam bank—Redshanks, Recce Boats, engines, packsaddles and other camp stores—and a few tents and stores on the Begemdir side.

"Welcome to Group P," said John, shaking hands all round, "You're walking straight into a political crisis."

I was too tired, at first, to care, but merely noted that there seemed to be many venerable men sitting about or standing on the approaches to the bridge. However, I soon learnt that a number of Gojjam chiefs among them wanted us to remove our camp from their end of the bridge. There was apparently a Begemdir chief who said that we might go on to his side of the river, but that our camp would have to be transported—boats, engines and all—up the cliff, on to the first terrace at least five hundred yards from the bridge. This we felt to be preposterous, but Mesfin Abebe, our patient, invaluable friend from the Department for the Conservation of Wild Life, was having difficulty, obviously, in his discussions with these elderly men.

There were some seventeen or eighteen of them, and on closer inspection they were of varying age. All were heavily armed with ancient Männlichers or Steyrs which dated from about the time of the Battle of Adowa in 1896. They wore the usual shirts, shorts and *shammas*, and were corseted with two or three rows of bullets in bandoliers. They were mostly bare-headed, but three or four wore a turban or the occasional plastic topee, which is *de rigueur* for the smarter sort of old man throughout the Empire.

We told them, *via* Mesfin, that it was out of the question to move the boats, and so they retired below the first arch of the bridge on the Gojjam side in secret conclave. There was peace for an hour, so the new arrivals erected *bashas*, brewed tea and rested. As the chiefs filed out, Mesfin spoke to them and we learned their verdict.

"They say that you must all move from this place and that you can go across onto the other bank, onto the land of this chief"—indicating a tall, wizened old man—"Ato Alamayo Teghen, from Begemdir."

"But this is ridiculous. We've been here quite peaceably since early yesterday. What's the problem?" asked John.

"They say there are people in Gojjam who are coming to attack you. They may be here tonight."

"And then again they might not," said "Johnny" Johnson.

We felt, quite reasonably, that if everything else in Ethiopia tended to arrive a day or two late, the same might apply to a bunch of angry villagers, which would give us time to get away as planned.

"If they say people are coming to attack us, why can't the chiefs tell them not to come? They must be powerful men in this area and they can see that we are friendly."

"Yes, they see this," replied Mesfin patiently, "but they say they have no control over the people who are coming, because they are from other villages."

"Who are they then? *Shifta*?"

Mesfin was embarrassed and turned his head away.

"Not exactly. They are people who have quarrelled with the government over their taxes. You see, there has been trouble recently in Gojjam and there are two sets of chiefs in many villages. The last Governor tried to change the system of tax assessment and appointed government chiefs in the villages to do it. But the people did not like this so they appointed their own chiefs, some of whom are these men here. The government chiefs went to live in Mota because they were unpopular in the villages."

"Well, if these chiefs are popularly elected, there should be no trouble with the people around here. Anyway, they must be able to see we are not revenue men, but only zoologists and *ferenji* soldiers."

"They know that, but they still fear you will be attacked by people who don't believe that, and they want you to move."

"Look, we'll post guards," said John, "it's only a narrow path down."

"They say there are two or three thousand who will come."

It was late afternoon now, and the sun had long ago dipped behind heavy storm clouds. Beyond the Choke Mountains some of us were preparing an early supper. Dusk was approaching and we were adjusting our tents as a slight wind got up. There was much discussion of the supposed threat. It was difficult to believe that this was anything but a piece of sheer obstructionism by a bunch of proud, puzzled Slenders and Shallows, apprehensive at the appearance of white men in large numbers, possibly for the first time ever, and anxious to seem resolute in each other's eyes.

"Look, we've got to try and get some agreement with these chaps," said John Blashford-Snell.

"We can't move now; it'll be dark in half an hour," said Martin Romilly. "Tell them that, Mesfin."

It began to rain. I thought I might go and sleep under one of the smaller arches on the Begemdir side, and as I was collecting my things together the chiefs pronounced again: "You must all move!"

"O.K.," said John with remarkable reasonableness, "let's take up this Begemdir chief's offer and get everything over to the other side quickly."

"Look, John," said Gavin, "it'll be bloody dangerous in the half light on that rickety centre section. I reckon someone will go in the river carrying the dinghies over that."

"We'll put up a guide line before taking any heavy stuff, and karabiner things on to it for safety," said John.

So reluctantly we planned to co-operate. Roger Chapman and I went for some of our kit and appeared on the approaches to the bridge with armfuls of bedding and clothes. As we were moving towards Menelik's gateway through a cluster of chiefs, one of them stopped us.

"It's all right," said Mesfin, "they say that you needn't move tonight, but you must go early in the morning!"

"You know," I said, "they just wanted to make us agree to go so that they could tell everyone we'd given in. It's a pure question of status, and I don't much care for being a pawn in some feudal power game."

"Being messed about like this, just to strengthen their *amour propre...*" And so grumbling we returned to our *bashas* under the fig tree and the chiefs filtered away in the darkness.

The night passed—without incident—and in the morning they reassembled, still surly and umbrageous. John hopefully offered some of them medical aid for themselves or their dependents, but this did not seem to cut any ice.

"They still want us—this man in particular—to move away from here this morning," said the imperturbable Mesfin, looking at a little chief whose face had worn a very unhelpful scowl for the last two days. "Johnny" Johnson, digging a spoon into a plateful of Corporal Henry's inimitable field "porridge", overheard this news and summed up all our irritation:

"I refuse to allow the normal tempo of my breakfast to be disturbed by a grizzle-headed old moron who is living in the fourteenth century."

"Tell them," said John, "that we intend in any case to go off in our boats tomorrow."

"It's no good; they say that many people will come and attack you before that."

The previous evening the belief that as many as three thousand men might be on the warpath had received support. Assefa, who had been chatting with a number of chiefs and making notes, reiterated the figure. He said he thought they were indeed *shifta,* that the village they came from was called Goncha,[1] and their leader, one Michu. He added that there were representatives from the *shifta* among the chiefs present. So the Fifth Column was in the camp!

"Well, if they are going to attack us today," said John, trying a new line, "we must send for some police aid."

"They know nothing of police here," said Mesfin.

"Might it not be stirring up a hornet's nest?" asked Garth.

"I don't know," mused John. "There's a very good police captain in Mota, with whom we are on good terms. He got Gage Williams released. As the helicopter is coming, I'll get them to fetch him." The helicopter, sympathetically despatched by the U.S. Mapping Mission, was flying, with a light plane in support, to Mota, to carry out a search for Ian Macleod's body.

So it was that Captain (Shambel) Mulena Alamu, Chief of Police of the town of Mota, was collected by the obliging helicopter, lowered from the skies, and produced like a *Deus ex Machina,* with shiny boots, black Sam Browne and a flashing smile. He walked slowly down the path—like the Emperor, a diminutive but authoritative figure—greeted the chiefs and moved among groups of them, talking and questioning. John spoke to him too, by way of Mesfin, as he strolled over the crazy bridge from Gojjam to Begemdir and back to Gojjam. Eventually, with a charming smile he gave us his opinion: "I'm afraid you must move!"

I already had moved, and was sheltering from the noisy hubbub on the bridge under an arch on the Begemdir side. Here I could stretch out a bed, unpack and dry my things, and make a few notes. Occasionally a bolder spirit among the now considerable crowd of Ethiopians on the approaches to the bridge would venture down and stand staring from a distance of four or five yards at me and my displayed possessions; but while normally tolerant of the curiosity of Ethiopian countryfolk, I waved them away. Here I could enjoy, despite all the *va-et-vient* above me, the first spell of peace, quiet and warm sun for days.

Amidst the highly-charged political atmosphere on top of the bridge, Group P and the residual land party got on with their preparations: the land party were to leave for Mota as soon as the hired donkeys were loaded, and Gavin Pike was supervising this operation. Group P were making ready their four boats: all being commissioned for the first time for this stretch of river. Much work was required on the two new Redshanks, which we named *Crookenden* and *Deane-Drummond* as a mark of respect to two generals who helped us immeasurably in the preparatory stages of the expedition. Boat crews bustled about with Bostik and neoprene as the chiefs hedged and haggled all around them and herdsmen unconcernedly drove goats across the bridge, through the midst of everything. Presently the donkey team left on their six-hour haul up to Mota. Occasionally a plane or helicopter droned overhead—which must have added to the bewilderment and alarm of the chiefs. One such moment of alarm could have been when the Beaver flew low up and down the valley and airdropped onto the flat terrace at the top of the Gojjam cliff the vital supplies for the penultimate stage of our river journey. Were there memories amongst the older men of Caproni divebombers and the 1930s?

We had accepted the fact that we should move over the bridge from the Gojjam end to the Begemdir, and this we did in the course of a sunny morning. But the new proposition, which Captain Mulena was unable to scotch before he went off back to Mota, was that we must now move everything from the Begemdir end of the bridge to some higher point towards the plateau at least 500 yards away.

"What's so wrong with our camp here, Mesfin?" asked Colin Chapman.

"They are worried now about their bridge: it is important to them."

"Of course it is. We aren't going to do anything to it. Do they suspect sabotage?"

"I don't know. They are very suspicious of all strangers. And don't forget they have never seen any *ferenji* before—or only once or twice."

This development had most of us baffled; and some of us—not yet so acclimatised as John to the illogicality of events in Ethiopia —were becoming angry. Why should such patently inoffensive do-gooders be so inconvenienced? It was a point to be made again with greater vehemence further down the river.

But again sweet reason prevailed. John said that we must play it their way.

"There's a rough platform of rocks 150 yards downstream and a couple of places where the Recce boats can be tethered in the water. We'll make camp there tonight."

So, under the beady eye of our "friendly" Begemdir chief, the second big move of the clay began in the late afternoon. Everything had to be carried along a contour path south of the bridge and then lowered down a 70° grass slope to the rocks by the Abbai. We rigged a line to lower the boats from the path and to pull ourselves up by. Then we carted our belongings downstream, until by evening we had brought everything down the steep slope (one or two things bouncing into the Abbai in the process) onto this infinitely less comfortable site on the black rocks. We perched our tents like guillemot nests on hard ledges and slabs, cheered only by the knowledge that they were one-night stands.

"We'll go on to central cooking now this part of Phase 2 is beginning and there are only ten of us," said John. "Richard, would you like to kick off?" I got two fires going in a sheltered depression among the rocks and emptied four tins of soup powder into two cooking pots. Into another I put the usual mess of curried beef and rice for those addicts who had had little else for seven weeks and were now firmly hooked. Finally—special delicacy—some potatoes which David and I had been peeling for about an hour: we thought they would go well with a tin of luncheon meat, which had been recovered from the afternoon's airdrop. They were softening up well, until with tropical savagery a storm broke over us and a heavy downpour lashed the rocks. The other nine scuttled for shelter to their tents. I crouched hopelessly amongst the opened tins and the other debris of a half-completed supper. But the fires were soon extinguished in clouds of blue smoke and the potato pan filled almost to the brim with cold rainwater. I stumbled—for it was now pitch dark—from tent to tent with the *plat du jour*—luncheon meat and parboiled potatoes. This was rounded off by quantities of newly issued chewing gum and soft-centred Spangles. And so to bed.

NOTES:

[1] This was later corroborated by the Governor-General of Gojjam as a well-known haunt of dissidents.

Chapter Fifteen
THE NORTHERN GORGE

THROUGHOUT the expedition so far we had tended to be afraid of all the wrong things. Or at any rate our concern had been about dangers which in the event proved to be secondary or even non-existent. On Phase 1 we were apprehensive of the crocodile menace. "What are your feelings about the presence of crocodiles in the Nile?" had been among the first questions put to me before the Expedition by the BBC and the *Camberley News*. Yet we had barely been menaced by a single one. The real problems here were the rise and fall of the water level, food shortage, insects. On Phase 2 the crocodile threat still mesmerised us. It was always our secret fear because of the recorded experiences of previous Nile explorers, and possibly because it represented the main danger in the minds of our families, friends and the general public. Yet apart from one horrific bankside encounter by Jim Masters and Peter O'Mahony, when a crocodile had appeared suddenly out of the undergrowth by their side as they lunched, there had really been no significant sightings of the creatures on this phase. We knew, of course, from our talks with Tony Crewe-Gee at the Hydro-Electric Station, that they were there in great numbers in the waters above, and to a lesser extent below the Tissisat Falls; but the problem here was first and foremost the fierce power of the river itself.

From the Portuguese Bridge southwards a depleted and shaken White Water Team, merged now into Group P, faced the prospects of going down the river again with real, though—we hoped—without evident trepidation. But once more our fears—this time of the water—were largely misplaced. Within twenty-four hours we were to learn how new were the dangers that still lay ahead of us.

Our apprehension at what the swirling Abbai might do to us round the furthest visible bend was mixed with a very pleasurable exhilaration. The ten of us were about to embark on a stretch of the river, about 140 miles of it, never before navigated. We were going to enter country hitherto unknown to white men, except in so far as the indefatigable

Major Cheesman had overlooked it from high on the Gojjam bank in January and February, 1927. He had descended from the plateau to the mouth of the Tammi River, to Melka Daga and Melka Dibo, and had observed the Abbai, "the river of my dreams", at low water at just these three points between the second Portuguese Bridge and Shafartak. Near Goncha, the gorge of the Tammi River had forced him to make a wide detour inland, and the Abbai he left is marked on his map for fifteen miles or so by a broken line. It was in this short stretch, "unseen by European eyes", that we so keenly wanted to survey.

Group P, as we were now called, were to be borne in four craft—two Army Recce Boats, each with a 9 1/2 h.p. outboard engine, and two Avon Redshank dinghies, guided as before solely by paddles. The Recce Boats, like the Redshanks, were air-filled, and the Redshanks were without some of the modifications of those used on the earlier stages; for example, their inflatable compartments were themselves not stuffed with inflated football bladders. We were arranged as follows:

RECCE BOAT		REDSHANK
Semper	escorting	*Crookenden*
John Blashford-Snell,		Chris Bonington
(OC and Gun)		(Helm)
Joe Ruston,		Alastair Newman
(Radio Operator, Helm)		Garth Brocksopp
		(Zoologist)

RECCE BOAT		REDSHANK
Ubique	escorting	*Deane-Drummond*
John Fletcher,		Roger Chapman
(Engineer, Helm)		(White Water expert,
Colin Chapman,		Archaeologist, Helm)
(Crocodile Survey)		Richard Snailham,
		David Bromhead,
		(Zoologist)

Our plan was that the Recce Boats would scout out the lie of the river ahead, would help with the difficult business of getting the dinghies into the bank and mooring up, and would generally be responsible for the safety of a Redshank apiece. A first reconnaissance suggested that

David Bromhead, Roger Chapman and the author in the Northern Gorge.

immediately below our rocky camp site there were a couple of quite fierce hydraulics. Roger Chapman, remembering his air recce of this stretch, said, "These two are the worst we've got to deal with; once we are over them we are home and dry."

Buoyed up considerably by this news (quite falsely, as it turned out), we made the last preparations on the damp rocks. The local peasantry, apprised of our intended departure, were gathering like vultures on the path above. Some of the bolder of them had already come down the grassy chute to us and were sizing up the prospect of imminent scavenging. Yesterday's rancour already blurred in our memory, we dished out to them the heavier and less vital stores with a liberal hand.

After Roger had briefed us on his elaborate plan for circumventing the first two obstacles, we pushed first the Recce Boats then the dinghies into the river. The stream pulled at them as it coursed down between its rocky banks. Brief farewells, and John gave the order to go at 10.30 a.m. *Semper* slipped away round the corner. In due course *Deane-Drummond* and *Ubique* followed, leaving *Crookenden* to bring up the rear. Immediately the plan misfired. We had hoped to negotiate the hydraulics and then stop after 150 yards or so, to reconnoitre the river further on, but, though the two great, curling waves were breasted safely, the rope from Joe Ruston on the bank fell short and *Deane-Drummond* spun on, making the shore in dead ground another 100 yards downstream. Only *Crookenden* still remained to come through the hydraulics. Now there was a considerable hiatus, the first of several, which revealed the difficulties of this mode of progress: we had not yet established proper communication between boats. The waving of arms was not always meaningful and sometimes we went out of sight of each other completely. Ultimately *Crookenden* came through the hydraulics and the three other boats slipped their temporary mooring and joined her. After this John tried to keep in front in *Semper,* pausing to assess river hazards as he came upon them, and signalling the rest of the flotilla forward with an Ethiopian flag.

The river was at its most sporting. There were many large waves, with rocks lurking under them and whirlpools beyond. But all were entirely manageable and the morning had all the ingredients of excitement, plus a dash of risk, that one could wish for. There were rocky ledges and abutments from the bank, which threw the stream about and us with it. In one place a prominent submerged rock in the centre of the river caused such a thundering turmoil beyond that we stopped to "line" the boats past it. This consisted of drawing the boats along the bank one by one, like horsedrawn canal barges—except that we had a "horse" aft as well as forward to stop the boats swinging out. This was the last time before the end of our journey at Shafartak that we had to resort to any manoeuvre other than straightforward drifting and paddling. There were no more cataracts or other impediments that we could not ride over with reasonable ease—except for one, which, for reasons that will become apparent later, we tackled in the middle of the night.

But we were not to know that we had a virtually clear run to Shafartak. The river was still in quite a beetling gorge and its convolutions gave very little warning of our approach to rapids. As we hit big waves we began to ship a good deal of water and had to stop two or three times to bale out. David Bromhead, whose first experience of the river this was, began the morning with enthusiasm, but in one of the severer stretches, when cataract followed cataract with increasing speed, apprehension began to show in his face. Roger Chapman, on the other hand, had started off the day rather nervously, rapping out quiet orders in military tones: "When I say kneel, kneel!", or "keep on paddling!" and "Concentrate!" when our gaze wandered to some Goliath heron or a soaring fish eagle, and he gradually grew more relaxed as he became reassured that the dinghy was taking it all well, and that his crew was responding to orders with fair alacrity.

Roger perfected the technique for getting the Redshanks into the bank which is called the "ferry glide". It seemed to be the safest and quickest way of freeing them from the grip of the stream. He or Chris Bonington, the other dinghy helmsman, would select a likely landing point as far as 100-150 yards downstream. Each squatted in the stern of his dinghy, wielding a paddle held freely in both hands in place of any kind of fixed rudder. To begin the "ferry glide" the paddle would be thrust into the water and forced firmly in the direction of the required bank. This would turn the dinghy sharply through about 135°, so that its nose was faced half upstream, in the manner of a yacht tacking into the wind. Then the imaginary whips would crack and the two crew members, kneeling side by side in the body of the dinghy, would dig at the water frenziedly but more or less in unison. And so, carried backwards downstream at a smart 8 to 10 knots, the dinghy would imperceptibly edge towards the side, more obviously as it became freed from the stream. Whether one reached one's chosen landing point was a measure of the helmsman's judgement of the stream or of his crew's muscle power. In fast water it was impossible to be too selective of one's actual landfall. Usually we grabbed what trees there were, held on, and then drifted down to a better site, using branches, bushes and reeds as temporary anchors. If we landed on a bank of rocks or on a sheltered beach of dark brown sand, the near-side crewman would leap ashore, paying out a prepared nylon line which was attached to the dinghy, and make it fast on some tree or rock. I suppose we were lucky that no one ever leapt out onto the private strand of a basking crocodile, though plenty of these creatures were seen in just the sort of creek that we usually aimed for. Quite often we jumped ashore near a startled herdsman or group of small boys watering their cattle at the river.

About noon we came to a point where the gorge appeared to be blocked by a great cliff with hills above. We seemed to be running into a cul-de-sac. The river level perceptibly dropped, so it was not until we were about 100 yards off that we could see what happened to the Abbai. We pulled into a bay of relatively slack water and then *Semper* set off and the rest of us waited to see what became of her. In fact, the river turned sharply at right-angles and then twisted the other way through a fearsome S-bend. Here was the usual water pattern—shallow shingle beds on the inside of the bend, and deep, broken water undercutting the bank on the outside—but here, alarmingly exaggerated. And on the outside bend were ledges of rock scattered with great boulders and enmeshed logs against which the water washed. *Semper*, with engine power, cut through quite easily. The two dinghies decided on a course and set off, paddling firmly. Immediately it was clear we could not hold the course and we were drawn crab-wise into the tangled waves. By now, we accepted the fact that, however prudent we were, we would be carried ineluctably into the middle of the turbulence. And so it was.

We emerged dripping but intact, and to prove our *sang froid*, carried out immediately one of the neatest of our landings: we were "ferry gliding" hopefully towards a bank of great boulders when Colin Chapman, in attendance in *Ubique*, threw a rope by which John Fletcher towed us quickly in.

Lunch—still sardines and Mars bars—was taken on boulders made barely tolerable by the noonday heat, and then we pressed on downriver with ever increasing confidence. We must have passed under the foot of the prominent mountain called Gumari. Here the river, in a ravine with 200-foot sides, is believed by Cheesman to be in a relatively new course. Originally it passed to the north of Gumari, but "long ago" as he records, it cut its way through to its present course. We think we saw the col on the Begemdir side over which the river may once have flowed. Then the ravine widened and we came upon odd patches of maize cultivation and heard the whooping cries of astonished farmers.

Roger was sometimes able skilfully to keep us out of the worst belts of waves, but just as often we had to plough on through a steep swell, like the sea in noise and movement, though not in taste: the Abbai, incidentally, was almost drinkable here unfiltered. Though still a *café-au-lait* colour, there was less sediment than before.

In the early afternoon we came out suddenly into a region of amazing natural grandeur. Here was the beginning of a gorge that made the Black Gorge of Phase 1 seem puny and dull. Across the line of the river from the Gojjam bank a great vertical slab of basalt reared up. It was 40-50 feet high and relatively smooth, with here and there a tree sprouting from it, festooned with the nests of busy, yellow weaver birds. The river passed smoothly down to the left of this rock slab, which also bent round and continued as far as the eye could see. The left hand bank was more familiar: sloping, broken ground covered with scrub. So here, if you like, was half a gorge, but magnificent in its clean lines and its extent. It was the most dramatic landscape we had ever encountered.

It was like driving into Bath through undistinguished bungaloid suburbs and suddenly coming to a street with a lofty, elegant, eighteenth-century terrace down one side. The cliff went on for some miles, increasing in height as we passed along it, first to 60 feet, then 80, and finally after some few miles to a cathedral-like scale of about 120 feet. At water level the basalt was constantly washed, revealing the classic "Giant's Causeway" formation. Was this the "amygdaloidal basaltic lava" that Cheesman speaks of at the mouth of the Tammi River? Once again the need for a qualified geologist was keenly felt. Above flood level the rock was soft and brown—an overlay of what looked like daub, scored with vertical bands like the exposed marks of a pneumatic drill. Now more than ever were we filled with the exhilaration of pioneers. The existence of the Northern Gorge had been noted from the air, but Cheesman had had to move a long way inland to bypass Goncha, and did not record it in his famous work. We fell silent and drifted along on a slowish current of five to six knots.

In all this majestic natural scenery it was a shock suddenly to see in the cliff face a man-made wall! There it was, looming up towards us, about twenty-five feet above the high-water level; an 8-foot wall closing off a niche in the cliff visible through an open doorway in the wall, which had wooden doorposts and lintel. What was this? A Gojjam frontier post? Religious site? *Shifta* hideout? The dwelling of an anchorite? Further investigation might reveal more clues. The line of the cliff was fortunately broken just upstream of the bastion containing the wall.

"We'll pull in here and take a look," said John, and soon he was following Joe Ruston through tangled trees and elephant grasses.

"Hey, there's a man up there," said Joe.

We froze and looked. High on the bastion above us, peering between the scrub on the lip of the cliff was a solitary figure. "*Tanastalin!* " shouted John. There was no response. "*Tanastalin!* " shouted Joe. Silence.

This was distinctly odd. Normally, bank dwellers had either fled in terror or returned our greetings cheerily. However, we moved forward to attempt a climb over the shoulders of a buttress towards the constructed wall.

Suddenly the man broke into a torrent of angry words, and swept his arm first upstream and then down in a clear gesture of rebuff. We felt that he was probably a lookout man for one of the parties of dissidents that are said to roam this area. However, we could see no rifle, only an axe crooked over his left arm; so gingerly, and glancing up now and then in case he might let fall a stone or two, Joe, Roger and I descended a gully and climbed a convenient tree which gave access to the basalt shoulder. Once up, we were disappointed to find that a traverse to the "fort" was impossible. At any rate, we could look over the wall and see into part of it.

There was no sign of steps from the doorway to the Abbai twenty-five feet below it. Entry might, therefore, be from the interior. On the floor inside stood a tall, narrow, drum-like vessel, probably a storage jar of some kind. Nothing else. Still somewhat mystified we climbed down to the boats.

Almost immediately round the next corner we saw ahead of us in the broad stream two huge, isolated pillars, slices of cliff cut off by the river. They soared, narrow and sheer to about 120 feet, beautifully shaped and crowned with trees and shrubs. One stood in the middle of the river like an island, the other was on the now more broken right-hand bank. I wondered if the Ethiopian Tourist Organisation, a very forward-looking institution, would ever arrange cruises for the more adventurous sort of holiday-maker down this particular piece of river. It certainly deserved a wider audience.

Marvelling at all this, we sat still and drifted silently but swiftly, now at about ten knots, over the smooth, broad Abbai. There were signs of cliffs now on the left bank; a vast, tilted slab with gaping bedding-plane below it, in front of which a large colony of hamadryad baboons was barking noisily.

Chris Bonington, one of his cameras permanently to his face, gyrated feverishly in the stern of his dinghy.

As the gorge narrowed again, with sheer cliffs for a time on both sides, the leading boat spotted further curious examples of the combined work of man and nature. On the same Gojjam cliff face and at the same height were the mouths of two large caves side by side, one triangular and one semicircular. The entrances of both were shored up to the horizontal by layers of regular stones. We saw quite large chambers within as we sped by; possibly there would be some interior access here, too.

Almost immediately, on the opposite Begemdir bank, we found a splendid place to make a night stop.[1] A fresh stream ran out into the Abbai over a broad shingle bank; above it, two shallow, sandy ledges amongst trees; a profusion of dry wood; no immediate villages and thus no inquisitive villagers; a superb prospect of the 120-foot cliff directly opposite, with the nest of a fish eagle in a tree and the tantalising caves near by. Behind us was the muffled thudding of a waterfall; this was, in fact, an 80-foot spout of water coming straight off the terrace some distance behind, and hidden from, the site of our camp, and pouring into a damp cleft, reminiscent of a pot-hole. In it was a pool, from which ran the fresh, warm stream in front of us.

It was an idyllic setting. Soon the boats were beached in a convenient creek, tents were up and fires crackling. There was even time to cook and eat a delectable curry before the inevitable torrential rain. We were somewhere near the mouth of the Tammi. We lay back in our tents, smoking, reading and watching the lightning. From the Portuguese Bridge it had been virgin river, and that day we had covered about seventeen and a half miles of it.

NOTES:

[1] See map p.214.

Chapter Sixteen
HIGH NOON AT THE
TAMMI RIVER

THE first sound I awoke to was the cry of the seagull. It did not seem to blend at all with the barking of baboons in the trees behind us, and actually it turned out to be the fish eagle's call, which is very similar. A dark fog lay over the chasm and it was quite cold. The sun always took time to penetrate the gorge bottom, but this morning it seemed uncomfortably long before the mists dispersed and the arc of blue between the overhanging cliff tops was revealed. In a leisurely way we got the burners going and put bedding out to dry on the shingle.

Since my first disastrous essay at "central cooking" we had messed in three groups—the two Recce Boats together, each Redshank separately. *Deane-Drummond*'s crew squatted rather sleepily on the sandy ledge outside David Bromhead's tent, and drank that first, marvellous morning brew.

After breakfast we turned to our various scientific tasks. Garth and David went off up a winding path behind us to carry out a lizard hunt with .22s. Chris and Roger dressed themselves in an array of equipment to cover river work, rock climbing and caving, and then got Joe to run them over to the caves in a Recce Boat. John Fletcher checked the engines, and John Blashford-Snell reminisced, sent a report of our situation over the radio, and, as always, planned ahead. Groups of us washed clothes, or themselves, in the stream, or sprawled on the shingle drying off and talking in the sunshine.

After a while I dressed and hung a few karabiners and slings on me and went over with Joe in a Recce Boat to the caves. We found the $9\frac{1}{2}$ h.p. engine could just beat upstream and it only took moments to reach the cliff wall where the other two had begun climbing. They were now in the caves but had left a fixed line for me. This proved unnecessary as the rough basalt, though vertical, offered many handholds. Joe very ably held the boat on full throttle against the stream and alongside the cliff as I felt for the first of these and pulled myself onto a stance. I proceeded diagonally up the face as he wheeled away on the current like a fighter pilot. Chris and Roger were most excited by their finds.

"There's masses of pottery and basketwork up here," shouted Chris.

It looked as if this might be of distinct archaeological interest. The first cave had a triangular mouth and we called it Cave A. It curved inwards, upwards and to the left for about twenty-five yards. It seemed to be a natural excavation by river erosion at a much earlier age. There was no access from inside the cliff; the only human modification had been the platform of dressed stone at the mouth. There was no sign of any permanent or even temporary arrangements for getting in and out of the cave. Yet the floor, which was liberally heaped with evil-smelling bat dung, showed many traces of human use: broken sherds, strips of rattan, fragments of old wickerwork, and in the furthest corner on a constructed stone platform, the bases and lower parts of two earthenware storage jars.

It was possible to move easily round and up to Cave B, with its semi-circular entrance and man-made platform. This cave was more regular and shallower in depth. On the floor, which was on two levels, we found a complete black pot and more fragments, some of which clearly fitted together.

We resolved to collect a few examples of what was there, rather than try to bring out everything. In any case, time was pressing. We knew we were due to leave the area after lunch. Accordingly, we signalled to Joe to fetch a rucksack which we hauled up and filled carefully with finds. These included a bat which Chris had shot. Roger had even found a piece of charred bone, which might have made radiocarbon dating possible. We let all this down the cliff face delicately, and reluctantly, despite the nauseous stink, left this strange habitat.

Back on the other bank we spread the artefacts on a poncho which was lying on the shingle. The sun shone warmly on clothes that were now dried. It was almost noon.

From beyond the top of the great cliff we presently heard a number of whooping cries: the sort often heard exchanged between travellers in the quiet of the Ethiopian countryside—but here, excited and in concert.

John said urgently, "Come on, just grab a Mars bar everyone, and then we'll get going!" and he strode off briskly up the stream bed to take one of his rare photographs—of the waterfall. The ululations above the cliff went on. Almost immediately he came back down the stream running—another rare event.

"Hurry up!" he shouted excitedly. "Get out of here!"

Whilst taking the photograph he had been shot at by a lone native on the top of the terrace, but the bullet had hit the cliff twenty feet above him.

The rest of us were steadily packing our kit when several short, strident blasts on a brass horn sounded from the invisible ground behind the opposite cliff top.

We were all slow to appreciate the significance of the whoops that were echoing back and forth across the gorge. Suddenly, our methodical preparations were disturbed by a fusillade of shots. I looked up and about seventy-five yards away along the rim of the cliff, amongst the fringe of trees and scrub, appeared a motley crowd of about twenty-five or thirty armed men, in shorts and vests, shouting angrily and gesticulating.

A long row of them loomed on the horizon, not quite with the precision of the well-drilled band of Apaches in a Western, but at all events they were there, all together, and had achieved a considerable surprise effect. As some local Geronimo gave the order, a rock plummeted down into the river, then another, and another. More shots rang out and spurts of water danced up in the stream by the camp.

Then a stone came bouncing down the hillside behind our ledge and struck a tree. Shouts indicated that there were hostile natives on the Begemdir side, too, and that John's sniper had not, in fact, been far from his fellows.

We were dumbfounded. Not only had the natural peace of this almost Arcadian vale lulled us into a state of relaxation, but utter disbelief that we were actually being attacked rooted us for the moment to the spot. How could it happen to us, a peaceful crowd of *ferenji* bent on discovery and zoological collection? Part of the fruits of this collection was, ironically, destined for the Haile Selassie I University in Addis Ababa, though of course our ragged assailants could know nothing of this. However, our stupefaction was only momentary.

Angry natives were picking up jagged pieces of basalt and flinging them down over the river towards our boats, which we were now feverishly packing. John strode out on to the tongue of shingle in his white Wolseley helmet.

"*Tanastalin! Tanastalin!*" he shouted, raising both arms in greeting. A crack and a little jet of water nearby was the answer. A few moments later he repeated this bold attempt at appeasement, but with the same result.

Any doubts about the serious intent of our attackers were dispelled when a vast boulder, two feet across, shook the ground as it plunged down among the trees behind us and bounded through the *Crookenden* tent area, now fortunately empty. We dashed about, plucking things off trees and picking gear up from the shingle, sometimes exposed to the hail of stones and bullets, sometimes sheltering on the sand ledge.

"Why don't we fire back, John?" someone asked.

So far we had just scurried about like rabbits.

"No, don't shoot yet," he said. "Let's try the minimum of force," and he strode out onto the beach to make his second attempt to pacify by salutation. Another answering shot ricocheted off the nearby shingle. We had, anyway, no real ability to retaliate—the 9.3 mm rifle was stowed away under a heap of kit in the most distant Recce Boat; apart from this, we had only .455 pistols, .22s and shotguns, and most of these were also inaccessible for the moment.

In the British Army officers are taught to tackle a military problem in the following sequence: AIM, FACTORS, COURSES OPEN, COURSE ADOPTED, PLAN. However, the manual adds helpfully: "A pl comd, when in contact with the en, will seldom have time for this procedure." How very true, I thought, as I dashed out with a last bundle of kit, which was now stacked high in the dinghies in no sort of order at all. No doubt, in John's mind the shortened form of appreciation—AIM, GROUND, PLAN—was being made.

"Let's get as quickly as we can to the boats and get them away," he said. The four boats were lying two in a shallow creek, two on the shingle spit—a long way from any cover in each case. Moving off down the river would mean running a most dangerous gauntlet: we would have to pass almost vertically below the Gojjam contingent of this troupe of bandits; rocks and bullets would surely perforate the inflated boats, if they did not, indeed, account for any of the ten members of the team. We wondered whether flight was the right answer. Behind this doubt, of course, lay the greater uncertainty of what the motives were for this vicious attack. We did not know whether they sought testicular trophies, in an expression of ancient Ethiopian custom, or whether they wanted our obviously desirable equipment—our weapons, our boats; or merely our departure from their scene. The lone figure on the cliff the day before had made it clear he wished us out of the area. Yet some of the bullets were obviously aimed to do more than just frighten us.

John later said it was just a bunch of ignorant villagers who perhaps thought we were devils. Yet this was not the work of really primitive savages. It had all the signs of an organised, premeditated assault, with some quite sophisticated staff work behind it. We had damaged no crops, nor given any provocation other than some .22 shots on a lizard hunt an hour before. But we had sailed on their river: although dreaded, the Abbai is also revered. Perhaps this had caused resentment. The theory that it was all part of a Gojjam fiscal dispute did not seem to be logical either; no one could mistake four boatloads of white men in black rubber suits for tax gatherers; though perhaps they tended to associate *any* intruders with Government agencies, and the fact that we were white men in boats—both of which they might never have seen before in this remote corner of the Empire —might not perhaps make any difference.

I believe, however, that this was an example of pure brigandage that could have come straight from the Europe of the Middle Ages. Perhaps we had strayed without realising it into the bounds of some petty *shifta* kingdom, where the writs of the Governors-General of Gojjam and Begemdir did not run. We might have met the same fate in the tenth century at the hands of the Saracens in the Alpine passes, or in the Marches of Wales before the Council of the West came to Ludlow.

In fact, four-fifths of the Empire was subjugated to Imperial rule by the Emperor Menelik II only as recently as the 1880s and 1890s. Gojjam, under the control of the wayward Ras Hailu until 1933, had a tradition of fierce independence, and there are still signs of separatism today. It is quite understandable that in an Empire as large as France and Germany together, and with only rudimentary communications, there should still be pockets of lawlessness in a province which has always been anti-establishment.

Rocks and boulders continued to rain down and, from time to time, bullets. Gunfire was fortunately restricted by the fact that a round of .303 costs about one Ethiopian dollar (3s. 4d. in 1968); and though many of these men were probably generously endowed with ammunition, indiscriminate fire could easily blaze away their social status. They did not seem to fear any return fire, for they stepped boldly to the skyline to take aim. This gave us a brief moment to run for cover. In the open, of course, the practice was to keep very much on the move. Happily their marksmanship was atrocious and their weapons were obviously ancient.

The situation, however, could easily worsen. Although the Abbai is usually a great social divide, this ingenious *shifta* leader had placed men, probably Gojjamis, on the Begemdir side also. We could not tell how many, for they were hidden behind and above us—but perhaps about twenty. We could not be sure whether they would content themselves with rolling boulders down. It seemed more likely that they would soon infiltrate through the trees and come amongst us. We would then be involved in hand-to-hand fighting on the beach, like the Persians evacuating Marathon. This we naturally wanted to avoid as there were only ten of us.

"Are we all completely ready now?" asked John.

"It'll be suicide to go out there," said David Bromhead. "Let's hold on here and radio for an air strike."

"It would take too long," said John. "These chaps could well be down here in half an hour. We must get to the boats and force our way out of here."

"I think we ought to wait and see if we can hold out until tonight," said Chris Bonington. "We'll only get shot down if we show ourselves."

These were the two possible courses: a few of us wanted to shelter and wait until help could be summoned; the majority wanted to make a concerted move for the boats, launch them and paddle downstream fast, with power assistance from the Recce Boats as soon as it could be given. An excited discussion broke out under the trees, but John gave a firm order to launch the boats. Still there was some hesitation as we made a last-minute inspection of the camp, and dodged in and out of the trees as we saw rifles raised to shoulders. Even for the Service members of the group, this was a baptism of fire.

"Right, get to the boats!" shouted John.

SITES OF THE TWO BANDIT ATTACKS

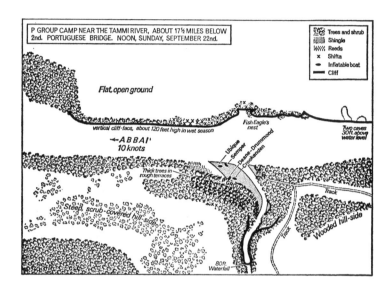

P GROUP CAMP NEAR THE TAMMI RIVER, ABOUT 17½ MILES BELOW 2nd. PORTUGUESE BRIDGE. NOON, SUNDAY, SEPTEMBER 22nd.

Trees and shrub
Shingle
Reeds
x   Shifta
Inflatable boat
Cliff

Flat, open ground

vertical cliff-face, about 120 feet high in wet season

Fish Eagle's nest

Two caves 30ft. above water level

ABBAI 10 knots

Ubique
Semper
Deane-Drummond
Crookenden

Thick trees in rough terraces

Track

Steep, scrub-covered hill-side

Wooded hill-side

Track

80ft. Waterfall

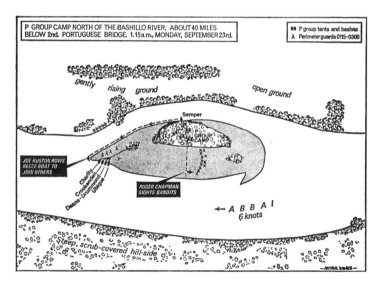

P GROUP CAMP NORTH OF THE BASHILLO RIVER, ABOUT 40 MILES BELOW 2nd. PORTUGUESE BRIDGE. 1.15a.m., MONDAY, SEPTEMBER 23rd.

P group tents and bashas
λ   Perimeter guards 0115–0300

gently rising ground

open ground

Semper

P GROUP CAMP

JOE RUSTON ROWS RECCE BOAT TO JOIN OTHERS

Chasty
Crookenden
Deane-Drummond
Ubique

ROGER CHAPMAN SIGHTS BANDITS

ABBAI 6 knots

Steep, scrub-covered hill-side

~ARTHUR BANKS~

I swallowed drily as a fleeting "going-over-the-top" feeling gripped me, and then Roger and I ran out to our Redshank and began manoeuvring it slowly into the creek leading to the Abbai. Inevitably we drew the fire. A rifle bullet struck the water a foot from the dinghy just before I reached it, and Roger heard the different sound of a revolver bullet as it spatted into the mud two yards from him. Apprehension and alarm took hold of the other eight also, as they sprinted urgently for their boats, casting their eyes upwards, whenever possible, so as to be able to dodge the hail of sharp rocks.

I had evolved the idea of hanging on to the lifeline on the side of the dinghy opposite the bandits, ignoring the crocodiles, and allowing the Abbai to carry the dinghy and its pendant crew slowly away. We then would see the falling rocks more easily and at the same time be sheltered from view. Therefore I stayed in the water as we pushed *Deane-Drummond* towards the mainstream. Soon David Bromhead and I were side by side and up to our chests in the water. But Roger had climbed inboard and taken up his paddle. We were unfortunately entangled in the bushes some way from the fast-moving water and making no progress. Plumes of spray shot up beyond us as rocks hit the river. I managed to clamber over the side as Roger roared, "Get into the boat!" Soon David was in too. We scrabbled for paddles and began to get under way, but not very effectively as our eyes were hardly ever on the river. Seven or eight stones could be observed in the air at any one time.

With great coolness, especially on the part of the helmsmen, who were a sitting target as they struggled to get the engines going, the other crews also got away. Last of all on the beach, Joe Ruston had to sit fast while John Blashford-Snell made a final dash for their fuel cans. One chunk of stone the size of a grapefruit hit the inflated side of the dinghy a yard in front of me and shot up in the air as from a trampoline. Another hit Chris Bonington on the back, making an ugly cut. Amazingly he was our only casualty.

As the Recce Boats hummed into motion, John thought it the moment to provide some covering fire and aimed three shots almost vertically at the cliff top. The last of these made a gunman reel back from the edge and may have killed him. Colin Chapman, also circling round in a Recce Boat, fired another, but most of us were too busy with the paddles, and soon the Abbai carried us away from the great bluff of rock from which the worst fire had come.

The title of Chris Bonington's first *Daily Telegraph Magazine* article—"Into the Last Unconquered Hell on Earth"—had provoked amused smiles during the more placid stretches of Phase 1; but it now seemed a pardonable piece of journalese.

Dazed and dishevelled we drifted slowly on, careless of the magnificent landscape which now presented sheer gorge walls on both sides. A fire on a hilltop ahead caused a stir, but there was no significance in it. Curiously, the cause of most annoyance, first of all, was the fact that we had left, neatly arranged on the shingle bank, all our archaeological finds from the caves.

Chapter Seventeen
HORRID NIGHT, THE CHILD
OF HELL

FOR a mile or so we sat, mute and disorganised, as the Recce Boats towed the dinghies away from danger. There were still sheer, basalt cliffs on both sides, but after a while the gorge opened out and the cliffs were replaced by sloping hillsides. These were dotted here and there with plantations of maize, guarded by ramshackle watchtowers on which small boys were set to protect the corn cobs from predatory baboons.

The mood in all boats was one of impotent rage, and it was turned, for want of a better target, on these distant wards on their high perches, who crouched, amazed at what they saw, a fold of *shamma* keeping the sun from their heads.

"Bloody gollies!" muttered David Bromhead, provoked by the assault into bitter xenophobia.

Slowly, however, the gall and the gloom dispersed and we recovered our spirits. Rather as after a cocktail party one always thinks of dazzling and witty retorts that one should have made, so now we began to consider more positively how things might have gone. Wishful thinking took over. The common regret was that we had not been able to return the fire with more suitable weapons.

"One machine gun and we could have fixed the lot of them," said Alastair, expressing everyone's subsequent dream. We visualised the bandits raked with fire, toppling from the cliff-edge and cartwheeling like stuntmen into the Abbai.

John Blashford-Snell was sitting in his Recce Boat *Semper*, bent over a signal pad; and soon our dreams of what might have been were interrupted by the voice of Joe Ruston—"Wonderful Radio Abbai"—sending the news to Debre Marcos of what actually did happen:

"SITREP. ATTACK ON CAMP BY 40 NATIVES FROM BOTH BANKS WITH RIFLES, ROCKS AND SLINGS. NO

SERIOUS CASUALTIES TO US. FIRE WAS RETURNED IN SELF DEFENCE. NO ENEMY CASUALTIES. BONINGTON MINOR CASUALTY. DO NOT CAUSE FLAP OVER THIS AND TELL D1[1] ALL OK BUT MUCH KIT LOST. DO NOT RELEASE TO PRESS. SUNRAY."[2]

A cool, matter-of-fact statement. And so the news spread, from Debre Marcos to Addis Ababa, to the zoologists in the Awash game park, to England. Two days later the *Daily Telegraph* ran the headlines: "Bandits fire on Blue Nile team—Boulder attack in gorge."

At the Second Portuguese Bridge three days before, two of our Redshanks, *Faith* and *Charity*, had slipped from the grasp of John Blashford-Snell and his team and drifted downriver. Now as we were motoring steadily on, Colin Chapman pointed excitedly ahead. There, caught by grasses in an inlet, was a dinghy. To everyone's pleasure, and Chris Bonington's positive joy, it was the indestructible *Charity*. On inspection, it was found to be very little damaged, and it was soon stripped of its floorboards and turned upside down. The *Semper-Crookenden* combine then took it in tow, with Alastair sprawled on top.

For background music we had the buzz of the two $9^1/2$ h.p. outboard engines on the Recce Boats and the wash of water against the dinghies. Occasionally there was a disconcerting note in the otherwise silent valley: a high-pitched whooping call from some distant baboon-scarer would be answered by a similar but faint call from far down the river. The news of our approach was being passed on: "*Ferenji* are coming down the Abbai." Although we might outstrip bandits, we could not escape being picked up by this Ethiopian Distant Early Warning System. Unseen eyes watched us all the time and at every bend we were anticipated.

By 5 p.m. we had put about twenty-five miles between us and the bandits and we felt it was probably safe to call a halt. However determined, they would have had to be a bunch of Abebe Bikilas to keep up with us—and the riverside terrain was no normal Marathon course. Major Cheesman in 1927 averaged only one and a half miles a day south of Tissisat.[3] At the end of the long afternoon, we saw another section of gorge ahead, far wider this time, with tall cliffs, limestone now, set well back from the river. It was as if a new Building Line had been fixed primevally by some divine law. Far down the river was an isolated pillar on the right, forming with the cliffs a strange, almost lunar landscape in the setting sun. We estimated that we were two or three miles north of the junction of the Bashillo River with the Abbai.

At the opportune moment, we came upon a large, flat, shingle island to the right of the stream. Here the river itself would provide some all-round protection and at its centre was a small clump of trees and bushes that would offer shelter for our camp. It was ideal. We drew up four of the boats on a shingle spit at the downstream tip of the island—we were now thinking much more defensively, and here they would be ready, if need be, for a quick getaway. We tethered them all to a single, 300-foot, nylon line, which we ran up the beach to the nearest large tree. *Semper*, which carried the A13 radio set, was moored half-way down the narrower channel which separated the island by about thirty yards from the right bank. The Recce Boat was thus near the Command tent and an aerial could be conveniently strung up in the surrounding trees. Our own tents and hammocks were erected around and under this central knot of vegetation.

As we lit fires and began to prepare a quick supper, we saw a figure swimming the broader Abbai channel from the Begemdir side. It emerged from the river and a well-built young man walked over the shingle towards us, naked, black and dripping. As he came up to us he grinned happily and seemed harmless enough. He was soon followed by three or four others, and we welcomed them all to our camp. The bitterness of the early afternoon had abated and we seized the chance of getting on good terms with some of the local people of this region. Aspirin tablets, chocolate, plastic bags were showered on them; they handled our weapons and examined our tents with evident interest and respect; John Blashford-Snell clapped his white Wolseley helmet on the head of the leading one, and there was much hilarity as he stood, otherwise naked, enjoying the whole game hugely. They were frank and open youngsters, but we could not really get through to them—we had no interpreter on this leg, and my pidgin Amarhinya seemed to make no obvious impression. No doubt this was because they spoke another of Ethiopia's eighty-odd languages. Soon they walked up to the top of the island to swim diagonally back to the left bank.

"O Group!" called John, and in a few minutes we were all gathered around the *basha* he and Joe Ruston had put up.

"Today has, of course, been Sunday, and so after this Orders Group meeting we will have a short Evening Service."

For a few moments John spoke of our noon "Battle of the Tammi River" as he already called it. Then he outlined a plan for the possible defence of the island and withdrawal from it. It began to rain and the O Group pressed under the edges of the *basha*.

John asked me to choose a hymn. I flicked through the Army Prayer Book, and as the rain pattered down, our ten-strong male voice choir, all very relieved to be alive to sing, opened the proceedings reasonably tunefully with:

> *"Now thank we all our God,*
> *With hearts and hands and voices…"*

Soon we were filtering back to our separate camp-fires. Roger, David and I sat round ours in the cool evening and mulled over the day's events.

"How the hell they missed us, I'll never know," said Roger, throwing some dry driftwood onto the fire.

"I reckon a mixture of good fortune and bad marksmanship saved us," I suggested.

David said, "God, I hated every minute of it. What a gorge to be caught in!"

"We'll be all right here," said Roger. "Good field of fire, river all round."

"Good job there were no Sunday papers," I added. "Wouldn't have had time to read them."

We wrote diaries, and I did a spell of guard duty from 8 to 10 p.m. Every quarter of an hour the guard had to inspect the boats and the mooring line to see that the river level had not suddenly risen or dropped. There was no moon; across the river the occasional red eyes of a crocodile reflected the torch's beam. As I walked back I collected an armful of driftwood and tossed it into the tent entrance to keep dry. "A quick fire for breakfast," I thought, "and a bowl of porridge. Lovely."

Roger moved an ember and the sparks flew upward. It was after midnight and now he was on guard. As the fire was dying, a candle had been set in front of our tent, and David lay in his sleeping-bag writing his diary by its light. I was asleep alongside him. After a while David, too, lay back and dozed off. Roger looked at his watch. 1.15 a.m. Time to go and check the boats again.

He picked up his revolver and torch and set off down the shingle. So as to see if there were any crocodiles about, he walked directly out towards the river and not diagonally down the beach to where the boats were moored 150 yards away. As he drew near the water, he heard a slight sound to his left. He shone his torch along the beach, and caught in the beam, not a crocodile, but two natives in shirts and shorts, frozen into immobility, pistols and knives in their hands. Roger panned round with his torch and picked out about ten more, crouched in a long line from the river's edge inwards. As all stood, momentarily transfixed, Roger noticed that they were dripping wet.

He called out *"Tanastalin!"* to them, as if it was the most normal thing to find a dozen armed men creeping down on one's camp in the small hours of the morning. A few seconds of excited jabbering followed, and then a flash of yellow light from two rifles and two dull cracks. Roger loosed off a round from his Webley .476, switched off his torch and sprinted back up to the camp.

"Stand by!" he shouted. "We're being attacked from the beach!" There was a quick stirring in all tents.

Everyone thought, "Oh, Christ! Not again."

Through the tent door I could see Roger standing four-square, revolver in hand. There was a dreadful whooping and howling from the natives, intended, no doubt, to shake morale, and not making too bad a job of it. Every now and then came the staccato cracks of ancient rifles. Roger turned and stamped on the candle. As I emerged from the tent all was pitch dark, except for the regular yellowish flashes from down the beach.

John Blashford-Snell had ordered that in an event of this sort, one person from each boat should take up a defensive position, while the others struck camp. David said to me, "You've no weapon, have you? I'll go out and fend them off. You grab the tent and all the kit and get it down to the boats."

He ran out with his .455 revolver and dropped down amongst the grasses. It was at this point that John Blashford-Snell shot off the first round of the secret weapon which was the factor that, next to Roger's vigilance, was to save all our lives—a red ministar made an arc through the trees into the sky and for five precious seconds illumined the beach and its ring of crouching gunmen. David saw two of them together, about fifteen yards from him, and with his first round brought the right-hand one to his knees.

I could hear more of them threading through the trees up the island above us. I grabbed a piece of the morning kindling and went beyond the tent, which was on the northern edge of the camp, to investigate. Then ensued one of those ridiculous moments which I am sure lighten the stories of most battles. Armed with my bit of wood I rushed straight into a tangled clump of thornbush and fell. Within seconds I was thoroughly enmeshed, and began slowly and painfully unhooking my tracksuit from the barbs. Reasoning that if we were so thickly encircled no bandit would be likely to come through that way, I came back and, extending my arms, enveloped David's tent in a bear-like hug and collapsed it.

A few moments before, Chris Bonington had cried out, "For Chrissake, someone go and look after the boats!" and Roger had run out of the camp and down the shingle towards the southern tip of the island. As he ran, with his torch picking out the long, white mooring rope and guiding him towards the boats, a volley of shots came from the Gojjam mainland to his right. A covering party of perhaps a dozen men had obviously been stationed to cut off our retreat. Roger flicked off his torch and ran on blindly. Near the boats he was more or less in dead ground, and putting on his torch again, he caught in its beam the two bandits that he had encountered at the very outset. Doubtless, their task had been to detach the boats with their knives and thus prevent our escape. Seeing a figure cut away from the camp, they, too, had run down the shingle, but Roger had beaten them to it. Now, forestalled, they checked and retreated.

Roger now decided that he should guard the boats and at the same time make them ready for a speedy withdrawal. Already armfuls of kit were arriving. An agitated Chris Bonington ran up, threw a stack of bedding into *Crookenden*, and ran off again for more. There was a tangle of cordage on the stones and a veritable Gordian knot where the separate lines joined the main rope. The other end was seventy yards away round the big tree. No time to pick at knots. Roger looked in the dinghies for a knife. No sign of one. Moments were slipping by. Influenced, no doubt, by many a boyhood Western, he took out his revolver to shoot the rope in two. Flouting the best traditions, however, he missed. Colin Chapman fortunately came up at that moment with some kit and cut the rope with his soft steel skinning knife.

Chris Bonington had now evacuated the camp area and Roger set him to guard the embarkation point. He lay on the shingle with his .455 and faced the enemy covering party about thirty yards away across the narrows. Roger was glad to see that despite his inclinations to pacifism he put at least five rounds over, which served to keep the enemy's head down whilst John Fletcher, Alastair and I tottered to and fro with kit.

Meanwhile, the battle was still in progress. Animal-like whoops and cries continued to fill the air, but the twelve gunmen seemed now to be in control only of the top half of the island; more fire was coming into the camp from the mainland opposite and sling shot was rattling through the trees. Every now and then John Blashford-Snell would send up a red or green flare and there would be a spirited exchange of shots while the artificial light lasted. Occasionally, he levelled a ministar horizontally at a group of riflemen, with very satisfactory results.

The impetus of the bandits' onrush was now obviously checked. They had crept up, clearly planning to murder us in our sleeping-bags; they had been most fortunately surprised, and were now bedazzled and halted by the mysterious flares and the spirited reply from our revolvers. Desultory firing went on from the bank and from the northern half of the island, but after a fifteen-minute fight they filtered away and seemed to swim to the Gojjam side.

It had all been grimly reminiscent of the fate of the Franco-Swiss Expedition led down the Abbai from Shafartak by Dr. Amoudruz in 1962. They had gone past Sirba and were near their terminus at Shogali when a similar bunch of *shifta* shot at them in the night as they slept. It had happened at much the same hour, 1.30 a.m. Six of them were on a similar islet, though only about fifteen yards from the right bank in their case. A full moon enabled the bandits to shoot and kill Dr. Walter and Henri Kadrnka outright. The marksmanship of these *shifta* must have been good; as the four survivors escaped, they wounded Michel Weber, holed the canoe, and smashed the paddle that Weber was wielding. Dr. Amoudruz's party, however, only had one revolver with six rounds, so no real battle developed.

While the bandits were retiring, John Blashford-Snell and Joe Ruston, under the central tree, were dismantling our short-lived H.Q.

Calmly, Joe was clambering about in the tree, unhitching the skywave dipole aerial that he had slung up only six hours previously. John, trying to help him, gave me his 9.3 mm rifle and white topee to take to the boats. The topee, a large, prominent symbol, had become for us like the Eagles for Roman legionaries, but, of course, it was just as likely to draw enemy fire. So as I walked over the familiar shingle with various bits of other kit, I held the white, luminous dome towards the distant Begemdir bank and the dark, leather lining to hostile Gojjam.

Joe loaded the radio gear into *Semper* and then stealthily, and right under the guns of the bandits thirty yards away, paddled in it down the narrow channel to the southern tip. It was a brave effort, for, although there was no obvious moon, it was possible, when acclimatised, to discern broad outlines at quite a fair distance.

I had plenty of time to discover this, for I soon found myself guarding the perimeter of our new position on the southern tip. When the camp had been cleared of all but minor, unseen oddments and we had fallen back on the boats, it was decided to hold this triangle of shingle until the first glimmerings of day, before pushing off into the river. This was because Roger, who had lately flown over the area, spoke of a considerable cataract at the north end of the broad section of gorge ahead of us. So Alastair and Chris covered the Gojjam bank, while Garth and I, with Colin's revolver, faced north up the island. The others attended to the boats, and David, for one, made an excellent job of resolving the chaos in *Deane-Drummond*. There was silence, save for the hiss of the river and the occasional clink of a dislodged pebble.

I lay at the apex of our little perimeter and stared out into blackness. An hour limped by heavily. Not even a distant parish church bell to mark the quarters, or a country cockerel. I fell to comparing our situation to that of the English army before Agincourt: of course, we had had our little battle—they knew theirs was to come...

> *Now entertain conjecture of a time*
> *When creeping murmur and the poring dark*
> *Fills the wide vessel of the universe...*

I groped for the next line. It was a stimulating pastime to try to put Shakespeare's famous Prologue together in my mind. I could remember almost all the pieces, but it was a matter of slotting them into their proper places in the jig-saw puzzle:

> *From camp to camp, through the foul womb of night,*
> *The hum of either army stilly sounds,*
> *That the fix'd sentinels almost receive*
> *The secret whispers of each other's watch.*

Movements could certainly be heard in the bandit nerve centre under a group of tall trees, and every so often a man would run along the far bank. Furthermore, all the normal hallucinations of a sentry afflicted me: I could hear the lap of the fast stream, and it sounded like someone swimming gently from Gojjam with the current; I could see a small thornbush, and inevitably it kept turning into a crouching figure. No matter, as long as it crouched there until dawn.

Presently I heard the mutter of deep voices from under the tall trees opposite, and I crept back to report the fact to John Blashford-Snell. Almost immediately, short, sharp blasts on a hunting horn—familiar to us from the Tammi River—broke on the night air.

"Right. Man the boats," John whispered loudly. "We're going." He knew that ammunition was running low—we now had an average of three rounds per revolver—and the second bandit assault promised to be a determined one. Cataract or no cataract, it was wiser to slip away—even with a leak in *Semper*'s forward compartment and a suspected one in *Ubique*. We fired off a flare and a few more shots and then in complete silence we closed in on the boats, waded out into the stream with them, and one by one rolled quietly inboard. The water lapped softly round us as we drifted quickly away from the island. It is fairly certain the robber band never sensed our departure, for ten minutes afterwards we heard a noisy attack going in on the abandoned site.

Now, in the black of night, we were at the mercy of a cruel river to which we had learnt to accord every respect by daylight. The fear of the unknown, which had already unnerved a number of us, was now horribly accentuated. We could not use engines for fear of alerting any bandits that may have moved down-river to cut us off. Nevertheless, *Semper* took *Crookenden* in tow, and *Ubique* threw a line to *Deane-Drummond*. This ensured some measure of cohesion. Swirling downstream at about six knots was a most eery sensation, for though it was happening, we were barely aware of it. We sat still, paddles ready in our hands, our ears twitching for clues like terriers.

Soon the towering monolith loomed up ahead. With alarming suddenness the noise of a cataract was heard. We could not tell whether it involved the whole river or only a part. Although by day it was impossible to avoid being sucked into turbulence, at least the boat could be directed towards the fringes of the rapid and trimmed to minimise the impact. We did not really know if it was a large rock round which the river swirled, or a general drop in the water level. Trying to pierce the gloom, we looked for *Semper* and *Crookenden* who were on a parallel course to our right; but we could barely even see *Ubique* to which we were tied.

With the rope between us sagging and tautening, *Ubique* and *Deane-Drummond* entered the hazard, trying desperately to keep their bows head on to the waves. As the noise increased, *Ubique* suddenly dipped down a chute of water and as suddenly climbed up the face of a broad, 10-foot wave beyond. *Deane-Drummond,* an unwilling child, was jerked along in its wake. As we climbed the wave a counter-wave seemed to strike us and the whole Redshank canted on to its beam ends, tipping to port. David Bromhead and I were shot out into the water. I caught a glimpse as I went, of *Ubique,* with John Fletcher and Colin Chapman still aboard, trapped in a churning sea ahead of us. One could be forgiven, I think, for regarding this as the end: the darkness was complete, neither of us was attached to the dinghy, the water was in tumult, and there must have been crocodiles beyond.

However, Roger Chapman in the stern had thrust his foot out at the moment of torque and wedged himself in the aft quarter of the boat. He stayed inboard, and *Deane-Drummond* did not capsize, but fell back on an even keel. David and I surfaced near the dinghy. In the earlier conflicts with cataracts above Tissisat the comforting phenomenon had been noted, that if thrown into the water one always came up more or less alongside the boat. I managed to hook my right foot under a lifeline on the port side, and within seconds Roger had grabbed it. He tried at first to haul me in by one leg, but it is not the simplest of manoeuvres and I swallowed a lot of Abbai water. So I shook free and was hauled in normally, and David, who had also grabbed a lifeline, was similarly fished out.

John Fletcher then started the engine in *Ubique* and drew the stricken *Deane-Drummond* out of the cataract. The two boats veered over to the right where they grounded on shingle not far from *Semper*, in which John Blashford-Snell and Joe had passed to the side of the worst turbulence, slipping easily into calmer water. This was as well, for the bows of their Recce Boat were now completely deflated. They had had to cast off the tow-rope to *Crookenden* and limp in on their engine to the western bank.

The crews of the three boats stood apprehensively thigh-deep in the Abbai and looked inland to the dark, Gojjam cliffs. We felt it was probably safe to wait here; we were, perhaps, two miles below the island, not far from the Bashillo River junction, and on the edge of an extensive piece of shingle, on which we partially beached our boats. This proved to be another island, for a stream separated it from the mainland 200 yards from us.

Unhappily, *Crookenden* was missing. They had been cast off by Joe in his extremity and had paddled for the right bank, but had been carried about half a mile downriver. In a few moments a point of light flickered in the blackness to the south: "O ... K," it spelled out.

We slowly unwound.

"Thanks, Roger," I said. "That's the second time today you've saved my life and it's only 4 a.m."

Now, for once, we were glad of the cloud blanketing the moon — on the island it had inhibited us in our action against the bandits; on the river it had hidden from us the extent of the cataract we had just come through; finally, it was to our advantage, and allowed us to stand and wait on this exposed shingle in reasonable security from the main shore.

We knew that we must wait for dawn before slipping off again onto the uncharted river, and two hours of the night still had to pass. It was an uncomfortable vigil. We were all wet, especially David and I, who had been ditched completely. The battle had caught us in the tracksuits in which we slept. There were no other dry clothes, no shelter. For warmth, we stripped and put on our rubber wet-suits and pooled any other garments that had remained dry in the dinghy thwarts, and then stood huddled together like moorland sheep.

John Fletcher and Joe Ruston, our two helmsmen, got on with the repair of their expiring Recce Boats. Soon John quietly approached

Roger Chapman.

"I say, Roger. Something terrible has happened. I've lost a nipple in the Abbai."

Roger looked at him. "You've what?"

"I've dropped it. The nipple. The nut that holds the propeller onto the shaft. The flow of water will just whizz the prop off unless I fix it."

John had already shown his resourcefulness when a Recce Boat had smashed its transom. He had purloined a cooking grid as a stiffener to the cracked stern-piece, and sealed it on with Araldite.

He and Roger tinkered about in the darkness with wire and nails, but nothing worked. His splendid, last-hope improvisation was to mix Araldite blindly in a tobacco tin and pour it all over the propeller and shaft. A polythene bag was tied over it to keep the spray off, if we were to move on before it had dried.

The rest of us stood about silently, ankle-deep in the Abbai, which was a good deal warmer than the surrounding air. We ate biscuits and Spangles, glanced at watches, and cursed

> the cripple tardy-gaited night
> Who like a foul and ugly witch doth limp
> So tediously away.

It was not yet dawn when we left. The darkness was less intense, however, and we could just see across the river when John Blashford-Snell said, "All right. Let's go," and we climbed wearily into our wet and disorganised craft and paddled off.

At first we concentrated on peering ahead for signs of the next cataract, and scrutinising every prominent bluff of rock for a possible ambush; but the river was broad and never more than gently undulating, and we saw no sign of life.

As it grew lighter an unimaginably beautiful landscape appeared around us: stark and arid, pink and brown, with towering cliffs, vast boulders, and natural arches high on the skyline. Basalt seemed to give way to sandstone and then to limestone.

We sat hunched and heavy-lidded in the four boats. It was a blessed moment when the sun climbed over the eastern cliff-top to warm our chilled bodies. The world seemed not only brighter but safer.

All praise and thanks to God
The Father now be given...

We had sung Catherine Winkworth's hymn a bit prematurely the first time, and I was probably not the only one of us to recall it now as, saving fuel, we drifted easily along, once again rejoicing to be alive.

There was a quickening of excitement when for a second time we found *Charity* on the left-hand bank. She had been cast away when we evacuated our first island at 3.30 a.m., and had been later pulled from the river by a cowherd, who stood, amazed, whilst we somewhat brusquely dispossessed him. *Faith* had never been recovered after the first release of the two dinghies from K2; she was almost certainly destroyed, for the Beaver had later in the day seen football bladders floating in the river. *Hope* had been packed away at Tissisat and was later lost, and so it was indeed *Charity* that sprang eternal and proved to be the greatest of the three.

As the sun climbed in the sky we saw further signs of human life, of which we were naturally wary. One man on the Gojjam bank saw us from afar and set off running down a long spur to the river. He sped along the beach and along a limestone shelf, and, astonishingly he kept pace with us as we moved silently along. He caused a tiny, irrational crumb of alarm, although he was alone and carried only a spear. Suddenly he stopped and stared at us as we slipped slowly out of his life.

Soon it was 8 a.m. We had been awake almost continuously for over twenty-four hours. We coiled round meanders, and slipped past banks of limestone that looked like the tumbled débris of pediments, columns and capitals from a string of Greek temples. The miles were being steadily eaten up and it would not be long—a radio call from Debre Marcos suggested—before we met Group J.

John Wilsey with Group J had set off from Shafartak on September 17th to proceed upstream in an Assault Boat to meet Group P on their way down. They were to provide an additional escort in an area particularly infested with crocodile. Certainly the saurian population did seem to have increased. They lay smugly sunbathing on almost every available long strip of exposed beach. All boats carried a sandbag full of stones to keep them at bay, and Garth Brocksopp, in particular, used his geological specimens to best effect, scoring a number of direct hits.

An impressive butte marks the junction of the Jamma River (right) with the Abbai.
Here P and J Groups lunched on the final day.

Suddenly, without the pleasurable doubt and anticipation of a long approach in sight of one another, Group J were there. We dropped down a rapid in the now much shallower river, and there, round the corner, tied up to a boulder beach was *Sandford*. John Wilsey's radio was out of action and he knew nothing of our battles and hasty getaway. There was a pleasant two hours of talk, laughter, recuperation and reorganisation, as we exchanged news, dried our clothes and drank tea.

After a disastrous free drop from the Beaver onto an ill-chosen stony beach, when more supplies perished than survived, we pressed on down the river. The mood was very relaxed now: even old White Water antagonisms were reconciled. It had been remarkable how the death of Ian Macleod had brought the incompatible together; and now shared dangers had cemented the union.

The two groups together made up an impressive flotilla: *Sandford* towed *Crookenden*, *Deane-Drummond* and *Charity* in line ahead, while *Semper* and *Ubique*, like frigates, buzzed hither and thither, showing their paces. The river was broad and easy, and tiredness could safely overcome us: Group P talked, sunbathed and dozed—freed from the cares of navigation. We moved at speed; John Huckstep, playfully wagging his "tail" of dinghies behind him, took us in seconds down cataracts that he had taken hours to surmount. The seventy or so miles between our rendezvous near the Dankoro River junction and Shafartak, which had occupied Group J for seven days, was covered in just thirty-six hours, with an intervening night stop at the Walaka River junction.

We paused for some time to allow Colin Chapman to shoot an eight-foot crocodile, the only one we killed. It clung tenaciously to life, for even with its head virtually severed, its jaws bit and held the axe we had used. Its skull is now in the Cromwell Road, at the British Museum (Natural History Department), where all our zoological specimens have been lodged. After Colin had examined its stomach, which contained a catfish, ten locusts, some feathers, some roots and the usual load of stones, we pushed on southwards, taking the crocodile's tail, which we later ate.

Tuesday, September 24th, was our last day on the river. The flotilla moved swiftly downstream into an increasingly deep gorge. The water remained entirely manageable: fast, brimming, and for the most part smooth; but the terraces of alternating scrub and cliff soared up above us like an opulent wedding cake. John amused himself with a little mobile game hunting. Standing on the quarter deck of his flagship with a 12-bore resting on the "dodger", he potted at guinea fowl and francolin, and the Recce Boats raced like busy retrievers to pick up the kill from among the bank-side trees.

The rest of us had time to think about the river, which we had now successfully descended. As Chris Bonington rightly concluded, no-one conquers the Blue Nile. The most that can be wrung from this powerful, turgid river is a grudging acceptance that some men and boats have passed over more or less all of it. But they do not do this without a mauling; they come away scarred; some do not come away at all. We had lost a precious life. The survivors were probably all scarred in some way, physically or mentally. And we knew it would be some time before the scars were healed.

Colin Chapman, Joe Ruston and David Bromhead dissect the only crocodile we shot.

Shortly before Shafartak we ran up British and Ethiopian flags and made rather ineffectual efforts to smarten up. Soon the welcome note of the Beaver was heard, and in moments it was roaring over us up the gorge in triumphal fly-past. Then the majestic structure of the Abbai bridge came into sight round a bend. From M to Z, and from A to L: apart from the odd impossible letter, we had now spelt out the whole alphabet. A small but enthusiastic reception committee—English,

Final leg of the journey to Shafartak.

Ethiopian and American, in about equal proportions—awaited us on the stony beach. Incredibly, we hove to at almost exactly the advertised hour—4 p.m.

There was, of course, no welcoming wail of ships' sirens, no cascading water from firefloats, no gun salute from the Yacht Club terrace. But Press and TV were gathered in some force with cameras and tape-recorders, and our Embassy was represented by its Chief Clerk, Mr. Hartley, and his wife. There was some slight confusion when the interviewer from Radio Voice of the Gospel addressed Joe Ruston as Brother Charles. We fleetingly thought that the strain of the river had been such that Joe had secretly joined an Order by radio, but it appeared that the interviewer had intercepted some of our messages and had misheard our call-sign codewords "Bravo, Charlie". Long interviews were given by some of us, as others unloaded our kit. Kay kissed everybody, bottles were passed round and champagne flowed.

NOTES:

[1] Lt.-Col. Philip Shepherd in Addis Ababa.
[2] Army parlance for "Leader" of formations of any size.
[3] Of course, he had a string of mules and a large entourage.

Chapter Eighteen
SKULLS, CROSSES AND BONES

ON my desk rests a monkey's skull with a large chunk of its occiput missing. A trophy picked up on an earlier Ethiopian expedition, it is a reminder not only of the impermanence of things, but of the central position that zoology held in our work in the Blue Nile region.

The scientific aim of the Expedition embraced a wider variety of studies, however: the archaeology of the region, and to a limited extent its geology; a survey of the crocodile population of the Great Abbai and of the ornithology of the area; an enquiry into the prevalence of Schistosomiasis (Bilharzia) among gorge dwellers or their nearest highland neighbours; the collection of ectoparasites from some mammals on the Wallega plateau. But the major part of our scientific work was to do with fauna, and the major interest of the zoologists was in the smaller vertebrate species of the region. We were working, in this respect, in the service of the Natural History Department of the British Museum, to enable them to build up a reference collection for the better understanding of Ethiopian wild life.

To a layman the essence of much zoological fieldwork today seems to be that it is comparative: our zoologists wanted to compare the livestock in the gorge with that of the surrounding plateau on both sides, and, as an even starker contrast, with that of the drier regions of eastern Ethiopia. The Blue Nile gorge was hot, dry and largely uninhabited, yet subject in the wet season to frequent sharp rainstorms and thus covered at this time with considerable vegetation. The surrounding highlands were flatter, cooler, wetter, muddier, densely populated, and covered with a thick soil and, in places, a scattering of rocks. The areas investigated in eastern Ethiopia were in one instance (near Harar) arid, stony ground, covered with thorn scrub, and in the other (in the Awash valley) a dry, thinly-grassed plain, spread with volcanic rubble and dust. At different times our zoologists operated in all these varied types of terrain. Their method was twofold: to observe, and where necessary to collect specimens.

Pat Morris, the Senior Scientist and an experienced field zoologist, had with him a talented support team. Dr. Derek Yalden, a twenty-eight-year-old Lecturer at Manchester University, had, in fact, taught Pat at an earlier stage. Dr. Malcolm Largen, tall and nordic, was a zoologist lecturing at Haile Selassie I University in Addis Ababa. Our link with this institution was an important one, one of our declared aims being ultimately to give the University a selection of zoological specimens to form the basis of a small reference collection there. They, in turn, helped the Expedition in a number of ways. The "baby" of the team was nineteen-year-old Hilary King; between school and university he had managed to study Soay sheep on St. Kilda, work in Chessington Zoo, do forestry work in the Gambia, and guard the nesting ospreys at Loch Garten. Slight and mop-headed, his special, somewhat macabre interest was skulls.

These four joined Group A to carry out the zoological investigation of the gorge between Shafartak and Sirba. Associated with them was a fifth zoologist, who was to conduct a crocodile survey of the whole river. This was Colin Chapman, stocky and blond and by birth South African, who had been in Ethiopia for some time and joined the Expedition in Addis Ababa. For over a year he had worked for Dofan, an Ethiopian Share Company supplying crocodile skins for the Parisian handbag trade. Colin was their adviser on conservation, and told them, in collaboration with the Ethiopian game control, how many reptiles they could slaughter each year. This was rather like being a dental consultant to a boiled sweet factory—the *parisiennes* wanted their handbags, Colin had to conserve. The dilemma caused him, in the end, to resign and return home after the Expedition, to read Medicine at Bristol.

As we moved down the Nile, we stopped for a few days every forty or fifty miles to enable this team to conduct their enquiries in the constantly changing habitat. When their tents had been set up, some would go off on a shoot and others lay traps. An open-air laboratory was constructed—the half dozen green zoological chests placed under a polythene rain-shelter. At dusk, mist-nets and headlamps would be brought out for the continuing war on the bat world; the traps would be inspected and the quarry overdosed with anaesthetic and bagged. Colin, by day, would roam the banks for his saurian friends, and, by night, would cruise up and down the river in an Assault Boat, sweeping the black mirror of water with his powerful beam, counting up the red eyes and dividing by two. Later still in the night, Pat and his men would sit on their uncomfortable boxes and carry out the vital other half of the work of collection: data sheets would be filled in with the details of each specimen: "*Tadarida,* ♂, weight x grammes, wingspan y centimetres…" The kill would then either be prepared for preservation in formalin solution, or delicately skinned with dissecting scissors. In both cases, the corpse or its skin would be meticulously labelled before being put away. Considerations of time and space made it fortunate that specimens in the gorge were few at first, and that only the smaller vertebrates were collected—mice, bats, lizards. Mice and bats were skinned—the mice pulled like finger-stalls onto a piece of card cut, appropriately, like a pointed tomb-stone; the bats displayed volant on a rectangle of similar card. Lizards were pumped full of preservative and dropped into plastic drums of formalin.

The conditions in which this exact work was done were far from ideal. And after two or three days, perhaps, the whole camp would be struck, the mobile laboratory put into the green chests and the team exposed once more to the rigours of cataract and whirlpool. Although John Blashford-Snell was as accommodating as possible, the state of the river ultimately dictated our movements, and they sometimes occurred before or after the zoologists were ready. Despite the frustration, the damp and dirt, all was safely conveyed to Sirba and eventually by air to Debre Marcos. Some specimens were carried from intermediate points on the river by returning re-supply columns.

At Base Camp Barbara Wells, our Zoological Secretary, was patiently waiting. Here she collated and stored the bizarre organs, strange skins and corpses that came in. In all, we netted over 1,000 specimens, which compared very favourably with the 260 brought back by the 1966 Expedition, and made ours the biggest collection ever to come out of Ethiopia.

For Phase 2, Pat's team, together with Barbara, moved north to Bahardar. Here they made camp a few miles south of the town in the wet fields by the Tissisat road. They did not join the boat party on the journey from Lake Tana to Shafartak, but there was nevertheless some zoological collecting done in the gorge at times, mainly by Garth Brocksopp and David Bromhead. These two experienced fieldworkers, stationed south of the Abbai at Ghimbi throughout most of Phase 1, had done much valuable hunting in the undulating highland country near by. For Phase 2 they were in the river party, and their amphibious career began at the 2nd Portuguese Bridge. It may be said of Pat's professional zoologists, meanwhile, that they literally left few stones unturned in the Tana-Tissisat area in their search for, frogs and snakes. It was here they captured our tiniest specimen—a fully-grown shrew 1 1/2 inches long and weighing less than a half-crown. After this they moved off to the drier regions near Harar and in the Awash National Park.

A few members, notably John Huckstep and Alec Murray, tried their hand at fishing in the Abbai and its tributaries. These proved not the best of waters; the strong currents made netting and trapping impossible and only line could be used. The Abbai was as inhospitable below as it was on the surface, and it was mainly the tributaries that yielded the occasional catfish or electric fish. The catfish, which were up to a metre in length, were well adapted to a life of ooze, having feelers rather than eyes to guide them about. The three large freshwater turtles fished out near Mabil were an additional interesting surprise.

Despite the thick scrub and tall grasses in the Black Gorge, it was found that the fauna was of the kind associated with dry, stony areas: Agamid lizards, orange bats, spiny mice, scorpions and sun spiders. Where neither migration out of the gorge nor burrowing away from the sun's heat would be easy, it seemed that the wild life of the river-bank had to be able to stand the scorching drought of February as well as the heavy rains of August. Further down the river, where there is always likely to be more vegetation, a wider variety of small mammals was found. Very few larger animals were encountered, however, apart from the numerous crocodiles and occasional hippo: klipspringer sprang about among the boulders of the Black Gorge, a young leopard was seen on a sandbank, a bushbuck at Mabil, a large pig at the Azir River—this was the meagre tally. To the east the gorge is too dry and forbidding, in the west the land is roamed by gun-toting Shankilla; these, perhaps, are the explanations for the virtual absence of large game.

Even the crocodile have begun to suffer from human depredations. Below the Western Cataracts their numbers thin. We heard numerous

A Fresh-water turtle, or *Trionyx*.

reports of poachers coming upriver from the Sudan in the early months of the year, and this may be why Colin Chapman noted mainly young specimens in this area. Above the Western Cataracts, a region more difficult to penetrate, crocodiles of all ages were found, though they became fewer again in the faster currents of the Black Gorge. Hunters have had their effect, too, in the reaches above the Tissisat Falls, though the dry season reveals that there are still plenty of crocodiles there. The thunderous waters of the Northern Gorge are, of course, too much for them, but from the Bashillo River downstream almost to Shafartak they are quite thick on the banks. It was in this area that Colin selected and shot his one and only specimen.

On an earlier expedition to Ethiopia led by John in 1964 there had been much talk, during a foray to the Lake Tana area, of the search for Osgood's swamp rat. Beds of waving papyrus by the lake had been hopefully combed for this rare creature, but the marshes had kept their mysterious secret. No such specialised aim excited Pat Morris and his zoologists, and indeed no Osgood's swamp rat was ever found, for it turned out to be a rodent equivalent of the gryphon or the giant roc, and quite imaginary. The fruits of our work in 1968, however, are already proving to be of dramatic zoological significance, and amongst them is clear evidence of new species discovered.

The herpetological report is a glowing one: we collected 368 reptiles and amphibians, including Colin's crocodile and John Huckstep's three specimens of freshwater turtle (Trionyx). Of the rest, only thirty-three were snakes, a surprisingly low total for an area where in popular imagination the trees are hung about with fiendish python and every boulder conceals its spitting cobra. We did take specimens of both these species, and a cobra and a Western Crowned snake had not been seen in Ethiopia before—not nearer, in fact, than 400 miles. Two other species of snake were also the first found in Ethiopia—one of them not previously known outside Southern Africa. It might have been this that was the only creature to fall victim to "Teeny-Weeny Airways", for Alan Calder ran over a snake whilst taxiing in the Beaver at Sirba. Snakes were rare, however, and I never saw a live one at all.

An agamid lizard.

We caught many skinks—smooth, shiny lizards—with confusing variations of colour and marking. Their full identification has been a slow and complex task. A caecilian (a wormlike amphibian with hidden eyes), found by the military zoologists at Ghimbi, was the first specimen of a whole group of species, and of more than 200 frogs and toads brought back to the Cromwell Road, one long-legged grass frog was of a sort thought to be purely West African and now discovered in the Ethiopian Highlands for the first time. Several other species of frog have been found to have broken their previous altitude records by as much as 7,000 feet. No fewer than twelve mature males were found of a species of tree frog that cannot so far be identified; of the genus *Leptopelis*, they may represent another new species. And a further example of the very rare frog *Rana beccarii is* now available to the British Museum, whose only two previous specimens were in poor condition.

The bat experts also have pronounced on our findings; we caught about ninety in all, of twenty-three different species. At least two were not known to be in Ethiopia and one is the first male of its species ever collected. More vespertilian wonders may well emerge even yet. Other mammals found include genets, mongooses, hares, duiker, bushbuck—mostly in the fields south of Bahardar, and the similar countryside around Ghimbi provided a rich harvest, too. But for the first three weeks of our work in the gorge below Shafartak, a squirrel was the largest mammal collected.

All the zoologists were interested in the birdlife of the river, which was plentiful and wonderfully polychrome; and "Johnny" Johnson made exhaustive notes on it. Hilary King managed to capture a live eagle owl near Bahardar, but birds were logged rather than bagged, except, of course, on the few occasions when we could get something for the pot. Spur-winged geese were quite plentiful in the highlands and at least two ended up as a satisfying supper. In this respect, there was happily little conflict between the requirements of scientists and the appetites of hunters; only on one or two occasions did a fish that should have been pickled in formalin end up spattering in a frying-pan.

A highly specialised collection of insects was made by our vet, Keith Morgan-Jones. During his weeks at Ghimbi, he picked over 200 ectoparasites from the bodies of bats, civet and serval cats, genets, rabbits, hyena and zebu cattle. He also carried out comparative tests on various kinds of commercial insect repellent. The insect life was, of course, varied and exotic, and the gorge, particularly, would have been an entomologist's paradise.

The scientist who found the gorge least paradisial was Mansel Spratling, Expedition Archaeologist. It was not until he reached the Western Cataracts at the end of two weeks on the river that he made

These gelada baboons were seen near the source of the Mugher River.

any significant find. Here, on a bed of boulders on which we camped, he turned up fragments of pottery and stone artefacts. This was on the northern shore of the Abbai at the foot of an 18-foot bank of black alluvium. The river, forced here between massive stone outcrops, was sinuous and fast-flowing. Since its last occupants had quitted the site, the Nile had grown broader and deeper for the alluvium to have been laid down over it. Now the river has dropped again, but when it is at its height in the rainy season, it cuts into the earth bank and reveals more of this erstwhile settlement.

Mansel found dolerite axeheads here, and smaller implements of translucent chalcedony, one of which has what appear to be sun-symbols cut on its surface. There was much pottery, some of it marked with incised patterns. Between two large boulders lay almost all the pieces of a shattered vessel. This must have been frequently covered by the swirling Nile, but was so lodged that it had not been carried away. Mansel thought his trouvailles compared closely with early Neolithic material of about 3,000 B.C. in the Khartoum area, and it is thus probable that the settlement—which seems to be the earliest in Ethiopia in which potsherds have been found—received influences from the Sudanese end of the Blue Nile valley.

This discovery apart, Mansel had to wait for Phase 2 for his greatest moments. Our journey from Shafartak to Sirba saw him grow increasingly depressed. It became clear that he was looking for archaeological evidence at quite the wrong time of year—the vegetation in August was thick, and obscured almost all signs of artefacts (on the other hand, of course, combing the arid rocks in the dry season would be physically almost unbearable). Furthermore, it became gradually more and more obvious that where very few people lived today, only very few had probably ever lived. When he stumbled on the site in the Western Cataracts, Mansel believed he had only twenty-four hours to uncover it. Accordingly, he dug, with help from Ian Macleod and many others, all day and all night. But the following morning the river level was found to have fallen and we could not leave, and so, dirty and weary, he sought the help of Spencer Lane-Jones in making a survey of the complete site.

These two spent a good deal of the rest of the expedition in useful partnership. Mansel, twenty-four, working for his doctorate at London University, was dark and pale, with a slight frame that became perceptibly gaunter as the lack of carbohydrates took its toll. Spencer was an Engineer from Shrivenham, a noted Army pistol shot, and Chief Surveyor for the Expedition. We had no intention of map-making on a grand scale, as this had all been adequately done from the air by the Americans. Various sites were surveyed and mapped by Spencer, however, and our position was regularly determined from the stars.

Based at Bahardar, where kind hospitality was offered by Dr. and Mrs. Uwe Brinkmann of the West German Hospital, he and Mansel carried out many journeys and surveys in the Lake Tana area. To the west of the town, at Shimbet Mikhael, they found—dating from the mid-seventeenth century reign of the Emperor Fasiladas—defence works which cut off a peninsula from the mainland. Here, a surviving moat, and a rampart seven or eight feet high, run up to a stone gatehouse of two storeys. What might be a royal mausoleum on a near by uninhabited island was investigated, together with a variety of decaying, drystone structures abandoned by the last monastic community.

On the north-east coast of Lake Tana and somewhat inland, Mansel and Spencer surveyed the sixteenth-century castle of Guzera. This had probably been built about 1570 by the warlike Emperor Sarsa

Mansel Spratling (above) and Ian Macleod at an archaeological "dig" in the Western Cataracts.

Dengel, who frequently sallied into the Agau country to subjugate the troublesome Galla. Its rectangular keep, once with round towers at all but one of the corners, seems to have been slighted; for a round tower, and the taller, square tower on the southern corner, is collapsed. An eight-foot rampart surrounds it. The castle antedates the famous imperial palaces of Gondar to the north, but is similar in style. The Portuguese, who began to penetrate Ethiopia in earnest in the early sixteenth century, could well have introduced influence from their own work in India and on the East African coast; their effect on bridge-building was considerable, too. Mansel examined the 1st Portuguese Bridge, or Agama Dildi, a few hundred yards downstream of the Tissisat Falls, and another in Shoa, just off the Addis Ababa-Shafartak road.

His interests towards the end broadened out to embrace many areas of traditional Ethiopian life: he made recordings of Coptic services in the new and beautiful church by the lake at Bahardar; and he acquired two of the distinctive *tankwas*, or reed boats, on which fishermen propel themselves about Lake Tana with bladeless bamboo poles. These safely made the journey back to England and one of them was shown on the Expedition's stand at the Great Outdoors Exhibition in the Kelvin Hall, Glasgow, and later on Thames TV.

Like many of us, he bought a number of the beautiful, silver, pectoral crosses worn on leather thongs round the necks of the Christian peasant women of the region. The design of these varies slightly in the different parts of the Empire, and I saw a good representative collection in the home of the Defence Attaché in Addis Ababa.

Towards the end of the expedition Mansel had quite recovered his health and enthusiasm, and with his small Group S (Tadesse Wolde and Claude joined in from time to time) he ferreted about tirelessly in the Lake Tana district. He seems to have been well pleased with what he found, and work to determine its full significance still goes on.[1]

It is perhaps appropriate to end with a reference to the work of Nigel Marsh, who carefully organised the collection of samples of human excrement from villagers by the river or on the fringes of the gorge. This was done to try to discover to what extent, if any, Bilharzia, highly endemic in the Nile valley, had gripped them. Specimens of faeces and urine in little screw-top bottles were to be preserved in formalin and sent to the Department of Parasitology at the University in Addis Ababa to see if Schistosoma eggs were present. Collecting this sort of sample is commonplace in a sophisticated society, but the amazed villagers were not quick to act until we told them that the Emperor would be pleased with their efforts. Even then, Nigel was never sure it was all their own work.

NOTES:

[1] The results given in this chapter are by no means complete. Final scientific reports from several sources arc not yet available. The zoological assessment is based upon forecasts made by Pat Morris in an article published in *The Daily Telegraph Magazine* in June, 1969, for the use of which I am much indebted to him. I am grateful, too, to the others in the scientific team whose reports I have read, and also to the staff of the British Museum (Natural History Department) whose painstaking work is gradually enabling an assessment of our collection to be made.

Chapter Nineteen
ENVOI

OUR last days in Addis Ababa and the journey home were inevitably tinged with a sense of aftermath and anticlimax. We had stumbled into the Ras Hotel with the abstracted air of a bunch of central European refugees, and it was some days before the comforts of civilisation seemed normal once again. Roger West maintained a busy surgery in his hotel bedroom for our lingering maladies, but our pain and fatigue was counter-balanced by the knowledge that we had successfully taken on a job far more formidable than many of us had light-heartedly assumed as we laid our plans at Chiseldon twelve months before. It was made clear to us in Addis Ababa that official Ethiopian opinion was wholly satisfied with all the aspects of our achievement. It would be months before all the scientists could assess the value of our work, but we had reason to think that our survey had been a useful one. From time to time a pixie smile would play on Pat Morris's face and the zoologists obviously had their lockers crammed with good things. But however favourable the ultimate scientific judgement of our survey of the gorge might be, we at all events felt that we had grappled with the awesome river itself and come out on top.

It was afterwards, too, that some of us began to realise how much the Blue Nile lies at the core of many of Ethiopia's current problems. Some 550 billion cubic metres of water flow down it each year, bearing an immense volume of eroded earth. This annual loss is as damaging to Ethiopia's agriculture as it has traditionally been vital to that of the Sudan and Egypt. For this reason these Arab lands have long opposed the idea of a Blue Nile barrage in Ethiopia. Now, however, they have dams of their own, from Roseires down to the vast Lake Nasser at Aswan, and they have realised that enormous quantities of silt build up behind a dam and shorten its life. So it is a strange reversal of historical attitudes that these Arab countries encourage Ethiopia in the construction of Blue Nile dams—although only for those producing hydro-electric power, for irrigation leads precious water away. Seven dams are projected in the Blue Nile area, though only one, near Sirba, will be over the Abbai itself. Others are to span various tributaries—the Fincha, the Didessa etc.

In fact, many of them will provide for irrigation, and efforts are being made in the area below Tissisat—where there is at present a great soil loss in tributaries like the Tul, the Yezzat and the Abaya—to educate villagers in the virtues of terrace farming. This will be a slow and painful process, however, for the Department concerned has already lost six of its men to *shifta*, who, as we too had learnt, resist any sort of intrusion.

The advent of barrages in the Abbai and its tributaries will probably mean a change in the seasonal rise and fall of the river as we know it. Before technological advances reach these distant valleys, there may, therefore, be only a brief opportunity to navigate the Blue Nile in its present state. From blueprint to barrage is a long haul, however, and so there will doubtless be time enough for our journey to be repeated—and repeated it should be, for there is still much scientific work to be done in the gorge.

Within a few months of our return home there were even some hints from John Blashford-Snell that he might consider going back into the gorge himself, perhaps in different vessels with more powerful engines. If this ever materialised he would be sure of a warm welcome by Ethiopians at the highest levels. The hospitality accorded to us and the kindness we received were remarkable. All will remember, for example, the Reception given for us by His Imperial Majesty, Haile Selassie I, at the Jubilee Palace.

Sunburnt, in some cases moustached or bearded, sticking-plastered and weary, we stood about looking rather incongruous in our dark suits, which Kay Thompson had carefully kept during our absence. Slowly we filed in under the brilliant chandeliers, each pausing three times to bow rather awkwardly as we drew near the Emperor. After the last obeisance, the thin, brown hand was gently held and then began the inelegant business of walking backwards to our places in the horseshoe around him. Soon footmen circled amongst us with plates of canapés, or refilled our glasses with the excellent imperial *tej*. I could not help thinking of the Army biscuit with its golden squirt of molten margarine, which was my mid-afternoon snack the previous week. The Emperor spoke at length to John Blashford-Snell and Philip Shepherd, expressing his interest in our work and his hopes for our return on some

His Imperial Majesty Haile Selassie I receives members of the expedition.

similar project. We were grateful for his encouragement, and indeed for his direct intercessions on our behalf. As some token of this, we presented him, as mentioned in an earlier chapter, with Lulette, a Chihuahua bitch, to share the basket of Lulu, his own much-loved dog.[1]

"The biggest little man I ever met," was "Hank" Mansley's comment, as we stood afterwards on the steps of the Palace talking to members of the Emperor's Cabinet.

Ethiopia, to our delight, ran true to form in every respect right to the very end. All the old, slightly comic shortcomings of a bureaucracy struggling to make a quick transformation from the Middle Ages to Modernity were there to dog us once again. Indeed, they even pursued us onto the tarmac. On the day before our departure from Addis Ababa, Philip Shepherd paid another of his many visits to the International

Airport. He wanted to find out the arrival time of the aircraft that was to carry us home. Nobody on the ground floor seemed to have any knowledge of the advent of a Transglobe charter flight. So with characteristic panache, and a boldness that would not cut much ice at Heathrow, he climbed up to the Control Tower. Inside, an Ethiopian official sat with his feet on an adjacent chair, quietly tidying his fingernails with a file.

"Good afternoon," said Philip, "I'd like to know when the charter plane from Gatwick, which is to pick up the Great Abbai Expedition, is expected to arrive."

The official flicked over some sheets of paper in front of him.

"It's a CL 44 of Transglobe Airways," added Philip helpfully.

"I'm afraid there's nothing like that expected in," the Ethiopian said.

"But there *must* be," Philip insisted, looking over the man's shoulder.

"No. Nothing due from London now, Sir."

Philip glanced through the large windows. Parked far across the tarmac, opposite the tower, was a large Transglobe airliner.

"What's that?" he cried.

"Oh, that one came in this morning," the airline man replied, "but it's not for you. It's for some Blue Nile Expedition."

Philip's verification of our plane's arrival was typical of the many exercises in detection, persuasion, attrition or improvisation that he performed in the capital on our behalf. His was a first-class, indeed an indispensable performance.

Primarily, of course, we all acknowledged John Blashford-Snell's ability in dealing with our tribulations in the field. With some modesty, John has always accounted for the Expedition's achievement by explaining its thorough preparations, its excellent equipment and its teamwork. He was, of course, himself ultimately responsible for all of these factors, and it was his inspiration and drive that made them so effective. But the success of the venture was also due far more to good leadership than is perhaps generally the case. Whilst we all understood the strategy of the Expedition pretty well, John alone could be relied upon to interpret its implications at any moment and in considerable detail. The interrelation of men, boats, mules, Land-Rovers, stores and air support was always crystal-clear to him. In an undertaking of such complexity and magnitude his fore-thought and organisational ability were remarkable. It was his brain-child and he guided it through all the problems of adolescence to a successful maturity.

As the CL 44 climbed up over the Red Sea, the brown Danakil desert slipped slowly past beneath us. The humidity was intense, and we slumped, bereft of air-conditioning, in damp immobility.

"I guess it's 'Thirteen Months of Sunshine' in this corner of the Empire," said Mansel, glancing out at the arid landscape.

"What do you mean, 'thirteen months'?" asked Hilary King.

"Well, that's the Tourist Organisation slogan; they have thirteen months in the Coptic calendar. One of them, *Pagume*, has only five days, but..."

"I believe it; I believe it. I believe anything in this extraordinary country," said Hilary.

After some time the unvarying brown of the sands of Nubia gave way to a dramatic belt of cultivation. We were passing over the Nile. Flanked by irrigated fields, the grey ribbon appeared broad and tranquil in the fading evening light. This was, of course, the joint product of Blue and White Niles, our own Blue, however, providing six-sevenths of the water at this time of year.

By and by, John began to try on his proconsular face. Gatwick was not far away and Press and Television would be waiting. Already there had been gratifying notices of our achievement in *Ethiopian Herald* and *Daily Telegraph* alike. There were personal plaudits, too, which we valued. On his estate at Mulu, the eighty-six-year-old Brigadier Daniel Sandford and his family had been most hospitable and had paid us pleasant tributes. He was amused to hear that the Assault Boat that we had named after him had been the only one to be safely extricated from Sirba, and had gone on to carry out the first ascent of the Abbai above Shafartak. After lunch he said to us: "It has been the very greatest pleasure to me to meet your group, who have done this wonderful trip. I think from what I know of the Blue Nile that the chances were against your getting through; but you have surmounted them all and had a thoroughly successful trip, on which I congratulate you."

The canvas "dodger" from *Sandford* now hangs on the wall of his verandah.

In similar vein was a signal which was handed to John by Major-General Napier Crookenden on our arrival at Gatwick. It read:

"I have been watching your Expedition's progress with great interest and admiration. There are undoubtedly easier rivers to cruise down and more comfortable ways to travel, but I can think of no task as challenging as the journey you undertook. I am full of respect for the way the Expedition overcame so many obstacles to achieve its object. My warmest congratulations to you all are only tempered by my sincerest sympathy on the loss of Corporal Ian Macleod.

Geoffrey Baker, Chief of the General Staff."

✳ ✳ ✳

On antique maps the Nile's source used to be set in highlands labelled "Lunae Montes". Now it is the real mountains of the moon which draw explorers. The kind of challenge which excites the astronauts of today, we were fortunate enough to find on our terrestrial globe.

"The course of the Blue Nile," wrote Cheesman in 1936, "might be considered as offering the only bit of pioneering exploration left in Africa."

The offer was still open as late as 1968, and it was this perhaps that all along had inspired most of us.

NOTES:

[1] It was reported the following April that relations between Lulu and Lulette had been warm, and that a family was expected.

APPENDIX

EXPEDITION MEMBERS

Capt. JOHN BLASHFORD-SNELL,* *R.E.*, Expedition Leader.
Capt. NIGEL SALE, *Royal Green Jackets*, Second-in-Command, Leader of B and N groups.
Lieut. JIM MASTERS, *R.E.*, * Chief Engineer; White Water Team.
Capt. ROGER CHAPMAN, *Green Howards*, * Leader of White Water Team; P Group.
Dr. PATRICK MORRIS, B.Sc.,* Director of Zoology.
Lieut.-Col. PHILIP SHEPHERD, B.Sc., *R.A.*, Senior Military Officer, Addis Ababa.
Capt. JOHN WILSEY, *Devonshire and Dorset Regiment*, Chief Reconnaissance Officer; Leader of J Group.
Capt. "BUCK" TAYLOR, *R.E.*, Quartermaster; Motor Transport Officer.
Lieut.-Col. ROGER WEST, O.B.E., T.D., M.R.C.S., M.R.C.P., D.P.H., R.A.M.C.(v), Senior Medical Officer.
Lieut. BARRY COOKE, B.Sc., *R. Signals*, Chief Signals Officer.
Lieut. MARTIN ROMILLY, B.Sc., *R. Anglian*,* Information Officer.
Major ALAN CALDER, *R.E.*, Head of Air Support Section (Pilot).
"JOHNNY" JOHNSON, Member of the British Ornithologists' Union; Associate of the Royal Photographic Society,* Director of Photography, Ornithology.
S/Sgt. "TICKY" WRIGHT, *R.E.*, Chief Mechanic; Assistant Q.M.; J Group.
JOHN FLETCHER,* Boatfitter; White Water Team; P Group.
Lieut. GARTH BROCKSOPP, *R. Irish Rangers*, Leader of C1 Group; at Ghimbi; P Group.
Lieut. DAVID BROMHEAD, *South Wales Borderers*, B Group; at Ghimbi; I and P Groups.
Lieut. GAVIN PIKE, 14th/20th *King's Hussars*, C1 Group; at Ghimbi; N Group.
Lieut. GAGE WILLIAMS, *Light Infantry*, Leader of C2 and C3 Groups.

Lieut. IAN CARRUTHERS, *R. Signals*, Signals Officer; C1 and I Groups.

Lieut. CHRIS EDWARDS, *Duke of Wellington's Regiment*, C2 and C3 Groups; White Water Team.

Lieut. RICHARD GREVATTE-BALL, *Royal Corps of Transport*, Air Support Section (Pilot).

Lieut. SPENCER LANE-JONES, B.Sc., *R.E.*,* Chief Surveyor; Leader of S Group.

Surgeon Sub-Lieut. NIGEL MARSH, M.B., Ch.B., *R.N.*,* Medical Officer.

Lieut. (J.G.) "TILLY" MAKONNEN, *Imperial Ethiopian Navy*,* Ethiopian Liaison Officer; N and J Groups.

Sub-Lieut. JOE RUSTON, *R.N.*,* Helmsman; Engineer; N and P Groups.

Warrant Officer I ALEC MURRAY, *R.E.*,* Helmsman; Engineer.

S/Sgt. "HANK" MANSLEY, *R.E.*,* Helmsman; Engineer; Leader of E Group.

S/Sgt. JOHN HUCKSTEP, *R.E.*,* Helmsman; Engineer; White Water Team and J Group.

Sgt. REX MATTHEWS, *Grenadier Guards*, B and N Groups; Signaller.

Dr. DEREK YALDEN, B.Sc.,* Zoologist.

Dr. MALCOLM LARGEN, B.Sc.,* Zoologist.

HILARY KING,* Zoologist.

COLIN CHAPMAN, B.Sc.,* Zoologist; Crocodile Survey; N and P Groups.

MANSEL SPRATLING, B.A.,* Archaeologist.

Capt. KEITH MORGAN-JONES, B. Vet. Med., M.R.C.V.S., R.A.V.C., Veterinary Surgeon.

ALASTAIR NEWMAN, B.Sc., Grad. Inst. P.,* Geologist; Meteorologist; White Water Team; P Group.

Cpl. IAN MACLEOD, *Black Watch* (Deceased),* Reconnaissance; White Water Team.

L/Cpl. MIKE HENRY, *R.E.*, Chief Clerk; C2 and C3 Groups.

Sgt. DAVID DAVIES, *R.E.M.E.*, Air Support Section (Mechanic).

Sgt. JOHN TOMANEY, *R.E.M.E.*, Air Support Section (Mechanic).

Cpl. PETER O'MAHONY, *R. Signals*, Signaller; White Water Team.

Cpl. DAVID FISHER, *R. Signals*, Signaller.

L/Cpl. TONY DAVIDSON, *R. Signals*, Signaller.

J/R.S.M., PETER HAMPSON, *R.E.,* Engineer; C2 and N Groups.

J/Sgt. CHRISTOPHER WHITWELL, *R.E.,** Engineer.

JOHN BLOWER, Adviser to Ethiopian Wild Life Conservation Department; B Group.

ALEM BERHANU, Assistant Game Warden; B Group.

ASSEFA GABRE YOHANNIS,* Water Resources Department.

MESFIN ABEBE, Assistant Game Warden; C2, C3 and I Groups.

TADESSE WOLDE GOSSA,* Haile Selassie I University, Addis Ababa; Interpreter.

RICHARD SNAILHAM, M.A.,* Secretary and Treasurer; N Group and White Water Team; P Group.

CHRISTIAN BONINGTON,* *The Daily Telegraph* Representative; White Water Team; N and P Groups.

Baron CLAUDE CHARNOTET (Deceased),* Deputy Director of Photography; C2 and S Groups.

Mrs. KAY THOMPSON, P.R.O.; Welfare.

Miss BARBARA WELLS, Zoological Secretary; Philatelic Section.

---

* There were 56 Expedition Members, not counting some 15 Ethiopian policemen who were attached to us from time to time. The 27 names marked with an asterisk were members also of Group A, and thus navigated the lower section of the Blue Nile, from the bridge at Shafartak to Sirba.

A SHORT BIBLIOGRAPHY

ALONE, Major J. P. H. M., and STOKES, D. E., *Short Manual of the Amharic Language* (Macmillan, 1966).

BRUCE, James, *Travels to Discover the Source of the Nile in the years 1768, 1769, 1770, 1771, 1772 and 1773*. Edited by Beckingham, C. F. (Edinburgh University Press, 1967).

CHEESMAN, Major R. E., *Lake Tana and the Blue Nile* (Frank Cass, 1968).

FORBES, Rosita, *From Red Sea to Blue Nile* (Penguin Books, 1939).

GREENFIELD, Richard, *Ethiopia: A New Political History* (Pall Mall Press, 1965).

JEŠMAN, Czeslaw, *Ethiopian Paradox* (O.U.P., 1963).

JESSEN, B. H., *W. N. McMillan's Expedition and Big-Game Hunting in Southern Sudan, Abyssinia and East Africa* (Marchant Singer, 1906).

LEVINE, Donald N., *Wax and Gold: Tradition and Innovation in Ethiopian Culture* (University of Chicago Press, 1965).

MATHEW, David, *Ethiopia: The Study of a Polity, 1540-1935* (Eyre and Spottiswoode, 1947).

MOOREHEAD, Alan, *The Blue Nile* (Hamish Hamilton, 1962).

MOSLEY, Leonard, *Haile Selassie* (Weidenfield and Nicolson, 1964).

PAKENHAM, Thomas, *The Mountains of Rasselas: An Ethiopian Adventure* (Weidenfeld and Nicolson, 1959).

PANKHURST, Richard, (Ed.) *Travellers in Ethiopia* (O.U.P., 1965).

PANKHURST, Sylvia, *Ethiopia: A Cultural History* (Lalibela House, Woodford Green, 1955).

PERHAM, Margery and SIMMONS, Jack, *African Discovery: an Anthology of Exploration* (Faber and Faber, 1942).

REID, J. M., *Traveller Extraordinary: The Life of James Bruce of Kinnaird* (History Book Club, 1968).

REY, C. F., *In the Country of the Blue Nile* (Duckworth, 1927). *The Real Abyssinia* (Seeley, Service and Co., 1935).

RITTLINGER, Herbert, *Schwarzes Abenteuer* (F. A. Brockhaus, Weisbaden, 1955).

RUBIN, Arne, *Ensam med Blå Nilen* (Forum, Stockholm, 1966).

SANDFORD, Christine, *Ethiopia under Haile Selassie* (Dent, 1946).

ULLENDORFF, Edward, *The Ethiopians: an Introduction to Country and People* (O.U.P., 1960).
WAUGH, Evelyn, *Remote People* (Duckworth, 1932).

INDEX

Many references to ADDIS ABABA, BAHARDAR, DEBRE MARCOS, GOJJAM, LAKE TANA, SHAFARTAK, SIRBA AND TISSISAT have been omitted, as they so often appear in the text only as start-points or end-points of journeys, or definitions of stretches of river, road or gorge.